Fodor's 2014

SOUTHERN CALIFORNIA

Portions of this book appear in *Fodor's California 2014*.

WELCOME TO SOUTHERN CALIFORNIA

Balmy weather, blissful beaches, Hollywood glamour—Southern California delivers fun and relaxation year-round. Outdoor enthusiasts revel in the natural beauty and excellent outdoor activities in the dramatic Mojave Desert and iconic Yosemite National Park, and at relaxing Palm Springs resorts. Beachgoers are drawn to the seemingly endless strands that line the stunning coast. For urban culture-vultures, trendy Los Angeles and sunny San Diego hold a wealth of treasures, including movie studio tours, America's preeminent zoo, and superb restaurants.

TOP REASONS TO GO

★ **Cool Cities:** San Diego's bay, Los Angeles's movie lore, Palm Springs' spa resorts.

★ **Beaches:** For swimming, surfing, or tanning, the beaches can't be beat.

★ **Feasts:** Cutting-edge cuisine, food trucks, fusion flavors, farmers' markets.

★ **Theme Parks:** From Disneyland to LEGOLAND, SoCal has some of the biggest and best.

★ **Outdoor Adventures:** Hiking, golfing, and national park excursions are all excellent.

★ **Road Trips:** The Pacific Coast Highway offers spectacular views and thrills aplenty.

Fodor's SOUTHERN CALIFORNIA 2014

Publisher: Amanda D'Acierno, *Senior Vice President*

Editorial: Arabella Bowen, *Executive Editorial Director*; Linda Cabasin, *Editorial Director*

Design: Fabrizio La Rocca, *Vice President, Creative Director*; Tina Malaney, *Associate Art Director*; Chie Ushio, *Senior Designer*; Ann McBride, *Production Designer*

Photography: Melanie Marin, *Associate Director of Photography*; Jessica Parkhill and Jennifer Romains, *Researchers*

Maps: Rebecca Baer, *Senior Map Editor*; David Lindroth and Mark Stroud *Cartographers*

Production: Linda Schmidt, *Managing Editor*; Evangelos Vasilakis, *Associate Managing Editor*; Angela L. McLean, *Senior Production Manager*

Sales: Jacqueline Lebow, *Sales Director*

Marketing & Publicity: Heather Dalton, *Marketing Director*; Katherine Fleming, *Senior Publicist*

Business & Operations: Susan Livingston, *Vice President, Strategic Business Planning*; Sue Daulton, *Vice President, Operations*

Fodors.com: Megan Bell, *Executive Director, Revenue & Business Development*; Yasmin Marinaro, *Senior Director, Marketing & Partnerships*

Copyright © 2014 by Fodor's Travel, a division of Random House LLC.

Writers: Tanvi Chheda, Seth Combs, Cheryl Crabtree, Maren Dougherty, Amanda Knoles, Kathy A. McDonald, Reed Parsell, Claire Deeks van der Lee, Christine Vovakes, Bobbi Zane

Editors: Luke Epplin (lead project editor), Salwa Jabado, Amanda Sadlowski

Editorial Contributors: Debbie Harmsen, Caroline Trefler

Production Editor: Evangelos Vasilakis

ISBN 978-0-7704-3264-5

ISSN 1543-1037

All details in this book are based on information supplied to us at press time. Always confirm information when it matters, especially if you're making a detour to visit a specific place. Fodor's expressly disclaims any liability, loss, or risk, personal or otherwise, that is incurred as a consequence of the use of any of the contents of this book.

SPECIAL SALES

This book is available at special discounts for bulk purchases for sales promotions or premiums. For more information, e-mail specialmarkets@randomhouse.com

PRINTED IN CHINA

10 9 8 7 6 5 4 3 2 1

CONTENTS

Fodor's Features

ABOUT THIS GUIDE

Fodor's Recommendations

Everything in this guide is worth doing—we don't cover what isn't—but exceptional sights, hotels, and restaurants are recognized with additional accolades. **Fodor's Choice★** indicates our top recommendations; and **Best Bets** call attention to notable hotels and restaurants in various categories. Care to nominate a new place? Visit Fodors.com/contact-us.

Trip Costs

We list prices wherever possible to help you budget well. Hotel and restaurant price categories from **$** to **$$$$** are noted alongside each recommendation. For hotels, we include the lowest cost of a standard double room in high season. For restaurants, we cite the average price of a main course at dinner or, if dinner isn't served, at lunch. For attractions, we always list adult admission fees; discounts are usually available for children, students, and senior citizens.

Hotels

Our local writers vet every hotel to recommend the best overnights in each price category, from budget to expensive. Unless otherwise specified, you can expect private bath, phone, and TV in your room. For expanded hotel reviews, facilities, and deals visit Fodors.com.

Restaurants

Unless we state otherwise, restaurants are open for lunch and dinner daily. We mention dress code only when there's a specific requirement and reservations only when they're essential or not accepted. To make restaurant reservations, visit Fodors.com.

Credit Cards

The hotels and restaurants in this guide typically accept credit cards. If not, we'll say so.

Top Picks	Hotels &
★ **Fodor's** Choice	**Restaurants**
	⊡ Hotel
Listings	⬱ Number of
⊠ Address	rooms
⬰ Branch address	⑂⊙⑂ Meal plans
☎ Telephone	✕ Restaurant
🖷 Fax	⬟ Reservations
⊕ Website	🏛 Dress code
✐ E-mail	⊟ No credit cards
🎫 Admission fee	⑤ Price
⊙ Open/closed	
times	**Other**
Ⓜ Subway	⇨ See also
⊹ Directions or	☞ Take note
Map coordinates	⅄ Golf facilities

EXPERIENCE SOUTHERN CALIFORNIA

WHAT'S NEW IN SOUTHERN CALIFORNIA

Foodie's Paradise

Great dining is a staple of the California lifestyle, and a new young generation of chefs is challenging old ideas about preparing and presenting great food. Food-truck frenzy has created a movable feast up and down the state. Esteemed chefs and urban foodies follow the trucks on Twitter as they move around cities 24/7 purveying delicious, cheap, fresh meals. In L.A., chef Roy Choi started the movement when he began serving up his Korean/Mexican Pacman burgers from his Kogi BBQ truck. In SoCal, you can find food-laden trucks at sports and entertainment venues, near parks and attractions, and on busy roads and boulevards—and the ensuing lines of hungry patrons.

California chefs continue to shop locally for produce and farmer-sourced meat. Tender Greens (with locations in Hollywood, Pasadena, and Walnut Creek) sets the bar high by serving hand-raised produce from an Oxnard farm; grain-fed, hormone-free beef; hand-raised chickens; and line-caught tuna.

Grape Expectations

Evidence that California wine culture is alive and well comes from Temecula, which is emerging as an exciting wine destination in the Inland Empire. The number and quality of the wineries continue to grow: Thornton, Ponte, and Mount Palomar wineries offer fine dining to pair with their delicious Rhône-style wines. Hotels are springing up among the vineyards, and events such as the Balloon and Wine Festival draw thousands of visitors to the region. In SoCal, vineyards are going up in unlikely places, such as in the hillsides of San Diego County, where Escondido-based Orfila keeps snagging awards, and on Catalina Island, where the Rusack family planted the first wine grapes ever on the historic Escondido Ranch. The Turkovich Family Winery opened in the Central Valley town of Winters just west of Sacramento.

Suite Dreams

Hotels are coming back to life in a big way. The luxurious new JW Marriott and Ritz-Carlton stand side by side in the burgeoning L.A. LIVE sports and entertainment complex. The W Hollywood now occupies the famed corner of Hollywood and Vine, another hot spot just steps from the Pantages Theatre.

All Aboard

Riding the rails can be a satisfying experience, particularly in California where the distances between destinations sometimes run into the hundreds of miles. Amtrak has frequent Pacific Surfliner service between San Diego and Los Angeles, and San Diego and Santa Barbara. These are coach cars, but many of the trains have been upgraded and are comfortable and convenient, especially if you want to get off and on the train at several destinations—Anaheim near Disneyland, downtown Los Angeles, coastal Ventura and Santa Barbara, San Luis Obispo, and Oakland (just a BART ride to San Francisco).

Kid-ding Around

California's theme parks work overtime to keep current and attract patrons of all ages. LEGOLAND California Resort keeps expanding with new attractions such as Pirate Reef and LEGOLAND Water Park. And LEGOLAND opened its 250-room LEGO-theme hotel in 2013.

Captain EO, a 3-D film starring Michael Jackson, is back at Disneyland. *Star Tours: The Adventures Continue*, also 3-D, has a new look, and World of Color in Disney California Adventure Park presents an outdoor light and water show.

State of the Arts

California's beauty-obsessed citizens aren't the only ones opting for a fresh look these days: its esteemed art museums are also having a bit of work done.

Following a trend set by the de Young Museum in San Francisco and the Getty Villa in L.A., Long Beach's Museum of Latin American Art doubled its exhibition space. Meanwhile, San Jose's Institute of Contemporary Art and the Museum of Contemporary Art in San Diego (MCASD Downtown) have both expanded into new digs. And the Palm Springs Museum of Art, a world-class showcase for contemporary work, has opened a satellite venue in Palm Desert. The L.A. County Museum of Art keeps expanding its Wilshire Boulevard campus; the latest addition is the Renzo Piano–designed Resnick Pavilion, which will hold special exhibits.

WHAT'S WHERE

The following numbers refer to chapters.

2 San Diego. Historic Gaslamp Quarter and Mexican-themed Old Town have a human scale—but it's big-ticket animal attractions like SeaWorld and the San Diego Zoo that pull in planeloads of visitors.

3 Orange County. The real OC is a diverse destination with premium resorts, first-rate restaurants, waterfront communities, and kid-friendly attractions.

4 Los Angeles. Go for the glitz of the entertainment industry, but stay for the rich cultural attributes and myriad communities of people from different cultures.

5 The Central Coast. Three of the state's top stops—swanky Santa Barbara, Hearst Castle, and Big Sur—sit along the scenic 200-mile route.

6 Channel Islands National Park. Only 60 miles northwest of Los Angeles, this park accessible only by boat seems worlds away.

7 Monterey Bay Area. Postcard-perfect Monterey, Victorian-flavored Pacific Grove, and surfer paradise Santa Cruz share this gorgeous stretch of coast.

8 The Inland Empire. The San Bernardino Mountains provide seasonal escapes at Lake Arrowhead and Big Bear Lake, and the Temecula Valley will challenge your ideas of "California Wine Country."

9 Palm Springs and the Desert Resorts. Golf on some of the West's most challenging courses, lounge at fabulous resorts and luxurious spas, check out midcentury-modern architectural gems, and experience the simple life at primitive desert parks.

10 Joshua Tree National Park. Proximity to major urban areas—as well as world-class rock climbing and nighttime celestial displays—help make this one of the most visited national parks in the United States.

11 The Mojave Desert. Material pleasures are in short supply, but Mother Nature's stark beauty more than compensates.

12 Death Valley National Park. America's second-largest national park isn't just vast—it's also very beautiful.

13 The Central Valley. Travelers along Highway 99 will enjoy attractions like Fresno's Forestiere Underground Gardens and the wineries of Lodi.

14 The Southern Sierra. Sawtooth mountains and deep powdery snowdrifts combine to create the state's premier conditions for skiing and snowboarding.

15 Yosemite National Park. The views immortalized by photographer Ansel Adams are still camera-ready.

16 Sequoia and Kings Canyon National Parks. The sight of ancient redwoods towering above jagged mountains is breathtaking.

PACIFIC OCEAN

NEVADA

UTAH

ARIZONA

MEXICO

Truckee
Reno
CARSON CITY
Lake Tahoe

Sonora
Bridgeport
Mono Lake
Mammoth Lakes
Bishop
Big Pine

Merced
Madera
Fresno
Visalia
Coalinga
McKittrick

Yosemite National Park
Kings Canyon National Park
Sequoia National Park
Porterville
Kernville
Tulare Lake Bed

SIERRA NEVADA

Stovepipe Wells
Furnace Creek
Death Valley Junction
Las Vegas
Lake Mead

Death Valley National Park
China Lake
Ridgecrest

Bakersfield
TEHACHAPI MTS.
Tejon Pass
Lancaster

MOJAVE DESERT
Barstow
Baker
Mojave National Preserve
Needles
Amboy

Santa Maria
Lompoc
Santa Barbara
Ojai
Oxnard
Ventura
Malibu
Santa Cruz

Santa Barbara Channel

CHANNEL ISLANDS NATIONAL PARK
Santa Rosa
Santa Barbara
San Nicolas
Santa Catalina
San Clemente

Victorville
Wrightwood
Lake Arrowhead
San Bernardino
Pasadena
LOS ANGELES
Long Beach
Huntington Beach
Santa Ana
Riverside
Temecula
Oceanside

Twentynine Palms
Joshua Tree National Park
Palm Springs
Indio
Desert Center
Blythe

Del Mar
La Jolla
SAN DIEGO
Tijuana
Julian
Brawley
El Centro
Mexicali
Yuma

Salton Sea

0   75 mi
0   75 km

SOUTHERN CALIFORNIA PLANNER

Air Travel

Around Los Angeles, the options grow exponentially. LAX, the world's fifth-busiest airport, gets most of the attention—and not usually for good reasons. John Wayne Airport (SNA), about 25 miles south in Orange County, is a solid substitute—especially if you're planning to visit Disneyland or Orange County beaches. Depending on which part of L.A. you're heading to, you might also consider Bob Hope Airport (BUR) in Burbank (close to Hollywood and its studios) or Long Beach Airport (LGB), convenient if you're catching a cruise ship. The smaller size of these airports means easier access and shorter security lines. Another advantage is that their lower landing costs often attract budget carriers (like Southwest and JetBlue).

Convenience is the allure of San Diego's Lindbergh International Airport (SAN), located minutes from the Gaslamp Quarter, Balboa Park and Zoo, Sea World, and the cruise ship terminal.

Car Travel

Driving may be a way of life in California, but it isn't cheap (gas prices here are usually among the highest in the nation). It's also not for the fainthearted; you've surely heard horror stories about L.A.'s freeways, but even the state's scenic highways and byways have their own hassles. For instance, on the dramatic coastal road between San Simeon and Carmel, twists, turns, and divinely distracting vistas frequently slow traffic; in rainy season, mud slides can close the road altogether. ⚠ **Never cross the double line to pass a slower car ahead of you. If you see that cars are backing up behind you, stop at the first available pullout to allow faster drivers to pass.**

On California's notorious freeways, other rules apply. Nervous Nellies must resist the urge to stay in the two slow-moving lanes on the far right, used primarily by trucks. To drive at least the speed limit, get yourself in a middle lane. If you're ready to bend the rules a bit, the second (lanes are numbered from 1 starting at the center) lane moves about 5 mph faster. But avoid the far-left lane (the one next to the carpool lane), where speeds range from 75 mph to 90 mph.

SOCAL DRIVING TIPS

Use your signal correctly. Here signaling is a must. Because of all the different lanes, people may try to merge into the same spot as you from three lanes away. Protect yourself and your space by always using your signal. And don't forget to turn your signal off when the lane change is complete.

Drive friendly. Here's how to avoid causing road rage: don't tailgate. Don't flail your arms in frustration. Don't glare at the driver of the car you finally have a chance to pass. And above all, don't fly the finger. Road rage is a real hazard.

Don't pull over on the freeway. Short of a real emergency, never, ever, pull over and stop on a freeway. So you took the wrong ramp and need to huddle with your map—take the next exit and find a safe, well-lighted public space to stop your car and get your bearings.

WHEN TO GO

Because they offer activities indoors and out, the top California cities rate as all-season destinations. Ditto for Southern California's coastal playgrounds. Dying to see Death Valley or Joshua Tree National Park? They are best appreciated in spring when desert blooms offset their austerity and temperatures are still manageable. Yosemite is ideal in the late spring because roads closed in winter are reopened, and the park's waterfalls—swollen with melting snow—run fast. Snowfall makes winter peak season for skiers in Mammoth Mountain, where runs typically open around Thanksgiving. (They sometimes remain in operation into June.)

Climate

It's difficult to generalize much about the state's weather beyond saying that precipitation comes in winter and summer is dry in most places. As a rule, inland regions are hotter in summer and colder in winter, compared with coastal areas, which are relatively cool year-round. Fog is a potential hazard any day of the year in coastal regions. As you climb into the mountains, seasonal variations are more apparent: winter brings snow (at elevations above 3,000 feet), autumn is crisp, spring can go either way, and summer is sunny and warm, with only an occasional thunder-shower in the southern part of the state.

Microclimates

Mountains separate the California coast-line from the state's interior, and the weather can sometimes vary dramatically within a 15-minute drive. Day and night-time temperatures can also vary greatly. In August, Palm Springs' thermometers can soar to 110°F at noon, and drop to 75°F at night. Temperature swings elsewhere can be even more extreme.

Forecasts
National Weather Service
⊕ *www.wrh.noaa.gov.*

°F LOS ANGELES °C

86 30
68 20
50 10
32 0
    J F M A M J J A S O N D

°F SAN DIEGO °C

86 30
68 20
50 10
32 0
    J F M A M J J A S O N D

SOUTHERN CALIFORNIA TODAY

The People

California is as much a state of mind as a state in the union—a kind of perpetual promised land that has represented many things to many people. In the 18th century, Spanish missionaries came seeking converts and gold. In the 19th, miners rushed here to search for gold. And, in the years since, a long line of Dust Bowl farmers, land speculators, Haight-Ashbury hippies, migrant workers, dotcommers, real estate speculators, and would-be actors has come chasing their own dreams.

The result is a population that leans toward idealism—without necessarily being as liberal as you might think. (Remember, this is Ronald Reagan's old stomping ground.) And despite the stereotype of the blue-eyed, blond surfer, California's population is not homogeneous either. Ten million people who live here (more than 28% of Californians) are foreign born—including former Governor Schwarzenegger. Almost half hail from Latin American countries; another third emigrated from Asia, following the waves of Chinese workers who arrived in the 1860s to build the railroads and subsequent waves of Indochinese refugees from the Vietnam War.

The Politics

What's blue and red and green all over? California: a predominantly Democratic state with an aggressive "go green" agenda. Democratic Governor Jerry Brown, who was elected to the office for the second time in 30 years, is moving the progressive agenda ahead with policies that make California the greenest state in the nation supporting more green construction, wind farms, and solar panels.

The Economy

Leading all other states in terms of the income generated by agriculture, tourism, and industrial activity, California has the country's most diverse state economy. Moreover, with a gross state product of more than $2 trillion, California would be one of the top 10 economies *in the world* if it were an independent nation. But due to its wealth ($65,476 median household income) and productivity, California took a large hit in the recession that began in 2007. This affected all levels of government from local to statewide and resulted in reduction of services that Californians have long taken for granted.

But the Golden State's economic history is filled with boom and bust cycles—beginning with the mid-19th-century gold rush that started it all. Optimists already have their eyes on the next potential boom: high-tech and bio research, "green companies" focused on alternative energy, renewables, electric cars, and the like.

The Culture

Cultural organizations thrive in California. San Francisco—a city with only about 812,000 residents—has well-regarded ballet, opera, and theater companies, and is home to one of the continent's most noteworthy orchestras. Museums like San Francisco Museum of Modern Art (SFMOMA) and the de Young also represent the city's ongoing commitment to the arts. Art and culture thrive farther south in San Diego as well. Balboa Park alone holds 15 museums, opulent gardens, and three performance venues, in addition to the San Diego Zoo. The Old Globe Theater and La Jolla Playhouse routinely originate plays that capture coveted Tony Awards in New York.

But California's *real* forte is pop culture, and L.A. and its environs are the chief arbiters. Movie, TV, and video production have been centered here since the early 20th century. Capitol Records set up shop in L.A. in the 1940s, and this area has been instrumental in the music industry ever since. And while these industries continue to influence national trends, today they are only part of the pop culture equation. Websites are also a growing part of that creativity—Facebook, YouTube, and Google are California creatures.

The Parks and Preserves

Cloud-spearing redwood groves, snow-tipped mountains, canyon-slashed deserts, primordial lava beds, and a seemingly endless coast: California's natural diversity is staggering—and efforts to protect it started early. The first national park here was established in 1890, and the National Park Service now oversees 30 sites in California (more than in any other state). When you factor in 278 state parks—which encompass underwater preserves, historic sites, wildlife reserves, dune systems, and other sensitive habitats—the number of acres involved is almost as impressive as the topography itself.

Due to encroaching development and pollution, keeping these natural treasures in pristine condition is an ongoing challenge. For instance, Sequoia and Kings Canyon (which is plagued by pesticides and other agricultural pollutants blown in from the San Joaquin Valley) has been named America's "smoggiest park" by the National Parks Conservation Association, and the Environmental Protection Agency has designated it as an "ozone non-attainment area with levels of ozone pollution that threaten human health."

There is no question that Californians love their 278 state parks, 70 of which were scheduled to close in July 2012 due to budget cuts. Nearly every park has its grass-roots supporters, who volunteer to raise money, volunteer as rangers, and work other jobs to keep the parks open.

The Cuisine

California gave us McDonald's, Denny's, Carl's Jr., Taco Bell, and, of course, In-N-Out Burger. Fortunately for those of us with fast-clogging arteries, the state also kick-started the organic food movement. Back in the 1970s, California-based chefs put American cuisine on the culinary map by focusing on freshly prepared seasonal ingredients.

Today, this focus has spawned the "locavore" or sustainable food movement—followers try to only consume food produced within a 100-mile radius of where they live, since processing and refining food and transporting goods over long distances is bad for both the body and the environment. This isn't much of a restriction in California, where a huge variety of crops grow year-round. Some 350 cities and towns have certified farmers' markets—and their stalls are bursting with a variety of goods. California has been America's top agricultural producer for the last 50 years, growing more fruits and vegetables than any other state. Dairies and ranches also thrive here, and fishing fleets harvest fish and shellfish from the rich waters offshore.

SOUTHERN CALIFORNIA TOP ATTRACTIONS

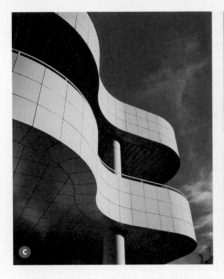

San Diego

(A) San Diego is a thoroughly modern metropolis set on the sunny Pacific, filled with tourist attractions (think the Balboa Park, Zoo, SeaWorld, and LEGO-LAND) and blissful beaches. But this is also a city steeped in history—in 1769 Spaniards established a settlement here near Old Town, site of the first Spanish outpost and now a state park dedicated to illustrating San Diego's raucous early days. The city's rousing Downtown dining and entertainment district, the Gaslamp Quarter, is a contemporary recreation of bawdy Stingaree of the late 1800s.

Channel Islands National Park

(B) This five-island park northwest of Los Angeles is a remote but accessible eco escape. There are no phones, no cars, and no services—but there are more than 2,000 species of plants and animals (among them blue whales and brown pelicans), plus ample opportunities for active pursuits. On land, hiking tops the itinerary. Underwater preserves surround the park, so snorkeling, scuba diving, fishing, and kayaking around lava tubes and natural arches are other memorable options.

Los Angeles

(C) Tinseltown, Lala Land, City of Angels: L.A. goes by many names and has many personas. Recognized as America's capital of pop culture, it also has highbrow appeal with arts institutions like the Getty Center, the Geffen Contemporary at MOCA, Walt Disney Concert Hall, the Norton Simon Museum, and Huntington Library. But you can go wild here, too—and not just on the Sunset Strip. Sprawling Griffith Park, Will Rogers State Historic Park, and Malibu Lagoon State Beach all offer a natural break from the concrete jungle.

Palm Springs and Beyond

(D) Celebrities used to flee to the desert for rest, relaxation, a few rays of sun, and to indulge in some high jinks beyond the watchful eyes of the media. You don't have to spend much time in Palm Springs to realize those days are *long* gone. In this improbably situated bastion of Bentleys and bling, worldly pleasures rule. Glorious golf courses, tony shops and restaurants, decadent spa resorts—they're all here. Solitude seekers can still slip away to nearby Joshua Tree National Park or Anza-Borrego Desert State Park.

Death Valley

(E) On the surface, a vacation in Death Valley sounds about as attractive as a trip to hell. Yet for well-prepared travelers, the experience is more awe-inspiring than ominous. Within the largest national park in the contiguous United States you'll find the brilliantly colored rock formations of Artists Palette, the peaks of the Panamint Mountains, and the desolate salt flats of Badwater, 282 feet below sea level. You can't get any lower than this in the Western Hemisphere—and, in summer, you can't get much hotter.

Yosemite National Park

(F) Nature looms large here, both literally and figuratively. In addition to hulking Half Dome, the park is home to El Capitan (the world's largest exposed granite monolith, rising 3,593 feet above the glacier-carved valley floor) and Yosemite Falls (North America's tallest cascade). In Yosemite's signature stand of giant sequoias—the Mariposa Grove—even the trees are Bunyanesque. Needless to say, crowds can be super-size, too.

SOUTHERN CALIFORNIA'S TOP EXPERIENCES

Hit the Road

Kings Canyon Highway, Tioga Pass, 17-Mile Drive, and the grand Pacific Coast Highway: California has some splendid and challenging roads. Most of these are well-traveled paths, but if you venture over the Sierras by way of Tioga Pass (through Yosemite in summer only), you'll see emerald green meadows, gray granite monoliths, and pristine blue lakes—and very few people.

Ride a Wave

Surfing—which has influenced everything from fashion to moviemaking to music— is a quintessential California activity. You can find great surf breaks in many places along the coast between Santa Cruz and San Diego. But one of the best places to try it is Huntington Beach. Lessons are widely available. If you're not ready to hang 10, you can hang out at "Surf City's" International Surfing Museum or stroll the Surfing Walk of Fame.

Think Globally, Eat Locally

Over the years California cuisine has evolved from a mere trend into a respected gastronomic tradition: one that pairs local, often organic or sustainable, ingredients with techniques inspired by European, Asian, and, increasingly, Indian and Middle Eastern cookery.

See Eccentric Architecture

California has always drawn creative and, well, eccentric people. And all that quirkiness has left its mark in the form of oddball architecture that makes for some fun sightseeing. Begin by touring Hearst Castle—the beautifully bizarre estate William Randolph Hearst built above San Simeon. Scotty's Castle, a Moorish confection in Death Valley, offers a variation on the theme, as does Marta Becket's one-woman Amargosa Opera House.

Get Behind the Scenes

In L.A. it's almost obligatory to do some Hollywood-style stargazing. Cue the action with a behind-the-scenes tour of one of the dream factories. (Warner Bros. Studios' five-hour deluxe version, which includes lunch in the commissary, is just the ticket for cinephiles.) Other must-sees include the Dolby Theater, permanent home to the Cirque du Soleil and Academy Awards; Grauman's Chinese Theatre, where celebs press feet and hands into cement for posterity's sake; Hollywood Boulevard's star-paved Walk of Fame; and the still-iconic Hollywood sign.

People-Watch

Opportunities for world-class people-watching abound in California. Just stroll the century-old boardwalk in time-warped, resiliently boho Santa Cruz. Better yet, hang around L.A.'s Venice Boardwalk, where chain-saw jugglers, surfers, fortune-tellers, and well-oiled bodybuilders take beachfront exhibitionism to a new high (or low, depending on your point of view). The result is pure eye candy.

FAQ

I'm not particularly active. Will I still enjoy visiting a national park? Absolutely, the most popular parks really do have something for everyone. Take Yosemite. When the ultrafit embark on 12-hour trail treks, mere mortals can hike Cook's Meadow—an easy 1-mile loop that's also wheelchair accessible. If even that seems too daunting, you can hop on a free shuttle or drive yourself to sites like Glacier Point or the Mariposa Grove of Giant Sequoias.

What's the single best place to take the kids? Well, that depends on your children's ages and interests, but for its sheer smorgasbord of activities, San Diego is hard to beat. Between the endless summer weather and sites such as SeaWorld, the San Diego Zoo, and LEGOLAND (about 30 minutes away), California's southernmost city draws families in droves. Once you've covered the mega-attractions, enjoy an easy-to-swallow history lesson in Old Town or the Maritime Museum. Want to explore different ecosystems? La Jolla Cove has kid-friendly tidal pools and cliff caves, while Anza-Borrego Desert State Park is a doable two-hour drive east.

That said, there are kid-friendly attractions all over the state—your kids are going to have to try really hard to be bored.

California sounds expensive. How can I save on sightseeing? CityPass (☎ *888/330–5008* ⊕ *www.citypass.com*) includes admission and some upgrades for main attractions in Hollywood and Southern California (Disneyland, Universal Studios, and SeaWorld). Also, many museums set aside free-admission days. Prefer the great outdoors? An America the Beautiful annual pass (☎ *888/275–8747* ⊕ *www. nps.gov*) admits you to every site under the National Park Service umbrella. Better yet, depending on the property, passengers in your vehicle get in free, too.

Any tips for a first-time trip into the desert? The desert's stark, sun-blasted beauty will strip your mind of everyday clutter. But it is a brutal, punishing place for anyone ill-prepared. So whether it's your first or 15th visit, the same dos and don'ts apply. Stick to a state or national park. Pick up pamphlets at its visitor center and *follow the instructions* they set out. Keep your gas tank full. Bring lots of water and drink at least two gallons a day—even if you're not thirsty. Wear a hat and sunscreen, and don't expect to move too fast at midday when the sun is kiln-hot.

QUINTESSENTIAL SOUTHERN CALIFORNIA

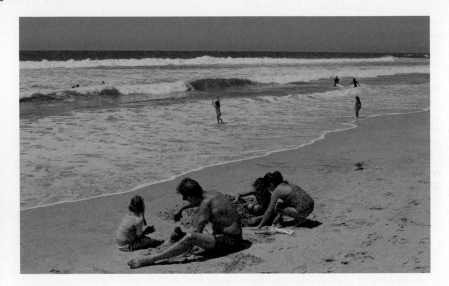

The Beach

California's beach culture is, in a word, legendary. Of course, it only makes sense that folks living in a state with a 1,264-mile coastline (a hefty portion of which sees the sun upward of 300 days a year) would perfect the art of beach-going. True aficionados begin with a reasonably fit physique, plus a stylish wardrobe consisting of flip-flops, bikinis, wet suits, and such. Mastery of at least one beach skill—surfing, boogie boarding, kayaking, Frisbee tossing, or looking fab while catching rays—is also essential. As a visitor, though, you need only a swimsuit and some rented equipment for most sports. You can then hit the beach almost anywhere, thanks to the California belief in coastal access as a birthright. The farther south you go, the wider, sandier, and sunnier the beaches become; moving north they are rockier and foggier, with colder and rougher surf.

The Automobile

Americans may have a love affair with the automobile, but Californians have an out-and-out obsession. Even when gas prices rev up and freeway traffic slows down, their passion burns as hot as ever. You can witness this ardor any summer weekend at huge classic- and custom-car shows held statewide. Even better, you can feel it yourself by taking the wheel. Drive to the sea following Laguna Canyon Road to Laguna Beach; trace an old stagecoach route through the mountains above Santa Barbara on Highway 154; track migrating whales up the coast to Big Sur; or take 17-Mile Drive along the precipitous edge of the Monterey Peninsula. Glorious for the most part, but authentically congested in some areas in the south, Highway 1 runs almost the entire length of the state, hugging the coast most of the way.

Californians live in such a large and splashy state that they sometimes seem to forget about the rest of the country. They've developed a distinctive culture all their own, which you can delve into by doing as the locals do.

The Unusual

Maybe the constantly perfect weather or the looming threat of earthquakes makes Southern Californians a little crazy. Whatever the reason, many have a pronounced appetite for the unusual, the off-center, even the bizarre. Witness the Integratron, a domed time machine with UFO landing strip, near Joshua Tree National Park (itself filled with natural oddities). Or San Luis Obispo's Madonna Inn, where you can sleep in a faux-cave and stir pink sugar into your coffee. Marta Becket performs solo in her Amargosa Opera House outside Death Valley National Park, where Scotty's Castle stands in pointless Moorish-style splendor way out in the desert. Idiosyncratic creations large and small litter the Southern California landscape—many of them designed to attract visitors, others simply personal expressions.

The Outdoors

One of California's greatest assets—the mild year-round weather enjoyed by most of the state—inspires residents to spend as much time outside as they possibly can. They have a tremendous enthusiasm for every imaginable outdoor sport, and, up north especially, fresh-air adventures are extremely popular (which may explain why everyone there seems to own at least one pair of hiking boots). But the California-alfresco creed is more broadly interpreted, and the general rule when planning any activity is "if it can happen outside, it will!" *Plein air* vacation opportunities include dining on patios, decks, and wharves; shopping in street markets or elaborate open-air malls; hearing almost any kind of music at moonlight concerts; touring the sculpture gardens that grace major art museums; and celebrating everything from gay pride to garlic at outdoor fairs.

GREAT ITINERARIES

SOUTHERN CALIFORNIA WITH KIDS, 7 DAYS

SoCal offers many opportunities to entertain the kids beyond the Magic Kingdom. LEGOLAND is a blast for kids 12 and under and families can't beat SeaWorld, the San Diego Zoo, and San Diego's historic Old Town.

Day 1–2: Disneyland

Get out of Los Angeles International Airport as fast as you can. Pick up your rental car and head south on the I-405 freeway, which can be congested day or night, toward Orange County and **Disneyland.** Skirt the lines at the box office with advance-purchased tickets in hand and storm the gates of the Magic Kingdom. You can cram the highlights into a single day, but if you get a 2-day ticket and stay the night you can see the parade and visit **Downtown Disney** before heading south. Highway 39, just west of Disneyland will take you all the way to the coast, just south of surfer's haven at **Huntington Beach,** where you can spend the night in one of several beachfront hotels.

Day 3: LEGOLAND

Get an early start for your next roller coaster ride at **LEGOLAND,** about an hour's drive south of Huntington Beach via the Pacific Coast Highway. Check into newly opened **LEGOLAND Hotel** or the **Sheraton Carlsbad Resort & Spa;** both offer direct access to the park. LEGOLAND has a water park and aquarium in addition to the LEGO-based rides, shows, and roller coasters. The little ones can live out their fairy-tale fantasies and bigger ones can spend all day on waterslides, shooting water pistols, driving boats, or water fighting with pirates.

Day 4: La Jolla and San Diego

Take a leisurely drive south to San Diego by using the "old road," the original Pacific Coast Highway that hugs the shore all the way. It's a slow drive through Leucadia, Encinitas, Solana Beach, and Del Mar, all of which are popular surfing beaches. When you get to **La Jolla,** swing around the cove to see one of the area's most beautiful beaches. Look, but don't go in the water at the children's pool, as it's likely to be filled with barking seals. The **Birch Aquarium at Scripps** here offers a look at how scientists study the oceans.

Hop onto I-5 and head for Downtown **San Diego.** Go straight for the city's nautical heart by exploring the restored ships of the **Maritime Museum** at the waterfront Downtown. Victorian buildings—and plenty of other tourists—surround you on a stroll through the **Gaslamp Quarter,** but the 21st century is in full swing at the **Westfield Horton Plaza** retail and entertainment complex. Plant yourself at a Downtown hotel and graze your way through the neighborhood's many restaurants.

Day 5: San Diego Zoo

Malayan tapirs in a faux-Asian rain forest, polar bears in an imitation Arctic, and pandas frolicking in the trees—the **San Diego Zoo** maintains a vast and varied collection of creatures in a world-renowned facility comprised of meticulously designed habitats. Come early, wear comfy shoes, and stay as long as you like.

Los Angeles
405
39
Anaheim
Disneyland
Huntington Beach
10
Joshua Tree
National Park
Twenty Nine Palms
Palm Springs
10
86S
Salton
Sea
Borrego
Springs
86
5
Catalina
Island
Carlsbad
LEGOLAND
Leucadia
Encinitas
Solana Beach
Del Mar
La Jolla
Sea World/
Old Town
San Diego/
San Diego Zoo
78
Anza-Borrego Desert
State Park

PACIFIC
OCEAN

MEXICO

Day 6: SeaWorld and Old Town

Resistance is futile: you're going to **Sea-World.** So what if it screams commercial? This humongous theme park, with its walk-through shark tanks and killer-whale shows, also screams fun. Surrender to the experience and try not to sit in anything sticky. Also touristy, but with genuine historical significance, **Old Town** drips with Mexican and early Californian heritage. Soak it up in the plaza at **Old Town San Diego State Historic Park;** have a bite at one of the Mexican restaurants here, then browse the stalls and shops at **Fiesta de Reyes** and along San Diego Avenue.

Day 7: Departure from San Diego or Los Angeles

Pack up your Mouseketeer gear and give yourself ample time to reach the airport. San Diego International Airport lies within a 10-minute drive from Old Town. Although you'll be driving on freeways the entire way to LAX, traffic is always heavy and you should plan for a full day to get there.

PALM SPRINGS AND THE DESERT, 5 DAYS

The Palm Springs area is paradise for many. Most go for more than a good tan or to play golf on championship courses. Expect fabulous and funky spas, a dog-friendly atmosphere, and sparkling stars at night.

Day 1: Palm Springs

Freeway traffic permitting, you can drive from the middle of L.A. to the middle of the desert in a couple of hours. Somehow in harmony with the harsh environment, midcentury-modern homes and businesses with clean, low-slung lines define the **Palm Springs** style. Although the desert cities comprise a trendy destination with beautiful hotels, fabulous multicultural food, abundant nightlife, and plenty of culture, a quiet atmosphere prevails. The city seems far away when you hike in hushed **Tahquitz** or **Indian Canyon;** cliffs and palm trees shelter rock art, irrigation works, and other remnants of Agua Caliente culture. If your boots aren't made for walking, you can always practice your golf game or indulge in some sublime or funky spa treatments at an area resort instead.

Day 2: Explore Palm Springs

If riding a tram up an 8,516-foot mountain for a stroll or even a snowball fight above the desert sounds like fun to you, then show up at the **Palm Springs Aerial Tramway** before the first morning tram leaves (later, the line can get discouragingly long). Afterward stroll through the **Palm Springs Art Museum** where you can see a shimmering display of contemporary studio glass, an array of enormous Native American baskets, and significant works of 20th-century sculpture by Henry Moore and others. After all that walking you may be ready for an early dinner. Nearly every restaurant in Palm Springs offers a happy hour, when you can sip a cocktail and nosh on a light entrée, usually for half price. Using your hotel as a base, take a few day trips to discover the natural beauty of the desert.

Day 3: Joshua Tree National Park

Due to its proximity to Los Angeles and the highway between Las Vegas and coastal cities, **Joshua Tree** is one of the most popular and accessible of the national parks. It's about an hour northeast of Palm Springs. You can see most of it in a day, entering the park at the town of Joshua Tree, exploring sites along **Park Boulevard**, and exiting at **Twentynine Palms**. With its signature trees, piles of rocks, glorious spring wildflowers, starlit skies, and colorful pioneer history, the experience is a bit more like the Wild West than Sahara sand dunes.

Day 4: Anza-Borrego Desert State Park and the Salton Sea

There are two worthwhile destinations about two hours south and east of the Palm Springs area, Salton Sea and Anza-Borrego State Park. The **Salton Sea**, about 60 miles south of Palm Springs via I-10

TIPS

No matter how carefully you plan your movements to avoid busy routes at peak hours, you will inevitably encounter heavy traffic in L.A., Orange County, and San Diego. All of these itineraries start at LAX. If your plans include a trip from L.A. to San Diego or O.C., you can save time (and maybe money) by booking your flight to L.A. and returning from San Diego, O.C., or LA/Ontario.

Allow yourself twice as much time as you think you'll need to negotiate LAX.

and Highway 86S, is one of the largest inland seas on earth. A new sea, formed by the flooding of the Colorado River in 1905, it attracts thousands of migrating birds and bird-watchers every fall. **Anza-Borrego Desert State Park** is the largest state park in California, with 600,000 acres of mostly untouched wilderness; it offers one of the best spring-wildflower displays in California and also displays a large collection of life-size bronze sculpture of animals that roamed this space millions of years ago. **Borrego Springs**, a tiny hamlet, lies in the center of it all. The desert is home to an archeological site, where scientists continue to uncover remnants of prehistoric animals ranging from mastodons to horses.

Day 5: Return to L.A.

If you plan to depart from LAX, plan for a full day of driving from the desert to the airport. Be prepared for heavy traffic at any time of day or night. If possible, opt to fly out of LA/Ontario International Airport instead.

HOORAY FOR HOLLYWOOD, 4 DAYS

If you are a movie fan, there's no better place to see it all than L.A. Always keep your eyes out for a familiar face: you never know when you might spot a celebrity.

Day 1: Los Angeles

As soon as you land at LAX, make like a local and hit the freeway. Even if L.A.'s top-notch art, history, and science museums don't tempt you, the hodgepodge of art deco, Beaux Arts, and futuristic architecture begs at least a drive-by. Heading east from Santa Monica, Wilshire Boulevard cuts through a historical and cultural cross section of the city. Two stellar sights on its Miracle Mile are the encyclopedic **Los Angeles County Museum of Art** and the fossil-filled **La Brea Tar Pits.** Come evening, the open-air **Farmers' Market** and its many eateries hum. Hotels in Beverly Hills or West Hollywood beckon, just a few minutes away.

Day 2: Hollywood and the Movie Studios

Every L.A. tourist should devote at least one day to the movies and take at least one studio tour in the San Fernando Valley. For fun, choose the special-effects theme park at **Universal Studios Hollywood;** for the nitty-gritty, choose **Warner Bros. Studios.** Nostalgic musts in Hollywood include the **Walk of Fame** along **Hollywood Boulevard** and the celebrity footprints cast in concrete outside **Grauman's Chinese Theatre.** When evening arrives, the Hollywood scene boasts a bevy of trendy restaurants and nightclubs.

Day 3 and 4: Beverly Hills and Santa Monica

Even without that extensive art collection, the **Getty Center's** pavilion architecture, hilltop gardens, and frame-worthy L.A. views make it a dazzling destination. Descend to the sea via Santa Monica Boulevard for lunch along **Third Street Promenade,** followed by a ride on the historic carousel on the pier. The buff and the bizarre meet at **Venice Beach Oceanfront Walk** (strap on some Rollerblades if you want to join them!). **Rodeo Drive** in Beverly Hills specializes in exhibitionism with a heftier price tag, but voyeurs are still welcome.

Splurge on breakfast or brunch at a posh café in **Farmers' Market,** then stroll through aisles and aisles of gorgeous produce and specialty food before you take a last look at the Pacific Ocean through the camera obscura at **Palisades Park** in Santa Monica.

THE ULTIMATE ROAD TRIP

CALIFORNIA'S LEGENDARY HIGHWAY 1

by Cheryl Crabtree

One of the world's most scenic drives, California's State Route 1 (also known as Highway 1, the Pacific Coast Highway, the PCH) stretches along the edge of the state for nearly 660 miles, from Southern California's Dana Point to its northern terminus near Leggett, about 40 miles north of Fort Bragg. As you travel south to north, the water's edge transitions from long, sandy beaches and low-lying bluffs to towering dunes, craggy cliffs, and ancient redwood groves. The ocean changes as well; the relatively tame and surfable swells lapping the Southern California shore give way to the frigid, powerful waves crashing against weatherbeaten rocks in the north.

HIGHWAY 1 TOP 10

- Santa Monica
- Santa Barbara
- Hearst San Simeon State Historical Monument
- Big Sur
- Carmel
- 17–Mile Drive
- Monterey
- San Francisco
- Marin Headlands
- Point Reyes National Seashore

Give yourself lots of extra time to pull off the road and enjoy the scenery

STARTING YOUR JOURNEY

You may decide to drive the road's entire 660-mile route, or bite off a smaller piece. In either case, a Highway 1 road trip allows you to experience California at your own pace, stopping when and where you wish. Hike a beachside trail, dig your toes in the sand, and search for creatures in the tidepools. Buy some artichokes and strawberries from a roadside farmstand. Talk to people along the way (you'll run into everyone from soul-searching meditators, farmers, and beatniks to city-slackers and working-class folks), and take lots of pictures. Don't rush—you could easily spend a lifetime discovering secret spots along this route.

To help you plan your trip, we've broken the road into three regions (Santa Monica to Carmel, Carmel to San Francisco, and San Francisco to Fort Bragg); each region is then broken up into smaller segments—many of which are suitable for a day's drive. If you're pressed for time, you can always tackle a section of Highway 1, and then head inland to U.S. 101 or I-5 to reach your next destination more quickly.

WHAT'S IN A NAME?

Though it's often referred to as the Pacific Coast Highway (or PCH), sections of Highway 1 actually have different names. The southernmost section (Dana Point to Oxnard) is the Pacific Coast Highway. After that, the road becomes the Cabrillo Highway (Las Cruces to Lompoc), the Big Sur Coast Highway (San Luis Obispo County line to Monterey), the North Coast Scenic Byway (San Luis Obispo city limit to the Monterey County line), the Cabrillo Highway again (Santa Cruz County line to Half Moon Bay), and finally the Shoreline Highway (Marin City to Leggett). To make matters more confusing, smaller chunks of the road have additional honorary monikers.

Just follow the green triangular signs that say "California 1."

HIGHWAY 1 DRIVING

- Rent a convertible. (You will not regret it.)
- Begin the drive north from Santa Monica, where congestion and traffic delays pose less of a problem.
- Take advantage of turnouts. Let cars pass you as you take in the ocean view and snap a picture.
- Mind your manners: Don't tailgate or glare at other drivers.
- If you're prone to motion sickness, take the wheel yourself. Focusing on the landscape outside should help you feel less queasy.
- If you're afraid of heights, drive from south to north so you'll be on the mountain rather than the cliff side of the road.
- Driving PCH is glorious during winter, but check weather conditions before you go as landslides are frequent after storms.

HIGHWAY 1: SANTA MONICA TO BIG SUR

Hearst Castle

THE PLAN

Distance: approx. 335 mi

Time: 3-5 days

Good Overnight Options: Malibu, Santa Barbara, Pismo Beach, San Luis Obispo, Cambria, Carmel

For more information on the sights and attractions along this portion of Highway 1, please see Los Angeles and Central Coast chapters

SANTA MONICA TO MALIBU (approx. 26 mi)

Highway 1 begins in Dana point, but it seems more appropriate to begin a PCH adventure in **Santa Monica.** Be sure to experience the beach culture, then balance the tacky pleasures of Santa Monica's amusement pier with a stylish dinner in a neighborhood restaurant.

MALIBU TO SANTA BARBARA (approx. 70 mi)

The PCH follows the curve of Santa Monica Bay all the way to **Malibu** and **Point Mugu,**

near **Oxnard.** Chances are you'll experience *déjà vu* driving this 27-mile stretch: mountains on one side, ocean on the other, opulent homes perched on hillsides; you've seen this piece of coast countless times on TV and film. Be sure to walk out on the **Malibu Pier** for a great photo opp, then check out **Surfrider Beach,** with three famous points where perfect waves ignited a worldwide surfing rage in the 1960s.

After Malibu you'll drive through miles of protected, largely unpopulated coastline. Ride a wave at **Zuma Beach,** scout for offshore whales at **Point Dume State Preserve,** or hike the trails at **Point Mugu State Park.** After skirting Point Mugu, Highway 1 merges with U.S. 101 for about 70 mi before reaching **Santa Barbara.** A mini-tour of the city includes a real Mexican lunch at **La Super-Rica,** a visit to the magnificent Spanish **Mission Santa Barbara,** and a walk down hopping **State Street** to Stearns Wharf.

SANTA BARBARA TO SAN SIMEON (approx. 147 mi)

North of Santa Barbara, Highway 1 morphs into the Cabrillo Highway, separating

Santa Barbara

from and then rejoining U.S. 101. The route winds through rolling vineyards and rangeland to **San Luis Obispo,** where any legit road trip includes a photo stop at the quirky **Madonna Inn.** Be sure to also climb the humungous dunes at **Guadalupe-Nipomo Dunes Preserve.**

In downtown San Luis Obispo, the **Mission San Luis Obispo de Tolosa** stands by a tree-shaded creek edged with shops and cafés. Highway 1 continues to **Morro Bay** and up the coast. About 4 mi north of Morro Bay, you'll reach **Cayucos,** a classic old California beach town with an 1875 pier, restaurants, taverns, and shops in historic buildings. The road continues through **Cambria** to solitary **Hearst San Simeon State Historical Monument**—the art-filled pleasure palace at **San Simeon.** Just four miles north of the castle, elephant seals grunt and cavort at the

Santa Monica

Big Sur

TOP 5 PLACES TO LINGER

- Point Dume State Preserve
- Santa Barbara
- Hearst San Simeon State Historical Monument
- Big Sur/Julia Pfeiffer Burns State Park
- Carmel

Piedras Blancas Elephant Seal Rookery, just off the side of the road.

SAN SIMEON TO CARMEL (approx. 92 mi) Heading north, you'll drive through **Big Sur,** a place of ancient forests and rugged shoreline stretching 90 mi from San Simeon to **Carmel.** Much of Big Sur lies within several state parks and the 165,000-acre **Ventana Wilderness,** itself part of the **Los Padres National Forest.** This famously scenic stretch of the coastal drive, which twists up and down bluffs above the ocean, can last hours. Take your time.

At **Julia Pfeiffer Burns State Park** one easy but rewarding hike leads to an iconic waterfall off a beach-front cliff. When you reach lovely **Carmel,** stroll around the picture-perfect town's mission, galleries, and shops.

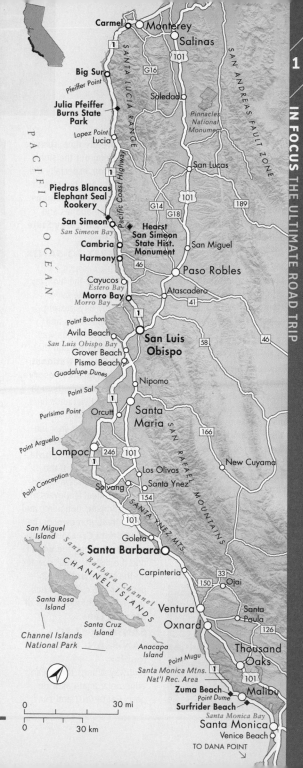

HIGHWAY 1: CARMEL TO SAN FRANCISCO

San Francisco

THE PLAN

Distance: approx. 123 mi

Time: 2-4 days

Good Overnight Options: Carmel, Monterey, Santa Cruz, Half Moon Bay, San Francisco

For more information on the sights and attractions along this portion of Highway 1, please see Monterey Bay.

CARMEL TO MONTEREY

(approx. 4 mi)

Between **Carmel** and **Monterey,** Highway 1 cuts across the base of the Monterey Peninsula. Pony up the toll and take a brief detour to follow famous **17-Mile Drive,** which traverses a surf-pounded landscape of cypress trees, sea lions, gargantuan estates, and the world famous **Pebble Beach Golf Links.** Take your time here as well, and be sure to allow lots of time for pulling off to enjoy the gorgeous views.

Monterey

If you have the time, spend a day checking out the sights in **Monterey,** especially the kelp forests and bat rays of the **Monterey Bay Aquarium** and the adobes and artifacts of **Monterey State Historic Park.**

MONTEREY TO SANTA CRUZ (approx. 42 mi)

From Monterey the highway rounds the gentle curve of Monterey Bay, passing through sand dunes and artichoke fields on its way to **Moss Landing** and the **Elkhorn Slough National Estuarine Marine Preserve.** Kayak near or walk through the protected wetlands here, or board a pontoon safari boat—don't forget your binoculars. The historic seaside villages of **Aptos, Capitola,** and **Soquel,** just off the highway near the bay's midpoint, are ideal stopovers for beachcombing, antiquing, and hiking through redwoods. In boho **Santa Cruz,** just 7 mi north, walk along the **wharf,** ride the historic roller coaster on the **boardwalk,** and perch on the cliffs to watch surfers peel through tubes at **Steamer Lane.**

SANTA CRUZ TO SAN FRANCISCO

(approx. 77 mi)

Highway 1 hugs the ocean's edge once again as it departs Santa Cruz and runs

Davenport cliffs, Devenport

northward past a string of secluded beaches and small towns. Stop and stretch your legs in the tiny, artsy town of **Davenport,** where you can wander through several galleries and enjoy sumptuous views from the bluffs. At **Año Nuevo State Reserve,** walk down to the dunes to view gargantuan elephant

FRIGID WATERS

If you're planning to jump in the ocean in Northern California, wear a wetsuit or prepare to shiver. Even in summer, the water temperatures warm up to just barely tolerable. The fog tends to burn off earlier in the day at relatively sheltered beaches near Monterey Bay's midpoint, near Aptos, Capitola and Santa Cruz. These beaches also tend to attract softer waves than those on the bay's outer edges.

Half Moon Bay

TOP 5 PLACES TO LINGER

- 17-Mile Drive
- Monterey
- Santa Cruz
- Año Nuevo State Reserve
- Half Moon Bay

seals lounging on shore, then break for a meal or snack in **Pescadero** or **Half Moon Bay.**

From Half Moon Bay to **Daly City,** the road includes a number of shoulderless twists and turns that demand slower speeds and nerves of steel. Signs of urban development soon appear: mansions holding fast to Pacific cliffs and then, as the road veers slightly inland to merge with Skyline Boulevard, boxlike houses sprawling across **Daly City** and **South San Francisco.**

HIGHWAY 1: SAN FRANCISCO TO FORT BRAGG

Mendocino Coast Botanical Garden

THE PLAN

Distance: 177 mi

Time: 2-4 days

Good Overnight Options: San Francisco, Olema, Bodega Bay, Gualala, Mendocino, Fort Bragg

SAN FRANCISCO

The official Highway 1 heads straight through **San Francisco** along 19th Avenue through **Golden Gate Park** and the **Presidio** toward the **Golden Gate Bridge.** For a more scenic tour, watch for signs announcing exits for 35 North/Skyline Boulevard, then Ocean Beach/The Great Highway (past Lake Merced). The Great Highway follows the coast along the western border of San Francisco; you'll cruise past entrances to the **San Francisco Zoo, Golden Gate Park,** and the **Cliff House.** Hike out to **Point Lobos** or **Land's End** for awesome vistas, then drive

through **Lincoln Park** and the **Palace of the Legion of Honor** and follow El Camino del Mar/Lincoln Boulevard all the way to the Golden Gate Bridge.

The best way to see San Francisco is on foot and public transportation. A **Union Square** stroll—complete with people-watching, window-shopping, and architecture-viewing—is a good first stop. In **Chinatown,** department stores give way to storefront temples, open-air markets, and delightful dim-sum shops. After lunch in one, catch a **Powell Street cable car** to the end of the line and get off to see the bay views and the antique arcade games at **Musée Mécanique** (the gem of otherwise mindless **Fisherman's Wharf**). For dinner and live music, try cosmopolitan **North Beach.**

SAN FRANCISCO TO OLEMA

(approx. 37 mi)

Leaving the city the next day, your drive across the Golden Gate Bridge and a stop at a **Marin Headlands** overlook will yield memorable views (if fog hasn't socked in the bay). So will a hike in **Point Reyes National Seashore,** farther up Highway 1 (now called Shoreline Highway).

Point Reyes National Seashore

On this wild swath of coast you'll likely be able to claim an unspoiled beach for yourself. You should expect company, however, around the lighthouse at the tip of Point Reyes because year-round views—and seasonal elephant seal- and whale-watching—draw crowds. If you have time, poke around tiny **Olema,** which has some excellent restaurants, and is home to the historic Olema Inn & Restaurant.

OLEMA TO MENDOCINO

(approx. 131 mi)

Passing only a few minuscule towns, this next stretch of Highway 1 showcases the northern coast in all its rugged glory. The reconstructed compound of eerily foreign buildings at **Fort Ross State Historic Park** recalls the era of Russian fur trading in California. Pull into **Gualala** for an espresso, a sandwich, and a little human contact

Golden Gate Bridge

Point Reyes National Seashore

TOP 5 PLACES TO LINGER

- San Francisco
- Marin Headlands
- Point Reyes National Seashore
- Fort Ross State Historic Park
- Mendocino

before rolling onward. After another 50 mi of tranquil state beaches and parks you'll return to civilization in **Mendocino.**

MENDOCINO TO FORT BRAGG

(approx. 9 mi)

Exploring Mendocino you may feel like you've fallen through a rabbit hole: the weather screams Northern California, but the 19th-century buildings—erected by homesick Yankee loggers—definitely say New England. Once you've browsed around the artsy shops, continue on to the **Mendocino Coast Botanical Gardens;** then travel back in time on the **Skunk Train,** which follows an old logging route from **Fort Bragg** deep into the redwood forest.

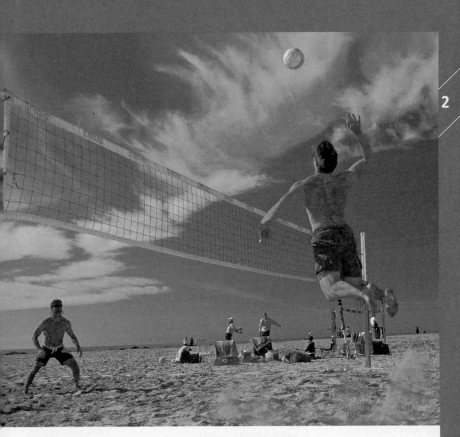

SAN DIEGO

WELCOME TO SAN DIEGO

TOP REASONS TO GO

★ **Beautiful beaches:** San Diego's shore shimmers with crystalline Pacific waters rolling up to some of the prettiest stretches of sand on the West Coast.

★ **Good eats:** Taking full advantage of the region's bountiful vegetables, fruits, herbs, and seafood, San Diego's chefs dazzle and delight diners with inventive California-colorful cuisine.

★ **History lessons:** The well-preserved and reconstructed historic sites in California's first European settlement help you imagine what the area was like when explorers first arrived.

★ **Stellar shopping:** Westfield Horton Plaza, the Gaslamp Quarter, Seaport Village, Coronado, Old Town, La Jolla . . . no matter where you go in San Diego, you'll find great places to do a little browsing.

★ **Urban oasis:** Balboa Park's 1,200 acres contain world-class museums and the San Diego Zoo, but also well-groomed lawns and gardens and wild, undeveloped canyons.

1 Downtown. San Diego's Downtown area is delightfully urban and accessible, filled with walkable A-list attractions like the Gaslamp Quarter, Horton Plaza, and the waterfront.

2 Balboa Park. San Diego's cultural heart is where you'll find most of the city's museums and its world-famous zoo.

3 Old Town and Uptown. California's first permanent European settlement is now preserved as a state historic park in Old Town. Uptown is composed of several smaller neighborhoods that showcase a unique blend of historical charm and modern urban community.

4 Mission Bay, Beaches, and SeaWorld. Home to 27 miles of shoreline, this 4,600 acre aquatic park is San Diego's monument to sports and fitness. SeaWorld, one of the city's most popular attractions, lies south of the bay.

5 La Jolla. This luxe, blufftop enclave fittingly means "the jewel" in Spanish. Come here for fantastic upscale shopping and unspoiled stretches of the coast.

6 Point Loma and Coronado. Home to the Hotel Del, Coronado's island-like isthmus is a favorite celebrity haunt. Visit the site of the first European landfall on Point Loma.

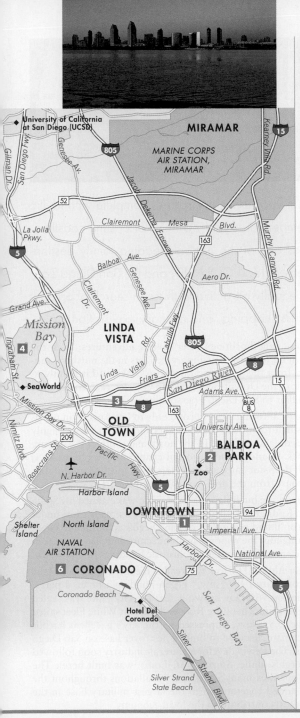

MIRAMAR

MARINE CORPS
AIR STATION,
MIRAMAR

University of California
at San Diego (UCSD)

805

52

Clairemont   Mesa   Blvd.

163

La Jolla
Pkwy.

5

Balboa   Ave.

Aero Dr.

Grand Ave.

LINDA
VISTA

805

Mission
Bay

4

Linda   Vista   Rd.

8

Friars

15

SeaWorld

San Diego River

Adams Ave.

Mission Bay Dr.

3   8

163

BUS
8

OLD
TOWN

University Ave.

209

Pacific   Hwy.

BALBOA
PARK

2

Zoo

N. Harbor Dr.

Harbor Island

5

DOWNTOWN

94

1

Shelter
Island

North Island

Imperial Ave.

NAVAL
AIR STATION

National Ave.

6   CORONADO

75

5

Coronado Beach

Hotel Del
Coronado

San Diego Bay

Silver Strand
State Beach

2

GETTING
ORIENTED

Exploring San Diego may
be an endless adventure,
but there are limitations,
especially if you don't
have a car. San Diego is
more a chain of separate
communities than a cohe-
sive city, and many of the
major attractions are miles
apart. Walking is good for
getting an up-close look
at neighborhoods like the
Gaslamp Quarter, but true
Southern Californians use
the freeways that crisscross
the county. Interstate 5
runs a direct north–south
route through the coastal
communities from Orange
County in the north to the
Mexican border. Interstates
805 and 15 do much the
same inland. Interstate 8 is
the main east–west route.
Routes 163, 52, and 94
serve as connectors.

San Diego is a vacationer's paradise, complete with idyllic year-round temperatures and 70 miles of pristine coastline. Recognized as one of the nation's leading family destinations, with SeaWorld, LEGOLAND, and the San Diego Zoo, San Diego is equally attractive to those in search of art, culture, world-class shopping, and culinary exploration.

San Diego's many neighborhoods offer diverse adventures: from the tony boutiques in La Jolla to the culinary delights in the northern suburb of Del Mar; from the authentic European charm of Little Italy to the nouveau-chic of the Downtown Gaslamp Quarter, each community adds flavor and flair to San Diego's personality.

San Diego is a big California city—second only to Los Angeles in population—with a small-town feel. It also covers a lot of territory, roughly 400 square miles of land and sea. To the north and south of the city are its famed beaches. Inland, a succession of chaparral-covered mesas is punctuated with deep-cut canyons that step up to forested mountains, separating the coast from the arid Anza-Borrego Desert.

The San Diego area, the birthplace of California, was claimed for Spain by explorer Juan Rodríguez Cabrillo in 1542 and eventually came under Mexican rule. You'll find reminders of San Diego's Spanish and Mexican heritage throughout the region—in architecture and place-names, in distinctive Mexican cuisine, and in the historic buildings of Old Town.

In 1867 developer Alonzo Horton, who called the town's bay front "the prettiest place for a city I ever saw," began building a hotel, a plaza, and prefab homes on 960 Downtown acres. The city's fate was sealed in 1908, when President Theodore Roosevelt's Great White Fleet sailed into the bay. The U.S. Navy, impressed by the city's excellent harbor and temperate climate, decided to build a destroyer base on San Diego Bay in the 1920s. The newly developed aircraft industry soon followed (Charles Lindbergh's plane, *Spirit of St. Louis,* was built here). The military, which operates many bases and installations throughout the county (which, added together, form the largest military base in the world), continues to contribute to the local economy.

PLANNING

Updated by
Bobbi Zane

2

WHEN TO GO

San Diego's weather is so ideal that most locals shrug off the high cost of living and relatively lower wages as a "sunshine tax." Along the coast, average temperatures range from the mid-60s to the high 70s, with clear skies and low humidity. Annual rainfall is minimal, less than 10 inches per year.

The peak season for sun seekers is July through October. In July and August, the mercury spikes and everyone spills outside. From mid-December to mid-March, whale-watchers can glimpse migrating gray whales frolicking in the Pacific. In spring and early summer, a marine layer hugs the coastline for much or all of the day (locals call it "June Gloom"), which can be dreary and disappointing for those who were expecting to bask in Southern California sunshine.

GETTING HERE AND AROUND

AIR TRAVEL

The major airport is San Diego International Airport (SAN), called Lindbergh Field locally. Major airlines depart and arrive at Terminal 1 and Terminal 2; commuter flights identified on your ticket with a 3000-sequence flight number depart from a third commuter terminal. A red shuttle bus provides free transportation between terminals.

Airport San Diego International Airport ⊠ *3225 N. Harbor Dr., off I-5* ☎ *619/400–2400* ⊕ *www.san.org.*

Airport Transfers Cloud 9 Shuttle/SuperShuttle ⊠ *123 Caminio de la Riena* ☎ *800/974–8885* ⊕ *www.cloud9shuttle.com.* **San Diego Transit** ☎ *619/233–3004* ⊕ *transit.511sd.com.*

BUS AND TROLLEY TRAVEL

Under the umbrella of the Metropolitan Transit System, there are two major transit agencies in the area: San Diego Transit and North County Transit District (NCTD). The bright-red trolleys of the San Diego Trolley light-rail system operate on three lines that serve Downtown San Diego, Mission Valley, Old Town, South Bay, the U.S. border, and East County. The trolley system connects with San Diego Transit bus routes—connections are posted at each trolley station.

San Diego Transit bus fares range from $2.25 to $5; North County Transit District bus fares are $1.75. You must have exact change in coins and/or bills. Pay upon boarding. Transfers are not included; the $5 day pass is the best option for most bus travel and can be purchased on board.

San Diego Trolley tickets cost $2.50 and are good for two hours, but for one-way travel only. Round-trip tickets are double the one-way fare.

Bus and Trolley Information North County Transit District ☎ *800/266–6883* ⊕ *www.gonctd.com.* **San Diego Transit** ☎ *619/233–3004, 800/234–5005* ⊕ *transit.511sd.com.* **Transit Store** ⊠ *102 Broadway* ☎ *619/234–1060* ⊕ *www.sdmts.com.*

CAR TRAVEL

A car is necessary for getting around greater San Diego on the sprawling freeway system and for visiting the North County beaches, mountains, and Anza Borrego Desert. Driving around San Diego County is pretty simple: most major attractions are within a few miles of the Pacific Ocean. Interstate 5, which stretches from Canada to the Mexican border, bisects San Diego. Interstate 8 provides access from Yuma, Arizona, and points east. Drivers coming from the Los Angeles area, Nevada, and the mountain regions beyond can reach San Diego on I–15. During rush hour there are jams on I–5 and on I–15 between I–805 and Escondido.

There are border inspection stations along major highways in San Diego County. Travel with your driver's license, and passport if you're an international traveler, in case you're asked to pull into one.

TAXI TRAVEL

Fares vary among companies. If you are heading to the airport from a hotel, ask about the flat rate, which varies according to destination; otherwise you'll be charged by the mile (which works out to $15 or so from any Downtown location). Taxi stands are at shopping centers and hotels; otherwise you must call and reserve a cab. The companies listed *below* don't serve all areas of San Diego County. If you're going somewhere other than Downtown, ask if the company serves that area.

Taxi Companies Orange Cab ☎ *619/291-3333* ⊕ *www.orangecabsandiego. com.* **Silver Cabs** ☎ *619/280-5555* ⊕ *www.sandiegosilvercab.com.* **Yellow Cab** ☎ *619/444-4444* ⊕ *www.driveu.com.*

TRAIN TRAVEL

Amtrak serves Downtown San Diego's Santa Fe Depot with daily trains to and from Los Angeles, Santa Barbara, and San Luis Obispo. Amtrak trains stop in San Diego North County at Solana Beach and Oceanside. Coaster commuter trains, which run between Oceanside and San Diego Monday–Saturday, stop at the same stations as Amtrak as well as others. The frequency is about every half hour during the weekday rush hour, with four trains on Saturday. One-way fares are $4 to $5.50, depending on the distance traveled. The Sprinter runs between Oceanside and Escondido, with many stops along the way.

Metrolink operates high-speed rail service between the Oceanside Transit Center and Union Station in Los Angeles.

Information Amtrak ☎ *800/872-7245* ⊕ *www.amtrak.com.* **Coaster** ☎ *760/966-6683* ⊕ *transit.511sd.com.* **Metrolink** ☎ *800/371-5465* ⊕ *www.metrolinktrains.com.*

TOURS

Bike Tours Bike Revolution ☎ *619/564-4843* ⊕ *www.thebikerevolution.com.* **Secret San Diego** ⊠ *611 K St., #B224* ☎ *619/917-6037* ⊕ *www.wheretours.com.*

Boat Tours Flagship Cruises and Events ☎ *855/955-9558* ⊕ *www.flagshipsd.com.* **H&M Landing** ⊠ *2803 Emerson St.* ☎ *619/222-1144* ⊕ *www.hmlanding.com.* **Hornblower Cruises & Events** ⊠ *1066. N. Harbor Dr.* ☎ *619/234-8687, 800/668-4322* ⊕ *www.hornblower.com.* **San Diego Seal Tours** ⊕ *www.sealtours.com.* **Seaforth Boat Rentals** ☎ *888/834-2628* ⊕ *www.seaforthboatrental.com.*

Bus and Trolley Tours DayTripper ☎ *619/299–5777, 800/679–8747*
⊕ *www.daytripper.com.* **Five Star Tours** ✉ *1050 Kettner Blvd.* ☎ *619/232–
5040* ⊕ *www.fivestartours.com.* **Old Town Trolley Tours** ✉ *2115 Kurtz St.*
☎ *619/298–8687* ⊕ *www.trolleytours.com/san-diego.* **San Diego Scenic Tours**
✉ *2255 Garnet Ave., #3* ☎ *858/273–8687* ⊕ *www.sandiegoscenictours.com.*

Walking Tours Coronado Walking Tours ✉ *1630 Glorietta Blvd.* ☎ *619/435–
5993* ⊕ *coronadowalkingtour.com.* **Gaslamp Quarter Historical Foundation**
✉ *410 Island Ave.* ☎ *619/233–4692* ⊕ *www.gaslampquarter.org.* **Offshoot
Tours** ☎ *619/239–0512* ⊕ *www.balboapark.org.* **Urban Safaris** ☎ *619/944–
9255* ⊕ *www.walkingtoursofsandiego.com.*

VISITOR INFORMATION

For general information and brochures before you go, contact the San
Diego Tourism Authority, which publishes the helpful *San Diego Visitors Planning Guide.* When you arrive, stop by one of the local visitor
centers for general information.

Citywide Contacts San Diego Convention & Visitors Bureau
☎ *619/232-3101* ⊕ *www.sandiego.org.* **San Diego Tourism Authority
International Visitor Information Center** ✉ *1140 N. Harbor Dr., Downtown*
☎ *619/243-1308* ⊕ *www.sandiego.org.*

EXPLORING SAN DIEGO

DOWNTOWN

Updated by
Claire Deeks
van der Lee

Nearly written off in the 1970s, today Downtown San Diego is a tes-
tament to conservation and urban renewal. Once derelict Victorian
storefronts now house the hottest restaurants, and the *Star of India,*
the world's oldest active sailing ship, almost lost to scrap, floats regally
along the Embarcadero. Like many modern U.S. cities, Downtown San
Diego's story is as much about its rebirth as its history. Although many
consider Downtown to be the 16½-block Gaslamp Quarter, it's actually
comprised of eight neighborhoods, including East Village, Little Italy,
and Embarcadero.

GASLAMP QUARTER

Considered the liveliest of the Downtown neighborhoods, the Gaslamp
Quarter's 4th and 5th avenues are peppered with trendy nightclubs,
swanky lounge bars, chic restaurants, and boisterous sports pubs. The
Gaslamp has the largest collection of commercial Victorian-style buildings in the country. Despite this, when the move for Downtown redevelopment gained momentum in the 1970s, there was talk of bulldozing
them and starting from scratch. In response, concerned history buffs,
developers, architects, and artists formed the Gaslamp Quarter Council to clean up and preserve the quarter. The majority of the quarter's
landmark buildings are on 4th and 5th avenues, between Island Avenue
and Broadway.

Gaslamp Museum at the William Heath Davis House. The oldest wooden house in San Diego houses the Gaslamp Quarter Historical Foundation, the district's curator. Before developer Alonzo Horton came to town, Davis, a prominent San Franciscan, had made an unsuccessful attempt to develop the waterfront area. In 1850 he had this prefab saltbox-style house, built in Maine, shipped around Cape Horn and assembled in San Diego (it originally stood at State and Market streets). Regularly scheduled two-hour walking tours of the historic district leave from the house on Saturday at 11 and cost $15. If you can't time your visit with the weekly tour, a self-guided tour map is available for purchase for $2. ✉ *410 Island Ave., at 4th Ave.* ☏ *619/233–4692* ⊕ *www. gaslampquarter.org* 🏷 *$5* ⊘ *Tues.–Sat. 10–5, Sun. noon–4.*

Westfield Horton Plaza. This Downtown shopping, dining, and entertainment mecca fronts Broadway and G Street from 1st to 4th avenues and covers more than six city blocks. Designed by Jon Jerde and completed in 1985, Westfield Horton Plaza is a collage of colorful tile work, banners waving in the air, and modern sculptures. The complex rises in uneven, staggered levels to five floors; great views of Downtown from the harbor to Balboa Park and beyond can be had here.

Macy's and Nordstrom department stores anchor the plaza housing more than 100 clothing, sporting-goods, jewelry, book, and gift shops in all. Other attractions include the country's largest Sam Goody music store, a movie complex, restaurants, and the respected San Diego Repertory Theatre below ground level. In 2008 the **Balboa Theater**, contiguous with the shopping center, reopened its doors after a $26.5 million renovation. The historic 1920s theater seats 1,400 and offers live arts and cultural performances throughout the week.

The mall has a multilevel parking garage; even so, lines to find a space can be long. ■TIP➔ **Entering the parking structure on G Street rather than 4th Avenue generally means less traffic and more parking space.** Parking validation is complimentary whether you spend a bundle or just window-shop. Validation machines throughout the center allow for three hours' free parking; after that it's $8 per hour (or $2 per 15-minute increment). If you use this notoriously confusing fruit-and-vegetable–themed garage, be sure to remember at which produce level you've left your car. If you're staying Downtown, the Old Town Trolley Tour will drop you directly in front of Westfield Horton Plaza. ✉ *324 Horton Plaza, Gaslamp Quarter* ☏ *619/238–1596* ⊕ *www.westfield. com/hortonplaza* ⊘ *Weekdays 10–9, Sat. 10–8, Sun. 11–6.*

EMBARCADERO

The Embarcadero cuts a scenic swath along the harbor front and connects today's Downtown San Diego to its maritime routes. The bustle of Embarcadero comes less these days from the activities of fishing folk than from the throngs of tourists, but this waterfront walkway, stretching from the Convention Center to the Maritime Museum, remains the nautical soul of the city. There are several seafood restaurants here, as well as sea vessels of every variety—cruise ships, ferries, tour boats, and Navy destroyers.

Be sure to enjoy a walk along San Diego's lovely waterfront sometime during your visit.

Maritime Museum. From sailing ships to submarines, the Maritime Museum is a must for anyone with an interest in nautical history. This collection of restored and replica ships affords a fascinating glimpse of San Diego during its heyday as a commercial seaport.

The jewel of the collection, the *Star of India*, is often considered a symbol of the city. An iron windjammer built in 1863, the *Star of India* made 21 trips around the world in the late 1800s, when it traveled the East Indian trade route, shuttled immigrants from England to New Zealand, and served the Alaskan salmon trade. Saved from the scrap yard and painstakingly restored, the *Star of India* is the oldest active iron sailing ship in the world.

The popular HMS *Surprise,* purchased in 2004, is a replica of an 18th-century British Royal Navy frigate and was used in the Academy Award–winning *Master and Commander: The Far Side of the World.*

The museum's headquarters are on the *Berkeley,* an 1898 steam-driven ferryboat, which served the Southern Pacific Railroad in San Francisco until 1958. Its ornate detailing carefully restored, the main deck serves as a floating museum, with permanent exhibits on West Coast maritime history and complementary rotating exhibits.

Two submarines are featured at the museum: a *Soviet B-39* "Foxtrot" class submarine and the USS *Dolphin* research submarine. Take a peek at the harbor from a periscope, get up close with the engine control room, and wonder at the tight living quarters onboard.

At Spanish Landing Park, about 2 miles to the west, the museum is constructing a full-scale working replica of the *San Salvador,* the first

European ship to land on the western coast of the future United States. To view this work-in-progress (daily 10–3:30), obtain directions at the Berkeley. Once complete, the San Salvador will be on display at the museum's main location. ⊠ *1492 N. Harbor Dr., Embarcadero* 🕾 *619/234–9153* ⊕ *www.sdmaritime.org* 🖃 *$15 includes entry to all ships except Californian, $3 more for Pilot Boat Bay Cruise* ⊙ *Daily 9–8.*

Fodor's Choice
★

Museum of Contemporary Art San Diego (MCASD). At the Downtown branch of the city's contemporary art museum (the original is in La Jolla), explore the works of international and regional artists in a modern, urban space. The Jacobs Building—formerly the baggage building at the historic Santa Fe Depot—features large gallery spaces, high ceilings, and natural lighting, giving artists the flexibility to create large-scale installations. MCASD's collection includes many pop art, minimalist, and conceptual works from the 1950s to the present. The museum showcases both established and emerging artists in temporary exhibitions, and has permanent, site-specific commissions by Jenny Holzer and Richard Serra. ■TIP➜ **Admission, good for seven days, includes the Downtown and La Jolla locations.** ⊠ *1100 and 1001 Kettner Blvd., Downtown* 🕾 *858/454–3541* ⊕ *www.mcasd.org* 🖃 *$10; free 3rd Thurs. of the month 5–7* ⊙ *Thurs.–Tues., 11–5; 3rd Thurs. until 7* ⊙ *Closed Wed.*

FAMILY
Fodor's Choice
★

The New Children's Museum (NCM). Opened in May 2008, NCM blends contemporary art with unstructured play to create an environment that appeals to children as well as adults. The 50,000-square-foot structure was constructed from recycled building materials, operates on solar energy, and is convection-cooled by an elevator shaft. It also features a nutritious and eco-conscious café. Interactive exhibits include designated areas for toddlers and teens, as well as plenty of activities for the entire family. Several art workshops are offered each day, as well as hands-on studios where visitors are encouraged to create their own art. The studio projects change frequently and the entire museum changes exhibits every 18 to 24 months, so there is always something new to explore. The adjoining 1-acre park and playground is conveniently located across from the convention center trolley stop. ⊠ *200 W. Island Ave., Embarcadero* 🕾 *619/233–8792* ⊕ *www.thinkplaycreate. org* 🖃 *$10; 2nd Sun. each month free 10–4* ⊙ *Mon., Tues., Fri., Sat. 10–4, Thurs. 10–6, Sun. noon–4.* ⊙ *Closed Wed. Sept.–June.*

FAMILY
Seaport Village. You'll find some of the best views of the harbor at Seaport Village, three bustling shopping plazas designed to reflect the New England clapboard and Spanish Mission architectural styles of early California. On a prime stretch of waterfront the dining, shopping and entertainment complex connects the harbor with hotel towers and the convention center. Specialty shops offer everything from a kite store and swing emporium to a shop devoted to hot sauces. You can dine at snack bars and restaurants, many with harbor views. Seaport Village's shops are open daily 10 to 9; a few eateries open early for breakfast, and venues many have extended nighttime hours, especially in summer. Restaurant prices here are high and the food is only average, so your best bet is to go elsewhere for a meal.

Live music can be heard daily from noon to 4 at the main food court. Additional free concerts take place every Sunday from 1 to 4 at the East Plaza Gazebo. If you happen to visit San Diego in late November or early December, you might be lucky enough to catch Surfing Santa's Arrival and even have your picture taken with Santa on his wave. In April the Seaport Buskers Fest presents an array of costumed street performers. The **Seaport Village Carousel** (rides $2) has 54 animals, hand-carved and hand-painted by Charles Looff in 1895. ⊠ *849 W. Harbor Dr., Downtown* ☎ *619/235–4014 office and events hotline* ⊕ *www.seaportvillage.com.*

Fodor's Choice

★

USS Midway Museum. After 47 years of worldwide service, the retired USS *Midway* began a new tour of duty on the south side of the Navy pier in 2004. Launched in 1945, the 1,001-foot-long ship was the largest in the world for the first 10 years of its existence. The most visible landmark on the north Embarcadero, it now serves as a floating interactive museum—an appropriate addition to the town that is home to one-third of the Pacific fleet and the birthplace of naval aviation. A free audio tour guides you through the massive ship while offering insight from former sailors. As you clamber through passageways and up and down ladder wells, you'll get a feel for how the *Midway*'s 4,500 crew members lived and worked on this "city at sea."

Though the entire tour is impressive, you'll really be wowed when you step out onto the 4-acre flight deck—not only the best place to get an idea of the ship's scale, but also one of the most interesting vantage points for bay and city skyline views. An F-14 Tomcat jet fighter is just one of many vintage aircraft on display. Free guided tours of the bridge and primary flight control, known as "the Island," depart every 10 minutes from the flight deck. Many of the docents stationed throughout the ship served in the Navy, some even on the *Midway*, and they are eager to answer questions or share stories. The museum also offers multiple flight simulators for an additional fee, climb-aboard cockpits, and interactive exhibits focusing on naval aviation. There are a gift shop and a café with pleasant outdoor seating. This is a wildly popular stop, with most visits lasting several hours. ⚠ **Despite efforts to provide accessibility throughout the ship, some areas can only be reached via fairly steep steps; a video tour of these areas is available on the hangar deck.** ⊠ *910 N. Harbor Dr., Embarcadero* ☎ *619/544–9600* ⊕ *www.midway.org* ⊠ *$18* ⊙ *Mid-Aug.–June, daily 10–5; July–mid-Aug., daily 9–5; last admission 4 pm.*

EAST VILLAGE

The most ambitious of the Downtown projects is East Village, not far from the Gaslamp Quarter, and encompassing 130 blocks between the railroad tracks up to J Street, and from 6th Avenue east to around 10th Street. Sparking the rebirth of this former warehouse district was the 2004 construction of the San Diego Padres' baseball stadium, PETCO Park. As the city's largest Downtown neighborhood, East Village is continually broadening its boundaries with its urban design of redbrick cafés, spacious galleries, rooftop bars, sleek hotels, and warehouse restaurants.

LITTLE ITALY

Unlike many tourist-driven communities, the charming neighborhood of Little Italy is authentic to its roots, from the Italian-speaking residents to the imported delicacies. The main thoroughfare—from India Street to Kettner Boulevard—is filled with lively cafés, gelato shops, bakeries, and restaurants. Art lovers can browse gallery showrooms, while shoppers adore the Fir Street cottages. Home to many in San Diego's design community, Little Italy exudes a sense of urban cool.

BALBOA PARK AND SAN DIEGO ZOO

Overlooking Downtown and the Pacific Ocean, 1,200-acre Balboa Park is the cultural heart of San Diego. Ranked as one of the world's best parks by the Project for Public Spaces, it's also where you can find most of the city's museums, art galleries, the Tony Award–winning Old Globe Theatre, and the world-famous San Diego Zoo. Often referred to as the "Smithsonian of the West" for its concentration of museums, Balboa Park is also a series of botanical gardens, performance spaces, and outdoor playrooms endeared in the hearts of residents and visitors alike.

Thanks to the "Mother of Balboa Park," Kate Sessions, who suggested hiring a landscape architect in 1889, wild and cultivated gardens are an integral part of the park, featuring 350 species of trees. What Balboa Park would have looked like had she left it alone can be seen at Florida Canyon (between the main park and Morley Field, along Park Boulevard)—an arid landscape of sagebrush, cactus, and a few small trees.

In addition, the captivating architecture of Balboa's buildings, fountains, and courtyards gives the park an enchanted feel. Historic buildings dating from San Diego's 1915 Panama–California International Exposition are strung along the park's main east–west thoroughfare, El Prado. The parkland across the Cabrillo Bridge, at the west end of El Prado, is set aside for picnics and athletics. East of Plaza de Panama, El Prado becomes a pedestrian mall and ends at a footbridge that crosses over Park Boulevard, to rose and desert gardens.

TOP ATTRACTIONS

Bea Evenson Fountain. A favorite of barefoot children, this fountain shoots cool jets of water upwards of 50 feet. Built in 1972 between the Fleet Center and Natural History Museum, the fountain offers plenty of room to sit and watch the crowds go by. ⊠ *East end of El Prado, Balboa Park* ⊕ *www.balboapark.org.*

Fodor's Choice
★

Botanical Building. The graceful redwood-lath structure, built for the 1915 Panama–California International Exposition, now houses more than 2,000 types of tropical and subtropical plants plus changing seasonal flower displays. Ceiling-high tree ferns shade fragile orchids and feathery bamboo. There are benches beside miniature waterfalls for resting in the shade. The rectangular pond outside, filled with lotuses and water lilies that bloom in spring and fall, is popular with photographers. ⊠ *1549 El Prado, Balboa Park* ☎ *619/239–0512* ⊕ *www. balboapark.org* ⊠ *Free* ☉ *Fri.–Wed. 10–4* ☉ *Closed Thurs.*

2

Cabrillo Bridge. The park's official (and pedestrian-friendly) gateway soars 120 feet above a canyon floor. Crossing the 1,500-foot bridge into the park provides awe-inspiring views of the California Tower and El Prado beyond. This is a great spot for a photo capturing a classic image of the park. ⊠ *On El Prado, at the 6th Ave. park entrance, Balboa Park* ⊕ *www.balboapark.org.*

FAMILY **Carousel.** Suspended an arm's length away on this antique merry-go-round is the brass ring that could earn you an extra free ride (it's one of the few carousels in the world that continue this bonus tradition). Hand-carved in 1910, the carousel features colorful murals, big-band music, and bobbing animals including zebras, giraffes, and dragons; real horsehair was used for the tails. ⊠ *1889 Zoo Pl., behind zoo parking lot, Balboa Park* ☎ *619/239–0512* ☞ *$2.50* ☉ *Mid-June–Labor Day, 11–5:30 daily; Labor Day–Mid-June, 11–5:30 weekends and school holidays.*

Fodor'sChoice **Inez Grant Parker Memorial Rose Garden and Desert Garden.** These neighboring gardens sit just across the Park Boulevard pedestrian bridge and offer gorgeous views over Florida Canyon. The formal rose garden contains 2,500 roses representing nearly 200 varieties; peak bloom is usually in April and May. The adjacent Desert Garden provides a striking contrast, with 2.5 acres of succulents and desert plants seeming to blend into the landscape of the canyon below. ⊠ *2525 Park Blvd., Balboa Park* ⊕ *www.balboapark.org.*

Japanese Friendship Garden. A koi pond with a cascading waterfall, a tea pavilion, and a large activity center are highlights of the park's authentic Japanese garden, designed to inspire contemplation and evoke tranquility. You can wander the various peaceful paths and meditate in the traditional stone and Zen garden. The development of an additional 9 acres is well underway and will include a traditional tea house and a cherry orchard. ⊠ *2215 Pan American Rd., Balboa Park* ☎ *619/232–2721* ⊕ *www.niwa.org* ☞ *$4* ☉ *Summer weekdays 10–5, weekends 10–4; rest of yr Tues.–Sun. 10–4.*

Mingei International Museum. All ages can enjoy the Mingei's colorful and creative exhibits of folk art, featuring toys, pottery, textiles, costumes, jewelry, and curios from around the globe. Traveling and permanent exhibits in the high-ceilinged, light-filled museum include everything from antique American carousel horses to the latest in Japanese ceramics. The name "Mingei" comes from the Japanese words *min,* meaning "all people," and *gei,* meaning "art." Thus the museum's name describes what you'll find under its roof: "art of all people." The gift shop carries artwork from cultures around the world, from Zulu baskets to Turkish ceramics to Mexican objects, plus special items related to major exhibitions. ⊠ *House of Charm, 1439 El Prado, Balboa Park* ☎ *619/239–0003* ⊕ *www.mingei.org* ☞ *$8* ☉ *Tues.–Sun. 10–4.*

Palm Canyon. Heading down into this lush canyon near the House of Charm provides an instant escape into another landscape. More than 450 palms are planted in two acres, with a small hiking trail emerging by the Balboa Park Club. ⊠ *South of the House of Charm, Balboa Park.*

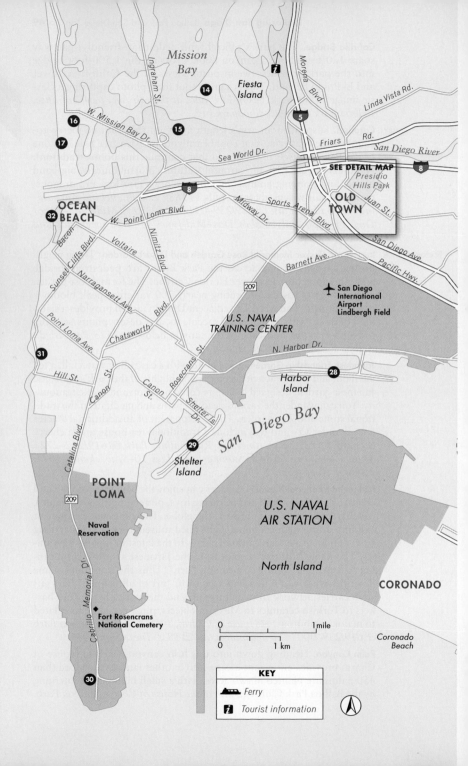

Mission
Bay

Fiesta
Island

14

16

W. Mission Bay Dr.

15

17

Ingraham St.

Moreña Blvd.

Linda Vista Rd.

5

Friars   Rd.

San Diego River

Sea World Dr.

8

SEE DETAIL MAP

Presidio
Hills Park

OLD
TOWN

8

Juan St.

**OCEAN
BEACH**

32

W. Point Loma Blvd.

Midway Dr.

Sports Arena   Blvd.

San Diego Ave.

Bacon

Voltaire

Nimitz Blvd.

Barnett Ave.

Pacific Hwy.

Sunset Cliffs Blvd.

Narragansett Ave.

Blvd.

209

✈ San Diego
International
Airport
Lindbergh Field

Point Loma Ave.

Chatsworth

**U.S. NAVAL
TRAINING CENTER**

31

Rosecrans St.

N. Harbor Dr.

Hill St.

Canon

St.

Canon
St.

Harbor
Island

28

Shelter Isl.
Dr.

San Diego Bay

29

Shelter
Island

Catalina Blvd.

**POINT
LOMA**

209

**U.S. NAVAL
AIR STATION**

Naval
Reservation

Cabrillo   Memorial   Dr.

North Island

CORONADO

◆ Fort Rosencrans
National Cemetery

0   1mile

0   1 km

Coronado
Beach

30

KEY	
🚢	*Ferry*
🛈	*Tourist information*

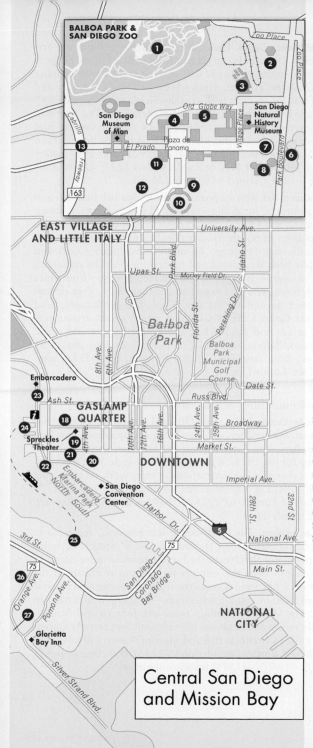

FAMILY **Reuben H. Fleet Science Center.** The center's interactive exhibits are artfully educational. Older kids can get hands-on with inventive projects in the Tinkering Studio, while Kid City entertains the five-and-under set. The IMAX Dome Theater, which screens exhilarating nature and science films, was the world's first, as is the Fleet's new "NanoSeam" (seamless) dome ceiling that doubles as a planetarium. The Nierman Challenger Learning Center—a realistic mock mission-control and futuristic space station—is a big hit. ⊠ *1875 El Prado, Balboa Park* ☏ *619/238–1233* ⊕ *www.rhfleet.org* ⬚ *Gallery exhibits $12, gallery exhibits and 1 IMAX film $16, or 2 IMAX films $22* ⊙ *Opens daily at 10; closing hrs vary from 5 to 9, so call ahead.*

San Diego Museum of Art. Known primarily for its Spanish baroque and Renaissance paintings, including works by El Greco, Goya, Rubens, and van Ruisdael, San Diego's most comprehensive art museum also has strong holdings of South Asian art, Indian miniatures, and contemporary California paintings. An outdoor Sculpture Court and Garden exhibits both traditional and modern pieces. The museum's exhibits tend to have broad appeal, and if traveling shows from other cities come to town, you can expect to see them here. Free docent tours are offered throughout the day. If you become hungry, head to the **Sculpture Court Café by Giuseppe,** which serves artisan pizzas, gourmet salads and sandwiches, and grilled burgers and steak. ⊠ *1450 El Prado, Balboa Park* ☏ *619/232–7931* ⊕ *www.sdmart.org* ⬚ *$12* ⊙ *Mon., Tues., and Thurs.–Sat. 10–5, Sun. noon–5; Fri. until 9 Memorial Day–Labor Day.*

FAMILY **San Diego Zoo.**
Fodor'sChoice ⇨ *See the highlighted listing in this chapter.*
★

Spanish Village Art Center. More than 250 local artists, including glassblowers, enamel workers, woodcarvers, sculptors, painters, jewelers, and photographers rent space in these red tile–roof studio-galleries that were set up for the 1935–36 exposition in the style of an old Spanish village, and they give demonstrations of their work on a rotating basis. Spanish Village is a great source for memorable gifts. ⊠ *1770 Village Pl., Balboa Park* ☏ *619/233–9050* ⊕ *www.spanishvillageart. com* ⬚ *Free* ⊙ *Daily 11–4.*

Spreckels Organ Pavilion. The 2,400-bench-seat pavilion, dedicated in 1915 by sugar magnates John D. and Adolph B. Spreckels, holds the 4,518-pipe Spreckels Organ, the largest outdoor pipe organ in the world. You can hear this impressive instrument at one of the year-round, free, 2 pm Sunday concerts, regularly performed by civic organist Carol Williams and guest artists—a highlight of a visit to Balboa Park. On Monday evenings from late June to mid-August, internationally renowned organists play evening concerts. At Christmastime the park's Christmas tree and life-size Nativity display turn the pavilion into a seasonal wonderland. ⊠ *2211 Pan American Rd., Balboa Park* ☏ *619/702–8138* ⊕ *www.sosorgan.org.*

Continued on page 60

Polar bear, San Diego Zoo

LIONS AND TIGERS AND PANDAS:
The World-Famous San Diego Zoo

From cuddly pandas and diving polar bears to 6-ton elephants and swinging great apes, San Diego's most famous attraction has it all. Nearly 4,000 animals representing 800 species roam the 100-acre zoo in expertly crafted habitats that replicate the animals' natural environments. While the pandas get top billing, there are plenty of other cool creatures to see here, from teeny-tiny mantella frogs to two-story-tall giraffes. But it's not all just fun and games. Known for its exemplary conservation programs, the zoo educates visitors on how to go green and explains its efforts to protect endangered species.

SAN DIEGO ZOO TOP ATTRACTIONS

Underwater viewing area at the Hippo Trail

❶ Children's Zoo (Discovery Outpost). Goats and sheep beg to be petted, and there is a viewer-friendly nursery where you may see baby animals bottle-feed and sleep peacefully in large cribs.

❷ Monkey Trails and Forest Tales (Lost Forest). Follow an elevated trail at treetop level and trek through the forest floor observing African mandrill monkeys, Asia's clouded leopard, the rare pygmy hippopotamus, and Visayan warty pigs.

❸ Orangutan and Siamang Exhibit (Lost Forest). Orangutans and siamangs climb and swing in this lush, tropical environment lined with 110-foot-long and 12-foot-high viewing windows.

Polar Bear Plunge

10

Skyfari West

PARK WAY

Express Bus Stop

PARK WAY

POLAR RIM

Arctic Trader

Express Bus Stop

Elephant Odyssey Entrance

Ituri Forest Outpost

PANDA CANYON

9

Giant Panda Research Station

Hippo Trail

LOST FOREST

Albert's Restaurant

PARK WAY

Panda Shop

6

Treehouse Trader

Treetops Room

Treehouse Cafe

Hua Mei Cafe

Hippo Trail

7

2

Monkey Trail

Gorilla Exhibit

Scripps Aviary

Parker Aviary

Owens Aviary

Hippo Trail

4

Greenzoo Coffee Co.

CENTER STREET

Tiger Trail

5

Monkey Trail

Hippo Trail

Monkey Trail

EASY STREET

Orangutan Trail

Feda Canyon

Tiger Trail

Wegeforth Bowl

First Aid & Nursing Station

Jungle Java

3

Orangutan and Siamang Exhibit

Fern Canyon Trail

DISCOVERY OUTPOST

Reptile House

Safari Kitchen

Bus Tour Loading

Clark Theater

Poppy's Patio

Zoofari Photos

Front St. Photos

Cinnamon Tree

FRONT STREET

Lagoon Terrace

Insect House

Front St. Cafe

Kidstore

Rondavel Room

Petting Zoo

Children's Zoo

Fisher Price Discovery Playground

Skyfari East

Zoofari Party Area

San Diego Zoo Store

Flamingo Sandwich Co.

Rondavel Room

1

Otto Center

ENTRANCE

Warner Administration Center

Balboa Park Railroad (MiniatureTrain)

P

4 Scripps, Parker, and Owens Aviaries (Lost Forest). Wandering paths climb through the enclosed aviaries where brightly colored tropical birds swoop between branches inches from your face.

5 Tiger Trail (Lost Forest). The mist-shrouded trails of this simulated rainforest wind down a canyon. Tigers, Malayan tapirs, and Argus pheasants wander among the exotic trees and plants.

6 Hippo Trail (Lost Forest). Glimpse huge but surprisingly graceful hippos frolicking in the water through an underwater viewing window and buffalo cavorting with monkeys on dry land.

7 Gorilla Exhibit (Lost Forest). The gorillas live in one of the zoo's bioclimatic zone exhibits modeled on their native habitat with waterfalls, climbing areas, and an open meadow. The sounds of the tropical rain forest emerge from a 144-speaker sound system that plays CDs recorded in Africa.

8 Sun Bear Forest (Asian Passage). Playful beasts claw apart the trees and shrubs that serve as a natural playground for climbing, jumping, and general merrymaking.

9 Giant Panda Research Station (Panda Canyon). An elevated pathway provides visitors with great access

Lories at Owen's Aviary

to the zoo's most famous residents in their side-by-side viewing areas. The adjacent discovery center features lots of information about these endangered animals and the zoo's efforts to protect them.

10 Polar Bear Plunge (Polar Rim). Watch polar bears take a chilly dive from the underwater viewing room. There are also Siberian reindeer, white foxes, and other Arctic creatures here. Kids can learn about the Arctic and climate change through interactive exhibits.

11 Elephant Odyssey. Get a glimpse of the animals that roamed Southern California 12,000 years ago and meet their living counterparts. The 7.5-acre, multispecies habitat features elephants, California condors, jaguars, and more.

12 Koala Exhibit (Outback). The San Diego Zoo houses the largest number of koalas outside Australia. Walk through the exhibit for photo ops of these marsupials from Down-Under curled up on their perches or dining on eucalyptus branches.

ASIAN PASSAGE

ELEPHANT ODYSSEY
11

Elephant Care Center

Express Bus Stop

PARK WAY

Big Cat Trail

Hunte Amphitheater

Big Cat Trail

Hunte Trail

8
Sun Bear Forest

URBAN JUNGLE

Sabertooth Grill

Sun Bear Trail

Big Cat Trail

AFRICA ROCKS

Tusker's Trunk

Express Bus Stop

PARK WAY

Elephant Odyssey Exit

Express Bus Stop

Bus Tour Unloading

Sydney's Grill

OUTBACK

FRONTSTREET

CENTER STREET

FRONTSTREET

12
Sydney's Shoppe

Koala Exhibit

MUST-SEE ANIMALS

❶ GORILLA

This troop of primates engages visitors with their human-like expressions and behavior. The youngsters are sure to delight, especially when hitching a ride on mom's back. Up-close encounters might involve the gorillas using the glass partition as a backrest while peeling cabbage. By dusk the gorillas head inside to their sleeping quarters, so don't save this for your last stop.

❷ ELEPHANT

Asian and African elephants coexist at the San Diego Zoo. The larger African elephant is distinguished by its big flapping ears—shaped like the continent of Africa—which it uses to keep cool. An elephant's trunk has over 40,000 muscles in it—that's more than humans have in their whole body.

❸ GIANT PANDA

The San Diego Zoo is well-known for its giant panda research and conservation efforts, and has had five successful panda births. You'll likely see parents Bai Yun ("White Cloud") and Gao-Gao ("Big-Big") with their youngest baby Xiao Liwu ("little gift").

❹ KOALA

While this collection of critters is one of the cutest in the zoo, don't expect a lot of activity from the koala habitat. These guys spend most of their day curled up asleep in the branches of the eucalyptus tree—they can sleep up to 20 hours a day. Although eucalyptus leaves are poisonous to most animals, bacteria in koalas' stomachs allow them to break down the toxins.

❺ POLAR BEAR

The trio of polar bears is one of the San Diego Zoo's star attractions, and their brand-new exhibit gets you up close and personal. Visitors sometimes worry about polar bears living in the warm San Diego climate, but there is no cause for concern. The San Diego-based bears eat a lean diet, thus reducing their layer of blubber and helping them keep cool.

DID YOU KNOW?

Bamboo is the panda's dietary staple—they can consume 84 pounds of it a day—and the zoo grows 69 species of bamboo to ensure they have plenty of variety.

PLANNING YOUR DAY AT THE ZOO

Left: Main entrance of the San Diego Zoo. Right: Sunbear

PLANNING YOUR TIME

Plan to devote at least a half-day to exploring the zoo, but with so much to see it is easy to stay a full day or more.

If you're on a tight schedule, opt for the guided **35 minute bus tour** that lets you zip through three-quarters of the exhibits. However, lines to board the busses can be long, and you won't get as close to the animals.

Another option is to take the **Skyfari Aerial Tram** to the far end of the park, choose a route, and meander back to the entrance. The Skyfari trip gives a good overview of the zoo's layout and a spectacular view.

The **Elephant Odyssey**, while accessible from two sides of the park, is best entered from just below the Polar Rim. The extremely popular **Panda exhibit** can develop long lines, so get there early.

The zoo offers several entertaining **live shows** daily. Check the website or the back of the map handed out at the zoo entrance for the day's offerings and showtimes.

BEFORE YOU GO	AT THE ZOO
■ To avoid ticket lines, purchase and print tickets online using the zoo's Web site.	■ Don't forget to explore at least some of the exhibits on foot—a favorite is the lush Tiger Trail.
■ To avoid excessive backtracking or a potential meltdown, plan your route along the zoo map before setting out. Try not to get too frustrated if you lose your way, as there are exciting exhibits around every turn and many paths intersect at several points.	■ If you visit on the weekend, find out when the Giraffe Experience is taking place. You can purchase leaf–eater biscuits to hand feed the giraffes!
■ The zoo offers a variety of program extras, including behind-the-scenes tours, backstage pass animal encounters, and sleepover events. Call in advance for pricing and reservations.	■ Splurge a little at the gift shop: your purchases help support zoo programs.
	■ The zoo rents strollers, wheelchairs, and lockers; it also has a first-aid office, a lost and found, and an ATM.

Fern Canyon, San Diego Zoo

GETTING HERE AND AROUND

The zoo is easy to get to, whether by bus or car.

Bus Travel: Take Bus No. 7 and exit at Park Boulevard and Zoo Place.

Car Travel: From Downtown, take Route 163 north through Balboa Park. Exit at Zoo/Museums (Richmond Street) and follow signs.

Several options help you get around the massive park: express buses loop through the zoo and the Skyfari Aerial Tram will take you from one end to the other. The zoo's topography is fairly hilly, but moving sidewalks lead up the slopes between some exhibits.

QUICK BITES

There is a wide variety of food available for purchase at the zoo from food carts to ethnic restaurants such as the Pan-Asian **Hua Mei Cafe**.

One of the best restaurants is **Albert's** ($), near the Gorilla exhibit, which features grilled fish, homemade pizza, and fresh pasta along with a full bar.

SERVICE INFORMATION

✉ 2920 Zoo Dr., Balboa Park

☎ 619/234–3153; 888/697–2632 Giant panda hotline

🌐 www.sandiegozoo.org

🎟 $42 adult, $32 children (3-11) includes Skyfari and bus tour; 2-Visit Pass ($76 adult, $56 children age 3-11); zoo parking free

💳 AE, D, MC, V

🕐 July–Sept., daily 9–9; Oct.–June, daily 9–dusk. Hours may be extended for holidays and special events, and Children's Zoo and Skyfari ride may have reduced hours—check

SAN DIEGO ZOO SAFARI PARK

online or call for details.

About 45 minutes north of the zoo in Escondido, the 1,800-acre San Diego Zoo Safari Park is an extensive wildlife sanctuary where animals roam free—and guests can get close in escorted caravans and on backcountry trails. This park and the zoo operate under the auspices of the San Diego Zoo's nonprofit organization; joint tickets are available. ➪ See Chapter 15: North County and Environs for more information.

OLD TOWN AND UPTOWN

San Diego's Spanish and Mexican roots are most evident in Old Town and the surrounding hillside of Presidio Park. Visitors can experience settlement life in San Diego from Spanish and Mexican rule to the early days of U.S. statehood. Nearby Uptown is composed of several smaller neighborhoods near Downtown and around Balboa Park that showcase a unique blend of historical charm and modern urban community.

OLD TOWN

As the first European settlement in Southern California, Old Town began to develop in the 1820s. However, its true beginnings took place on a nearby hillside in 1769 with the establishment of a Spanish military outpost and the first of California's missions, San Diego de Alcalá. In 1774 the hilltop was declared a presidio reál, a fortress built by the Spanish empire, and the mission was relocated along the San Diego River. Over time, settlers moved down from the presidio to establish Old Town. A central plaza was laid out, surrounded by adobe and, later, wooden structures. San Diego became an incorporated U.S. city in 1850, with Old Town as its center. In the 1860s, however, the advent of Alonzo Horton's New Town to the southeast caused Old Town to wither. Efforts to preserve the area began early in the 20th century, and Old Town became a state historic park in 1968.

Today Old Town is a lively celebration of history and culture. The Old Town San Diego State Historic Park re-creates life during the early settlement, while San Diego Avenue buzzes with art galleries, gift shops, festive restaurants, and open-air stands selling inexpensive Mexican handicrafts.

FAMILY

Fodor's Choice

★

Fiesta de Reyes. North of San Diego's Old Town Plaza lies the area's unofficial center, built to represent a colonial Mexican plaza. This collection of shops and restaurants around a central courtyard in blossom with magenta bougainvillea, scarlet hibiscus, and other flowers in season reflect what it might have looked like in the early California days, from 1821 to 1872, complete with shops stocked with items reminiscent of that era. More than a dozen shops and restaurants line the plaza (Casa de Reyes is a great stop for a margarita and some chips and guacamole), and if you are lucky, you might catch a mariachi band or folklorico dance performance on the plaza stage—check the website for times and upcoming special events. ⊠ *4016 Wallace St.* ☎ *619/297–3100* ⊕ *www. fiestadereyes.com* ⊗ *Shops 10–9 daily.*

FAMILY

Fodor's Choice

★

Old Town San Diego State Historic Park. The six square blocks on the site of San Diego's original pueblo are the heart of Old Town. Most of the 20 historic buildings preserved or re-created by the park cluster around **Old Town Plaza,** bounded by Wallace Street on the west, Calhoun Street on the north, Mason Street on the east, and San Diego Avenue on the south. The plaza is a pleasant place to rest, plan your tour of the park, and watch passersby. San Diego Avenue is closed to vehicle traffic here.

Some of Old Town's buildings were destroyed in a fire in 1872, but after the site became a state historic park in 1968, reconstruction and

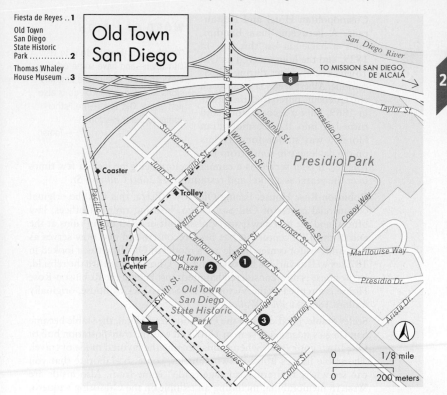

Old Town
San Diego

TO MISSION SAN DIEGO,
DE ALCALÁ

restoration of the remaining structures began. Five of the original adobes are still intact. The tour pamphlet available at Robinson-Rose House gives details about all the historic houses on the plaza and in its vicinity; *a few of the more interesting ones are noted ⇨ below.* Several reconstructed buildings serve as restaurants or as shops purveying wares reminiscent of those that might have been available in the original Old Town; **Racine & Laramie**, a painstakingly reproduced version of San Diego's first (1868) cigar store, is especially interesting. Free tours depart daily from the Robinson-Rose House at 11 and 2.

Casa de Estudillo. San Diego's first County Assessor, Jose Antonio Estudillo, built this home in 1827 in collaboration with his father, the commander of the San Diego Presidio, José Maria Estudillo. The largest and most elaborate of the original adobe homes, it was occupied by members of the Estudillo family until 1887. It was purchased and restored in 1910 by sugar magnate and developer John D. Spreckels, who advertised it in bold lettering on the side as "Ramona's Marriage Place." Spreckels's claim that the small chapel in the house was the site of the wedding in Helen Hunt Jackson's popular novel *Ramona* had no basis; that didn't stop people from coming to see it, however. ⊠ *4001 Mason St.*

Cosmopolitan Hotel and Restaurant. A Peruvian, Juan Bandini, built a hacienda on this site in 1829, and the house served as Old Town's social center during Mexican rule. Albert Seeley, a stagecoach entrepreneur, purchased the home in 1869, built a second story, and turned it into the Cosmopolitan Hotel, a way station for travelers on the daylong trip south from Los

Angeles. It later served as a cannery before being revived (a few times over the years) as a hotel and restaurant. ⊠ *2660 Calhoun St.*

Robinson-Rose House. Facing Old Town Plaza, this was the original commercial center of Old San Diego, housing railroad offices, law offices, and the first newspaper press. Built in 1853 but in ruins at the end of the 19th century, it has been reconstructed and now serves as the park's visitor center. Inside are a model of Old Town as it looked in 1872 as well as various historic exhibits. Ghosts came with the rebuild, as the house is now considered haunted. Just behind the Robinson-Rose House is a replica of the Victorian-era Silvas-McCoy house, originally built in 1869. ⊠ *4002 Wallace St.*

Seeley Stable. Next door to the Cosmopolitan Hotel, the stable became San Diego's stagecoach stop in 1867 and was the transportation hub of Old Town until 1887, when trains became the favored mode of travel. The stable houses horse-drawn vehicles, some so elaborate that you can see where the term "carriage trade" came from. Also inside are Western memorabilia, including an exhibit on the California vaquero, the original American cowboy, and a collection of Native American artifacts. ⊠ *2630 Calhoun St.*

Also worth exploring: The San Diego Union Museum, Mason Street School, Wells Fargo History Museum, First San Diego Courthouse, Casa de Machado y Silvas Commercial Restaurant Museum, and the Casa de Machado y Stewart. Ask at the visitor center for locations. ⊠ *Visitor Center (Robinson-Rose House), 4002 Wallace St.* ☎ *619/220–5422* ⊕ *www.parks.ca.gov* ⊠ *Free* ☉ *Oct.–Apr., daily 10–4; May–Sept., daily 10–5; hrs may vary at individual sites.*

Thomas Whaley House Museum. Thomas Whaley was a New York entrepreneur who came to California during the gold rush. He wanted to provide his East Coast wife with all the comforts of home, so in 1857 he had Southern California's first two-story brick structure built, making it the oldest double-story brick building on the West Coast. The house, which served as the county courthouse and government seat during the 1870s, stands in strong contrast to the Spanish-style adobe residences that surround the nearby historic plaza and marks an early stage of San Diego's "Americanization." A garden out back includes many varieties of prehybrid roses from before 1867. The place is perhaps most famed, however, for the ghosts that are said to inhabit it. Starting at 5 pm, admission is by guided tour offered every half hour with the last tour departing at 9:30 pm. The nighttime tours are geared more toward the supernatural aspects of the house than the daytime self-guided tour. ✉ 2476 San Diego Ave. ☎ 619/297–7511 ⊕ www.whaleyhouse.org ⊠ $6 before 5 pm, $10 after 5 ⊘ Sept.–May, Sun.–Tues. 10–5, Thurs.– Sun. 10–9:30; June–Aug., daily 10–9:30 ⊘ Closed Weds. Sept.–May.

HILLCREST

The large retro Hillcrest sign over the intersection of University and 5th avenues makes an excellent landmark at the epicenter of this vibrant section of Uptown. Strolling along University Avenue between 4th and 6th avenues from Washington Street to Robinson Avenue will reveal a mixture of retail shops and restaurants. A few blocks east, another interesting stretch of stores and restaurants runs along University Avenue to Normal Street. Long established as the center of San Diego's gay community, the neighborhood bustles both day and night with a mixed crowd of shoppers, diners, and partygoers.

MISSION VALLEY

Although Mission Valley's charms may not be immediately apparent, it offers many conveniences to visitors and residents alike. The Mission Basilica San Diego de Alcalá provides a tranquil refuge from the surrounding suburban sprawl.

Mission Basilica San Diego de Alcalá. It's hard to imagine how remote California's earliest mission once must have been; these days, it's accessible by major freeways (I–15 and I–8) and by the San Diego Trolley. Mission San Diego de Alcalá, the first of a chain of 21 missions stretching northward along the coast, was established by Father Junípero Serra on Presidio Hill in 1769 and moved to this location in 1774. There was no greater security from enemy attack here: Padre Luis Jayme, California's first Christian martyr, was clubbed to death by the Kumeyaay Indians he was trying to convert in 1775. The present church is the fifth built on the site; it was reconstructed in 1931 following the outline of the 1813 church. It measures 150 feet long but only 35 feet wide because, without easy means of joining beams, the mission buildings were only as wide as the trees that served as their ceiling supports were tall. Father Jayme is buried in the sanctuary; a small museum named for him documents mission history and exhibits tools and artifacts from the early days. From the peaceful palm-bedecked gardens out back you can gaze at the 46-foot-high *campanario* (bell tower), the mission's most distinctive feature; one of its five bells was cast in 1802. ✉ 10818 San Diego Mission Rd. ✛ From I–8 east, exit and turn left on Mission Gorge Rd., turn left on Twain Rd. and the mission will be on the right ☎ 619/281–8449 ⊕ www.missionsandiego. com ⊠ $3 suggested donation, $2 audio tour ⊘ Daily 9–4:45.

NORTH PARK

Named for its location north of Balboa Park, this evolving neighborhood is home to an exciting array of restaurants, bars, and shops. High-end condominiums and local merchants are often cleverly disguised behind historic signage from barbershops, bowling alleys, and theater marquees. The stretch of Ray Street near University Avenue is home to several small galleries. With a steady stream of new openings in the neighborhood, North Park is one of San Diego's top dining and nightlife destinations.

MISSION BAY, BEACHES, AND SEAWORLD

Mission Bay and the surrounding beaches are the aquatic playground of San Diego. The choice of activities available is astonishing, and the perfect weather makes you want to get out there and play. At the south end of the bay lies SeaWorld, one of San Diego's most popular attractions. If you're craving downtime after all the activity, there are plenty of peaceful spots to relax and simply soak up the sunshine.

Mission Bay welcomes visitors with its protected waters and countless opportunities for fun. The 4,600-acre Mission Bay Park is the place for water sports like sailing, stand-up paddleboarding, and water-skiing. With 19 miles of beaches and grassy areas, it's also a great place for a picnic. One Mission Bay caveat: swimmers should note signs warning about water pollution; on occasions when heavy rains or other events cause pollution, swimming is dangerous.

Mission Beach is a famous and lively fun zone for families and young people both; if it isn't party time at the moment, it will be five minutes from now. The pathways in this area are lined with vacation homes, many for rent by the week or month.

North of Mission Beach is the college-packed party town of Pacific Beach, or "PB" as locals call it. The laid-back vibe of this surfer's mecca draws in free-spirited locals who roam the streets on skateboards and beach cruisers. The energy level peaks during happy hour, when PB's cluster of nightclubs, bars, and 150 restaurants open their doors to those ready to party.

FAMILY **Belmont Park.** The once-abandoned amusement park between the bay and Mission Beach Boardwalk is now a shopping, dining, and recreation complex. Twinkling lights outline the **Giant Dipper,** an antique wooden roller coaster on which screaming thrill-seekers ride more than 2,600 feet of track and 13 hills (riders must be at least 4 feet, 2 inches tall). Created in 1925 and listed on the National Register of Historic Places, this is one of the few old-time roller coasters left in the United States. The **Plunge,** an indoor swimming pool, also opened in 1925, and was the largest—60 feet by 125 feet—saltwater pool in the world at the time (it's had freshwater since 1951). Johnny Weismuller and Esther Williams are among the stars who were captured on celluloid swimming here. Other Belmont Park attractions include a video arcade, a submarine ride, bumper cars, a tilt-a-whirl, and an antique carousel. The rock wall challenges both junior climbers and their elders. Belmont Park also has the most consistent wave in the county at the **Wave House,** where the FlowRider provides surfers and bodyboarders a near-perfect simulated wave on which to practice their skills. ⊠ *3146 Mission Blvd., Mission Bay* 🕾 *858/488–1549 for rides, 858/228–9300 for pool* ⊕ *www.belmontpark.com* 🖃 *Unlimited ride day package $27 for 48 inches and over, $16 for under 48 inches; pool $7; pool and fitness center $15* ⊙ *Park opens at 11 daily, ride operation varies seasonally; pool open weekdays noon–4 pm and 8–10 pm, weekends noon–8 pm.*

Mission Bay Park. Mission Bay Park is San Diego's monument to sports and fitness. This 4,600-acre aquatic park has 27 miles of shoreline including 19 miles of sandy beaches. Playgrounds and picnic areas abound on the beaches and low grassy hills. On weekday evenings, joggers, bikers, and skaters take over. In the daytime, swimmers, water-skiers, windsurfers, anglers, and boaters—some in single-person kayaks, others in crowded powerboats—vie for space in the water. ⊠ *2688 E. Mission Bay Dr., off I–5 at Exit 22 East Mission Bay Drive, Mission Bay* ☎ *858/581–7602 Park Ranger's Office* ⊕ *www.sandiego. gov/park-and-recreation/parks/ missionbay* ⊠ *Free.*

WORD OF MOUTH

"We got [to SeaWorld] for opening. Park was quiet and we got to ride Atlantis 3 times with no wait. My 3-year-old LOVED this ride. We got to 'pet' some lizards and check out some parrots. Then we just slowly meandered through the park... We had reservations for the 12:30 Dine with Shamu. The lunch was actually pretty good, and I really enjoyed the Shamu cookies."

—rizzo0904

Mission Beach Boardwalk. The cement pathway lining the sand from the southern end of Mission Beach north to Pacific Beach is always bustling with activity. Cyclists ping the bells on their beach cruisers to pass walkers out for a stroll alongside the oceanfront homes. Vacationers kick back on their patios, while friends play volleyball in the sand. The activity picks up alongside Belmont Park and the Wavehouse, where people stop to check out the action on the Flow-Rider wave. ⊠ *Alongside the sand from Mission Beach Park to Pacific Beach, Mission Beach.*

FAMILY
Fodor's Choice
★

SeaWorld San Diego. One of the world's largest marine-life amusement parks, SeaWorld is spread over 189 tropically landscaped bay-front acres—and it seems to be expanding into every available square inch of space with new exhibits, shows, and activities. The park offers a variety of amusement rides, some on dry land and others that will leave riders soaking wet.

The majority of SeaWorld's exhibits are walk-through marine environments. Kids get a particular kick out of the **Shark Encounter,** where they come face-to-face with sand, tiger, nurse, bonnethead, black-tipped, and white-tipped reef sharks by walking through a 57-foot clear acrylic tube that passes through the 280,000-gallon shark habitat. **Turtle Reef** offers an incredible up-close encounter with the green sea turtle, while the moving sidewalk at **Penguin Encounter** whisks you through a colony of nearly 300 macaroni, gentoo, Adelie, and emperor penguins. Various **freshwater and saltwater aquariums** hold underwater creatures from around the world.

SeaWorld's highlights are its large-arena entertainments. You can get front-row seats if you arrive 30 minutes in advance, and the stadiums are large enough for everyone to get a seat in the off-season. **One Ocean,** Sea World's headlining Shamu show, stars a synchronized team of orca whales who leap out of the water to the tunes of surround-sound music, illuminated by brilliantly colored lights. **Blue Horizons**

TIP SHEET: SEAWORLD SAN DIEGO

SEAWORLD IN A DAY

The highlights of any visit to Sea-World are the shows, so review the current performance schedule (available online or when you arrive at the park) and plan accordingly. Shows are fairly short—about 20 minutes—so you can see several.

SeaWorld is busiest in the middle of the day, so tackle the adventure rides either at the beginning or end of your visit. Coaster lovers will want to carve out time for the popular new **Manta** ride. Unless it's very hot, consider braving the soakers—**Journey to Atlantis, Shipwreck Rapids,** and sitting in the arenas' **Splash Zones**—in close secession, and then changing into dry clothes.

For an interactive experience, focus on the feeding stations and touch pools. The friendly bottlenose dolphins at **Dolphin Point** just might let you pet them while the hands-on **California Tide Pool** features San Diego's indigenous marine life. At the **Bat Ray Feeding** pool, the friendly rays pop up to the surface for snacks and a gentle pat on the head, while hungry sea lions await you at **Pacific Point.**

The standouts among the walk-through marine exhibits are the **Penguin** and **Shark Encounters, Turtle Reef,** and **Wild Arctic.** Those with tots 42 inches and under should head to the **Sesame Street Bay of Play.**

It's easy for your SeaWorld visit to become a very full day. Although saving either **One Ocean** or **Blue Horizons** for a finale can be great, if you get too tired you might end up missing a main attraction.

POPULAR ADD-ONS

The 30-minute **Dolphin Interaction Program** ($215) lets you feed, touch, and give behavior signals to bottlenose dolphins. A less expensive treat ($39 adults, $19 children) is the **Dine with Shamu** package, which includes a buffet lunch or dinner. The one-hour **Sea World Up Close Tour** ($16 adults, $14 children) takes you into backstage training areas.

TIPS

■ Pack a change of clothes for after the soaker rides and shows; you can rent lockers to stow belongings. And bring sunscreen and hats.

■ If you get your hand stamped when exiting the park, you can return later that same day.

■ Arrive at shows at least 30 minutes early to get front-row seats, and be prepared to get wet.

■ Steer kids to the **Under the Sun** gift shop, near the Calypso Smoke House, where all items are $10 or less.

■ Eating options include dining with Shamu next to the pool, or casual spots like the Seaside Coffee and Bakery or the Seaport Market.

Elmo's Flying Fish, in SeaWorld's Sesame Street Bay of Play.

Acrobatic dolphins perform in SeaWorld's Dolphin Discovery show.

combines dolphins, pilot whales, tropical birds, and aerialists in a spectacular performance.

The **Dolphin Interaction Program** gives guests the chance to interact with SeaWorld's bottlenose dolphins in the water. The hour-long program (20 minutes in the water), during which visitors can feed, touch, and give behavior signals, costs $215. You can also **Breakfast with Shamu** ($26) or **Dine with Shamu** ($39), buffet meals with great views of the whales at play.

The San Diego Zoo Combo Ticket ($135 for adults, $105 for children ages 3 to 9) offers seven consecutive days of unlimited admission to SeaWorld, the San Diego Zoo, and the San Diego Zoo's Safari Park. This is a good idea, because if you try to get your money's worth by fitting everything in on a single day, you're likely to end up tired and cranky. Many hotels, especially those in the Mission Bay area, also offer SeaWorld specials that may include rate reductions or two-day entry for the price of one.

There is no shortage of dining options inside SeaWorld, from sandwiches at the Seaport Market, to Italian fare at Mama Stella's Pizza Kitchen, BBQ at the Calypso Bay Smokehouse, or baked goods at Seaside Coffee and Bakery. ✉ *500 SeaWorld Dr., near west end of I–8, Mission Bay* ☎ *800/257–4268* ⊕ *www.seaworldparks.com* 🎟 *$78 adults, $70 kids; parking $15* ⊙ *Daily 10–dusk; extended hrs in summer.*

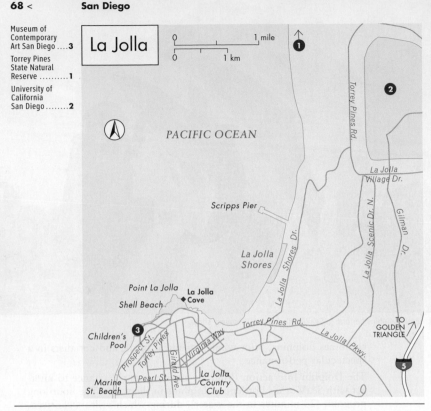

LA JOLLA

La Jollans have long considered their village to be the Monte Carlo of California, and with good cause. Its coastline curves into natural coves backed by verdant hillsides covered with homes worth millions. La Jolla is both a natural and cultural treasure trove. The upscale shops, galleries, and restaurants of La Jolla Village satisfy the glitterati, while secluded trails, scenic overlooks, and abundant marine life provide balance and refuge.

Although La Jolla is a neighborhood of the city of San Diego, it has its own postal zone and a coveted sense of class; the ultrarich from around the globe own second homes here—the seaside zone between the neighborhood's bustling Downtown and the cliffs above the Pacific has a distinctly European flavor—and old-money residents maintain friendships with the visiting film stars and royalty who frequent the area's exclusive luxury hotels and private clubs.

The Native Americans called the site La Hoya, meaning "the cave," referring to the grottoes that dot the shoreline. The Spaniards changed the name to La Jolla (same pronunciation as La Hoya), "the jewel," and its residents have cherished the name and its allusions ever since.

Fodor's Choice ★ **Museum of Contemporary Art San Diego.** Driving along Coast Boulevard, it is hard to miss the mass of watercraft jutting out from the rear of the Museum of Contemporary Art San Diego (MCASD) La Jolla location. *Pleasure Point* by Nancy Rubins is just one example of the mingling of art and locale at this spectacular oceanfront setting.

The oldest section of La Jolla's branch of San Diego's contemporary art museum was originally a residence, designed by Irving Gill for philanthropist Ellen Browning Scripps in 1916. In the mid-1990s the compound was updated and expanded by architect Robert Venturi, who respected Gill's original geometric structure and clean Mission-style lines while adding his own distinctive touches. The result is a striking contemporary building that looks as though it's always been here.

The light-filled Axline Court serves as the museum's entrance and does triple duty as reception area, exhibition hall, and forum for special events, including the glittering Monte Carlo gala each September, attended by the town's most fashionable folk. Inside, the museum's artwork gets major competition from the setting: you can look out from the top of a grand stairway onto a landscaped garden that contains permanent and temporary sculpture exhibits as well as rare 100-year-old California plant specimens and, beyond that, to the Pacific Ocean.

California artists figure prominently in the museum's permanent collection of post-1950s art, but the museum also includes examples of every major art movement through the present—works by Andy Warhol, Robert Rauschenberg, Frank Stella, Joseph Cornell, and Jenny Holzer, to name a few. Important pieces by artists from San Diego and Tijuana were acquired in the 1990s. The museum also gets major visiting shows. ⊠ *700 Prospect St.* ☎ *858/454–3541* ⊕ *www.mcasd.org* ⊠*$10, good for one visit here and at MCASD Downtown within 7 days; free 3rd Thurs. of the month 5–7* ⊙ *Thurs.–Tues. 11–5; 3rd Thurs. of month 11–7* ⊙ *Closed Wed.*

Fodor's Choice ★ **Torrey Pines State Natural Reserve.** *Pinus torreyana*, the rarest native pine tree in the United States, enjoys a 1,700-acre sanctuary at the northern edge of La Jolla. About 6,000 of these unusual trees, some as tall as 60 feet, grow on the cliffs here. The park is one of only two places in the world (the other is Santa Rosa Island, off Santa Barbara) where the Torrey pine grows naturally. The reserve has several hiking trails leading to the cliffs, 300 feet above the ocean; trail maps are available at the park station. Wildflowers grow profusely in spring, and the ocean panoramas are always spectacular. When in this upper part of the park, respect the restrictions. Not permitted: picnicking, smoking, leaving the trails, dogs, alcohol, or collecting plant specimens.

You can unwrap your sandwiches, however, at Torrey Pines State Beach, just below the reserve. When the tide is out, it's possible to walk south all the way past the lifeguard towers to Black's Beach over rocky promontories carved by the waves (avoid the bluffs, however; they're unstable). **Los Peñasquitos Lagoon** at the north end of the reserve is one of the many natural estuaries that flow inland between Del Mar and

A surfer prepares to head out before sunset at La Jolla's Torrey Pines State Beach and Reserve.

Oceanside. It's a good place to watch shorebirds. Volunteers lead guided nature walks at 10 and 2 on most weekends. ⊠ *N. Torrey Pines Rd. exit off I–5 onto Carmel Valley Rd. going west, then turn left (south) on Coast Hwy. 101, 12600 N. Torrey Pines Rd.* ☎ *858/755–2063* ⊕ *www. torreypine.org* ▨ *Parking $10–$15* ◷ *Daily 9–dusk.*

University of California at San Diego. The campus of one of the country's most prestigious research universities spreads over 1,200 acres of coastal canyons and eucalyptus groves, where students and faculty jog, bike, and rollerblade to class. If you're interested in contemporary art, check out the **Stuart Collection of Sculpture**—18 thought-provoking, site-specific works by artists such as Nam June Paik, William Wegman, Niki de St. Phalle, Jenny Holzer, and others arrayed around the campus. UCSD's **Price Center** has a well-stocked, two-level bookstore—the largest in San Diego—and a good coffeehouse, Perks. Look for the postmodern **Geisel Library**, named for longtime La Jolla residents Theodor "Dr. Seuss" Geisel and his wife, Audrey. For campus culture, political views, vegan dishes, and live music, head to the **Che Café** located in Building 161, painted in bright murals. Bring quarters for the parking meters, or cash or a credit card for the parking structures, since free parking is only available on weekends. ⊠ *Exit I–5 onto La Jolla Village Dr. going west; take Gilman Dr. off-ramp to right and continue on to information kiosk at campus entrance on Gilman Dr.* ☎ *858/534–4414 campus tour information* ⊕ *www.ucsd.edu* ◷ *90-min campus tours Sun. at 2 from South Gilman Information Pavilion; reserve before noon Thurs.*

POINT LOMA AND CORONADO WITH HARBOR AND SHELTER ISLANDS, AND OCEAN BEACH

Although Coronado is actually an isthmus, easily reached from the mainland if you head north from Imperial Beach, it has always seemed like an island and is often referred to as such. To the west, Point Loma protects the San Diego Bay from the Pacific's tides and waves. Both Coronado and Point Loma have stately homes, sandy beaches, private marinas, and prominent military installations. Nestled between the two, Harbor and Shelter islands owe their existence to dredging in the bay.

POINT LOMA

The hilly peninsula of Point Loma curves west and south into the Pacific and provides protection for San Diego Bay. Its high elevations and sandy cliffs provide incredible views, and make Point Loma a visible local landmark. Its maritime roots are evident, from its longtime ties to the U.S. Navy to its bustling sport fishing and sailing marinas. The funky community of Ocean Beach coexists alongside the stately homes of Sunset Cliffs and the honored graves at Fort Rosecrans National Cemetery.

FAMILY
Fodor's Choice
★

Cabrillo National Monument. This 160-acre preserve marks the site of the first European visit to San Diego, made by 16th-century explorer Juan Rodríguez Cabrillo. Cabrillo landed at this spot on September 15, 1542. Today the site, with its rugged cliffs and shores and outstanding overlooks, is one of the most frequently visited of all the national monuments.

The **visitor center** presents films and lectures about Cabrillo's voyage, the sea-level tide pools, and migrating gray whales. **Interpretive stations** have been installed along the walkways that edge the cliffs. The moderately steep **Bayside Trail,** 2½ miles round-trip, winds through coastal sage scrub, curving under the cliff-top lookouts and taking you ever closer to the bay-front scenery. You cannot reach the beach from this trail, and must stick to the path to protect the cliffs from erosion and yourself from thorny plants and snakes—including rattlers. You'll see prickly pear cactus and yucca, black-eyed Susans, fragrant sage, and maybe a lizard, rabbit, or hummingbird. The climb back is long but gradual, leading up to the **Old Point Loma Lighthouse.**

The western and southern cliffs of Cabrillo National Monument are prime whale-watching territory. A sheltered **viewing station** has wayside exhibits describing the great gray whales' yearly migration from Baja California to the Bering and Chukchi seas near Alaska. High-powered telescopes help you focus on the whales' waterspouts. Whales are visible on clear days from late December through early March, with the highest concentration in January and February. More-accessible sea creatures (starfish, crabs, anemones) can be seen in the **tide pools** at the foot of the monument's western cliffs. Drive north from the visitor center to Cabrillo Road, which winds down to the Coast Guard station and the shore. ⊠ *1800 Cabrillo Memorial Dr.* ☎ *619/557–5450* ⊕ *www.nps. gov/cabr* ⊠ *$5 per car, $3 per person on foot/bicycle, entry good for 7 days* ☉ *Daily 9–5.*

2

Sunset Cliffs. As the name suggests, the 60-foot-high bluffs on the western side of Point Loma south of Ocean Beach are a perfect place to watch the sun set over the sea. To view the tide pools along the shore, use the staircase off Sunset Cliffs Boulevard at the foot of Ladera Street.

The dramatic coastline here seems to have been carved out of ancient rock. The impact of the waves is very clear: each year more sections of the cliffs are posted with caution signs. Don't ignore these warnings—it's easy to slip in the crumbling sandstone, and the surf can be extremely rough. The small coves and beaches that dot the coastline are popular with surfers drawn to the pounding waves. The homes along the boulevard—pink stucco mansions beside shingled Cape Cod–style cottages—are fine examples of Southern California luxury. ⊠ *Sunset Cliffs Blvd., Point Loma.*

OCEAN BEACH

At the northern end of Point Loma lies the chilled-out, hippyesque town of Ocean Beach, commonly referred to as "OB." The main thoroughfare of this funky neighborhood is dotted with dive bars, coffeehouses, surf shops, and 1960s diners. OB is a magnet for everyone from surfers to musicians and artists. Fans of OB applaud its resistance to "selling out" to upscale development, whereas detractors lament its somewhat scruffy edges.

SHELTER ISLAND

In 1950 San Diego's port director decided to raise the shoal that lay off the eastern shore of Point Loma above sea level with the sand and mud dredged up during the course of deepening a ship channel in the 1930s and '40s. The resulting peninsula, **Shelter Island,** became home to several marinas and resorts, many with Polynesian details that still exist today, giving them a retro flair. This reclaimed peninsula now supports towering palms and resorts, restaurants, and side-by-side marinas. A long sidewalk runs past boat brokerages to the hotels and marinas that line the inner shore, facing Point Loma. On the bay side, fishermen launch their boats and families relax at picnic tables along the grass, where there are fire rings and permanent barbeque grills.

HARBOR ISLAND

Following the successful creation of Shelter Island, in 1961 the U.S. Navy used the residue from digging berths deep enough to accommodate aircraft carriers to build **Harbor Island.** Restaurants and high-rise hotels dot the inner shore of this 1½-mile-long man-made peninsula adjacent to the airport. The bay's shore is lined with pathways, gardens, and scenic picnic spots. The east end point, has killer views of the Downtown skyline.

CORONADO

As if freeze-framed in the 1950s, Coronado's quaint appeal is captured in its old-fashioned storefronts, well-manicured gardens, and charming **Ferry Landing Marketplace.** The streets of Coronado are wide, quiet, and friendly, and many of today's residents live in grand Victorian homes handed down for generations. Naval Air Station North Island was established in 1911 on Coronado's north end, across from Point Loma, and was the site of Charles Lindbergh's departure on the transcontinental flight that preceded his famous solo flight across the Atlantic. Coronado's long relationship with the U.S. Navy and its desirable real estate have made it an enclave for military personnel; it's said to have more retired admirals per capita than anywhere else in the United States.

Coronado is accessible via the arching blue 2.2-mile-long San Diego–Coronado Bay Bridge, which handles some 68,000 cars each day. The view of the harbor, Downtown, and the island is breathtaking, day and night. Until the bridge was completed in 1969, visitors and residents relied on the Coronado Ferry, which today has become quite popular with bicyclists, who shuttle their bikes across the harbor and ride Coronado's wide, flat boulevards for hours.

FAMILY **Coronado Ferry Landing.** This collection of shops at Ferry Landing is on a smaller scale than the Embarcadero's Seaport Village, but you do get a great view of the Downtown San Diego skyline. The little bayside shops and restaurants resemble the gingerbread domes of the Hotel Del Coronado. **Bikes and Beyond** (☎ 619/435–7180 ⊕ hollandsbicycles. com) rents bikes and surreys, perfect for riding through town and along Coronado's scenic bike path. ✉ 1201 1st St., at B Ave. ☎ 619/435–8895 ⊕ www.coronadoferrylandingshops.com.

Coronado Museum of History and Art. The neoclassical First Bank of Commerce building, constructed in 1910, holds the headquarters and archives of the Coronado Historical Association, a museum, the Coronado Visitor Center, the Coronado Museum Store, and Tent City Restaurant. The museum's collection celebrates Coronado's history with photographs and displays of its formative events and major sights. *Promenade Through the Past: A Brief History of Coronado and its Architectural Wonders*, available at the museum store, traces a 60-minute walking tour of the area's architecturally and historically significant buildings. A guided tour of them departs from the museum lobby on Wednesday mornings at 10:30 and costs $10 (reservations required). ✉ 1100 Orange Ave., at Park Pl. ☎ 619/435–7242, 619/437–8788 walking tour reservations ⊕ www.coronadohistory.org ✉ $4 suggested donation ⊙ Mon.–Fri. 9–5, Sat.–Sun. 10–5.

Fodor's Choice **Hotel Del Coronado.** The Del's distinctive red-tile roofs and Victorian gin-
★ gerbread architecture have served as a set for many movies, political meetings, and extravagant social happenings. It's speculated that the Duke of Windsor may have first met Wallis Simpson here. Eleven presidents have been guests of the Del, and the film *Some Like It Hot*—starring Marilyn Monroe, Jack Lemmon, and Tony Curtis—used the hotel as a backdrop.

The Hotel Del, as locals call it, was the brainchild of financiers Elisha Spurr Babcock Jr. and H. L. Story, who saw the potential of Coronado's virgin beaches and its view of San Diego's emerging harbor. It opened in 1888 and became a National Historic Landmark in 1977.

Although the pool area is reserved for hotel guests, several surrounding dining patios make great places to sit back and imagine the scene during the 1920s, when the hotel rocked with good times. Behind the pool area, an attractive shopping arcade features a classic candy shop as well as several fine clothing and accessories stores. A lavish Sunday brunch is served in the Crown Room, from 9:30 to 1 pm. During the

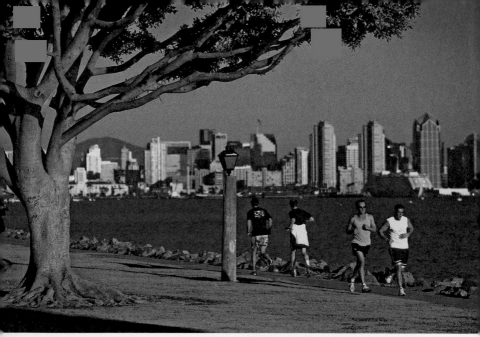
San Diego's myriad coastal trails and paths provide great views of natural and man-made wonders alike.

holidays, the hotel hosts Skating by the Sea, an outdoor beachfront ice-skating rink open to the public. ■TIP→ **Even if you don't happen to be staying at the Del, gazing out over the ocean while enjoying a drink at the Sun Deck Bar and Grill makes for a great escape. If it's chilly, the fire pits and sofa seating are very inviting.**

The History Gallery displays photos from the Del's early days, and books elaborating on its history and that of Kate Morgan, the hotel's resident ghost, are sold along with logo apparel and gifts in the hotel's 15-plus shops. Tours of the Del take place on Tuesday and Friday at 10:30, Saturday and Sunday at 2. Reservations are required. ⊠ *1500 Orange Ave., at Glorietta Blvd.* ☎ *619/435–6611, 619/437–8788 tour reservations (through Coronado Visitor Center)* ⊕ *www.hoteldel.com* ☎ *Tours $15.*

Orange Avenue. Coronado's business district and its villagelike heart, this street is surely one of the most charming spots in Southern California. Slow-paced and very "local" (the city fights against chain stores), it's a blast from the past, although entirely up to date in other respects. The military presence—Coronado is home to the U.S. Navy Sea, Air and Land (SEAL) forces—is reflected in shops selling military gear and places like **McP's Irish Pub,** at No. 1107. A family-friendly stop for a good, all-American meal, it's the unofficial SEALs headquarters. Many clothing boutiques, home-furnishings stores, and upscale restaurants cater to visitors with deep pockets, but you can buy plumbing supplies, too, or get a genuine military haircut at **Crown Barber Shop,** at No. 947. If you need a break, stop for a latte at the sidewalk café of **Bay Books,** San Diego's largest independent bookstore, at No. 1029. ⊠ *Orange Avenue, near 9th St.*

BEACHES

Updated
by Amanda
Knoles

San Diego's beaches have a different vibe from their northern counterparts in neighboring Orange County and glitzy Los Angeles farther up the coast. San Diego is more laid-back and less of a scene. Cyclists on cruiser bikes whiz by as surfers saunter toward the waves and sunbathers bronze under the sun, be it July or November.

Even at summer's hottest peak, San Diego's beaches are cool and breezy. Ocean waves are large, and the water will be colder than what you experience at tropical beaches—temperatures range from 55°F to 65°F from October through June, and 65°F to 73°F from July through September.

Finding a parking spot near the ocean can be hard in summer, but for the time being, unmetered parking is available at all San Diego city beaches.

Pay attention to signs listing illegal activities; undercover police often patrol the beaches. Smoking and alcoholic beverages are completely banned on city beaches. Drinking in beach parking lots, on boardwalks, and in landscaped areas is also illegal. Glass containers are not permitted on beaches, cliffs, and walkways, or in park areas and adjacent parking lots. Littering is not tolerated, and skateboarding is prohibited at some beaches. Fires are allowed only in fire rings or elevated barbecue grills. Although it may be tempting to take a sea creature from a tide pool as a souvenir, it may upset the delicate ecological balance, and it's illegal, too.

Lifeguards are stationed at city beaches from Sunset Cliffs up to Black's Beach in the summertime, but coverage in winter is provided by roving patrols only. When swimming in the ocean be aware of rip currents, which are common in California shores.

San Diego's beaches are well maintained and very clean during summertime, when rainfall is infrequent. Pollution is generally worse near river mouths and storm-drain outlets, especially after heavy rainfall. Call San Diego's Lifeguard Services at ☎ *619/221–8824* for a recorded message that includes pollution reports along with surfing and diving conditions.

Beaches are listed geographically, south to north.

CORONADO

FAMILY **Silver Strand State Beach.** This quiet Coronado beach is ideal for families. The water is relatively calm, lifeguards and rangers are on duty year-round, and there are places for boating, water sports, biking, volleyball, and fishing. Picnic tables, grills, and fire pits are available, and the Silver Stand Beach Cafe is open during the summer. The beach sits across the street from Loews Coronado Bay Resort and the Coronado Cays, an exclusive community popular with yacht owners and celebrities. You can reserve RV sites ($50 beach; $35 inland) at ⊕ *www.reserveamerica. com.* Four day-use parking lots provide room for more than 1,000 cars. Foot tunnels under Route 75 lead to a bayside beach with great views of the San Diego skyline. **Amenities:** food and drink; lifeguards; parking (fee); showers; toilets. **Best for:** walking; swimming; surfing. ⊹ *From San*

Diego–Coronado Bridge, turn left onto Orange Ave., which becomes Rte. 75, and follow signs ☎ *619/435–5184* ⊕ *www.parks.ca.gov/silverstrand* 🅿 *Parking $10; $15 peak weekends and holidays.*

FAMILY
Fodor's Choice
★

Coronado Beach. With the famous Hotel Del Coronado as a backdrop, this sandy white beach is one of San Diego County's largest and most picturesque strands. It's perfect for sunbathing, people-watching, and Frisbee tossing. Exercisers might include Navy SEAL teams or other military units that conduct training runs on beaches in and around Coronado. There are picnic tables, grills and fire rings, a playground, and (on the northern end) a dog run. Free parking is available along Ocean Boulevard, though it's often hard to snag a space. **Amenities:** food and drink; lifeguards; showers; toilets. **Best for:** swimming; walking ⊹ *From the San Diego–Coronado bridge, turn left on Orange Ave. and follow signs.*

POINT LOMA, MISSION BAY, AND LA JOLLA

POINT LOMA

Sunset Cliffs. Semisecluded Sunset Cliffs is popular with surfers and locals but offers little in the way of amenities. A few miles long, it lies beneath jagged cliffs on the Point Loma Peninsula's western side. Low tide at the southern end, near Cabrillo Point, reveals tide pools teeming with small sea creatures. Farther north the waves lure surfers, and the lonely coves attract sunbathers. Stairs at the foot of Pescadero and Bermuda avenues provide beach access, as do some cliff trails, which are treacherous at points. Osprey Point offers good fishing off the rocks. A visit here is more enjoyable at low tide or at sunset when the views are sensational. Check WaveCast (⊕ *wavecast.com/tides*) for tide schedules. **Amenities:** parking (no fee). **Best for:** solitude; sunset. ⊹ *Take I–8 west to Sunset Cliffs Blvd. and head west.*

Ocean Beach. Much of this mile-long beach south of Mission Bay's channel entrance is a haven for volleyball players, sunbathers, and swimmers. The area around the municipal pier at the southern end is a hangout for surfers and transients. The pier stays open 24 hours a day for fishing and walking. There's a restaurant about halfway out, and more places to grab a snack can be found on the streets near the beach. Swimmers should beware of strong rip currents around the main lifeguard tower. There's a dog beach at the northern end; during summer there can be as many as 100 dogs running in the sand. For picnic areas (with fire rings) and a paved path, check out Ocean Beach Park, across from Dog Beach. **Amenities:** lifeguards; parking (no fee); showers; toilets. **Best for:** surfing; swimming; walking. ⊹ *Take I–8 west to Sunset Cliffs Blvd. and head west; a right turn off Sunset Cliffs Blvd. takes you to the water.*

MISSION BAY

FAMILY
Mission Beach. San Diego's most popular beach draws huge crowds on hot summer days, but it's lively year-round. The 2-mile-long stretch extends from the northern entrance of Mission Bay to Pacific Beach. A wide boardwalk paralleling the beach is popular with walkers, joggers, roller skaters, rollerbladers, and bicyclists. Surfers, swimmers, and volleyball players congregate at the southern end. Scantily clad volleyball players practice on Cohasset Court. Toward its northern end, near the

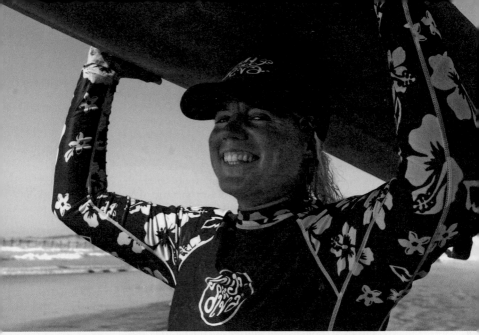
Experts and beginners alike head to San Diego for its excellent surfing.

Belmont Park roller coaster, the beach narrows and the water becomes rougher. The crowds grow thicker and somewhat rougher as well. For parking, you can try for a spot on the street, but your best bets are the two big lots at Belmont Park. **Amenities:** lifeguards; parking (no fee); showers; toilets. **Best for:** surfing; swimming; walking. ✢ *Exit I–5 at Grand Ave. and head west to Mission Blvd.; turn south and look for parking near roller coaster at West Mission Bay Dr.*

Pacific Beach/North Pacific Beach. The boardwalk of Mission Beach turns into a sidewalk here, but there are still bike paths and picnic tables along the beach. Pacific Beach runs from the northern end of Mission Beach to Crystal Pier. The scene here is lively on weekends, with nearby restaurants, beach bars, and nightclubs providing a party atmosphere. North Pacific Beach, extending north from the pier, attracts families. There are designated swimming and surfing areas, and fire rings are available, as are places to eat. Parking can be a challenge. **Amenities:** food and drink; lifeguards; parking (no fee); showers; toilets. **Best for:** partiers; surfing; swimming. ✢ *Exit I–5 at Grand Ave. and head west to Mission Blvd. Turn north and look for parking.*

Tourmaline Surfing Park. Offering slow waves and frequent winds, this is one of the most popular beaches for beginning surfers, longboarders, windsurfers, and kiteboarders. Separate areas designated for swimmers and surfers are strictly enforced. The 175-space parking lot at the foot of Tourmaline Street normally fills to capacity by midday. **Amenities:** lifeguards; parking (no fee); showers,; toilets. **Best for:** surfing; windsurfing. ⊠ *600 Tourmaline St.* ✢ *Take Mission Blvd. north (it turns into La Jolla Blvd.) and turn west on Tourmaline St.*

LA JOLLA

Windansea Beach. Named for a hotel that burned down in the late 1940s, Windansea Beach has become famous for the unusual A-frame waves the reef break here creates—and for the eclectic group of surfers those waves attract. This is one of San Diego County's most popular surf spots, and with its incredible views and secluded sunbathing spots set among sandstone rocks, Windansea is also one of the most romantic of West Coast beaches, especially at sunset. You can usually find nearby street parking. **Amenities:** lifeguards. **Best for:** solitude; sunset; surfing. ✛ *Take Mission Blvd. north (it turns into La Jolla Blvd.) and turn west on Nautilus St.*

WORD OF MOUTH

"The cove at La Jolla…reminds one of the South of France. From there you can easily wander around the very cute/upscale village of La Jolla."

—Tomsd

Marine Street Beach. A wide expanse of white sand, this beach often teems with sunbathers, swimmers, walkers, joggers, and folks just out for the incredible views. This is a great spot for bodysurfing, but be aware that the waves break in extremely shallow water. You'll also need to watch out for riptides. Picnic tables, showers, and toilets are available at the nearby cove. **Amenities:** lifeguards. **Best for:** solitude; swimming; walking. ⊠ *Accessible from Marine St., off La Jolla Blvd.*

FAMILY
Fodor'sChoice
★

La Jolla Cove. This shimmering blue inlet is what first attracted everyone to La Jolla, from Native Americans to the glitterati; it's the secret to the village's enduring cachet. You'll find "the cove"—as locals refer to it, as though it were the only one in San Diego—beyond where Girard Avenue dead-ends into Coast Boulevard, marked by towering palms that line a promenade where people strolling in designer clothes are as common as Frisbee throwers. Ellen Browning Scripps Park sits atop cliffs formed by the incessant pounding of the waves and offers a great spot for picnics with a view. At low tide, the pools and cliff caves are a destination for explorers. Divers, snorkelers, and kayakers can check out the underwater delights of the **San Diego–La Jolla Underwater Park Ecological Reserve.** The cove is also a favorite of rough-water swimmers. **Amenities:** lifeguards; showers; toilets. **Best for:** snorkeling; swimming; walking. ✛ *Follow Coast Blvd. north to signs, or take La Jolla Village Dr. exit from I–5, head west to Torrey Pines Rd., turn left, and drive downhill to Girard Ave.; turn right and follow signs.*

FAMILY
La Jolla Shores. This is one of San Diego's most popular beaches, so get here early on summer weekends. The lures are an incredible view of La Jolla peninsula, a wide sandy beach, a grassy park that's adjacent to **San Diego La Jolla Underwater Park Ecological Reserve,** and the gentlest waves in San Diego. Several surf and scuba schools teach here, and kayak rentals are nearby. A concrete boardwalk parallels the beach, and a boat launch for small vessels lies 300 yards south of the lifeguard station at Avenida de Playa. Arrive early to get a parking spot in the lot at the foot of Calle Frescota. **Amenities:** lifeguards; parking (no fee); showers; toilets. **Best for:** surfing; swimming; walking. ⊠ *8200 Camino del Oro* ✛ *From I–5 take La Jolla Village Dr. west and turn left onto La Jolla Shores Dr.; head west to Camino del Oro or Vallecitos St., turn right.*

Black's Beach. The powerful waves at this beach, officially known as Torrey Pines City Park beach, attract world-class surfers, and the strand's relative isolation appeals to nudist nature lovers (although by law nudity is prohibited) as well as gays and lesbians. Backed by cliffs whose colors change with the sun's angle, Black's can be accessed from Torrey Pines State Beach to the north, or by a narrow path descending the cliffs from Torrey Pines Glider Port. Access to parts of the shore coincides with low tide. Lifeguards patrol the area only between spring break and mid-October. Strong rip currents are common—only experienced swimmers should take the plunge. Storms have weakened the cliffs in the past few years; they're dangerous to climb and should be avoided. Part of the fun here is watching hang gliders and paragliders ascend from atop the cliffs. Parking is available at the Torrey Pines Glider Port and La Jolla Farms. **Amenities:** None. **Best for:** nudists; solitude; surfing. ✛ *Take Genesee Ave. west from I–5 and follow signs to Torrey Pines Glider Port; easier access, via a paved path, available on La Jolla Farms Rd., but parking is limited to 2 hrs.*

Torrey Pines State Beach and Reserve. One of San Diego's best beaches encompasses 2,000 acres of bluffs and bird-filled marshes. A network of meandering trails leads to the wide, sandy shoreline below. Along the way enjoy the rare Torrey pine trees, found only here and on Santa Rosa Island, offshore. Guides conduct tours of the nature preserve on weekends. Torrey Pines tends to get crowded in summer, but you'll find more isolated spots heading south under the cliffs leading to Black's Beach. **Amenities:** lifeguards; parking (fee); showers; toilets. **Best for:** surfing; swimming; walking. ✉ *12600 N. Torrey Pines Rd.* ✛ *Take Carmel Valley Rd. exit west from I–5, turn left on Rte. S21* ☎ *858/755–2063* ⊕ *www.torreypine.org* 🅿 *Parking $12–$15 per vehicle depending on day and season.*

NORTH COUNTY BEACHES

DEL MAR

Del Mar Beach. The numbered streets of Del Mar, from 15th north to 29th, end at a wide beach popular with volleyball players, surfers, and sunbathers. The portion of Del Mar south of 15th Street is lined with cliffs and rarely crowded. Leashed dogs are permitted on most sections of the beach, except Main Beach, where they are prohibited from June 15th through Labor Day. For the rest of the year, dogs may run under voice control at North Beach, also known as Dog Beach. Food, hotels, and shopping are all within an easy walk of Del Mar beach. Parking costs from $1.50 to $3 per hour at meters and pay lots on Coast Boulevard and along Camino Del Mar. **Amenities:** food and drink; lifeguards; parking (fee); showers; toilets. **Best for:** swimming; walking. ✛ *Take Via de la Valle exit from I–5 west to Rte. S21 (also known as Camino del Mar in Del Mar) and turn left.*

ENCINITAS

Swami's. The palms and the golden lotus-flower domes of the nearby Self-Realization Center temple and ashram earned this picturesque beach, also a top surfing spot, its name. Extreme low tides expose tide pools that harbor anemones, starfish, and other sea life. The only access is by a long stairway leading down from the cliff-top Seaside Roadside Park, where there's free parking. On big winter swells, the bluffs are lined with gawkers watching the area's best surfers take on—and be taken down by—some of the county's best big waves. Offshore, divers do their thing at North County's underwater park, Encinitas Marine Life Refuge. **Amenities:** lifeguards; parking (no fee); showers; toilets. **Best for:** snorkeling; surfing; swimming. ✢ *Follow Rte. S21 north from Cardiff, or Exit I–5 at Encinitas Blvd., go west to Rte. S21, and turn left.*

WHERE TO EAT

Updated
by Maren
Dougherty

San Diego's proximity to Mexico makes it an attractive destination for anything wrapped in a tortilla, but there's so much more. While most of the top restaurants offer seasonal California fare, San Diego also boasts excellent ethnic cuisines available at all prices.

As elsewhere in the United States, the San Diego dining scene has moved toward using sustainable, locally sourced meat, seafood, and produce—and providing good value. This emphasis on affordability is often presented as early or late-night dining specials, but also extends to the wine lists, where smart sommeliers are offering more wines from value regions like France's Loire and Languedoc, and countries like Chile and South Africa.

Use the coordinate (✢ A1) at the end of each listing to locate a site on the corresponding map.

RESTAURANT COSTS

Prices in the restaurant reviews are the average cost of a main course at dinner or, if dinner is not served, at lunch (excluding sales tax).

DOWNTOWN

GASLAMP QUARTER

$$

SPANISH

Fodor's Choice

★

✕ **Café Sevilla.** Sevilla moved into new digs in 2011, allowing a fresh look for this tapas bar, nightclub, and restaurant. Thursday through Sunday evenings, it's packed with youthful throngs who crowd the ground-floor bar for drinks, tapas, and live music. Others head to the downstairs club for classics from the Spanish kitchen and, on Saturday nights, professional flamenco dancing. The kitchen does a respectable job with the traditional shellfish and chicken paella (there are meat and other seafood versions, too); other good choices are the highly flavorful baked rabbit and the roasted pork tenderloin. A new favorite is a trio of dramatically presented *brochetas,* or skewers, of spiced shrimp, Spanish sausage, and steak with mushrooms and onions. ⑤ *Average main: $20* ✉ *353 5th Ave.* ☎ *619/233–5979* ⊕ *www.cafesevilla.com* ☾ *No lunch* ✢ *H3.*

$$$

AMERICAN

✕ **Searsucker.** The much-hyped first restaurant from *Top Chef* finalist Brian Malarkey opened in summer 2010 and has maintained its buzz ever since, attracting patrons with its fun urban decor and experimental dishes like swordfish with drunken cherries and beef cheeks over goat cheese dumplings. The flavor combinations are mostly successful, particularly when paired with comfort-food sides like bacon grits and grilled asparagus. Chef Malarkey adds to the lively vibe when he makes his rounds to chat with diners. ⑤ *Average main: $30* ⊠ *611 5th Ave.* ☎ *619/233–7327* ⊕ *www.searsucker.com* ⌕ *Reservations essential* ⊹ *H2.*

$$ ✕ **Taka.** It may be on a prominent corner, but the pristine fish imported
JAPANESE from around the world and the creative presentations are what attracts
Fodor'sChoice the crowds each night. Start with one of the sushi chef's appetizers,
★ perhaps the monkfish liver with ponzu, some slices of tender hamachi sashimi, or a special box-press sushi with shrimp, tuna, and crab topped with pickled seaweed and caviar. Hot dishes include salmon teriyaki and an East-meets-West-style New York steak. The restaurant is a favorite with Japanese visitors. ⑤ *Average main: $20* ⊠ *555 5th Ave.* ☎ *619/338–0555* ⊕ *www.takasushi.com* ☾ *No lunch* ⊹ *H2.*

EAST VILLAGE

$$ ✕ **Café Chloe.** The intersection of 9th and G is the meeting point for San
FRENCH Diego's café society, thanks to the superchic and friendly Café Chloe.
Fodor'sChoice Surrounded by luxury high-rises, hotels, and boutiques, this pretty Parisian spot is frequented by the locals for breakfast, lunch, dinner, and
★ weekend brunch. Whole-wheat pancakes with sour-cherry sauce are an excellent way to start the day; lunch might mean a smoked trout and apple salad or a casserole of macaroni, pancetta, and Gorgonzola; and dinner highlights include duck confit or steak frites. Enjoy wines by the glass, imported teas, and coffee with desserts like seasonal fruit tarts or chocolate pot de crème. It's a particularly lovely place to spend the afternoon. ⑤ *Average main: $21* ⊠ *721 9th Ave.* ☎ *619/232–3242* ⊕ *www.cafechloe.com* ⊹ *E5.*

$$$ ✕ **Cowboy Star.** Executive chef Victor Jimenez cooks up porterhouses
STEAKHOUSE for two and grass-fed fillets along with fluffy mashed potatoes, glazed
Fodor'sChoice carrots, and garlic-sautéed spinach at this modern, urban steak house
★ with a tongue-in-cheek cowboy theme. It's not a place for line dancing or peanut shelling: servers wear stylish plaid shirts and the wood-and-brick decor has leather accents and photography that recalls the Old West. Non–steak eaters can tuck into dishes like scallops with spiced kumquats and halibut with summer squash. The high-back booths are comfy; so are the chef's counter and the bar, where mixologists shake up strong bourbon cocktails. The drink selections include artisanal brews paired with the steaks. Street parking is usually available. ⑤ *Average main:* ☾ ⊠ *640 10th Ave.* ☎ *619/450–5880* ⊕ *www.thecowboystar. com* ☾ *Closed Mon. No lunch Sun.* ⊹ *H2*

$ ✕ **The Kebab Shop.** Easy to find in Europe but rare in San Diego are
GREEK kebab shops: fast-food Mediterranean eateries where roasted meats and
Fodor'sChoice falafel are served on plates of rice or wrapped in flatbread for consumption at all hours of the day. This East Village shop doesn't have much
★ competition, but that doesn't mean it's not first-rate. The lamb is spicy and filling, and fresh tabouli and Greek salads round out the meals. For a delicious meal on the go, order the *döner* box: a choice of spiced lamb, marinated chicken, or falafel, accompanied by fries or rice, fresh veggies, and creamy garlic yogurt sauce. ⑤ *Average main: $7* ⊠ *630 9th Ave.* ☎ *619/525–0055* ⊕ *www.thekebabshop.com* ⌕ *Reservations not accepted* ⊹ *H2.*

BEST BETS FOR SAN DIEGO DINING

With hundreds of restaurants to choose from, how will you decide where to eat? We've selected our favorite restaurants by price, cuisine, and experience in the Best Bets list below. In the first column, Fodor's Choice properties represent the "best of the best" in every price category. Bon appétit!

Fodor's Choice★

A.R. Valentien, $$$$, p. 87
Bali Hai, $$, p. 90
Barrio Star, $, p. 83
Bencotto, $$, p. 83
Bread & Cie, $, p. 86
Café Chloe, $$, p. 81
Café Sevilla, $$, p. 80
Cowboy Star, $$$, p. 81
Cucina Urbana, $$$, p. 83
El Pescador, $, p. 88
George's at the Cove, $$$$, p. 88
Jimmy's Famous American Tavern, $, p. 90
The Kebab Shop, $, p. 81
Lucha Libre, $, p. 86
Mistral, $$, p. 91
Nine-Ten, $$$$, p. 88
Ortega's Bistro, $$, p. 86
Phil's BBQ, $, p. 90
Sushi on the Rock, $, p. 89
Sushi Ota, $$$, p. 87
Taka, $$, p. 81
Tender Greens, $, p. 90
Wisknladle, $$, p. 89

By Price

$

Bread & Cie, p. 86
Lucha Libre, p. 86
Tender Greens, p. 90
URBN Coal Fired Pizza, p. 87

$$

Benecotto, p. 83
Café Chloe, p. 81
Mistral, p. 91
Taka, p. 81

$$$

Cowboy Star, p. 81
Searsucker, p. 80
Sushi Ota, p. 87

$$$$

1500 Ocean, p. 90
A.R. Valentien, p. 87
George's at the Cove, p. 88
Nine-Ten, p. 88

Best by Cuisine

AMERICAN

A.R. Valentien, $$$$, p. 87
Jimmy's Famous American Tavern, $, p. 90
Nine-Ten, $$$$, p. 88
Searsucker, $$$, p. 80

CAFÉS

Bread & Cie, $, p. 86
Café Chloe, $$, p. 81

ITALIAN

Bencotto, $$, p. 83
Cucina Urbana, $$$, p. 83

JAPANESE

Sushi Ota, $$$, p. 87
Taka, $$, p. 81

LATIN/MEXICAN

El Agave, $$$, p. 86
Lucha Libre, $, p. 86
Ortega's Bistro, $$, p. 86

PIZZA

Cucina Urbana, $$$, p. 83

URBN Coal Fired Pizza, $, p. 87

VEGETARIAN

Tender Greens, $, p. 90

Best By Experience

BRUNCH

Café Chloe, $$, p. 81
JRDN, $$$, p. 87
Nine-Ten, $$$$, p. 88

DINING WITH KIDS

Ortega's Bistro, $$, p. 86
Tender Greens, $, p. 90
URBN Coal Fried Pizza, $, p. 87

GOOD FOR GROUPS

Barrio Star, $, p. 83
Café Sevilla, $$, p. 80
URBN Coal Fired Pizza, $, p. 87

ROMANTIC

George's at the Cove, $$$$, p. 88
Mistral, $$, p. 91

WATER VIEWS

Bali Hai, $$, p. 90
George's at the Cove, $$$$, p. 88
Mistral, $$, p. 91

LITTLE ITALY

$$
ITALIAN
Fodor's Choice
★

✕ **Bencotto.** The Northern Italian team behind Bencotto opened a fine-dining restaurant in Milan and a bistro called Salumeria Rosi in New York before developing this sophisticated addition to Little Italy. Diners linger over wine and meat platters at the friendly bar and the more intimate upstairs dining room. Small plates designed for sharing include fried saffron risotto balls and sliced cantaloupe with prosciutto, but the real draws are the fresh pastas made daily in-house that include Gorgonzola-filled gnocchi, various ravioli, and squid-ink fettuccine. The pastas can be topped with a choice of sauces and chicken, shrimp, or meatballs. ■TIP→ **Parking can be challenging but the Little Italy valet service is available after 6 pm.** ⑤ *Average main: $18* ⊠ *750 W. Fir St.* ☎ *619/450–4786* ⊕ *www.lovebencotto.com* ⊗ *Closed Mon. (except in summer)* ✛ *E5.*

BALBOA PARK AND BANKERS HILL

BALBOA PARK

$$$
ECLECTIC

✕ **The Prado.** The striking Spanish-Moorish interior of this lovely restaurant in the historic House of Hospitality on Balboa Park's museum row has painted ceilings and elaborate glass sculptures. It also brings a contemporary menu to an area where picnic lunches or hot dogs from a nearby cart are the usual options. The bar is a fashionable pre- and post-theater destination for light nibbles with Latin, Italian, and Asian flavors and creative drinks; in the dining room, reliable dishes range from lunchtime grilled mahimahi tacos and a fancy pressed salad of baby arugula, strawberries, dried figs, and asiago cheese to saffron-scented lobster paella and roasted sea bass. ⑤ *Average main: $30* ⊠ *1549 El Prado* ☎ *619/557–9441* ⊕ *www.pradobalboa.com* ⊗ *No dinner Mon.* ✛ *E5.*

BANKERS HILL

$
MEXICAN
Fodor's Choice
★

✕ **Barrio Star.** In a colorful, airy Bankers Hill space, chef Isabel Cruz of Isabel's Cantina and up-and-coming chef Todd Camburn put a fresh, distinctive, and rather refined spin on classic Mexican fare. After an afternoon at nearby Balboa Park, swing by for happy-hour margaritas and tacos or feast on grilled sweet corn slathered in spicy lime butter, tortilla soup with cotija cheese, slow-roasted pork carnitas tacos with house-made tortillas, flourless Mexican chocolate cake, and Latin-inspired cocktails. On weekends, Barrio Star opens at 9 am for breakfasts of tamales, tortas, and blackberry pancakes. ⑤ *Average main: $12* ⊠ *2706 5th Ave.* ☎ *619/501–7827* ⊕ *www.barriostar.com* ✛ *E5.*

$$$
ITALIAN
Fodor's Choice
★

✕ **Cucina Urbana.** Proprietor Tracy Borkum's casual and stylish Cal-Italian spot remains one of the most popular tables in town. Everything is reasonably priced, and diners can pop into the retail wine room, select a bottle, and drink it with dinner for a modest corkage fee. The ricotta gnudi bathed in brown butter and fried sage are the best yet; fried squash blossoms sing; and polenta boards mixed tableside are creative and satisfying. Also good are the lasagna, the short rib pappardelle, and the goat cheese and toasted almond ravioli. Sit at the cozy bar and watch the chefs turn out bubbly, thin-crust pizzas topped

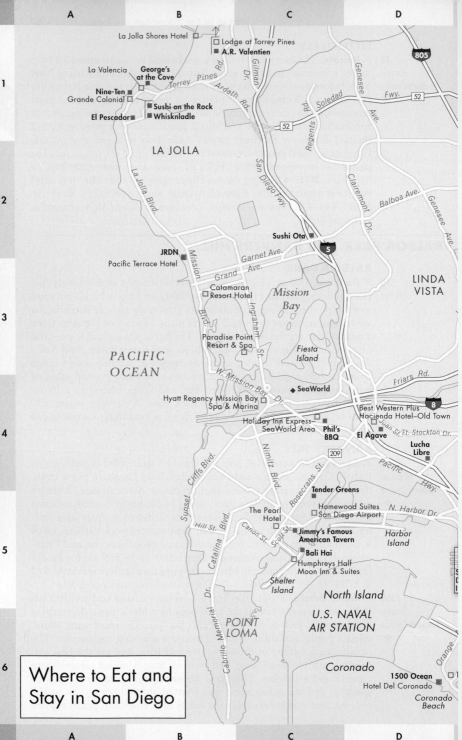

Where to Eat and Stay in San Diego

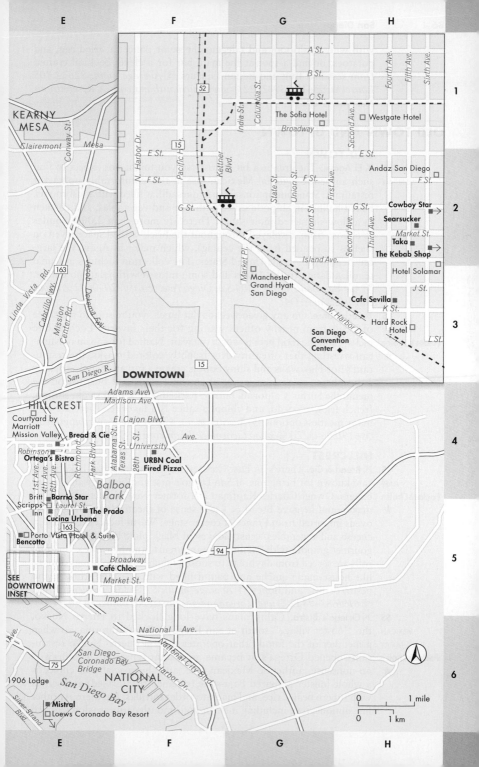

with wild mushroom and taleggio cheese or pancetta, fried egg, and potatoes, or find a spot at the main bar for a clever cocktail crafted from seasonal fruit and Italian liqueurs. $ *Average main: $26* ⊠ *505 Laurel St.* ☎ *619/239–2222* ⊕ *www.cucinaurbana.com* ⌕ *Reservations essential* ✛ *E5.*

OLD TOWN AND UPTOWN

OLD TOWN

$$$ ✕ **El Agave.** The area is a bit touristy so you might not expect to find
MEXICAN such authentic regional Mexican fare at this comfortably upmarket restaurant. Standout options include quesadillas filled with mushrooms, baked halibut in chipotle sauce with rice and vegetables, and chicken in a slow-simmered mole sauce. There are more than 2,000 tequilas to choose from, displayed throughout the brick-walled space (even on shelves suspended from the ceiling), which make El Agave the largest "tequileria" in the United States. The collection includes artisanal tequilas dating to the 1930s and some infused with jalapeño chilies. $ *Average main: $30* ⊠ *2304 San Diego Ave.* ☎ *619/220–0692* ⊕ *www. elagave.com* ✛ *D4.*

$ ✕ **Lucha Libre.** On any given weekday at lunch, you're sure to see a line
MEXICAN of locals from nearby offices waiting for their favorite Lucha Libre
Fodor's Choice picks—and the food here is worth the wait. Named for a form of Mexi-
★ can wrestling that often involves brightly colored masks, the restaurant's hot-pink walls and shiny booths create a fun and family-friendly atmosphere. There is an array of gourmet tacos and burritos on the menu; the Surfin' California burrito packed with grilled steak, shrimp, french fries, avocado, and chipotle sauce is a favorite. There are also many meatless options. $ *Average main: $7* ⊠ *1810 W. Washington St.* ☎ *619/296–8226* ⊕ *www.tacosmackdown.com* ✛ *D4.*

HILLCREST

$ ✕ **Bread & Cie.** There's an East Coast air to this artsy urban bakery and
CAFÉ café known for being one of San Diego's first and best artisanal bread
Fodor's Choice bakers. Owner Charles Kaufman is a former New Yorker and a film-
★ maker, and he gave Bread & Cie a sense of theater by putting bread ovens imported from France at center stage. Warm focaccia covered in cheese and vegetables, crusty loaves of black olive bread, bear claws, gourmet granola with Mediterranean yogurt, and first-rate cinnamon rolls are served from daybreak to sunset; lunch time also brings options like house-made quiche and panini filled with pastrami, turkey, and pesto, or Brie and honey. $ *Average main: $7* ⊠ *350 University Ave.* ☎ *619/683–9322* ⊕ *www.breadandcie.com* ☉ *No dinner* ✛ *E4.*

$$ ✕ **Ortega's Bistro.** Californians have long flocked to Puerto Nuevo,
MEXICAN the "lobster village" south of San Diego in Baja California, so when
FAMILY a member of the family that operates several Puerto Nuevo restau-
Fodor's Choice rants opened Ortega's, it became an instant sensation. The draw is
★ no-nonsense, authentic Mexican fare, and the specialty of choice is a whole lobster prepared Baja-style (steamed then grilled) and served with superb beans, rice, and made-to-order tortillas. But there are other fine options, too, including melt-in-your-mouth carnitas (slow-cooked

pork), made-at-the-table guacamole, and grilled tacos filled with *huitlacoche* corn mushrooms and Mexican herbs. The pomegranate margaritas are a must, as is the special red salsa if you like authentic spice. ⑤ *Average main: $18* ✉ *141 University Ave.* ☎ *619/692–4200* ⊕ *www. ortegasbistro.com* ✛ *E4.*

NORTH PARK

$ ✕ **URBN Coal Fired Pizza.** A few blocks east of 30th Street (North Park's
PIZZA restaurant row), this 5,000-square-foot warehouse is a chic and casual pizza spot. Hip young locals chow down on coal-fired New Haven–style pies, fresh salads, and cheese boards. Try the carbalicious mashed potato pizza pie topped with pancetta, fresh mozzarella, and Parmesan. Linger with a local brew or a craft cocktail off the extensive drink list. It's a good space for groups so the atmosphere can get quite festive. ⑤ *Average main: $8* ✉ *3085 University Ave.* ☎ *619/255–7300* ⊕ *www. urbnnorthpark.com* ⊗ *No lunch on Mondays.* ✛ *F4.*

PACIFIC BEACH

$$$ ✕ **JRDN.** With some 300 seats, this ocean-facing restaurant (pronounced
AMERICAN Jordana), in the beach-chic, boutique-style Tower23 Hotel might sound overwhelming, but the seating is divided between a long, narrow outdoor terrace and a series of relatively intimate indoor rooms. Chef David Warner prepares modern steak house fare including chops and steaks with sauces of the diner's choosing, lightened with lots of seasonal produce and a raw bar menu. Weekend brunch and lunch have a similar appeal, with dishes like crab cake eggs Benedict with citrus hollandaise, a blackened mahi mahi sandwich, and a summer melon salad. On Fridays and Saturdays, the bar is the place to see and be seen in Pacific Beach for under-30 types, and it's jammed after 9 pm. ⑤ *Average main: $33* ✉ *Tower 23 Hotel, 723 Felspar St.* ☎ *858/270–5736* ⊕ *www.jrdn.com* ✛ *B3.*

$$$ ✕ **Sushi Ota.** Wedged into a minimall between a convenience store and
JAPANESE a looming medical building, Sushi Ota's location might seem less than
Fodor'sChoice auspicious but it helps to know that San Diego–bound Japanese busi-
★ nesspeople frequently call for reservations before boarding their trans-Pacific flights. Look at the expressions on customers' faces as they leave and you can see the satisfied glows that result from dining on San Diego's best sushi. Besides the usual California roll and tuna and shrimp sushi, there are specialties that change daily such as sea urchin or surf clam sushi, a soft-shell crab roll, or the *omakase* tasting menu. Note that Japanese speakers tend to get the best spots, and servers can be abrupt. ■ TIP➔ There's additional parking behind the mall. ⑤ *Average main: $30* ✉ *4529 Mission Bay Dr.* ☎ *858/270–5670* ⚐ *Reservations essential* ⊗ *No lunch Sat.–Mon.* ✛ *C2.*

LA JOLLA

$$$$ ✕ **A. R. Valentien.** Known for his insistence on in-season, fresh-today
AMERICAN produce and seafood, chef Jeff Jackson writes menus daily for this cozy
Fodor'sChoice room in the luxurious, Craftsman-style Lodge at Torrey Pines. His take
★ on food combinations is simultaneously simple and inventive, as demonstrated in appetizers of smoked trout with potatoes and turnips, and

porcini mushroom and chestnut soup with bacon and apple. In addition to the à la carte menu, a nightly three-course tasting menu explores the day's market through the eyes of the talented chef. At lunch on the outdoor terrace, consider the "Drugstore" hamburger: a grilled patty is placed on top of lettuce, tomato, and condiments, and is then topped with cheese before being steamed to perfection on its sesame seed bun. $ *Average main: $35* ✉ *11480 N. Torrey Pines Rd.* ☎ *858/777–6635* ⊕ *www.arvalentien.com* ◷ *No breakfast Mon.–Fri.* ✛ *B1.*

$
SEAFOOD
Fodor's Choice
★

✕ **El Pescador.** This low-key fish market and café in the heart of La Jolla village is popular with locals for its simply prepared fresh fish. Try a filet—maybe halibut, swordfish, salmon, or tuna—lightly grilled and perched on a soft torta roll with shredded lettuce, tomato, and onions. Other choices include ceviche, sashimi plates, Dungeness crab salad, sautéed mussels with sourdough bread, and excellent fish tacos. Seats are few, and tables often end up being shared, but the food is worth the wait. ■**TIP→** Order fish sandwiches to go for a tasty oceanfront picnic at La Jolla Cove. $ *Average main: $15* ✉ *627 Pearl St.* ☎ *858/456–2526* ⊕ *www.elpescadorfishmarket.com* ⩟ *Reservations not accepted* ✛ *B1.*

$$$$
AMERICAN
Fodor's Choice
★

✕ **George's at the Cove.** La Jolla's oceanfront destination restaurant includes three dining areas: **California Modern** on the bottom floor, **George's Bar** in the middle, and **Ocean Terrace** on the roof. Hollywood types and other visiting celebrities can be spotted at California Modern, the sleek main dining room with its wall of windows. Simple preparations of fresh seafood, beef, and lamb reign on the menu, which chef Trey Foshee enlivens with produce from local specialty growers. Give special consideration to roasted Niman Ranch pork loin with maitake mushrooms, smoked Maine lobster with squash blossoms, and the legendary fish tacos. For a more casual and inexpensive experience, go to the indoor/outdoor George's Bar, where you can get tacos and watch a sports game, or head upstairs to the outdoor-only Ocean Terrace for spectacular views of La Jolla Cove. $ *Average main: $39* ✉ *1250 Prospect St.* ☎ *858/454–4244* ⊕ *www.georgesatthecove.com* ⩟ *Reservations essential* ✛ *B1.*

$$$$
AMERICAN
Fodor's Choice
★

✕ **Nine-Ten.** In the sleek, contemporary dining room that occupies the ground floor of the Grande Colonial Hotel, acclaimed chef (and 2011 *Iron Chef* challenger) Jason Knibb serves satisfying seasonal fare at breakfast, lunch, and dinner. The Downtown La Jolla location is ideal for travelers but it's just as much a locals spot, attracting professionals for power lunches and foodies for the excellent food. At night the perfectly executed menu may include tantalizing appetizers like Jamaican jerk pork belly or lamb sugo and mains such as a roasted leg of rabbit stuffed with Swiss chard, lemons, raisins, and cumin, or beef short ribs braised with Alesmith stout and served with root vegetables. Stand-out desserts include cilantro basil cake and strawberry sorbet with candied kumquats. Three- and five-course prix-fixe menus are available for the whole table. $ *Average main: $36* ✉ *Grande Colonial Hotel, 910 Prospect St.* ☎ *858/964–5400* ⊕ *www.nine-ten.com* ✛ *B1.*

The quality of the food complements the spectacular views at George's at the Cove.

$ **⚔ Sushi on the Rock.** There's something fun about Sushi on the Rock,
SUSHI from the young, friendly chefs to the comically named California-style
Fodor'sChoice sushi specialties, like the Slippery When Wet roll featuring tempura
★ shrimp, eel, crab, and cucumber. There are many original rolls to choose
from, including the Barrio Roll stuffed with tuna, cilantro, and spicy
tomato salsa; the Ashley Roll that pairs seared tuna with soft-shell
crab and tangy whole-grain mustard sauce; and the Bruce Lee, with
spicy crab, tuna, and avocado. The Japanese-inspired dishes, including pot stickers and an Asian-style Caesar salad are also good, as is
the lobster mac and cheese. This popular spot, which has a patio with
an ocean view, gets busy in the late afternoon with people wanting to
grab a seat for the daily happy hour (5–6:30 pm). ⑤ *Average main: $16*
✉ *1025 Prospect St., #250* ☎ *858/459–3208* ⊕ *www.sushiontherock.*
com ⌘ *Reservations not accepted* ✣ *B1.*

$$ **⚔ Whisknladle.** This hip, popular eatery that doubles as a fashion show
SEAFOOD of La Jolla ladies who lunch has earned national acclaim with its com-
Fodor'sChoice bination of casual comfort and a menu of ever-changing local fare. In
★ nice weather, request a patio table when reserving. Appetizers include
dishes like heirloom tomato salad and savory flatbreads that change
daily. Larger plates feature local halibut with Chino Farms vegetables or
crab tortellini. And the bar is worth a visit, too, with its original menu
of cocktails like the tamarind margarita, cucumber honey mimosa, and
pomegranate mojito. ⑤ *Average main: $23* ✉ *1044 Wall St.* ☎ *858/551–*
7575 ⊕ *www.whisknladle.com* ⌘ *Reservations essential* ✣ *B1.*

POINT LOMA, SHELTER ISLAND, AND CORONADO

POINT LOMA

$ ✕ **Jimmy's Famous American Tavern.** Jimmy's is a standout in the wave
AMERICAN of recent gastropubs, and while the food is the main draw here, the
FAMILY decor—industrial meets Americana—has an appealing straightfor-
Fodor'sChoice wardness, too. Head through the garage-style doors for a patio seat
★ with a water view or opt for a cozy booth. The menu features elevated
takes on backyard BBQ that include the Jimmy, a 10-ounce burger
topped with pimento cheese, applewood smoked bacon, and jalapeño
jelly. The buttermilk fried chicken breast and jalapeño deviled eggs
are also worth a try. The short rib hash at Sunday brunch is stellar. $ *Average main: $16 ✉ 4990 N. Harbor Dr.* ☎ *619/226–2103*
⊕ *www.j-fat.com* ✢ *C5.*

$ ✕ **Phil's BBQ.** At peak dining hours, the line can be hours long for din-
BARBECUE ers craving Phil's baby back ribs, the pulled pork, or the huge, crispy
Fodor'sChoice onion rings. Adding to the restaurant's reputation and allure is the fact
★ that one of the specialties, the El Toro trI–tip sandwich, was included
in Travel Channel celebrity Adam Richman's 2012 list of America's
best sandwiches. But don't let the crowds dissuade you: phone in for
carry-out, sit at the bar, or bring the family during midafternoon for a
messy, char-grilled introduction to barbecue heaven. $ *Average main:*
$14 ✉ 3750 Sports Arena Blvd. ☎ *619/226–6333* ⊕ *www.philsbbq.net*
⚖ *Reservations not accepted* ⊗ *Closed Mon.* ✢ *C4.*

$ ✕ **Tender Greens.** "Farm-fresh ingredients served up with little fuss" is
AMERICAN the ethos behind this casual cafeteria-style spot in Liberty Station. It's
FAMILY very popular at lunch but the line moves quickly. Expect big salads like
Fodor'sChoice seared tuna Niçoise; Fra' Mani salami with shaved fennel, pecorino, and
★ arugula; or chipotle chicken salad. Naturally raised beef and chicken
are roasted and then tucked into sandwiches or served as a dinner plate
with vegetables. Wine and house-made desserts round out the menu.
$ *Average main: $13 ✉ 2400 Historic Decatur Rd.* ☎ *619/226–6254*
⊕ *tendergreensfood.com* ✢ *C4.*

SHELTER ISLAND

$$ ✕ **Bali Hai.** This kitschy-classy waterfront restaurant is loved as much
HAWAIIAN for the strong, sugary drinks served in tiki mugs as it is for the gorgeous
Fodor'sChoice views of the San Diego Bay and the Downtown skyline. One of few
★ restaurants within walking distance of Shelter Island hotels, Bali Hai's
menu has Hawaiian, Asian, and Californian influences, with an empha-
sis on seafood. Standouts include the Hawaiian tuna poke stack, crispy
spring rolls, and seared diver scallops with glazed pork belly. Lounge
seating accommodates groups while tables by the window are ideal for
quiet, romantic dinners. $ *Average main: $23 ✉ 2230 Shelter Island*
Dr. ☎ *619/222–1181* ⊕ *www.balihairestaurant.com* ✢ *C5.*

CORONADO

$$$$ ✕ **1500 Ocean.** The fine-dining restaurant at Hotel Del Coronado, right
AMERICAN on the beach, offers a memorable evening showcasing the best organic
and naturally raised ingredients the region has to offer. Select ingre-
dients come straight from the hotel's herb and produce garden. Sub-
limely subtle dishes include the colorful succotash with sweet corn,

heirloom tomatoes, squash blossoms, and Sauvignon Blanc; and diver scallops with roasted corn, grilled apricots, and Chardonnay. The elegant interior of the restaurant evokes a posh cabana; the terrace has ocean views. An excellent international wine list and clever desserts and artisanal cheeses complete the experience. $ *Average main: $36* ⊠ *Hotel Del Coronado, 1500 Orange Ave.* ☎ *619/522–8490* ⊕ *www. hoteldel.com/1500-ocean.aspx* ⚑ *Reservations essential* ⊘ *Closed. Sun. and Mon. No lunch* ✢ *D6.*

$$

INTERNATIONAL

Fodor's Choice

★

✕ **Mistral.** Named after the warm wind that blows across southern France and Italy, the fine-dining, dinner-only restaurant at Loews Coronado Bay Resort focuses on southern French and northern Italian cuisine built around naturally raised meats and organic local produce. Fifth-generation French chef Patrick Ponsaty presents a menu that ranges from arugula salad with figs and lavender honey, to grilled prime beef tenderloin and salmon with lobster emulsion. A well-edited wine list and house-made desserts like profiteroles with Valrhona chocolate sauce and vanilla ice cream complete the experience. The decor plays up the sweeping views of the bay visible from every table. $ *Average main: $24* ⊠ *Loews Coronado Bay Resort, 4000 Coronado Bay Rd.* ☎ *619/424–4000* ⊕ *www.dineatmistral.com* ⊘ *Closed Sun. and Mon., no lunch* ✢ *E6.*

WHERE TO STAY

Updated
by Maren
Dougherty

In San Diego, you could plan a luxurious vacation, staying at a hotel with 350-thread-count sheets, wall-mounted flat screens, and panoramic Pacific views. But with some flexibility—maybe opting for a partial-view room with standard TVs—it's possible to experience the city's beauty at half the price.

Any local will tell you two things about San Diego: No. 1, the weather really is perfect; and No. 2, the area's neighborhoods and beach communities offer great diversity, from lively urban vacations to laid-back beachfront escapes. You'll need a car if you stay outside Downtown, but the coastal communities are rich with lodging options. For families, Uptown, Mission Valley, and Old Town are close to SeaWorld and the San Diego Zoo, offering good-value accommodations with extras like sleeper sofas and video games.

Many hotels promote discounted weekend packages to fill rooms after convention and business customers leave town. You can save on hotels and attractions by visiting the San Diego Convention and Visitors Bureau website (⊕ *www.sandiego.org*) for a free Vacation Planning Kit with a Travel Value Coupon booklet.

Use the coordinate (✢ A1) at the end of each listing to locate a site on the corresponding map.

PRICES

Prices in the reviews are the lowest cost of a standard double room in high season. For expanded hotel reviews, facilities, and current deals, visit Fodors.com.

DOWNTOWN

For expanded reviews, facilities, and current deals, visit Fodors.com.

GASLAMP QUARTER

$$
HOTEL
Fodor's Choice
★

▦ **Andaz San Diego.** The former Ivy Hotel was rebranded in 2010 as the luxury, Hyatt-managed Andaz, whose new owners nixed the snobbery but kept the style. **Pros:** luxurious rooms; thriving nightlife scene; friendly service. **Cons:** noisy on weekends; not a good choice for families. ⑤ *Rooms from: $288* ⊠ *600 F St.* ☎ *619/849–1234* ⊕ *www.sandiego.andaz.hyatt.com* ⚲ *142 rooms, 17 suites* ⏺⏺ *No meals* ✥ *H2.*

$$
HOTEL
Fodor's Choice
★

▦ **Hard Rock Hotel.** Self-billed as a hip playground for rock stars and people who want to party like them, the Hard Rock is conveniently located near PETCO Park overlooking glimmering San Diego Bay. **Pros:** central location; great scene; luxurious rooms. **Cons:** pricey drinks; some attitude. ⑤ *Rooms from: $204* ⊠ *207 5th Ave.* ☎ *619/702–3000, 866/751–7625* ⊕ *www.hardrockhotelsd.com* ⚲ *244 rooms, 176 suites* ⏺⏺ *No meals* ✥ *H3.*

$$
HOTEL
FAMILY
Fodor's Choice
★

▦ **Hotel Solamar.** The hip Solamar is best known for its poolside rooftop bar, LoungeSix, and stylish lobby decor. **Pros:** great restaurant; attentive service; upscale rooms. **Cons:** busy valet parking; bars are crowded and noisy on weekends. ⑤ *Rooms from: $242* ⊠ *435 6th Ave.* ☎ *619/819–9500, 877/230–0300* ⊕ *www.hotelsolamar.com* ⚲ *217 rooms, 16 suites* ⏺⏺ *No meals* ✥ *H2.*

$$
HOTEL
Fodor's Choice
★

▦ **The Sofia Hotel.** This stylish and centrally located boutique hotel has small rooms, but clever details help guests feel pampered. **Pros:** upscale room amenities; historic building; near shops and restaurants. **Cons:** busy area; small rooms. ⑤ *Rooms from: $209* ⊠ *150 W. Broadway* ☎ *619/234–9200, 800/826–0009* ⊕ *www.thesofiahotel.com* ⚲ *211 rooms, 4 suites* ⏺⏺ *No meals* ✥ *G1.*

$$
HOTEL
Fodor's Choice
★

▦ **Westgate Hotel.** A modern high-rise near Horton Plaza hides San Diego's most opulent old-world-style hotel. **Pros:** elegant rooms; grand lobby, near shopping. **Cons:** formal atmosphere; mandatory facility fee. ⑤ *Rooms from: $280* ⊠ *1055 2nd Ave.* ☎ *619/238–1818, 800/221–3802* ⊕ *www.westgatehotel.com* ⚲ *215 rooms, 8 suites* ⏺⏺ *No meals* ✥ *H1.*

LITTLE ITALY

$
HOTEL

▦ **Porto Vista Hotel & Suites.** A $15 million renovation turned this former budget motel into a contemporary hotel-motel with two additional buildings, a stylish restaurant and lounge, and a fitness center. **Pros:** new decor in common areas, some guest rooms, and the fitness center; airport shuttle. **Cons:** spotty service; small rooms, some still in need of updating. ⑤ *Rooms from: $145* ⊠ *1835 Columbia St.* ☎ *619/544–0164, 855/504–8986* ⊕ *www.portovistasandiego.com* ⚲ *189 rooms, 22 suites* ⏺⏺ *No meals* ✥ *E5.*

EMBARCADERO

$$
HOTEL
FAMILY

▦ **Manchester Grand Hyatt San Diego.** Primarily for business travelers, this hotel between Seaport Village and the convention center is San Diego's largest, and its 33- and 40-story towers make it the West Coast's tallest waterfront hotel. **Pros:** great views; conference facilities; good location.

BEST BETS FOR SAN DIEGO LODGING

Fodor's offers a selective listing of quality lodging experiences. Here we've compiled our top recommendations. The very best properties—in other words, those that provide a particularly remarkable experience in their price range—are designated in the listings with a Fodor's Choice logo.

Fodor's Choice★

1906 Lodge at Coronado Beach, $$, p. 98

Andaz San Diego, $$, p. 92

Britt Scripps Inn, $$, p. 94

Catamaran Resort Hotel, $, p. 97

Courtyard by Marriott Mission Valley, $, p. 94

Grande Colonial, $$, p. 97

Hard Rock Hotel, $$, p. 92

Homewood Suites San Diego Airport, $, p. 98

Hotel Del Coronado, $$$, p. 98

Hotel Solamar, $$, p. 92

Lodge at Torrey Pines, $$$, p. 97

The Pearl Hotel, $, p. 98

The Sofia Hotel, $$, p. 92

Westgate Hotel, $$, p. 92

Best by Price

$

Best Western Plus Hacienda Hotel-Old Town, p. 94

Catamaran Resort Hotel, p. 97

Courtyard by Marriott Mission Valley, p. 94

Homewood Suites San Diego Airport, p. 98

The Pearl Hotel, p. 98

Porto Vista Hotel & Suites, p. 92

$$

Andaz San Diego, p. 92

Grande Colonial, p. 97

Hard Rock Hotel, p. 92

Hotel Solamar, p. 92

Paradise Point Resort & Spa, p. 94

The Sofia Hotel, p. 92

$$$

Hotel Del Coronado, p. 98

La Valencia, p. 97

Lodge at Torrey Pines, p. 97

$$$$

Pacific Terrace Hotel, p. 97

Best by Experience

BEST BEACH

Catamaran Resort Hotel, $, p. 97

Hotel Del Coronado, $$$, p. 98

La Jolla Shores Hotel, $$, p. 97

Paradise Point Resort & Spa, $$, p. 94

BEST POOL

Andaz San Diego, $$, p. 92

Hotel Solamar, $$, p. 92

Hyatt Regency Mission Bay Spa & Marina, $$, p. 94

Loews Coronado Bay Resort, $$, p. 98

Manchester Grand Hyatt San Diego, $$, p. 92

BEST FOR ROMANCE

1906 Lodge, $$, p. 98

Hotel Del Coronado, $$$, p. 98

Hotel Solamar, $$, p. 92

The Lodge at Torrey Pines, $$$, p. 97

2

Cons: very busy; some rooms dated. $ *Rooms from: $235* ✉ *1 Market Pl.* ☎ *619/232–1234, 800/233–1234* ⊕ *www.manchestergrand.hyatt. com* ⟿ *1,530 rooms, 95 suites* �‖*No meals* ✛ *G3.*

OLD TOWN, MISSION VALLEY, AND NORTH PARK

For expanded reviews, facilities, and current deals, visit Fodors.com.

OLD TOWN

$ 🏨 **Best Western Plus Hacienda Hotel–Old Town.** Perched on a hill in the heart
HOTEL of Old Town, this hotel is known for its expansive courtyards, out-
FAMILY door fountains, and maze of stairs that connect eight buildings of guest rooms. **Pros:** airport shuttle; well-maintained outdoor areas. **Cons:** some rooms need renovating; complicated layout. $ *Rooms from: $149* ✉ *4041 Harney St.* ☎ *619/298–4707* ⊕ *www.haciendahotel-oldtown. com* ⟿ *178 rooms, 21 suites* �‖*No meals* ✛ *D4.*

MISSION VALLEY

$ 🏨 **Courtyard by Marriott Mission Valley.** Amenities abound for families
HOTEL seeking a fun and casual base for trips to SeaWorld and the zoo. **Pros:**
FAMILY easy freeway access to area attractions; good value; nice perks for
Fodor'sChoice families and business travelers. **Cons:** few stores and restaurants in
★ walking distance; halls can be noisy with kids. $ *Rooms from: $134* ✉ *595 Hotel Circle S* ☎ *619/291–5720* ⊕ *www.courtyardsd.com* ⟿ *309 rooms, 8 suites* �‖*No meals* ✛ *E4.*

NORTH PARK

$$ 🏨 **Britt Scripps Inn.** A block west of Balboa Park, this inn occupies the
B&B/INN former mansion of the Scripps newspaper family. **Pros:** intimate; his-
Fodor'sChoice toric building; upscale amenities. **Cons:** far from nightlife; some street
★ noise. $ *Rooms from: $255* ✉ *406 Maple St.* ☎ *888/881–1991* ⊕ *www. brittscripps.com* ⟿ *9 rooms* �‖*Breakfast* ✛ *E5.*

MISSION BAY AND BEACHES

For expanded hotel reviews, visit Fodors.com.

MISSION BAY

$$ 🏨 **Hyatt Regency Mission Bay Spa & Marina.** This modern property has
RESORT many desirable amenities, including balconies with excellent views of
FAMILY the garden, bay, ocean, or swimming pool courtyard. **Pros:** modern decor; great pet program; water views; 120-foot waterslides in pools, plus kiddie slide. **Cons:** slightly hard to navigate surrounding roads; thin walls; not centrally located. $ *Rooms from: $209* ✉ *1441 Quivira Rd.* ☎ *619/224–1234, 800/233–1234* ⊕ *www.missionbay.hyatt.com* ⟿ *354 rooms, 76 suites* �‖*No meals* ✛ *C4.*

$$ 🏨 **Paradise Point Resort & Spa.** The beautiful landscape of this 44-acre
RESORT resort on Vacation Isle has been the setting for a number of movies.
FAMILY **Pros:** water views; pools; good service. **Cons:** not centrally located; sum-
mer minimum stays; motel-thin walls; parking and resort fees. $ *Rooms from: $250* ✉ *1404 Vacation Rd.* ☎ *858/274–4630, 800/344–2626* ⊕ *www.paradisepoint.com* ⟿ *462 cottages* �‖*No meals* ✛ *C3.*

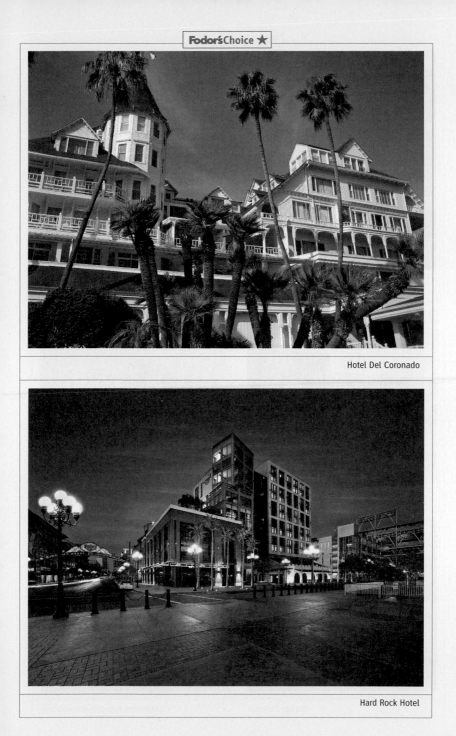

Hotel Del Coronado

Hard Rock Hotel

Lodge at Torrey Pines

Hotel Solamar

Hotel Solamar

Grande Colonial

Catamaran Resort Hotel and Spa

MISSION BEACH

$ **Catamaran Resort Hotel.** Tiki torches light the way through grounds
RESORT thick with tropical foliage to the six two-story buildings and the
Fodor'sChoice 14-story high-rise in Mission Bay. **Pros:** spa; bay views; many activities
★ for kids. **Cons:** not centrally located; dated room decor. [$] *Rooms from:*
FAMILY *$189 ⊠ 3999 Mission Blvd.* ☎ *858/488–1081, 800/422–8386* ⊕ *www.
catamaranresort.com* ↪ *262 rooms, 50 suites* ❘❍❘ *No meals* ✛ *B3.*

PACIFIC BEACH

$$$$ **Pacific Terrace Hotel.** Travelers love this terrific beachfront hotel and
RESORT the ocean views from most rooms; it's a perfect place for watching sunsets over the Pacific. **Pros:** beach views; large rooms; friendly service.
Cons: busy and sometimes noisy area; lots of traffic. [$] *Rooms from:
$400 ⊠ 610 Diamond St.* ☎ *858/581–3500, 800/344–3370* ⊕ *www.
pacificterrace.com* ↪ *61 rooms, 12 suites* ❘❍❘ *No meals* ✛ *B3.*

LA JOLLA

For expanded hotel reviews, visit Fodors.com.

$$ **Grande Colonial.** This white wedding cake–style hotel in the heart of
HOTEL La Jolla village has ocean views and charming European details that
Fodor'sChoice include chandeliers, mahogany railings, and French doors. **Pros:** near
★ shopping; near beach; superb restaurant. **Cons:** somewhat busy street;
no fitness center. [$] *Rooms from: $229 ⊠ 910 Prospect St.* ☎ *858/454–
2181, 877/792–8053* ⊕ *www.thegrandecolonial.com* ↪ *52 rooms, 41
suites* ❘❍❘ *No meals* ✛ *B1.*

$$ **La Jolla Shores Hotel.** One of San Diego's few hotels actually on the
HOTEL beach, this property is part of La Jolla Beach and Tennis Club. **Pros:**
FAMILY on beach; great views; quiet area. **Cons:** not centrally located; some
rooms are dated. [$] *Rooms from: $289 ⊠ 8110 Camino del Oro*
☎ *858/459–8271, 877/346–6714* ⊕ *www.ljshoreshotel.com* ↪ *127
rooms, 1 suite* ✛ *B1.*

$$$ **La Valencia.** This pink Spanish-Mediterranean confection drew Hol-
HOTEL lywood film stars in the 1930s and '40s with its setting and views of
La Jolla Cove. **Pros:** upscale rooms; views; near beach. **Cons:** standard
rooms are tiny; lots of traffic outside. [$] *Rooms from: $320 ⊠ 1132
Prospect St.* ☎ *858/454–0771, 800/451–0772* ⊕ *www.lavalencia.com*
↪ *82 rooms, 15 villas, 15 suites* ❘❍❘ *No meals* ✛ *B1.*

$$$ **Lodge at Torrey Pines.** This beautiful Craftsman-style lodge sits on
RESORT a bluff between La Jolla and Del Mar and commands a coastal view.
Fodor'sChoice **Pros:** spacious upscale rooms; good service; Torrey Pines Golf Club on
★ property. **Cons:** not centrally located; expensive. [$] *Rooms from: $400
⊠ 11480 N. Torrey Pines Rd.* ☎ *858/453–4420, 800/995–4507* ⊕ *www.
lodgetorreypines.com* ↪ *164 rooms, 6 suites* ❘❍❘ *No meals* ✛ *B1.*

POINT LOMA AND CORONADO WITH HARBOR AND SHELTER ISLANDS

For expanded hotel reviews, visit Fodors.com.

POINT LOMA

$ **⊡ Homewood Suites San Diego Airport.** Families and business trav-
HOTEL elers on long trips will benefit from the space and amenities at this
FAMILY all-suites hotel. **Pros:** warm staff; free parking; close to paths for jog-
Fodor's Choice gers and bikers. **Cons:** often crowded dining room; far from nightlife.
★ ⑤ *Rooms from: $185 ⊠ 2576 Laning Rd.* ☎ *619/222-0500 ⊕ www.*
homewoodsuites.com ↝ 150 suites ⚏ *Multiple meal plans ✛ C5.*

$ **⊡ The Pearl Hotel.** This previously vintage motel received a makeover,
HOTEL turning it into a retro-chic beach hangout decorated with kitschy lamps
Fodor's Choice and original art by local children. **Pros:** near marina; restaurant on-site
★ (dinner only). **Cons:** not centrally located; one bed in rooms. ⑤ *Rooms*
from: $119 ⊠ 1410 Rosecrans St. ☎ *619/226-6100 ⊕ www.thepearlsd.*
com ↝ 23 rooms ⚏ *No meals ✛ C5.*

SHELTER ISLAND

$ **⊡ Humphreys Half Moon Inn & Suites.** This sprawling South Seas–style
RESORT resort has grassy open areas with palms and tiki torches; many of the
rooms have water views. **Pros:** water views; near marina; free admission to Backstage Live music club. **Cons:** vast property; not centrally
located. ⑤ *Rooms from: $159 ⊠ 2303 Shelter Island Dr.* ☎ *619/224-*
3411, 800/542-7400 ⊕ www.halfmooninn.com ↝ 128 rooms, 54
suites ⚏ *No meals ✛ C5.*

CORONADO

$$ **⊡ 1906 Lodge at Coronado Beach.** Smaller but no less luxurious than the
B&B/INN sprawling beach resorts of Coronado, this lodge welcomes couples for
Fodor's Choice romantic retreats two blocks from the ocean. **Pros:** welcoming staff;
★ historic property; free underground parking. **Cons:** too quiet for fami-
lies; no pool. ⑤ *Rooms from: $209 ⊠ 1060 Adella Ave.* ☎ *619/437-*
1900, 866/435-1906 ⊕ www.1906lodge.com ↝ 6 rooms, 11 suites
⚏ *Some meals ✛ D6.*

$$$ **⊡ Hotel Del Coronado.** The Victorian-style "Hotel Del" is as much of a
RESORT draw today as it was when it opened in 1888. **Pros:** romantic; on the
FAMILY beach; hotel spa. **Cons:** some rooms are small; expensive dining; hectic
Fodor's Choice public areas. ⑤ *Rooms from: $310 ⊠ 1500 Orange Ave.* ☎ *800/468-*
★ *3533, 619/435-6611 ⊕ www.hoteldel.com ↝ 679 rooms, 43 villas, 35*
cottages ⚏ *No meals ✛ D6.*

$$ **⊡ Loews Coronado Bay Resort.** You can park your boat at the 80-slip
RESORT marina of this romantic retreat set on a secluded 15-acre peninsula
FAMILY on the Silver Strand. **Pros:** great restaurants; lots of activities; lobby
worth lingering in. **Cons:** far from anything; confusing layout. ⑤ *Rooms*
from: $219 ⊠ 4000 Coronado Bay Rd. ☎ *619/424-4000, 800/815-*
6397 ⊕ www.loewshotels.com/Coronado-Bay-Resort ↝ 402 rooms,
37 suites ⚏ *No meals ✛ E6.*

NIGHTLIFE

Updated by
Seth Combs

A couple of decades ago, San Diego scraped by on its superb daytime offerings. Those sleepy-after-dark days are over; San Diego now sizzles when the sun goes down. Of particular interest to beer lovers, the city has become internationally acclaimed for dozens of breweries, beer pubs, and festivals.

The most obvious destination for visitors is the Gaslamp Quarter, a 16-block former red-light district gone glam. The debauchery is slightly more modest these days—or at least legal, anyway. Between the Gaslamp and neighboring East Village, there's truly something for everyone, from secretive speakeasies to big, bangin' dance clubs and chic rooftop lounges to grimy dives. If you're staying in the Gaslamp, it's the perfect place to party. If you're driving from elsewhere, prepare to pay. Your best options: parking lots (prices start at $20) or valet (at some restaurants and clubs).

The epicenter of gay culture is Hillcrest, where you'll find bars and clubs catering primarily to the LGBT crowd—though everyone is welcome. East of Hillcrest is North Park, where hip twenty- and thirtysomethings hang out at edgy scenester hotspots. Nearby South Park and University Heights also have a few cool offerings. A cab from Downtown to any of these 'hoods costs about $15.

Pacific Beach tends to draw college kids who don't know when to say when, while Ocean and Mission beaches pull laid-back surfers and their cohorts. La Jolla, for the most part, is a snooze if you're in the mood to booze late at night.

DOWNTOWN

GASLAMP QUARTER

BARS

Fodor'sChoice ★ **Ivy Rooftop and Ivy Nightclub.** Here are lively and chill versions of San Diego nightlife on the same premises. Thrill seekers should head to the chicly cavernous Ivy Nightclub, while those in search of romance should head straight to the Ivy Rooftop, where they can sip cocktails poolside while gazing at gorgeous people or views of the city—both are abundant. ⊠ 600 F St. ☎ 619/814-2055 ⊕ ivyentertainmentsandiego.com.

WINE BARS

Fodor'sChoice ★ **Vin de Syrah.** This "spirit and wine cellar" sends you down a rabbit hole (or at least down some stairs) to a whimsical spot straight out of Alice in Wonderland. Behind a hidden door (look for a handle in the grass wall), you'll find visual delights (grapevines suspended from the ceiling, vintage jars with flittering "fireflies," cozy chairs nestled around a faux fireplace and pastoral vista) that rival the culinary ones—the wine list is approachable and the charcuterie boards are exquisitely curated. ■TIP→ It's worth it to try the cocktails, especially if bar manager Adam Stemmler is on duty. ⊠ 901 5th Ave., Gaslamp Quarter ☎ 619/234-4166 ⊕ www.syrahwineparlor.com.

DANCE CLUBS

Stingaree. One could argue that Stingaree was the Gaslamp's first mega-club and, almost a decade later, it's still going strong. Guests can enjoy electro and Top 40 in the main nightclub, a smashing three-story space with translucent "floating" staircases and floor-to-ceiling water walls. Dress nicely. The air of exclusivity at this hangout is palpable, and to reinforce the point, the drink prices are steep. ⊠ *454 6th Ave., at Island St.* ☎ *619/544–9500* ⊕ *www.stingsandiego.com.*

Fodor's Choice ★ **Voyeur.** This tiny club will leave you gasping for air—and loving it. The space may be small and stifling, but compensations include the creepy-cool decor (a mashup of skull/guns/gothic weird stuff), a can't-hide bathroom in line with the club's name, a mesmerizing LED wall, gorgeous go-go girls, and cutting-edge electronic acts like MSTRKRFT and Bloody Beetroots. ⊠ *755 5th Ave.* ☎ *619/756–7678* ⊕ *voyeursd.com.*

MUSIC CLUBS

House of Blues. The local branch of the renowned music chain is decorated floor to ceiling with colorful folk art and features three different areas to hear music. There's something going on here just about every night of the week, and Sunday's gospel brunch is one of the most praiseworthy events in town. Can we get a hallelujah? ⊠ *1055 5th Ave.* ☎ *619/299–2583* ⊕ *www.houseofblues.com.*

OFF THE BEATEN PATH

The Casbah. This small club near the airport, the unofficial headquarters of the city's indie music scene, has a national reputation for showcasing up-and-coming acts of all genres. Nirvana, Smashing Pumpkins, and the White Stripes all played here on the way to stardom. ⊠ *2501 Kettner Blvd., Middletown* ☎ *619/232–4355* ⊕ *www.casbahmusic.com.*

PIANO BARS

Fodor's Choice ★ **Westgate Hotel Plaza Bar.** The old-money surroundings, including leather-upholstered seats, marble tabletops, and a grand piano, supply one of the most elegant and romantic settings for a drink in San Diego. ⊠ *1055 2nd Ave.* ☎ *619/557-3650* ⊕ *www.westgatehotel.com.*

EAST VILLAGE
PIANO BARS

Fodor's Choice ★ **Noble Experiment.** Speakeasy-style bars have been popping up all over San Diego, and the trend is impeccably realized in this quaint but decidedly swank cocktail lounge hidden in the back of a burger restaurant. Once customers find the hidden door (hint: look for the stack of kegs), they can bask in one of the plush leather booths while enjoying intricately crafted drinks that are second to none in the city. ⚠ **Warning: Reservations are almost always a must, so be sure to call ahead.** ⊠ *777 G St.* ☎ *619/888–4713* ⊕ *nobleexperimentsd.com.*

LITTLE ITALY
BARS

Fodor's Choice ★ **The Waterfront Bar & Grill.** It isn't really *on* the waterfront, but San Diego's oldest bar was once the hangout of Italian fishermen. Most of the collars are now white, and patrons enjoy an excellent selection of beers, along with chili, burgers, fish-and-chips, and other great-tasting grub, including fish tacos. Get here early, as there's almost always a crowd. ⊠ *2044 Kettner Blvd.* ☎ *619/232–9656* ⊕ *www.waterfrontbarandgrill.com.*

COFFEEHOUSES

Extraordinary Desserts. A delicious visual treat, with a lacy, laser-cut metal façade and elegant teak patio, also satisfies every sort of culinary craving, from savory to sweet and everything in between. The wine, beer, and bubbly list is très chic, too. ✉ *1430 Union St.* ☎ *619/294–7001* ⊕ *www.extraordinarydesserts.com.*

JAZZ CLUBS

Fodor'sChoice ★ **Anthology.** The Rat Pack would love the fine-tuned acoustics in this classy, three-floor joint, one of the best-sounding music clubs in the city. Jazz acts are the mainstay, although the repertoire also includes folk and rock, and the club has hosted Ozomatli as well as Herb Alpert. ✉ *1337 India St.* ☎ *619/595–0300* ⊕ *www.anthologysd.com.*

OLD TOWN AND UPTOWN

HILLCREST

GAY NIGHTLIFE

Fodor'sChoice ★ **Baja Betty's.** Although it draws plenty of gay customers, this low-key but elegant space with chandeliers and soft lighting is popular with just about everyone in the Hillcrest area (and their pets are welcome, too). The bar staff stocks more than 100 brands of tequila and mixes plenty of fancy cocktails. ✉ *1421 University Ave.* ☎ *619/269–8510* ⊕ *bajabettyssd.com.*

Urban Mo's Bar and Grill. Cowboys gather for line dancing and two-stepping on the wooden dance floor—but be forewarned, yee-hawers, it can get pretty wild on Western nights. There are also Latin, hip-hop, and drag revues but the real allure is in the creative drinks ("Gone Fishing"—served in a fishbowl, for example) and the breezy patio where love (or something like it) is usually in the air. ✉ *308 University Ave.* ☎ *619/491–0400* ⊕ *www.urbanmos.com.*

MISSION HILLS

PIANO BARS

Fodor'sChoice ★ **Starlite.** Bargoers are dazzled by Starlite's award-winning interior design, which includes rock walls, luxe leather booths, and a massive mirror-mounted chandelier. A hexagonal wood-plank entryway leads to a sunken white bar, where sexy tattooed guys and girls mix creative cocktails, such as the signature Starlite Mule, served in a copper mug. An iPod plays eclectic playlists ranging from old-timey jazz and blues to obscure vintage rock (and DJs are on hand on certain evenings). During warmer months, procuring a spot on the outside wood-decked patio is an art form. ✉ *3175 India St.* ☎ *619/358–9766* ⊕ *www.starlitesandiego.com.*

NORTH PARK

BARS

Toronado. One of San Diego's favorite gathering spots for hop-heads is named in honor of the San Francisco beer bar of the same name. The beer list—both on tap and by the bottle—is hard to beat. The place can get noisy, but the food—a mix of burgers and American-style comfort food—more than makes up for it. ✉ *4026 30th St.* ☎ *619/282–0456* ⊕ *www.toronadosd.com.*

CLOSE UP

San Diego On Tap

The secret is out: San Diego is the nation's best beer town. In addition to more than 30 local breweries, San Diego has a stretch of beer-nerd heaven nicknamed the Belgian Corridor (30th Street in North/South Park). You can find all styles of beer in San Diego, from the meek to the mighty, but many local brewers contend that the specialty is the big, bold Double IPA (also called an Imperial IPA). It's an India Pale Ale with attitude—and lots of hops. Nearly every local brewery has its own version.

Bars with the best microbrew selection: Blind Lady Ale House, Hamilton's Tavern, Live Wire, O'Brien's, Toronado.

Best fests: Want one location and a seemingly endless supply of beer? Try the Belgian Beer Fest (March), the San Diego Festival of Beers (September ⊕ www.sdbeerfest.org), San Diego Beer Week (November ⊕ www.sdbw. org), and the Strong Ale Fest (December). ⊕ www.sandiegobrewersguild.org has more listings.

Best way to sample it all: Sign up for Brewery Tours of San Diego (⊕ www.brewerytoursofsandiego.com) to sample the best craft beers without a second thought about directions or designated drivers.

SAN DIEGO'S BEST BREWERIES
You can also head to the source, where beer is brewed. These are outside the city center, but worth the trek for beer aficionados.

AleSmith Brewing Co. This artisanal microbrewery offers tastings at its out-of-the-way locale in the Miramar area. Just how artisanal is it? The "Kopi Luwak" special edition of Ale-Smith's popular Speedway Stout is

brewed with Civet coffee from Indonesia, made from rare and expensive coffee berries that have been eaten—and passed, undigested—by the Asian Palm Civet. Visitors can tour the entire brewery for free on the last Saturday of every month. ⊠ 9368 Cabot Dr., Scripps Ranch ☎ 858/549–9888 ⊕ alesmith.com.

Fodor's Choice★ Alpine Brewing Co. Well worth the mountain drive, this family-owned operation may be itty-bitty, but it's also a big champ: brewmaster Pat McIlhenney, a former fire captain, has won national and international kudos for his hopped-up creations and took the title of the fifth-best brewery in the nation from Beer Advocate. Tasters are only a buck each, or fill a growler, which holds a half gallon, for future imbibing. If they're on tap, don't pass up Duet, Pure Hoppiness, or Exponential Hoppiness. Alpine recently opened a pub a few doors down where you can taste flights of their various beers. ⊠ 2351 Alpine Blvd., Alpine ☎ 619/445–2337 ⊕ www.alpinebeerco.com.

Stone Brewing World Gardens and Bistro. The Big Daddy of San Diego craft brewing was founded by a couple of basement beer tinkerers in 1996; the company now exports its aggressively hoppy beers—instantly identifiable by their leering gargoyle labels—to bars and stores across the nation. Stone's monumental HQ is off the beaten path, but totally worth a visit for its free tours (with free tasters at the end!), vast on-tap selection (not just Stone beers), and hard-to-beat bistro eats. ⊠ 1999 Citracado Pkwy., Escondido ☎ 760/294-7866 ⊕ www.stonebrew.com.

MISSION BAY AND THE BEACHES

PACIFIC BEACH

BARS

JRDN. This contemporary lounge (pronounced "Jordan") occupies the ground floor of Pacific Beach's chicest boutique hotel, Tower23, and offers a more sophisticated vibe in what is a very party-happy neighborhood. Sleek walls of windows and an expansive patio overlook the boardwalk. ⊠ *723 Felspar St.* ☎ *858/270–5736* ⊕ *www.t23hotel.com.*

THE ARTS

Updated by
Seth Combs

TICKETS

Arts Tix. You can buy advance tickets, many at half price, to theater, music, and dance events at Arts Tix. ⊠ *28 Horton Plaza, 3rd Ave. and Broadway* ☎ *858/381–5595* ⊕ *www.sdartstix.com.*

DANCE

California Ballet Company. The company performs high-quality contemporary and classical works September–May at the **Civic Theatre** (*3rd Ave. and B St., Downtown* ☎ *619/570–1100*). The *Nutcracker* is staged annually around the holiday season. ⊕ *www.californiaballet.org.*

Balboa Theatre. This historic landmark hosts ballet, music, plays and even stand-up comedy performances. ⊠ *868 4th Ave., Downtown* ☎ *619/570–1100* ⊕ *www.sandiegotheatres.org*

MUSIC

Fodor'sChoice
★

Copley Symphony Hall. The great acoustics here are surpassed only by the incredible Spanish baroque interior. Not just the home of the San Diego Symphony Orchestra, the renovated 2,200-seat 1920s-era theater has also hosted major stars like Elvis Costello, Leonard Cohen, and Sting. ⊠ *750 B St., Downtown* ☎ *619/235–0804* ⊕ *www.sandiegosymphony.org.*

San Diego Symphony Orchestra. The orchestra's events include classical concerts and summer and winter pops, nearly all of them at Copley Symphony Hall. The outdoor Summer Pops series is held on the Embarcadero, on North Harbor Drive beyond the convention center. ⊠ *Box office, 750 B. St., Downtown* ☎ *619/235–0800* ⊕ *www. sandiegosymphony.org.*

Spreckels Organ Pavilion. Home of a giant outdoor pipe organ donated to the city, the beautiful Spanish baroque pavilion hosts concerts by civic organist Carol Williams and guest organists on most Sunday afternoons and on Monday evenings in summer. Local military bands, gospel groups, and barbershop quartets also perform here. All shows are free. ⊠ *Balboa Park* ☎ *619/702–8138* ⊕ *sosorgan.com.*

THEATER

Fodor'sChoice   **La Jolla Playhouse.** Under the artistic direction of Christopher Ashley, the
★   playhouse presents exciting and innovative plays and musicals on three
stages. Many Broadway shows—among them *Memphis, Tommy,* and
Jersey Boys—have previewed here before their East Coast premieres.
✉ *University of California at San Diego, 2910 La Jolla Village Dr., La
Jolla* ☎ *858/550–1010* ⊕ *www.lajollaplayhouse.org.*

Fodor'sChoice   **The Old Globe.** This complex, comprising the Sheryl and Harvey White
★   Theatre, the Lowell Davies Festival Theatre, and the Old Globe Theatre,
offers some of the finest theatrical productions in Southern California. Theater classics such as *The Full Monty* and *Dirty Rotten Scoun-
drels,* both of which went on to Broadway, premiered on these famed
stages. The Old Globe presents the family-friendly *How the Grinch
Stole Christmas* around the holidays, as well as a renowned summer
Shakespeare Festival with three to four plays in repertory. ✉ *1363 Old
Globe Way, Balboa Park* ☎ *619/234–5623* ⊕ *www.oldglobe.org.*

SPORTS AND THE OUTDOORS

PARTICIPATION SPORTS

Updated by
Claire Deeks
van der Lee

BICYCLING

San Diego offers bountiful opportunities for bikers, from casual boardwalk cruises to strenuous rides into the hills. The mild climate makes
biking in San Diego a year-round delight. Bike culture is respected here,
and visitors are often impressed with the miles of designated bike lanes
running alongside city streets and coastal roads throughout the county.

Cheap Rentals Mission Beach. Right by the boardwalk, this place has good
daily and weekly prices for bike rentals, which include beach cruisers, tandems, hybrids, and two-wheeled baby carriers. ✉ *3689 Mission Blvd., Mission Beach* ☎ *858/488–9070, 800/941–7761* ⊕ *www.
cheap-rentals.com.*

Hike Bike Kayak San Diego. This outfitter offers a wide range of guided
bike tours, from easy excursions around Mission Bay and Coronado
Island to slightly more rigorous trips through coastal La Jolla. Moun-
tain-biking tours are also available, and the company also rents bikes of
all types (and can deliver them to your hotel). ✉ *2246 Ave. de la Playa,
La Jolla* ☎ *858/551–9510* ⊕ *www.hikebikekayak.com.*

Holland's Bicycles. This great bike rental source on Coronado Island
has another store (**Bikes and Beyond** ☎ *619/435–7180)* located at the
ferry landing, so you can jump on your bike as soon as you cross the
harbor from Downtown San Diego. ✉ *977 Orange Ave., Coronado*
☎ *619/435–3153* ⊕ *www.hollandsbicycles.com.*

Route S21. On many summer days, Route S21, aka Old Highway 101,
from La Jolla to Oceanside looks like a freeway for cyclists. About 24
miles long, it's easily the most popular and scenic bike route around,
never straying far from the beach. Although the terrain is fairly easy,
the long, steep Torrey Pines grade is famous for weeding out the weak.

Another Darwinian challenge is dodging slow-moving pedestrians and cars pulling over to park in towns like Encinitas and Del Mar.

DIVING

Ocean Enterprises Scuba Diving. Stop in for everything you need to plan a diving adventure, including equipment, advice, and instruction. ⊠ *7710 Balboa Ave., Suite 101, Clairemont Mesa* ☎ *858/565–6054* ⊕ *www. oceanenterprises.com.*

San Diego–La Jolla Underwater Park Ecological Preserve. Diving enthusiasts the world over come to San Diego to snorkel and scuba dive off La Jolla at the underwater preserve. Because all sea life is protected here, this 533-acre preserve (all of La Jolla Cove to La Jolla Shores) is the best place to see large lobster, sea bass, and sculpin (scorpion fish), as well as numerous golden garibaldi damselfish, the state marine fish. It's common to see hundreds of beautiful (and harmless) leopard sharks schooling at the north end of the cove, near La Jolla Shores, especially in summer.

Scuba San Diego. This center is well regarded for its top-notch instruction and certification programs, as well as for guided dive tours. Trips include dives to kelp reefs in La Jolla Cove, night diving at La Jolla Canyon, and unguided charter boat trips to Mission Bay's Wreck Alley or to the Coronado Islands (in Mexico, just south of San Diego). ⊠ *San Diego Hilton Hotel, 1775 E. Mission Bay Dr., Mission Bay* ☎ *619/260–1880* ⊕ *www.scubasandiego.com.*

FISHING

Fisherman's Landing. You can book space on a fleet of luxury vessels from 57 feet to 124 feet long and embark on multiday trips in search of yellowfin tuna, yellowtail, and other deep-water fish. Half-day fishing and whale-watching trips are also available. ⊠ *2838 Garrison St., Point Loma* ☎ *619/221–8500* ⊕ *www.fishermanslanding.com.*

H&M Landing. Join up for fishing trips, plus whale-watching excursions from December through March. ⊠ *2803 Emerson St., Point Loma* ☎ *619/222–1144* ⊕ *www.hmlanding.com.*

GOLF

Balboa Park Municipal Golf Course. In the heart of Balboa Park, this course is convenient for Downtown visitors. ⊠ *2600 Golf Course Dr., Balboa Park* ☎ *619/235–1184* ⮕ *18 holes. 6,281 yds. Par 72. Greens fees: $40/$50* ⤳ *Facilities: Driving range, putting green, pitching area, golf carts, pull carts, rental clubs, pro shop, golf academy/lessons, restaurant, bar.*

Coronado Municipal Golf Course. Views of San Diego Bay and the Coronado Bridge from the front 9 make this course popular—it's difficult to get on unless you reserve a tee time, 3 to 14 days in advance, for an additional $60. ⊠ *2000 Visalia Row, Coronado* ☎ *619/435–3121* ⊕ *www.golfcoronado.com* ⮕ *18 holes. 6,590 yds. Par 72. Greens fees: $30/$35. Reservations essential* ⤳ *Facilities: Driving range, putting green, pitching area, golf carts, pull carts, rental clubs, pro shop, golf academy/lessons, restaurant, bar.*

La Costa Resort and Spa. One of the premier golf resorts in Southern California, La Costa is home to the PGA Tour Golf Academy, whose instructors include past and present touring pros and coaches. The resort recently remodeled its Champions Course, host to more than three dozen PGA events. After a day on the links you can wind down with a massage, steam bath, and dinner at the resort. ✉ *2100 Costa del Mar Rd., Carlsbad* ☎ *800/854-5000* ⊕ *www.lacosta.com* ⚑ *Champions: 18 holes, 6608 yds. Par 72. Greens fees: $225/$250. South: 18 holes, 6524 yds. Par 72. Greens fees: $175/$185. Reservations essential ☞ Facilities: Driving range, putting green, pitching area, golf carts, caddies, rental clubs, pro shop, golf academy/lessons, restaurant, bar.*

FodorsChoice
★
Park Hyatt Aviara Golf Club. Designed by Arnold Palmer, this top-quality course includes views of the protected adjacent Batiquitos Lagoon and the Pacific Ocean. The carts, which are fitted with GPS systems that tell you the distance to the pin, are included in the cost. ✉ *7447 Batiquitos Dr., Carlsbad* ☎ *760/603–6900* ⊕ *www.golfaviara.com* ⚑ *18 holes. 7,007 yds. Par 72. Greens fees: $215/$235* ☞ *Facilities: Driving range, putting green, pitching area, golf carts, rental clubs, pro shop, golf academy/lessons, restaurant, bar.*

FodorsChoice
★
Torrey Pines Golf Course. One of the best public golf courses in the United States, Torrey Pines was the site of the 2008 U.S. Open and has been the home of the Buick Invitational (now the Farmers Insurance Open) since 1968. The par-72 South Course receives rave reviews from the touring pros. Redesigned by Rees Jones in 2001, it's longer, more challenging, and more expensive than the North Course. Tee times may be booked from 8 to 90 days in advance at ☎ *877/581–7171* and are subject to an advance booking fee ($43). A full-day or half-day instructional package includes cart, greens fee, and a golf-pro escort for the first 9 holes. ✉ *11480 N. Torrey Pines Rd., La Jolla* ☎ *858/452–3226, 800/985–4653* ⊕ *www.torreypinesgolfcourse.com* ⚑ *36 holes. South: 7,227 yds., North: 6874 yds. North and South: Par 72. Greens fees: South: $183/$229, North: $100/$125* ☞ *Facilities: Driving range, putting green, pitching area, golf carts, pull carts, caddies upon request in advance, rental clubs, pro shop, golf academy/lessons, restaurant, bar.*

HIKING AND NATURE TRAILS

FodorsChoice
★
Bayside Trail at Cabrillo National Monument. Driving here is a treat in itself, as a vast view of the Pacific unfolds before you. The view is equally enjoyable on Bayside Trail (2 miles round-trip), which is home to the same coastal sagebrush that Juan Rodriguez Cabrillo saw when he first discovered the California coast in the 16th century. After the hike, you can explore nearby tide pools, the monument statue, and the Old Point Loma Lighthouse. ✉ *1800 Cabrillo Memorial Dr., from I–5, take the Rosecrans exit and turn right on Canon St. then left on Catalina Blvd.; continue following signs to the park, Point Loma* ☎ *619/557–5450* ⊕ *www.nps.gov/cabr.*

Torrey Pines State Reserve. Hiking aficionados will appreciate this park's many winning features: a number of modest trails that descend to the sea, an unparalleled view of the Pacific, and a chance to see the Torrey pine tree, one of the rarest pine breeds in the United States. The reserve hosts guided nature walks as well. All food is prohibited at the reserve so save the picnic until you reach the beach below. Parking is $12.

✉ *12600 N. Torrey Pines Rd., exit I–5 at Carmel Valley Rd. and head west toward Coast Hwy. 101 until you reach Torrey Pines State Beach; turn left, La Jolla* ☎ *858/755–2063* ⊕ *www.torreypine.org.*

KAYAKING, SAILING, AND BOATING

Hike Bike Kayak San Diego. This shop offers several kayak tours, from easy excursions in Mission Bay that are well suited to families and beginners on to more advanced jaunts. Tours include kayaking the caves off La Jolla coast, whale-watching (from a safe distance) December through March, moonlight and sunset trips, and a cruise into the bay to see SeaWorld's impressive fireworks shows over the water in the summer. Tours last two to three hours and cost between $50 and $70 per person; cost includes kayak, paddle, life vest, and guide. ✉ *2246 Ave. de la Playa, La Jolla* ☎ *858/551–9510* ⊕ *www.hikebikekayak.com.*

Seaforth Boat Rentals. You can book charter tours and rent kayaks, Jet Skis, fishing skiffs, powerboats and sailboats at Seaforth's five locations around town. They also can hook you up with a skipper for a deep-sea fishing trip. Seaforth also rents paddleboards at their Mission Bay location, and surfboards at the Coronado location. ✉ *1715 Strand Way, Coronado* ☎ *619/437–1514, 888/834–2628* ⊕ *www.seaforthboatrentals.com.*

SURFING

If you're a beginner, consider paddling in the waves off Mission Beach, Pacific Beach, Tourmaline Surfing Park, La Jolla Shores, Del Mar, or Oceanside. More experienced surfers usually head for Sunset Cliffs, La Jolla reef breaks, Black's Beach, or Swami's in Encinitas. All necessary equipment is included in the cost of all surfing schools. Beach-area Y's offer surf lessons and surf camp in the summer months and during spring break.

Cheap Rentals Mission Beach. Many local surf shops rent both surf and bodyboards. Cheap Rentals Mission Beach is right off the boardwalk, just steps from the waves. They rent wet suits, bodyboards, and skimboards in addition to soft surfboards and long and short fiberglass rides. They also have good hourly to weekly pricing on paddleboards and accessories. ✉ *3689 Mission Blvd., Mission Beach* ☎ *858/488–9070, 800/941–7761* ⊕ *www.cheap-rentals.com.*

Hansen's. A short walk from Swami's beach, Hansen's is one of San Diego's oldest and most popular surf shops. It has an extensive selection of boards, wet suits, and clothing for sale, and a rental department as well. ✉ *1105 S. Coast Hwy. 101, Encinitas* ☎ *760/753–6595, 800/480–4754* ⊕ *www.hansensurf.com.*

Surf Diva Surf School. Check out clinics, surf camps, surf trips, and private lessons especially formulated for girls and women. Most clinics and trips are for women only, but there are some co-ed options. Guys can also book private lessons from the nationally recognized staff. ✉ *2160 Ave. de la Playa, La Jolla* ☎ *858/454–8273* ⊕ *www.surfdiva.com.*

SPECTATOR SPORTS

BASEBALL

Fodor's Choice ★ Long a favorite spectator sport in San Diego, where games are rarely rained out, baseball gained even more popularity in 2004 with the opening of PETCO Park, a stunning 42,000-seat facility in the heart of Downtown. In March 2006, the semifinals and the final game of the first-ever World Baseball Classic, scheduled to be a quadrennial event fielding teams from around the world, took place here.

San Diego Padres. The Padres slug it out for bragging rights in the National League West from April into October. Tickets are usually available on game day, but games with such rivals as the Los Angeles Dodgers and the San Francisco Giants often sell out quickly. For an inexpensive day at the ballpark, go for the park pass ($5–$12, depending on demand, available for purchase at the park only) and have a picnic on the grass, while watching the game on one of several giant-screen TVs. ⊠ *100 Park Blvd., East Village* ☎ *619/795–5000, 877/374–2784* ⊕ *sandiego.padres.mlb.com.*

FOOTBALL

San Diego Chargers. The Chargers play their NFL home games at Qualcomm Stadium. Games with AFC West rivals the Oakland Raiders are particularly intense. ⊠ *9449 Friars Rd., Mission Valley* ☎ *858/874–4500 Charger Park, 877/242–7437 Season Tickets* ⊕ *www.chargers.com.*

SHOPPING

Updated by Amanda Knoles

San Diego's retail venues are as diverse as the city's vibrant neighborhoods. From La Jolla's tony boutiques to the outlet malls at San Ysidro, you'll find stores that appeal to every taste and budget.

DOWNTOWN

The Gaslamp Quarter, Downtown's trendy hot spot, is where you'll find independent shops selling urban apparel, unique home decor items, and vintage treasures. If you can't find it in the boutiques, head for Westfield Horton Plaza, the Downtown mall with more than 130 stores and 26 eateries.

Just a hop, skip, and a jump from the Gaslamp Quarter, the 130-block East Village neighborhood contains shops catering to local hipsters and visitors looking for edgy street wear, novelty T-shirts, and offbeat accessories. Some of the best shopping can be found from 8th to 10th avenues between Broadway and J Street.

Nearby, Little Italy is the place to find contemporary art, clothing from local designers, and home-decor items. Kettner Boulevard and India Street from Laurel to Date Street are the heart of the Art and Design District.

Into kitschy gifts and souvenirs? Downtown's Seaport Village has an abundance of quirky shops that won't disappoint, plus you'll be able to enjoy the coastal breezes while you shop for that Coronado Bridge snow globe.

Spanning 14 acres and offering more than 50 shops and 18 restaurants, Seaport Village is by far the most popular destination in waterfront Embarcadero neighborhood.

OLD TOWN AND UPTOWN

OLD TOWN

Tourist-focused Old Town, north of Downtown off I–5 has a festival-like ambience that also makes it a popular destination for locals. At Old Town Historic Park, you'll feel like a time traveler as you visit shops housed in restored adobe buildings. Farther down the street you'll find stores selling Mexican blankets, piñatas, and glassware. Old Town Market offers live entertainment, local artists selling their wares from carts, and a market crammed with unique apparel, home-decor items, toys, jewelry, and food.

Fodor'sChoice
★
Bazaar del Mundo Shops. An arcade with a Mexican villa theme, the Bazaar hosts riotously colorful gift shops such as **Ariana,** for ethnic and artsy women's fashions; **Artes de Mexico,** which sells handmade Latin American crafts and Guatemalan weavings; and **The Gallery,** which carries handmade jewelry, Native American crafts, collectible glass, and original serigraphs by John August Swanson. The **Laurel Burch Gallerita** carries the complete collection of the northern California artist's signature jewelry, accessories, and totes. ⊠ *4133 Taylor St., at Juan St.* ☏ *619/296–3161* ⊕ *www.bazaardelmundo.com.*

UPTOWN

Hillcrest has a large gay community and boasts many avant-garde apparel shops alongside gift, book, and music stores. North Park, east of Hillcrest, is a retro buff's paradise with many resale shops, trendy boutiques, and stores that sell a mix of old and new. South Park's 30th, Juniper, and Fern streets have everything from the hottest new denim lines to baby gear and craft supplies. The shops and art galleries in upscale Mission Hills, west of Hillcrest, have a modern and sophisticated ambience that suits the well-heeled residents.

MISSION VALLEY

Northeast of Downtown near I–8 and Route 163, Mission Valley holds two major shopping centers and a few smaller strip malls.

Fodor'sChoice
★
Fashion Valley. San Diego's best and most upscale mall has a contemporary Mission theme, lush landscaping, and more than 200 shops and restaurants. Acclaimed retailers like Bloomingdale's, Neiman Marcus, and Tiffany are here, along with boutiques from fashion darlings like Michael Kors, Jimmy Choo, Tory Burch, and James Perse. H&M is a favorite of fashionistas in search of edgy and affordable styles. ∎ **TIP→ Free wireless Internet service is available throughout the mall. Select "Simon WiFi" from any Wi-Fi–enabled device to log onto the network.** ⊠ *7007 Friars Rd.* ☏ *619/688–9113* ⊕ *www.simon.com/mall/fashion-valley.*

LA JOLLA

Known as San Diego's answer to Rodeo Drive in Beverly Hills, La Jolla has chic boutiques, art galleries, and gift shops and plenty of celebrity sightings. Prospect Street and Girard Avenue are the primary shopping stretches, and North Prospect is chockablock with art galleries. Parking is tight in the village. Most shops on Prospect Street stay open until 10 pm on weeknights to accommodate evening strollers.

CORONADO

Coronado's resort hotels attract tourists in droves, but somehow the town has managed to avoid being overtaken by chain stores. Friendly shopkeepers make the boutiques lining Orange Avenue, Coronado's main drag, a good place to browse for clothes, home-decor and gift items, and gourmet foods.

Fodor's Choice   **Coronado Ferry Landing.** A staggering view of San Diego's Downtown
★   skyline across the bay and a dozen boutiques make this a delightful place to shop while waiting for a ferry. **La Camisa** (☎ 619/435–8009) is a fun place to pick up kitschy souvenirs, T-shirts, fleece jackets, and postcards. **The French Room** (☎ 619/889–9004) specializes in comfy women's shoes and affordable casual wear. **Men's Island Sportswear** (☎ 619/437–4696) sells hats, tropical sportswear, and accessories to complete your seaside getaway outfit. Get in touch with your Celtic roots at **Scottish Treasures** (☎ 619/435–1880), purveyor of apparel, gifts, tableware, and jewelry from Ireland, Scotland, England, and Wales. ☒ 1201 1st St. ☎ 619/435–8895 ⊕ www.coronadoferrylandingshops.com ☯ Shops daily 10–7 ☞ Farmers' market Tues. 2:30–6; some restaurants daily late-afternoon happy hour.

Fodor's Choice   **Hotel Del Coronado.** At the dozen gift shops within the peninsula's main
★   historic attraction, you can purchase sportswear, designer handbags, jewelry, and antiques. **Babcock & Story Emporium** (☎ Ext. 7265) carries an amazing selection of home-decor items, garden accessories, and classy gifts. **Blue Octopus** (☎ Ext. 7330) is a children's store featuring creative toys, gifts, and apparel. **Spreckels Sweets & Treats** (☎ Ext. 7627) offers old-time candies, freshly made fudge, and decadent truffles. Women will appreciate the stylish fashions and accessories at **Kate's** (☎ Ext. 7601) and **Isabel B** (☎ Ext. 7384), while well-dressed men can't go wrong with a shirt or jacket from **Brady's** (☎ Ext. 7339). For those celebrating a special occasion, **Del Coronado Jewels** (☎ Ext. 7340) features vintage, traditional, and modern jewelry. ☒ 1500 Orange Ave. ☎ 619/435–6611 plus extension ⊕ www.hoteldel.com/shopping.

SIDE TRIPS TO NORTH COUNTY

DEL MAR

Updated by
Bobbi Zane

23 miles north of Downtown San Diego on I–5, 9 miles north of La Jolla on Rte. S21.

Del Mar is best known for its quaint old section west of Interstate 5 marked with a glamorous racetrack, half-timber buildings, chic shops, tony restaurants, celebrity visitors, and wide beaches.

FAMILY **Del Mar Fairgrounds.** The Spanish Mission–style fairground is the home of the **Del Mar Thoroughbred Club** (☎ 858/755–1141 ⊕ *www.dmtc. com*). Crooner Bing Crosby and his Hollywood buddies—Pat O'Brien, Gary Cooper, and Oliver Hardy, among others—organized the club in the 1930s, and the racing here (usually July–September, Wednesday–Monday, post time 2 pm) remains a fashionable affair. Del Mar Fairgrounds hosts more than 100 different events each year, including the San Diego County Fair, which draws more than a million visitors annually. ⊠ *2260 Jimmy Durante Blvd.* ☎ *858/793–5555* ⊕ *www. delmarfairgrounds.com.*

WHERE TO EAT

$$$$ ✕ **Addison.** The sophisticated and stylish dining room and adjacent bar
FRENCH feel Italian and clubby, with intricately carved dark-wood motifs, and
Fodor's Choice the tables, by contrast, are pure white, adorned with a single flower.
★ Acclaimed chef William Bradley serves up explosive flavors in his four-course prix-fixe dinners, such as Prince Edward Island mussels with champagne sabayon and lemon verbena jus or foie gras de canard with Le Puy lentils, port wine, and smoked bacon mousse. Entrées might include spring lamb *persille* (parsley and garlic topping) with pistachio pâté brisée and caramelized garlic purée or wild Scottish salmon with sauce *vin jaune* (white wine from France's Jura region). Addison challenges wine lovers with 160 pages of choices. ⑤ *Average main: $158* ⊠ *5200 Grand Del Mar Way* ☎ *858/314–1900* ⊕ *www.addisondelmar. com* ⬥ *Reservations essential* ⊘ *Closed Sun. and Mon. No lunch.*

$$$ ✕ **Market Restaurant + Bar.** Carl Schroeder, one of California's hottest
AMERICAN young chefs, draws well-heeled foodies to sample his creative and fun
Fodor's Choice California fare, much of it with an Asian flare. The menu changes
★ regularly depending upon what's fresh. Schroeder's seasonally inspired dishes have a playful spirit, whether it's a blue cheese soufflé with seasonal fruit, a Maine lobster salad with mango, or a local black cod with soba noodles. A well-edited wine list offers food-friendly wines by the best and brightest young winemakers around the world. Desserts are exquisite, such as the lemon soufflé tart with buttermilk ice cream or the milk chocolate panna cotta with espresso caramel. ⑤ *Average main: $30* ⊠ *3702 Via de la Valle* ☎ *858/523–0007* ⊕ *www.marketdelmar. com* ⬥ *Reservations essential* ⊘ *No lunch.*

WHERE TO STAY
For expanded hotel reviews, visit Fodors.com.

$$$$
HOTEL
FAMILY
Fodor'sChoice
★

☰ **The Grand Del Mar.** Mind-blowing indulgence in serene surroundings, from drop-dead beautiful guest accommodations to outdoor adventures, sets the opulent Mediterranean-style Grand Del Mar apart from any other luxury hotel in San Diego. **Pros:** ultimate luxury; secluded, on-site golf course. **Cons:** service can be slow; hotel is not on the beach. ⑤ *Rooms from: $425* ✉ *5200 Grand Del Mar Ct., San Diego* ☎ *858/314–2000, 888/314–2030* ⊕ *www.thegranddelmar.com* ⇆ *218 rooms, 31 suites.*

CARLSBAD

6 miles north of Encinitas on Rte. S21, 36 miles north of Downtown San Diego on I–5.

Once-sleepy Carlsbad has long been popular with beachgoers and sun seekers. On a clear day in this village, you can take in sweeping ocean views that stretch from La Jolla to Oceanside by walking the 2-mile-long seawalk running between the Encina power plant and Pine Street. En route, you'll find several stairways leading to the beach and quite a few benches. Inland are LEGOLAND California and other attractions in its vicinity.

FAMILY
Fodor'sChoice
★

Flower Fields at Carlsbad Ranch. In spring the hillsides are abloom on this, the largest bulb production farm in Southern California, when thousands of Giant Tecolote ranunculus produce a stunning 50-acre display of color against the backdrop of the blue Pacific Ocean. Other knockouts include the rose gardens—with examples of every All-American Rose Selection award-winner since 1940—and a historical display of Paul Ecke poinsettias. Family activities include a LEGO Flower Garden and a kids' playground. ✉ *5704 Paseo del Norte, east of I–5* ☎ *760/431–0352* ⊕ *www.theflowerfields.com* ▦ *$11* ◷ *Mar.–May, daily 9–6.*

FAMILY
Fodor'sChoice
★

LEGOLAND California Resort. The centerpiece of a development that includes resort hotels, a designer discount shopping mall, an aquarium, and a waterpark, LEGOLAND has rides and diversions geared toward kids ages 2 to 12. Bring bathing suits; there are lockers at the entrance and at Pirate Shores. The main events are as follows:

Lost Kingdom Adventure: Armed with a laser blaster, you'll journey through ancient Egyptian ruins in a desert roadster, scoring points as you hit targets.

Star Wars **Miniland:** Follow the exploits of Yoda, Princess Leia, ObI–Wan, Anakin, R2, Luke, and the denizens of the six *Star Wars* films. Some kids loop back several times to take it all in.

Miniland U.S.A.: This miniature, animated, interactive collection of U.S. icons was constructed out of 24 million LEGO bricks!

Soak-N-Sail: Hundreds of gallons of water course through 60 interactive features including a pirate shipwreck–theme area. You'll need your swimsuit for this one.

WORD OF MOUTH

"Ranunculus flowers explode into color every spring at the Flower Fields in Carlsbad. While taking a detour from the freeway, I caught these two sisters admiring the view."   —photo by mlgb, Fodors.com member

A LEGOLAND model worker puts the finishing touches on the San Francisco portion of Miniland U.S.A.

Dragon Coaster: Little kids love this popular indoor/outdoor steel roller coaster that goes through a castle. Don't let the name frighten you—the motif is more humorous than scary.

Volvo Driving School: Kids 6–13 can drive speed-controlled cars (not on rails) on a miniature road; driver's licenses are awarded after the course. Volvo Junior is the pint-sized version for kids 3–5.

■**TIP→** The best value is one of the Hopper Tickets that give you one admission to LEGOLAND plus Sea Life Aquarium and/or the LEGOLAND Water Park. These can be used on the same day or on different days. Go midweek to avoid the crowds.

LEGOLAND Hotel: Set to open in May 2013, this is the place to immerse your family in everything LEGO. Family rooms are themed Pirate, Adventure, and Kingdom, with corresponding LEGO-style decor. Each suite has sleeping quarters for up to three kids. The hotel has interactive play areas, a restaurant, bar, and swimming pool but best of all, guests get early admission to the park. For more information, go to ⊕ *www.legolandtravel.com.*

Be sure to try Granny's Apple Fries, Castle Burgers, and Pizza Mania for pizzas and salads. The Market near the entrance has excellent coffee, fresh fruit, and yogurt. ⊠ *1 Legoland Dr., Exit I–5 at Cannon Rd. and follow signs east ¼ mile* ☎ *760/918–5346* ⊕ *california.legoland. com* ⊠*LEGOLAND $72 adults, $62 children; parking $12* ◷ *Late May–early Sept. daily (hrs vary), early Sept.–late May closed Tues. and Wed. except holiday weeks. Water Park closed Nov. to spring; check website or call for specifics.*

2

WHERE TO EAT

$$$
MEDITERRANEAN
Fodor's Choice
★

✕ **BlueFire Grill.** Fire and water drama defines this signature restaurant that's part of La Costa resort complex. The centerpiece of the resort's entrance plaza, the grill holds an outdoor patio with fire pits, fountains, and a year-round floral display. Inside is a contemporary Mission-style room surrounding a green bottle glass fountain that extends the length of the main dining room. The menu features local seafood and vegetables combined in exciting ways. As a starter, try the Carlsbad mussels and Manila clams in a Riesling broth, followed by a prime flatiron steak with white truffle and lobster mac and cheese. Tantalizing desserts include luscious Carlsbad strawberries marinated in balsamic and lemon herb crème brûlée. ⑤ *Average main: $27* ✉ *2100 Costa Del Mar Rd.* ☎ *760/929–6306* ⊕ *www.dinebluefire.com* ⚫ *Reservations essential* ⊘ *Closed Sun.–Tues. No lunch.*

WHERE TO STAY

$$
RESORT
FAMILY
Fodor's Choice
★

⚟ **La Costa Resort and Spa.** A legendary '50s-style resort is a chic Spanish colonial oasis, where ample guest rooms, in shades of brown and sand with oversize chairs and sofas, are spread among a collection of handsome two-story buildings. **Pros:** huge glamorous spa; excellent kids' facilities; popular restaurant. **Cons:** very spread out, making long walks necessary; lots of kids, so if you're not in the market for a family-friendly stay, look elsewhere. ⑤ *Rooms from: $259* ✉ *2100 Costa del Mar Rd.* ☎ *760/438–9111, 800/854–5000* ⊕ *www.lacosta.com* ➫ *610 rooms, 120 villas.*

$$
RESORT
FAMILY
Fodor's Choice
★

⚟ **Park Hyatt Aviara Resort.** The quietly elegant hilltop retreat is one of the most luxurious hotels in the San Diego area, where rooms have every possible amenity (including private terraces and deep soaking tubs) and one of the most sublime views in Southern California, overlooking Batiquitos Lagoon and the Pacific. **Pros:** unbeatable location; many nature trails; beach butler service. **Cons:** a little stiff; some complaints about service; $25 resort fee. ⑤ *Rooms from: $285* ✉ *7100 Four Seasons Point* ☎ *800/233–1234, 760/448–1234* ⊕ *www.parkhyattaviara. com* ➫ *329 rooms, 44 suites.*

OCEANSIDE

8 miles north of Carlsbad on Rte. S21, 37 miles north of Downtown San Diego on I–5.

FAMILY
Fodor's Choice
★

Old Mission San Luis Rey. Known as the King of the Missions, the 18th and largest and most prosperous of California's missions was built in 1798 by Franciscan friars under the direction of Father Fermin Lasuen to help educate and convert local Native Americans. The *sala* (parlor), the kitchen, a friar's bedroom, a weaving room, and a collection of religious art and old Spanish vestments convey much about early mission life. A location for filming Disney's 1950's *Zorro* TV series, the well-preserved mission is still owned by the Franciscans. ✉ *4050 Mission Ave.* ☎ *760/757–3651* ⊕ *www.sanluisrey.org* ✎ *$5* ⊘ *Weekdays 9:30–5; weekends 10–5.*

ESCONDIDO

8 miles north of Rancho Bernardo on I–15, 31 miles northeast of Downtown San Diego on I–15.

FAMILY

Fodor's Choice

★

San Diego Zoo Safari Park. A branch of the San Diego Zoo, 35 miles to the south, the 1,800-acre preserve in the San Pasqual Valley is designed to protect endangered species from around the world. Exhibit areas have been carved out of the dry, dusty canyons and mesas to represent the animals' natural habitats in various parts of Africa, the Australian rain forest, and Asian swamps and plains.

The best way to see these preserves is to take the 45-minute, 2½-mile Africa tram safari, included with admission. As you pass in front of the large, naturally landscaped enclosures, you can see animals bounding across prairies and mesas as they would in the wild. More than 3,500 animals of more than 400 species roam or fly above the expansive grounds. Predators are separated from prey by deep moats, but only the elephants, tigers, lions, and cheetahs are kept in enclosures. Photographers with zoom lenses can get spectacular shots of zebras, gazelles, and rhinos. In summer, when the park stays open late, the trip is especially enjoyable in the early evening, when the heat has subsided and the animals are active and feeding. When the bus travels through the park after dark, sodium-vapor lamps illuminate the active animals.

For a more focused view of the park, you can take one of several other safaris at an extra charge. You can choose from several behind-the-scenes safaris, fly above it all via the zipline safari, or get up close to giraffes and rhinos on a caravan safari. Rental camcorders, strollers, and wheelchairs are available. You can also arrange to stay overnight in the park in summer on a Roar and Snore Sleepover (adults $140–$262, kids 8–11 $152–$192, plus admission). ⊠ *15500 San Pasqual Valley Rd.* ✚ *Take I–15 north to Via Rancho Pkwy. and follow signs, 6 miles* ⊕ *www.sdzsafaripark.org* ⊠ *$44 for basic one-day pass; multipark and multiday passes are available; special safaris are extra; parking $10* ⊙ *Daily 9–dusk, later in summer.*

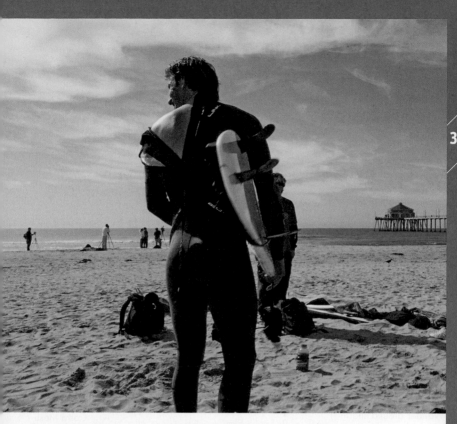

ORANGE COUNTY AND CATALINA ISLAND

With Disneyland and Knott's Berry Farm

WELCOME TO ORANGE COUNTY AND CATALINA ISLAND

TOP REASONS TO GO

★ **Disney magic:** Walking down Main Street, U.S.A., with Cinderella's Castle straight ahead, you really will feel like you're in one of the happiest places on Earth.

★ **Beautiful beaches:** Surf, swim, sail, or just relax on one of the state's most breathtaking stretches of coastline. Keep in mind, the water may be colder than you expect.

★ **Island getaways:** Just a short hydrofoil away, Catalina Island feels 1,000 miles away from California. Wander around charming Avalon, or explore the unspoiled beauty of the island's wild interior.

★ **The fine life:** Some of the state's wealthiest communities are in coastal Orange County, so spend at least part of your stay here experiencing how the other half lives.

★ **Family fun:** Spend some quality time with the kids riding roller coasters, eating ice cream, fishing off ocean piers, and bodysurfing.

1 Disneyland Resort. Southern California's top family destination has expanded from the humble park of Walt Disney's vision to a megaresort with more attractions spilling over into Disney's California Adventure. But kids (and many adults) still consider it the happiest place on Earth.

2 Knott's Berry Farm. Amusement park lovers should check out this Buena Park attraction, with thrill rides, the *Peanuts* gang, and lots of fried chicken and boysenberry pie.

3 Coastal Orange County. The OC's beach communities may not be quite as glamorous as seen on TV, but coastal spots like Huntington Beach, Newport Harbor, and Laguna Beach are perfect for chilling out in a beachfront hotel.

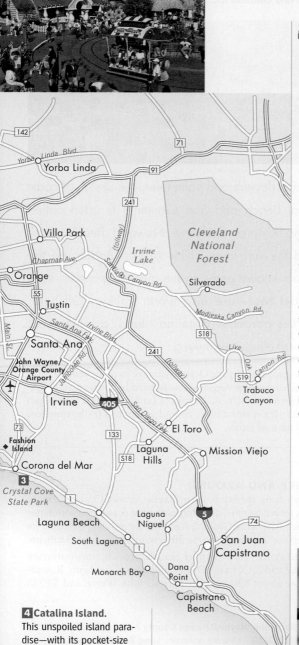

GETTING ORIENTED

3

Like Los Angeles, Orange County stretches over a large area, lacks a singular focal point, and has limited public transportation. You'll need a car and a sensible game plan to make the most of your visit. Try staying at a midpoint location such as Irvine or Costa Mesa, both equidistant from inland tourist attractions and the coast. These towns are less crowded than Anaheim and less expensive than the beach cities. Of course, if you can afford it, staying at the beach is always recommended.

4 Catalina Island. This unspoiled island paradise—with its pocket-size town, Avalon, and large nature preserve—is just off the Orange County coast.

Updated
by Kathy A.
McDonald

With its tropical flowers and palm trees, the stretch of coast between Seal Beach and San Clemente is often called the California Riviera. Exclusive Newport Beach, artsy Laguna, and the surf town of Huntington Beach are the stars, but lesser-known gems on the glistening coast—such as Corona del Mar—are also worth visiting. Offshore, meanwhile, lies gorgeous Catalina Island, a terrific spot for diving, snorkeling, and hiking.

Few of the citrus groves that gave Orange County its name remain. This region south and east of Los Angeles is now ruled by tourism and high-tech business instead of farmers. Despite a building boom that began in the 1990s, the area is still a place to find wilderness trails, canyons, greenbelts, and natural parks.

PLANNING

GETTING HERE AND AROUND

Orange County's main facility is John Wayne Airport Orange County (SNA), which is served by ten major domestic airlines and two commuter lines. Long Beach Airport (LGB) is served by four airlines, including its major player, JetBlue. It's roughly 20 to 30 minutes by car from Anaheim.

Airport Bus and Prime Time Airport Shuttle provide transportation from John Wayne and LAX to the Disneyland area of Anaheim. Round-trip fares average about $20 per person from John Wayne and $30 to $34 from LAX.

AIR TRAVEL

Airport Information John Wayne/Orange County Airport (SNA). ⊠ 18601 Airport Way ☎ 949/252–5006 ⊕ www.ocair.com. **Long Beach Airport** (LGB). ⊠ 4100 Donald Douglas Dr. ☎ 562/570–2600 ⊕ www.lgb.org.

BUS TRAVEL

The Orange County Transportation Authority will take you virtually anywhere in the county, but it will take time; OCTA buses go from Knott's Berry Farm and Disneyland to Huntington Beach and Newport Beach. Bus 1 travels along the coast; buses 701 and 721 provide express service to Los Angeles.

Information Orange County Transportation Authority (OCTA) ☎ 714/560–6282 ⊕ www.octa.net.

CAR TRAVEL

The San Diego Freeway (Interstate 405), the coastal route, and the Santa Ana Freeway (Interstate 5), the inland route, run north–south through Orange County. South of Laguna, Interstate 405 merges into Interstate 5 (called the San Diego Freeway south from this point). A toll road, Highway 73, runs 15 miles from Newport Beach to San Juan Capistrano; it costs $5.25–$6.25 (lower rates are for weekends and off-peak hours) and is usually less jammed than the regular freeways. Do your best to avoid all Orange County freeways during rush hours (6–9 am and 3:30–6:30 pm). Highway 55 leads to Newport Beach. The Pacific Coast Highway (Highway 1) allows easy access to beach communities and is the most scenic route.

FERRY TRAVEL

There are two ferries that service Catalina Island; Catalina Express runs from Long Beach (about 90 minutes) and from Newport Beach (about 75 minutes). Reservations are advised for summers and weekends. During the winter months, ferry crossings are not as frequent as in the summer high season.

TRAIN TRAVEL

When planning train travel, consider where the train stations are in relation to your ultimate destination. You may need to make extra transportation arrangements once you've arrived in town. Amtrak makes daily stops in Orange County at all major towns. Metrolink is a weekday commuter train that runs to and from Los Angeles and Orange County.

Information Amtrak ☎ 800/872–7245 ⊕ www.amtrak.com. **Metrolink** ☎ 800/371–5465 ⊕ www.metrolinktrains.com.

For more information on Getting Here and Around, see Travel Smart California.

RESTAURANTS

Much like L.A., restaurants in Orange County are generally casual, and you'll rarely see men in jackets and ties. However, at top resort hotel dining rooms, many guests choose to dress up.

Of course, there's also a swath of supercasual places along the beach-fronts—fish-taco takeout, taquerias, burger joints—that won't mind if you wear flip-flops. Reservations are recommended for the nicest restaurants.

Many places don't serve past 11 pm, and locals tend to eat early. Remember that according to California law, smoking is prohibited in all enclosed areas.

Prices in the restaurant reviews are the average cost of a main course at dinner or, if dinner is not served, at lunch (excluding sales tax).

HOTELS

Along the coast there are remarkable luxury resorts; if you can't afford a stay, pop in for the view at Laguna Beach's Montage or the always welcoming Ritz-Carlton at Dana Point. For a taste of the OC glam life, have lunch overlooking the yachts of Newport Bay at the Balboa Bay Resort.

As a rule, lodging prices tend to rise the closer the hotels are to the beach. If you're looking for value, consider a hotel that is inland along the Interstate 405 freeway corridor.

In most cases, you can take advantage of some of the facilities of the high-end resorts, such as restaurants and spas, even if you aren't an overnight guest.

Prices in the hotel reviews are the lowest cost of a standard double room in high season. Prices do not include taxes (as high as 15%, depending on the region).

VISITOR INFORMATION

The Anaheim-Orange County Visitor and Convention Bureau is an excellent resource for both leisure and business travelers and can provide materials on many area attractions. It's on the main floor of the Anaheim Convention Center.

The Orange County Tourism Council's website is also a useful source of information.

Information Anaheim/Orange County Visitor & Convention Bureau
✉ *Anaheim Convention Center, 800 W. Katella Ave., Anaheim* ☎ *714/765–8888*
⊕ *www.anaheimoc.org.* **Orange County Tourism Council** ⊕ *www.visittheoc.com.*

DISNEYLAND RESORT

26 miles southeast of Los Angeles, via I–5.

The snowcapped Matterhorn, the centerpiece of the Magic Kingdom, punctuates the skyline of Anaheim. Since 1955, when Walt Disney chose this once-quiet farming community for the site of his first amusement park, Disneyland has attracted more than 600 million visitors and tens of thousands of workers, and Anaheim has been their host.

To understand the symbiotic relationship between Disneyland and Anaheim, you need only look at the $4.2 billion spent in a combined effort to revitalize Anaheim's tourist center and run-down areas, and to expand and renovate the Disney properties into what is known now as Disneyland Resort.

The resort is a sprawling complex that includes Disney's two amusement parks; three hotels; and Downtown Disney, a shopping, dining, and entertainment promenade. Anaheim's tourist center includes Angel Stadium of Anaheim, home of baseball's 2002 World Series Champion Los Angeles Angels of Anaheim; the Honda Center (formerly the Arrowhead Pond), which hosts concerts and the Anaheim Ducks hockey team; and the enormous Anaheim Convention Center.

GETTING THERE

Disney is about a 30-mile drive from either LAX or Downtown. From LAX, follow Sepulveda Boulevard south to the Interstate 105 freeway and drive east 16 miles to the Interstate 605 north exit. Exit at the Santa Ana Freeway (Interstate 5) and continue south for 12 miles to the Disneyland Drive exit. Follow signs to the resort. From Downtown, follow Interstate 5 south 28 miles and exit at Disneyland Drive. **Disneyland Resort Express** (☎ *714/978–8855* ⊕ *graylineanaheim.com*) offers daily nonstop bus service between LAX, John Wayne Airport, and Anaheim. Reservations are not required. The cost is $20 one-way for adults, $17 for children for LAX; and $15 and $12 one-way for John Wayne Airport.

DISNEY'S TOP ATTRACTIONS

Finding Nemo: Board a yellow submarine and view a 3-D animated adventure.

Haunted Mansion: A "doombuggy" takes you through a spooky old plantation mansion.

Matterhorn Bobsleds: At the center of the Magic Kingdom, this roller coaster simulates bobsleds.

Pirates of the Caribbean: Watch buccaneers wreak havoc as you float along in a rowboat.

Space Mountain: This scary-but-thrilling roller coaster is indoors—and mostly in the dark.

SAVING TIME AND MONEY

If you plan to visit for more than a day, you can save money by buying two- three-, four-, and five-day Park Hopper tickets that grant same-day "hopping" privileges between Disneyland and Disney's California Adventure. You get a discount on the multiple-day passes if you buy online through the Disneyland website.

A one-day Park Hopper pass costs $137 for anyone 10 or older, $131 for kids ages 3–9. Admission to either park (but not both) is $92 or $86 for kids 3–9; kids 2 and under are free.

In addition to tickets, parking is $15–$22 (unless your hotel has a shuttle or is within walking distance), and meals in the parks and at Downtown Disney range from $10 to $30 per person.

DISNEYLAND

FAMILY

Fodor's Choice

★

Disneyland. One of the biggest misconceptions people have about Disneyland is that they've "been there, done that" if they've visited either Florida's mammoth Walt Disney World or one of the Disney parks overseas. But Disneyland, which opened in 1955 and is the only one of the parks to be overseen by Walt himself, has a genuine historic feel and occupies a unique place in the Disney legend. Expertly run, with polite and helpful staff ("cast members" in the Disney lexicon), the park has plenty that you won't find anywhere else—such as the Indiana Jones Adventure ride and Storybook Land, with its miniature replicas of animated Disney scenes from classics such as *Pinocchio* and *Alice in Wonderland*. Characters appear for autographs and photos throughout the day; guidebooks at the entrances give times and places. (Some visitors download the Disney Park mobile app). Live shows, strolling musicians, and endless snack choices add to the carnival atmosphere. You can also meet some of the animated icons at one of the character meals served at the three Disney hotels (open to the public). Belongings can be stored in lockers just off Main Street; stroller rentals at the entrance gate are a convenient option for families with small tykes. ⊠ *1313 S. Disneyland Dr., between Ball Rd. and Katella Ave., Anaheim* ☎ *714/781–4565 Guest information* ⊕ *www.disneyland.com* ✉ *$87; kids 3–9 $81; parking $15* ⊗ *Hrs. vary.*

PARK NEIGHBORHOODS
Neighborhoods for Disneyland are arranged in geographic order.

MAIN STREET, U.S.A. Walt's hometown of Marceline, Missouri, was the inspiration behind this romanticized image of small-town America, circa 1900. The sidewalks are lined with a penny arcade and shops that sell everything from tradable pins to Disney-theme clothing, an endless supply of sugar confections, and a photo shop that offers souvenirs created via Disney's PhotoPass (onsite photographers capture memorable moments digitally—you can access in person or online). Main Street opens half an hour before the rest of the park, so it's a good place to explore if you're getting an early start to beat the crowds (it's also open an hour after the other attractions close, so you may want to save your shopping for the end of the day). **Main Street Cinema** offers a cool respite from the crowds and six classic Disney animated shorts, including *Steamboat Willie*. There's rarely a wait to enter. Grab a cappuccino and fresh-made pastry at the Jolly Holiday bakery to jump-start your visit. Board the **Disneyland Railroad** here to save on walking; it tours all the lands plus offers unique views of Splash Mountain and the Grand Canyon and Primeval World dioramas.

NEW ORLEANS SQUARE This mini–French Quarter, with narrow streets, hidden courtyards, and live street performances, is home to two iconic attractions and the Cajun-inspired Blue Bayou restaurant. **Pirates of the Caribbean** now features Jack Sparrow and the cursed Captain Barbossa, in a nod to the blockbuster movies of the same name, plus enhanced special effects and battle scenes (complete with cannonball explosions). Nearby **Haunted Mansion** continues to spook guests with its stretching room and "doombuggy" rides (plus there's now an expanded storyline for the beating-heart bride). Its *Nightmare Before Christmas* holiday overlay is an annual tradition. This is a good area to get a casual bite to eat; the clam chowder in sourdough bread bowls, sold at the French Market Restaurant and Royal Street Veranda, is a popular choice. Food carts offer everything from just-popped popcorn to churros, and even fresh fruit.

FRONTIERLAND Between Adventureland and Fantasyland, Frontierland transports you to the wild, wild West with its rustic buildings, shooting gallery, mountain range, and foot-stompin' dance hall. The marquee attraction, **Big Thunder Mountain Railroad,** is a relatively tame roller coaster ride (no steep descents) that takes the form of a runaway mine car as it rumbles past desert canyons and an old mining town; in 2013 it underwent a complete makeover. Tour the Rivers of America on the **Mark Twain Riverboat** in the company of a grizzled old river pilot or circumnavigate the globe on the **Sailing Ship Columbia,** though its operating hours are

BEST TIPS FOR DISNEYLAND

Buy entry tickets in advance.
Many nearby hotels sell park admission tickets; you can also buy them through the Disney website. If you book a package deal, such as those offered through AAA, tickets are included, too.

The lines at the ticket booths can take more than an hour on busy days, so you'll definitely save time by buying in advance, especially if you're committed to going on a certain day regardless of the weather.

Come midweek. Weekends, especially in summer, are a mob scene. Holidays are crowded, too. A rainy winter weekday is often the least crowded time to visit.

Plan your times to hit the most popular rides. Fodorites recommend to get to the park as early as possible. If you're at the park when the gates open, make a beeline for the top rides before the crowds reach a critical mass. Another good time is the late evening, when the hordes thin out somewhat, and during a parade or other show. Save the quieter attractions for midafternoon.

Use FASTPASS. These passes allow you to reserve your place in line at some of the most crowded attractions (only one at a time). Distribution machines are posted near the entrances of each attraction. Feed in your park admission ticket, and you'll receive a pass with a printed time frame (generally up to 1–1½ hours later) during which you can return to wait in a much shorter line.

Plan your meals to avoid peak mealtime crowds. Start the day with a big breakfast so you won't be too hungry at noon, when restaurants and vendors get swarmed. Wait to have lunch until after 1.

If you want to eat at the **Blue Bayou** in New Orleans Square, you can make a reservation up to six months in advance online. Another (cheaper) option is to bring your own food. There are areas just outside the park gates with picnic tables set up for this. And it's always a good idea to bring water and a few melt-resistant snacks with you. (No bottles or coolers allowed.)

Check the daily events schedule online or at the park entrance. During parades, fireworks, and other special events, sections of the parks clog with crowds. This can work for you or against you. An event could make it difficult to get around a park—but if you plan ahead, you can take advantage of the distraction to hit popular rides.

Send the Teens Next Door. Disneyland's newer sister park, California Adventure, features more intense rides suitable for older kids (Park Hopper passes include admission to both parks).

3

usually limited to weekends. From here, you can raft over to Pirate's Lair on **Tom Sawyer Island,** which now features pirate-theme caves, treasure hunts, and music, along with plenty of caves and hills to climb and explore. If you don't mind tight seating, have a snack at the Golden Horseshoe Restaurant while enjoying the always-entertaining comedy and bluegrass show of Billy Hill and the Hillybillies. Children won't want to miss **Big Thunder Ranch,** a small petting zoo featuring pigs, goats, and cows, beyond Big Thunder Mountain.

CRITTER COUNTRY Down-home country is the theme in this shady corner of the park, where Winnie the Pooh and Davy Crockett make their homes. Here you can find **Splash Mountain,** a classic flume ride accompanied by music and appearances by Brer Rabbit and other characters from *Song of the South.* Don't forget to check out your photo (the camera snaps close-ups of each car just before it plunges into the water) on the way out. The patio of the popular Hungry Bear Restaurant has great views of Tom Sawyer's Island and Davy Crockett's Explorer Canoes.

ADVEN-TURELAND Modeled after the lands of Africa, Polynesia, and Arabia, this tiny tropical paradise is worth braving the crowds that flock here for the ambience and better-than-average food. Sing along with the animatronic birds and tiki gods in the **Enchanted Tiki Room,** sail the rivers of the world with joke-cracking skippers on **Jungle Cruise,** and climb the Disneyodendron semperflorens (aka always-blooming Disney tree) to **Tarzan's Treehouse,** where you can walk through scenes, some interactive, from the 1999 animated film. Cap off the visit with a wild Jeep ride at **Indiana Jones Adventure,** where the special effects and decipherable hieroglyphics distract you while you're waiting in line. The skewers (some vegetarian options available) at Bengal Barbecue and pineapple whip at Tiki Juice Bar are some of the best fast-food options in the park.

FANTASYLAND Sleeping Beauty Castle marks the entrance to Fantasyland, a visual wonderland of princesses, spinning teacups, flying elephants, and other classic storybook characters. Rides and shops (such as the princess-theme Once Upon a Time and Gepetto's Toys and Gifts) take precedence over restaurants in this area of the park, but outdoor carts sell everything from churros to turkey legs. Tots love the **King Arthur Carousel, Casey Jr. Circus Train,** and **Storybook Land Canal Boats.** This is also home to **Mr. Toad's Wild Ride, Peter Pan's Flight,** and **Pinocchio's Daring Journey,** classic, movie-theater-dark rides that immerse riders in Disney fairy tales and appeal to adults and kids alike. The Abominable Snowman pops up on the **Matterhorn Bobsleds,** a roller coaster that twists and turns up and around on a made-to-scale model of the real Swiss mountain. Anchoring the east end of Fantasyland is **It's a Small World,** a smorgasbord of dancing animatronic dolls, cuckoo clock–covered walls, and variations of the song everyone knows, or soon *will* know, by heart. Beloved Disney characters like Ariel from *Under the Sea* are also part of the mix. New in 2013: A Fantasy Faire village that collects the Disney princesses together and offers storytelling at the Royal Theatre.

MICKEY'S TOONTOWN Geared toward small fries, this lopsided cartoonlike downtown, complete with cars and trolleys that invite exploring, is where Mickey, Donald, Goofy, and other classic Disney characters hang their hats. One of the most popular attractions is **Roger Rabbit's Car Toon Spin,** a twisting, turning cab ride through the Toontown of *Who Framed Roger Rabbit?* You can also walk through **Mickey's House** to meet and be photographed with the famous mouse, take a low-key ride on **Gadget's Go Coaster,** or bounce around in the fenced-in playground in front of **Goofy's House.**

DID YOU KNOW?

Apparently, the plain purple teacup in Disneyland's Mad Tea Party ride spins the fastest—though no one knows why.

TOMOR-
ROWLAND
This popular section of the park continues to tinker with its future, adding and enhancing rides regularly. One of the newest attractions, Star Tours, is a 3-D immersive experience in the world of Star Wars. **Finding Nemo's Submarine Voyage** updates the old Submarine Voyage ride with the exploits of Nemo, Dory, Marlin, and other characters from the Disney Pixar film. Try to visit this popular ride early in the day if you can and be prepared for a wait. The interactive **Buzz Lightyear Astro Blasters** lets you zap your neighbors with laser beams and compete for the highest score. Hurtle through the cosmos on **Space Mountain** or check out mainstays like the futuristic **Astro Orbiter** rockets, **Innoventions,** a self-guided tour of the latest toys and gadgets of tomorrow, and **Caption EO,** a 3-D film featuring the music and talents of the late Michael Jackson. Disneyland Monorail and Disneyland Railroad both have stations here. There's also a video arcade and dancing water fountain that makes a perfect playground for kids on hot summer days. The Jedi Training Academy spotlights future Luke Skywalkers in the *Star Wars*-themed show's crowd.

Besides the eight lands, the daily live-action shows and parades are always crowd-pleasers. **Fantasmic!** is a musical, fireworks, and laser show in which Mickey and friends wage a spellbinding battle against Disneyland's darker characters. ■TIP→ Arrive early to secure a good view; if there are two shows scheduled for the day, the second one tends to be less crowded. A fireworks display sparks up most evenings. Brochures with maps, available at the entrance, list show and parade times.

DISNEY CALIFORNIA ADVENTURE

FAMILY
Fodor's Choice
★
Disney California Adventure. The sprawling Disney California Adventure, adjacent to Disneyland (their entrances face each other), pays tribute to the Golden State with eight themed areas that recreate vintage architectural styles and embrace several hit Pixar films via engaging attractions. In 2012, the park's entrance was revamped—visitors now enter through the art deco–style Buena Vista Street—and the 12-acre Cars Land and Radiator Springs Racers, an immediate blockbuster hit (FASTPASS tickets for the ride run out early most days) was added. Other popular attractions include *World of Color*, a nighttime water-effects show, and Toy Story Mania!, an interactive adventure ride hosted by Woody, Buzz Lightyear, and friends. At night, the park takes on neon-colored hues as neon signs light up Route 66 in Cars Land and Mickey's Fun Wheel, a mega-sized Ferris wheel on the Paradise Pier. Unlike at Disneyland, cocktails, beer, and wine are available, and there's even an outdoor dance spot, the Mad T Party. Live nightly entertainment also features a 1930s jazz troupe that arrives in a vintage jalopy. ⊠ *1313 S. Disneyland Dr., between Ball Rd. and Katella Ave., Anaheim* ☎ *714/781–4565 Guest information* ⊕ *www.disneyland.com* ✉ *$87; kids 3–9 $81; parking $15* ☉ *Hrs. vary.*

PARK NEIGHBORHOODS

BUENA VISTA STREET California Adventure's grand entryway re-creates the lost 1920s of Los Angeles that Walt Disney encountered when he moved to the Golden State. There's a **Red Car trolley** (modeled after Los Angeles's bygone streetcar line); hop on for the brief ride to Hollywood Land. Buena Vista Street is also home to a Starbucks outlet—within the Fiddler, Fifer & Practical Café—and the upscale Carthay Circle Restaurant and Lounge, which serves modern craft cocktails and beer.

CONDOR FLATS Dive into California's history and natural beauty with nature trails, a winery, and a tortilla factory (with free samples). Condor Flats has **Soarin' Over California,** a spectacular simulated hang-glider ride over California terrain.

GRIZZLY PEAK Test your outdoorsman skills on the **Redwood Creek Challenge Trail,** a challenging trek across net ladders and suspension bridges. **Grizzly River Run** mimics the river rapids of the Sierra Nevadas; be prepared to get soaked.

HOLLYWOOD LAND With a main street modeled after Hollywood Boulevard, a fake blue-sky backdrop, and real soundstages, this area celebrates California's most famous industry. **Disney Animation** gives you an insider's look at the work of animators and how they create characters. **Turtle Talk with Crush** lets kids have an unrehearsed talk with computer-animated Crush, a sea turtle from *Finding Nemo.* The Hyperion Theater hosts **Aladdin—A Musical Spectacular,** a 45-minute live performance with terrific visual effects. ■TIP➜ Plan on getting in line about half an hour in advance: the show is worth the wait. On the film-inspired ride, **Monsters, Inc. Mike & Sulley to the Rescue,** you climb into taxis and travel the streets of Monstropolis on a mission to safely return Boo to her bedroom. A major draw for older kids is the looming **Twilight Zone Tower of Terror,** which drops riders 13 floors. Their screams can be heard throughout the park!

A BUG'S LAND Inspired by the 1998 film *A Bug's Life,* this section skews its attractions to an insect's point of view. Kids can spin around in giant takeout Chinese food boxes on **Flik's Flyers,** and hit the bug-shaped bumper cars on **Tuck and Roll's Drive 'Em Buggies.** The short show *It's Tough to Be a Bug!* gives a 3-D look at insect life.

CARS LAND Amble down Route 66, the main thoroughfare of Cars Land, a pitch-perfect re-creation of the vintage highway. Quick eats are found at the Cozy Cone Motel (in a teepee-shaped motor court) while Flo's V8 café serves hearty comfort food. Start your day at Radiator Springs Racers, the park's most popular attraction, where waits can be two hours or longer. Strap into a nifty sports car and meet the characters of Pixar's *Cars;* the ride ends in a speedy auto race through the red rocks and desert of Radiator Springs.

PACIFIC WHARF The Wine Country Trattoria at the Golden Vine Winery is a great place for Italian specialties paired with California wine; relax outside on the restaurant's terrace for a casual bite. Mexican cuisine and potent margaritas are available at the Cocina Cucamonga Mexican Grill and Rita's Baja Blenders.

PARADISE PIER This section re-creates the glory days of California's seaside piers. If you're looking for thrills, the **California Screamin'** roller coaster takes its riders from 0 to 55 mph in about four seconds and proceeds through scream tunnels, steeply angled drops, and a 360-degree loop. **Goofy's Sky School** is a rollicking roller coast ride that goes up three stories and covers more than 1,200 feet of track. **Mickey's Fun Wheel,** a giant Ferris wheel, provides a good view of the grounds at a more leisurely pace. There are also carnival games, a fish-theme carousel, and Ariel's Grotto, where future princesses can dine with the mermaid and her friends (reservations are a must). Get a close-up look at Ariel's world on the **Little Mermaid— Ariel's Undersea Adventure.** The best views of the nighttime music, water and light show, **World of Color,** are from the paths along Paradise Bay. Book a picnic dinner at the Golden Vine Winery that includes a ticket to a viewing area to catch all the show's stunning visuals.

OTHER ATTRACTIONS

Downtown Disney. Downtown Disney is a 20-acre promenade of dining, shopping, and entertainment that connects the Disneyland Resort hotels and theme parks. Restaurant-nightclub **House of Blues** spices up its Delta-inspired ribs and seafood with various live music acts on an intimate two-story stage. At **Ralph Brennan's Jazz Kitchen** you can dig into New Orleans–style food and music. Sports fans gravitate to **ESPN Zone,** a sports bar–restaurant–entertainment center with American grill food, interactive video games, and 175 video screens telecasting worldwide sports events. An **AMC** multiplex movie theater with stadium-style seating plays the latest blockbusters and, naturally, a couple of kid flicks. Promenade shops sell everything from Disney goods to antique jewelry— don't miss **Vault 28,** a hip boutique that sells one-of-a-kind vintage and couture clothes and accessories from Disney, Harajuku Lovers, and other designers. At the megasized **LEGO Store,** there are hands-on demonstrations and space to play with the latest LEGO creations. Parking is a deal: the first three hours are free; an additional two hours are free with validation. ⊠ *Disneyland Dr., between Ball Rd. and Katella Ave., Anaheim* ☎ *714/300–7800* ⊕ *disneyland.disney.go.com/downtown-disney* ⊠ *Free* ☺ *Daily 7 am–2 am; hrs at shops and restaurants vary.*

WHERE TO EAT

$$$$ ✕ **Anaheim White House.** Several small dining rooms are set with crisp lin-
ITALIAN ens and candles in this flower-filled 1909 mansion. The northern Italian menu includes steak, rack of lamb, and fresh seafood. Try the signature Ravioli Arragosta, lobster-filled pasta on a bed of ginger and citrus. A three-course prix-fixe low-calorie lunch, served weekdays, costs $23. ⑤ *Average main: $35* ⊠ *887 S. Anaheim Blvd., Anaheim* ☎ *714/772–1381* ⊕ *www.anaheimwhitehouse.com* ☺ *No lunch Sat.*

$$$ ✕ **Catal Restaurant & Uva Bar.** Famed chef Joachim Splichal of L.A.'s
MEDITERRANEAN Patina empire and his pro culinary staff take a more relaxed approach at this bi-level Mediterranean spot—with tapas breaking into the finger-food territory. People-watch at the colorful, outdoor Uva (Spanish for "grape") bar on the ground level in the center of Downtown Disney's action, where there are specialty cocktails, craft beers, and more than 40 wines by the glass. Burgers here are crowd-pleasers, as are the diverse selection of appetizers from corn *arepas* with pickled onions to

3

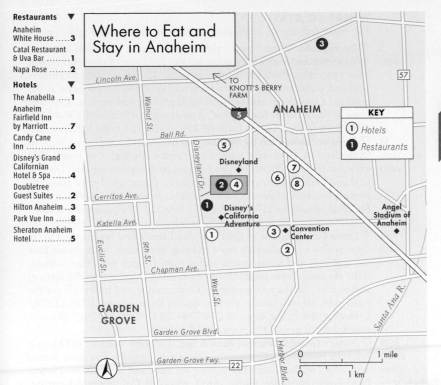

Where to Eat and Stay in Anaheim

KEY

① *Hotels*

❶ *Restaurants*

hummus. Upstairs, Catal's menu has tapas, a variety of flavorful paellas (lobster is worth the splurge), and charcuterie. ■TIP→ Reserve a table for dinner on Catal's second floor outdoor terrace for an awesome view of the Disneyland fireworks. ⑤ *Average main: $30* ✉ *Downtown Disney, 1580 S. Disneyland Dr., Suite 103, Anaheim* ☎ *714/774–4442* ⊕ *www.patinagroup.com.*

$$$$

AMERICAN

✕ **Napa Rose.** In sync with its host hotel, Disney's Grand Californian, this restaurant is done in a lovely Arts and Crafts–style and overlooks a woodsy corner of the California Adventure Park. The contemporary cuisine here is matched with an extensive wine list (1,000 labels on hand). For a look into the open kitchen, sit at the counter and watch the chefs as they whip up signature dishes such as pan-roasted diver scallops in a sauce of lemon, lobster, and vanilla and slowly braised beef short rib in a Cabernet jus. There are 80 wines available by the glass; the restaurant's lounge is a casual place to taste dishes from the seasonal menu. A drink on the outdoor patio with fire pit is a pleasant way to end the night. The four-course, $100 prix-fixe menu changes weekly; with wine pairings, it's $145. ⑤ *Average main: $40* ✉ *Disney's Grand Californian Hotel, 1600 S. Disneyland Dr., Anaheim* ☎ *714/300–7170, 714/381–3463 Disney dining* ⊕ *disneyland.disney. go.com/grand-californian-hotel/napa-rose* ⚘ *Reservations essential.*

WHERE TO STAY

For expanded reviews, facilities, and current deals, visit Fodors.com.

$ 🎬 **The Anabella.** On the convention center campus, a Spanish Mission–
HOTEL style exterior and leafy landscaping sets this hotel apart from other budget
basic properties. **Pros:** landscaped grounds; 15-minute walk to Disneyland and California Adventure entrance; extended happy hour at the
hotel bar. **Cons:** some say the room walls are thin; add-on fees. ⑤ *Rooms
from: $99* ⊠ *1030 W. Katella Ave., Anaheim* ☎ *714/905–1050, 800/863–
4888* ⊕ *www.anabellahotel.com* ⊃ *234 rooms, 124 suites* ⼳*No meals.*

$$ 🎬 **Anaheim Fairfield Inn by Marriott.** Attentive service and proximity to
HOTEL Disneyland (a 10-minute walk away) make this high-rise hotel a big
FAMILY draw for families. **Pros:** free Wi-Fi; close to many restaurants; Disney-
land and Park Hopper passes are available. **Cons:** small pool abuts the
parking lot; lack of green space. ⑤ *Rooms from: $139* ⊠ *1460 S. Har-
bor Blvd., Anaheim* ☎ *714/772–6777, 800/228–2800* ⊕ *www.marriott.
com* ⊃ *463 rooms, 4 suites* ⼳*No meals.*

$$ 🎬 **Candy Cane Inn.** One of the Disneyland area's first hotels, the Candy
HOTEL Cane is one of Anaheim's most relaxing properties, with rooms that
are spacious and understated and a palm-fringed pool that is especially inviting. **Pros:** proximity to everything Disney; friendly service;
well-lighted, landscaped property. **Cons:** rooms and lobby are on the
small side; all rooms face parking lot. ⑤ *Rooms from: $149* ⊠ *1747
S. Harbor Blvd., Anaheim* ☎ *714/774–5284, 800/345–7057* ⊕ *www.
candycaneinn.net* ⊃ *171 rooms* ⼳*Breakfast.*

$$$$ 🎬 **Disney's Grand Californian Hotel & Spa.** The most opulent of Disney's
RESORT Anaheim hotels, this Craftsman-style luxury property has guest rooms
FAMILY with views of the California Adventure Park and Downtown Disney.
Fodor'sChoice **Pros:** large, gorgeous lobby; direct access to California Adventure.
★ **Cons:** the self-parking lot is across the street from the hotel; standard
rooms are on the small side. ⑤ *Rooms from: $471* ⊠ *1600 S. Dis-
neyland Dr., Anaheim* ☎ *714/635–2300, 714/956–6425 reservations*
⊕ *disneyland.disney.go.com/grand-californian-hotel* ⊃ *904 rooms, 44
suites, 50 villas* ⼳*No meals.*

$$ 🎬 **Doubletree Guest Suites Anaheim Resort-Convention Center.** This upscale
HOTEL hotel near the Convention Center and a 20-minute walk from Disney-
land caters to business travelers and families alike. **Pros:** huge suites;
elegant lobby; within walking distance of a variety of restaurants.
Cons: some say the hotel seems far-removed from Disneyland; pool
area is small. ⑤ *Rooms from: $139* ⊠ *2085 S. Harbor Blvd., Ana-
heim* ☎ *714/750–3000, 800/215–7316* ⊕ *doubletree3.hilton.com* ⊃ *50
rooms, 202 suites.*

$$ 🎬 **Hilton Anaheim.** Next to the Anaheim Convention Center, this busy
HOTEL Hilton is one of the largest hotels in Southern California, with a res-
FAMILY taurant and food court, cocktail lounges, a full-service gym, and its
own Starbucks. **Pros:** friendly, efficient service; great seasonal kids'
programs; some rooms have views of Disneyland's nightly fireworks.
Cons: huge size can be daunting; $16 fee per day to use health club.
⑤ *Rooms from: $159* ⊠ *777 Convention Way, Anaheim* ☎ *714/750–
4321, 800/445–8667* ⊕ *www.anaheim.hilton.com* ⊃ *1,479 rooms, 93
suites* ⼳*No meals.*

$$ **Park Vue Inn.** This bougainvillea-trimmed two-story Spanish-style inn
HOTEL is one of the closest hotels you can find to the main entrance of the
Disneyland Resort. **Pros:** easy walk to Disneyland, Downtown Disney,
and California Adventure; good value; some rooms have bunk beds.
Cons: all rooms face the parking lot; some complain about early-morn-
ing street noise. $ *Rooms from: $163* ⊠ *1570 S. Harbor Blvd., Ana-
heim* ☎ *714/772–3691, 800/334–7021* ⊕ *www.parkvueinn.com* ➾ *76
rooms, 8 suites* ⊙*No meals.*

$$ **Sheraton Anaheim Hotel.** If you're hoping to escape from the commer-
HOTEL cial atmosphere of the hotels near Disneyland and California Adventure,
FAMILY consider this sprawling replica of a Tudor castle. **Pros:** large, attractive
lobby; game room; spacious rooms with comfortable beds. **Cons:** confusing layout; hotel sits close to a busy freeway. $ *Rooms from: $139*
⊠ *900 S. Disneyland Dr., Anaheim* ☎ *714/778–1700, 866/716-8130*
⊕ *www.starwoodhotels.com* ➾ *460 rooms, 29 suites* ⊙*No meals.*

SPORTS

Anaheim Ducks. The National Hockey League's Anaheim Ducks, winners of the 2007 Stanley Cup, play at Honda Center (formerly Arrowhead Pond). ⊠ *Honda Center, 2695 E. Katella Ave.* ☎ *877/945–3946*
⊕ *ducks.nhl.com.*

Los Angeles Angels of Anaheim. Pro baseball's Los Angeles Angels of Anaheim play at Angel Stadium of Anaheim. An "Outfield Extravaganza"
celebrates great plays on the field, with fireworks and a geyser exploding
over a model evoking the California coast. ⊠ *Angel Stadium, 2000 E.
Gene Autry Way* ☎ *714/940–2200* ⊕ *www.angelsbaseball.com* Ⓜ *Metrolink Angels Express.*

KNOTT'S BERRY FARM

25 miles south of Los Angeles, via I–5, in Buena Park.

FAMILY **Knott's Berry Farm.** The land where the boysenberry was invented (by
crossing red raspberry, blackberry, and loganberry bushes) is now
occupied by Knott's Berry Farm. In 1934 Cordelia Knott began serving chicken dinners on her wedding china to supplement her family's
income—or so the story goes. The dinners and her boysenberry pies
proved more profitable than husband Walter's berry farm, so the two
moved first into the restaurant business and then into the entertainment
business. The park is now a 160-acre complex with 100-plus rides,
dozens of restaurants and shops, and even a brick-by-brick replica of
Philadelphia's Independence Hall. Although it has some good attractions for small children, the park is best known for its roster of awesome thrill rides. And, yes, you can still get that boysenberry pie (and
jam, juice—you name it). Look for the only O.C. outlet of L.A. favorite
Pink's hot dogs, in the Knott's Marketplace. At this writing, new roller
coasters and an upgrade to the boardwalk are scheduled to open in
summer 2013. ⊠ *8039 Beach Blvd.* ✛ *Between La Palma Ave. and Crescent St., 2 blocks south of Hwy. 91* ☎ *714/220–5200* ⊕ *www.knotts.
com* ⊟ *$59.99; kids 3 years or older and under 48 inches tall $30.99.*

PARK NEIGHBORHOODS

THE
BOARDWALK
Not-for-the-squeamish thrill rides and skill-based games dominate the scene at the **boardwalk**. New roller coasters were added to the section in 2013. Go head over heels on the **Boomerang** roller coaster, then do it again—backward. The boardwalk is also home to a string of test-your-skill games that are fun to watch whether you're playing or not, and Johnny Rockets, the park's newest restaurant.

CAMP SNOOPY
It can be gridlock on weekends, but small fries love this miniature High Sierra wonderland where the *Peanuts* gang hangs out. Tykes can push and pump their own minI–mining cars on **Huff and Puff**, zip around a pint-size racetrack on **Charlie Brown Speedway**, and hop aboard **Woodstock's Airmail**, a kids' version of the park's Supreme Scream ride. Most of the rides here are geared toward kids only, leaving parents to cheer them on from the sidelines. **Sierra Sidewinder**, a roller coaster near the entrance of Camp Snoopy, is aimed at older children, with spinning saucer-type vehicles that go a maximum speed of 37 mph.

FIESTA
VILLAGE
Over in **Fiesta Village** are three more musts for adrenaline junkies: **Montezooma's Revenge**, a roller coaster that goes from 0 to 55 mph in less than five seconds, and **Jaguar!**, which simulates the motions of a cat stalking its prey, twisting, spiraling, and speeding up and slowing down as it takes you on its stomach-dropping course. **Windseeker**, which opened in 2011, whisks passengers on an unforgettable gondola ride 301 feet above the park, but is sometimes closed due to maintenance issues. There's also **Hat Dance**, a version of the spinning teacups but with sombreros, and a 100-year-old **Dentzel Carousel**, complete with an antique organ and menagerie of hand-carved animals.

GHOST TOWN
Clusters of authentic old buildings relocated from their original mining-town sites mark this section of the park. You can stroll down the street, stop and chat with a blacksmith, pan for gold (for a fee), crack open a geode, check out the chalkboard of a circa-1875 schoolhouse, and ride an original Butterfield stagecoach. Looming over it all is **GhostRider**, Orange County's first wooden roller coaster. Traveling up to 56 mph and reaching 118 feet at its highest point, the park's biggest attraction is riddled with sudden dips and curves, subjecting riders to forces up to three times that of gravity. On the Western-theme **Silver Bullet**, riders are sent to a height of 146 feet and then back down 109 feet. Riders spiral, corkscrew, fly into a cobra roll, and experience overbanked curves. The **Calico Mine** ride descends into a replica of a working gold mine. The **Timber Mountain Log Ride** is a visitor favorite—the flume ride underwent a complete renovation in 2013. Also found here is the park's newest thrill ride, the **Pony Express**, a roller coaster that lets riders saddle up on packs of "horses" tethered to platforms that take off on a series of hairpin turns and travel up to 38 mph. Don't miss the **Western Trails Museum**, a dusty old gem full of Old West memorabilia, plus menus from the original chicken restaurant, and Mrs. Knott's antique button collection. **Calico Railroad** departs regularly from Ghost Town station for a round-trip tour of the park (bandit holdups notwithstanding).

This section is also home to **Big Foot Rapids**, a splash-fest of white-water river rafting over towering cliffs, cascading waterfalls, and wild rapids. Don't miss the visually stunning show at **Mystery Lodge**, which tells the story of Native Americans in the Pacific Northwest with lights, music, and beautiful images.

INDIAN LANDS Celebrate Native American traditions through interactive exhibits like tepees and daily dance and storytelling performances.

Knott's Soak City Water Park is directly across from the main park on 13 acres next to Independence Hall. It has a dozen major water rides; the latest is **Pacific Spin**, an oversize waterslide that drops riders 75 feet into a catch pool. There's also a children's pool, 750,000-gallon wave pool, and funhouse. Soak City is open daily after Memorial Day; weekends only after Labor Day.

WHERE TO EAT AND STAY
For expanded hotel reviews, visit Fodors.com.

$$

AMERICAN ✕ **Mrs. Knott's Chicken Dinner Restaurant.** Cordelia Knott's fried chicken and boysenberry pies drew crowds so big that Knott's Berry Farm was built to keep the hungry customers occupied while they waited. The restaurant's current incarnation (outside the park's entrance) still serves crispy fried chicken, along with fluffy biscuits, corn, mashed potatoes, and Mrs. Knott's signature chilled cherry-rhubarb compote. The wait, unfortunately, can be an hour or more on weekends; another option is to order a bucket of the same tasty chicken from the adjacent takeout counter and have a picnic at the duck pond next to Independence Hall across the street. Jump-start a visit to the park with a hearty breakfast here. ⓢ *Average main: $17* ✉ *Knott's Berry Farm Marketplace Area, 8039 Beach Blvd.* ☎ *714/220–5080.*

$$$$

AMERICAN ✕ **Pirate's Dinner Adventure.** During this interactive pirate-theme dinner show, 150 actors/singers/acrobats (some quite talented) perform on a galleon while you eat a three-course meal. Food—barbecue pork, roast chicken, salad, veggies, rice, and unlimited soda and coffee—is mediocre and seating is tight, but kids love making a lot of noise to cheer on their favorite pirate, and the action scenes are breathtaking. ⓢ *Average main: $38* ✉ *7600 Beach Blvd.* ☎ *866/439–2469.*

$

RESORT
FAMILY ▦ **Knott's Berry Farm Hotel.** Knott's Berry Farm runs this convenient high-rise hotel on park grounds, complete with a Camp Snoopy motif in the second-floor "camp rooms," which come with telephone bedtime stories. **Pros:** easy access to Knott's Berry Farm; plenty of kids' activities; basketball court. **Cons:** lobby and hallways can be noisy and chaotic. ⓢ *Rooms from: $79* ✉ *7675 Crescent Ave.* ☎ *714/995–1111, 866/752–2444* ⊕ *www.knottshotel.com* ⤳ *320 rooms* ❏❘ *No meals.*

THE COAST

Running along the Orange County coastline is scenic Pacific Coast Highway (Highway 1, known locally as the PCH). Older beachfront settlements, with their modest bungalow-style homes, are joined by posh gated communities. The pricey land between Newport Beach and Laguna Beach is where Laker Kobe Bryant, novelist Dean Koontz, and a slew of Internet and finance moguls live.

Though the coastline is rapidly being filled in, there are still a few stretches of beautiful, protected open land. And at many places along the way you can catch an idealized glimpse of the Southern California lifestyle: surfers hitting the beach, boards under their arms.

LONG BEACH AND SAN PEDRO

About 25 miles southeast of Los Angeles, via I–110 south.

EXPLORING

FAMILY **Aquarium of the Pacific.** Sea lions, nurse sharks, and octopuses, oh my!—this aquarium focuses primarily on ocean life from the Pacific Ocean, with a detour into Australian birds. The main exhibits include lively sea lions, penguins, large tanks of various sharks and stingrays, and ethereal sea dragons, which the aquarium has successfully bred in captivity. Welcoming visitors to the aquarium's Great Hall is the multimedia attraction *Penguins,* a panoramic film that captures the world of this endangered species. Be sure to say hello to the newest rescued sea otter, Betty, at the engaging sea otter exhibit. For a nonaquatic experience, go to Lorikeet Forest, a walk-in aviary full of the friendliest parrots from Down Under. Buy a cup of nectar and smile as you become a human bird perch. If you're a true tropical animal lover, book an up-close-and-personal Animal Encounters Tour ($100) to learn about and assist in the care and feeding of the animals; or find out how the aquarium functions with the extensive Behind the Scenes Tour ($39.95). Certified divers can book a supervised dive in the aquarium's Tropical Reef Habitat ($299). Twice daily whale-watching trips on the *Harbor Breeze* depart from the dock adjacent to the aquarium; summer sightings of blue whales are an unforgettable thrill. ⊠ *100 Aquarium Way, Long Beach* 🕾 *562/590–3100* ⊕ *www.aquariumofpacific.org* 🖾 *$25.95* ☉ *Daily 9–6.*

Cabrillo Marine Aquarium. Dedicated to the marine life that flourishes off the Southern California coast, this Frank Gehry–designed center gives an intimate and instructive look at local sea creatures. Head to the Exploration Center and S. Mark Taper Foundation Courtyard for kid-friendly interactive exhibits and activity stations. Especially fun is the "Crawl In" aquarium, where you can be surrounded by fish without getting wet. ■TIP→ From March through July the aquarium organizes a legendary grunion program, when you can see the small, silvery fish as they come ashore at night to spawn on the beach. After visiting the museum, you can stop for a picnic or beach stroll along Cabrillo Beach. ⊠ *3720 Stephen M. White Dr., San Pedro, Los Angeles* 🕾 *310/548–7562* ⊕ *www.cabrilloaq.org* 🖾 *$5 suggested donation, parking $1 per hour* ☉ *Tues.–Fri. noon–5, weekends 10–5.*

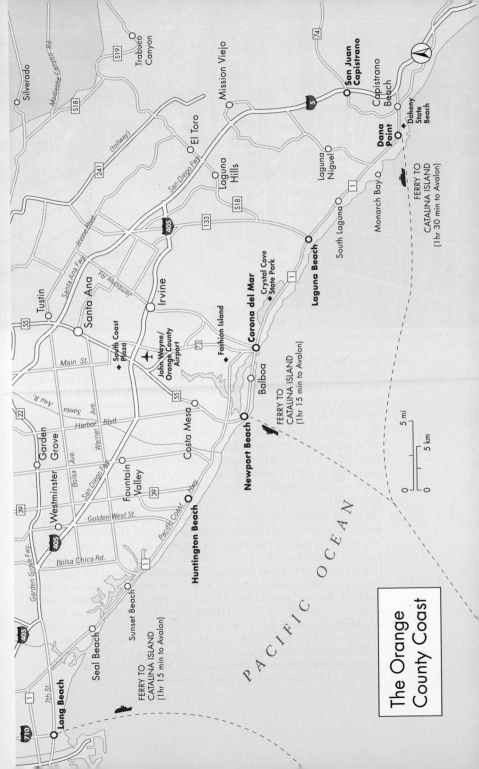

The Orange County Coast

A mural at Huntington Beach

FAMILY **Queen Mary.** The reason to see this impressive example of 20th-century cruise ship opulence is because it's the last of its kind. And there's a saying among staff members that the more you get to know the *Queen Mary*, the more you realize she has an endearing personality to match her wealth of history.

The beautifully preserved art deco–style ocean liner was launched in 1936 and made 1,001 transatlantic crossings before finally berthing in Long Beach in 1967. It has gone through many periods of renovations since, and in 2011, Evolution Hospitality Group took over management adding the popular Princess Diana exhibit and a daily British-style high tea.

On board, you can take one of a dozen tours, such as the informative Behind the Scenes walk or the downright spooky Haunted Encounters tour. (Spirits have reportedly been spotted in the pool and engine room.) You could stay for dinner at one of the ship's restaurants, listen to live jazz in the original first-class lounge, or even spend the night in one of the wood-paneled cabins. The ship's neighbor, a geodesic dome originally built to house Howard Hughes's *Spruce Goose* aircraft, now serves as a terminal for Carnival Cruise Lines, making the *Queen Mary* the perfect pit stop before or after a cruise. And anchored next to the *Queen* is the *Scorpion*, a Russian submarine you can tour for a look at Cold War history. ⊠ *1126 Queens Hwy., Long Beach* ☎ *877/342–0742* ⊕ *www.queenmary.com* ⛴ *Tours $25–$75, includes a self-guided audio tour* ☉ *Call for times and frequency of guided tours.*

HUNTINGTON BEACH

40 miles southeast of Los Angeles, I–5 south to I–605 south to I–405 south to Beach Blvd.

Once a sleepy residential town with little more than a string of rugged surf shops, Huntington Beach has transformed itself into a resort destination. The town's appeal is its broad white-sand beaches with often-towering waves, complemented by a lively pier, shops, and restaurants on Main Street and a growing collection of resort hotels.

A draw for sports fans and partiers of all stripes is the U.S. Open professional surf competition, which brings a festive atmosphere to town annually in late July. There's even a Surfing Walk of Fame, with plaques set in the sidewalk around the intersection of PCH and Main Street.

ESSENTIALS

Huntington Beach Marketing and Visitors Bureau ✉ *301 Main St., Suite 208* ☎ *714/969–3492, 800/729–6232* ⊕ *www.surfcityusa.com.*

EXPLORING

Bolsa Chica Ecological Reserve. Wildlife lovers and bird-watchers flock to Bolsa Chica Ecological Reserve, which has a 1,180-acre salt marsh where 321 out of Orange County's 420 bird species—including great blue herons, snowy and great egrets, and brown pelicans—have been spotted in the past decade. Throughout the reserve are trails for bird-watching, including a comfortable 1½-mile loop. Free guided tours depart from the walking bridge on the second Saturday of each month at 10 am. There are two entrances: one close to the Interpretive Center and a second 1 mile south on Warner Avenue, opposite Bolsa Chica State Beach. ✉ *Bolsa Chica Wetlands Interpretive Center, 3842 Warner Ave.* ☎ *714/846–1114* ⊕ *www.bolsachica.org* 🎟 *Free* ⊙ *Daily dawn–dusk.*

Huntington Pier. This pier stretches 1,800 feet out to sea, well past the powerful waves that made Huntington Beach reach for the title of "Surf City U.S.A." A farmers' market is held on Friday afternoons; an informal arts fair sets up most weekends.

NEED A BREAK?

Ruby's. At the end of the pier sits Ruby's, part of a California chain of 1940s-style burger joints. ✉ *1 Main St.* ☎ *714/969–7829* ⊕ *www.rubys.com.*

International Surfing Museum. Just up Main Street from the pier, the International Surfing Museum pays tribute to the sport's greats with the Surfing Hall of Fame, which has an impressive collection of surfboards and related memorabilia. They've even got the Bolex camera used to shoot the 1966 surfing documentary *The Endless Summer.* ✉ *411 Olive Ave.* ☎ *714/960–3483* ⊕ *www.surfingmuseum.org* 🎟 *Free, donations accepted* ⊙ *Sun. noon–5, Mon. and Wed.–Fri. noon–7, Tues. noon–9, Sat. 11–7.*

BEACHES

Bolsa Chica State Beach. At the northern section of the city, Bolsa Chica State Beach has barbecue pits and RV campsites and is usually less crowded than its southern neighbors. Sand is somewhat gritty and not the cleanest, but swells make it a hot surfing spot. Picnic sites can be reserved in advance. **Amenities:** food and drink; lifeguards; parking;

showers; toilets. **Best for:** sunset; surfing; swimming; walking. ⊠ *Off PCH, between Seapoint St. and Warner Ave.* ☎ *714/846–3460* ⊕ *www. parks.ca.gov/?page_id=642* ⊠ *$15 parking.*

Huntington City Beach. Stretching for 3½ miles north and south of the pier from Bolsa Chica State Beach to Huntington State Beach on the south, Huntington City Beach is most crowded around the pier; amateur and professional surfers brave the waves daily on its north side. RV camping is permitted October through May. Fire pits, the numerous concession stands, dog beach area, and well-raked white sand make this a very popular beach come summertime. **Amenities:** food and drink; lifeguards; parking; showers; toilets. **Best for:** sunset; surfing; swimming; walking. ⊠ *PCH, from Beach Blvd. to Seapoint St.* ☎ *714/536–5281* ⊕ *www.ci.huntington-beach.ca.us* ⊠ *Parking $15 weekdays, $17 weekends, $20–$27 holidays.*

Huntington State Beach. As you continue south, Huntington State Beach parallels Pacific Coast Highway. On the state and city beaches, there are changing rooms, concessions, lifeguards, Wi-Fi, and ample parking; the state beach also has 200 fire pits for bonfires. A 6-mile bike path connects Huntington State Beach to the city beach and Bolsa Chica to the north. Picnic areas can be reserved in advance for a $150 fee, otherwise it's first come, first served. On hot days, expect crowds at this broad, soft sandy beach. Busy PCH separates the beach from the town. **Amenities:** food and drink; lifeguards; parking; showers; toilets. **Best for:** sunset; surfing; swimming; walking. ⊠ *PCH, from Beach Blvd. south to Santa Ana River* ☎ *714/536–1454* ⊕ *www.parks.ca.gov/?page_id=643* ⊠ *$15 parking Apr.–Sept., $10 Oct.–Mar.*

WHERE TO EAT

$$$$
SEAFOOD

✕ **Duke's.** Oceanfront vistas and fresh-caught seafood reign supreme at this homage to surfing legend Duke Kahanamoku; it's also a prime people-watching spot right at the beginning of the pier. Choose from several fish-of-the-day selections—many Hawaiian—prepared in one of five ways. Or try the crispy coconut shrimp or tuna tacos with Maui onions. Duke's mai tai is not to be missed. ⑤ *Average main: $34* ⊠ *317 PCH* ☎ *714/374–6446* ⊕ *www.dukeshuntington.com.*

$$
AMERICAN

✕ **Lou's Red Oak BBQ.** You won't find any frills at Lou's Red Oak BBQ—just barbecue pork, grilled linguica, rotisserie chicken, and a lot of beef. Try the tri-tip (either as an entrée or on a toasted bun smothered with traditional Santa Maria–style salsa) or a Hawaiian teriyaki plate to get into the surfing spirit. ⑤ *Average main: $17* ⊠ *21501 Brookhurst St.* ☎ *714/965–5200* ⊕ *www.lousbbq.com.*

SPORTS AND THE OUTDOORS

SURFING

Corky Carroll's Surf School. This surf school organizes lessons, weeklong workshops, and surfing trips. ☎ *714/969–3959* ⊕ *www.surfschool.net.*

Dwight's. You can rent wet suits as well as surf and boogie boards at Dwight's, one block south of the pier. ⊠ *201 PCH* ☎ *714/536–8083.*

SHOPPING

HSS Pierside. The best surf-gear source is HSS Pierside, across from the pier, staffed by true surf enthusiasts. ⊠ *300 Pacific Coast Hwy.* ☎ *714/841–4000* ⊕ *www.hsssurf.com*

Riding the waves at Newport Beach

NEWPORT BEACH

6 miles south of Huntington Beach, PCH.

Newport Beach has evolved from a simple seaside village to an icon of chic coastal living. Its ritzy reputation comes from megayachts bobbing in the harbor, boutiques that rival those in Beverly Hills, and spectacular homes overlooking the ocean.

Newport is said to have the highest per-capita number of Mercedes-Benzes in the world; inland Newport Beach's concentration of high-rise office buildings, shopping centers, and luxury hotels drive the economy. But on the city's Balboa Peninsula, you can still catch a glimpse of a more innocent, down-to-earth beach town scattered with taco spots, tackle shops, and sailor bars.

ESSENTIALS

Visitor and Tour Information Visit Newport Beach Inc.
✉ *1600 Newport Center Dr., Suite 120* ☎ *949/719–6100, 800/942–6278*
⊕ *www.visitnewportbeach.com.*

EXPLORING

Balboa Island. This sliver of terra firma in Newport Harbor boasts quaint streets tightly packed with impossibly charming, multimillion-dollar cottages. The island's main drag, Marine Avenue, is lined with equally picturesque cafés and shops.

Olive Oil & Beyond. At Olive Oil & Beyond, you can sample and purchase premium oils from around the globe. There's also a lineup of unique balsamic vinegars—some flavored with fig or tangerine—

and other gourmet goodies. ⊠ *210 Marine Ave., Balboa Island* ☎ *949/566–9380* ⊕ *www.oliveoilandbeyond.com.*

Sugar & Spice. Stop by ice cream parlor Sugar & Spice for a Balboa Bar—a slab of vanilla ice cream dipped first in chocolate and then in a topping of your choice such as hard candy or Oreo crumbs. Other parlors serve the concoction, but Sugar & Spice claims to have invented it back in 1945. ■TIP→ Cash only. ⊠ *310 Marine Ave., Balboa Island* ☎ *949/673–8907.*

Balboa Pavilion. Located on the bay side of the peninsula, the Balboa Pavilion was built in 1905 as a bath- and boathouse. Today it is home to a restaurant and shops; it also serves as a departure point for Catalina Island and harbor- and whale-watching cruises. Look for it on Main Street, off Balboa Boulevard. Adjacent to the pavilion is the three-car ferry that connects the peninsula to Balboa Island. In the blocks around the pavilion, you can find restaurants, beachside shops, and the small **Fun Zone**—a local kiddie hangout with a Ferris wheel and Explor-Ocean, an interactive nautical museum. On the other side of the narrow peninsula is **Balboa Pier.** On its end is the original branch of Ruby's, a 1940s-esque burger-and-shake joint. ⊠ *400 Main St.* ☎ *949/675–1905* ⊕ *www.balboapavilion.com.*

Balboa Peninsula. Newport's best beaches are on Balboa Peninsula, where many jetties pave the way to ideal swimming areas. The most intense bodysurfing place in Orange County and arguably on the West Coast, known as the **Wedge,** is at the south end of the peninsula. Created by accident in the 1930s when the Federal Works Progress Administration built a jetty to protect Newport Harbor, the break is pure euphoria for highly skilled bodysurfers. ■TIP→ Since the waves generally break very close to shore and rip currents are strong, lifeguards strongly discourage visitors from attempting it—but it sure is fun to watch an experienced local ride it.

FAMILY **ExplorOcean/Newport Harbor Nautical Museum.** The ExplorOcean/Newport Harbor Nautical Museum, in the Balboa Fun Zone (a small, historic amusement park), has exhibits on the history of the harbor, ocean explorers, and scientific aspects of the Pacific Ocean. There's a fleet of ship models: some date to 1798, and one is made entirely of gold and silver. Another fun feature is a touch tank holding local sea creatures. ⊠ *600 E. Bay Ave., Newport Beach* ☎ *949/675–8915* ⊕ *www.explorocean.org* 🎟 *$4* ⊗ *Mon.–Thurs. 11–3, Fri. and Sat. 11–6, Sun. 11–5.*

Fashion Island. Shake the sand out of your shoes to head inland to the ritzy Fashion Island outdoor mall, a cluster of arcades and courtyards complete with koi pond, fountains, and a family-friendly trolley—plus some awesome ocean views. Although it doesn't have quite the international-designer clout of South Coast Plaza, it has the luxe department stores Neiman Marcus and Bloomingdale's plus expensive spots like L'Occitane, Kate Spade, Kitson, and Michael Stars. Chains, restaurants, and the requisite multiplex fill out the rest. ⊠ *401 Newport Center Dr., between Jamboree and MacArthur Blvds., off PCH* ☎ *949/721–2000, 855/658–8527* ⊕ *www.shopfashionisland.com.*

Newport Harbor. Newport Harbor, which shelters nearly 10,000 small boats, may seduce even those who don't own a yacht. Spend an afternoon exploring the charming avenues and surrounding alleys. Within Newport Harbor are eight small islands, including Balboa and Lido. The houses framing the shore may seem modest, but this is some of the most expensive real estate in the world. Several grassy areas on primarily residential Lido Isle have views of Newport Harbor.

Orange County Museum of Art. The Orange County Museum of Art (OCMA) gathers a collection of modernist paintings and sculpture by California artists (Richard Diebenkorn, Ed Ruscha, Robert Irwin, and Chris Burden) and cutting-edge, international contemporary works. OCMA also sponsors a triennial contemporary international art exhibition and showcases avant garde films. ⊠ *850 San Clemente Dr.* ☎ *949/759–1122* ⊕ *www.ocma.net* ⊡ *$12* ⊙ *Wed. and Fri.–Sun. 11–5, Thurs. 11–8.*

WHERE TO EAT

$$$
AMERICAN

✕ **3-Thirty-3.** If there's a nightlife "scene" to be had in Newport Beach, this is it. This stylish eatery attracts a convivial crowd—both young and old—for midday, sunset, and late-night dining; a long list of small, shareable plates heightens the camaraderie. Pair a cocktail with Chinese-spiced lollipop lamb chops or chicken satay while you check out the scene, or settle in for a dinner of Kobe flatiron steak or potato-crusted halibut. ⑤ *Average main: $25* ⊠ *333 Bayside Dr., at PCH* ☎ *949/673–8464* ⊕ *www.3thirty3nb.com.*

$$$
BRASSERIE

✕ **Basilic.** This intimate French-Swiss bistro adds a touch of old-world elegance to the island with its white linen and flower-topped tables. Chef-owner Bernard Althaus grows the herbs used in his classic French dishes. Head here for charcuterie, steak au poivre, and a fine Bordeaux. ⑤ *Average main: $28* ⊠ *217 Marine Ave., Balboa Island* ☎ *949/673–0570* ⊕ *www.basilicrestaurant.com* ⊙ *Closed Sun. and Mon.*

$$$$
SEAFOOD

✕ **The Cannery.** This 1920s cannery building still teems with fish, but now they go into dishes on the eclectic Pacific Rim menu rather than being packed into crates. Settle in at the sushi bar, dining room, or patio before choosing between sashimi, bouillabaisse, or halibut served with black truffle risotto. The menu includes a selection of steaks, ribs, and seafood from the world's waters. Fodor's readers recommend the milk chocolate crème brûlée for dessert. ⑤ *Average main: $35* ⊠ *3010 Lafayette Rd.* ☎ *949/566–0060* ⊕ *www.cannerynewport.com.*

WHERE TO STAY

For expanded reviews, facilities, and current deals, visit Fodors.com.

$$$$
RESORT

🛏 **Balboa Bay Resort.** Sharing the same frontage as the private Balboa Bay Club where Humphrey Bogart, Lauren Bacall, and the Reagans hung out, this hotel has one of the best bay views around. **Pros:** exquisite bayfront views; comfortable beds; romantic. **Cons:** service is helpful but can be slow; not much within walking distance; $20 hospitality fee per night. ⑤ *Rooms from: $309* ⊠ *1221 W. Coast Hwy.* ☎ *949/645–5000* ⊕ *www.balboabayresort.com* ⇆ *149 rooms, 10 suites* ⦿❘ *No meals.*

$$$$
HOTEL

🛏 **The Island Hotel.** A suitably stylish hotel in a very chic neighborhood (it's across the street from the Fashion Island shopping center), this 20-story tower caters to luxury seekers by offering weekend golf packages in conjunction with the nearby Pelican Hill golf course. **Pros:** proximity to Fashion Island; 24-hour exercise facilities; first-class spa. **Cons:** steep valet parking prices; some rooms have views of mall; pricey. ⑤ *Rooms from: $259* ✉ *690 Newport Center Dr.* ☎ *949/759–0808, 866/554–4620* ⊕ *www.theislandhotel.com* ⇥ *295 rooms, 83 suites* ⦿ *No meals.*

SPORTS AND THE OUTDOORS
BOAT RENTALS
Balboa Boat Rentals. You can tour Lido and Balboa isles by renting kayaks ($15 an hour), sailboats ($45 an hour), small motorboats ($75 an hour), and electric boats ($75–$90 an hour) at Balboa Boat Rentals. You must have a driver's license, and some knowledge of boating is helpful; rented boats must stay in the bay. ✉ *510 E. Edgewater Ave.* ☎ *949/673–7200* ⊕ *www.boats4rent.com.*

BOAT TOURS
Catalina Flyer. The Catalina Flyer, at the Balboa Pavilion, operates a 90-minute daily round-trip passage to Catalina Island for $70. Reservations are required. ✉ *400 Main St.* ☎ *800/830–7744 reservations* ⊕ *www.catalinainfo.com.*

Hornblower Cruises & Events. This operator books three-hour weekend dinner cruises with dancing for $82; the two-hour Sunday brunch cruise is $61. ✉ *2431 West Coast Hwy.* ☎ *949/650–2412, 888/979–6942* ⊕ *www.hornblower.com.*

GOLF
Newport Beach Golf Course. An 18-hole executive course, Newport Beach Golf Course is also lighted for night play. Rates start at $20 (Mon.–Thurs. and twilight). Reservations are accepted up to one week in advance, but walk-ins are accommodated when possible. ✉ *3100 Irvine Ave.* ☎ *949/852–8681* ⊕ *www.npbgolf.com* ⚑ *18 holes. 3180 yards. Par 59. Greens fees: $20/$27* ⊂ *Facilities: Driving range, putting green, pitching area, pull carts, rental clubs, pro shop, golf academy/lessons, restaurant, bar.*

SPORTFISHING
Davey's Locker. In addition to a complete tackle shop, Davey's Locker operates sportfishing trips starting at $46.50 (half-day) as well as private charters and whale-watching trips for $36. ✉ *Balboa Pavilion, 400 Main St.* ☎ *949/673–1434* ⊕ *www.daveyslocker.com.*

CORONA DEL MAR

2 miles south of Newport Beach, via PCH.

A small jewel on the Pacific Coast, Corona del Mar (known by locals as "CDM") has exceptional beaches that some say resemble their majestic Northern California counterparts. South of CDM is an area referred to as the Newport Coast or Crystal Cove—whatever you call it, it's another dazzling spot on the California Riviera.

ESSENTIALS
Visitor and Tour Information Visit Newport Beach Inc. ✉ *1600 Newport Center Dr., Suite 120, Newport Beach* ☎ *949/719–6100, 800/942–6278* ⊕ *www.visitnewportbeach.com.*

A whimbrel hunts for mussels at Crystal Cove State Park.

EXPLORING

Crystal Cove Promenade. Further adding to Orange County's overwhelming supply of high-end shopping and dining is Crystal Cove Promenade, which might be described as the toniest strip mall in America. The storefronts of this Mediterranean–inspired center are lined up across the street from Crystal Cove State Park, with the shimmering Pacific waters in plain view. There is plenty of sidewalk and courtyard seating at this center that is both a regional destination and dog-friendly neighborhood hangout for the lucky locals. ⊠ *7772–8112 E. Coast Hwy.* ⊕ *www.crystalcove.com/beach-living/shopping.*

FAMILY
Fodor's Choice
★

Crystal Cove State Park. Midway between Corona del Mar and Laguna, stretching along both sides of Pacific Coast Highway, Crystal Cove State Park is a favorite of local beachgoers and wilderness trekkers. It encompasses a 3.2-mile stretch of unspoiled beach and has some of the best tide pooling in southern California. Here you can see starfish, crabs, and other sea life on the rocks. The park's 2,400 acres of back-country are ideal for hiking, horseback riding, and mountain biking, but stay on the trails to preserve the beauty. Hike-in, backcountry camping is allowed in one of the three campgrounds. Bring water, food, and other supplies; there's a pit toilet but no shower. Open fires and pets are forbidden. **Crystal Cove Historic District** holds a collection of 46 handmade historic cottages (17 of which are available for overnight rental), decorated and furnished to reflect the 1935–1955 beach culture that flourished here. On the sand above the high-tide line and on a bluff above the beach, the cottages offer a funky look at beach life 50 years ago. Reservations are essential for cottage overnight stays. ☎ 949/494–3539, 800/444–7275 Reserve America ⊕ www.crystalcovestatepark.com ☒ $15 parking ☉ Daily 6–dusk.

NEED A BREAK? **Bluefin.** This is the area's most renowned sushi bar because of its superlative selection of fresh fish, authentic Japanese presentation, and wide selection of Japanese sake. ✉ 7952 E. Coast Hwy. ☎ 949/715–7373 ⊕ www.bluefinbyabe.com.

BEACHES

Corona del Mar State Beach. This beach is actually made up of two beaches, Little Corona and Big Corona, separated by a cliff. Both have soft, golden-hued sand. Facilities include fire pits and volleyball courts. ■ TIP→ Two colorful reefs (and the fact that it's off-limits to boats) make Corona del Mar great for snorkelers and for beachcombers who prefer privacy. Parking in the lot is a steep $15 and $25 on holidays, but you can often find a spot on the street on weekdays. **Amenities:** lifeguards; parking; showers; toilets. **Best for:** snorkeling; sunset; swimming. ✉ Iris St. and Ocean Blvd. ☎ 949/644–3151 ⊕ www.parks.ca.gov.

LAGUNA BEACH

10 miles south of Newport Beach on PCH, 60 miles south of Los Angeles, I–5 south to Hwy. 133, which turns into Laguna Canyon Rd.

Fodor'sChoice ★ Even the approach tells you that Laguna Beach is exceptional. Driving in along Laguna Canyon Road from the Interstate 405 freeway gives you the chance to cruise through a gorgeous coastal canyon, large stretches of which remain undeveloped. You'll arrive at a glistening wedge of ocean, at the intersection with PCH.

Laguna's welcome mat is legendary. For decades in the mid-20th century a local booster, Eiler Larsen, greeted everyone downtown (there's now a statue of him on the main drag). On the corner of Forest and Park avenues you can see a 1930s' gate proclaiming, "This gate hangs well and hinders none, refresh and rest, then travel on." A gay community has long been established here; until relatively recently, this was quite the exception in conservative Orange County. The Hare Krishnas have a temple where they host Sunday vegetarian feasts, environmentalists' rallies, and numerous artists—there seems to be room for everyone.

There's a definite creative slant to this tight-knit community. The California plein air art movement coalesced here in the early 1900s; by 1932 an annual arts festival was established. Art galleries now dot the village streets, and there's usually someone daubing up in Heisler Park, overlooking the beach. The town's main street, Pacific Coast Highway, is referred to as either South Coast or North Coast Highway, depending on the address. From this waterfront, the streets slope up steeply to the residential areas. All along the highway and side streets, you'll find dozens of fine art and crafts galleries, clothing boutiques, jewelry shops, and cafés.

ESSENTIALS

Visitor and Tour Information Laguna Beach Visitors Center ✉ 381 Forest Ave. ☎ 949/497–9229, 800/877–1115 ⊕ www.lagunabeachinfo.com.

EXPLORING

Laguna Art Museum. The Laguna Art Museum displays American art, with an emphasis on California artists from all periods. Special exhibits change quarterly. ■TIP→ On the first Thursday of each month, the museum and galleries throughout the city stay open until 9 for Art Walk (⊕ *www.firstthursdaysartwalk.com*). A free shuttle service runs from the museum to galleries and studios (except in July and August). ⊠ *307 Cliff Dr.* ☎ *949/494–8971* ⊕ *www.lagunaartmuseum.org* ⊠ *$7* ⊗ *Fri.–Tues. 11–5, Thurs. 11–9* ⊗ *Closed Wed.*

BEACHES

There are a handful of lovely beaches around town besides the Main Beach.

1,000 Steps Beach. Off South Coast Highway at 9th Street, 1,000 Steps Beach is a hard-to-find locals' spot tucked away in a neighborhood with great waves and hard-packed, white sand. There aren't really 1,000 steps down (but when you hike back up, it'll certainly feel like it). **Amenities:** parking. **Best for:** sunset; surfing; swimming. ⊠ *South Coast Hwy. at 9th St.*

FAMILY **Main Beach Park.** Laguna's central beach gives you a perfect slice of local life. A stocky 1920s lifeguard tower marks Main Beach Park, at the end of Broadway at South Coast Highway. A wooden boardwalk separates the sand from a strip of lawn. Walk along this soft-sand beach, or hang out on one of its benches, to watch people bodysurfing, playing sand volleyball, or scrambling around one of two half-basketball courts. The beach also has children's play equipment. Across the street is a historic Spanish Renaissance movie theater. Most of Laguna's hotels are within a short (but hilly) walk. **Amenities:** lifeguards; (limited) parking; showers; toilets. **Best for:** sunset; swimming; walking. ⊠ *Broadway at PCH.*

Wood's Cove. Wood's Cove, off South Coast Highway at Diamond Street, is especially quiet during the week. Big rock formations hide lurking crabs. This is a prime scuba diving spot. At high tide much of the beach is underwater; plan accordingly. Climbing the steps to leave, you can see a Tudor-style mansion that was once home to Bette Davis. Parking, which is on the street, is limited. **Amenities:** none. **Best for:** scuba diving; snorkeling; sunset. ⊠ *Diamond St. and Ocean Way.*

WHERE TO EAT

$ ✕ **Café Zinc & Market.** Families flock to this small Laguna Beach insti-
VEGETARIAN tution for well-priced breakfast and lunch. Try the signature quiches or poached egg dishes in the morning, or swing by later in the day for healthy salads, quesadillas, house-made soup, or a pizzette. The café also has great artisanal cheese and gourmet goodies to go, and your four-legged friends are welcome in the outdoor patio area. Dinner is served Wednesday through Sunday in summer. ⑤ *Average main: $12* ⊠ *350 Ocean Ave.* ☎ *949/494–6302* ⊕ *www.zinccafe.com.*

$$$$ ✕ **Studio.** In a nod to Laguna's art history, this restaurant has house-
AMERICAN made specialties that entice the eye as well as the palate. You can't beat the location, on a 50-foot bluff overlooking the Pacific Ocean— every table has an ocean view. And because the restaurant occupies its own Craftsman-style bungalow, it doesn't feel like a hotel dining room.

Looking for shells on Laguna Beach, one of the nicest stretches of sand in Southern California

Under the deft direction of chef Craig Strong, the menu changes seasonally to reflect the finest seafood and the freshest local ingredients on hand. You might begin with Kumamoto oysters or black pepper seared hamachi before moving on to a perfectly cooked John Dory or lamb chops topped with eggplant caponata. The wine list here is bursting with nearly 2,500 labels. $ *Average main: $55* ⊠ *Montage Laguna Beach, 30801 S. Coast Hwy.* ☎ *949/715–6420* ⊕ *www.studiolagunabeach.com* ⊘ *Reservations essential* ☉ *Closed Mon. No lunch.*

WHERE TO STAY

For expanded reviews, facilities, and current deals, visit Fodors.com.

$$$
HOTEL

▦ **La Casa del Camino.** This historic Spanish-style hotel opened in 1929 and was once a favorite of Hollywood stars. **Pros:** breathtaking views from rooftop lounge; personable service; close to beach. **Cons:** some rooms front traffic-filled highway; frequent on-site events can make hotel busy and noisy. $ *Rooms from: $224* ⊠ *1289 S. Coast Hwy.* ☎ *949/497–2446, 888/367–5232* ⊕ *www.lacasadelcamino.com* ⊅ *26 rooms, 10 suites* ⊙| *No meals.*

$$$$
RESORT
Fodors Choice
★

▦ **Montage Laguna Beach.** Laguna's connection to the Californian plein air artists is mined for inspiration at this head-turning, lavish hotel. **Pros:** per Fodorites, top-notch, enthusiastic service; idyllic coastal location; special programs for all interests, from art to marine biology. **Cons:** pricey; food inconsistent given the prices; $36 valet parking. $ *Rooms from: $495* ⊠ *30801 S. Coast Hwy.* ☎ *949/715–6000, 866/271-6943* ⊕ *www.montagelagunabeach.com* ⊅ *188 rooms, 60 suites* ⊙| *No meals.*

$$$$ ⛺ **Surf & Sand Resort.** One mile south of downtown, this Laguna Beach
RESORT   property has been made over and is now even more fantastic than
longtime locals remember. **Pros:** easy beach access; intimate property;
central location slightly removed from Main Street crowds. **Cons:** $30
valet parking; surf is quite loud. ⑤ *Rooms from: $425* ⊠ *1555 S. Coast
Hwy.* ☎ *949/497–4477, 888/869–7569* ⊕ *www.surfandsandresort.com*
☞ *155 rooms, 13 suites* ⦿ *No meals.*

NIGHTLIFE AND THE ARTS
Laguna Playhouse. Dating to the 1920s, the Laguna Playhouse mounts
a variety of productions, from classics to youth-oriented plays. ⊠ *606
Laguna Canyon Rd.* ☎ *949/497–2787* ⊕ *www.lagunaplayhouse.com.*

SPORTS AND THE OUTDOORS
HIKING
Laguna Coast Wilderness Park. The Laguna Coast Wilderness Park is spread
over 19 acres of fragile coastal territory, including the canyon. The trails
are great for hiking and mountain biking and are open daily, weather
permitting. Docent-led hikes are given regularly; call for information.
☎ *949/923–2235* ⊕ *www.ocparks.com/parks/lagunac* ⊠ *$3 parking.*

WATER SPORTS
Hobie Sports. Because its entire beach area is a marine preserve, Laguna
Beach is ideal for snorkelers. Scuba divers should head to the Marine
Life Refuge area, which runs from Seal Rock to Diver's Cove. In sum-
mer, rent bodyboards at Hobie Sports. ⊠ *294 Forest Ave.* ☎ *949/497–
3304* ⊕ *www.hobiesurfshop.com.*

DANA POINT

10 miles south of Laguna Beach, via PCH.

Dana Point's claim to fame is its small-boat marina tucked into a dramatic natural harbor and surrounded by high bluffs.

ESSENTIALS
Visitor and Tour Information Dana Point Chamber of Commerce. You'll find
a useful visitor's guide here. ☎ *949/496–1555* ⊕ *www.danapointchamber.com.*

EXPLORING
Dana Point Harbor. The harbor was first described more than 100 years
ago by its namesake, Richard Henry Dana, in his book *Two Years
Before the Mast*. At the marina are docks for private boats and yachts,
marine-oriented shops, restaurants, and boat, kayak, stand-up paddle-
board and bike rentals. ⊠ *Dana Point Harbor Dr.* ☎ *949/923–2255*
⊕ *www.danapointharbor.com.*

    Dana Point Festival of Whales. This early-March festival celebrates
the passing gray whale migration with two weekends full of activities
that include concerts, 40-foot-long balloon whales on parade, films,
sports competitions, and a street fair. ⊠ *Dana Point Harbor* ☎ *949/496–
1045, 888/440–4309* ⊕ *www.festivalofwhales.org*

BEACHES

Doheny State Beach. The beach at the south end of Dana Point is one of Southern California's top surfing destinations, but there's a lot more to do within this 61-acre area. There are five indoor tanks and an interpretive center devoted to the wildlife of the Doheny Marine Refuge, as well as food stands and shops, picnic facilities, volleyball courts, and a pier for fishing. Divers and anglers hang out at the beach's western end, and during low tide, the tide pools beckon both young and old. The beachfront campground, with 120 no-hookup sites that rent for $35 (inland) or $60 (beachfront) per night, is one of the most popular in the state; reservations are essential and should be made through Reserve America. ■TIP➜ Be aware that the waters here periodically do not meet health standards established by California (warning signs are posted if that's the case). **Amenities:** food and drink; lifeguards; parking; showers; toilets. **Best for:** partiers; sunset; surfing; swimming; walking. ⊠ *25300 Dana Point Harbor Dr.* ☎ *949/496–6172, 714/433–6400 water quality information, 800/444–7275 Reserve America* ⊕ *www. dohenystatebeach.org* ⊡ *$15 parking.*

WHERE TO EAT

$$
ITALIAN

✕ **Luciana's Ristorante.** This intimate family-owned eatery serves simply prepared, tasty Italian food. Try one of the homemade soups or gnocchi classico—Grandma's homemade potato dumplings with marinara sauce. If you don't have a reservation, be prepared to wait at the bar with a glass of one of the many reasonably priced Italian wines, chatting with the predominantly local clientele. ⑤ *Average main: $19* ⊠ *24312 Del Prado Ave.* ☎ *949/661–6500* ⊕ *www.lucianas.com* ☾ *No lunch.*

$$$
AMERICAN

✕ **Wind & Sea.** An unblocked marina view makes this a particularly great place for lunch or a sunset dinner. The Sunday breakfast buffet is good value at $15 per person. Among the entrées, the macadamia-crusted mahi-mahi and the grilled teriyaki shrimp stand out. On warm days, patio tables beckon you outside, and looking out on the Pacific might put you in the mood for a retro cocktail like a mai tai. ⑤ *Average main: $25* ⊠ *34699 Golden Lantern St.* ☎ *949/496–6500* ⊕ *www. windandsearestaurants.com.*

WHERE TO STAY

For expanded reviews, facilities, and current deals, visit Fodors.com.

$$$
B&B/INN

🏨 **Blue Lantern Inn.** Combining New England–style architecture with a Southern California setting, this white-clapboard B&B rests on a bluff overlooking the harbor and ocean. **Pros:** bikes to borrow; one room welcomes pets; free Wi-Fi and parking; gas fireplaces; amazing harbor views from Room 304; breakfast buffet. **Cons:** nearby restaurant can be noisy; service gets mixed reviews; best for adults. ⑤ *Rooms from: $185* ⊠ *34343 Blue Lantern St.* ☎ *949/661–1304, 800/950–1236* ⊕ *www. bluelanterninn.com* ➪ *29 rooms* ⦿ *Breakfast.*

$$$$
RESORT
FAMILY
Fodor's Choice
★

🏨 **Ritz-Carlton, Laguna Niguel.** Take Ritz-Carlton's top-tier level of service coupled with an unparalleled view of the Pacific and you're in the lap of complete luxury at this ocean-side resort. **Pros:** beautiful grounds and views; luxurious bedding; seamless service. **Cons:** some rooms are small for the price; culinary program has room to grow. ⑤ *Rooms from:*

$475 ⊠ 1 Ritz-Carlton Dr. ☎ *949/240–2000, 800/241–3333* ⊕ *www. ritzcarlton.com* ⊅ *367 rooms, 29 suites* ⦿ *No meals.*

SPORTS AND THE OUTDOORS

Rental stands for surfboards, paddleboards, windsurfers, small power-boats, and sailboats can be found near most of the piers.

Capt. Dave's Dolphin & Whale Watching Safari. You have a good chance of getting a water's-eye view of resident dolphins and migrating whales if you take one of these tours on a 35-foot catamaran. Dave, a marine naturalist–filmmaker, and his wife run the safaris year-round. The endangered blue whale is sometimes seen in summer. Reservations are required for the safaris, which last 2½ hours and cost $55. ⊠ *24440 Dana Point Harbor Dr.* ☎ *949/488–2828* ⊕ *www.dolphinsafari.com.*

Dana Wharf Sportfishing & Whale Watching. Charters and whale-watching excursions are offered by Dana Wharf Sportfishing & Whale Watching from early November to late April. Tickets cost $45; reservations are required. ⊠ *34675 Golden Lantern St.* ☎ *949/496–5794* ⊕ *www. danawharf.com.*

SAN JUAN CAPISTRANO

5 miles north of Dana Point, Hwy. 74, 60 miles north of San Diego, I–5.

San Juan Capistrano is best known for its historic mission, where the swallows traditionally return each year, migrating from their winter haven in Argentina, but these days they are more likely to choose other local sites for nesting. St. Joseph's Day, March 19, launches a week of fowl festivities. After summering in the arches of the old stone church, the swallows head south on St. John's Day, October 23. Charming antiques stores, which range from pricey to cheap, line Camino Capistrano.

If you arrive by train, which is far more romantic and restful than battling freeway traffic, you'll be dropped off across from the mission at the San Juan Capistrano depot. With its appealing brick café and preserved Santa Fe cars, the depot retains much of the magic of early American railroads. If driving, park near Ortega and Camino Capistrano, the city's main streets.

ESSENTIALS

Visitor and Tour Information San Juan Capistrano Chamber of Commerce and Visitors Center ⊠ *31421 La Matanza St.* ☎ *949/493–4700* ⊕ *www.sanjuanchamber.com.*

EXPLORING

FAMILY

Fodor's Choice

★

Mission San Juan Capistrano. The mission, founded in 1776 by Father Junípero Serra, was one of two Roman Catholic outposts between Los Angeles and San Diego. The Great Stone Church, begun in 1797, is the largest structure created by the Spanish in California. Many of the mission's adobe buildings have been preserved to illustrate mission life, with exhibits of an olive millstone, tallow ovens, tanning vats, metal-working furnaces, and the padres' living quarters. The gardens, with their fountains, are a lovely spot in which to wander. The bougainvillea-covered Serra Chapel is believed to be the oldest church still standing in

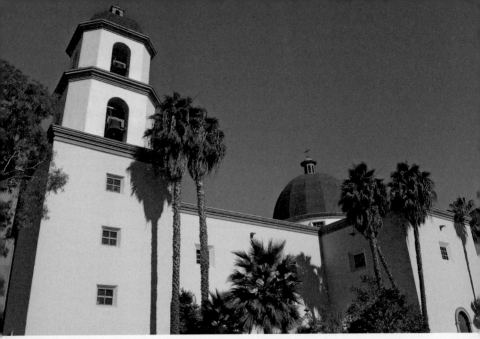
Mission San Juan Capistrano

California and is the only building remaining in which Fr. Serra actually led Mass. Mass takes place weekdays at 7 am in the chapel. ⊠ *Camino Capistrano and Ortega Hwy.* ☎ *949/234–1300* ⊕ *www.missionsjc.com* ✉ *$9* ⊙ *Daily 9–5.*

WHERE TO EAT

$ **✕ The Ramos House Cafe.** It may be worth hopping the Amtrak to San
AMERICAN Juan Capistrano just for the chance to have breakfast or lunch at one of Orange County's most beloved restaurants. Here's your chance to visit one of Los Rios Historic District's simple, board and batten homes dating back to 1881. This café sits practically on the railroad tracks across from the depot—nab a table on the patio and dig into a hearty breakfast, such as the smoked bacon scramble. The $35 weekend brunch includes champagne, memorable mac-and-cheese with wild mushrooms, and huckleberry coffee cake. Every item on the menu illustrates chef-owner John Q. Humphreys' creative hand. ⑤ *Average main: $15* ⊠ *31752 Los Rios St.* ☎ *949/443–1342* ⊕ *www.ramoshouse.com* ⊙ *Closed Mon. No dinner.*

CATALINA ISLAND

Fodor'sChoice Just 22 miles out from the L.A. coastline, across from Newport Beach
★ and Long Beach, Catalina has virtually unspoiled mountains, canyons, coves, and beaches; best of all, it gives you a glimpse of what undeveloped Southern California once looked like.

Water sports are a big draw, as divers and snorkelers come for the exceptionally clear water surrounding the island. Kayakers are attracted to the calm cove waters and thrill seekers have made the eco-themed zip line so popular, there are nighttime tours via flashlight in summer. The main town, Avalon, is a charming, old-fashioned beach community, where yachts and pleasure boats bob in the crescent bay. Wander beyond the main drag and find brightly painted little bungalows fronting the sidewalks; golf carts are the preferred mode of transport.

Perhaps it's no surprise that Catalina has long been a destination for filmmakers and movie stars. In its earlier past, however, the island also sheltered Russian fur trappers (seeking sea-otter skins), pirates, gold miners, and bootleggers (carrier pigeons were used to communicate with the mainland).

In 1919, William Wrigley Jr., the chewing-gum magnate, purchased a controlling interest in the company developing Catalina Island, whose most famous landmark, the Casino, was built in 1929 under his orders. Because he owned the Chicago Cubs baseball team, Wrigley made Catalina the team's spring training site, an arrangement that lasted until 1951.

In 1975, the Catalina Island Conservancy, a nonprofit foundation, acquired about 88% of the island to help preserve the area's natural flora and fauna, including the bald eagle and the Catalina Island fox. These days the conservancy is restoring the rugged interior country with plantings of native grasses and trees. Along the coast you might spot oddities like electric perch, saltwater goldfish, and flying fish.

GETTING HERE AND AROUND

FERRY TRAVEL Two companies offer ferry service to Catalina Island. The boats have both indoor and outdoor seating and snack bars. Excessive baggage is not allowed, and there are extra fees for bicycles and surfboards. The waters around Santa Catalina can get rough, so if you're prone to seasickness, come prepared.

Catalina Express makes an hourlong run from Long Beach or San Pedro to Avalon and a 90-minute run from Dana Point to Avalon with some stops at Two Harbors. Round-trip fares begin at $72.50, with discounts for seniors and kids. On busy days, a $15 upgrade to the Commodore Lounge, when available, is worth it. Service from Newport Beach to Avalon is available through the Catalina Flyer. Boats leave from Balboa Pavilion at 9 am (in season), take 75 minutes to reach the island, and cost $70 round-trip. Return boats leave Catalina at 4:30 pm. Reservations are advised in summer and on weekends for all trips. ■TIP➔ Keep an eye out for dolphins, which sometimes swim alongside the ferries.

GOLF CARTS Golf carts constitute the island's main form of transportation for sightseeing in the area, however some parts of town are off limits as is the island's interior. You can rent them along Avalon's Crescent Avenue and Pebbly Beach Road for about $40 per hour with a $40 deposit, payable via cash or traveler's check only.

HELICOPTER TRAVEL Island Express helicopters depart hourly from San Pedro and Long Beach (8 am–dusk). The trip takes about 15 minutes and costs $125 one-way, $250 round-trip (plus tax). Reservations a week in advance are recommended (☎ 800/228-2566).

Catalina Island

TO DANA POINT
1 hr 30mn

TO NEWPORT BEACH
1 hr 15mn

TO SAN PEDRO AND LONG BEACH
1 hr 15mn

1 hr 15mn

Casino Point
Underwater Park
Avalon Bay

Underwater Marine Park

Avalon

Wrigley Memorial and Botanical Garden

East Mtn.
East Peak
Church Rock

PALISADES

Toyon Bay

Long Point

Whites Landing
Echo Lake

SILVER CANYON

MIDDLE CANYON

Black Jack Mtn.

Mt. Orizaba

Cactus Peak

SALTA VERDE

Catalina Airport

Escondido Rd.

Middle Canyon Trail

Empire Landing Rd.

Little Harbor Rd.

Little Harbor
Overlook

Ben Weston Beach
Ben Weston Point

China Point

Salta Verde Point

SAN PEDRO CHANNEL

Isthmus Cove

West End Rd.

Two Harbors

Lobster Bay

Catalina Harbor
Catalina Head

Silver Peak Trail

Silver Peak

Emerald Bay

Starlight Beach

West End

Star Bay

Iron Bound Bay

PACIFIC OCEAN

0   4 mi
0   4 km

TIMING

Although Catalina can be seen in one very hectic day, several inviting hotels make it worth extending your stay for one or more nights. A short itinerary might include breakfast on the pier, a tour of the interior, a snorkeling excursion at Casino Point, or beach day at the Descanso Beach Club and a romantic waterfront dinner in Avalon.

After late October, rooms are much easier to find on short notice, rates drop dramatically, and many hotels offer packages that include transportation from the mainland and/or sightseeing tours.

3

TOURS

Santa Catalina Island Company runs the following Discovery Tours: a summer-only coastal cruise to Seal Rocks; the *Flying Fish* boat trip (summer evenings only); a comprehensive inland motor tour; a tour of Skyline Drive; several Casino tours; a scenic tour of Avalon; a glass-bottom-boat tour; an undersea tour on a semisubmersible vessel; an eco-themed zip line tour that traverses a scenic canyon; and a tour of the Botanical Garden. Reservations are highly recommended for the inland tours. Tours cost $10 to $178. There are ticket booths on the Green Pleasure Pier, at the Casino, in the plaza, and at the boat landing. Catalina Adventure Tours, which has booths at the boat landing and on the pier, arranges similar excursions at comparable prices.

The Catalina Island Conservancy organizes custom ecotours and hikes of the interior. Naturalist guides drive open Jeeps through some gorgeously untrammeled parts of the island. Tours start at $70 per person for a two-hour trip (two-person minimum); you can also book half- and full-day tours. The tours run year-round.

ESSENTIALS

Ferry Contacts Catalina Express ☎ *800/481–3470* ⊕ *www.catalinaexpress.com.* **Catalina Flyer** ☎ *949/673–5245, 800/830–7744* ⊕ *www.catalinainfo.com.*

Golf Cart Rentals Island Rentals ⊠ *125 Pebbly Beach Rd., Avalon* ☎ *310/510–1456* ⊕ *www.catalinagolfcartrentals.com.*

Visitor and Tour Information Catalina Adventure Tours ☎ *877/510–2888* ⊕ *www.catalinaadventuretours.com.* **Catalina Island Chamber of Commerce & Visitors Bureau** ⊠ *#1 Green Pleasure Pier, Avalon* ☎ *310/510–1520* ⊕ *www. catalinachamber.com.* **Santa Catalina Island Company** ☎ *310/510–2000, 877/778–8322* ⊕ *www.visitcatalinaisland.com.* **Catalina Island Conservancy** ⊠ *125 Claressa Ave., Avalon* ☎ *310/510–2595* ⊕ *www.catalinaconservancy.org.*

AVALON

A 1- to 2-hour ferry ride from Long Beach, Newport Beach, or San Pedro; a 15-minute helicopter ride from Long Beach or San Pedro.

Avalon, Catalina's only real town, extends from the shore of its natural harbor to the surrounding hillsides. Its resident population is about 3,800, but it swells with tourists on summer weekends. Most of the city's activity, however, is centered on the pedestrian mall on Crescent Avenue, and most sights are easily reached on foot. Private cars are restricted and rental cars aren't allowed, but taxis, trams, and shuttles can take you anywhere you need to go. Bicycles, electric bikes, and golf carts can be rented from shops along Crescent Avenue.

EXPLORING

Fodor's Choice
★
Casino. On the northwest point of Avalon Bay (looking to your right from Green Pleasure Pier) is the majestic landmark Casino. This circular white structure is one of the finest examples of art deco architecture anywhere. Its Spanish-inspired floors and murals gleam with brilliant blue and green Catalina tiles. In this case, *casino*, the Italian word for "gathering place," has nothing to do with gambling. Rather, Casino life revolves around the magnificent ballroom and equally impressive 1,184-seat movie theater.

Santa Catalina Island Company leads two tours of the Casino—the basic tour ($10), and the behind-the-scenes tour ($32.75), which leads visitors through the green room and into the Wrigleys' private lounge and includes entrance to the quaint **Catalina Island Museum,** in the lower level of the Casino; each lasts about 55 minutes. Museum exhibits chronicle 7,000 years of island history. First-run movies are screened nightly at the **Avalon Theatre,** noteworthy for its classic 1929 theater pipe organ and art deco wall murals. ⊠ *1 Casino Way* 🕾 *310/510–2414 Museum, 310/510–0179 Avalon Theatre* ⊕ *www. catalinamuseum.org* 🖃 *Museum $5* ☉ *Daily 10–5.*

Casino Point Underwater Park. In front of the Casino are the crystal clear waters of the Casino Point Underwater Park, a marine preserve protected from watercraft where bright orange Garibaldi, moray eels, bat rays, spiny lobsters, harbor seals, and other sea animals cruise around kelp forests and along the sandy bottom. It's a terrific site for scuba diving, with some shallow areas suitable for snorkeling. Scuba and snorkeling equipment can be rented on and near the pier. The shallow waters of **Lover's Cove,** east of the boat landing, are also good for snorkeling.

Crescent Avenue. A walk along Crescent Avenue is a nice way to begin a tour of the town. Vivid art deco tiles adorn the avenue's fountains and planters—fired on the island by the now-defunct Catalina Clay Products company, the tiles are coveted collectibles.

Green Pleasure Pier. Head to the pier at the center of Crescent Avenue for a good vantage point of Avalon. At the top of the hill spot a white and green-shuttered mansion, the Inn at Mt. Ada, now a top-of-the-line B&B but originally built by William Wrigley Jr. for his wife. On the pier you can find the Catalina Island Chamber of Commerce, snack stands, the Harbor Patrol, Catalina Divers Supply, and scads of squawking seagulls. It's also the landing where visiting cruise ship passengers catch tenders back out to their ship.

Wrigley Memorial and Botanic Garden. Two miles south of the bay via Avalon Canyon Road is Wrigley Memorial and Botanic Garden, home to plants native to Southern California, including several that grow only on Catalina Island—Catalina ironwood, wild tomato, and rare Catalina mahogany. The Wrigley family commissioned the garden as well as the monument, which has a grand staircase and a Spanish mausoleum inlaid with colorful Catalina tile. (The mausoleum was never used by the Wrigleys, who are buried in Pasadena.) Taxi service from

Avalon is available, or you can take a tour bus from the downtown Tour Plaza or ferry landing during the summer and on weekends other times of the year. ⊠ *Avalon Canyon Rd.* ☎ *310/510–2897* ⊕ *www. catalinaconservancy.org* ☜ *$7* ⊘ *Daily 8–5.*

WHERE TO EAT

$ ╳ **Descanso Beach Club.** Set on an expansive deck overlooking the scenic AMERICAN Descanso cove and the Casino beyond, this place has quick bites and a FAMILY full bar. Hamburgers, peel-and-eat shrimp, salads, nachos, and wraps are part of the selection. There's a small kids' menu (grilled cheese). Watch the harbor seals frolic just offshore while sipping the island's supersweet signature cocktail, the Buffalo Milk, a mix of fruit liqueurs, vodka, and whipped cream. Fire pits and colorful beach cabanas add to the scene, as does the sound of happy and terrified screams from the zip-liners in the canyon above the beach. ⑤ *Average main: $15* ⊠ *Descanso Beach, 1 Descanso Ave.* ☎ *310/510–7410.*

$ ╳ **Eric's on the Pier.** This little snack bar has been an Avalon family–run AMERICAN institution since the 1920s. It's a good place to people-watch while drinking a draft beer and munching on a breakfast burrito, hot dog, or signature buffalo burger. The seating is outside, where you can grab a bowl of homemade clam chowder in a baked bread bowl, an order of fish-and-chips, or tacos. ⑤ *Average main: $10* ⊠ *Green Pier No. 2* ☎ *310/510–0894* ⊘ *Closed Mon. No dinner.*

$$$ ╳ **The Lobster Trap.** Seafood rules here—the restaurant's owner has his AMERICAN own boat and fishes for the catch of the day and, in season, Pacific Spiny lobster. Ceviche is a great starter and is fresh and brightly flavored. Pastas, steaks, and tacos are served and locals (and you'll see many at the small counter) come for the relaxed atmosphere, large portions, draft beers and live music on weekend nights. ⑤ *Average main: $24* ⊠ *128 Catalina St.* ☎ *310/510–8585* ⊕ *catalinalobstertrap.com.*

WHERE TO STAY

For expanded reviews, facilities, and current deals, visit Fodors.com.

$$$ 🏨 **Hotel Villa Portofino.** Steps from the beach and the Pleasure Pier, this HOTEL hotel has a European flair and creates an intimate feel with brick court-yards and walkways and suites named after Italian cities. **Pros:** romantic; close to beach; incredible sun deck. **Cons:** though quiet in general, ground floor rooms can be noisy; some rooms are on small side; no elevator. ⑤ *Rooms from: $250* ⊠ *111 Crescent Ave.* ☎ *310/510–0555, 800/346–2326* ⊕ *www.hotelvillaportofino.com* ↪ *35 rooms* ⦿⊙ *Breakfast.*

$$$ 🏨 **Hotel Vista del Mar.** In the middle of Main Street, this third-floor prop-HOTEL erty is just steps from the beach, where complimentary towels, chairs, and umbrellas await guests. **Pros:** comfortable king beds; central; modern decor. **Cons:** no restaurant or spa facilities; only the two pricier suites have ocean views or balconies; no elevator. ⑤ *Rooms from: $225* ⊠ *417 Crescent Ave.* ☎ *310/510–1452, 800/601–3836* ⊕ *www.hotel-vistadelmar.com* ↪ *12 rooms, 2 suites* ⦿⊙ *Breakfast.*

$$$$ 🏨 **Inn on Mt. Ada.** If you stay in the mansion where Wrigley Jr. once lived, B&B/INN you can enjoy all the comforts of a millionaire's home—at a millionaire's **Fodor's**Choice prices. **Pros:** timeless charm; shuttle from heliport and dock; first-class ★ service. **Cons:** smallish rooms and bathrooms; expensive. ⑤ *Rooms*

from: $430 ✉ *398 Wrigley Rd.* ☎ *310/510–2030, 800/608–7669*
⊕ *www.innonmtada.com* ⫘ *6 rooms* ⊘ *Closed Jan.* 🍽 *Some meals.*

$$$$
HOTEL   🛏 **Pavilion Hotel.** The two-story, midcentury modern–style hotel (built in 1960) underwent a total makeover in 2010 and is now Avalon's most citified spot with a large welcoming fire pit and trellised patio at the entrance right across from the water. **Pros:** steps from the water; friendly staff; plush bedding. **Cons:** no pool. ⑤ *Rooms from: $255* ✉ *513 Crescent Ave.* ☎ *310/510–1788* ⊕ *www.visitcatalinaisland.com* ⫘ *69 rooms, 2 suites* 🍽 *Breakfast.*

SPORTS AND THE OUTDOORS
BICYCLING
To bike beyond the paved roads of Avalon, you must join the Catalina Island Conservancy. Individual passes start at $35; family passes cost $125. You may not ride on hiking paths.

Bike rentals are widely available in Avalon starting at $8 per hour and $20 per day. Beach cruisers and electric and mountain bikes are at the ready.

Brown's Bikes. Look for rentals on Crescent Avenue and Pebbly Beach Road, where this shop is located. ✉ *107 Pebbly Beach Rd., next to Island Rentals* ☎ *310/510–0986* ⊕ *www.catalinabiking.com.*

DIVING AND SNORKELING
The Casino Point Underwater Park, with its handful of wrecks, is best suited for diving. Lover's Cove is better for snorkeling (no scuba diving allowed, but you'll share the area with glass-bottom boats). Both are protected marine preserves.

Catalina Divers Supply. Head here to rent equipment, take guided scuba and snorkel tours, and attend certification classes. It also has an outpost at Casino Point. ✉ *#7 Green Pleasure Pier* ☎ *800/353–0330* ⊕ *www.catalinadiverssupply.com.*

LOS ANGELES

WELCOME TO LOS ANGELES

TOP REASONS TO GO

★ **Hollywood magic:** A massive chunk of the world's entertainment is developed, written, filmed, edited, distributed, and sold here; you'll hear people discussing "the Industry" wherever you go.

★ **The beach:** Getting some sand on the floor of your car is practically a requirement here, and the beach is an integral part of the SoCal lifestyle.

★ **Chic shopping:** From Beverly Hills's Rodeo Drive and Downtown's Fashion District to the funky boutiques of Los Feliz, Silver Lake, and Echo Park, L.A. is a shopper's paradise.

★ **Trendy restaurants:** Celebrity is big business here, so it's no accident that the concept of the celebrity chef is a key part of the city's dining scene.

★ **People-watching:** Celeb-spotting in Beverly Hills, trying to get past the velvet rope at hip clubs, hanging out on the Venice Boardwalk . . . there's always something (or someone) interesting to see.

1 Hollywood. Glitzy and tarnished, good and bad—Hollywood is just like the entertainment business itself. The Walk of Fame, Grauman's Chinese Theatre, Paramount Pictures studio, and the Hollywood Bowl keep the neighborhood's romantic past alive. Universal Studios Hollywood, Warner Bros., and NBC Television Studios are in the Valley.

2 Beverly Hills and the Westside. Go for the glamour, the restaurants, and the scene. Rodeo Drive is particularly good for a look at wretched or ravishing excess. But don't forget the Westside's cultural attractions—especially the dazzling Getty Center. West Hollywood's an area for urban indulgences—shopping, restaurants, nightspots—rather than sightseeing. Its main arteries are the Sunset Strip (Sunset Boulevard), and Melrose Avenue, lined with shops ranging from punk to postmodern.

3 Downtown Los Angeles. Downtown L.A. shows off spectacular modern architecture with the swooping Walt Disney Concert Hall and the stark Cathedral of Our Lady of the Angels. The Music Center and the Museum of Contemporary Art anchor a world-class arts scene, while Olvera Street, Chinatown, and Little Tokyo reflect the city's history and diversity.

4 Santa Monica, Venice, and Malibu. These desirable beach communities move from ultrarich, ultracasual Malibu to bohemian/transitioning Venice, with liberal, Mediterranean-style Santa Monica in between.

5 Pasadena Area. Its own separate city, Pasadena is a quiet area with outstanding Arts and Crafts homes, good dining, and a pair of exceptional museums.

Sepulveda Dam Recreation Area
Ventura Fwy.
101
VAN NUYS
Mulholland Dr.
SHERMAN OAKS
SANTA MONICA MTS.
405
Topanga State Park
Getty Center
BEVERLY HILLS
2
BRENTWOOD
WESTWOOD
← TO MALIBU
Sunset Blvd.
1
PACIFIC PALISADES
4
2
10
SANTA MONICA
1
PACIFIC
Venice Boardwalk
VENICE
MARINA DEL REY
OCEAN
Santa Monica

GETTING ORIENTED

Looking at a map of sprawling Los Angeles, first-time visitors are sometimes overwhelmed. Where to begin? What to see first? And what about all those freeways? Here's some advice: relax. Begin by setting your priorities—movie and television buffs should first head to Hollywood, Universal Studios, and a taping of a television show. Beach lovers and nature types might start out in Santa Monica, Venice, or Malibu, or spend an afternoon in Griffith Park, one of the largest city parks in the country. Culture vultures should make a beeline for the twin Gettys (the center in Brentwood and the villa near Malibu), the Los Angeles County Museum of Art (LACMA), or the Norton Simon Museum. And urban explorers might begin with Downtown L.A.

SOUTH-OF-THE-BORDER FLAVOR

From Cal-Mex burritos to Mexico City–style tacos, Southern California is a top stateside destination for experiencing Mexico's myriad culinary styles.

Many Americans are surprised to learn that the Mexican menu goes far beyond Tex-Mex (or Cal-Mex) favorites like burritos, chimichangas, enchiladas, fajitas, and nachos—many of which were created or popularized stateside. Indeed, Mexico has rich, regional food styles, like the complex *mole* sauces of Puebla and Oaxaca and the fresh *ceviches* of Veracruz, as well as the trademark snack of Mexico City: tacos.

In Southern California, tacos are an obsession, with numerous blogs and websites dedicated to the quest for the perfect taco. They're everywhere—in ramshackle taco stands, roving taco trucks, and strip-mall taquerias. Whether you're looking for a cheap snack or a lunch on-the-go, SoCal's taco selection can't be beat. But be forewarned: there may not be an English menu. Here we've noted unfamiliar taco terms, along with other potentially new-to-you items from the Mexican menu.

THIRST QUENCHERS

Spanish for "fresh water," *agua fresca* is a nonalcoholic Mexican drink made from fruit, rice, or seeds that are blended with sugar and water. Fruit flavors like lemon, lime, and watermelon are common. Other varieties include *agua de Jamaica*, flavored with red hibiscus petals; *agua de horchata*, a cinnamon-scented rice milk; and *agua de tamarindo*, a bittersweet variety flavored with tamarind. If you're looking for something with a little more kick, try a *Michelada*, a beer that has been enhanced with a mixture of lime juice, chili sauce, and other savory ingredients. It's typically served in a salt-rimmed glass with ice.

DECODING THE MENU

Ceviche—Citrus-marinated seafood appetizer from the Gulf shores of Veracruz. Often eaten with tortilla chips.

Chile relleno—Roasted poblano pepper that is stuffed with ingredients like ground meat or cheese, then dipped in egg batter, fried, and served in tomato sauce.

Clayuda—A Oaxacan dish similar to pizza. Large corn tortillas are baked until hard, then topped with ingredients like refried beans, cheese, and salsa.

Fish taco—A specialty in Southern California, the fish taco is a soft corn tortilla stuffed with grilled or fried white fish (mahimahi, tilapia, or wahoo), pico de gallo, *crema*, and shredded cabbage.

Gordita—"Little fat one" in Spanish, this dish is like a taco, but the cornmeal shell is thicker, similar to pita bread.

Mole—A complex, sweet sauce with Aztec roots made from more than 20 ingredients, including chilis, cinnamon, cumin, anise, black pepper, sesame seeds, and Mexican chocolate. There are many types of mole using various chilis and ingredient combinations, but the most common is *mole poblano* from the Puebla region.

Quesadilla—A snack made from a fresh tortilla that is folded over and stuffed with simple fillings like cheese, then toasted on a griddle. Elevated versions

of the quesadilla may be stuffed with sautéed *flor de calabaza* (squash blossoms) or *huitlacoche* (corn mushrooms).

Salsa—A class of cooked or raw sauces made from chilis, tomatoes, and other ingredients. Popular salsas include *pico de gallo*, a fresh sauce made from chopped tomatoes, onions, chilis, cilantro, and lime; *salsa verde*, made with tomatillos instead of tomatoes; and *salsa roja*, a cooked sauce made with chilis, tomatoes, onion, garlic, and cilantro.

Sopes—A small, fried corn cake topped with ingredients like refried beans, shredded chicken, and salsa.

Taco—In Southern California, as in Mexico, tacos are made from soft, palm-sized corn tortillas folded over and filled with meat, chopped onion, cilantro, and salsa. Common taco fillings include *al pastor* (spiced pork), *barbacoa* (braised beef), *carnitas* (roasted pork), *cecina* (chili-coated pork), *carne asada* (roasted, chopped beef), *chorizo* (spicy sausage), *lengua* (beef tongue), *sesos* (cow brain), and *tasajo* (spiced, grilled beef).

Tamales—Sweet or savory corn cakes that are steamed, and may be filled with cheese, roasted chilis, shredded meat, or other fillings.

Torta—A Mexican sandwich served on a crusty sandwich roll. Fillings often include meat, refried beans, and cheese.

Updated by
Tanvi Chheda

Los Angeles is as much a fantasy as it is a physical city. A mecca for face-lifts, film noir, shopping starlets, beach bodies, and mind-numbing traffic, it is a true urban mash-up, equal parts glamour and grit.

Yes, you'll encounter traffic-clogged freeways, but there are also palm tree–lined, walkable pockets like Venice's Abbot Kinney, voted the coolest block in America by GQ magazine in 2012. You'll drive past Beverly Hills mansions and spy palaces perched atop hills, but you'll also see the roots of midcentury modern architecture in Silver Lake. You'll soak up the sun in Santa Monica and then find yourself barhopping in the city's revitalized Downtown while chomping on scrumptious fish tacos along the way.

You might think that you'll have to spend most of your visit in a car, but that's not the case. In fact, getting out of your car is the only way to really get to know the various entertainment-industry-centered financial, beachfront, wealthy, and fringe neighborhoods and mini-cities that make up the vast L.A. area. But remember, no single locale—whether it be Malibu, Downtown, Beverly Hills, or Burbank—fully embodies Los Angeles. It's in the mix that you'll discover the city's character.

PLANNING

WHEN TO GO

Almost any time of the year is the right time to go to Los Angeles; the climate is mild and pleasant year-round. Winter brings crisp, sunny, unusually smogless days from about November to May (expect brief rains from December to April). Los Angeles summers, which are virtually rainless, can lead to air-quality alerts. Prices skyrocket and reservations are a must when tourism peaks from July through early October.

GETTING HERE AND AROUND

AIR TRAVEL

It's generally easier to navigate the secondary airports than to get through sprawling LAX, the city's major gateway. Bob Hope Airport in Burbank is closest to Downtown L.A., and domestic flights to it can be cheaper than flights to LAX—it's definitely worth checking out. From

Long Beach Airport it's equally convenient to go north to central Los Angeles or south to Orange County. Flights to Orange County's John Wayne Airport are often more expensive than those to the other secondary airports. Parking at the smaller airports is cheaper than at LAX.

Airports Bob Hope Airport (*BUR*). ☎ 818/840–8840 ⊕ www.bobhopeairport. com. **John Wayne/Orange County Airport** (*SNA*). ✉ 18601 Airport Way ☎ 949/252–5006 ⊕ www.ocair.com.

Long Beach Airport (*LGB*). ✉ 4100 Donald Douglas Dr. ☎ 562/570–2600 ⊕ www.lgb.org. **Los Angeles International Airport** (*LAX*). ☎ 310/646–5252 ⊕ www.lawa.org. **Ontario International Airport** (*ONT*). ☎ 909/937–2700 ⊕ www.lawa.org/welcomeont.aspx.

Shuttles Prime Time ☎ 800/733–8267 ⊕ www.primetimeshuttle.com. **SuperShuttle** ☎ 323/775–6600, 310/782–6600, 800/258–3826 ⊕ www.supershuttle.com. **Express by ExecuCar** ☎ 800/427–7483 ⊕ www.execucarexpress.com.

BUS TRAVEL

Inadequate public-transportation systems have been an L.A. problem for decades. That said, many local trips can be made, with time and patience, by bus. In certain cases, such as visiting the Getty Center or going to Universal Studios and/or the adjacent CityWalk, the bus may actually be your best option. The Metropolitan Transit Authority DASH (Downtown Area Short Hop) minibuses cover nine different circular routes in Hollywood, Mid-Wilshire, and Downtown. The buses stop every two or so blocks. The Santa Monica Municipal Bus Line, also known as the Big Blue Bus, is a pleasant and inexpensive way to move around the Westside, where the MTA lines leave off. There's also an express bus to and from Downtown L.A., and a shuttle bus, the Tide Shuttle, which runs between Main Street and the Third Street Promenade and stops at hotels along the way. Culver CityBus Lines runs seven routes through Culver City.

Bus Information Commute Smart ⊕ www.commutesmart.info. **Culver City-Bus Lines** ☎ 310/253–6000 ⊕ www.culvercity.org. **DASH** ☎ 310/808–2273 ⊕ www.ladottransit.com/dash. **Los Angeles County Metropolitan Transit Authority (LACMTA)** ☎ 323/466–3876 ⊕ www.metro.net. **Santa Monica Municipal Bus Line** ☎ 310/451–5444 ⊕ www.bigbluebus.com.

CAR TRAVEL

Most freeways are known by a name and a number; for example, the San Diego Freeway is Interstate 405, the Hollywood Freeway is U.S. 101, the Ventura Freeway is a different stretch of U.S. 101, the Santa Monica Freeway is Interstate 10, and the Harbor Freeway is Interstate 110. It helps, too, to know which direction you're traveling; say, west toward Santa Monica or east toward Downtown Los Angeles. Distance in miles doesn't mean much, depending on the time of day you're traveling: the short 10-mile drive between the San Fernando Valley and Downtown Los Angeles might take an hour to travel during rush hour but only 20 minutes at other times.

Be aware that a number of major streets have similar-sounding names (Beverly Drive and Beverly Boulevard, or numbered streets north to south Downtown and east to west in Hollywood, West Hollywood, and Beverly Hills) or exactly the same name (such as San Vicente Boulevard in West L.A., Brentwood, Santa Monica, and West Hollywood). Also, some smaller streets seem to exist intermittently for miles, so unless you have good directions, you should use major streets rather than try for an alternative that is actually blocked by a dead end or detours, like the side streets off Sunset Boulevard. Try to get clear directions and stick to them.

If you get discombobulated while on the freeway, remember the rule of thumb: even-numbered freeways run east and west, odd-numbered freeways run north and south.

Information California Highway Patrol ☎ 800/427–7623 for road conditions. **City of Los Angeles** ⊕ www.sigalert.com.

Emergency Services Metro Freeway Service Patrol ☎ 213/922–2957 general information, 323/982–4900 for breakdowns ⊕ www.mta.net.

METRO RAIL TRAVEL
Metro Rail covers a limited area of L.A.'s vast expanse, but what exists is helpful and frequent. The underground Red Line runs from Union Station Downtown through Mid-Wilshire, Hollywood, and Universal City on its way to North Hollywood, stopping at the most popular tourist destinations along the way. The light commuter rail Green Line stretches from Redondo Beach to Norwalk, while the partially underground Blue Line goes from Downtown to the South Bay (Long Beach/San Pedro). The Green and Blue lines are not often used by visitors, though the Green is gaining popularity as an alternative, albeit time-consuming, way to reach LAX. The monorail-like Gold Line begins at Union Station and heads northeast to Pasadena and Sierra Madre. The Orange Line, a 14-mile bus corridor, connects the North Hollywood subway station with the western San Fernando Valley. The new Expo line to Culver City began operations in 2012.

The website is the best way to get info on Metro Rail.

Metro Rail Information Los Angeles County Metropolitan Transit Authority (LACMTA) ☎ 323/466–3876 ⊕ www.metro.net.

TAXI AND LIMOUSINE TRAVEL
Don't even try to hail a cab on the street in Los Angeles. Instead, phone one of the many taxi companies. The metered rate is $2.85 per mile. Taxi rides from LAX have an additional $4 surcharge. Be aware that distances between sights in L.A. are vast, so cab fares add up quickly. On the other end of the price spectrum, limousines come equipped with everything from a full bar and telephone to a hot tub. If you open any L.A.–area yellow pages, the number of limo companies will astound you. Most charge by the hour, with a three-hour minimum.

Limousine Companies ABC Limousine & Sedan Service ☎ 818/980–6000, 888/753–7500. **American Executive** ☎ 800/927–2020. **Black & White Transportation Services** ☎ 800/924–1624. **Chauffeur's Unlimited** ☎ 888/546–6019. **Dav El Chauffeured Transportation Network** ☎ 800/922–0343 ⊕ www.davel.com. **First Class Limousine Service by Norman Lewis** ☎ 800/400–9771 ⊕ www.first-classlimo.com. **ITS** ☎ 800/487–4255 ⊕ www.itslimo.com.

Taxi Companies Beverly Hills Cab Co. ☎ *800/398–5221.*
Checker Cab ☎ *800/300–5007.* **Independent Cab Co.** ☎ *800/521–8294*
⊕ *www.taxi4u.com.* **United Independent Taxi** ☎ *800/822–8294.*
Yellow Cab/LA Taxi Co-Op ☎ *800/200–1085, 800/200–0011.*

TRAIN TRAVEL

Union Station in Downtown Los Angeles is one of the great American railroad stations. The interior is well kept and includes comfortable seating, a restaurant, and snack bars. As the city's rail hub, it's the place to catch an Amtrak train. Among Amtrak's Southern California routes are 12 daily trips to San Diego and four to Santa Barbara. Amtrak's luxury *Coast Starlight* travels along the spectacular coastline from Seattle to Los Angeles in just a day and a half (though it's often a little late). The *Sunset Limited* goes to Los Angeles from Florida (via New Orleans and Texas), and the *Southwest Chief* from Chicago. You can make reservations in advance by phone or at the station. As with airlines, you usually get a better deal the farther in advance you book. You must show your ticket and a photo ID before boarding. Smoking is not allowed on Amtrak trains.

Information Amtrak ☎ *800/872–7245* ⊕ *www.amtrak.com.*
Union Station ✉ *800 N. Alameda St.* ☎ *213/683–6979.*

VISITOR INFORMATION

Contacts Beverly Hills Conference and Visitors Bureau ☎ *310/248–1000, 800/345–2210* ⊕ *www.lovebeverlyhills.com.* **California Office of Tourism** ☎ *916/444–4429, 800/862–2543* ⊕ *www.visitcalifornia.com.* **Hollywood Chamber of Commerce Info Center** ☎ *323/469–8311* ⊕ *www.hollywoodchamber. net.* **L.A. Inc./The Convention and Visitors Bureau** ☎ *213/624–7300, 800/228–2452* ⊕ *www.discoverlosangeles.com.* **Pasadena Convention and Visitors Bureau** ☎ *626/795–9311* ⊕ *www.pasadenacal.com.* **Redondo Beach Chamber of Commerce and Visitors Bureau** ☎ *310/376–6911, 800/282–0333* ⊕ *www.redondochamber.org.* **Santa Monica Convention & Visitors Bureau** ☎ *310/393–7593, 800/544–5319* ⊕ *www.santamonica.com.*
West Hollywood Marketing and Visitors Bureau ☎ *310/289–2525, 800/368–6020* ⊕ *www.visitwesthollywood.com.*

EXPLORING LOS ANGELES

Star-struck . . . excessive . . . smoggy . . . superficial. There's a modicum of truth to each of the adjectives regularly applied to L.A. But Angelenos—and most objective visitors—dismiss their prevalence as signs of envy from people who hail from places less blessed with fun and sun.

Pop culture, for instance, *does* permeate life in LaLaLand: A massive economy employing millions of Southern Californians is built around it. However, this city also boasts highbrow appeal, having amassed an impressive array of world-class museums and arts venues. Moreover, it has burgeoning neighborhoods that bear little resemblance to those featured on *The Real Housewives of Beverly Hills* or *Entourage.* America's second-largest city has more depth than paparazzi shutters can ever capture.

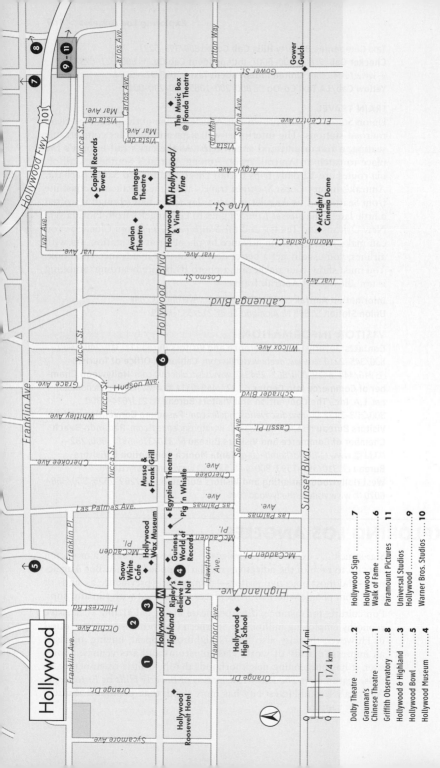

Hollywood

1/4 mi

1/4 km

HOLLYWOOD AND THE STUDIOS

The Tinseltown mythology of Los Angeles was born in Hollywood. Daytime attractions can be found on foot around the home of the Academy Awards at the Dolby Theatre, part of the Hollywood & Highland entertainment complex. The adjacent Grauman's Chinese Theatre delivers silver screen magic with its cinematic facade and ornate interiors from a bygone era. Walk the renowned Hollywood Walk of Stars to find your favorite celebrities' hand- and footprints. In summer, visit the crown jewel of Hollywood, the Hollywood Bowl, which features shows by the Los Angeles Philharmonic.

The San Fernando Valley gets a bad rap. There are even some Angelenos who swear, with a sneer, that they will never set foot in "the Valley." Despite all the snickering, it's where the majority of studios that have made Los Angeles famous are located.

4

TOP ATTRACTIONS

Grauman's Chinese Theatre. A place that inspires the phrase "only in Hollywood," these stylized Chinese pagodas and temples have become a shrine to stardom. Although you have to buy a movie ticket to appreciate the interior trappings, the courtyard is open to the public. The main theater itself is worth visiting, if only to see a film in the same seats as hundreds of celebrities who have attended big premieres here.

And then, of course, outside in front are the oh-so-famous cement hand- and footprints. This tradition is said to have begun at the theater's opening in 1927, with the premiere of Cecil B. DeMille's *King of Kings,* when actress Norma Talmadge just happened to step into wet cement. Now more than 160 celebrities have contributed imprints for posterity, including some oddball specimens, such as ones of Whoopi Goldberg's dreadlocks. ⊠ *6925 Hollywood Blvd., Hollywood* ☎ *323/464–8111* ⊕ *www.tclchinesetheatres.com.*

Griffith Observatory. High on a hillside overlooking the city, the Griffith Observatory is one of the most celebrated icons of Los Angeles. And now, its interior is as impressive as its exterior after a massive expansion and cosmic makeover. Highlights of the building include the Foucoult's pendulum hanging in the main lobby, the planet exhibitions on the lower level, and the playful wall display of galaxy-themed jewelry along the twisty indoor ramp.

In true L.A. style, the Leonard Nimoy Event Horizon Theater presents guest speakers and shows on current space-related topics and discoveries. The planetarium now features a new dome, laser digital projection system, theatrical lighting, and a stellar sound system. Shows are $7.

Grab a meal at the Café at the End of the Universe, which serves up dishes created by celebrity chef Wolfgang Puck. For a fantastic view, come at sunset to watch the sky turn fiery shades of red with the city's skyline silhouetted. ⊠ *2800 E. Observatory Rd., Griffith Park* ☎ *213/473–0800* ⊕ *www.griffithobservatory.org* �l *Wed.–Fri. noon–10, Sat.–Sun. 10–10.*

Fodor's Choice
★ **Hollywood Museum.** Lovers of Hollywood's glamorous past will be singing "Hooray for Hollywood" when they stop by this gem of cinema history. It's inside the Max Factor Building, purchased in 1928. Factor's

famous makeup was made on the top floors and on the ground floor was a salon. After its renovation, this art deco landmark now holds more than 10,000 bits of film memorabilia.

The extensive exhibits inside include those dedicated to Marilyn Monroe and Bob Hope and to costumes and set props from such films as *Moulin Rouge, The Silence of the Lambs,* and *Planet of the Apes.* There's an impressive gallery of photos showing movie stars frolicking at such venues as the Brown Derby, Ciro's, the Trocadero, and the Mocambo.

Hallway walls are covered with the stunning autograph collection of ultimate fan Joe Ackerman; aspiring filmmakers will want to check out an exhibit of early film equipment. The museum's showpiece, however, is the Max Factor exhibit, where separate dressing rooms are dedicated to Factor's "color harmony": creating distinct looks for "brownettes" (Factor's term), redheads, and of course, bombshell blondes. You can practically smell the peroxide of Marilyn Monroe getting her trademark platinum look here, and see makeup cases owned by Lucille Ball, Lana Turner, Ginger Rogers, Bette Davis, Rita Hayworth, and others who made the makeup as popular as the starlets who wore it. ⊠ *1660 N. Highland Ave., Hollywood* ☎ *323/464-7776* ⊕ *www. thehollywoodmuseum.com* ✍ *$15* ☽ *Wed.–Sun. 10–5.*

Hollywood Walk of Fame. Along Hollywood Boulevard runs a trail of affirmations for entertainment-industry overachievers. On this mile-long stretch of sidewalk, inspired by the concrete handprints in front of Grauman's Chinese Theatre, names are embossed in brass, each at the center of a pink star embedded in dark-gray terrazzo. They're not all screen deities; many stars commemorate people who worked in a technical field. The first eight stars were unveiled in 1960 at the northwest corner of Highland Avenue and Hollywood Boulevard: Olive Borden, Ronald Colman, Louise Fazenda, Preston Foster, Burt Lancaster, Edward Sedgwick, Ernest Torrence, and Joanne Woodward (some of these names have stood the test of time better than others). Since then, more than 2,000 others have been immortalized, though that honor doesn't come cheap—upon selection by a special committee, the personality in question (or more likely his or her movie studio or record company) pays about $30,000 for the privilege. To aid you in spotting celebrities you're looking for, stars are identified by one of five icons: a motion-picture camera, a radio microphone, a television set, a record, or a theatrical mask. Contact the **Hollywood Chamber of Commerce** (⊠ *7018 Hollywood Blvd.* ☎ *323/469–8311*) for celebrity-star locations and information on future star installations. ⊕ *www.walkoffame.com.*

Fodor's Choice
★

Paramount Pictures. With a history dating to the early 1920s, this studio was home to some of Hollywood's most luminous stars, including Rudolph Valentino, Mae West, Mary Pickford, and Lucille Ball, who filmed episodes of *I Love Lucy* here. The lot still churns out memorable movies and TV shows, such as *Forrest Gump, Titanic,* and *Star Trek.* You can take a studio tour (reservations required; ages 12 and up) led by guides who walk and trolley you around the back lots. As well as gleaning some gossipy history (see the lawn where Lucy and Desi broke up), you'll spot the sets of TV and film shoots in progress. You can also be part of the audience for live TV tapings. Tickets are free; call for listings and times. ✉ *5555 Melrose Ave., Hollywood* ☎ *323/956–1777* ⊕ *www. paramountstudiotour.com* 🖃 *$48* ☯ *Tours daily by reservation only.*

FAMILY **Universal Studios Hollywood.** While most first-time Los Angeles visitors consider this to be a must-see stop, bear in mind there are many other attractions that define Hollywood that aren't a tourist trap with steep prices. ■**TIP**➔ **If you get here when the park opens, you'll likely save yourself from long waits in line.**

The first-timer favorite is the tram tour, during which you can experience the parting of the Red Sea; duck from spitting creatures in Jurassic Park; visit Dr. Seuss's "Whoville"; see the airplane wreckage of *War of the Worlds* and the still-creepy *Psycho* house; be attacked by the ravenous killer shark of *Jaws* fame. The trams have audiovisual monitors that play video clips of TV shows and movies shot on the sets you pass. ■**TIP**➔ **This tram ride is usually the best place to start, since it's on the lower level of the park, which gets really crowded in the afternoon.**

Many attractions are based on Universal films and TV shows, designed to give you a thrill in one form or another. Take your pick from the bone-rattling roller coaster Revenge of the Mummy, The Ride; or see Shrek 4-D, a 15-minute trailer of 3-D animation shown in an action simulation theater. Fear Factor Live and the House of Horrors are guaranteed to provide screams, while the Animal Actors show offers milder entertainment courtesy of some talented furry friends. The attraction based on *The Simpsons* animated series takes you on a journey like no other through their Springfield neighborhood in a ride that only the beloved, albeit cantankerous, Krusty the Klown could dream up. Look for the most recent thrill ride based on the popular *Transformers* movies.

Throughout the park you can wander through prop-style settings of a French village or travel back in time to the 1950s, as costumed characters mingle with guests and pose for photos. Aside from the park, City-Walk is a separate venue, with shops, restaurants, nightclubs, and movie theaters, including IMAX 3-D. ✉ *100 Universal City Plaza, Universal City* ☎ *818/622–3801* ⊕ *www.universalstudioshollywood.com* 🖃 *$80, parking $15 ($10 after 3)* ☯ *Contact park for seasonal hrs.*

Warner Bros. Studios. This major studio center wins hands down for the most authentic behind-the-scenes look at how films and TV shows are made.

You start with a short film on Warner Bros. movies and TV shows, then hop into a tram for a ride through the sets and soundstages of such favorites as *Casablanca* and *Rebel Without A Cause*. You'll see the bungalows where icons such as Marlon Brando and Bette Davis spent time between shots, and the current production offices for Clint Eastwood and George Clooney. You might even spot a celeb or see a shoot in action—tours change from day to day depending on the productions taking place on the lot.

Reservations are required. Call at least one week in advance and ask about provisions for people with disabilities; children under 8 are not admitted. Tours are given at least every hour, more frequently from May to September, and last 2 hours and 15 minutes. A five-hour deluxe tour, $250 including a VIP lunch, allows visitors to spend more time on the sets, with more ops for behind-the-scenes peeks and star spotting. ✉ *3400 W. Riverside Dr., Burbank* ☎ *877/492–8687* ⊕ *vipstudiotour. warnerbros.com* ✉ *$52 for the VIP tour, $250 for the Deluxe tour* ⊙ *Mon.–Sat. 8:15–4, limited availability on Sun.*

WORTH NOTING

Dolby Theatre. Formerly the Kodak Theatre, the Dolby's interior design was inspired by European opera houses, but underneath all the trimmings, the space has one of the finest technical systems in the world. The half-hour tour of this theater that hosts the Academy Awards is a worthwhile expense for movie buffs who just can't get enough insider information. Tour guides share plenty of behind-the-scenes tidbits about Oscar ceremonies as they take you through the theater. You'll get to step into the VIP lounge, where celebrities mingle on the big night, and get a bird's-eye view from the balcony seating. ■ **TIP➜ If you have the Hollywood CityPass, the tour is included.** Another way to get a glimpse of the inside is by attending a concert or musical held here. In 2013, for example, Kathy Griffin and Scooby-Doo each had their night on the stage. ✉ *6801 Hollywood Blvd., Hollywood* ☎ *323/308–6300* ⊕ *www. dolbytheatre.com* ✉ *Free; tours $17* ⊙ *Daily 10:30–4.*

Hollywood & Highland. Bringing some glitz, foot traffic, and commerce back to Hollywood, the hotel-retail-entertainment complex here has become a huge tourist magnet. The design pays tribute to the city's film legacy with a grand staircase leading up to a pair of white stucco 33-foot-high elephants, a nod to the 1916 movie *Intolerance.* (Something tells us that the reference is lost on most visitors.) ■ **TIP➜ Pause at the entrance arch, Babylon Court, which frames the "Hollywood" sign in the hills above for a picture-perfect view.**

There are plenty of clothing stores and eateries, and you may find yourself ducking into these for a respite from the crowds and street artists. In the summer and during Christmas vacation—when the complex is at its busiest—special music programs and free entertainment keep strollers entertained.

A Metro Red Line station provides easy access to and from other parts of the city, and there's plenty of underground parking accessible from Highland Avenue. ✉ *Hollywood Blvd. and Highland Ave., Hollywood* ☎ *323/467–6412 visitor center* ⊕ *www.hollywoodandhighland.com* ✉ *Parking $2 with validation* ⊙ *Mon.–Sat. 10–10, Sun. 10–7.*

Hollywood Bowl. Classic Hollywood doesn't get better than this. Summer-evening concerts have been a tradition since 1922 at this amphitheater cradled in the Hollywood Hills. The bowl is the summer home of the Los Angeles Philharmonic, but the musical fare also includes pop and jazz. A new, much larger shell arrived in 2004, improving the acoustics and allowing the occasional dance and theater performance on stage with the orchestra.

Evoking the 1929 shell structure, the revised shell ripples out in a series of concentric rings. The 17,000-plus seating capacity ranges from boxes (where alfresco preconcert meals are catered) to concrete bleachers in the rear. Most of the box seats are reserved for season ticket holders, but the ideally located Super Seats, with comfortable armrests and great sight lines, are a great alternative. Dollar tickets are available for some weeknight classical and jazz performances. Come early to picnic on the grounds. ✉ *2301 N. Highland Ave., Hollywood* ☎ *323/850–2000* ⊕ *www.hollywoodbowl.com* ✉ *museum free* ☉ *Grounds daily dawn–dusk, call or check online for performance schedule.*

Hollywood Bowl Museum. Before the concert, or during the day, visit the Hollywood Bowl Museum for a time-capsule version of the bowl's history. The microphone used during Frank Sinatra's 1943 performance is just one of the pieces of rare memorabilia on display.

Throughout the gallery, drawers open to reveal vintage programs or letters written by fans tracing their fondest memories of going to the bowl. Headphones let you listen to recordings of such great bowl performers as Amelita Galli-Curci, Ella Fitzgerald, and Paul McCartney, and videos give you a tantalizing look at performances by everyone from the Beatles to Esa-Pekka Salonen. Be sure to pick up a map and take the "Bowl Walk" to explore the park-like grounds of this beautiful setting. During the summer, the store stays open until show time. ☎ *323/850–2058* ☉ *Tues.–Fri. 10–5, Sat. by appointment*

Hollywood Sign. With letters 50 feet tall, Hollywood's trademark sign can be spotted from miles away. The sign, which originally read "Hollywoodland," was erected on Mt. Lee in the Hollywood Hills in 1923 to promote a real-estate development. In 1949 the "land" portion of the sign was taken down. By 1973, the sign had earned landmark status, but since the letters were made of wood, its longevity came into question. A makeover project was launched and the letters were auctioned off (rocker Alice Cooper bought the "o" and singing cowboy Gene Autry sponsored an "l") to make way for a new sign made of sheet metal. Inevitably, the sign has drawn pranksters who have altered it over the years, albeit temporarily, to spell out "Yollyweed" (in the 1970s, to commemorate lenient marijuana laws), "go navy" (before a Rose Bowl game), and "Perotwood" (during the 1992 presidential election). A fence and surveillance equipment have since been installed to deter intruders. Use caution if driving up to the sign on residential streets since many cars speed around the blind corners. ⊕ *www.hollywoodsign.org.*

BEVERLY HILLS AND THE WESTSIDE

If you only have a day to see L.A., see Beverly Hills. Love it or hate it, it delivers wealth and excess on a dramatic, cinematic scale. West Hollywood is not a place to see things (like museums or movie studios) as much as it is a place to *do* things—like go to a nightclub, eat at a world-famous restaurant, or attend an art gallery opening.

The three-block stretch of Wilshire Boulevard known as Museum Row, east of Fairfax Avenue, features five intriguing museums and a prehistoric tar pit to boot. Only a few blocks away are the historic Farmers Market and The Grove shopping mall, a great place to people-watch over breakfast. Wilshire Boulevard itself is something of a cultural monument—it begins its grand 16-mile sweep to the sea in Downtown L.A.

A mural depicting Hollywood's legends (John Wayne, Elvis Presley, and Marilyn Monroe) adorns a wall of West Hollywood's Stella Adler Academy on Highland Avenue.

For some privileged Angelenos, the city begins west of La Cienega Boulevard, where keeping up with the Joneses becomes an epic pursuit. Chic, attractive neighborhoods with coveted postal codes—Bel Air, Brentwood, Westwood, West Los Angeles, and Pacific Palisades—are home to power couples pushing power kids in power strollers. Still, the Westside is rich in culture—and not just entertainment-industry culture. It's home to UCLA, the monumental Getty Center, and the engrossing Museum of Tolerance.

TOP ATTRACTIONS

Fodor's Choice **Farmers Market and The Grove.** The saying "Meet me at 3rd and Fairfax"
★ became a standard line for generations of Angelenos who ate, shopped, and spotted the stars who drifted over from the studios for a breath of unpretentious air. Starting back in 1934, when two entrepreneurs persuaded oil magnate E. B. Gilmore to open a vacant field for a bare-bones market, this spot became a humble shop for farmers selling produce out of their trucks. From this seat-of-the-pants situation grew a European-style open-air market and local institution at the corner of 3rd Street and Fairfax Avenue.

Now the market includes 110 stalls and more than 30 restaurants, plus the landmark 1941 Clock Tower. The Grove celebrated its 10th anniversary in 2012, and the outdoor mall, with its pseudo-European facade, cobblestones, marble mosaics, and pavilions has never been more popular or packed, especially on weekends and holidays.

Los Angeles history gets a nod with the electric steel-wheeled Red Car trolley, which shuttles two blocks through the Farmers Market and The Grove. If you hate crowds, try visiting The Grove before noon for the most comfortable shopping experience. By afternoon, it bustles with shoppers and teens hitting the movie theaters and chain stores such as Banana Republic, Crate & Barrel, Barnes & Noble, and J. Crew. Fashionistas find a haven at the Barney's Co-Op store. The parking structure on the east side for The Grove handles the cars by monitoring the number of spaces available as you go up each level, combined with the first hour free and a second hour free if you get your ticket validated, which helps to make parking less of a pain. Surface parking for the Farmers Market is 2 hours free with validation. ■TIP➔ The Grove really dazzles around Christmas, with an enormous Christmas tree and a nightly faux snowfall until New Year's Day. ✉ *Farmers Market, 6333 W. 3rd St.; The Grove, 189 The Grove Dr., Fairfax District* ☎*323/965–9594 Farmers Market, 323/900–8080 The Grove* ⊕ *www.farmersmarketla. com; www.thegrovela.com* ☺ *Farmers Market, Mon.–Fri. 9–9, Sat. 9–8, Sun. 10–7; The Grove, Mon.–Thurs. 10–9, Fri.–Sat. 10–10, Sun. 10–8.*

FAMILY
Fodor's Choice
★

The Getty Center. With its curving walls and isolated hilltop perch, the Getty Center resembles a pristine fortified city of its own. You may have been lured up by the beautiful views of L.A. (on a clear day stretching all the way to the Pacific Ocean), but the architecture, uncommon gardens, and fascinating art collections will be more than enough to capture and hold your attention. When the sun is out, the complex's rough-cut travertine marble skin seems to soak up the light.

J. Paul Getty, the billionaire oil magnate and art collector, began collecting Greek and Roman antiquities and French decorative arts in the 1930s. He opened the J. Paul Getty Museum at his Malibu estate in 1954, and in the 1970s, he built a re-creation of an ancient Roman village to house his initial collection. When Getty died in 1976, the museum received an endowment of $700 million that grew to a reported $4.5 billion. The Malibu villa, reopened in 2006, is devoted to the antiquities. The Getty Center, designed by Richard Meier, opened in 1998 and pulled together the rest of the collections, along with the museum's affiliated research, conservation, and philanthropic institutes.

Getting to the center involves a bit of anticipatory lead-up. At the base of the hill, a pavilion disguises the underground parking structure. From there you either walk or take a smooth, computer-driven tram up the steep slope, checking out the Bel Air estates across the humming 405 freeway. The five pavilions that house the museum surround a central courtyard and are bridged by walkways. From the courtyard, plazas, and walkways, you can survey the city from the San Gabriel Mountains to the ocean.

In a ravine separating the museum and the Getty Research Institute, conceptual artist Robert Irwin created the playful Central Garden in stark contrast to Meier's mathematical architectural geometry.

Inside the pavilions are the galleries for the permanent collections of European paintings, drawings, sculpture, illuminated manuscripts, and decorative arts, as well as American and European photographs. The Getty's collection of French furniture and decorative arts, especially from the early years of Louis XIV (1643–1715) to the end of the reign of Louis XVI (1774–92), is renowned for its quality and condition; you

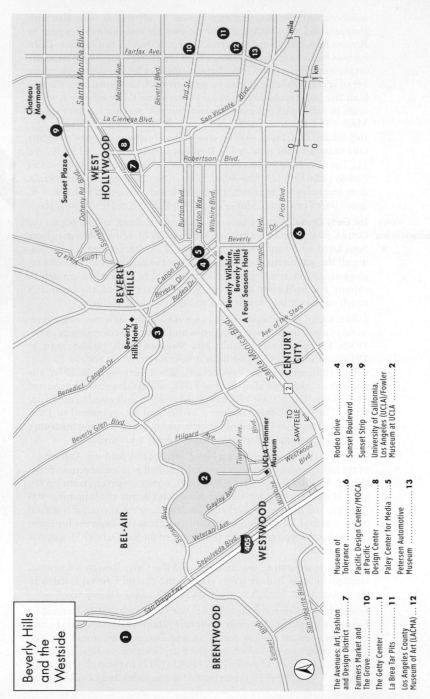

Beverly Hills and the Westside

Chateau Marmont ◆

Sunset Plaza ◆

Santa Monica Blvd.

Fairfax Ave.

Melrose Ave.

La Cienega Blvd.

WEST HOLLYWOOD

Doheny Rd. Blvd.

Sunset

Loma Vista Dr.

Beverly Blvd.

3rd St.

San Vicente Blvd.

Robertson Blvd.

Burton Blvd.

Canon Dr.

Beverly Dr.

Rodeo Dr.

Dayton Way

Wilshire Blvd.

BEVERLY HILLS

Beverly Hills Hotel ◆

Benedict Canyon Dr.

Beverly Glen Blvd.

Beverly Wilshire, Beverly Hills A Four Seasons Hotel

Beverly

Santa Monica Blvd.

Ave. of the Stars

CENTURY CITY

Olympic

Pico Blvd.

Dr.

1 mile

1 km

0

0

BEL-AIR

Sunset Blvd.

Hilgard Ave.

Gayley Ave.

Tiverton Ave.

Veteran Ave.

Westwood Blvd.

Blvd.

TO SAWTELLE

WESTWOOD

UCLA-Hammer Museum ◆

Wilshire

405

Sepulveda Blvd.

San Diego Fwy.

BRENTWOOD

Sunset

Blvd.

San Vicente Blvd.

can see a pair of completely reconstructed salons. In the paintings galleries, a computerized system of louvered skylights allows natural light to filter in, creating a closer approximation of the conditions in which the artists painted. Notable among the paintings are Rembrandt's *The Abduction of Europa*, Van Gogh's *Irises*, Monet's *Wheatstack, Snow Effects*, and *Morning*, and James Ensor's *Christ's Entry into Brussels*.

If you want to start with a quick overview, pick up the brochure in the entrance hall that guides you to 15 highlights of the collection. There's also an instructive audio tour ($5) with commentaries by art historians. Art information rooms with multimedia computer stations contain more details about the collections. The Getty also presents lectures, films, concerts, and special programs for kids and families. The complex includes an upscale restaurant and downstairs cafeteria with panoramic window views, and two outdoor coffee bar cafés. ■TIP➜ On-site parking is subject to availability and can fill up by late afternoon on holidays and summer weekends, so try to come early in the day. You may also take public transportation (MTA Bus 761). ⊠ *1200 Getty Center Dr., Brentwood* ☎ *310/440–7300* ⊕ *www.getty.edu* ⊠ *Free, parking $15* ☺ *Tues.–Fri. 10–5:30, Sat. 10–9, Sun. 10–5:30.*

FAMILY **La Brea Tar Pits.** Do your children have pre-historic animals on the brain? Show them where Ice Age fossils come from by taking them to the stickiest park in town. The area formed when deposits of oil rose to the earth's surface, collected in shallow pools, and coagulated into asphalt. In the early 20th century, geologists discovered that all that goo contained the largest collection of Pleistocene, or Ice Age, fossils ever found at one location: more than 600 species of birds, mammals, plants, reptiles, and insects. Roughly 100 tons of fossil bones have been removed in excavations during the last 100 years, making this one of the world's most famous fossil sites. You can see most of the pits through chain-link fences. (They can be a little smelly, but your kids are sure to love it.) Pit 91 and Project 23 are ongoing excavation projects; tours are available, and you can volunteer to help with the excavations in summer. There are several pits scattered around Hancock Park and the surrounding neighborhood; construction in the area has often had to accommodate them, and in nearby streets and along sidewalks, little bits of tar occasionally ooze up, unstoppable. The nearby **Page Museum at the La Brea Tar Pits** displays fossils from the tar pits and has a "Fishbowl Lab," which is a glass-walled laboratory that allows visitors a rare look behind-the-scenes of the museum where paleontologists and volunteers work on specimens. ⊠ *5801 Wilshire Blvd., Hancock Park, Miracle Mile* ☎ *323/934–7243* ⊕ *www.tarpits.org* ⊠ *$7, Children under 5 free, free on 1st Tues. of each month* ☺ *Daily 9:30–5.*

Fodor's Choice **Los Angeles County Museum of Art (LACMA).** Without a doubt, LACMA is ★ the focal point of the museum district that runs along Wilshire Boulevard. Chris Burden's *Urban Light* sculpture, composed of more than two hundred restored cast iron antique street lamps, elegantly illuminates the building's facade.

Inside, visitors will find one of the country's most comprehensive collections of more than 100,000 objects dating from ancient times to the present. Since opening in 1965, the museum has grown into a complex of several different buildings interconnected via walkways, stretching across a 20-acre campus.

Works from the museum's rotating permanent collection include Latin American artists such as Diego Rivera and Frida Kahlo, prominent Southern California artists, collections of Islamic and European art, paintings by Henri Matisse and Rene Magritte, as well as works by Paul Klee and Wassily Kandinsky. There's also a solid collection of art representing the ancient civilizations of Egypt, the Near East, Greece, and Rome, plus a vast costume and textiles collection dating back to the 16th century.

As part of an ambitious 10-year face-lift plan that is becoming a work of art on its own, entitled "Transformation: The LACMA Campaign," the museum is adding buildings and exhibition galleries, and redesigning public spaces and gardens.

In early 2008, the impressive Broad Contemporary Art Museum (BCAM) opened. With three vast floors, BCAM integrates contemporary art into LACMA's collection, exploring the interplay of current times with that of the past. In 2010, the Lynda and Stewart Resnick Exhibition Pavilion was added, a stunning, light-filled space designed by Renzo Piano.

■TIP→ Temporary exhibits sometimes require tickets purchased in advance, so check the calendar ahead of time. ⊠ *5905 Wilshire Blvd., Miracle Mile* ☎ *323/857–6000* ⊕ *www.lacma.org* ⊠ *$15* ☉ *Mon., Tues., and Thurs. noon–8, Fri. noon–9, weekends 11–8.*

FAMILY **Museum of Tolerance.** Using interactive technology, this important museum (part of the Simon Wiesenthal Center) challenges visitors to confront bigotry and racism. One of the most affecting sections covers the Holocaust, with film footage of deportation scenes and simulated sets of concentration camps. Each visitor is issued a "passport" bearing the name of a child whose life was dramatically changed by the German Nazi rule and by World War II; as you go through the exhibit, you learn the fate of that child. Anne Frank artifacts are part of the museum's permanent collection as is Wiesenthal's Vienna office, set exactly as the famous "Nazi hunter" had it while performing his research that brought more than 1,000 war criminals to justice. Interactive exhibits include the "Millennium Machine," which engages visitors in finding solutions to human rights abuses around the world; Globalhate.com, which examines hate on the Internet by exposing problematic sites via touch-screen computer terminals; and the "Point of View Diner," a re-creation of a 1950s diner, red booths and all, that "serves" a menu of controversial topics on video jukeboxes. Renovations brought a new youth action floor and revamped 300-seat theater space. To ensure a visit to this popular museum, make reservations in advance (especially for Friday, Sunday, and holidays) and plan to spend at least three hours here. Testimony from Holocaust survivors is offered at specified times. Museum entry stops at least two hours before the actual closing time. Although every exhibit may not be appropriate for children, school tours regularly visit the museum. ⊠ *9786 W. Pico Blvd., just south of Beverly Hills* ☎ *310/553–8403* ⊕ *www.museumoftolerance.com* ⊠ *$15.50* ☉ *Sun. 11–5 year-round; Mon.–Fri.10–5 Apr.–Oct. and 10–3 Nov.–Mar.*

FAMILY **Petersen Automotive Museum.** You don't have to be a gearhead to appreciate this building full of antique and unusual cars. The Petersen is likely to be one of the coolest museums in town with its take on some of the most unusual creations on wheels and rotating exhibits of the icons who drove them. Lifelike dioramas and street scenes spread through the ground floor help to establish a local context for the history of the automobile. The second floor may include displays of Hollywood-celebrity and movie cars, "muscle" cars (like a 1969 Dodge Daytona 440 Magnum), alternative-powered cars, motorcycles, and a showcase of the Ferrari. You can also learn about the origins of our modern-day car-insurance system, as well as the history of L.A.'s formidable freeway network. A children's interactive Discovery Center illustrates the mechanics of the automobile and fun child-inspired creations; there is also a gift shop. ⊠ *6060 Wilshire Blvd., Miracle Mile* ☎ *323/930–2277* ⊕ *www.petersen.org* 🖃 *$10* ⊙ *Tues.–Sun. 10–6.*

Sunset Boulevard. One of the most fabled avenues in the world, Sunset Boulevard began humbly enough in the 18th century as a route from El Pueblo de Los Angeles (today's Downtown L.A.) to the ranches in the west and then to the Pacific Ocean. Now as it winds its way across the L.A. basin to the ocean, it cuts through gritty urban neighborhoods and what used to be the working center of Hollywood's movie industry. In West Hollywood, it becomes the sexy and seductive Sunset Strip, then slips quietly into the tony environs of Beverly Hills and Bel Air, twisting and winding past gated estates. Continuing on past UCLA in Westwood, through Brentwood and Pacific Palisades, Sunset finally descends to the beach, the edge of the continent, and the setting sun.

Sunset Strip. For 80 years the Hollywood's night owls have headed for the 1¾-mile stretch of Sunset Boulevard between Crescent Heights Boulevard on the east and Doheny Drive on the west, known as the Sunset Strip. In the 1930s and '40s, stars such as Tyrone Power, Errol Flynn, Norma Shearer, and Rita Hayworth came for wild evenings of dancing and drinking at nightclubs like Trocadero, Ciro's, and Mocambo. By the '60s and '70s, the Strip had become the center of rock and roll for acts like Johnny Rivers, the Byrds, and the Doors. The '80s punk riot gave way to hair metal lead by Mötley Crüe and Guns N' Roses on the stages of the Whisky A Go-Go (⊠ *8901 Sunset Blvd.* ☎ *310/652–4202* ⊕ *www.whiskyagogo.com*) and The Roxy (⊠ *9009 Sunset Blvd.* ☎ *310/278–9457* ⊕ *www.theroxyonsunset.com*). Nowadays it's the Viper Room (⊠ *8852 Sunset Blvd.* ☎ *310/358–1881* ⊕ *www.viperroom.com*), the House of Blues (⊠ *8430 Sunset Blvd.* ☎ *323/848–5100* ⊕ *www.hob.com*), and the Key Club (⊠ *9039 Sunset Blvd.* ☎ *310/274–5800* ⊕ *www.keyclub.com*), where you'll find on-the-cusp actors, rock stars, club-hopping regulars, and out-of-towners all mingling over drinks and live music. Parking and traffic around the Strip can be tough on weekends, expect to pay around $10–$25 to park, which can take a bite out of your partying budget, but the time and money may be worth it if you plan to make the rounds—most clubs are within walking distance of each other. ■TIP→ Do not drink and drive: the Strip is heavily patrolled by the L.A. County sheriffs, especially on weekends. A taxi is the best bet.

4

WORTH NOTING

The Avenues: Art, Fashion, and Design District. Established in 1996, the area defined by Melrose Avenue and Robertson and Beverly boulevards is The Avenues: Art, Fashion, and Design District. More than 300 businesses including art galleries, antiques shops, contemporary furniture and interior design stores, high-end boutiques, and about 40 restaurants are clustered here. Note that some showrooms are reserved for design professionals and require trade credentials, and are not open to the public. ✉ *Melrose Ave. and Robertson and Beverly Blvds.* ☎ *310/289–2534* ⊕ *www.avenueswh.com.*

Pacific Design Center. World-renowned architect Cesar Pelli's original vision for the Pacific Design Center was three buildings that together housed designer showrooms, office buildings, parking, and more—a virtual multibuilding shrine to design. These architecturally intriguing buildings were built years apart: the building sheathed in blue glass (known as the Blue Whale) opened in 1975; the green building opened in 1988. In 2013 the final "Red" building is scheduled to open, completing Pelli's grand vision all of these many years later. All together the 1.2 million-square-foot vast complex covers more than 14 acres, housing more than 120 design showrooms as well as 2,100 interior product lines; it's the largest interior design complex in the western United States. You'll also find restaurants such as Red Seven by Wolfgang Puck, the Silverscreen movie theater, an outpost of the Museum of Contemporary Art, as well as a myriad of special events. Focused on the professional trade, some showrooms are open only to professionals such as credentialed decorators, but many other showrooms are open to the public. The PDC also has a designer service to help nonprofessionals shop and get access to certain designers and showrooms. ✉ *8687 Melrose Ave., West Hollywood* ☎ *310/657–0800* ⊕ *www. pacificdesigncenter.com* ☾ *Mon.–Fri. 9–5.*

MOCA at Pacific Design Center. The Downtown Museum of Contemporary Art has a small satellite MOCA Gallery here that shows works from current artists and designers and hosts exhibit-related talks. ✉ *8687 Melrose Avenue, West Hollywood* ☎ *310/657–0800* ⊕ *www.moca.org*

Paley Center for Media. Formerly the Museum of Television and Radio, this institution changed its name in 2007 with a look toward a future that encompasses all media in the ever-evolving world of entertainment and information. Reruns are taken to a curated level in this sleek stone-and-glass building, designed by Getty architect Richard Meier. A sister to the New York location, the Paley Center carries a duplicate of its collection: more than 100,000 programs spanning eight decades. Search for your favorite commercials and television shows on easy-to-use computers. A radio program listening room provides cozy seats supplied with headphones playing snippets of a variety of programming from a toast to Dean Martin to an interview with John Lennon. Frequent seminars with movers 'n' shakers from the film, television, and radio world are big draws, as well as screenings of documentaries and short films. Free parking is available in the lot off Santa Monica Boulevard. ✉ *465 N. Beverly Dr., Beverly Hills* ☎ *310/786–1000* ⊕ *www.paleycenter.org* ☾ *Wed.–Sun. noon–5.*

Rodeo Drive. The ultimate shopping indulgence—Rodeo Drive is one of Southern California's bona fide tourist attractions. The art of window-shopping is prime among the retail elite: Tiffany & Co., Gucci, Jimmy Choo, Valentino, Harry Winston, Prada—you get the picture. Several nearby restaurants have patios where you can sip a drink while watching career shoppers in their size 2 threads saunter by with shopping bags stuffed with superfluous delights. At the southern end of Rodeo Drive (at Wilshire Boulevard), **Via Rodeo,** a curvy cobblestone street designed to resemble a European shopping area, makes the perfect backdrop to strike a pose for that glamour shot. The holidays bring a special magic to Rodeo and the surrounding streets with twinkling lights, swinging music, and colorful banners. ✉ *Beverly Hills.*

University of California, Los Angeles (UCLA). With spectacular buildings such as a Romanesque library, the park-like UCLA campus makes for a fine stroll through one of California's most prestigious universities. In the heart of the north campus, the **Franklin Murphy Sculpture Garden** contains more than 70 works by artists such as Henry Moore and Gaston Lachaise. The **Mildred E. Mathias Botanic Garden,** which contains some 5,000 species of plants from all over the world in a 7-acre outdoor garden, is in the southeast section of the campus and is accessible from Tiverton Avenue. West of the main-campus bookstore, the **J.D. Morgan Center and Athletic Hall of Fame** displays the sports memorabilia and trophies of the university's athletic departments and championship teams.

Campus maps and information are available at drive-by kiosks at major entrances daily, and free 90-minute walking tours of the campus are given most weekdays at 10:15 and 2:15, and Saturday at 10:15. Call ☎ *310/825–8764* for reservations, which are required three to four weeks in advance. The campus has cafés, plus bookstores selling UCLA Bruins paraphernalia. The main-entrance gate is on Westwood Boulevard. Campus parking costs $11. ✉ *Bordered by Le Conte, Hilgard, and Gayley Aves. and Sunset Blvd., Westwood* ⊕ *www.ucla.edu.*

Fowler Museum at UCLA. Many visitors head straight to the Fowler Museum at UCLA, which presents exhibits on the world's diverse cultures and visual arts, especially those of Africa, Asia, the Pacific, and Native and Latin America. The museum is open Wednesday through Sunday from noon to 5 and Thursday until 8 pm. ☎ *310/825–4361* ⊕ *www.fowler.ucla.edu* 🖅 *Free; parking $11, use lot 4 off Sunset Blvd.*

DOWNTOWN AND LOS FELIZ

Once the lively heart of Los Angeles, Downtown was a no man's land until a few decades ago, when high-rise condos starting going up and urban renewal followed. While certain sections can still be gritty, some of the city's most talked about restaurants, bars, and cultural attractions, including the Frank Gehry–designed Walt Disney Concert Hall, reside Downtown. In 2014, the debut of the Broad Museum will complete the neighborhood's transformation. While first-timers tend to stick with Hollywood and the Westside, it's worth exploring the fringe neighborhoods of Los Feliz and Silver Lake, which maintain a bohemian vibe.

There you'll find hipsters, bloggers, and creative types caffeinating at corner cafés while typing away on their iPads.

TOP ATTRACTIONS

Fodor'sChoice **Cathedral of Our Lady of the Angels.**
★ A half-block away from the giant rose-shaped steel grandeur of Frank Gehry's curvaceous Disney Concert Hall sits Cathedral of Our Lady of the Angels. It is both a spiritual draw as well as an architectural attraction. The exterior is all strict soaring angles and the building is as heavy, solid, and hunkering as the Gehry building is feminine and ethereal.

Controversy surrounded Spanish architect José Rafael Moneo's unconventional, costly, austere design for the seat of the Archdiocese of Los Angeles. But judging from the swarms of visitors and the standing-room-only holiday masses, the church has carved out a niche for itself in Downtown L.A.

Opened in 2002, the ocher-concrete cathedral looms up by the Hollywood Freeway. The plaza in front is relatively austere, glaringly bright on sunny days; a children's play garden with bronze animals helps relieve the stark space. Imposing bronze entry doors, designed by local artist Robert Graham, are decorated with multicultural icons and New World images of the Virgin Mary. The canyon-like interior of the church is spare, polished, and airy. By day, sunlight illuminates the sanctuary through translucent curtain walls of thin Spanish alabaster, a departure from the usual stained glass.

Artist John Nava used residents from his hometown of Ojai, California, as models for some of the 135 figures in the tapestries that line the nave walls. Make sure to go underground to wander the bright, maze-like white-marble corridors of the mausoleum.

Free, guided tours start at the entrance fountain at 1 pm on weekdays. Check for free concerts inside the Cathedral on Wednesdays at 12:45 p.m. There's plenty of underground visitor parking; the vehicle entrance is on Hill Street. ■ TIP➔ The café in the plaza has become one of Downtown's favorite lunch spots. You can pick up a fresh, reasonably priced meal to eat at one of the outdoor tables. ✉ *555 W. Temple St., Downtown* ☎ *213/680–5200* ⊕ *www.olacathedral.org* ✉ *Free, parking $4 every 15 min, $18 maximum* ⊙ *Weekdays 6–6, Sat. 9–6, Sun. 7–6.*

The Geffen Contemporary at MOCA. Frank Gehry transformed what was a 40,000-square-foot former police warehouse in Little Tokyo into this top-notch museum, originally built as a temporary exhibit hall while the **Museum of Contemporary Art** (MOCA) was under construction at California Plaza. Thanks to its popular reception, it remains one of two satellite museums of MOCA (the other is outside the Pacific Design Center in West Hollywood) and houses a sampling of its permanent collection. In addition, it puts on one or two special exhibits yearly. Call before you visit because the museum sometimes closes for installations.

Downtown
Los Angeles

CHINATOWN

4

Union
Station

Walt Disney
Concert Hall

Watercourt

Bunker Hill
Steps

Grand Central
Market

Central
Library

Pershing
Square

LITTLE TOKYO

TO
EXPOSITION
PARK

FASHION
DISTRICT

TO
WATTS
TOWERS

Flower
Market

0   1/2 mi
0   800 meters

KEY
Ⓜ Metro stops

✉ *152 N. Central Ave., Downtown* ☎ *213/626–6222* ⊕ *www.moca-la. org* 🖳 *$10, free with MOCA admission on same day and on Thurs. evenings.* ⊙ *Mon. 11–5, Thurs. 11–8, Fri. 11–5, Sat.–Sun. 11–6.*

Fodor's Choice **The Museum of Contemporary Art (MOCA).** The MOCA's permanent
★ collection of American and European art from 1940 to the present divides itself between three spaces: this linear red-sandstone building at California Plaza, the **Geffen Contemporary,** in nearby Little Tokyo, and the satellite gallery at West Hollywood's **Pacific Design Center.** Likewise, its exhibitions are split between the established and the cutting edge.

Heavy hitters such as Mark Rothko, Franz Kline, Susan Rothenberg, Diane Arbus, and Robert Frank are part of the permanent collection that's rotated into the museum exhibits at different times, while additional theme shows are featured annually. It's a good idea to check the schedule in advance, as some galleries occasionally close for exhibit installations. ✉ *250 S. Grand Ave., Downtown* ☎ *213/626– 6222* ⊕ *www.moca.org* 🖳 *Grand Ave. and Geffen Contemporary $10, free Thurs. 5–8; Pacific Design Center free* ⊙ *Mon. and Fri. 11–5, Thurs. 11–8, Sat.–Sun. 11–6; Pacific Design Center, Tues.–Fri. 11–5, Sat.–Sun. 11–6.*

The Music Center. Serving as L.A.'s major performing arts venue since its opening in 1964, this was where the Academy Awards was held until it moved to what is now called the Dolby Theatre.

The Music Center is reminiscent of New York's Lincoln Center because the buildings that house the Los Angeles Philharmonic, the Los Angeles Opera, the Center Theater Group, and the Los Angeles Master Chorale all surround a large courtyard. Glorya Kaufman presents Dance at the Music Center is another program that features the best of dance, from global to traditional ballet. At intermission, patrons spill into the plaza to drink wine, enjoy the lighted "dancing" fountain or occasional art exhibits, adding magic to an evening already filled with artistic excellence.

The largest of the center's four theaters is the **Dorothy Chandler Pavilion,** named after the philanthropic wife of former *Los Angeles Times* publisher Norman Chandler. The **Ahmanson,** at the north end, is a flexible venue for major musicals and plays. In between these two sits the round **Mark Taper Forum,** an intimate 700-seat theater.

Activity isn't limited to merely ticketed events; free tours of the entire Music Center campus are available by volunteer docents who provide a wealth of architectural and behind-the-scenes information while escorting you through elaborate, art-punctuated VIP areas. ✉ *135 N. Grand Ave., at 1st St., Downtown* ☎ *213/972–7211, 213/972–4399 for tour information* ⊕ *www.musiccenter.org.*

Walt Disney Concert Hall. L.A.'s crown jewel, designed by Frank Gehry, opened in 2003 and instantly became a stunning icon of the city. The gorgeous stainless-steel-clad exterior soars upward, seeming to defy the laws of engineering.

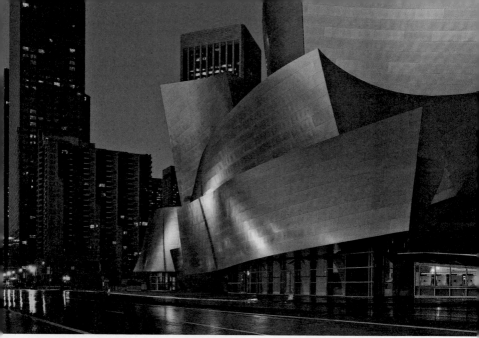
Frank Gehry's Walt Disney Concert Hall is the crown jewel of the Music Center, if not all of Downtown Los Angeles.

Inside, the hall has a billowing ceiling of Douglas fir and an enormous pine-clad organ centerpiece said to have been inspired by a box of McDonald's french fries. The carpet, named "Lily," is a wild collage of petals inspired by Lillian Disney's love of flowers, as is the "Rose for Lily" fountain—made entirely of bits of Delftware, Mrs. Disney's favorite collectible—in the tranquil outdoor public garden.

Docent-led and self-guided audio tours of the hall are available free to the public for parties of 14 and fewer, but note that entry to the performance space is subject to rehearsal schedules. Your chances are better in summer when the Philharmonic moves to the Hollywood Bowl.

Additional children's performances, lectures, and experimental works are held in surrounding smaller theater spaces: the indoor BP Hall, two outdoor mini-amphitheaters, and CalArts's intimate 266-seat REDCAT Theatre. ✉ *111 South Grand Avenue, Downtown* ☏ *323/850–2000* ⊕ *www.laphil.com*

Olvera Street Visitors Center. For information, stop by the Olvera Street Visitors Center, in the Sepulveda House, a Victorian building built in 1887 as a hotel and boardinghouse. The center is open weekdays and weekends 9–4. Free hour-long walking tours leave here at 10, 11, and noon Tuesday through Saturday. ✉ *622 N. Main St., Downtown* ☏ *213/628–1274* ⊕ *www.lasangelitas.org.*

Union Station. Once the key entry point into Los Angeles prior to LAX, Union Station is worth a visit even if you don't plan to go anywhere but merely want to wallow in the ambience of one of the country's last great rail stations.

Evoking an era when travel and style went hand in hand, Union Station will transport you to another destination, and another time. Built in 1939 and designed by City Hall architects John and Donald Parkinson, it combines Spanish colonial revival and art deco styles that have retained their classic warmth and quality.

The waiting hall's commanding scale and enormous chandeliers have provided the setting for countless films, TV shows, and music videos. The indoor restaurant, **Traxx**, offers a glamorous vintage setting for lunch and dinner. ⊠ *800 N. Alameda St., Downtown.*

WORTH NOTING

Bradbury Building. Stunning wrought-iron railing, blond-wood and brick interior, ornate moldings, pink marble staircases, Victorian-style skylighted atrium that rises almost 50 feet, and a birdcage elevator: it's easy to see why the Bradbury leaves visitors awestruck.

Designed in 1893 by a novice architect who drew his inspiration from a science-fiction story and a conversation with his dead brother via a Ouija board, the office building was originally the site of turn-of-the-20th-century sweatshops, but now houses a variety of business that try to keep normal working conditions despite the barrage of daily tourist visits and filmmakers. *Blade Runner, Chinatown,* and *Wolf* were filmed here.

For that reason, visits (and photo-taking) are limited to the lobby and the first-floor landing. The building is open daily 9–5 for a peek, as long as you don't wander beyond visitor-approved areas. ⊠ *304 S. Broadway, southeast corner Broadway and 3rd St., Downtown* ☎ *213/626–1893.*

California African American Museum. Works by 20th-century African-American artists and contemporary art of the African Diasporas are the backbone of this museum's permanent collection. Its exhibits document the African-American experience from Emancipation and Reconstruction through the 20th century, especially as expressed by artists in California and elsewhere in the West. ⊠ *600 Exposition Park, Exposition Park* ☎ *213/744–7432* ⊕ *www.caamuseum.org* ⊠ *Free, parking $10* ⊙ *Tues.–Sat. 10–5, Sun. 11–5.*

FAMILY **California Science Center.** You're bound to see excited kids running up to the dozens of interactive exhibits here that illustrate the relevance of science to everyday life, from bacteria to airplanes. Clustered in different "Worlds," this center provides opportunities to examine such topics as structures and communications. Be an architect and design your own building and learn how to make it earthquake-proof, or watch Tess, the 50-foot animatronic star of the exhibit "Body Works," dramatically demonstrate how the body's organs work together. Air and Space Exhibits show what it takes to go to outer space with Gemini 11, a real capsule flown into space by Pete Conrad and Dick Gordon in September 1966. An IMAX theater shows large-format releases.

New in 2013, the museum is now home to NASA's Space Shuttle Endeavor. The Samuel Oschin Air and Space Center, which will be the shuttle's permanent home, is currently under construction, but visitors can view the spacecraft (as well as view exhibits about it) in the temporary Endeavor Display Pavilion. ■TIP→ You will need a timed ticket to view the space craft; see the website for details. ⊠ *700 State Dr., Exposition Park* ☎ *213/744–7400, 323/724–3623* ⊕ *www. californiasciencecenter.org* ✎ *Free, except for Endeavor timed ticket ($2–$3 service fee if purchased online or by phone) and IMAX (prices vary); parking $10* ☉ *Daily 10–5.*

Japanese American National Museum. What was it like to grow up on a sugar plantation in Hawaii? How difficult was life for Japanese-Americans interned in concentration camps during World War II? These questions are addressed by changing exhibits at this museum in Little Tokyo. Insightful volunteer docents are on hand to share their own stories and experiences. The museum occupies an 85,000-square-foot adjacent pavilion as well as its original site in a renovated 1925 Buddhist temple. ⊠ *100 North Central Ave., off E. 1st St., next to Geffen Contemporary, Downtown* ☎ *213/625–0414* ⊕ *www.janm.org* ✎ *$9, free Thur. 5–8 and 3rd Thurs. of month* ☉ *Tues.–Wed., and Fri.–Sun. 11–5; Thurs. noon–8.*

FAMILY **Natural History Museum of Los Angeles County.** This 1913-built Beaux Arts museum has the same quaint feel of many natural history museums, with enclosed dioramas of animals in their natural habitats. But it mixes it up with interactive displays such as a seasonal Butterfly Pavilion in a separate small building in front of the museum; the Discovery Center, where kids can touch real animal pelts; the Insect Zoo; and the Dino Lab, where you can watch actual paleontologists work on dinosaur fossils. In addition, there are exhibits typifying various cultural groups, including pre-Columbian artifacts and a display of crafts from the South Pacific, as well as marine-life exhibits. Dinosaur Hall features more than 300 fossils, 20 full-body specimens, manual and digital interactivity, and large-format video, as well as a *T. rex* series that includes adult, juvenile, and baby specimens. And at the time of this writing, a new gardens complex was set to debut. ⊠ *900 Exposition Blvd., Exposition Park* ☎ *213/763–3466* ⊕ *www.nhm.org* ✎ *$12, free 1st Tues. of month except July and Aug.* ☉ *Daily 9:30–5.*

SANTA MONICA, VENICE, AND MALIBU

Hugging the Santa Monica Bay in an arch, the desirable communities of Malibu, Santa Monica, and Venice move from ultrarich, ultracasual Malibu to bohemian, borderline seedy Venice. What they have in common is cleaner air, mild temperatures, horrific traffic, and an emphasis on the beach-focused lifestyle that many people consider the hallmark of Southern California.

TOP ATTRACTIONS

Fodor's Choice ★ **Getty Villa Malibu.** Feeding off the cultures of ancient Rome, Greece, and Etruria, the remodeled Getty Villa opened in 2006 with much fanfare—and some controversy concerning the acquisition and rightful ownership of some of the Italian artifacts on display. The antiquities are astounding, but on a first visit even they take a backseat to their environment. This megamansion sits on some of the most valuable coastal property in the world. Modeled after an Italian country home, the Villa dei Papiri in Herculaneum, the Getty Villa includes beautifully

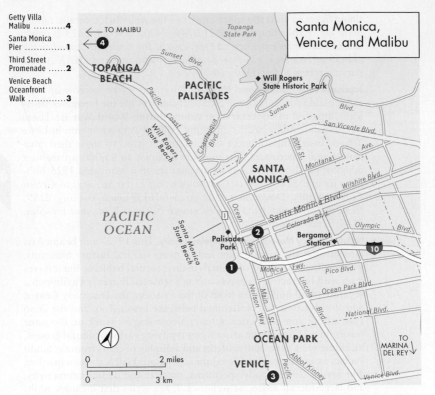

TO MALIBU

Santa Monica,
Venice, and Malibu

Topanga
State Park

Sunset Blvd.

TOPANGA
BEACH

PACIFIC
PALISADES

Pacific Coast Hwy.

Will Rogers
State Historic Park

Will Rogers
State Beach

Chautauqua Blvd.

Sunset Blvd.

San Vicente Blvd.

20th St.

Montana Ave.

SANTA
MONICA

Montana

Wilshire Blvd.

PACIFIC
OCEAN

Ocean Ave.

Santa Monica State Beach

Palisades
Park

Santa Monica Blvd.

Colorado Blvd.

Bergamot
Station

Olympic Blvd.

10

Santa
Monica Fwy.

Pico Blvd.

Lincoln Blvd.

Ocean Park Blvd.

Neilson Way

Main St.

National Blvd.

0   2 miles
0   3 km

OCEAN PARK

VENICE

Abbot Kinney

Pacific

TO
MARINA
DEL REY

Venice Blvd.

manicured gardens, reflecting pools, and statuary. The largest and most
lovely garden, the Outer Peristyle, gives you glorious views over a rectangular reflecting pool and geometric hedges to the Pacific. The new
structures blend thoughtfully into the rolling terrain and significantly
improve the public spaces, such as the new outdoor amphitheater,
gift store, café, and entry arcade. Talks and educational programs are
offered at an indoor theater. ■TIP→ An advance timed entry ticket is
required for admission. Tickets are free and may be ordered from the
website or by phone. ⊠ 17985 *Pacific Coast Hwy., Pacific Palisades*
☎ 310/440–7300 ⊕ *www.getty.edu* ⊠ *Free, tickets required. Parking
$15, cash or credit card* ⊗ *Wed.–Mon. 10–5.*

Third Street Promenade. Stretch your legs along this pedestrians-only
three-block stretch of 3rd Street, just a whiff away from the Pacific,
lined with jacaranda trees, ivy-topiary dinosaur fountains, strings of
lights, and branches of nearly every major U.S. retail chain. Outdoor
cafés, street vendors, movie theaters, and a rich nightlife make this
a main gathering spot for locals, visitors, as well as street musicians
and performance artists. Plan a night just to take it all in or take an
afternoon for a long people-watching stroll. There's plenty of parking in city structures on the streets flanking the promenade. **Santa
Monica Place** reopened in 2010 at the south end of the promenade

as a sleek outdoor mall and foodie haven. Its three stories are home to Bloomingdale's, Burberry, Coach, and other upscale retailers. Don't miss the ocean views from the rooftop food court. ⊠ *Third St., between Colorado and Wilshire Blvds., Santa Monica* ⊕ *www. thirdstreetpromenade.com.*

Venice Beach Oceanfront Walk. The surf and sand of Venice are fine, but the main attraction here is the boardwalk scene, which is a cosmos all its own. Go on weekend afternoons for the best people-watching experience. There are also swimming, fishing, surfing, skateboarding, basketball (it's the site of some of L.A.'s most hotly contested pickup games), racquetball, handball, and shuffleboard. You can rent a bike or some in-line skates and hit the Strand bike path. ⊠ *1800 Ocean Front Walk, west of Pacific Ave., Venice* ☎ *310/392–4687* ⊕ *www. westland.net/venice.*

WORTH NOTING

FAMILY **Santa Monica Pier.** Souvenir shops, carnival games, arcades, eateries, an outdoor trapeze school, **Pacific Park,** and more are all part the festive atmosphere of this truncated pier at the foot of Colorado Boulevard below Palisades Park. The pier's indoor trademark 46-horse Looff Carousel, built in 1922, has appeared in several films, including *The Sting.* Free concerts are held on the pier in summer. ⊠ *Colorado Ave. and the ocean, Santa Monica* ☎ *310/458–8900* ⊕ *www.santamonicapier. org* ⊗ *Hrs vary by season; check website before visiting.*

PASADENA AREA

Although seemingly absorbed into the general Los Angeles sprawl, Pasadena is a separate and distinct city. Noted for its Tournament of Roses, seen around the world each New Year's Day, the city brims with noteworthy spots, from its gorgeous Craftsman homes to its exceptional museums, particularly the Norton Simon and the Huntington Library, Art Collections, and Botanical Gardens. Where else can you see a Chaucer manuscript and rare cacti in one place?

TOP ATTRACTIONS

Fodor's Choice **Huntington Library, Art Collections, and Botanical Gardens.** If you have time
★ for only one stop in the Pasadena area, it should be the Huntington, built in the early 1900s as the home of railroad tycoon Henry E. Huntington. Wandering the ground's 150 acres, just over the Pasadena line in San Marino, you can truly forget you're in a city. Henry and his wife, Arabella (who was his aunt by marriage), voraciously collected rare books and manuscripts, botanical specimens, and 18th-century British art. The institution they established became one of the most extraordinary cultural complexes in the world. ■**TIP**➔ Ongoing gallery renovations occasionally require some works from the permanent collection to be shifted to other buildings for display.

Among the highlights are John Constable's intimate *View on the Stour near Dedham* and the monumental *Sarah Siddons as the Tragic Muse,* by Joshua Reynolds. In the Virginia Steele Scott Gallery of American

Art, you can see paintings by Mary Cassatt, Frederic Remington, and more.

The library contains more than 700,000 books and 4 million manuscripts, including such treasures as a Gutenberg Bible, the Ellesmere manuscript of Chaucer's *Canterbury Tales,* George Washington's genealogy in his own handwriting, scores of works by William Blake, and a world-class collection of early editions of Shakespeare. You'll find some of these items in the Library Hall with more than 200 important works on display. In 2006 the library acquired more than 60,000 rare books and reference volumes from the Cambridge, Massachusetts–based Bundy Library, making the Huntington the source of one of the biggest history-of-science collections in the world.

Although the art collections are increasingly impressive here, don't resist being lured outside into the stunning Botanical Gardens. From the main buildings, lawns and towering trees stretch out toward specialty areas. The 10-acre Desert Garden, for instance, has one of the world's largest groups of mature cacti and other succulents, arranged by continent. ■TIP➔ Visit this garden on a cool morning or in the late afternoon, or a hot midday walk may be a little too authentic. ⊠ *1151 Oxford Rd., San Marino* ☎ *626/405–2100* ⊕ *www.huntington.org* ⬩*$15 Mon.–Fri., $20 Sat.–Sun., free 1st Thurs. of month (reservations required)* ☾ *Mon. and Wed.–Fri. noon–4:30, Sat.–Sun. 10:30–4:30; call for summer hours.*

Fodor'sChoice ★ **Norton Simon Museum.** Long familiar to TV viewers of the New Year's Day Rose Parade, this low-profile brown building is more than just a background for the passing floats. It's one of the finest small museums anywhere, with an excellent collection that spans more than 2,000 years of Western and Asian art. It all began in the 1950s when Norton Simon (Hunt-Wesson Foods, McCalls Corporation, and Canada Dry) started collecting the works of Degas, Renoir, Gauguin, and Cézanne. His collection grew to include old masters, impressionists, and modern works from Europe as well as Indian and Southeast Asian art. After he retired, Simon reorganized the failing Pasadena Art Institute and continued to assemble one of the world's finest collections.

Today the Norton Simon Museum is richest in works by Rembrandt, Goya, Picasso, and, most of all, Degas—this is one of the only two U.S. institutions to hold the complete set of the artist's model bronzes (the other is New York's Metropolitan Museum of Art). Renaissance, baroque, and rococo masterpieces include Raphael's profoundly spiritual *Madonna with Child with Book* (1503), Rembrandt's *Portrait of a Bearded Man in a Wide-Brimmed Hat* (1633), and a magical Tiepolo ceiling, *The Triumph of Virtue and Nobility Over Ignorance* (1740–50). The museum's collections of impressionist (Van Gogh, Matisse, Cézanne, Monet, Renoir) and cubist (Braque, Gris) works are extensive. Several Rodin sculptures are placed throughout the museum. Head down to the bottom floor to see rotating exhibits and phenomenal Southeast Asian and Indian sculptures and artifacts, where graceful pieces like a Ban Chiang blackware vessel date to well before 1000 BC. Don't miss a living artwork outdoors: the garden, conceived by noted southern California landscape designer Nancy Goslee Power. The tranquil pond was inspired by Monet's gardens at Giverny. ⊠ *411 W. Colorado Blvd., Pasadena* ☎ *626/449–6840* ⊕ *www.nortonsimon.org* 🔳 *$10, free 1st Fri. of month 6–9 pm* ⊘ *Wed., Thurs., and Sat.–Mon. noon–6, Fri. noon–9.*

WORTH NOTING

Gamble House. Built by Charles and Henry Greene in 1908, this is a spectacular example of American Arts and Crafts bungalow architecture. The term *bungalow* can be misleading, since the Gamble House is a huge three-story home. To wealthy Easterners such as the Gambles (as in Procter & Gamble), this type of vacation home seemed informal compared with their mansions back home. What makes admirers swoon is the incredible amount of handcraftsmanship, including a teak staircase and cabinetry, Greene and Greene–designed furniture, and an Emil Lange glass door. The dark exterior has broad eaves, with sleeping porches on the second floor. An hour-long, docent-led tour of the Gamble's interior will draw your eye to the exquisite details. If you want to see more Greene and Greene homes, buy a self-guided tour map of the neighborhood in the bookstore. ⊠ *4 Westmoreland Pl., Pasadena* ☎ *626/793-3334* ⊕ *www. gamblehouse.org* 🔳 *$10* ⊘ *Thur.–Sun. noon–3; tickets go on sale Thur.– Sat. at 10, Sun. at 11:30. 1-hr tour every 15–30 min.*

Old Town Pasadena. Once the victim of decay, the area was revitalized in the 1990s as a blend of restored 19th-century brick buildings with a contemporary overlay. A phalanx of chain stores has muscled in, but there are still some homegrown shops and plenty of tempting cafés and restaurants. In the evening and on weekends, streets are packed with people, and Old Town crackles with energy. The 12-block historic district is anchored along Colorado Boulevard between Pasadena Avenue and Arroyo Parkway.

Rose Bowl. With an enormous rose, the city of Pasadena's logo, adorned on its exterior, it's hard to miss this 100,000-seat stadium, host of many Super Bowls and home to the UCLA Bruins. Set in Brookside Park at the wide bottom of an arroyo, the facility is closed except during games and special events. ⊠ *1001 Rose Bowl Dr., at Rosemont Ave., Pasadena* ☎ *626/577–3100* ⊕ *www.rosebowlstadium.com.*

Rose Bowl Flea Market. One such special event is the monthly Rose Bowl Flea Market, which is considered the granddaddy of West Coast flea markets. If you want the best selection of items, show up early. People start arriving here at the crack of dawn, but note you will also pay a higher entry fee for having first dibs on the selection. The best bargaining takes place at the end of the day when vendors would rather settle for a little less cash than have to lug their goods home. ⊠ *Pasadena* ⊕ *www.rgcshows.com* ⊡ *$8 from 9 am on, $10 for 8–9 am entrance, $15 for 7–8 am entrance* ☉ *Flea market 2nd Sun. of month 9–3.*

BEACHES

Los Angeles County beaches (and state beaches operated by the county) have lifeguards on duty year-round, with expanded forces during the summer. Public parking is usually available, though fees can range anywhere from $8 to $20; in some areas, it's possible to find free street and highway parking. Both restrooms and beach access have been brought up to the standards of the Americans with Disabilities Act. Generally, the northernmost beaches are best for surfing, hiking, and fishing, and the wider and sandier southern beaches are better for tanning and relaxing. ■TIP➔ **Almost all are great for swimming in warmer months, but beware: pollution in Santa Monica Bay sometimes approaches dangerous levels, particularly after storms.**

Redondo Beach. The Redondo Beach Pier marks the starting point of this wide, sandy, busy beach along a heavily developed shoreline community. Restaurants and shops flourish along the pier, excursion boats and privately owned crafts depart from launching ramps, and a reef formed by a sunken ship creates prime fishing and snorkeling conditions. If you're adventurous, you might try to kayak out to the buoys and hobnob with pelicans and sea lions. A series of free rock and jazz concerts takes place at the pier every summer. **Amenities:** food and drink; lifeguards; parking; showers; toilets; water sports. **Best for:** snorkeling; sunset; swimming; walking. ⊠ *Torrance Blvd. at Catalina Ave., Redondo Beach* ☎ *310/372–2166.*

CLOSE UP

Surf City

Nothing captures the laid-back cool of California quite like surfing. Those wanting to sample the surf here should keep a few things in mind before getting wet. First, surfers can be notoriously territorial. Beginners should avoid Palos Verdes and Third Point, at the north end of Malibu Lagoon State Beach, where veterans rule the waves. Once in the water, be as polite and mellow as possible. Give other surfers plenty of space—do *not* cut them off—and avoid swimmers. Beware of rocks and undertows. Surfing calls for caution: that huge piece of flying fiberglass beneath you could kill someone. If you're not a strong swimmer, think twice before jumping in; fighting the surf to where the waves break is a strenuous proposition. The best and safest way to learn

is by taking a lesson. A wet suit is a must most of the year.

When you hit the surfing hot spots, surf shops with rentals will be in long supply. Competition keeps prices comparable; most rent long and short boards and miniboards (kid-size surfboards) from $20 per day and wet suits from $10 per day (some give discounts for additional days).

Learners should never surf in a busy area; look for somewhere less crowded where you'll catch more waves anyway. Good beaches for beginners are Santa Monica State Beach, Malibu Lagoon State Beach, and Huntington City Beach north of the pier, but you should always check conditions, which change throughout the day, before heading into the water.

Fodor's Choice
★ **Robert H. Meyer Memorial State Beach.** Part of Malibu's most beautiful coastal area, this beach is made up of three minibeaches: El Pescador, La Piedra, and El Matador—all with the same spectacular view. Scramble down the steps to the rocky coves via steep, steep stairways; all food and water needs to be toted as there are no services. Portable toilets at the trailhead are the only restrooms. "El Mat" has a series of caves, Piedra some nifty rock formations, and Pescador a secluded feel; but they're all picturesque and fairly private. **Amenities:** lifeguards (summer weekends); parking; toilets. **Best for:** solitude; sunset; surfing; walking. ■**TIP→** One warning: watch the incoming tide and don't get trapped between those otherwise scenic boulders. ⊠ *32350, 32700, and 32900 PCH, Malibu* ☎ *818/880–0363* ⊕ *www.parks.ca.gov.*

Santa Monica State Beach. It's the first beach you'll hit after the Santa Monica Freeway (I–10) runs into the PCH, and it's one of L.A.'s best known. Wide and sandy, Santa Monica is *the* place for sunning and socializing: be prepared for a mob scene on summer weekends, when parking becomes an expensive ordeal. Swimming is fine (with the usual post-storm pollution caveat); for surfing, go elsewhere. For a memorable view, climb up the stairway over the PCH to Palisades Park, at the top of the bluffs. Free summer-evening concerts are held Thursday nights on the pier. **Amenities:** food and drink; lifeguards; parking; showers; toilets; water sports. **Best for:** sunset; surfing; swimming; walking. ⊠ *1642 Promenade, PCH at California Incline, Santa Monica* ☎ *310/458–8573* ⊕ *www.smgov.net/Portals/Beach* ▨ *$10 parking* ☞ *Parking, lifeguard (year-round), restrooms, showers.*

Will Rogers State Beach. This clean, sandy, 3-mile beach, with a dozen volleyball nets, gymnastics equipment, and playground equipment for kids, is an all-around favorite. The surf is gentle, perfect for swimmers and beginning surfers. However, it's best to avoid the place after a storm, when untreated water flows from storm drains into the sea. **Amenities:** food and drink; lifeguards; parking; showers; toilets. **Best for:** sunset; swimming; walking. ⊠ *17700 PCH, 2 miles north of Santa Monica Pier, Pacific Palisades* 🕾 *310/305–9503* ⊕ *www.parks.ca.gov* ⊒ *$12 parking.*

Zuma Beach Park. This 2-mile stretch of white sand, usually dotted with tanning teenagers, has it all: from fishing and kite surfing to swings for the kids to volleyball courts. Beachgoers looking for quiet or privacy should head elsewhere. Stay alert in the water: the surf is rough and inconsistent. **Amenities:** food and drink; lifeguards; parking; showers; toilets. **Best for:** partiers; sunset; swimming; walking. ⊠ *30000 Pacific Coast Highway, Malibu* 🕾 *310/305–9503* ⊕ *beaches.lacounty.gov* ⊒ *$10 parking.*

WHERE TO EAT

Dining out in Los Angeles tends to be a casual affair, and even at some of the most expensive restaurants you're likely to see customers in jeans (although this is not necessarily considered in good taste). Despite its veneer of decadence, L.A. is not a particularly late-night city for eating (the reenergized Hollywood dining scene is emerging as a notable exception). The peak dinner times are from 7 to 9, and most restaurants won't take reservations after 10 pm. Generally speaking, restaurants are closed either Sunday or Monday; a few are shuttered both days. Most places—even the upscale spots—are open for lunch on weekdays, when Hollywood megadeals are conceived.

Prices in the restaurant reviews are the average cost of a main course at dinner or, if dinner is not served, at lunch (excluding sales tax). Use the coordinate (✛ 1:A1) at the end of each listing to locate a site on the corresponding map.

DOWNTOWN WITH LOS FELIZ AND SILVER LAKE

DOWNTOWN

$ ✕ **Baco Mercat.** Chef Josef Centeno, previously at Lazy Ox Canteen,
AMERICAN originally came up with the baco, a flatbread sandwich, as a late-night snack for friends. The once off-menu, carnitas-stuffed dish now steals the spotlight at this brilliant Downtown newcomer; so does the mint and basil-dusted okra, cocà flatbread pizza topped with mushrooms and fontina, and housemade orange-juniper soda pop. Centeno recently opened a second spot, Bar Ama, also in Downtown. ⑤ *Average main: $14* ⊠ *408 S. Main St.* 🕾 *213/687-8808* ⊕ *www.bacomercat.com* ⩜ *Reservations essential* ✛ *1:C3.*

$$ ✕ **Bottega Louie.** This former Brooks Brother's suit store was reincarnated
ITALIAN into a lively Italian restaurant and gourmet market in 2008 and quickly
Fodor's Choice crowned Downtown's new culinary darling. Vast open space, stark
★ white walls and long windows that stretch from floor to ceiling give it

a grand and majestic appeal. An army of stylish servers weave in-and-out of the crowds carrying bowls of pasta, trays of bubbly Prosecco and thin-crust pizzas. Pick and choose from a bevy of salads, pastas, pizzas and entrées that range from shrimp scampi to a hearty New York strip steak. Or simply order from its small plates menu with favorites: asparagus with fried egg, burrata and roasted vine tomatoes, tomato bruschetta, and fried calamari. Don't let the crowd of people waiting for a table deter you, order a cocktail from the bar, peruse the gourmet *patisserie*, and nibble on a brightly colored macaroon. $ *Average main: $18 ⊠ 700 S. Grand Ave. ☎ 213/802–1470 ⊕ www.bottegalouie.com ⌂ Reservations not accepted ⊕ 1:A3.*

$$$$
FRENCH
✕ **Patina.** Formed by chef Joachim Splichal, the Patina Group's flagship restaurant has Downtown's most striking address: inside the Frank Gehry–designed Walt Disney Concert Hall. The contemporary space, surrounded by a rippled "curtain" of rich walnut, is an elegant, dramatic stage for the acclaimed restaurant's contemporary French cuisine. Seasonally changing specialties include copious amounts of foie gras, butter-poached lobster, and medallions of venison served with lady apples. Finish with a hard-to-match cheese tray (orchestrated by a genuine *maître fromager*) and the elegant fromage blanc soufflé served with house-made bourbon ice cream. $ *Average main: $46 ⊠ Walt Disney Concert Hall, 141 S. Grand Ave. ☎ 213/972–3331 ⊕ www. patinagroup.com ⌂ Reservations essential ⊗ Closed Mon. ⊕ 1:B2*

$ ✕ **Philippe the Original.** L.A.'s oldest restaurant (1908), Philippe claims
AMERICAN that the French dip sandwich originated here. You can get one made
FAMILY with beef, pork, ham, lamb, or turkey on a freshly baked roll; the house
Fodor'sChoice hot mustard is as famous as the sandwiches. Its reputation is earned by
★ maintaining traditions, from sawdust on the floor to long communal
tables where customers debate the Dodgers or local politics. The home
cooking—orders are taken at the counter where some of the motherly
servers have managed their long lines for decades—includes huge breakfasts, chili, pickled eggs, and a generous pie selection. The best bargain:
a cup of java for 49¢. ⑤ *Average main: $7* ⊠ *1001 N. Alameda St.*
☎ *213/628–3781* ⊕ *www.philippes.com* ⚘ *Reservations not accepted*
⊟ *No credit cards* ✣ *1:D3.*

LOS FELIZ

$$ ✕ **Little Dom's.** With a $15 Monday night supper, a vintage bar with a bar-
ITALIAN keep who mixes up seasonally inspired retro cocktails, and an attached
Fodor'sChoice Italian deli where one can pick up a pork cheek sub, it's not surprising
★ why Little Dom's is a neighborhood favorite. Cozy and inviting with big
leather booths one can sink into for the night, Little Dom's has a menu
that blends classic Italian fare with a modern sensibility, with dishes like
the baked ricotta and wild boar soppressatta, rigatoni with homemade
sausage, whitefish picatta, and a New York strip steak with fennel béar-
naise. This is a terrific spot for weekend brunch; order a bottle of the
well-priced house wine and take a seat in the sidewalk patio. ⑤ *Average
main: $24* ⊠ *2128 Hillhurst Ave.* ☎ *323/661–0055* ⊕ *www.littledoms.
com* ⚘ *Reservations essential* ✣ *2:F1.*

$ ✕ **Yuca's Hut.** Blink and you can miss this place, whose reputation far
MEXICAN exceeds its size (it may be the tiniest place to have ever won a James
FAMILY Beard award). It's known for *carne asada*, carnitas, and *cochinita pibil*
Fodor'sChoice (Yucatán-style roasted pork) tacos, burritos, and banana leaf–wrapped
★ tamales (Sat. only). This is a fast-food restaurant in the finest tradition—
independent, family-owned, and sticking to what it does best. The liquor
store next door sells lots of Coronas to Yuca's customers soaking up the
sun on the makeshift parking-lot patio. There's no chance of satisfying a
late-night craving, though; it closes at 6 pm. ⑤ *Average main: $10* ⊠ *2056
N. Hillhurst Ave.* ☎ *323/662–1214* ⊕ *www.yucasla.com* ⚘ *Reservations
not accepted* ⊟ *No credit cards* ☽ *Closed Sun. No dinner* ✣ *2:F1.*

SILVER LAKE

$ ✕ **Sqirl.** This little jam company that could, by self-taught owner Jes-
AMERICAN sica Koslow, took its pickle and preserves business brick and mortar in
December 2012. Foodies are now driving across town to Silver Lake
merely to have toast and jam there. That's saying a lot. The menu also
features brioche toasts with tomatillo purée, greens, and hot sauce, as
well as sweets like hazelnut cake and lemon meringue tarts. And who
doesn't love edible souvenirs such as strawberry rose geranium jam?
⑤ *Average main: $10* ⊠ *720 N Virgil Ave., Suite 4* ☎ *213/394–6526*
⊕ *sqirlla.com* ✣ *2:F2.*

4

BEST BETS FOR LOS ANGELES DINING

With thousands of restaurants to choose from, how will you decide where to eat? Fodor's writers and editors have selected their favorite restaurants by price and cuisine in the Best Bets lists below. You can also search by neighborhood—just peruse the following pages to find specific details about a restaurant in the full reviews later in the chapter.

Fodor'sChoice★

Angelini Osteria, $$$, p. 204
A.O.C. $$$, p. 205
The Apple Pan, $, p. 206
Bouchon Bistro, $$$, p. 203
Bottega Louie, $$, p. 195
Cube Café and Marketplace, $$, p. 201
Little Dom's, $$, p. 197
Philippe the Original, $, p. 197
Pizzeria Mozza, $$, p. 201
Providence, $$$$, p. 202
Urasawa, $$$$, p. 204
Yuca's Hut, $, p. 197

By Price

$

The Apple Pan, p. 206
Artisan Cheese Gallery, p. 202
Father's Office, p. 207
Little Flower Candy Company, p. 208
Philippe the Original, p. 197
Pink's Hot Dogs, p. 201
Porto's Bakery, p. 199
Venice Beach Wines, p. 208
Yuca's Hut, p. 197
Zankou Chicken, p. 202

$$

Bottega Louie, p. 195
Cube Café and Marketplace, p. 201
Gjelina, p. 208
Little Dom's, p. 197
Pizzeria Mozza, p. 201

$$$

Angelini Osteria, p. 204
Animal, p. 199
A.O.C., p. 205
Bouchon Bistro, p. 203
Oliverio, p. 204
Osteria Mozza, p. 201

$$$$

The Bazaar by José Andrés, p. 202
Gordon Ramsay at The London, p. 205
Providence, p. 202
Urasawa, p. 204

By Cuisine

AMERICAN

The Apple Pan, $, p. 206
Gjelina, $$, p. 208
Philippe the Original, $, p. 197
Pink's Hot Dogs, $, p. 201

CHINESE

Mandarette, $, p. 206

ITALIAN

Angelini Osteria, $$$, p. 204
Cube Café and Marketplace, $$, p. 201
Osteria Mozza, $$$, p. 201
Pizzeria Mozza, $$, p. 201
Valentino, $$$$, p. 208

JAPANESE

Urasawa, $$$$, p. 204

MEDITERRANEAN

A.O.C., $$$, p. 205
Cleo, $$$, p. 199

MEXICAN

Yuca's Hut, $, p. 197

SPANISH

The Bazaar by José Andrés, $$$$, p. 202

SEAFOOD

Providence, $$$$, p. 202

HOLLYWOOD, BURBANK, AND STUDIO CITY

BURBANK

$ ✕ **Porto's Bakery.** Waiting in line at Porto's is as much as part of the
CUBAN experience as is indulging in a roasted pork sandwich and chocolate-
FAMILY dipped croissant. Locals love this neighborhood bakery and café that
has been an L.A. staple for more than 50 years. This is its second location, just minutes away from the studios; it's a great spot to take a
stroll and peruse the consignment shops run by former movie stylists.
The crowded café bustles with an ambitious lunch crowd, but counter
service is quick and efficient. Go for one of its tasty Cuban sandwiches
like the *medianoche* or the *pan con lechon* (roasted pork) sandwich,
or try the filling *ropa vieja* (shredded beef) plate. Skipping dessert here
would just be wrong. Your sweet tooth will thank you later. ⑤ *Average main: $10* ⊠ *3614 W. Magnolia Blvd.* ☎ *818/846–9100* ⊕ *www.
portosbakery.com* ✢ *2:E1.*

HOLLYWOOD

$$$ ✕ **Animal.** When foodies in Los Angeles need a culinary thrill, they come
AMERICAN to this minimalist restaurant in the Fairfax District, which is light on
the flash but heavy on serious food. The James Beard award–winning
restaurant is owned by Jon Shook and Vinny Dotolo, two young chefs
who shot to fame with a stint on *Iron Chef* and later with their own
Food Network show, *Two Dudes Catering.* With a closing time of 1 am,
the small restaurant is an L.A. anomaly. The restaurant's diverse clien-
tele ranges from neighborhood dwellers to young Hollywood celebrities
to food snobs in search of their new favorite dish. The changing daily
menu consists of small plates and entrées that make it easy to explore
many items, like barbecue pork belly sandwiches, *poutine* with oxtail
gravy, foie gras *loco moco* (a hamburger topped with foie gras, quail
egg, and Spam), and grilled quail served with plum *char-siu.* For des-
sert, the house specialty is a multilayered bacon-chocolate crunch bar.
⑤ *Average main: $25* ⊠ *435 N. Fairfax Ave.* ☎ *323/782–9225* ⊕ *www.
animalrestaurant.com* ⚑ *Reservations essential* ◯ *No lunch* ✢ *2:C2.*

$$$ ✕ **Cleo.** Hollywood's nightlife and revitalized dining landscape continues
MEDITERRANEAN to thrive, especially with spots like this hip Mediterranean restaurant
that pays homage to Cleopatra. Tucked away in the newly revamped
Redbury Hotel, Cleo bumps with energy and life in both its ambience
as well as its fresh approach to Mediterranean cuisine. Small-plate offerings allow for plenty of sampling. Start with a trio of dips including
hummus with tahini, *lebaneh* (thick yogurt) with feta, and *muhammara*
(walnut garlic spread) that comes with fresh-from-the-oven flatbread.
Chicken and lamb kebabs are an ideal segue into the proteins, as is a
perfectly roasted lamb shank or moussaka made with eggplant, beef
ragù, and feta, and sprinkled with pine nuts. Get your veggie allowance
with the Brussels sprouts made with capers, parsley, and almonds, or
mushrooms with hazelnuts and dates. The thoughtful cocktail menu,
decent wine list, and enthusiastic staff make Cleo a great place to spend
the evening—Hollywood style. ⑤ *Average main: $30* ⊠ *1717 Vine St.*
☎ *323/962–1711* ⊕ *www.cleorestaurant.com* ◯ *No lunch* ✢ *2:E1.*

4

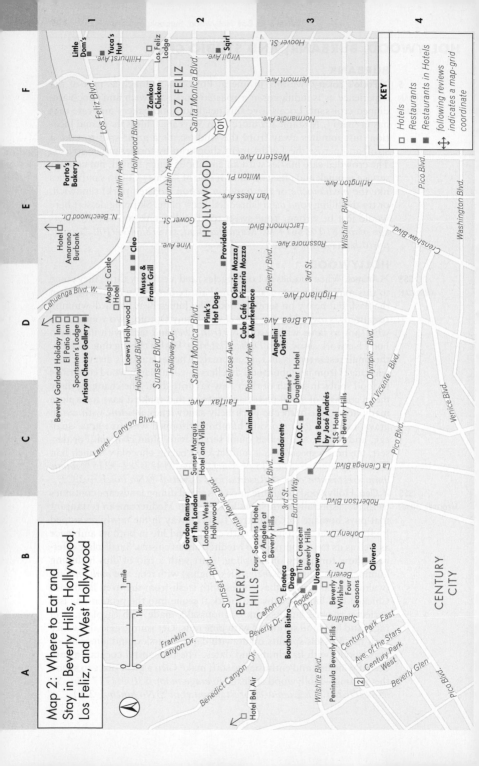

Map 2: Where to Eat and Stay in Beverly Hills, Hollywood, Los Feliz, and West Hollywood

KEY

☐ Hotels
■ Restaurants
■ Restaurants in Hotels
↔ following reviews indicates a map-grid coordinate

1 mile
1 km

Franklin Canyon Dr.

BEVERLY HILLS

CENTURY CITY

HOLLYWOOD

LOZ FELIZ

Benedict Canyon Dr.

Hotel Bel Air

Sunset Blvd.

Gordon Ramsay at The London
London West Hollywood

Santa Monica Blvd.

Laurel Canyon Blvd.

Cahuenga Blvd. W.

Beverly Garland Holiday Inn
El Patio Inn
Sportsmen's Lodge
Artisan Cheese Gallery

Hotel Amarano Burbank

Porto's Bakery

N. Beechwood Dr.

Franklin Ave.

Magic Castle Hotel
Loews Hollywood

Hollywood Blvd.

Cleo
Musso & Frank Grill

Hollywood Dr.

Holloway Dr.

Sunset Blvd.

Sunset Marquis Hotel and Villas

Santa Monica Blvd.

Four Seasons Hotel, Los Angeles at Beverly Hills

3rd St.

Burton Way

The Crescent Beverly Hills

Beverly Dr.

Cañon Dr.

Rodeo Dr.

Enoteca Drago
Bouchon Bistro
Urasawa

Beverly Wilshire Four Seasons

Spalding

Wilshire Blvd.

Peninsula Beverly Hills

Century Park East
Ave. of the Stars
Century Park West

Oliverio

Beverly Glen

Pico Blvd.

Beverly Blvd.

3rd St.

Animal

Mandarette

A.O.C.

The Bazaar by José Andrés
SLS Hotel at Beverly Hills

La Cienega Blvd.

Robertson Blvd.

Doherty Dr.

Beverly Dr.

San Vicente Blvd.

Olympic Blvd.

Pico Blvd.

Venice Blvd.

Fairfax Ave.

Melrose Ave.

Rosewood Ave.

Farmer's Daughter Hotel

Pink's Hot Dogs

Osteria Mozza/ Pizzeria Mozza

Cube Café & Marketplace

Angelini Osteria

La Brea Ave.

Highland Ave.

Beverly Blvd.

Rossmore Ave.

Larchmont Blvd.

3rd St.

Arlington Ave.

Wilshire Blvd.

Crenshaw Blvd.

Washington Blvd.

Pico Blvd.

Vine Ave.

Gower St.

N. Beechwood Dr.

Providence

Zankou Chicken

Hollywood Blvd.

Santa Monica Blvd.

Fountain Ave.

Van Ness Ave.

Wilton Pl.

Western Ave.

Normandie Ave.

Vermont Ave.

Hoover St.

101

Virgil Ave.

Squirl

Los Feliz Blvd.

Los Feliz Lodge

Little Dom's
Yuca's Hut
Hillhurst Ave.

$$
ITALIAN
Fodor'sChoice
★

✕ **Cube Café & Marketplace.** Cheese, charcuterie, and pasta lovers take heed: this dark and cozy Italian restaurant will ruin you for all the others. With more than 30 varieties of cheese, an enviable salami selection, pasta made in-house, and a passionate and earnest staff, this former pasta company turned upscale café and gourmet market is one of L.A.'s more affordable culinary gems. Take a seat at the cheese bar, order the cheesemonger's choice, and pair it with a glass of Italian wine. For dinner, order the antipasti of braised octopus, and then move onto the seasonally driven pasta dishes, like the English pea tortellini. $ *Average main: $22* ✉ *615 N. La Brea Blvd.* ☎ *323/939–1148* ⊕ *www.eatatcube.com* ☾ *Closed Sun.–Mon.* ✥ *2:D2.*

$$$
AMERICAN

✕ **Musso & Frank Grill.** Liver and onions, lamb chops, shrimp Louie salad, dry gin martinis, gruff waiters—you'll find all of the old favorites here in Hollywood's oldest restaurant. A film-industry hangout since it opened in 1919, Musso & Frank still attracts the working studio set to its maroon faux-leather booths, along with tourists and locals nostalgic for Hollywood's golden era. Great breakfasts are served all day, but the kitchen's famous "flannel cakes" (pancakes) are served only until 3 pm. $ *Average main: $30* ✉ *6667 Hollywood Blvd.* ☎ *323/467–7788* ⊕ *www.mussoandfrank.com* ☾ *Closed Sun.–Mon.* ✥ *2:D1.*

$$$
ITALIAN

✕ **Osteria Mozza.** Born from the immensely popular collaboration between celebrated bread maker Nancy Silverton (founder of L.A.'s La Brea Bakery), restaurateur Joe Bastianich, and Iron Chef Mario Batali, Osteria Mozza features candlelit, linen-clad tables surrounding a central marble-topped mozzarella bar, ideal for solo diners. From that bar come several presentations of velvety *burrata* cheese and perfectly dressed salads, while the kitchen turns out an oversize *raviolo* oozing ricotta and egg in brown butter sauce, blissful sweetbreads piccata, and grilled whole *orata* (Mediterranean sea bream), capped off with Italian cheeses and delicious rosemary–olive oil cakes. If you can't score a reservation here, treat yourself to the partners' pizzeria next door. $ *Average main: $34* ✉ *6602 Melrose Ave.* ☎ *323/297–0100* ⊕ *www.mozzarestaurantgroup.com* ⌦ *Reservations essential* ☾ *No lunch* ✥ *2:D2.*

$
AMERICAN
FAMILY

✕ **Pink's Hot Dogs.** Orson Welles ate 18 of these hot dogs in one sitting, and you, too, will be tempted to order more than one. The chili dogs are the main draw, but the menu has expanded to include a Martha Stewart Dog (a 10-inch frank topped with mustard, relish, onions, tomatoes, sauerkraut, bacon, and sour cream). Since 1939, Angelenos and tourists alike have been lining up to plunk down some modest change for one of the greatest guilty pleasures in L.A. Pink's is open until 3 am on weekends. $ *Average main: $4* ✉ *709 N. La Brea Ave.* ☎ *323/931–4223* ⊕ *www.pinkshollywood.com* ⌦ *Reservations not accepted* ▭ *No credit cards* ✥ *2:D2.*

$$
ITALIAN
Fodor'sChoice
★

✕ **Pizzeria Mozza.** The other, more casual half of Batali, Bastianich, and Silverton's partnership (the first being Osteria Mozza), this casual venue gives newfound eminence to the humble "pizza joint." With traditional Mediterranean items like white anchovies, lardo, squash blossoms, and Gorgonzola, Mozza's pies—thin-crusted delights with golden, blistered edges—are much more Campania than California, and virtually every

4

one is a winner. Antipasti include simple salads, roasted bone marrow, and platters of *salumi*. All sing with vibrant flavors thanks to superb market-fresh ingredients, and daily specials may include favorites like lasagna. Like the menu, the Italian-only wine list is both interesting and affordable. Walk-ins are welcomed for dining at the bar. Ⓢ *Average main: $20* ⊠ *641 N. Highland Ave.* ☎ *323/297–0101* ⊕ *www.pizzeriamozza.com* ⌕ *Reservations essential* ✛ *2:D2.*

$$$$
SEAFOOD
Fodor'sChoice
★

✗**Providence.** Chef-owner Michael Cimarusti has elevated Providence to the ranks of America's finest seafood restaurants. The elegant dining room, outfitted with subtle nautical accents, is smoothly overseen by co-owner–general manager Donato Poto. Obsessed with quality and freshness, the meticulous chef maintains a network of specialty purveyors, some of whom tip him off to their catch before it even hits the dock. This exquisite seafood then gets the Cimarusti treatment of French technique, traditional American themes, and Asian accents, often presented in elaborate tasting menus. Pastry chef David Rodriguez's exquisite desserts are not to be missed; consider the six-course dessert tasting menu. Ⓢ *Average main: $43* ⊠ *5955 Melrose Ave.* ☎ *323/460–4170* ⊕ *www.providencela.com* ⌕ *Reservations essential* ◷ *No lunch Mon.–Thurs. and weekends* ✛ *2:D2.*

$
MIDDLE EASTERN
FAMILY

✗**Zankou Chicken.** Forget the Colonel. Zankou's aromatic, Armenian-style rotisserie chicken with perfectly crisp, golden skin is one of L.A.'s truly great budget meals. It's served with pita bread, veggies, hummus, and unforgettable garlic sauce. If this doesn't do it for you, try the kebabs, falafel, or sensational *shawarma* (spit-roasted lamb or chicken) plates. Ⓢ *Average main: $9* ⊠ *5065 W. Sunset Blvd.* ☎ *323/665–7845* ⌕ *Reservations not accepted* ✛ *2:F2.*

STUDIO CITY

$
DELI
FAMILY

✗**Artisan Cheese Gallery.** Taste your way through triple creams, blues, goat's milk, and stinky cheeses from all over the globe at this charming locale that offers cheese and charcuterie plates, sandwiches, oversize salads, and hot panini sandwiches. Taste testing is encouraged, so don't be shy to ask. Grab a table on the small outdoor patio and enjoy the neighborhood scenery; it's a great way to experience the Valley. Ⓢ *Average main: $10* ⊠ *12023 Ventura Blvd.* ☎ *818/505–0207* ⊕ *www.artisancheesegallery.com* ⌕ *Reservations not accepted* ✛ *2:D1.*

BEVERLY HILLS AND THE WESTSIDE

BEVERLY HILLS

$$$$
SPANISH

✗**The Bazaar by José Andrés.** Celebrity Spanish chef José Andrés conquers L.A. with a multifaceted concept that includes two dining rooms (one classic, one modern, each with a tapas bar), a cocktail bar stocked with liquid nitrogen, and a flashy *pâtisserie*. There are even roaming pushcarts dispensing foie gras wrapped in cotton candy. Half the menu is dedicated to traditional Spanish tapas: creamy chicken *croquetas*, *bacalao* (salt cod) fritters with honey aïoli, and plates of chorizo or prized *jamón Ibérico* (Iberian ham). The other half involves some wild inventions of molecular gastronomy inspired by Andrés' mentor Ferran Adrià of world-famous El Bulli restaurant in Spain.

A feeling of refined elegance comes through in the food (and decor) at Patina, in Downtown Los Angeles.

Among the latter are "liquid" olives (created through a technique called spherification), and an ethereal version of the traditional tortilla Española in which an egg is cooked slowly at 63 degrees, just short of coagulation. A splendid list of Spanish wines is offered. For dessert, items like beet meringue with pistachios and chocolate lollipops await. $ *Average main: $36* ✉ *SLS Hotel at Beverly Hills, 465 S. La Cienega Blvd.* ☎ *310/246–5555* ⊕ *www.thebazaar.com* ⚏ *Reservations essential* ✛ *2:C3.*

$$$
FRENCH
Fodor's Choice
★

✕ **Bouchon Bistro.** Famed chef Thomas Keller finally made it back to Los Angeles and has set-up his French bistro in swanky Beverly Hills. Grand and majestic, but still casual and friendly, there is nothing about an afternoon or night at Bouchon that doesn't make you feel pampered. With little details that separate it from the pack, there's filtered Norwegian water served at every table, a twig-shaped baguette made fresh in the kitchen, and an expansive wine list celebrating California and French wines. It's a foodie scene that welcomes L.A.'s high-profile chefs, celebrities, and locals. Start with its classic onion soup that arrives with a bubbling lid of cheese or the salmon rillettes, which are big enough to share. For dinner, there's a traditional steak and frites, roasted chicken, steamed Maine mussels, and a delicious grilled *croque madame*. Bouchon Bistro is also known for its beautiful French pastries. For a sweet bite, order an espresso and the profiteroles or the Bouchons (bite-size brownies served with homemade vanilla ice cream). Special dining menus can come with a tour of the multimillion dollar kitchen. $ *Average main: $27* ✉ *235 N. Canon Dr.* ☎ *310/271–9910* ⊕ *www. bouchonbistro.com* ⚏ *Reservations essential* ✛ *2:B3.*

$ ✗ **Enoteca Drago.** High-flying Sicilian chef Celestino Drago scores with
ITALIAN this sleek but unpretentious version of an *enoteca* (a wine bar serving small snacks). It's an ideal spot for skipping through an Italian wine list—more than 50 wines are available by the glass—and enjoying a menu made up of small plates such as stuffed olives, an assortment of cheeses and *salumi,* ricotta-stuffed zucchini flowers, or *crudo* (Italy's answer to ceviche) from the raw bar. Although the miniature mushroom-filled ravioli bathed in foie gras–truffle sauce is a bit luxurious for an enoteca, it's one of the city's best pasta dishes. Larger portions and pizzas are also available here, but the essence of an enoteca is preserved. ⑤ *Average main: $17* ✉ *410 N. Cañon Dr.* ☎ *310/786–8236* ⊕ *www. celestinodrago.com* ⌖ *Reservations essential* ⊘ *Closed Sun.* ✛ *2:B3.*

$$$ ✗ **Oliverio.** This restaurant in the Avalon Hotel, an eco-friendly prop-
ITALIAN erty in a renovated 1950s apartment complex, feels straight out of the *Valley of the Dolls* movie. Midcentury design gives vintage appeal that blends in with the restaurant's modern Italian cuisine and Californian sensibility. Fresh food concepts are created by chef Mirko Paderno who favors seasonal ingredients. Enjoy a starter of fritto misto or a cauliflower soufflé; for dinner try the classic chicken diavolo, beef short ribs, or a risotto Milanese. Private poolside cabanas are a favorite for celebratory occasions. ⑤ *Average main: $25* ✉ *9400 W. Olympic Ave.* ☎ *310/277–5221* ⊕ *www.avalonbeverlyhills.com* ✛ *2:B4.*

$$$$ ✗ **Urasawa.** Shortly after celebrated sushi chef Masa Takayama packed
JAPANESE his knives for the Big Apple, his soft-spoken protégé Hiroyuki Urasawa
Fodor's Choice settled into the master's former digs. The understated sushi bar has few
★ precious seats, resulting in incredibly personalized service. At a minimum of $375 per person for a strictly *omakase* (chef's choice) meal, Urasawa remains the priciest restaurant in town, but the endless parade of masterfully crafted, exquisitely presented dishes renders few regrets. The maple sushi bar, sanded daily to a satin-like finish, is where most of the action happens. You might be served velvety bluefin toro paired with beluga caviar, slivers of foie gras to self-cook *shabu shabu* style, or egg custard layered with *uni* (sea urchin), glittering with gold leaf. This is also the place to come during *fugu* season, when the legendary, potentially deadly blowfish is artfully served to adventurous diners. ⑤ *Average main: $375* ✉ *2 Rodeo, 218 N. Rodeo Dr.* ☎ *310/247–8939* ⌖ *Reservations essential* ⊘ *Closed Sun. and Mon. No lunch.* ✛ *2:B3.*

WEST HOLLYWOOD

$$$ ✗ **Angelini Osteria.** You might not guess it from the modest, rather con-
ITALIAN gested dining room, but this is one of L.A.'s most celebrated Italian
Fodor's Choice restaurants. The key is chef-owner Gino Angelini's thoughtful use of
★ superb ingredients, evident in dishes such as a salad of baby greens, Gorgonzola, and pear; and pumpkin tortelli with butter, sage, and asparagus. An awesome lasagna verde, inspired by Angelini's grandmother, is not to be missed. Whole branzino, crusted in sea salt, and boldly flavored rustic specials (e.g., tender veal kidneys, rich oxtail stew) consistently impress. An intelligent selection of mostly Italian wines complements the menu. ⑤ *Average main: $32* ✉ *7313 Beverly Blvd.* ☎ *323/297–0070* ⊕ *www.angeliniosteria.com* ⌖ *Reservations essential* ⊘ *Closed Mon. No lunch weekends* ✛ *2:D3.*

CLOSE UP

Local Chains Worth Stopping For

It's said that the drive-in burger joint was invented in L.A., probably to meet the demands of an ever-mobile car culture. Burger aficionados line up at all hours outside **In-N-Out Burger** (⊕ www.in-n-out.com, multiple locations), still a family-owned operation whose terrific made-to-order burgers are revered by Angelenos. Visitors may recognize the chain as the infamous spot where Paris Hilton got nabbed for drunken driving, but locals are more concerned with getting their burger fix off the "secret" menu, with variations like "Animal Style" (mustard-grilled patty with grilled onions and extra spread), a "4 x 4" (four burger patties and four cheese slices, for big eaters) or the bun-less "Protein Style" that comes wrapped in Bibb lettuce. The company's website lists explanations for other popular secret menu items.

Tommy's sells a delightfully sloppy chili burger; the original location

(✉ 2575 Beverly Blvd., Westlake ☎ 213/389–9060) is a no-frills 24/7 culinary landmark. For rotisserie chicken that will make you forget the Colonel forever, head to **Zankou Chicken** (✉ 5065 Sunset Blvd., Hollywood ☎ 323/665–7845), noted for its golden crispy-skinned birds, potent garlic sauce, and Armenian specialties. Homesick New Yorkers will appreciate **Jerry's Famous Deli** (✉ 10925 Weyburn Ave., Westwood ☎ 310/208–3354 ⊕ www.jerrysfamousdeli.com), where the massive menu includes all the classic deli favorites. With a lively bar scene, good barbecued ribs, and contemporary takes on old favorites, the more upscale **Houston's** (✉ 202 Wilshire Blvd., Santa Monica ☎ 310/576–7558 ⊕ www.hillstone.com) is a popular local hangout. And **Señor Fish** (✉ 422 E. 1st St., Downtown ☎ 213/625–0566 ⊕ www.senor-fish.net) is known for its healthy Mexican seafood specialties, such as scallop burritos and seviche tostadas.

4

$$$
MEDITERRANEAN
Fodor'sChoice
★

✗ **A.O.C.** Since it opened in 2002, this restaurant and wine bar has revolutionized dining in L.A., pioneering the small-plate format that has now swept the city. The space is dominated by a long, candle-laden bar serving more than 50 wines by the glass. There's also a charcuterie bar, an L.A. rarity. The tapas-like menu is perfectly calibrated for the wine list; you could pick duck confit, lamb roulade with mint pistou, an indulgent slice of ricotta tartine, or just plunge into one of the city's best cheese selections. Named for the acronym for Appellation d'Origine Contrôlée, the regulatory system that ensures the quality of local wines and cheeses in France, A.O.C. upholds the standard of excellence. ⑤ *Average main: $35* ✉ *8022 W. 3rd St.* ☎ *323/653–6359* ⊕ *www.aocwinebar.com* ⚐ *Reservations essential* ⊗ *No lunch Mon.–Fri.* ✛ *2:C3.*

$$$$
FRENCH

✗ **Gordon Ramsay at the London.** The foul-mouthed celebrity chef from Fox's *Hell's Kitchen* demonstrates why he nevertheless ranks among the world's finest chefs at this fine-dining restaurant in a West Hollywood boutique hotel. Two pastel-color dining rooms with city views flank a formidable white marble bar, creating a space that feels trendy yet surprisingly unpretentious. A menu of small plates accommodates both light suppers and indulgent feasts alike. Highlights include Ramsay's signature

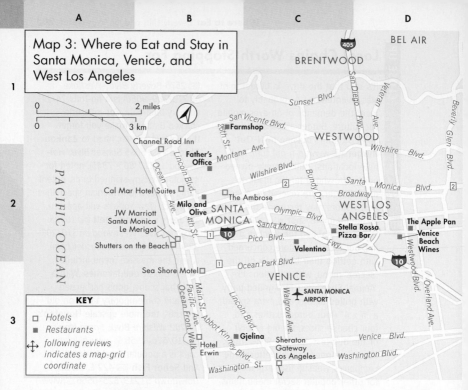

Map 3: Where to Eat and Stay in
Santa Monica, Venice, and
West Los Angeles

KEY

☐ *Hotels*

■ *Restaurants*

✛ *following reviews
indicates a map-grid
coordinate*

beef Wellington for two, filet mignon and braised short ribs, and a Maine lobster with coconut froth and mushroom ravioli. To maximize the experience, consider one of the flexible tasting menus ($120 on average), artfully crafted by Ramsay's local culinary team and orchestrated by a polished, gracious serving staff. ⑤ *Average main: $38* ⊠ *The London, 1020 N. San Vicente Blvd.* ☎ *310/358–7788* ⊕ *www.thelondonwesthollywood.com/gordon-ramsay* ♨ *Reservations essential* ✛ 2:C2.

$ ✕ **Mandarette.** Clad in warm wood and copper finishes, this inviting café

CHINESE began as a casual spin-off of the Mandarin in Beverly Hills, but the casual

FAMILY concept has outlasted its high-end originator. Start with chicken salad with red ginger, scallion pancakes, or shrimp dumplings before indulging in *kung pao* scallops or crispy sesame beef. ⑤ *Average main: $17* ⊠ *8386 Beverly Blvd.* ☎ *323/655–6115* ⊕ *www.mandarettecafe.com* ✛ 2:C3.

WEST LOS ANGELES

$ ✕ **The Apple Pan.** A burger-insider haunt since 1947, this unassuming joint

AMERICAN with a horseshoe-shaped counter—no tables here—turns out one heck of

Fodor's Choice a good burger topped with Tillamook cheddar, plus an excellent hickory

★ burger with barbecue sauce. You can also find great fries and, of course, an apple pie indulgent enough to christen the restaurant (although many regulars argue that the banana cream deserves the honor). Be prepared to wait, but the veteran countermen turn the stools at a quick pace. In the meantime, grab a cup of Sanka and enjoy a little L.A. vintage. ⑤ *Average main: $10* ⊠ *10801 W. Pico Blvd.* ☎ *310/475–3585* ♨ *Reservations not accepted* ▭ *No credit cards* ⊘ *Closed Mon.* ✛ 3:D2.

SANTA MONICA AND VENICE

SANTA MONICA

$ | AMERICAN

✗ Farmshop. Tucked away inside the Brentwood Country Mart, the new seasonal and California-inspired culinary darling Farmshop was invented by Jeffrey Cerciello, formerly the culinary director of Thomas Keller's casual restaurants. The Southern California native brought a little Napa Valley home with this classic spot that pays attention to the details but also keeps things refreshingly simple. Breads and pastries are made on-site daily, which is one detail that makes breakfast epic. Order the buttermilk biscuits served with quince preserves, French toast with pear marmalade and raisins, and the shirred eggs with wild greens, fennel cream, and flavorful sourdough toast. Lunch is an assortment of farm-fresh salads, soups, and sandwiches. Try the warm Dungeness crab salad made with butter lettuce, sunchokes, and curly mustard greens, or the smoked salmon tartine dressed with caper berries and pickled vegetables on rye bread. $ *Average main: $14* ✉ *225 26th St.* ☎ *310/566–2400* ⊕ *www.farmshopla.com* ✛ *3:B2.*

$ | AMERICAN

✗ Father's Office. With a facade distinguished only by a vintage neon sign, Father's Office is a congested, gentrified pub famous for hand-crafted beers and what has been called L.A.'s best burger. Topped with Gruyère and Maytag blue cheeses, arugula, caramelized onions, and applewood-smoked bacon compote, the "Office Burger" is a guilty pleasure worth waiting in line for (which is usually required). Other options include steak frites and Spanish tapas, with side orders of addictive sweet potato fries served in a miniature shopping cart with aioli—don't even think of asking for ketchup, because FO enforces a strict no-substitutions policy. So popular is the Office Burger that chef-owner Sang Yoon opened a second location in Culver City. Note: Because Father's Office is a bar, it's strictly 21 and older. $ *Average main: $15* ✉ *1018 Montana Ave.* ☎ *310/393–2337* ⊕ *www.fathersoffice.com* ✍ *Reservations not accepted* ◷ *No lunch weekdays* ✛ *3:B2.*

$ | AMERICAN

✗ Milo and Olive. The latest project by husband-wife team Josh Loeb and Zoe Nathan (behind Rustic Canyon Wine Bar & Seasonal Kitchen, Huckleberry Cafe & Bakery, and Sweet Rose Creamery), this 30-seat bakery-cum-restaurant in Santa Monica has locals lining up for breakfast (think dill crème fraîche-smeared bagels topped with cucumbers and cherry tomatoes) and lunch (chopped salads, wood-fired pizzas). Leave room for a sweet finish, including maple walnut sticky buns and pistachio olive oil cake. ■TIP➜ **There's usually a 10-to-40-minute wait for a table.** $ *Average main: $16* ✉ *2723 Wilshire Blvd.* ☎ *310/453-6776* ⊕ *www.miloandolive.com* ✍ *Reservations not accepted* ✛ *3:B2.*

$ | PIZZA

✗ Stella Rossa Pizza Bar. The loft-like interior and open kitchen at this artisanal pizza joint lend ample casualness, the location along Main Street can't be beat, and the food—from crusty shaved mushroom with Gruyère and the housemade sausage with oregano pies—really makes a statement. It's no surprise the restaurant goes through 300 pounds of dough each day (you'll see jars of dough fermenting on the white-brick, open-kitchen counter). Don't leave without ordering their signature grilled grapes with burrata side. Wines are paired well and priced fairly. $ *Average main: $15* ✉ *2000 Main St.* ☎ *310/396–9250* ⊕ *www. stellarossapizzabar.com* ✛ *3:C2.*

$$$$
ITALIAN

✘ **Valentino.** Renowned as one of the country's top Italian restaurants, Valentino has a truly awe-inspiring wine list. With nearly 2,800 labels consuming 130 pages, backed by a cellar overflowing with more than 80,000 bottles, this restaurant is nothing short of heaven for serious oenophiles. In the 1970s, suave owner Piero Selvaggio introduced L.A. to his exquisite modern Italian cuisine, and he continues to impress guests with dishes like a timballo of wild mushrooms with rich Parmigiano-Reggiano–saffron *fonduta*, a fresh risotto with farmers' market vegetables, a memorable osso buco, and sautéed branzino with lemon emulsion. A welcome addition to this exalted venue is its more casual wine bar for wine tasting and nibbles like *crudo* and carpaccio. $ *Average main: $40* ✉ *3115 Pico Blvd.* ☎ *310/829–4313* ⊕ *www. valentinosantamonica.com* ⌂ *Reservations essential* ⊘ *No lunch Sat. and Mon.–Thurs. Closed Sun.* ✛ *3:C2.*

VENICE

$$
AMERICAN

✘ **Gjelina.** This handsome restaurant comes alive with personality the minute you walk through its oversize, rustic wooden door. There are long communal tables, hanging light fixtures that soften the room and make it glow, and an outdoor patio. The menu is smart and seasonal with small plates, cheese and charcuterie, pastas, and pizza. Begin with a mushroom, goat cheese, and truffle oil pizza, heirloom spinach salad, mussels with chorizo, or grilled squid with lentils and salsa verde. For the main course, there's the duck leg confit or the Niman Ranch hanger steak with watercress salsa verde. Typically crowded and noisy, the outdoor patio is the spot. However, service is not on par with the setting. $ *Average main: $22* ✉ *1429 Abbot Kinney Blvd.* ☎ *310/450–1429* ⊕ *www.gjelina.com* ⌂ *Reservations essential* ⊘ *Open until midnight daily* ✛ *3:B3.*

$
DELI

✘ **Venice Beach Wines.** Locals pack into this casual wine shop-cum-deli to share plates of charcuterie, cheese, and plenty of reds from all over the Golden State. It's a great spot to visit before a meal, after a meal, or *for* a meal. The menu features pressed sandwiches such as Brie and grape, chopped salads, and dozens of small starters such as mint pesto–infused hummus and bacon-wrapped dates. $ *Average main: $10* ✉ *529 Rose Ave.* ☎ *310/606–2529* ⊕ *www.venicebeachwines.com* ✛ *3:C2.*

PASADENA

$
CAFÉ
FAMILY

✘ **Little Flower Candy Co.** Just off-the-beaten-path of Old Town Pasadena sits this quaint café that charms the hearts and tastebuds of locals with its seasonally driven menu of sandwiches, salads, fresh soups, and incredible baked goods. The café is owned by Christine Moore, who made a name for herself in the candy world as a creator of addicting sea salt caramels and oversize sugar marshmallows. She opened shop a few years ago to sell her sweets and ended up also creating a neighborhood hub for northeast Los Angeles. The café is nestled up against the sloping hills for a small-town feel (even though Downtown L.A. is a few miles away). It's a terrific place to grab a coffee, a fresh berry pastry, or a light lunch before heading out for an afternoon of shopping. $ *Average main: $10 ⊠ 1424 W. Colorado Blvd.* ☎ *626/304–4800* ⊕ *www. littleflowercandyco.com* ⊙ *Closed Sun.* ✛ *1:B1.*

WHERE TO STAY

When looking for a hotel, don't write off the pricier establishments immediately. Price categories are determined by "rack rates"—the list price of a hotel room, which is usually discounted. Specials abound, particularly Downtown on the weekends. Many hotels have packages that include breakfast, theater tickets, spa services, or exotic rental cars. Pricing is very competitive, so always check out the hotel website in advance for current special offers. When making reservations, particularly last-minute ones, check the hotel's website for exclusive Internet specials or call the property directly.

Prices in the hotel reviews are the lowest cost of a standard double room in high season. Prices do not include taxes (as high as 14%, depending on the region). Use the coordinate (✛ 1:B2) at the end of each listing to locate a site on the corresponding map. For expanded reviews, facilities, and current deals, visit Fodors.com.

DOWNTOWN WITH LOS FELIZ

DOWNTOWN

$ 🏨 **Figueroa Hotel.** On the outside, it feels like Spanish colonial; on
HOTEL   the inside, this 12-story hotel, built in 1926, is a mix of Mexican, Mediterranean, and Moroccan styles, with earth tones, hand-glazed walls, and wrought-iron beds. **Pros:** a short walk to Nokia Theatre, L.A. Live, Convention Center; well-priced, great poolside bar. **Cons:** somewhat funky room decor; small bathrooms; gentrifying neighborhood. $ *Rooms from: $148 ⊠ 939 S. Figueroa St.* ☎ *213/627–8971, 800/421–9092* ⊕ *www.figueroahotel.com* ⚓ *285 rooms, 6 suites* ⊚ *No meals* ✛ *1:A3.*

$ 🏨 **Hilton Checkers Los Angeles.** Opened as the Mayflower Hotel in 1927,
HOTEL   Checkers retains much of its original character; its various-size rooms
Fodor's Choice   all have charming period details, although it also has contemporary
★   luxuries like pillow-top mattresses, coffeemakers, 24-hour room service, and plasma TVs. **Pros:** historic charm; business-friendly; rooftop pool and spa. **Cons:** no on-street parking; some rooms compact; urban setting. $ *Rooms from: $189 ⊠ 535 S. Grand Ave.* ☎ *213/624–0000, 800/445–8667* ⊕ *www.hiltoncheckers.com* ⚓ *188 rooms, 5 suites* ⊚ *No meals* ✛ *1:B2.*

$$$ 🏨 **Millennium Biltmore Hotel.** One of Downtown L.A.'s true treasures,
HOTEL   the gilded 1923 Beaux Arts masterpiece exudes ambience and history. **Pros:** historic character; famed filming location; club-level rooms have many hospitable extras. **Cons:** pricey ($40) valet parking; standard rooms are truly compact. $ *Rooms from: $359 ⊠ 506 S. Grand Ave.* ☎ *213/624–1011, 866/866–8086* ⊕ *www.millenniumhotels.com* ⚓ *635 rooms, 48 suites* ⊚ *No meals* ✛ *1:B3.*

$$ 🖭 **The Standard, Downtown L.A.** Built in 1955 as Standard Oil's company's
HOTEL headquarters, the building was completely revamped under the sharp
eye of owner André Balazs, giving it a sleek, cutting-edge feel. **Pros:**
on-site Rudy's barbershop for grooming; 24/7 coffee shop for dining;
rooftop pool and lounge for fun. **Cons:** disruptive party scene week-
ends and holidays; street noise; pricey valet parking. ⑤ *Rooms from:*
$245 ✉ *550 S. Flower St.* ☎ *213/892–8080* ⊕ *www.standardhotels.com*
↪ *171 rooms, 36 suites* ⦿ *No meals* ✛ *1:B2.*

LOS FELIZ

$ 🖭 **Los Feliz Lodge.** Checking into this bungalow-style lodge is like crash-
RENTAL ing at an eco-minded and artsy friend's place: you let yourself into
an apartment with fully stocked kitchen, washer and dryer, and a
communal patio. **Pros:** homey feel; walking distance to restaurants.
Cons: no on-site restaurant or pool. ⑤ *Rooms from: $150* ✉ *1507 N.*
Hoover St. ☎ *323/660–4150* ⊕ *www.losfelizlodge.com* ↪ *4 rooms*
⦿ *No meals* ✛ *2:F2.*

HOLLYWOOD AND THE STUDIOS

BURBANK

$$$ 🖭 **Hotel Amarano Burbank.** Close to Burbank's TV and movie studios,
HOTEL the smartly designed Amarano feels like a Beverly Hills boutique hotel.
Pros: boutique style in a Valley location; pleasant breakfast room. **Cons:**
Pass Avenue street noise. ⑤ *Rooms from: $365* ✉ *322 N. Pass Ave.*
☎ *818/842–8887, 888/956–1900* ⊕ *www.hotelamarano.com* ↪ *108*
rooms, 24 suites ⦿ *No meals* ✛ *2:E1.*

HOLLYWOOD

$$ 🖭 **Farmer's Daughter Hotel.** A favorite of *The Price Is Right* and *Ameri-*
HOTEL *can Idol* hopefuls (both TV shows tape at the CBS studios nearby), this
Fodor'sChoice motel has a tongue-in-cheek country style: rooms are upholstered in
★ blue gingham with denim bedspreads, and farm tools serve as art. **Pros:**
great central city location; across from the cheap eats of the Farmers
Market and The Grove's shopping and entertainment mix. **Cons:** pricey
restaurant; roadside motel-size rooms; shaded pool; less than stellar
service. ⑤ *Rooms from: $229* ✉ *115 S. Fairfax Ave., Farmers Market*
☎ *323/937–3930, 800/334–1658* ⊕ *www.farmersdaughterhotel.com*
↪ *63 rooms, 2 suites* ⦿ *No meals* ✛ *2:C3.*

$$ 🖭 **Magic Castle Hotel.** Close to the action (and traffic) of Hollywood,
HOTEL this former apartment building faces busy Franklin Avenue and is
FAMILY a quick walk to the nearby Red Line stop at Hollywood & High-
land. **Pros:** remarkably friendly and able staff; free Wi-Fi; good value.
Cons: traffic-y locale; no elevator; small bathrooms. ⑤ *Rooms from:*
$224 ✉ *7025 Franklin Ave.* ☎ *323/851–0800, 800/741–4915* ⊕ *www.*
magiccastlehotel.com ↪ *7 rooms, 36 suites* ⦿ *Breakfast* ✛ *2:D1.*

$$ 🖭 **Loews Hollywood.** Part of the massive Hollywood & Highland shop-
HOTEL ping and entertainment complex, this 20-story Renaissance is at the
FAMILY center of Hollywood's action. **Pros:** large rooms with new contempo-
Fodor'sChoice rary-styled furniture; Red Line Metro–station adjacent. **Cons:** corpo-
★ rate feeling; very touristy. ⑤ *Rooms from: $299* ✉ *1755 N. Highland*

The Rooftop Bar at The Standard, Downtown L.A., is a swanky place to enjoy a nightcap with a view.

Ave. ☎ *323/856–1200, 800/769–4774* ⊕ *www.loewshotels.com/en/ Hollywood-Hotel* ↩ *604 rooms, 33 suites* ⦿ *No meals* ✛ *2:D1.*

NORTH HOLLYWOOD

$
HOTEL
FAMILY

🖵 **The Beverly Garland Holiday Inn.** The Hollywood connection at this family-run, lodge-like hotel on seven acres starts in the lobby, where framed photos of hotel namesake actress Beverly Garland line the walls. **Pros:** large pool and play area; unpretentious and friendly feel; on-site Wi-Fi café. **Cons:** small bathrooms; touristy; $15 self-parking lot charge. $ *Rooms from: $159* ✉ *4222 Vineland Ave.* ☎ *818/980–8000, 800/238–3759* ⊕ *www.beverlygarland.com* ↩ *238 rooms, 17 suites* ⦿ *No meals* ✛ *2:D1.*

STUDIO CITY

$
HOTEL

🖵 **El Patio Inn.** Behind a classic hacineda-style adobe and neon-lighted facade, within sight of Universal Studios, El Patio Inn is a throwback to 1960s-era roadside motels. **Pros:** close to Universal Studios and a Metro line stop; Ventura Boulevard has an endless supply of restaurants; low rates. **Cons:** no pool; service matches the low rates; zero amenities. $ *Rooms from: $94* ✉ *11466 Ventura Blvd.* ☎ *818/508–5828* ⊕ *www. elpatioinn.com* ↩ *16 rooms* ⦿ *Breakfast* ✛ *2:D1.*

$$
HOTEL
FAMILY

🖵 **Sportsmen's Lodge.** The sprawling five-story hotel, an L.A. landmark with a good location, is under new ownership and management and thus has a new contemporary look. **Pros:** close to Ventura Boulevard's plentiful restaurants; free shuttle and discounted tickets to Universal Hollywood; garden-view rooms are quietest. **Cons:** $11 daily self-parking fee. $ *Rooms from: $249* ✉ *12825 Ventura Blvd.* ☎ *818/769–4700, 800/821–8511* ⊕ *www.sportsmenslodge.com* ↩ *177 rooms, 13 suites* ⦿ *No meals* ✛ *2:D1.*

BEST BETS FOR LOS ANGELES LODGING

Fodor's offers a selective listing of lodging experiences at every price range. Here, we've compiled our top recommendations by price and experience. The very best properties are designated in the listings with the Fodor's Choice logo.

Fodor'sChoice★

Channel Road Inn, $$, p. 215

The Crescent Beverly Hills, $$, p. 213

Farmer's Daughter Hotel, $$, p. 210

Hilton Checkers Los Angeles, $, p. 209

Hotel Bel-Air, $$$, p. 213

The Langham Huntington, Pasadena, $$, p. 216

Loews Hollywood, $$, p. 210

Peninsula Beverly Hills, $$$$, p. 213

Shutters on the Beach, $$$$, p. 216

Sunset Marquis Hotel & Villas, $$$, p. 215

By Price

$

The Beverly Garland Holiday Inn, p. 211

El Patio Inn, p. 211

Figueroa Hotel, p. 209

Hilton Checkers Los Angeles, p. 209

Los Feliz Lodge, p. 210

Sea Shore Motel, p. 216

$$

The Ambrose, p. 215

Cal Mar Hotel Suites, p. 215

Channel Road Inn, p. 215

The Crescent Beverly Hills, p. 213

Farmer's Daughter Hotel, p. 210

Hotel Erwin, p. 216

The Langham Huntington, Pasadena, p. 216

The London West Hollywood, p. 215

Magic Castle Hotel, p. 210

Sheraton Gateway Los Angeles, p. 215

Sportsmen's Lodge, p. 211

The Standard, Downtown L.A., p. 210

$$$

Hotel Amarano Burbank, p. 210

JW Marriott Santa Monica Le Merigot, p. 216

Millennium Biltmore Hotel, p. 209

Sunset Marquis Hotel & Villas, p. 215

$$$$

Beverly Wilshire, a Four Seasons Hotel, p. 213

Four Seasons Hotel, Los Angeles at Beverly Hills, p. 213

Peninsula Beverly Hills, p. 213

Shutters on the Beach, p. 216

SLS Hotel at Beverly Hills, p. 213

By Experience

BEST DESIGN

Figueroa Hotel, $, p. 209

The Standard, Downtown L.A., $$, p. 210

BEST SPAS

Four Seasons Hotel, Los Angeles at Beverly Hills, $$$$, p. 213

Shutters on the Beach, $$$$, p. 216

GREEN FOCUS

The Ambrose, $$, p. 215

Los Feliz Lodge, $, p. 210

MOST KID-FRIENDLY

Magic Castle Hotel, $$, p. 210

Shutters on the Beach, $$$$, p. 216

BEVERLY HILLS AND THE WESTSIDE

BEL AIR

$$$
HOTEL
Fodor's Choice
★

⌂ Hotel Bel-Air. Set on 12 acres of lush gardens, this legendary Spanish Mission-style icon—a discreet hillside retreat for celebrities and society types since 1946—recently reopened its pink doors to unveil an updated look courtesy of star designers Alexandra Champalimaud and David Rockwell. **Pros:** country-club feel; lovely pool; spacious rooms. **Cons:** attracts society crowd; hefty price tag; a car is essential. *⑤ Rooms from: $395 ⊠ 701 Stone Canyon Rd. ☎ 310/472–1211, 800/648–4097 ⊕ www.hotelbelair.com ↝ 52 rooms, 39 suites ⊙ No meals ⊹ 2:A2.*

BEVERLY HILLS

$$$$
HOTEL

⌂ Beverly Wilshire, a Four Seasons Hotel. Built in 1928, the Italian Renaissance–style Wilshire wing of this fabled hotel is replete with elegant details: crystal chandeliers, oak paneling, walnut doors, crown moldings, and marble. **Pros:** chic location; top-notch service; refined vibe. **Cons:** small lobby; valet parking backs up at peak times; expensive dining options. *⑤ Rooms from: $475 ⊠ 9500 Wilshire Blvd. ☎ 310/275–5200, 800/427–4354 ⊕ www.fourseasons.com/beverlywilshire ↝ 258 rooms, 137 suites ⊙ No meals ⊹ 2:B3.*

$$
HOTEL
Fodor's Choice
★

⌂ The Crescent Beverly Hills. Built in 1926 as a dorm for silent film actors, the Crescent is now a sleek boutique hotel with a great location—within the Beverly Hills shopping triangle. **Pros:** the on-site restaurant CBH's tasty cuisine and convivial happy hour; the lobby is fashionista central. **Cons:** dorm-size rooms; gym an additional fee and only accessed outside hotel via Sports ClubLA; no elevator. *⑤ Rooms from: $224 ⊠ 403 N. Crescent Dr. ☎ 310/247–0505 ⊕ www.crescentbh.com ↝ 35 rooms ⊙ No meals ⊹ 2:B3.*

$$$$
HOTEL

⌂ Four Seasons Hotel, Los Angeles at Beverly Hills. High hedges and patio gardens make this hotel a secluded retreat that even the hum of traffic can't permeate. **Pros:** expert concierge; deferential service; celebrity magnet. **Cons:** Hollywood scene in bar and restaurant means rarefied prices. *⑤ Rooms from: $455 ⊠ 300 S. Doheny Dr. ☎ 310/273–2222, 800/332–3442 ⊕ www.fourseasons.com/losangeles ↝ 185 rooms, 100 suites ⊙ No meals ⊹ 2:B3.*

$$$$
HOTEL
Fodor's Choice
★

⌂ Peninsula Beverly Hills. This French Rivera–style palace is a favorite of Hollywood bold-face names, but all kinds of visitors consistently describe their stay as near perfect—though expensive. **Pros:** central, walkable Beverly Hills location; stunning flowers; one of the best concierges in the city. **Cons:** serious bucks required to stay here. *⑤ Rooms from: $555 ⊠ 9882 S. Santa Monica Blvd. ☎ 310/551–2888, 800/462–7899 ⊕ www.beverlyhills.peninsula.com ↝ 142 rooms, 36 suites, 16 villas ⊙ No meals ⊹ 2:A3.*

$$$$
HOTEL

⌂ SLS Hotel at Beverly Hills. Imagine dropping into Alice in Wonderland's rabbit hole: this is the colorful, textured, and tchotke-filled lobby of the SLS from design maestro Philippe Starck. **Pros:** a vibrant newcomer with lofty ambitions; excellent design and cuisine. **Cons:** standard rooms are compact, but you pay for the scene; pricey hotel dining. *⑤ Rooms from: $599 ⊠ 465 S. La Cienega Blvd. ☎ 310/247–0400 ⊕ www.slshotels.com ↝ 236 rooms, 61 suites ⊙ No meals ⊹ 2:C3.*

4

Farmer's Daughter Hotel

The Langham Huntington, Pasadena

The Crescent Beverly Hills

Peninsula Beverly Hills

Channel Road Inn

WEST HOLLYWOOD

$$ ⌂ **The London West Hollywood.** Just off the Sunset Strip, cosmopolitan
HOTEL   and chic in design, the London WeHo is a remake of 1984-built Bel
Age. **Pros:** perfectly designed interiors; hillside and city views in gen-
erous-size suites all with balconies and steps from the strip. **Cons:** too
refined for kids to be comfortable; lower floors have mundane views.
⑤ *Rooms from: $249* ⊠ *1020 N. San Vicente Blvd.* ☎ *310/854–1111,
866/282–4560* ⊕ *www.thelondonwesthollywood.com* ⌁ *200 suites*
⫮❂⫯ *No meals* ✛ *2:B2.*

$$$ ⌂ **Sunset Marquis Hotel & Villas.** If you're in town to cut your new hit
HOTEL   single, you'll appreciate the two on-site recording studios here. **Pros:**
Fodor's Choice superior service; discreet setting just off the Strip; clublike atmosphere;
★   free passes to Equinox nearby. **Cons:** standard suites are somewhat
small. ⑤ *Rooms from: $315* ⊠ *1200 N. Alta Loma Rd.* ☎ *310/657–
1333, 800/858–9758* ⊕ *www.sunsetmarquis.com* ⌁ *102 suites, 52 villas* ⫮❂⫯ *No meals* ✛ *2:C2.*

SANTA MONICA, VENICE, AND LAX

LOS ANGELES INTERNATIONAL AIRPORT

$$ ⌂ **Sheraton Gateway Los Angeles.** LAX's coolest-looking hotel is so
HOTEL   swank that guests have been known to ask to buy the black-and-
white photos hanging behind the front desk. **Pros:** weekend rates
significantly lower; free LAX shuttle. **Cons:** convenient to airport
but not much else. ⑤ *Rooms from: $219* ⊠ *6101 W. Century Blvd.*
☎ *310/642–1111, 800/325–3535* ⊕ *www.sheratonlosangeles.com*
⌁ *714 rooms, 88 suites* ✛ *3:C3.*

SANTA MONICA

$$ ⌂ **The Ambrose.** An air of tranquillity pervades the four-story Ambrose,
HOTEL   which blends right into its mostly residential Santa Monica neighbor-
hood. **Pros:** L.A.'s most eco-conscious hotel with nontoxic housekeeping
products and recycling bins in each room. **Cons:** quiet, residential area
of Santa Monica; no restaurant on-site. ⑤ *Rooms from: $225* ⊠ *1255
20th St.* ☎ *310/315–1555, 877/262–7673* ⊕ *www.ambrosehotel.com*
⌁ *77 rooms* ⫮❂⫯ *Breakfast* ✛ *3:B2.*

$$ ⌂ **Cal Mar Hotel Suites.** On a residential street one block from the Third
HOTEL   Street Promenade and within a short walk to the beach, this low-pro-
FAMILY   file, two-story, all-suites hotel is a comparative bargain. **Pros:** lower
off-season rates; full kitchens; low-key vibe. **Cons:** street noise; no air-
conditioning but ocean breeze is present; three-night minimum stay
in summer. ⑤ *Rooms from: $224* ⊠ *220 California Ave.* ☎ *310/395–
5555, 800/776–6007* ⊕ *www.calmarhotel.com* ⌁ *36 suites* ⫮❂⫯ *No
meals* ✛ *3:B2.*

$$ ⌂ **Channel Road Inn.** A quaint surprise in Southern California, the Chan-
B&B/INN   nel Road Inn is every bit the country retreat B&B lovers adore, with
Fodor's Choice four-poster beds with fluffy duvets and a cozy living room with fire-
★   place. **Pros:** quiet residential neighborhood close to beach; free Wi-Fi
and evening wine and hors d'oeuvres. **Cons:** no pool. ⑤ *Rooms from:
$235* ⊠ *219 W. Channel Rd.* ☎ *310/459–1920* ⊕ *www.channelroadinn.
com* ⌁ *15 rooms* ⫮❂⫯ *Breakfast* ✛ *3:B2.*

$$$

HOTEL

⊡ **JW Marriott Santa Monica Le Merigot.** Steps from Santa Monica's expansive beach, with panoramic views of the Santa Monica Pier and the Pacific from the upper floors, Le Merigot caters largely to a corporate clientele. **Pros:** steps from the beach and pier; welcoming to international travelers; walk to Third Street Promenade. **Cons:** small shaded pool; $35 valet parking. ⑤ *Rooms from: $349* ⊠ *1740 Ocean Ave.* ☎ *310/395–9700, 877/637–4468* ⊕ *www.lemerigothotel.com* ⇨ *173 rooms, 2 suites* ⦿*No meals* ✛ *3:B2.*

$

HOTEL

⊡ **Sea Shore Motel.** On Santa Monica's busy Main Street, the Sea Shore is a throwback to Route 66 and to '60s-style, family-run, roadside motels. **Pros:** close to beach and great restaurants; free Wi-Fi and parking. **Cons:** street noise; motel-style decor and beds. ⑤ *Rooms from: $160* ⊠ *2637 Main St.* ☎ *310/392–2787* ⊕ *www.seashoremotel.com* ⇨ *19 rooms, 5 suites* ⦿*No meals* ✛ *3:B3.*

$$$$

HOTEL

FAMILY

Fodor's Choice

★

⊡ **Shutters on the Beach.** Set right on the sand, this gray-shingle inn has become synonymous with in-town escapism, and while the hotel's service gets mixed reviews from some readers, the beachfront location and show-house decor make this one of SoCal's most popular luxury hotels. **Pros:** romantic; discreet; residential vibe. **Cons:** service not as good as it should be. ⑤ *Rooms from: $575* ⊠ *1 Pico Blvd.* ☎ *310/458–0030, 800/334–9000* ⊕ *www.shuttersonthebeach.com* ⇨ *186 rooms, 12 suites* ✛ *3:B2.*

VENICE

$$

HOTEL

⊡ **Hotel Erwin.** Formerly a Best Western, this now bonafide boutique hotel just off the Venice Beach boardwalk has a happening rooftop bar and lounge, appropriately named High, that even attracts locals (weather permitting). **Pros:** great location, great food; close to Santa Monica without hefty prices. **Cons:** some rooms face a noisy alley; no pool. ⑤ *Rooms from: $229* ⊠ *1697 Pacific Ave.* ☎ *310/452–1111, 800/786–7789* ⊕ *www.hotelerwin.com* ⇨ *119 rooms* ⦿*No meals* ✛ *3:B3.*

PASADENA

$$

HOTEL

FAMILY

Fodor's Choice

★

⊡ **The Langham Huntington, Pasadena.** An azalea-filled Japanese garden and the unusual Picture Bridge, with murals celebrating California's history, are just two of the picturesque attributes of this grande dame that opened in 1907 and has long been a mainstay of Pasadena's social history. **Pros:** great for romantic escape; excellent restaurant; top-notch spa. **Cons:** set in a suburban neighborhood far from local shopping and dining. ⑤ *Rooms from: $269* ⊠ *1401 S. Oak Knoll Ave.* ☎ *626/568–3900* ⊕ *www.pasadena.langhamhotels.com* ⇨ *342 rooms, 38 suites* ⦿*No meals* ✛ *1:B1.*

NIGHTLIFE AND THE ARTS

Hollywood and West Hollywood, where hip and happening nightspots liberally dot Sunset and Hollywood boulevards, are the epicenter of L.A. nightlife. The city is one of the best places in the world for seeing soon-to-be-famous rockers as well as top jazz, blues, and classical performers. Movie theaters are naturally well represented here, but the worlds of dance, theater, and opera have flourished in the past few years as well.

For a thorough listing of local events, ⊕ *www.la.com* and *Los Angeles Magazine* are both good sources. The Calendar section of the *Los Angeles Times* (⊕ *www.latimes.com*) also lists a wide survey of Los Angeles arts events, especially on Thursday and Sunday, as does the more irreverent publication, *LA Weekly* (free; published every Thursday ⊕ *www.laweekly.com*). Call ahead to confirm that what you want to see is ongoing.

THE ARTS

CONCERT HALLS

Fodor's Choice
★
Dolby Theatre. This jewel in the crown of the Hollywood & Highland Center, this theater (formerly the Kodak Theatre) was created as the permanent host of the Academy Awards, and the lavish 3,500-seat center is now also home to the Cirque du Soleil's *Iris* (except for a months-long hiatus in prepartion for and just after the awards). Via jaw-dropping acrobatics, inventive costumes, and music, *Iris* tells the story of cinema with humor and panache. Seeing a show in this setting is worthwhile just to witness the gorgeous, crimson-and-gold interior, with its box seating and glittering chandeliers. ⊠ *6801 Hollywood Blvd., Hollywood* ☎ *323/308–6300* ⊕ *www.dolbytheatre.com.*

Fodor's Choice
★
Dorothy Chandler Pavilion. One of the Music Center's most cherished and impressive music halls, the 3,200-seat landmark remains an elegant space to see performances with its plush red seats and giant gold curtain. It presents an array of music programs and L.A. Opera's classics from September through June. Music director Plácido Domingo encourages fresh work (in 2006, for instance, he ushered in *Grendel*, a new opera staged by the hypercreative director Julie Taymor) as much as old favorites (the 2010 season marked the world renown production of Wagner's *Der Ring des Nibelungen* or *Ring Cycle* that ran in conjunction with *Ring Festival L.A.*—a celebration of the arts and L.A. style). There's also a steady flow of touring ballet and modern ballet companies. ⊠ *135 N. Grand Ave., Downtown* ☎ *213/972–7211* ⊕ *www.musiccenter.org.*

Gibson Amphitheater. Adjacent to Universal Studios, this 6,189-seat space hosts more than 100 performances a year, including star-studded benefit concerts and all-star shindigs for local radio station KROQ 106.7. ⊠ *100 Universal City Plaza, Universal City* ☎ *818/622–4440.*

Greek Theatre. In the beautiful tree-enclosed setting of Griffith Park, this open-air auditorium in Los Feliz is in the company of stunning Hollywood Hills' homes and the nearby Griffith Observatory shining atop the hill. The Greek has hosted some of the biggest names in entertainment across all genres. Go for the laid-back California experience and the unique opportunity to experience your favorite performers in the warm western air with a view of the sparkling lights of the city flats splayed at your feet. After the concert, go for a later-night snack or cocktail in the hipster neighborhood hot spots nearby.

4

Open from May through November. The theater celebrated its 82nd year in 2013. ⊠ *2700 N. Vermont Ave., Los Feliz* ☎ *323/665–5857* ⊕ *www.greektheatrela.com.*

Fodor's Choice ★ **Hollywood Bowl.** Ever since it opened in 1920, in a park surrounded by mountains, trees, and gardens, the Hollywood Bowl has been one of the world's largest and most atmospheric outdoor amphitheaters. Its season runs from May through September; the L.A. Philharmonic spends its summers here. There are performances daily except Monday (and some Sundays); the program ranges from jazz to pop to classical. Concertgoers usually arrive early and bring picnic suppers (picnic tables are available). Additionally, a moderately priced outdoor grill and a more upscale restaurant are among the dining options operated by the Patina Group. ■ TIP➔ Be sure to bring a sweater—it gets chilly here in the evening. You might also bring or rent a cushion to apply to the wood seats. Avoid the hassle of parking by taking one of the Park-and-Ride buses, which leave from various locations around town; call the Bowl for information. ⊠ *2301 Highland Ave., Hollywood* ☎ *323/850–2000* ⊕ *www.hollywoodbowl.com.*

Shrine Auditorium. Former home of the Oscars, the 6,300-seat Arabic-inspired space was built in 1926 as Al Malaikah Temple. Touring companies from all over the world perform here, as do assorted gospel choirs, choral groups, and other musical acts. High-profile awards shows, including SAG and NAACP Image Awards, are still televised on-site. ⊠ *665 W. Jefferson Blvd., Downtown* ☎ *213/748–5116* ⊕ *www.shrineauditorium.com.*

Fodor's Choice ★ **Walt Disney Concert Hall.** Built in 2003 as a grand addition to L.A.'s Music Center, the 2,265-seat architectural wonder is now the home of the Los Angeles Master Chorale as well as the Los Angeles Philharmonic, under the direction of passionate, new Music Director Gustavo Dudamel, an international celebrity conductor in his own right. The theater, a sculptural monument of gleaming, curved steel designed by master architect Frank Gehry, is part of a complex that includes a public park, gardens, and shops as well as two outdoor amphitheaters for children's and preconcert events. ■ TIP➔ In the main hall, the audience completely surrounds the stage, so it's worth checking the seating chart when buying tickets to gauge your view of the performers. ⊠ *111 S. Grand Ave., Downtown* ☎ *323/850–2000* ⊕ *www.laphil.org.*

FILM

The American Cinémathèque Independent Film Series. Screen classics are shown here, and so are recent independent films, sometimes with question-and-answer sessions with the filmmakers. The main venue is the Lloyd E. Rigler Theater, within the 1922 Egyptian Theater, which combines an exterior of pharaoh sculptures and columns with a modern, high-tech design inside. ⊠ *6712 Hollywood Blvd., Hollywood* ☎ *323/466–3456* ⊕ *www.americancinematheque.com.*

Aero Theater. The Cinémathèque also screens movies at the 1940 Aero Theater. ⊠ *1328 Montana Ave., Santa Monica* ☎ *323/466–3456* ⊕ *www.americancinematheque.com*

Cinefamily at The Silent Movie Theatre.
A treasure of pretalkies, nonsilent films (the artier the better), and sneak previews of upcoming independent films are screened here. Live musical accompaniment and shorts precede some films. Each show is made to seem like an event in itself, and it's just about the only theater of its kind. The schedule—which also offers occasional DJ and live music performances—varies, but you can be sure to catch silent screenings every week. ⊠ *611 N. Fairfax Ave., Fairfax District* ☎ *323/655–2510* ⊕ *www.cinefamily.org.*

UCLA and the Hammer Museum. The museum, part of the university, presents several fine film series, including those curated by the UCLA Film & Television archive. ⊠ *10899 Wilshire Blvd.*

Billy Wilder Theater. The programs of the Billy Wilder Theater might cover the works of major directors, documentaries, children's films, horror movies—just about anything. ⊠ *10899 Wilshire Blvd., Westwood* ☎ *310/206–8013* ⊕ *www.cinema.ucla.edu/billy-wilder-theater.*

School of Film & Television. With its own program of newer, avant-garde films, the School of Film & Television uses the James Bridges Theater (⊠ *Melnitz Hall, Sunset Blvd. and Hilgard Ave., Westwood* ☎ *310/206–8365* ⊕ *www.cinema.ucla.edu/james-bridges-theater*). Enter the campus at the northeasternmost entrance. Street parking is available on Loring Avenue (a block east of the campus) after 6 pm, or park for a fee in Lot 3 (go one entrance south to Wyton Drive to pay at the kiosk before 7 pm, after 7 pm at the lot itself). ⊕ *www.cinema.ucla.edu.*

THEATER

Geffen Playhouse. Jason Robards and Nick Nolte got their starts here. This acoustically superior, 522-seat theater offers five new plays each season from September to July—both contemporary works and classics are mixed in with musicals and comedies, and many of the productions are on their way to or from Broadway. ⊠ *10886 Le Conte Ave., Westwood* ☎ *310/208–5454* ⊕ *www.geffenplayhouse.com.*

John Anson Ford Amphitheater. In addition to theater performances, this 1,250-seat outdoor venue in the Hollywood Hills hosts a wide variety of other events, including lectures, children's programs, summer jazz, dance, cabaret, and occasionally Latin and rock concerts. Winter shows are typically staged at the smaller indoor theater, **Inside the Ford.** ⊠ *2580 Cahuenga Blvd. E, Hollywood* ☎ *323/461–3673* ⊕ *www.fordamphitheater.org.*

LA Stage Alliance. Providing information on what's playing in Los Angeles, albeit with blurbs that are either noncommittal or overly enthusiastic, LA Stage Alliance also has an LAStageTIX service that allows you to buy tickets online the day of the performance at roughly half price. ⊕ *www.lastagealliance.com.*

The Music Center. Three theaters are part of this big Downtown complex. ⊠ *135 N. Grand Ave., Downtown* 🕾 *213/972–7211* ⊕ *www. musiccenter.org.*

Ahmanson Theatre. The 2,140-seat Ahmanson Theatre presents both classics and new plays. 🕾 *213/628–2772* ⊕ *www.centertheatregroup.org.*

Dorothy Chandler Pavilion. The 3,200-seat Dorothy Chandler Pavilions shows a smattering of plays between the more prevalent musical performances. ⊕ *www.musiccenter.org.*

Mark Taper Forum. The 760-seat Mark Taper Forum presents new works that often go on to Broadway, such as Bruce Norris's *Clybourne Park.* 🕾 *213/628–2772* ⊕ *www.centertheatregroup.org.*

Pantages Theatre. The home of the Academy Awards telecast from 1949 to 1959, this is a massive (2,600-seat) and splendid example of high-style Hollywood art deco, presenting large-scale Broadway musicals such as *The Lion King* and *Wicked.* ⊠ *6233 Hollywood Blvd., Hollywood* 🕾 *323/468–1770* ⊕ *www.broadwayla.org.*

Ricardo Montalbán Theatre. There's an intimate feeling here despite its 1,038-seat capacity. Plays, concerts, seminars, and workshops with an emphasis on Latin culture are all presented. ⊠ *1615 N. Vine St., Hollywood* 🕾 *323/871–2420* ⊕ *www.themontalban.com.*

NIGHTLIFE

Although the ultimate in velvet-roped vampiness and glamour used to be the Sunset Strip, in the past couple of years the glitz has shifted to Hollywood Boulevard and its surrounding streets. The lines are as long as the skirts are short outside the Hollywood club du jour (which changes so fast, it's often hard to keep track). But the Strip still has plenty going for it, with comedy clubs, hard-rock spots, and restaurants. West Hollywood's Santa Monica Boulevard bustles with gay and lesbian bars and clubs. For less conspicuous—and congested—alternatives, check out the events in Downtown L.A.'s performance spaces and galleries. Silver Lake and Echo Park are best for boho bars and live music clubs.

Note that parking, especially after 7 pm, is at a premium in Hollywood. In fact, it's restricted on virtually every side street along the "hot zone" of West Hollywood (Sunset Boulevard from Fairfax to Doheny). Posted signs indicate the restrictions, but these are naturally harder to notice at night. Paying $6 to $20 for valet or lot parking is often the easiest way to go.

HOLLYWOOD

BARS

Three Clubs. This casually hip club is in a strip mall, beneath a sign that simply reads "cocktails." The DJs segue through the many faces and phases of rock-and-roll and dance music. With dark-wood paneling, lamp-lighted tables, and even some sofas, you could be in a giant basement rec room from decades past—no fancy dress required, but fashionable looks suggested. ⊠ *1123 Vine St.* 🕾 *323/462–6441* ⊕ *www. threeclubs.com.*

Yamashiro. A lovely L.A. tradition is to meet here for cocktails at sunset. In the elegant restaurant, waitresses glide by in kimonos, and entrées can zoom up to $42; on the terrace, a spectacular hill-top view spreads out before you. ■TIP→ Valet parking is mandatory and runs $8. ⊠ *1999 N. Sycamore Ave.* ☎ *323/466–5125* ⊕ *www. yamashirorestaurant.com.*

COMEDY
Groundlings Theatre. For close to forty years, this renowned theater company has been a breeding ground for *Saturday Night Live* performers; alumni include Will Ferrell, Lisa Kudrow, and *Bridesmaids'* Melissa McCarthy. The primarily sketch and improv comedy shows run Wednesday–Sunday, costing $13–$19. ⊠ *7307 Melrose Ave.* ☎ *323/934–4747* ⊕ *www.groundlings.com.*

Upright Citizens Brigade. New York's UCB marched in with a mix of sketch comedy and wild improvisations skewering pop culture. Members of the L.A. Brigade include VH1 commentator Paul Scheer and *Mad TV*'s Andrew Daly. ⊠ *5919 Franklin Ave.* ☎ *323/908–8702* ⊕ *www.ucbtheatre.com.*

DANCE CLUBS
Boardner's. This bar has a multidecade history (in the '20s it was a speak-easy), but with the adjoining ballroom, which was added a couple of years ago, it's now a state-of-the-art dance club. DJs may be spinning electronica, funk, or something else depending on the night—at the popular Saturday Goth event "Bar Sinister," patrons must wear black or risk not getting in. The cover here ranges from $3–$20. ⊠ *1652 N. Cherokee Ave.* ☎ *323/462–9621* ⊕ *www.boardners.com.*

LIVE MUSIC
Avalon. The multilevel art deco building opposite Capitol Records, the Avalon, formerly known as the Palace, has a fabulous sound system, four bars, and a balcony. Big-name rock and pop concerts hit the stage during the week, but on weekends the place becomes a dance club, with the most popular night the DJ-dominated Avaland on Saturday. Upstairs, but with a separate entrance, you can find celeb hub **Bardot,** a glamorous tribute to Old Hollywood where stars and their entourages are frequent visitors. ⊠ *1735 N. Vine St.* ☎ *323/462–8900* ⊕ *www. avalonhollywood.com.*

Largo. Musician-producer Jon Brion (Fiona Apple, Aimee Mann, and others) shows off his ability to play virtually any instrument and any song in the rock lexicon—and beyond—as host of a popular evening of music some Fridays at Largo. Other nights, low-key rock and singer-songwriter fare is offered at this cozy venue. And when comedy comes in, about one night a week, it's usually one of the best comedy nights in town, with folks like Sarah Silverman. Cash only. ⊠ *366 N. La Cienega Blvd.* ☎ *310/855–0350* ⊕ *www.largo-la.com.*

WEST HOLLYWOOD
BARS
Bar Marmont. As at so many other nightspots in this neck of the woods, the popularity and clientele of this hotel bar bulged—and changed—after word got out that it was a favorite of celebrities. Lately, it's gotten

a second wind thanks to a strong DJ selection and luscious cocktails. The bar is next to the inimitable hotel Chateau Marmont, which boldface names continue to haunt. ⊠ *8171 Sunset Blvd.* ☏ *323/650–0575* ⊕ *www.chateaumarmont.com.*

Rainbow Bar & Grill. In the heart of the Strip and next door to the legendary Roxy, the Rainbow is a landmark in its own right as *the* drinking spot of the '80s hair-metal scene—and it still attracts a music-industry crowd. ⊠ *9015 Sunset Blvd.* ☏ *310/278–4232* ⊕ *www. rainbowbarandgrill.com.*

The Standard. This smart, brash-looking hotel for the young, hip, and connected in the happening part of Sunset Strip was formerly a nursing home—how's that for a classic Hollywood makeover? (Check out the live model in the lobby's terrarium.) The bar, at the hotel's 24/7 restaurant, is popular with those in the biz. There is also a Standard in Downtown L.A. *(⇨ Downtown)* ⊠ *8300 Sunset Blvd.* ☏ *323/650–9090* ⊕ *www.standardhotels.com.*

COMEDY

Comedy Store. A nightly premiere comedy showcase, this venue has been going strong for more than two decades, with three stages (with covers ranging from free to $20) to supply the yucks. Famous comedians occasionally make unannounced appearances. ⊠ *8433 Sunset Blvd.* ☏ *323/650–6268* ⊕ *www.thecomedystore.com.*

Improv. Richard Pryor got his start at this renowned stand-up comedy establishment that has venues throughout the country. Reservations are recommended. Cover is $11–$21, and you need to order a minimum of two items off the menu. ⊠ *8162 Melrose Ave.* ☏ *323/651–2583* ⊕ *www. improv.com.*

Laugh Factory. Look for top stand-ups—and frequent celeb residents— like Bob Saget, or unannounced drop-ins, like Chris Rock. The club has shows Sunday through Thursday nights at 8 pm and 10 pm, plus an additional show on Friday and Saturday at midnight; the cover is $20–$45 plus a two-drink minimum. ⊠ *8001 Sunset Blvd.* ☏ *323/656– 1336* ⊕ *www.laughfactory.com.*

GAY AND LESBIAN CLUBS

Some of the most popular gay and lesbian "clubs" are weekly theme nights at various venues, so read the preceding list of clubs, *LA Weekly* listings, and gay publications such as *Odyssey* in addition to the following recommendations.

The Palms. A long-running gay-gal fave, this club continues to thrive thanks to great DJs spinning dance tunes as well as karaoke and comedy shows. There are also pool tables, an outdoor patio, and an occasional live performance. ⊠ *8572 Santa Monica Blvd.* ☏ *310/652–1595* ⊕ *www.thepalmsbar.com.*

Rage. This spot is a longtime favorite of the "gym boy" set, with DJs following a different musical theme every night of the week (alternative rock, house, dance remixes, etc.). The cover ranges from free to $12. ⊠ *8911 Santa Monica Blvd.* ☏ *310/652–7055* ⊕ *www.theragenightclub.com.*

LIVE MUSIC

Key Club. This flashy, multitier rock club offers four bars presenting current artists of all genres (some on national tours, others local aspirants). After the concerts, there's often dancing with DJs spinning techno and house. ⊠ *9039 Sunset Blvd.* ☎ *310/274–5800.*

The Roxy Theatre. A Sunset Strip fixture for decades, this live music club hosts local and touring rock, alternative, blues, and rockabilly bands. The Roxy's not the comfiest club around, but it's the site of many memorable shows. ⊠ *9009 Sunset Blvd.* ☎ *310/278–9457* ⊕ *www. theroxyonsunset.com.*

The Troubadour. One of the best and most comfortable clubs in town, this wood-paneled, live music venue has a rich history dating back to the late 1950s when it was a folk club. After surviving the '80s heavy-metal scene, Troubadour caught a second (third? fourth?) wind by booking hot alternative rock acts. There's valet parking, but if you don't mind walking up Doheny a block or three, there's usually ample street parking (check the signs carefully). ⊠ *9081 Santa Monica Blvd.* ⊕ *www.troubadour.com.*

Viper Room. Actor Johnny Depp sold his share of the infamous rock venue in 2004, but the place continues to rock with a motley live music lineup, if a less stellar crowd. ⊠ *8852 W. Sunset Blvd.* ☎ *310/358–1881* ⊕ *www.viperroom.com.*

Whisky-A-Go-Go. The Whisky, as locals call it, is the most famous rock-and-roll club on the Strip, where back in the '60s, Johnny Rivers cut hit singles and the Doors, Love, and the Byrds cut their musical eyeteeth. It's still going strong, with up-and-coming alternative, hard rock, and punk bands, though mostly of the unknown variety. ⊠ *8901 Sunset Blvd.* ☎ *310/652–4202* ⊕ *www.whiskyagogo.com.*

ECHO PARK AND SILVER LAKE

BARS

Cha Cha Lounge. Seattle's coolest rock bar aims to repeat its success with this colorful, red-lighted space. Think part tiki hut, part tacky Tijuana party palace. The tabletops pay homage to the lounge's former performers; they've got portraits of Latin drag queens. ⊠ *2375 Glendale Blvd., Silver Lake* ☎ *323/660–7595* ⊕ *www.chachalounge.com.*

The Echo. This Echo Park mainstay sprang from the people behind the Silver Lake rock joint Spaceland. Most evenings this dark and divey space's tiny dance floor and well-worn booths attract artsy local bands and their followers, but things rev up when DJs spin reggae, rock, and funk. ⊠ *1154 Glendale Blvd.* ☎ *213/413–8200* ⊕ *www. attheecho.com.*

Tiki-Ti. This tiny Hawaiian-theme room is one of the most charming drinking huts in the city. You can spend hours just looking at the Polynesian artifacts strewn all about the place, but be careful—time flies in this tropical bar, and the colorful drinks can be so potent that you may have to stay marooned for a while. ⊠ *4427 Sunset Blvd., Silver Lake* ☎ *323/669–9381* ⊕ *www.tiki-ti.com.*

4

Rocking out at the Roxy.

LIVE MUSIC

The Satellite. The hottest bands of tomorrow, surprises from yesteryear, and unclassifiable bands of today perform at this low-key Silver Lake venue (formerly known as Spaceland), which has two bars, a jukebox, and a pool table. Monday is always free, with monthlong gigs by the indie fave du jour. There is a nice selection of beers. ✉ *1717 Silver Lake Blvd., Silver Lake* ☎ *323/661–4380* ⊕ *www.thesatellitela.com.*

Silver Lake Lounge. Neighborhoody and relaxed, this lounge draws a mixed collegiate and boho crowd. The club is very unmainstream "cool," the booking policy an adventurous mix of local and touring alt-rockers. Bands play three to five nights a week; covers vary but are low. ✉ *2906 Sunset Blvd., Silver Lake* ☎ *323/663–9636.*

DOWNTOWN

BARS

Fodor's Choice ★ **Downtown L.A. Standard.** This futuristic hotel has a groovy lounge with pink sofas and DJs, as well as an all-white restaurant that looks like something out of *2001: A Space Odyssey.* But it's the rooftop bar and *biergarten,* with an amazing view of the city's illuminated skyscrapers, a heated swimming pool, and private, podlike water-bed tents, that's worth waiting in line to get into. And wait you probably will, especially on weekends and in summer. On Friday and Saturday nights there's a $20 cover charge after 7 pm. ✉ *550 S. Flower St., at Sixth St.* ☎ *213/892–8080* ⊕ *www.standardhotels.com.*

SANTA MONICA

LIVE MUSIC

McCabe's Guitar Shop. This famous guitar shop is rootsy-retro-central, where all things earnest and (preferably) acoustic are welcome—chiefly folk, blues, bluegrass, and rock. It *is* a guitar shop (so no liquor license), with a room full of folding chairs for concert-style presentations. Shows on weekends only. Make reservations well in advance. ⊠ *3101 Pico Blvd.* ☎ *310/828–4497 for concert information* ⊕ *www.mccabes.com.*

SPORTS AND THE OUTDOORS

4

BASEBALL

Dodgers. You can watch the Dodgers take on its National League rivals while munching on pizza, tacos, or a foot-long "Dodger dog" at one of the game's most comfortable ball parks, Dodger Stadium. ⊠ *Dodger Stadium, 1000 Elysian Park Ave., exit off I–110, Pasadena Fwy.* ☎ *866/363–4377 ticket information* ⊕ *www.dodgers.com.*

Los Angeles Angels of Anaheim. The Los Angeles Angels of Anaheim made headlines when they acquired home-run hitter Josh Hamilton from the Texas Rangers for $125 million in late 2012. In 2002, the Angels won the World Series, the first time since the team formed in 1961. ⊠ *Angel Stadium of Anaheim, 2000 Gene Autry Way, Anaheim* ☎ *714/663–9000* ⊕ *www.angelsbaseball.com.*

Several colleges in the area also have baseball teams worth watching, especially USC, which has been a perennial source of major-league talent.

BASKETBALL

L.A.'s pro basketball teams play at the Staples Center.

Clippers. L.A.'s "other" team, the much maligned but newly revitalized Clippers, sells tickets that are sometimes cheaper and easier to get than those for Lakers games. ☎ *888/895–8662* ⊕ *www.nba.com/clippers.*

Los Angeles Lakers. See where Magic Johnson once strutted his stuff. It's not easy to get tickets, but if you can, don't miss the chance to see this championship-winning team—especially if the Lakers are playing their rivals, the Boston Celtics. ⊠ *STAPLES Center, 1111 S. Figueroa St., Downtown* ☎ *310/426–6000* ⊕ *www.nba.com/lakers.*

Los Angeles Sparks. After the 2010 retirement of WNBA superstar Lisa Leslie, the Los Angeles Sparks have put the spotlight on forward Candace Parker. ☎ *310/426–6031* ⊕ *www.wnba.com/sparks.*

GOLF

Griffith Park. Griffith Park has two splendid 18-hole courses along with a challenging 9-hole course. **Harding Municipal Golf Course** and **Wilson Municipal Golf Course** (⊠ *4900 Griffith Park Dr., Los Feliz*

The Santa Monica Pier is packed with fun diversions and hosts free concerts in summer.

☎ 323/663–2555) are about 1½ miles inside the park entrance, at Riverside Drive and Los Feliz Boulevard. Bridle paths surround the outer fairways, and the San Gabriel Mountains make a scenic background. ⊕ *www.golf.lacity.org.*

Los Verdes Golf Course. If you want a scenic course, the county-run, par-71 Los Verdes Golf Course has fierce scenery. You get a cliff-top view of the ocean—time it right and you can watch the sun set behind Catalina Island. ⊠ *7000 W. Los Verdes Dr., Rancho Palos Verdes* ☎ *310/377–7370* ⊕ *www.americangolf.com/los-verdes-golf-course* ⚑ *18 holes. Par 71. 6,262 yds. Slope 122. Greens fee: $40* ⚲ *Facilities: Driving range, putting green, rental clubs, golf carts, lessons, restaurant and bar.*

Rancho Park Golf Course. The City Parks and Recreation Department lists seven public 18-hole courses in Los Angeles, and L.A. County runs some good ones, too. Rancho Park Golf Course is one of the most heavily played links in the country. It's a beautifully designed course, but the towering pines present an obstacle for those who slice or hook. There's a two-level driving range, a 9-hole pitch 'n' putt, a snack bar, and a pro shop where you can rent clubs. ⊠ *10460 W. Pico Blvd., West L.A.* ☎ *310/838–7373* ⊕ *www.golf.lacity.org* ⚑ *18 holes. Par 71. 6,630 yds. Slope 126. Greens fee: $40* ⚲ *Facilities: Driving range, putting green, golf carts, rental clubs, lessons, café.*

Roosevelt Municipal Golf Course. The 9-hole Roosevelt Municipal Golf Course can be reached through the park's Vermont Avenue entrance. ⊠ *2650 N. Vermont Ave.* ☎ *323/665–2011* ⊕ *www.golf.lacity.org* ⚑ *9 holes. Par 33. 2,478 yds. Slope 108. Greens fees: $17.50/$22* ⚲ *Facilities: putting green, rental clubs, golf carts, café.*

SHOPPING

HOLLYWOOD

From records to lingerie to movie memorabilia, this area is a mixed bag when it comes to shopping.

Fodor's Choice ★ **Amoeba Records.** Touted as the "World's Largest Independent Music Store," Amoeba is a playground for music lovers with a knowledgeable staff and a "Homegrown" display to highlight local artists. Catch in-store appearances by artists and bands that play sold-out shows at venues down the road several times a week. Find a rich stock of used CDs and DVDs, an impressive cache of rarities and collectibles (like the Beatles' "Butcher" cover), an encyclopedic range of indie releases, and walls filled with posters for sale. ⊠ *6400 W. Sunset Blvd., at Cahuenga Blvd.* ☎ *323/245–6400.*

Hollywood & Highland. Dozens of stores, eateries, a bowling alley, and the Dolby Theatre fill this outdoor complex, which mimics cinematic glamour. Find designer shops (Coach, Louis Vuitton) and chain stores (Victoria's Secret, Fossil, Sephora, and the Hard Rock Café).

From the upper levels, there's a camera-perfect view of the famous "Hollywood" sign. On the second level, next to the Dolby Theatre, is a **Visitor Information Center** (☎ *323/467–6412*) with a multilingual staff, maps, attraction brochures, and information about services.

The streets nearby provide the setting for the Sunday Hollywood Farmers' Market, where you're likely to spot a celebrity or two picking up fresh produce or stopping to eat breakfast from the food vendors. ⊠ *Hollywood Blvd. and Highland Ave.* ☎ *323/817–0220.*

BEVERLY HILLS AND THE WESTSIDE

The shops of Beverly Hills, particularly Rodeo Drive, are a big draw for window-shopping, and leave visitors awestruck by L.A.'s glitz and excess. It's easy to stroll this area on foot, stopping into big-name luxury jewelers and department stores such as Barneys New York and Cartier.

BEVERLY HILLS

All Saints Spitalfields. The British store recently invaded Robertson Boulevard, bringing with it a rock and roll edge mixed with a dash of Downton Abbey. Look for furry vests, tough shoes, skull embellishments, and denim and khaki skirts, which, worn correctly, let them know you're with the band. ⊠ *100 N. Robertson Blvd., Beverly Hills* ☎ *310–432-8484* ⊕ *www.us.allsaints.com.*

Beverly Center. This is one of the more traditional malls you can find in L.A., with eight levels of stores, including Macy's, Bloomingdale's, and the newer addition: luxury retailer Henri Bendel. Fashion is the biggest draw and there's a little something for everyone, from D&G to H&M, and many shops in the midrange, including Banana Republic, Club Monaco, and Coach. Look for accessories at Aldo and inexpensive accessories and fun fashion at Forever 21; there's even a destination for the race car–obsessed at the Ferrari Store. Inside there are casual dining choices at the top-floor food court, and several popular chain restaurants are outside on the ground floor. Next door is Loehmann's, which offers a huge selection of discounted designer wear. ✉ *8500 Beverly Blvd., bounded by Beverly, La Cienega, and San Vicente Blvds. and 3rd St., between Beverly Hills and West Hollywood* ☎ *310/854–0071* ⊕ *www.beverlycenter.com.*

Kitson. Stars that want to be seen (and seen shopping) come here to choose from piles of jeans, tops, hoodies, graphic T-shirts, Pucci scarves, sequined Converse, thongs with "naughty" bejeweled across the front, and unusual pampering products. It's pure girly glitz. ✉ *115 S. Robertson Blvd., between Beverly Hills and West Hollywood* ☎ *310/859–2652.*

MAC. Not just your ordinary MAC store, this beauty emporium is what's called a "professional" MAC store, with products not available at the chain's regular outlets. This is also a place to book an appointment for makeup lessons or all-out makeovers, or even to prepare for red carpet or other special events. The artists here are fashion show and award-season veterans. ✉ *133 N. Robertson Blvd., West Hollywood* ☎ *310/271–9137.*

Rodeo Drive. New York City has Fifth Avenue, but L.A. has famed Rodeo Drive (pronounced Ro-DAY-o). The triangle, between Santa Monica and Wilshire boulevards and Beverly Drive, is one of the city's biggest tourist attractions and is lined with shops featuring the biggest names in fashion.

You can see well-coiffed, well-heeled ladies toting multiple packages to their Mercedes and paparazzi staking out street corners. Although the dress code in L.A. is considerably laid-back, with residents wearing flip-flops year-round, you might find them jewel-encrusted on Rodeo.

Steep price tags on designer labels make it a "just looking" experience for many residents and tourists alike, but salespeople are used to the ogling and window-shopping. In recent years, more midrange shops have opened up on the strip and surrounding blocks. Keep in mind that some stores are by appointment only. ✉ *Beverly Hills* ⊕ *www.rodeodrive-bh.com.*

Taschen. Philippe Starck designed the space to evoke a cool 1920s Parisian salon—a perfect showcase for the coffee-table books about architecture, travel, culture, and (often racy) photography. A suspended glass-cube gallery space in back shows rotating art, photo exhibits, and limited edition books. ✉ *354 N. Beverly Dr., Beverly Hills* ☎ *310/274–4300.*

WEST HOLLYWOOD AND MELROSE AVENUE

This is prime shopping real estate, with everything from bridal couture design shops to furnishing stores sharing sidewalk space along posh streets like Melrose Place and Robertson Boulevard. It's worth strolling West 3rd Street as well, which is lined with independent but affordable boutiques and several of the city's hottest restaurants and cafés.

Fodor's Choice
★
American Rag Cie. Half the store features new clothing from established and emerging labels and of-the-moment denim lines, and the other side is stocked with well-preserved vintage clothing, neatly organized by color and style. Also find shoes and accessories. Adjoining store World Denim Bar stocks jeans galore. ⊠ *150 S. La Brea Ave., Beverly–La Brea* ☎ *323/935–3154.*

Fodor's Choice
★
Farmers Market and The Grove. The granddaddy of L.A. markets dates to 1935, and the amazing array of clapboard stalls (selling everything from candy to hot sauce, fresh fruit to fresh lamb), wacky regulars, and a United Nations of food choices must be experienced to be appreciated.

Employees from the nearby CBS studios mingle with hungover clubbers and elderly locals at dozens of eateries, movie theaters, and shops under one huge roof. The green trolley shuttles visitors between the Farmers Market and the nearby **Grove**, a wildly popular outdoor mall with an ersatz European feel and a fabulous people-watching scene.

Although many of the stores are familiar in any mall (Nordstrom, Abercrombie & Fitch, the Apple Store, American Girl Place), the elaborate setting with cheerful winding tile walkways, the central fountain that has "dancing" water choreographed to music, and during the holidays even man-made "snow" (!) that falls accompanied by holiday music, put this shopping center over the top.

Oh, and if you happen to be in the Glendale area of Los Angeles, the same development team that brought you this temple to shopping and the easy–breezy outdoor California lifestyle opened a bright, shiny complex called the Americana at Brand that is very similar. ⊠ *6333 W. 3rd St., at Fairfax Ave., Fairfax District* ☎ *323/933–9211 Farmers Market, 323/900–8080 The Grove.*

Fodor's Choice
★
Fred Segal. The ivy-covered building and security guards in the parking lot might tip you off that this is *the* place to be. Go during the lunch hour to stargaze at the super-trendy café. This longtime L.A. fashion landmark is subdivided into miniboutiques that range from couture clothing to skateboard fashions. The entertainment industry's fashion fiends are addicted to the exclusive goods here, some from overseas, others from cult L.A. designers just making their marks. ⊠ *8118 Melrose Ave., at Crescent Heights Blvd., near West Hollywood* ☎ *323/651–4129.*

James Perse. The soft cotton tees (and sweaters and fleece) are quintessentially L.A. Find them here in an immaculate gallery-like space, with sleek white- and light-wood furnishings. ⊠ *8914 Melrose Ave., West Hollywood* ☎ *310/276–7277* ⊕ *www.jamesperse.com.*

OK. An über–gift shop, OK stocks the classy (such as Scandinavian stemware and vintage candelabras) and specializes in architecture and design books. There's also a second Silver Lake location. ⊠ *8303 W. 3rd St., near West Hollywood* ☎ *323/653–3501* ⊕ *okthestore.com.*

WEST LOS ANGELES

H.D. Buttercup. The renovated and expanded art deco Helms Bakery space is a shopping mecca that's more like a showroom than a traditional store. Manufacturers offer furniture, home decor, gifts, fashion accessories, antiques, books, artwork, bedding and textiles, lighting, candles and soaps, and more. Across the street, a newly opened **Backroom at Buttercup** features outlet prices on remainder stock. ⊠ *3225 Helms Ave., between Venice and Washington Blvds., Culver City* ☎ *310/558–8900.*

Surfas. You're likely to rub elbows with area chefs in their work whites at this spacious and well-organized restaurant supply store that's open to the public. Find aisles of spices (priced wholesale) and jarred delicacies along with all the pots, pans, bowls, and tools you'll need to be your own Top Chef. The adjoining café serves salads, sandwiches, hot specials, gourmet teas, and baked goods. ⊠ *8777 Washington Blvd., at National Blvd., Culver City* ☎ *310/559–4770.*

DOWNTOWN

As Downtown revitalizes, a handful of edgy and avant-garde shops have moved in; but you'll also find ethnic pockets, with their own trinket shops and markets, that testify to L.A.'s diversity.

Clare Vivier. Clare Vivier's chic handbags are classic French glamour by way of laid-back California, and her eponymous Silver Lake boutique, designed by Barbara Bestor, follows the same aesthetic. Inside, find her full line of messenger bags, foldover clutches, and iPad cases, all of them made locally in Los Angeles. ⊠ *3339 Sunset Blvd., Downtown* ☎ *323/665–2476* ⊕ *www.clarevivier.com.*

Heath Ceramics. This loft-like outpost of the beloved Sausalito-based ceramics company stocks everything from Coupe dishes, a line created by founder Edith Heath herself in the 1940s, to glass tumblers handblown in West Virginia. Also look for table linens, bud vases, and speciality foods like artisanal jams from Pasadena. ⊠ *7525 Beverly Blvd., Downtown* ☎ *323/965–0800* ⊕ *www.heathceramics.com.*

The Jewelry District. With the crowded sidewalks, diverse aromas, and haggling bargain hunters, this area resembles a slice of Manhattan. Expect to save 50% to 70% off retail price for everything from wedding bands to sparkling belt buckles. The more upscale stores are along Hill Street between 6th and 7th streets. There's a parking structure next door on Broadway. ⊠ *Between Olive St. and Broadway from 5th to 8th St., Downtown.*

Fodor's Choice ★ **Olvera Street.** Historic buildings line this redbrick walkway overhung with grape vines. At dozens of clapboard stalls you can browse south-of-the-border goods—leather sandals, bright woven blankets, devotional candles, and the like—as well as cheap toys and tchotchkes. With the musicians and cafés providing background noise, the area is constantly lively. ⊠ *Between Cesar Chavez Ave. and Arcadia St., Downtown.*

Topshop. This beloved high street British retailer opened its fourth U.S. outpost in L.A. last year at the outdoor shopping mall, The Grove, moving into a gargantuan 30,000-square-foot space spread across two floors. The upper floor is dedicated to the brand's men's division, TopMan, with plenty of tailored jackets, slim-fitting shirts, and leather accessories. ⊠ *189 The Grove Dr.* ☎ *323/938–1085* ⊕ *us.topshop.com.*

LOS FELIZ, SILVER LAKE, AND ECHO PARK

There's a hipster rock-and-roll vibe to this area, though its edge has softened in recent years. Come for homegrown, funky galleries, vintage shops, and local designers' boutiques. Shopping areas are concentrated along Vermont Avenue and Hollywood Boulevard in Los Feliz; Sunset Boulevard in both Silver Lake (known as Sunset Junction) and Echo Park; and Echo Park Avenue in Echo Park. ■**TIP→** Keep in mind that things are spread out enough to necessitate a couple of short car trips, and many shops in these neighborhoods don't open until noon but stay open later, so grab dinner or drinks in the area after shopping.

SANTA MONICA AND VENICE

The breezy beachside communities of Santa Monica and Venice are ideal for leisurely shopping. Scads of tourists (and some locals) gravitate to Santa Monica Place and the Third Street Promenade, a popular pedestrians-only shopping area that is within walking distance of the beach and historic Santa Monica Pier. A number of modern furnishings stores are nearby on 4th and 5th streets. Main Street between Pico Boulevard and Rose Avenue offers upscale chain stores, cafés, and some original shops, while Montana Avenue is a great source for distinctive clothing boutiques and child-friendly shopping, especially between 7th and 17th streets. ■**TIP→** Parking in Santa Monica is next to impossible on Wednesday, when some streets are blocked off for the farmers' market, but there are several parking structures with free parking for an hour or two. In Venice, Abbot Kinney Boulevard is abuzz with midcentury furniture stores, art galleries and boutiques, and cafés.

Malibu Lumberyard. This newer Malibu shopping complex is yet another window into luxe, beachfront California living. Emblematic Malibu lifestyle stores include James Perse, Alice + Olivia, celebrity magnet Maxfield, and one of the chicest boutiquelike J.Crew stores you've ever seen.

Before shopping, pick up a sandwich or salad at Malibu Country Mart across the way—another spot for star spotting—or drive further up the PCH and pay a visit to in-the-know El Matador beach and feast on fresh seafood at Neptune's Net, a shack that's one part biker stop, one part Vogue spread, and one part hangout for surfers. Not that you ever actually eat—that is, if you want to be a local for the day. ⌧ *3939 Cross Creek Rd., Malibu* ⊕ *www.themalibulumberyard.com.*

Third Street Promenade. Whimsical dinosaur-shaped, ivy-covered fountains, and buskers of every stripe set the scene along this pedestrians-only shopping stretch. Stores are mainly the chain variety (Restoration Hardware, Urban Outfitters, Apple), but there are also Quiksilver and Rip Curl outposts for cool surf attire. Movie theaters, bookstores, pubs, and restaurants ensure that virtually every need is covered. ⌧ *3rd St., between Broadway and Wilshire Blvd.*

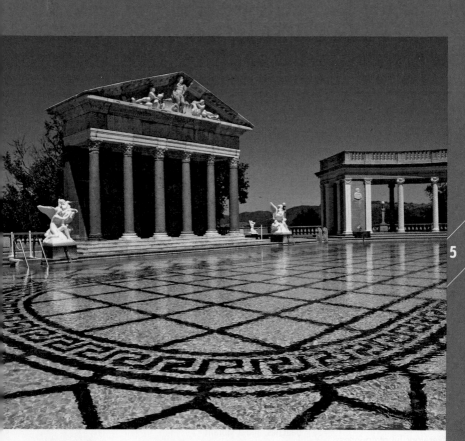

THE CENTRAL COAST

From Ventura to Big Sur

WELCOME TO THE CENTRAL COAST

TOP REASONS TO GO

★ **Incredible nature:** Much of the Central Coast looks as wild and wonderful as it did centuries ago. The area is home to Channel Islands National Park, two national marine sanctuaries, state parks and beaches, and the vast and rugged Los Padres National Forest.

★ **Edible bounty:** Land and sea provide enough fresh regional foods to satisfy even the most sophisticated foodies—grapes, strawberries, seafood, olive oil . . . the list goes on and on. Get your fill at countless farmers' markets, wineries, and restaurants.

★ **Outdoor activities:** Kick back and revel in the casual California lifestyle. Surf, golf, kayak, hike, play tennis—or just hang out and enjoy the gorgeous scenery.

★ **Small-town charm, big-city culture:** Small, friendly, uncrowded towns offer amazing cultural amenities. With all the art and history museums, theater, music, and festivals, you might start thinking you're in L.A. or San Francisco.

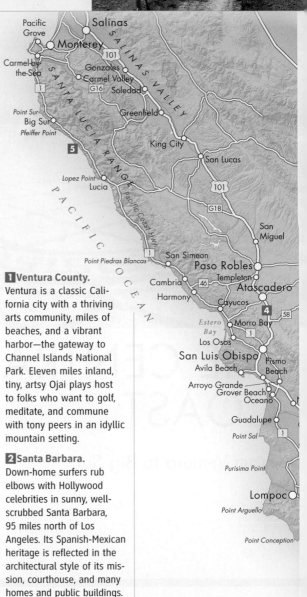

1 Ventura County. Ventura is a classic California city with a thriving arts community, miles of beaches, and a vibrant harbor—the gateway to Channel Islands National Park. Eleven miles inland, tiny, artsy Ojai plays host to folks who want to golf, meditate, and commune with tony peers in an idyllic mountain setting.

2 Santa Barbara. Down-home surfers rub elbows with Hollywood celebrities in sunny, well-scrubbed Santa Barbara, 95 miles north of Los Angeles. Its Spanish-Mexican heritage is reflected in the architectural style of its mission, courthouse, and many homes and public buildings.

3 Santa Barbara County.
Wineries, ranches, and
small villages dominate the
quintessentially Californian
landscape here.

**4 San Luis Obispo
County.** Friendly college
town San Luis Obispo serves
as the hub of a burgeoning
wine region that stretches
nearly 100 miles from Pismo
Beach north to Paso Robles;
the 230-plus wineries here
have earned reputations
for high-quality vintages
that rival those of Northern
California.

**5 The Big Sur Coast-
line.** Rugged cliffs meet
the Pacific for more than
60 miles—one of the most
scenic and dramatic drives
in the world.

**6 Channel Islands
National Park.** Home to
145 species of plants and
animals found nowhere
else on Earth, this relatively
undiscovered gem of a park
encompasses five islands
and a mile of surrounding
ocean. ⇨ *See Chapter 6 for
more information.*

GETTING ORIENTED

The Central Coast region
begins about 60 miles
north of Los Angeles,
near the seaside city of
Ventura. North along
the sinuous coastline
from here lie the cities of
Santa Barbara and San
Luis Obispo, and beyond
them the smaller towns
of Morro Bay, Cambria,
and Big Sur. The nearly
300-mile drive through
this region, especially
the section of Highway
1 from San Simeon to
Big Sur, is one of the
most scenic in the state.

5

```
0                    20 miles
|----|----|----|
0                         30 kilometers
```

Updated
by Cheryl
Crabtree

Balmy weather, glorious beaches, crystal clear air, and serene landscapes have lured people to the Central Coast since prehistoric times. It's an ideal place to relax, slow down, and appreciate the good things in life.

Along the Pacific coast, the scenic variety is stunning—everything from dramatic cliffs and grass-tufted bluffs to wildlife estuaries and miles of dunes. Offshore, a pristine national park and a vast marine sanctuary protect the wild, wonderful underwater resources of this incredible corner of the planet. But not all of the Central Coast's top attractions are natural: Ventura, Santa Barbara, and San Luis Obispo are filled with sparkling examples of Spanish-Mediterranean architecture, bustling shopping districts, and first-rate restaurants showcasing regional foods and wines.

PLANNING

WHEN TO GO
The Central Coast climate is mild year-round. If you like to swim in warmer (if still nippy) ocean waters, July and August are the best months to visit. Be aware that this is also high season. Fog often rolls in along the coastal areas in early summer; you'll need a jacket, especially after sunset, close to the shore. It usually rains from December through March. From April to early June and in early fall the weather is almost as fine as in high season, and the pace is less hectic.

GETTING HERE AND AROUND
AIR TRAVEL
Alaska Air, American, Frontier, United, and US Airways fly to Santa Barbara Airport (SBA), 9 miles from downtown. United and US Airways provide service to San Luis Obispo County Regional Airport (SBP), 3 miles from downtown San Luis Obispo.

Santa Barbara Airbus shuttles travelers between Santa Barbara and Los Angeles for $48 one-way and $90 round-trip. The Santa Barbara Metropolitan Transit District Bus 11 ($1.75) runs every 30 minutes from the airport to the downtown transit center. A taxi between the airport and the hotel districts costs between $20 and $38.

Airport Contacts San Luis Obispo County Regional Airport ⊠ *903 Airport Dr., off Hwy. 227, San Luis Obispo* ☎ *805/781-5205* ⊕ *www.sloairport.com.* **Santa Barbara Airport** ⊠ *500 Fowler Rd., off U.S. 101 Exit 104B, Santa Barbara* ☎ *805/683-4011* ⊕ *www.flysba.com.* **Santa Barbara Airbus** ☎ *805/964-7759, 800/423-1618* ⊕ *www.sbairbus.com.* **Santa Barbara Metropolitan Transit District** ☎ *805/963-3366* ⊕ *www.sbmtd.gov.*

BUS TRAVEL

Greyhound provides service from Los Angeles and San Francisco to San Luis Obispo, Ventura, and Santa Barbara. Local transit companies serve these three cities and several smaller towns. Buses can be useful for visiting some urban sights, particularly in Santa Barbara; they're less so for rural ones.

Bus Contact Greyhound ☎ *800/231-2222* ⊕ *www.greyhound.com.*

CAR TRAVEL

Driving is the easiest way to experience the Central Coast. U.S. 101 and Highway 1, which run north–south, are the main routes to and through the Central Coast from Los Angeles and San Francisco. Highly scenic Highway 1 hugs the coast, and U.S. 101 runs inland. Between Ventura County and northern Santa Barbara County, the two highways are the same road. Highway 1 again separates from U.S. 101 north of Gaviota, then rejoins the highway at Pismo Beach. Along any stretch where these two highways are separate, U.S. 101 is the quicker route.

The most dramatic section of the Central Coast is the 70 miles between San Simeon and Big Sur. The road is narrow and twisting, with a single lane in each direction. In fog or rain the drive can be downright nerve-racking; in wet seasons mudslides can close portions of the road.

Other routes into the Central Coast include Highway 46 and Highway 33, which head, respectively, west and south from Interstate 5 near Bakersfield.

Road Conditions Caltrans ☎ *800/427-7623, 888/836-0866 Hwy. 1 Visitor Hotline (Cambria north to Carmel)* ⊕ *www.dot.ca.gov.*

TRAIN TRAVEL

The Amtrak *Coast Starlight,* which runs between Los Angeles and Seattle via Oakland, stops in Paso Robles, San Luis Obispo, Santa Barbara, and Oxnard. Amtrak runs several *Pacific Surfliner* trains and buses daily between San Luis Obispo, Santa Barbara, Los Angeles, and San Diego. Metrolink Regional Rail Service trains connect Ventura and Oxnard with Los Angeles and points between.

Train Contacts Amtrak ☎ *800/872-7245, 805/963-1015 in Santa Barbara, 805/541-0505 in San Luis Obispo* ⊕ *www.amtrak.com.* **Metrolink** ☎ *800/371-5465* ⊕ *www.metrolinktrains.com.*

RESTAURANTS

The cuisine in Ventura and Santa Barbara is every bit as eclectic as it is in California's bigger cities; fresh seafood is a standout. A foodie renaissance has overtaken the entire region from Ventura to Paso Robles, spawning dozens of new restaurants touting locavore cuisine made with fresh organic produce and meats. Dining attire on the Central Coast is generally casual, though slightly dressy casual wear is the custom at pricier restaurants. *Prices in the reviews are the average cost of a main course at dinner or, if dinner is not served, at lunch.*

HOTELS

Lodging options abound in the Central Coast, but expect to pay top dollar for rooms along the shore, especially in summer. Moderately priced hotels and motels do exist—most just a short drive inland from their higher-price counterparts. Make your reservations as early as possible and take advantage of midweek specials to get the best rates. It's common for lodgings to require two-day minimum stays on holidays and some weekends, especially in summer, and to double rates during festivals and other events. Hot Spots provides room reservations and tourist information. *Prices in the reviews are the lowest cost of a standard double room in high season. For expanded reviews, facilities, and current deals, visit Fodors.com.*

Hot Spots ☎ *800/793–7666, 805/564–1637* ⊕ *www.hotspotsusa.com.*

TOUR OPTIONS

Central Coast Food Tours conducts walking tours ($69) of shops, restaurants, wineries, and other food-oriented spots in downtown San Luis Obispo, Paso Robles, and other Central Coast destinations. Cloud Climbers Jeep and Wine Tours offers four types of daily tours ($89–$129): wine tasting, mountain, sunset, and a discovery tour for families. These trips to the Santa Barbara/Santa Ynez mountains and Wine Country are conducted in open-air, six-passenger jeeps. The company also offers a four-hour All Around Ojai Tour ($109) and arranges biking, horseback riding, and trap-shooting tours and Paso Robles wine tours.

Wine Edventures operates guided wine tours ($105) in the Santa Ynez Valley in vans, minicoaches, and other vehicles. The Grapeline Wine Country Shuttle leads daily wine and vineyard picnic tours ($99–$119) in Paso Robles and the Santa Ynez Valley.

Santa Barbara Wine Country Cycling Tours leads half- and full-day tours ($80–$120) of the Santa Ynez wine region. The company also conducts half-day hiking tours ($100–$110) and custom and multiday cycling tours. Spencer's Limousine & Tours offers customized tours of Santa Barbara and the Wine Country via sedan, limousine, or van. A five-hour basic tour with at least four participants costs about $90 per person. Stagecoach Wine Tours runs daily wine-tasting excursions ($129) through the Santa Ynez Valley in vans, minicoaches, and SUVs. Sustainable Vine Wine Tours specializes in eco-friendly wine tours ($125) of the valley in nine-passenger Mercedes Sprinter vans. Trips include tastings at green-minded wineries, and a gourmet organic picnic lunch.

Many of the tour companies described above will pick you up at your hotel or central locations; ask about this when booking.

Tour Contacts Central Coast Food Tours ☎ *800/979–3370, 212/209–3370* ⊕ *www.centralcoastfoodtours.com.* **Cloud Climbers Jeep and Wine Tours** ☎ *805/646–3200* ⊕ *www.ccjeeps.com.* **The Grapeline Wine Country Shuttle** ☎ *888/894–6379* ⊕ *www.gogrape.com.* **Santa Barbara Wine Country Cycling**

Tours ✉ *3630 Sagunto St., Santa Ynez* ☎ *888/557–8687, 805/686–9490*
⊕ *www.winecountrycycling.com.* **Spencer's Limousine & Tours** ☎ *805/884–9700* ⊕ *www.spencerslimo.com.* **Stagecoach Wine Tours** ✉ *Solvang*
☎ *805/686–8347* ⊕ *www.winetourssantaynez.com.* **Sustainable Vine Wine Tours** ☎ *805/698–3911* ⊕ *www.sustainablevine.com.* **Wine Edventures**
✉ *Santa Barbara* ☎ *805/965–9463* ⊕ *www.welovewines.com.*

VISITOR INFORMATION

Contact Central Coast Tourism Council ⊕ *www.centralcoast-tourism.com.*

VENTURA COUNTY

Ventura County was first settled by the Chumash Indians. Spanish missionaries were the first Europeans to arrive, followed by Americans and other Europeans, who established bustling towns, transportation networks, and highly productive farms. Since the 1920s, agriculture has been steadily replaced as the area's main industry—first by the oil business and more recently by tourism.

5

VENTURA

60 miles north of Los Angeles.

Like Los Angeles, the city of Ventura enjoys gorgeous weather and sun-kissed beaches—but without the smog and congestion. The miles of beautiful beaches attract athletes—bodysurfers and boogie boarders, runners and bikers—and those who'd rather doze beneath an umbrella all day. Ventura Harbor is home to myriad fishing boats, restaurants, and water-activity centers where you can rent boats and take harbor cruises. Foodies can get their fix all over Ventura—dozens of upscale cafés and wine and tapas bars have opened in recent years. Arts and antiques buffs have long trekked downtown to browse the galleries and shops there.

GETTING HERE AND AROUND

Amtrak and Metrolink trains serve the area from Los Angeles area. Greyhound buses stop in Ventura; Gold Coast Transit serves the city and the rest of Ventura County.

U.S. 101 is the north–south main route into town, but for a scenic drive, take Highway 1 north from Santa Monica. The highway merges with U.S. 101 just south of Ventura. ■TIP➜ Traveling north to Ventura from Los Angeles on weekdays it's best to depart before 6 am, between 10 and 2, or after 7, or you'll get caught in the extended rush-hour traffic. Coming south from Santa Barbara, depart before 1 or after 6. On weekends, traffic is generally fine except southbound on U.S. 101 between Santa Barbara and Ventura.

ESSENTIALS

Bus Contact Gold Coast Transit ☎ *805/643-3158* ⊕ *www.goldcoasttransit.org.*

Visitor Information Ventura Visitors and Convention Bureau
✉ *Downtown Visitor Center, 101 S. California St.* ☎ *805/648-2075, 800/483-6214* ⊕ *www.ventura-usa.com.*

EXPLORING

FAMILY   **Lake Casitas Recreation Area.** Lunker largemouth bass, rainbow trout, crappie, redears, and channel catfish live in the waters at this park, one of the country's best bass-fishing areas. Nestled below the Santa Ynez Mountains' Laguna Ridge, Lake Casitas is also a beautiful spot for pitching a tent or having a picnic. The Casitas Water Adventure, which has two water playgrounds and a lazy river for tubing and floating, provides kids with endless diversions in summer. ⊠ *11311 Santa Ana Rd., off Hwy. 33, 13 miles northwest of Ventura* ☎ *805/649–2233, 805/649–1122 campground reservations* ⊕ *www.casitaswater.org* ⊡ *$10–$15 per vehicle, $13 per boat; Water Adventure $12 ($6 5–7 pm)* ☉ *Daily.*

Mission San Buenaventura. The ninth of the 21 California missions, Mission San Buenaventura was established in 1782 but burned to the ground in the 1790s. It was rebuilt and rededicated in 1809. A self-guided tour takes you through a small museum, a quiet courtyard, and a chapel with 250-year-old paintings. ⊠ *211 E. Main St., at Figueroa St.* ☎ *805/643–4318* ⊕ *www.sanbuenaventuramission.org* ⊡ *$4* ☉ *Weekdays 10–5, Sat. 9–5, Sun. 10–4.*

Museum of Ventura County. Exhibits in a contemporary complex of galleries and a sunny courtyard plaza tell the story of Ventura County from prehistoric times to the present. A highlight is the gallery that contains Ojai artist George Stuart's historical figures, dressed in exceptionally detailed, custom-made clothing reflecting their particular eras. In the courtyard, eight panels made with 45,000 pieces of cut glass form a historical timeline. ⊠ *100 E. Main St., at S. Ventura Ave.* ☎ *805/653–0323* ⊕ *venturamuseum.org* ⊡ *$4, free first Sun. of the month* ☉ *Tues.–Sun. 11–5.*

Ventura Oceanfront. Four miles of gorgeous coastline stretch from the county fairgrounds at the northern border of the city of San Buenaventura, through San Buenaventura State Beach, down to Ventura Harbor in the south. The main attraction here is the San Buenaventura City Pier, a landmark built in 1872 and restored in 1993. Surfers rip the waves just north of the pier, and sunbathers relax on white-sand beaches on either side. The mile-long promenade and the Omer Rains Bike Trail north of the pier attract scores of joggers, surrey cyclers, and bikers throughout the year. ⊠ *California St., at ocean's edge.*

WHERE TO EAT

$$ ✕ **Brophy Bros.** The Ventura outpost of this wildly popular Santa Barbara
SEAFOOD   restaurant provides the same fresh seafood-oriented meals in a spacious second-story setting overlooking the harbor. Feast on everything from fish and chips and crab cakes to chowder and delectable fish—often straight from the boats moored below. ⑤ *Average main: $22* ⊠ *1559 Spinnaker Dr., in Ventura Harbor Village* ☎ *805/639–0865* ⊕ *www. brophybros.com* ⚎ *Reservations not accepted.*

$ ✕ **Lure Fish House.** Fresh, sustainably caught seafood charbroiled over a
SEAFOOD   mesquite grill, a well-stocked oyster bar, specialty cocktails, and a wine list heavy on local vintages lure diners into this slick, nautical-themed space downtown. The menu, which changes daily, centers on the mostly local catch and organic veggies, and also includes tacos, sandwiches, and salads. Grilled entrées come with a choice of unusual farm-to-table

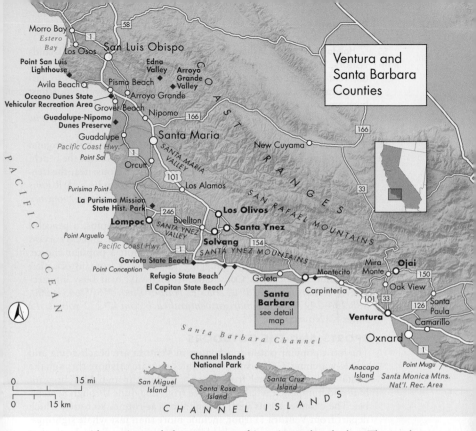

Ventura and
Santa Barbara
Counties

sides: quinoa salad, sweet-potato fries, pineapple cole slaw. The regulars rave about the shrimp-and-chips, cioppino, and citrus crab-cake salad. $ *Average main: $15* ⊠ *60 S. California St.* ☎ *805/567–4400* ⊕ *www.lurefishhouse.com.*

WHERE TO STAY

For expanded reviews, facilities, and current deals, visit Fodors.com.

$$ **Crowne Plaza Ventura Beach.** A 12-story hotel with an enviable location
HOTEL on the beach and next to a historic pier, the Crowne Plaza is also within walking distance of downtown restaurants and nightlife. **Pros:** on the beach; near downtown; steps from waterfront. **Cons:** early-morning train noise; waterfront crowded in summer; most rooms on the small side. $ *Rooms from: $169* ⊠ *450 E. Harbor Blvd.* ☎ *800/842–0800, 805/648–2100* ⊕ *cpventura.com* ⤳ *254 rooms, 4 suites* ⏐⊙⏐ *No meals.*

$$ **Four Points by Sheraton Ventura Harbor Resort.** An on-site restaurant,
RESORT spacious rooms, and a slew of amenities make this 17-acre property—which includes sister hotel Holiday Inn Express—a popular and practical choice for Channel Islands visitors. **Pros:** close to island transportation; mostly quiet; short drive to historic downtown. **Cons:** not in the heart of downtown; noisy seagulls sometimes congregate nearby. $ *Rooms from: $145* ⊠ *1050 Schooner Dr.* ☎ *805/658–1212* ⊕ *www.fourpoints.com/ventura* ⤳ *102 rooms, 4 suites* ⏐⊙⏐ *No meals.*

$$ ⌕ **Holiday Inn Express Ventura Harbor.** A favorite among Channel Islands
HOTEL   visitors, this quiet, comfortable, lodge-inspired property sits right at
the Ventura Harbor entrance. **Pros:** quiet at night; easy access to har-
bor restaurants and activities; five-minute drive to downtown. **Cons:**
busy area on weekends; complaints of erratic service. ⑤ *Rooms from:*
$130 ✉ *1080 Navigator Dr.* ☎ *805/856–9533, 800/315–2621* ⊕ *www.*
holidayinnexpress.com/venturaca ⇥ *69 rooms* ❑ *Breakfast.*

$$ ⌕ **Pierpont Inn.** Back in 1910, Josephine Pierpont-Ginn built the original
HOTEL   Pierpont Inn on a hill overlooking Ventura Beach. **Pros:** near the beach;
lush gardens; Tempur-Pedic mattresses and pillows. **Cons:** near the freeway and train tracks; difficult to walk downtown from here. ⑤ *Rooms*
from: $125 ✉ *550 Sanjon Rd.* ☎ *805/643–6144* ⊕ *www.pierpontinn.*
com ⇥ *65 rooms, 9 suites, 2 cottages* ❑ *No meals.*

$$$ ⌕ **Ventura Beach Marriott.** Spacious, contemporary rooms, a peaceful
HOTEL   location just steps from San Buenaventura State Beach, and easy access
to downtown arts and culture make the Marriott a popular choice.
Pros: walk to beach and biking/jogging trails; a block from historic pier;
great value for location. **Cons:** close to highway; near busy intersec-
tion. ⑤ *Rooms from: $189* ✉ *2055 E. Harbor Blvd.* ☎ *805/643–6000,*
888/236–2427 ⊕ *www.marriottventurabeach.com* ⇥ *272 rooms, 12*
suites ❑ *No meals.*

SPORTS AND THE OUTDOORS

The most popular outdoor activities in Ventura are beach-going and
whale-watching. California gray whales migrate offshore through the
Santa Barbara Channel from late December through March; giant
blue and humpback whales feed here from mid-June through Septem-
ber. The channel teems with marine life year-round, so tours, which
depart from Ventura Harbor, include more than just whale sightings.
To learn about the spectacular hiking trails on the five islands that
comprise Channel Islands National Park, check out its visitor center,
also at the harbor.

Island Packers. A cruise through the Santa Barbara Channel with Island
Packers will give you the chance to spot dolphins and seals—and some-
times even whales—throughout the year. ✉ *Ventura Harbor, 1691 Spin-*
naker Dr. ☎ *805/642–1393* ⊕ *www.islandpackers.com.*

OJAI

15 miles north of Ventura.

The Ojai Valley, which director Frank Capra used as a backdrop for
his 1936 film *Lost Horizon,* sizzles in the summer when temperatures
routinely reach 90°F. The acres of orange and avocado groves here
evoke postcard images of long-ago agricultural Southern California.
Many artists and celebrities have sought refuge from life in the fast
lane in lush Ojai.

GETTING HERE AND AROUND

From northern Ventura, Highway 33 veers east from U.S. 101 and
climbs inland to Ojai. From Santa Barbara, exit U.S. 101 at Highway
150 in Carpinteria, then travel east 20 miles on a twisting, two-lane

road that is not recommended at night or during poor weather. You can also access Ojai by heading west from Interstate 5 on Highway 126. Exit at Santa Paula and follow Highway 150 north for 16 miles to Ojai. Gold Coast Transit provides service to Ojai from Ventura.

Ojai can be easily explored on foot; you can also hop on the Ojai Trolley ($1, or $2 day pass), which until about 5 pm follows two routes around Ojai and neighboring Miramonte on weekdays and one route on weekends. Tell the driver you're visiting and you'll get an informal guided tour.

ESSENTIALS

Bus Contacts Gold Coast Transit ☎ *805/643–3158* ⊕ *www.goldcoasttransit. org.* **Ojai Trolley** ☎ *805/646–5581* ⊕ *www.ojaitrolley.com.*

Visitor Information Ojai Visitors Bureau ⊠ *206 N. Signal St., at E. Ojai Ave.* ☎ *888/652–4669* ⊕ *www.ojaivisitors.com* ☾ *Weekdays 9–4.*

EXPLORING

Ojai Art Center. California's oldest nonprofit, multipurpose arts center exhibits visual art from various disciplines and presents theater, dance, and other performances. ⊠ *113 S. Montgomery St., near E. Ojai Ave.* ☎ *805/646–0117* ⊕ *www.ojaiartcenter.org* ☾ *Tues.–Sun. noon–4.*

Ojai Avenue. The work of local artists is displayed in the Spanish-style shopping arcade along the avenue downtown. Organic and specialty growers sell their produce on Sundays between 9 and 1 at the outdoor market behind the arcade.

Ojai Valley Museum. The museum has many Native American artifacts and mounts exhibits documenting local history. Walking tours of Ojai depart from here. ⊠ *130 W. Ojai Ave.* ☎ *805/640–1390* ⊕ *www. ojaivalleymuseum.org* 🖾 *Musuem $4, walking tour $5* ☾ *Tues.–Sat. 10–4, Sun. noon–4; tour Oct.–July, Sat. 10:30.*

Ojai Valley Trail. The 18-mile trail is open to pedestrians, joggers, equestrians, bikers, and others on nonmotorized vehicles. You can access it anywhere along its route. ⊠ *Parallel to Hwy. 33 from Soule Park in Ojai to ocean in Ventura* ☎ *888/652–4669* ⊕ *www.ojaivisitors.com.*

WHERE TO EAT

$$$
MEDITERRANEAN

✗**Azu.** Delectable tapas, a full bar, slick furnishings, and piped jazz music draw diners to this artsy Mediterranean bistro. You can also order soups, salads, and bistro fare such as steak frites and paella. Save room for the homemade gelato. ⑤ *Average main: $24* ⊠ *457 E. Ojai Ave.* ☎ *805/640–7987* ⊕ *www.azuojai.com.*

$
ITALIAN

✗**Boccali's.** Edging a ranch, citrus groves, and a seasonal garden that provides produce for menu items, the modest but cheery Boccali's attracts many loyal fans. When it's warm, you can dine alfresco in the oak-shaded patio and lawn area and sometimes listen to live music. The family-run operation, best known for hand-rolled pizzas and home-style pastas (don't miss the eggplant lasagna), also serves a popular seasonal strawberry shortcake. ⑤ *Average main: $15* ⊠ *3277 Ojai Ave., about 2 miles east of downtown* ☎ *805/646–6116* ⊕ *www.boccalis.com* 🖃 *No credit cards* ☾ *No lunch Mon. and Tues.*

5

$$$ ✕ **The Ranch House.** This elegant yet laid-back eatery has been around
AMERICAN   for decades. Main dishes such as the broiled-and-roasted rack of lamb
with pineapple guava chutney and the grilled diver scallops with cur-
ried sweet-corn sauce are not to be missed. The verdant patio is a
wonderful place to have Sunday brunch. $ *Average main: $29* ⊠ *500
S. Lomita Ave.* ☎ *805/646–2360* ⊕ *www.theranchhouse.com* ⊙ *Closed
Mon. No lunch.*

$$$ ✕ **Suzanne's Cuisine.** Peppered filet mignon, linguine with steamed clams,
EUROPEAN   and pan-roasted salmon with a roasted mango sauce are among the
offerings at this European-style restaurant. Game, seafood, and vegetarian dishes dominate the dinner menu, and salads and soups star
at lunchtime. All the breads and desserts are made on the premises.
$ *Average main: $24* ⊠ *502 W. Ojai Ave.* ☎ *805/640–1961* ⊕ *www.
suzannescuisine.com* ⊙ *Closed Tues.*

WHERE TO STAY

For expanded reviews, facilities, and current deals, visit Fodors.com.

$$ ⌂ **The Blue Iguana Inn & Suites.** Artists run this Southwestern-style hotel,
B&B/INN   and their work (which is for sale) decorates the rooms. **Pros:** colorful
art everywhere; secluded. **Cons:** 2 miles from downtown; on a highway;
small. $ *Rooms from: $129* ⊠ *11794 N. Ventura Ave.* ☎ *805/646–
5277* ⊕ *www.iguanainnsofojai.com* ⇆ *4 rooms, 8 suites, 8 cottages*
†⊙† *Breakfast.*

$$$ ⌂ **Oaks at Ojai.** Rejuvenation is the name of the game at this destination
RESORT   spa. **Pros:** great place to get fit; peaceful retreat; healthful meals. **Cons:**
basic rooms; on main highway through town. $ *Rooms from: $199*
⊠ *122 E. Ojai Ave.* ☎ *805/646–5573, 800/753–6257* ⊕ *www.oaksspa.
com* ⇆ *44 rooms, 2 suites* †⊙† *All meals* ⌖ *2-night minimum stay.*

$$$$ ⌂ **Ojai Valley Inn & Spa.** This outdoorsy, golf-oriented resort and spa
RESORT   is set on beautifully landscaped grounds, with hillside views in nearly
Fodor's Choice   all directions. **Pros:** gorgeous grounds; exceptional outdoor activities;
★   romantic yet kid-friendly. **Cons:** expensive; areas near restaurants can
be noisy. $ *Rooms from: $400* ⊠ *905 Country Club Rd.* ☎ *805/646–
1111, 888/697–8780* ⊕ *www.ojairesort.com* ⇆ *231 rooms, 77 suites*
†⊙† *No meals.*

$$$ ⌂ **Su Nido Inn.** A short walk from downtown Ojai sights and restau-
B&B/INN   rants, this posh Mission revival–style inn sits in a quiet neighborhood
a few blocks from Libbey Park. **Pros:** walking distance from down-
town; homey feel. **Cons:** no pool; can get hot during summer. $ *Rooms
from: $189* ⊠ *301 N. Montgomery St.* ☎ *805/646–7080, 866/646–7080*
⊕ *www.sunidoinn.com* ⇆ *3 rooms, 9 suites* †⊙† *No meals* ⌖ *2-night
minimum stay on weekends.*

SANTA BARBARA

27 miles northwest of Ventura and 29 miles west of Ojai.

Santa Barbara has long been an oasis for Los Angelenos seeking respite from big-city life. The attractions begin at the ocean and end in the foothills of the Santa Ynez Mountains. A few miles up the coast east and west—but still very much a part of Santa Barbara—are the exclusive residential districts of Montecito and Hope Ranch. Santa Barbara is on a jog in the coastline, so the ocean is actually to the south, instead of the west; for this reason, directions can be confusing. "Up" the coast toward San Francisco is west, "down" toward Los Angeles is east, and the mountains are north.

GETTING HERE AND AROUND

U.S. 101 is the main route into Santa Barbara. If you're staying in town, a car is handy but not essential; the beaches and downtown are easily explored by bicycle or on foot. Visit the Santa Barbara Car Free website for bike-route and walking-tour maps and car-free vacation packages with substantial lodging, dining, activity, and transportation discounts.

Santa Barbara Metropolitan Transit District's Line 22 bus serves major tourist sights. Several bus lines connect with the very convenient electric shuttles that cruise the downtown and waterfront every 10 to 15 minutes (50¢ each way).

Santa Barbara Trolley Co. operates a motorized San Francisco–style cable car that loops past major hotels, shopping areas, and attractions from 10 to 4. Get off whenever you like, and pick up another trolley (they come every hour) when you're ready to move on. The fare is $19 for the day.

TOURS

Land and Sea Tours. This outfit conducts 90-minute narrated tours in an amphibious 49-passenger vehicle nicknamed the Land Shark. The adventure begins with a drive through the city, followed by a plunge into the harbor for a cruise along the coast. ⊠ *State St., at Stearns Wharf* ☎ *805/683–7600* ⊕ *www.out2seesb.com* ✉ *$25* ⊙ *Tours May–Oct., daily noon, 2, and 4; Nov.–Apr., daily noon and 2.*

Segway Tours of Santa Barbara. After a brief training session, a guide leads you around town on electric-powered personal balancing transporters. Tour options include the waterfront (1¼ hours), Butterfly Beach and Montecito (2 hours), historic downtown Santa Barbara (2½ hours), and through town to the mission (3 hours). This outfit also rents electric bikes. ⊠ *16 Helena Ave., at Cabrillo Blvd.* ☎ *805/963–7672* ⊕ *www. segwayofsb.com* ✉ *$65–$110.*

ESSENTIALS

Transportation Contacts Santa Barbara Car Free ☎ *805/696–1100* ⊕ *www.santabarbaracarfree.org.* **Santa Barbara Metropolitan Transit District** ☎ *805/963–3366* ⊕ *www.sbmtd.gov.* **Santa Barbara Trolley Co.** ☎ *805/965–0353* ⊕ *www.sbtrolley.com.*

Visitor Information Santa Barbara Visitor Center ⊠ *1 Garden St., at Cabrillo Blvd.* ☎ *805/965–3021, 805/568–1811* ⊕ *www.sbchamber.org* ⊙ *Mon.–Sat. 9–5, Sun. 10–5.* **Santa Barbara Conference and Visitors Bureau** ⊠ *500 E. Montecito St.* ☎ *805/966–9222* ⊕ *www.santabarbaraca.com.*

Continued on page 252

ON A MISSION

Their soul may belong to Spain, their heart to the New World, but the historic missions of California, with their lovely churches, beckon the traveler on a soulful journey back to the very founding of the American West.

by Cheryl Crabtree and Robert I.C. Fisher

California history changed forever in the 18th century when Spanish explorers founded a series of missions along the Pacific coast. Believing they were following God's will, they wanted to spread the gospel and convert as many natives as possible. The process produced a collision between the Hispanic and California Indian cultures, resulting in one of the most striking legacies of Old California: the Spanish mission churches. Rising like mirages in the middle of desert plains and rolling hills, these saintly sites transport you back to the days of the Spanish colonial period.

GOD AND MAN IN CALIFORNIA

The Alta California territory came under pressure in the 1760s when Spain feared foreign advances into the territory explorer Juan Rodríguez Cabrillo had claimed for the Spanish crown back in 1542. But how could Spain create a visible and viable presence halfway around the world? They decided to build on the model that had already worked well in Spain's Mexico colony. The plan involved establishing a series of missions, to be operated by the Catholic Church and protected by four of Spain's *presidios* (military outposts). The native Indians— after quick conversion to Christianity—would provide the labor force necessary to build mission towns.

FATHER OF THE MISSIONS

Father Junípero Serra is an icon of the Spanish colonial period. At the behest of the Spanish government, the diminutive padre—then well into his fifties, and despite a chronic leg infection— started out on foot from Baja California to search for suitable mission sites, with a goal of reaching Monterey. In 1769 he helped establish Alta California's first mission in San Diego and continued his travels until his death, in 1784, by which time he had founded eight more missions.

The system ended about a decade after the Mexican government took control of Alta California in the early 1820s and began to secularize the missions. The church lost horses and cattle, as well as vast tracts of land, which the Mexican government in turn granted to private individuals. They also lost laborers, as the Indians were for the most part free to find work and a life beyond the missions. In 1848, the Americans assumed control of the territory, and California became part of the United States. Today, these missions stand as extraordinary monuments to their colorful past.

Mission Santa Barbara Museum

MISSION ACCOMPLISHED

California's Mission Trail is the best way to follow in the fathers' footsteps. Here, below, are its 21 settlements, north to south.

Amazingly, all 21 Spanish missions in California are still standing—some in their pristine historic state, others with modifications made over the centuries. Many are found on or near the "King's Road"—El Camino Real—which linked these mission outposts. At the height of the mission system the trail was approximately 600 miles long, eventually extending from San Diego to Sonoma. Today the road is commemorated on portions of routes 101 and 82 in the form of roadside bell markers erected by CalTrans every one to two miles between San Diego and San Francisco.

San Francisco Solano, Sonoma (1823; this was the final California mission constructed.)

San Rafael, San Rafael (1817)

San Francisco de Asís (aka Mission Dolores), San Francisco (1776). Situated in the heart of San Francisco,

Mission Santa Clara de Asís

these mission grounds and nearby Arroyo de los Dolores (Creek of Sorrows) are home to the oldest intact building in the city.

Santa Clara de Asís, Santa Clara (1777). On the campus of Santa Clara University, this beautifully restored mission contains original paintings, statues, a bell, and hundreds of artifacts, as well as a spectacular rose garden.

San José, Fremont (1797)

Santa Cruz, Santa Cruz (1791)

San Juan Bautista, San Juan Bautista (1797). Immortalized in Hitchcock's *Vertigo*, this remarkably preserved pueblo contains the largest church of all the California missions, as well as 18th- and 19th-century buildings and a sprawling plaza.

San Carlos Borromeo del Río Carmelo, Carmel (1770). Carmel Mission was head-

Painting from 1818, San Juan Bautista.

quarters for the California mission system under Father Serra and the Father Presidents who succeeded him; the on-site museum includes Serra's tiny sleeping quarters (where he died in 1784).

Nuestra Señora de la Soledad, Soledad (1791)

San Antonio de Padua, Jolon (1771)

San Miguel Arcángel, San Miguel (1797). San Miguel boasts the only intact original interior wall painting in any of the missions, painted in 1821 by Native American converts under the direction of Spanish artist Esteban Muras.

Mission Santa Inés

Mission San Fernando Rey de España

now a living-history museum with a church and nearly forty craft and residence rooms.

Santa Inés, Solvang (1804). Home to one of the most significant pieces of religious art created by a California mission Indian.

Santa Bárbara, Santa Barbara (1786). The "Queen of the Missions" has twin bell towers, gorgeous gardens with heirloom plant varietals, a massive collection of rare artworks and artifacts, and lovely stonework.

San Buenaventura, Ventura (1782). This was the last mission founded by Father Serra; it is still an active parish in the Archdiocese of Los Angeles.

San Luis Obispo de Tolosa, San Luis Obispo (1772). Bear meat from grizzlies captured here saved the Spaniards from starving, which helped convince Father Serra to establish a mission.

La Purísima Concepción, Lompoc (1787). La Purísima is the nation's most completely restored mission complex. It is

San Fernando Rey de España, Mission Hills (1797)

San Gabriel Arcángel, San Gabriel (1771)

San Luis Rey de Francia, Oceanside (1798)

San Juan Capistrano, San Juan Capistrano (1776). This mission is famed for its Saint Joseph's Day (March 19) celebration of the return of swallows in the springtime. The mission's adobe walls enclose acres of lush gardens and historic buildings.

San Diego de Alcalá, San Diego (1769). This was the first California missions constructed, although the original was destroyed in 1775 and rebuilt over a number of years.

5

IN FOCUS ON A MISSION

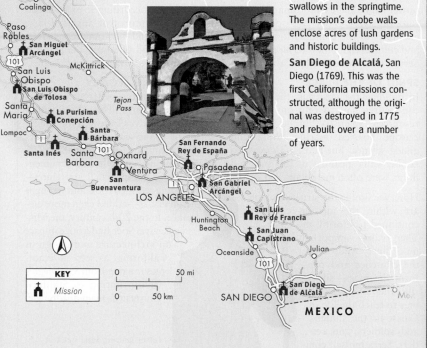

Coalinga

Paso Robles

San Miguel Arcángel

McKittrick

San Luis Obispo

San Luis Obispo de Tolosa

Tejon Pass

Santa Maria

La Purísima Conepción

Lompoc

Santa Bárbara

Santa Inés

Santa Barbara

Oxnard

San Fernando Rey de España

Ventura

Pasadena

San Buenaventura

San Gabriel Arcángel

LOS ANGELES

Huntington Beach

San Luis Rey de Francia

San Juan Capistrano

Oceanside

Julian

KEY

| 🕈 | Mission |

0   50 mi

0   50 km

San Diego de Alcalá

SAN DIEGO

MEXICO

SPANISH MISSION STYLE

(left) Mission San Luis Rey de Francia; (right) Mission San Antonio de Padua

The Spanish mission churches derive much of their strength and enduring power from their extraordinary admixture of styles. They are spectacular examples of the combination of races and cultures that bloomed along Father Serra's road through Alta California.

SPIRIT OF THE PLACE

In building the missions, the Franciscan padres had to rely on available resources. Spanish churches back in Europe boasted marble floors and gilded statues. But here, whitewashed adobe walls gleamed in the sun and floors were often merely packed earth.

However simple the structures, the art within the mission confines continued to glorify the Church. The padres imported much finery to decorate the churches and perform the mass—silver, silk and lovely paintings to teach the life of Christ to the Indians and soldiers and settlers. Serra himself com-

missioned fine artists in Mexico to produce custom works using the best materials and according to exact specifications. Sculptures of angels, Mary, Joseph, Jesus and the Franciscan heroes and saints—and of course the Stations of the Cross—adorned all the missions.

AN ENDURING LEGACY

Mission architecture reflects a gorgeous blend of European and New World influences. While naves followed the simple forms of Franciscan Gothic, cloisters (with beautiful arcades) adopted aspects of the Romanesque style, and ornamental touches of the Spanish Renaissance—including red-tiled roofs and wrought-iron grilles—added even more elegance. In the 20th century, the Mission Revival Style had a huge impact on architecture and design in California, as seen in examples ranging from San Diego's Union Station to Stanford University's main quadrangle.

Father Junípero Serra statue at Mission San Gabriel

FOR WHOM THE BELLS TOLLED

Perhaps the most famous architectural motif of the Spanish Mission churches was the belltower. These took the form of either a campanile—a single tower called a campanario—or, more spectacularly, of an open-work espedaña, a perforated adobe wall housing a series of bells (notable examples of this form are at San Miguel Arcángel and San Diego de Alcalá). Bells were essential to maintaining the routines of daily life at the missions.

MISSION LIFE

Morning bells summoned residents to chapel for services; noontime bells introduced the main meal, while the evening bells sounded the alert to gather around 5 pm for mass and dinner. Many of the natives were happy with their new faith, and even enjoyed putting in numerous hours a week working as farmers, soapmakers, weavers, and masons.

Others, however, were less willing to abandon their traditional culture, but were coerced to abide by the new Spanish laws and mission rules. Natives were sometimes mistreated by the friars, who used a system of punishments to enforce submission to the new culture.

NATIVE TRAGEDY

In the end, mission life proved extremely destructive to the Native Californian population. European diseases and contaminated water caused the death of nearly a third, with some tribes—notably the Chumash—being virtually decimated.

Despite these losses, small numbers did survive. After the Mexican government secularized the missions in 1833, a majority of the native population was reduced to poverty. Some stayed at the missions, while others went to live in the pueblos, ranchos, and countryside.

Many Native Californian people today still work and live near the missions that are monuments to their artistry skills.

FOR MORE INFORMATION

California Missions Foundation

✉ 26555 Carmel Rancho Blvd., Ste. 7 Carmel, CA 93923

☎ 831/622-7500

🌐 www.california missionsfoundation.org

Top, Mission San Gabriel Arcángel
Bottom, Mission San Miguel Arcángel

5

IN FOCUS ON A MISSION

EXPLORING

Santa Barbara's waterfront is beautiful, with palm-studded promenades and plenty of sand. In the few miles between the beaches and the hills are downtown, the old mission, and the botanic gardens.

EXPLORING

TOP ATTRACTIONS

El Presidio State Historic Park. Founded in 1782, El Presidio was one of four military strongholds established by the Spanish along the coast of California. The park encompasses much of the original site in the heart of downtown. El Cuartel, the adobe guardhouse, is the oldest building in Santa Barbara and the second oldest in California. ⊠ *123 E. Canon Perdido St., at Anacapa St.* ☎ *805/965–0093* ⊕ *www.sbthp.org* ☒ *$5* ⊘ *Daily 10:30–4:30.*

FAMILY
Fodor'sChoice
★

Lotusland. The 37-acre estate called Lotusland once belonged to the Polish opera singer Ganna Walska, who purchased it in the late 1940s and lived here until her death in 1984. Many of the exotic trees and other subtropical flora were planted in 1882 by horticulturist R. Kinton Stevens. On the two-hour guided tour—the only option for visiting unless you're a member; reserve well ahead in summer—you'll see an outdoor theater, a topiary garden, a huge collection of rare cycads (an unusual plant genus that has been around since the time of the dinosaurs), and a lotus pond. ■TIP➜ Child-friendly family tours are available for groups with children under the age of 10; contact Lotusland for scheduling. ⊠ *695 Ashley Rd., off Sycamore Canyon Rd. (Hwy. 192), Montecito* ☎ *805/969–9990* ⊕ *www.lotusland.org* ☒ *$35* ⊘ *Mid-Feb.–mid-Nov., Wed.–Sat. at 10 and 1:30 by appointment only.*

Fodor'sChoice
★

Mission Santa Barbara. Widely referred to as the "Queen of Missions," this is one of the most beautiful and frequently photographed buildings in coastal California. Dating to 1786, the architecture evolved from adobe-brick buildings with thatch roofs to more permanent edifices as the mission's population burgeoned. An earthquake in 1812 destroyed the third church built on the site. Its replacement, the present structure, is still a functioning Catholic church. Mission Santa Barbara has a splendid Spanish/Mexican colonial art collection, as well as Chumash sculptures and the only Native American–made altar and tabernacle left in the California missions. Docents lead 90-minute tours ($8 adult) Thursday and Friday at 11 and Saturday at 10:30. ⊠ *2201 Laguna St., at E. Los Olivos St.* ☎ *805/682–4149, 805/682–4713* ⊕ *www. santabarbaramission.org* ☒ *$5* ⊘ *Daily 9:30–4:30.*

Santa Barbara Botanic Garden. Scenic trails meander through the garden's 78 acres of native plants. The Mission Dam, built in 1806, stands just beyond the redwood grove and above the restored aqueduct that once carried water to Mission Santa Barbara. More than a thousand plant species thrive in various themed sections, including mountains, deserts, meadows, redwoods, and Channel Islands. ⊠ *1212 Mission Canyon Rd., north of Foothill Rd. (Hwy. 192)* ☎ *805/682–4726* ⊕ *www.sbbg. org* ☒ *$8* ⊘ *Mar.–Oct., daily 9–6; Nov.–Feb., daily 9–5. Guided tours weekends at 11 and 2, Mon. at 2.*

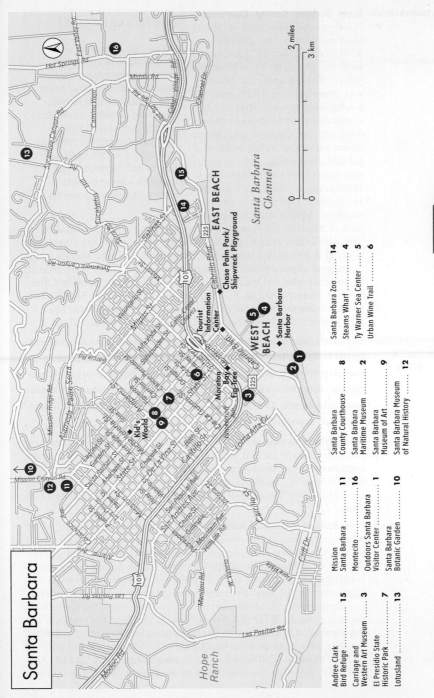

Santa Barbara

Fodor's Choice
★

Santa Barbara County Courthouse. Hand-painted tiles and a spiral staircase infuse the courthouse, a National Historic Landmark, with the grandeur of a Moorish palace. This magnificent building was completed in 1929, part of a rebuilding process after a 1925 earthquake destroyed many downtown structures. At the time, Santa Barbara was also in the midst of a cultural awakening, and the trend was toward an architectural style appropriate to the area's climate and history. The result is the harmonious Mediterranean–Spanish look of much of the downtown area, especially the municipal buildings. An elevator rises to an arched observation area in the courthouse tower that provides a panoramic view of the city. The murals in the ceremonial chambers on the courthouse's second floor were painted by an artist who did backdrops for some of Cecil B. DeMille's films. ⊠ *1100 Anacapa St., at E. Anapamu St.* ☎ *805/962–6464* ⊕ *www. santabarbaracourthouse.org* ☉ *Weekdays 8–4:45, weekends 10–4:30. Free guided tours Mon., Tues., Weds., and Fri. at 10:30, daily at 2.*

> ### SANTA BARBARA STYLE
>
> After a 1925 earthquake demolished many buildings, the city seized a golden opportunity to assume a Spanish-Mediterranean style. It established an architectural board of review, which, along with city commissions, created strict building codes for the downtown district: red tile roofs, earthtone facades, arches, wrought-iron embellishments, and height restrictions (about four stories).

QUICK BITES

Jeannine's. Take a break from State Street shopping at Jeannine's, revered locally for its wholesome sandwiches, salads, and baked goods, made from scratch with organic and natural ingredients. Pick up a turkey berry or chicken pesto sandwich to go, and picnic in the courthouse gardens a block away. ⊠ *La Arcada, 15 E. Figueroa St., at State St.* ☎ *805/687–8701* ⊕ *jeannines.com/downtown* ☉ *Daily 6:30–3:30.*

Santa Barbara Museum of Art. The highlights of this museum's permanent collection include ancient sculpture, Asian art, impressionist paintings, contemporary art, photography, and American works in several media. ⊠ *1130 State St., at E. Anapamu St.* ☎ *805/963–4364* ⊕ *www.sbma. net* ☒ *$10, free Thurs. 5–8* ☉ *Tues., Wed., Fri. and weekends 11–5, Thurs. 11–8.*

FAMILY **Santa Barbara Museum of Natural History.** The gigantic skeleton of a blue whale greets you at the entrance of this complex. The major draws include the planetarium, space lab, and a gem and mineral display. A room of dioramas illustrates Chumash Indian history and culture. Startlingly alive-looking stuffed specimens, complete with nests and eggs, roost in the bird diversity room. Many exhibits have interactive components. Outdoors, nature trails wind through the serene oak-studded grounds. ■TIP➔ A Nature Pass, available at the museum and the associated Ty Warner Sea Center, is good for discounted unlimited two-day admission to both facilities. ⊠ *2559 Puesta del Sol Rd., off E. Los Olivos St.* ☎ *805/682–4711* ⊕ *www.sbnature.org* ☒ *$12 Oct.–Apr., $13 May–Sept.; free third Sun. of month Sept.–May* ☉ *Daily 10–5.*

FAMILY **Santa Barbara Zoo.** The grounds of this smallish zoo are so gorgeous people book their weddings here long in advance. The palm-studded lawns on a hilltop overlooking the beach are perfect spots for family picnics. The natural settings of the zoo shelter elephants, gorillas, exotic birds like the California condor, and big cats such as the rare snow leopard, a thick-furred, high-altitude dweller from Asia. For small children, there's a scenic railroad and barnyard petting zoo. Duncan, an amazingly lifelike dinosaur, stars in the live stage show *How to Train Your Dinosaur* (free with zoo admission, daily in summer, on weekends the rest of the year). Duncan, designed by one of Hollywood's top creature shops, demonstrates the special techniques trainers use to care for animals. ⊠ *500 Niños Dr., off El Cabrillo Blvd.* ☎ *805/962–5339 main line, 805/962–6310 information* ⊕ *www.santabarbarazoo.org* 🖼*Zoo $14, parking $6* ⊙ *Daily 10–5.*

Stearns Wharf. Built in 1872, Stearns Wharf is Santa Barbara's most visited landmark. Expansive views of the mountains, cityscape, and harbor unfold from every vantage point on the three-block-long pier. Although it's a nice walk from the Cabrillo Boulevard parking areas, you can also park on the pier and then wander through the shops or stop for a meal at one of the wharf's restaurants. ⊠ *Cabrillo Blvd. and State St.* ⊕ *www.stearnswharf.org.*

FAMILY **Ty Warner Sea Center.** A branch of the Santa Barbara Museum of Natural History, the center specializes in Santa Barbara Channel marine life and conservation. Though small compared to aquariums in Monterey and Long Beach, this is a fascinating, hands-on marine science laboratory that lets you participate in experiments, projects, and exhibits, including touch tanks. Two-story glass walls here open to stunning ocean, mountain, and city views. You can purchase a Nature Pass, which includes discounted two-day admission to the natural history museum and the Sea Center. Ty Warner, the Beanie Baby mogul and a local resident, is a major donor. ⊠ *211 Stearns Wharf* ☎ *805/962–2526* ⊕ *www.sbnature. org* 🖼*$8* ⊙ *Daily 10–5.*

WORTH NOTING

Andree Clark Bird Refuge. This peaceful lagoon and its gardens sit north of East Beach. Bike trails and footpaths, punctuated by signs identifying native and migratory birds, skirt the lagoon. ⊠ *1400 E. Cabrillo Blvd., near the zoo* 🖼*Free.*

FAMILY **Carriage and Western Art Museum.** The country's largest collection of old horse-drawn vehicles—painstakingly restored—is exhibited here, everything from polished hearses to police buggies to old stagecoaches and circus vehicles. In August the Old Spanish Days Fiesta borrows many of the vehicles for a jaunt around town. This is one of the city's hidden gems. ⊠ *Pershing Park, 129 Castillo St.* ☎ *805/962–2353* ⊕ *www. carriagemuseum.org* 🖼*Free* ⊙ *Weekdays 9–3, 3rd Sun. of month 1–4 for docent tours.*

Montecito. Since the late 1800s the tree-studded hills and valleys of this town have attracted the rich and famous: Hollywood icons, business tycoons, dot-commers who divested before the crash, and old-money families who installed themselves here years ago. Shady roads wind through the community, which consists mostly of gated estates. Swank boutiques line **Coast Village Road,** where well-heeled residents such as Oprah Winfrey sometimes browse for truffle oil, picture frames, and designer jeans. Residents also hang out in the Upper Village, a chic shopping area with restaurants and cafés at the intersection of San Ysidro and East Valley roads. ⊠ *3 miles east of Santa Barbara off U.S. 101.*

Outdoors Santa Barbara Visitor Center. The small office provides maps and information about Channel Islands National Park, Channel Islands National Marine Sanctuary, and the Santa Barbara Maritime Museum, which occupies the same harbor building. ⊠ *113 Harbor Way, off Shoreline Dr.* ☎ *805/884–1475* ⊕ *outdoorsb.noaa.gov* ⊠ *Free* ☉ *Daily 11–5.*

FAMILY **Santa Barbara Maritime Museum.** California's seafaring history is the focus here. High-tech, hands-on exhibits, such as a sportfishing activity that lets participants catch a "big one" and a local surfing history retrospective make this a fun stop for families. On display beginning fall 2013 is the museum's shining star: an extremely rare, 17-foot-tall First Order Fresnel lens from the historic Point Conception Lighthouse. ⊠ *113 Harbor Way, off Shoreline Dr.* ☎ *805/962–8404* ⊕ *www.sbmm.org* ⊠ *$7* ☉ *June–Aug., Thurs.–Tues. 10–6; Sept.–May, Thurs.–Tues. 10–5.*

Urban Wine Trail. More than a dozen winery tasting rooms form the Urban Wine Trail; most are within walking distance of the waterfront and the lower State Street shopping and restaurant district. **Santa Barbara Winery,** at 202 Anacapa Street, and **Au Bon Climat,** at 813 Anacapa Street, are good places to start your oenological trek. ⊕ *urbanwinetrailsb.com.*

BEACHES

Santa Barbara's beaches don't have the big surf of the shoreline farther south, but they also don't have the crowds. You can usually find a solitary spot to swim or sunbathe. In June and July, fog often hugs the coast until about noon.

Arroyo Burro Beach. The beach's usually gentle surf makes it ideal for families with young children. It's a local favorite, since you can walk for miles in both directions when tides are low. Leashed dogs are allowed on the main stretch of beach and westward; they are allowed to romp off-leash east of the slough at the beach entrance. The parking lots fill early on weekends and throughout the summer, but the park is relatively quiet at other times. Walk along the beach just a few hundreds yards away from the main steps at the entrance to escape crowds on warm-weather days. Surfers, swimmers, standup paddlers, and boogie boarders regularly ply the waves, and photographers come often to catch the vivid sunsets. **Amenities:** food and drink; lifeguard in summer; parking; showers, toilets. **Best for:** sunset; surfing; swimming; walking. ⊠ *Cliff Dr. and Las Positas Rd.* ⊕ *www.countyofsb.org/parks.*

FAMILY **East Beach.** The wide swath of sand at the east end of Cabrillo Boulevard is a great spot for people-watching. East Beach has sand volleyball courts, summertime lifeguard and sports competitions, and arts-and-crafts shows on Sundays and holidays. You can use showers, a weight

Santa Barbara's downtown is attractive, but be sure also to visit its beautiful—and usually uncrowded—beaches.

room, and lockers (bring your own towel) and rent umbrellas and boogie boards at the Cabrillo Bathhouse. Next door, there's an elaborate jungle-gym play area for kids. Hotels line the boulevard across from the beach. **Amenities:** food and drink; lifeguards in summer; parking (fee); showers; toilets; water sports. **Best for:** surfing; swimming; walking. ✉ *1118 Cabrillo Blvd., at Ninos Dr.* ☎ *805/897–2680.*

WHERE TO EAT

$$ ✕ **Arigato Sushi.** You might have to wait for a table at this trendy, two-story restaurant and sushi bar—locals line up early for the wildly creative combination rolls and other delectables. Fans of authentic Japanese food sometimes disagree about the quality of the seafood, but all dishes are fresh and artfully presented. The menu includes traditional dishes as well as innovative creations such as shellfish sushi pizza and Hawaiian sashimi salad. ⑤ *Average main: $22* ✉ *1225 State St., near W. Victoria St.* ☎ *805/965–6074* ⊕ *www.arigatosantabarbara. com* ☖ *Reservations not accepted* ☉ *No lunch.*

JAPANESE

$$ ✕ **Brophy Bros.** The outdoor tables at this casual harborside restaurant have perfect views of the marina and mountains. Staffers serve enormous, exceptionally fresh fish dishes—don't miss the seafood salad and chowder—and provide guests with a pager if there's a long wait for a table. Stroll along the waterfront until the beep lets you know your table's ready. Hugely popular, Brophy Bros. can be crowded and loud, especially on weekend evenings. ⑤ *Average main: $22* ✉ *119 Harbor Way, off Shoreline Dr.* ☎ *805/966–4418* ⊕ *www.brophybros.com.*

SEAFOOD

$
INDIAN
✕ **Flavor of India.** Feast on authentic northern Indian dishes like tandoori chicken, lamb biryani, and a host of curries at this local favorite in a residential neighborhood. Best bets include the combination dinners served in a traditional Indian tray and the all-you-can-eat lunch buffet ($9). Ⓢ *Average main: $13* ✉ *3026 State St., at De La Vina St.* ☎ *805/682–6561* ⊕ *www.flavorofindiasb.com* ✆ *Closed Sun.*

$$$
SEAFOOD
✕ **The Hungry Cat.** The hip Santa Barbara sibling of a famed Hollywood eatery, run by chefs David Lentz and his wife Suzanne Goin, dishes up savory seafood in a small but lively nook in the downtown arts district. Feast on sea urchin, addictive peel-and-eat shrimp, and creative cocktails made from farmers' market fruits and veggies. A busy nightspot on weekends, the Cat also awakens for a popular brunch on Sunday. Night or day, come early or be prepared for a wait. Ⓢ *Average main: $30* ✉ *1134 Chapala St., near W. Figueroa St.* ☎ *805/884–4701* ⊕ *www.thehungrycat.com* ✆ *Closed Mon. Sept.–April.*

$
MEXICAN
✕ **La Super-Rica.** Praised by Julia Child, this food stand on the east side of town serves some of the spiciest and most authentic Mexican dishes between Los Angeles and San Francisco. Fans fill up on the soft tacos served with yummy spicy or mild sauces and legendary beans. Three specials are offered daily. Portions are on the small side; order several dishes and share. Ⓢ *Average main: $10* ✉ *622 N. Milpas St., at Alphonse St.* ☎ *805/963–4940* ⊟ *No credit cards* ✆ *Closed Wed.*

$$$
ITALIAN
✕ **Olio e Limone.** Sophisticated Italian cuisine (with an emphasis on Sicily) is served at this restaurant near the Arlington Center. The juicy veal chop is popular, but surprises abound here; be sure to try unusual dishes such as ribbon pasta with quail and sausage in a mushroom ragout, or the duck ravioli. Tables are placed close together, so this may not be the best spot for intimate conversations. Next door is the more casual Olio Pizzeria, a combination pizzeria and wine bar. Ⓢ *Average main: $30* ✉ *17 W. Victoria St., at State St.* ☎ *805/899–2699* ⊕ *www.olioelimone.com* ✆ *No lunch Sun.*

$$$
SOUTHERN
✕ **Palace Grill.** Mardi Gras energy, team-style service, lively music, and great food have made the Palace a Santa Barbara icon. Acclaimed for its Cajun and creole dishes such as blackened redfish and jambalaya with dirty rice, the Palace also serves Caribbean fare, including a delicious coconut-shrimp dish. If you're spice-phobic, you can choose pasta, soft-shell crab, or filet mignon. Be prepared to wait for a table on Friday and Saturday nights (when reservations are taken for a 5:30 seating only), though the live entertainment and free appetizers, sent out front when the line is long, will whet your appetite for the feast to come. Ⓢ *Aver-*

age main: $29 ⊠ 8 E. Cota St., at State St. ☎ *805/963–5000* ⊕ *www. palacegrill.com.*

$$$
ECLECTIC

✗ **Roy.** Owner-chef Leroy Gandy serves a fixed-price dinner (selections $25 and $30)—a real bargain—that includes a small salad, fresh soup, homemade organic bread, and a rotating selection of contemporary American main courses. If you're lucky, the entrée choices might include grilled local fish with a mandarin beurre blanc, or bacon-wrapped filet mignon. You can also choose from an à la carte menu of inexpensive appetizers and entrées, plus local wines. Roy is a favorite spot for late-night dining—it's open until midnight and has a full bar. ⑤ *Average main: $25 ⊠ 7 W. Carrillo St., near State St.* ☎ *805/966–5636* ⊕ *www.restaurantroy.com* ☾ *No lunch.*

$$$$
AMERICAN
Fodor's Choice
★

✗ **The Stonehouse.** The elegant Stonehouse is inside a century-old granite former farmhouse at the San Ysidro Ranch resort. Executive chef Matt Johnson creates outstanding regional cuisine centered around herbs and veggies from the on-site garden and top-quality local ingredients. The menu changes constantly but typically includes favorites such as crab cake with persimmon relish appetizer and local spiny lobster with mascarpone risotto. Dine on the radiant-heated ocean-view deck with stone fireplace, next to a fountain under a canopy of loquat trees, or in the romantic, candlelit dining room overlooking a creek. The Plow & Angel pub, downstairs, offers more casual bistro fare. ⑤ *Average main: $48 ⊠ 900 San Ysidro La., off San Ysidro Rd., Montecito* ☎ *805/565–1700* ⊕ *www. sanysidroranch.com* ⌂ *Reservations essential* ☾ *No lunch Sun.–Wed.*

$$$
AMERICAN

✗ **Wine Cask.** A reinvention of a same-named local favorite that closed a few years back, the Wine Cask serves bistro-style meals—many of them made with ingredients from a nearby farmers' market—in a comfortable and classy dining room. The dishes are paired with wines from Santa Barbara's most extensive wine list. The more casual bar-café, Intermezzo, across the courtyard, serves pizzas, salads, small plates, wines, and cocktails and is open late. ⑤ *Average main: $29 ⊠ El Paseo, 813 Anacapa St., at E. De La Guerra St.* ☎ *805/966–9463* ⊕ *www.winecask. com* ⌂ *Reservations essential.*

WHERE TO STAY

For expanded reviews, facilities, and current deals, visit Fodors.com.

$$$$
RESORT

⊞ **Bacara Resort & Spa.** A luxury resort with four restaurants and a 42,000-square-foot spa and fitness center with 36 treatment rooms, the Bacara provides a gorgeous setting for relaxing retreats. **Pros:** serene natural setting; nature trails; first-rate spa; three zero-edge pools. **Cons:** pricey; not close to downtown; sand on beach not pristine enough for some. ⑤ *Rooms from: $450 ⊠ 8301 Hollister Ave., Goleta* ☎ *805/968–0100, 877/422–4245 toll-free reservations* ⊕ *www.bacararesort.com* ⇥ *306 rooms, 45 suites* ⧠ *No meals.*

$$$$ **⊡ Canary Hotel.** The only full-service hotel in the heart of downtown,
HOTEL this Kimpton property blends a casual, beach-getaway feel with urban
sophistication. **Pros:** easy stroll to museums, shopping, dining; friendly,
attentive service; adjacent fitness center. **Cons:** across from transit center; some rooms feel cramped. $ *Rooms from: $450* ⊠ *31 W. Carrillo
St.* ☎ *805/884–0300, 877/468–3515* ⊕ *www.canarysantabarbara.com*
⇥ *77 rooms, 20 suites* ¶⊙ *No meals.*

$$$$ **⊡ El Encanto.** Stunning vistas magically unfold from nearly every van-
HOTEL tage point at this luxurious getaway in the hills above Mission Santa
Barbara. **Pros:** serene residential setting; authentic historic restoration;
lavish spa facility. **Cons:** long walk to downtown; pricey. $ *Rooms
from: $595* ⊠ *800 Alvarado Pl.* ☎ *805/845–5800, 800/393–5315*
⊕ *elencanto.com* ⇥ *70 rooms, 22 suites* ¶⊙ *No meals.*

$$$$ **⊡ Four Seasons Resort The Biltmore Santa Barbara.** Surrounded by lush,
RESORT perfectly manicured gardens and across from the beach, Santa Barbara's
Fodor'sChoice grande dame has long been a favorite for quiet, California-style luxury.
★ **Pros:** first-class resort; historic Santa Barbara character; personal service; steps from the beach. **Cons:** back rooms are close to train tracks;
expensive. $ *Rooms from: $425* ⊠ *1260 Channel Dr.* ☎ *805/969–2261,
800/332–3442* ⊕ *www.fourseasons.com/santabarbara* ⇥ *181 rooms,
26 suites* ¶⊙ *No meals.*

$$ **⊡ Franciscan Inn.** Part of this Spanish-Mediterranean motel, a block
HOTEL from the harbor and West Beach, dates back to the 1920s. **Pros:** walk-
ing distance from waterfront and harbor; family-friendly; great value.
Cons: busy lobby; pool can be crowded. $ *Rooms from: $160* ⊠ *109
Bath St.* ☎ *805/963–8845, 800/663–5288* ⊕ *www.franciscaninn.com*
⇥ *48 rooms, 5 suites* ¶⊙ *Breakfast.*

$$$ **⊡ Hotel Indigo.** The closest hotel to the train station, artsy Hotel Indigo
HOTEL (opened in 2012) is a great choice for travelers who appreciate contem-
porary art and want easy access to dining, nightlife, and the beach. **Pros:**
multilingual staff; a block from Stearns Wharf; great value for location.
Cons: showers only (no bathtubs); train whistles early morning; rooms
on small side. $ *Rooms from: $189* ⊠ *121 State St.* ☎ *805/966–6586,
877/270–1392 toll-free* ⊕ *www.indigosantabarbara.com* ⇥ *41 rooms*
¶⊙ *No meals.*

$$$ **⊡ Hyatt Santa Barbara.** A complex of four buildings on three landscaped
HOTEL acres, the Hyatt provides an appealing lodging option in a prime loca-
tion right across from East Beach. **Pros:** steps from the beach; many
room types and rates; walk to the zoo and waterfront shuttle. **Cons:**
motelish vibe; busy area in summer. $ *Rooms from: $229* ⊠ *1111 E.
Cabrillo Blvd.* ☎ *805/882–1234, 800/643–1994* ⊕ *www.santabarbara.
hyatt.com* ⇥ *171 rooms, 3 suites* ¶⊙ *No meals.*

$ **⊡ Motel 6 Santa Barbara Beach.** A half block from East Beach amid fan-
HOTEL cier hotels sits this basic but comfortable motel, which was the first
Motel 6 in existence. **Pros:** very close to zoo and beach; friendly staff;
clean. **Cons:** no frills; motel-style rooms; no breakfast. $ *Rooms from:
$119* ⊠ *443 Corona Del Mar Dr.* ☎ *805/564–1392, 800/466–8356*
⊕ *www.motel6.com* ⇥ *51 rooms* ¶⊙ *No meals.*

$$$$
RESORT
Fodor's Choice
★

⊞ **San Ysidro Ranch.** At this romantic hideaway on an historic property in the Montecito foothills—where John and Jackie Kennedy spent their honeymoon and Oprah sends her out-of-town visitors—guest cottages are scattered among groves of orange trees and flower beds. **Pros:** ultimate privacy; surrounded by nature; celebrity hangout; pet-friendly. **Cons:** very expensive; too remote for some. ⑤ *Rooms from: $695* ⊠ *900 San Ysidro La., Montecito* ☎ *805/565–1700, 800/368–6788* ⊕ *www. sanysidroranch.com* ↪ *23 rooms, 4 suites, 14 cottages* ⦿*No meals* ↪ *2-day minimum stay on weekends, 3 days on holiday weekends.*

$$$$
B&B/INN
Fodor's Choice
★

⊞ **Simpson House Inn.** If you're a fan of traditional B&Bs, this property, with its beautifully appointed Victorian main house and acre of lush gardens, is for you. **Pros:** impeccable landscaping; walking distance from everything downtown; ranked among the nation's top B&Bs. **Cons:** some rooms in main building are small; two-night minimum stay on weekends. ⑤ *Rooms from: $255* ⊠ *121 E. Arrellaga St.* ☎ *805/963–7067, 800/676–1280* ⊕ *www.simpsonhouseinn.com* ↪ *11 rooms, 4 cottages* ⦿*Breakfast.*

$$$$
B&B/INN

⊞ **Spanish Garden Inn.** A half block from the Presidio in the heart of downtown, this elegant Spanish-Mediterranean retreat celebrates Santa Barbara style, from the tile floors, wrought-iron balconies, and exotic plants, to the original art by local plein-air artists. **Pros:** walking distance from downtown; classic Spanish-Mediterranean style; caring staff. **Cons:** far from the beach; not much here for kids. ⑤ *Rooms from: $369* ⊠ *915 Garden St.* ☎ *805/564–4700, 866/564–4700* ⊕ *www. spanishgardeninn.com* ↪ *23 rooms* ⦿*Breakfast.*

NIGHTLIFE AND THE ARTS

Most major hotels present entertainment nightly during the summer and on weekends all year. The bar, club, and live-music scene centers on lower State Street, between the 300 and 800 blocks. The thriving arts district, with theaters, restaurants, and cafés, starts around the 900 block of State Street and continues north to the Arlington Center for the Performing Arts, in the 1300 block. The proximity to the University of California at Santa Barbara assures an endless stream of visiting artists and performers. To see what's scheduled around town, pick up a copy of the free weekly *Santa Barbara Independent* newspaper or visit its website ⊕ *www.independent.com.*

NIGHTLIFE

Blue Agave. Leather couches, a crackling fire in chilly weather, a cigar balcony, and pool tables draw a fancy crowd here for good food and designer martinis. ⊠ *20 E. Cota St., near State St.* ☎ *805/899–4694* ⊕ *www.blueagavesb.com.*

Dargan's. Lively Dargan's pub has pool tables, great draft beers and Irish whiskeys, and serves a full menu of traditional Irish dishes. ⊠ *18 E. Ortega St., at Anacapa St.* ☎ *805/568–0702* ⊕ *darganssb.com.*

James Joyce. A good place to have a few beers and while away an evening, the James Joyce sometimes hosts folk and rock performers. ⊠ *513 State St., at W. Haley St.* ☎ *805/962–2688* ⊕ *www.sbjamesjoyce.com.*

5

Joe's Cafe. Steins of beer accompany hearty bar food at Joe's. It's a fun, if occasionally rowdy, collegiate scene. ⊠ *536 State St., at E. Cota St.* ☎ *805/966–4638* ⊕ *www.joescafesb.com.*

Lucky's. A slick sports bar attached to an upscale steak house owned by the maker of Lucky Brand dungarees, this place attracts hip patrons hoping to see and be seen. ⊠ *1279 Coast Village Rd., near Olive Mill Rd., Montecito* ☎ *805/565–7540* ⊕ *www.luckys-steakhouse.com/bar.*

Milk & Honey. Artfully prepared tapas, coconut-mango mojitos, and exotic cocktails lure trendy crowds to swank M&H, despite high prices and a reputation for inattentive service. ⊠ *30 W. Anapamu St., at State St.* ☎ *805/275–4232* ⊕ *milknhoneytapas.com.*

SOhO. A hip restaurant, bar, and music club, SOhO books bands, from jazz to blues to rock, nightly. ⊠ *1221 State St., at W. Victoria St.* ☎ *805/962–7776* ⊕ *www.sohosb.com.*

THE ARTS

Arlington Theatre. This Moorish-style auditorium hosts events during the two-week Santa Barbara International Film Festival every winter and presents touring performers and films throughout the year. ⊠ *1317 State St., at Arlington Ave.* ☎ *805/963–4408* ⊕ *www.thearlingtontheatre.com.*

Granada. A restored, modernized landmark that dates to 1924, the Granada hosts Broadway touring shows and dance, music, and other cultural events. ⊠ *1214 State St., at E. Anapamu St.* ☎ *805/899–2222 box office* ⊕ *www.granadasb.org.*

Lobero Theatre. A state landmark, the Lobero hosts community theater groups and touring professionals. ⊠ *33 E. Canon Perdido St., at Anacapa St.* ☎ *805/963–0761* ⊕ *www.lobero.com.*

Santa Barbara International Film Festival. The hottest ticket in town in late January, the 11-day festival attracts film enthusiasts and major stars to various downtown venues for screenings, industry panels, and celebrity tributes.⊕ *sbiff.org.*

SPORTS AND THE OUTDOORS

BICYCLING

Cabrillo Bike Lane. The level, two-lane, 3-mile Cabrillo Bike Lane passes the Santa Barbara Zoo, the Andree Clark Bird Refuge, beaches, and the harbor. There are restaurants along the way, and you can stop for a picnic along the palm-lined path looking out on the Pacific.

Wheel Fun Rentals. You can rent bikes, quadricycles, and skates here. ⊠ *23 E. Cabrillo Blvd.* ☎ *805/966–2282* ⊕ *www.wheelfunrentalssb.com.*

BOATS AND CHARTERS

Channel Islands Outfitters. A full-service paddle sports center in the harbor, this outfit rents kayaks, stand-up paddleboards, surfboards, boogie boards, and watersports gear, and conducts guided tours and excursions. ⊠ *117 B Harbor Way, off Shoreline Dr.* ☎ *805/899–4925* ⊕ *www. channelislandso.com.*

Condor Express. From SEA Landing, the *Condor Express,* a 75-foot high-speed catamaran, whisks up to 149 passengers toward the Channel Islands on dinner cruises, whale-watching excursions, and pelagic-bird trips. ☎ *805/882–0088, 888/779–4253* ⊕ *condorexpress.com.*

Santa Barbara Sailing Center. The center offers sailing instruction, rents and charters sailboats, and organizes dinner and sunset champagne cruises, island excursions, and whale-watching trips. ✉ *Santa Barbara Harbor launching ramp* ☎ *805/962–2826, 800/350–9090* ⊕ *www.sbsail.com.*

FAMILY **Santa Barbara Water Taxi.** Children beg to ride *Lil' Toot*, a cherry yellow water taxi that cruises from the harbor to Stearns Wharf and back again. The fare for kids is $1 each way. ✉ *Santa Barbara Harbor and Stearns Wharf* ☎ *805/896–6900, 888/316–9363* ⊕ *sbwatertaxi.com* 🍴 *$4 one-way* ⏱ *June–Aug., daily noon–6, Sept.–May, Fri.–Sun. noon–sunset.*

Truth Aquatics. Truth runs kayaking, paddle boarding, hiking, and scuba excursions to the National Marine Sanctuary and Channel Islands National Park. ✉ *Departures from SEA Landing, Santa Barbara Harbor* ☎ *805/962–1127* ⊕ *www.truthaquatics.com.*

> **EARTH DAY**
>
> In 1969, 200,000 gallons of crude oil spilled into the Santa Barbara Channel, causing an immediate outcry from residents. The day after the spill, Get Oil Out (GOO) was established; the group helped lead the successful fight for legislation to limit and regulate offshore drilling in California. The Santa Barbara spill also spawned Earth Day, which is still celebrated across the nation today.

GOLF

Sandpiper Golf Club. This super-scenic course sits on the ocean bluffs and combines stunning views with a challenging game. ✉ *7925 Hollister Ave., 14 miles north of downtown off U.S. 101* ☎ *805/968–1541* ⊕ *www.sandpipergolf.com* 🏌 *18 holes. 7,000 yds. Par 72. Greens fees: $139/$159* ⛳ *Facilities: Driving range, putting green, pitching area, golf carts, rental clubs, pro shop, lessons, restaurant, bar.*

Santa Barbara Golf Club. The well-maintained public club—among the area's most affordable—occupies a hilltop site with sweeping views of mountains, ocean, and islands. Hotel guests receive greens-fee discounts by showing a room keycard. ✉ *3500 McCaw Ave., at Las Positas Rd.* ☎ *805/687–7087* ⊕ *www.thesantabarbaragolfclub.com* 🏌 *18 holes. 6,037 yds. Par 70. Greens fees: $48/$58* ⛳ *Facilities: Driving range, putting green, pitching area, golf carts, pull carts, rental clubs, pro shop, lessons, restaurant, bar.*

TENNIS

Many hotels in Santa Barbara have courts.

City of Santa Barbara Parks and Recreation Department. The City of Santa Barbara Parks and Recreation Department operates public courts with lighted play until 9 pm weekdays. You can purchase day permits ($8) at the courts, or call the department. ☎ *805/564–5573* ⊕ *www.santabarbaraca.gov/visitor.*

Municipal Tennis Center. The center's 12 hard courts include an enclosed stadium court and three that are lighted on weekdays. ⊠ *1414 Park Pl., near Salinas St. and U.S. 101.*

Pershing Park. The eight lighted courts here are available for public play after 5 pm weekdays and all day on weekends and some holidays. ⊠ *100 Castillo St., near Cabrillo Blvd.*

SHOPPING

SHOPPING AREAS

Brinkerhoff Avenue. Antiques and gift shops are clustered in restored Victorian buildings on Brinkerhoff Avenue. ⊠ *2 blocks west of State St., at W. Cota St.*

El Paseo. Shops, art galleries, and studios share the courtyard and gardens of El Paseo, a historic arcade. ⊠ *Canon Perdido St., between State and Anacapa Sts.*

State Street. State Street, roughly between Cabrillo Boulevard and Sola Street, is a shopper's paradise. Chic malls, quirky storefronts, antiques emporia, elegant boutiques, and funky thrift shops abound here. You can shop on foot or ride a battery-powered trolley (50¢) that runs between the waterfront and the 1300 block. Nordstrom and Macy's anchor **Paseo Nuevo,** an open-air mall in the 700 block. Shops, restaurants, galleries, and fountains line the tiled walkways of **La Arcada,** a small complex of landscaped courtyards in the 1100 block designed by famed architect Myron Hunt in 1926.

Summerland. Serious antiques hunters head southeast of Santa Barbara to Summerland, which is full of shops and markets. Several good ones are along Lillie Avenue and Ortega Hill Road. ⊠ *Summerland.*

BOOKS

Book Den. Bibliophiles have browsed for new, used, and out-of-print books at this independent shop since 1933. ⊠ *15 E. Anapamu St., at State St.* ☎ *805/962–3321* ⊕ *www.bookden.com.*

Chaucer's Bookstore. This well-stocked independent shop is a favorite bookstore of many residents. ⊠ *Loreto Plaza, 3321 State St., at Los Positas Rd.* ☎ *805/682–6787* ⊕ *www.chaucersbooks.com.*

CLOTHING

Diani. This upscale, European-style women's boutique dresses clients in designer clothing from around the world. A sibling shoe shop is nearby. ⊠ *1324 State St., at Arlington Ave.* ☎ *805/966–3114, 805/966–7175 shoe shop* ⊕ *www.dianiboutique.com.*

Surf N Wear's Beach House. This shop carries surf clothing, gear, and collectibles; it's also the home of Santa Barbara Surf Shop and the exclusive local dealer of Surfboards by Yater. ⊠ *10 State St., at Cabrillo Blvd.* ☎ *805/963–1281* ⊕ *surfnwear.com.*

Wendy Foster. This store sells casual-chic women's fashions. ⊠ *833 State St., at W. Canon Perdido St.* ☎ *805/966–2276* ⊕ *www.wendyfoster.com.*

EN
ROUTE If you choose to drive north via U.S. 101 without detouring to the Solvang/Santa Ynez area, you will drive right past some good beaches. In succession from east to west, **El Capitan, Gaviota, and Refugio state beaches** all have campsites, picnic tables, and fire rings.

SANTA BARBARA COUNTY

Residents refer to the glorious 30-mile stretch of coastline from Carpinteria to Gaviota as the South Coast. The Santa Ynez Mountains divide the county geographically; U.S. 101 passes through a mountain tunnel leading inland. Northern Santa Barbara County used to be known for its sprawling ranches and strawberry and broccoli fields. Today its 100-plus wineries and 22,000 acres of vineyards dominate the landscape from the Santa Ynez Valley in the south to Santa Maria in the north. The hit film *Sideways* was filmed almost entirely in the North County Wine Country; when the movie won Golden Globe and Oscar awards in 2005, it sparked national and international interest in visits to the region.

GETTING HERE AND AROUND

Two-lane Highway 154 over San Marcos Pass is the shortest and most scenic route from Santa Barbara into the Santa Ynez Valley. You can also drive along U.S. 101 north 43 miles to Buellton, then 7 miles east through Solvang to Santa Ynez. Santa Ynez Valley Transit shuttle buses serve Santa Ynez, Los Olivos, Ballard, Solvang, and Buellton. COLT Wine Country Express buses connect Lompoc, Buellton, and Solvang weekdays except holidays.

ESSENTIALS

Bus Contacts COLT Wine Country Express ✉ *Lompoc* ☎ *805/736–7666* ⊕ *www.cityoflompoc.com/transit.* **Santa Ynez Valley Transit** ☎ *805/688–5452* ⊕ *www.syvt.com.*

Visitor Information Santa Barbara County Vintners' Association ☎ *805/688–0881* ⊕ *www.sbcountywines.com.* **The Santa Barbara Conference & Visitors Bureau** ☎ *805/966–9222* ⊕ *www.santabarbaraca.com.* **Santa Ynez Valley Visitors Association** ☎ *805/686–0053* ⊕ *www.visitthesantaynezvalley.com.*

SANTA YNEZ

31 miles north of Goleta.

Founded in 1882, the tiny town of Santa Ynez still has many of its original frontier buildings. You can walk through the three-block downtown area in a few minutes, shop for antiques, and hang around the old-time saloon. At some of the eponymous valley's best restaurants, you just might bump into one of the celebrities who own nearby ranches.

GETTING HERE AND AROUND

Take Highway 154 over San Marcos Pass or U.S. 101 north 43 miles to Buellton, then 7 miles east.

WHERE TO EAT AND STAY

For expanded reviews, facilities, and current deals, visit Fodors.com.

$$
ITALIAN
✗ **Trattoria Grappolo.** Authentic Italian fare, an open kitchen, and festive, family-style seating make this trattoria equally popular with celebrities from Hollywood and ranchers from the Santa Ynez Valley. Thin-crust pizza, homemade ravioli, risottos, and seafood linguine are among the menu favorites. The noise level tends to rise in the evening, so this isn't the best spot for a romantic getaway. ⑤ *Average main: $22* ✉ *3687-C Sagunto St.* ☎ *805/688–6899* ⊕ *www.trattoriagrappolo.com* ⊘ *No lunch Mon.*

$$$
B&B/INN
⛱ **Santa Ynez Inn.** This posh two-story Victorian inn in downtown Santa Ynez was built from scratch in 2002, and the owners have furnished all the rooms with authentic historical pieces. **Pros:** near restaurants; unusual antiques; spacious rooms. **Cons:** high price for location; building not historic. ⑤ *Rooms from: $245* ✉ *3627 Sagunto St.* ☎ *805/688–5588, 800/643–5774* ⊕ *www.santaynezinn.com* ⇱ *20 rooms* ⦿ *Breakfast.*

LOS OLIVOS

4 miles north of Santa Ynez.

This pretty village was once on Spanish-built El Camino Real (Royal Road) and later a stop on major stagecoach and rail routes. It's so sleepy today, though, that the movie *Return to Mayberry* was filmed here. Tasting rooms, art galleries, antiques stores, and country markets line Grand Avenue and intersecting streets for several blocks.

GETTING HERE AND AROUND

From U.S. 101 north or south, exit at Highway 154 and drive east about 8 miles. From Santa Barbara, travel 30 miles northwest on Highway 154.

EXPLORING

Carhartt Vineyard Tasting Room. Pinot Noir, Sauvignon Blanc, and Syrah are among the small-lot vintages produced by owner-winemakers Mike and Brooke Carhartt. You'll often find the duo pouring at their intimate tasting room. ✉ *2990-A Grand Ave.* ☎ *805/693–5100* ⊕ *www.carharttvineyard.com* ☞ *Tasting $10* ⊙ *Daily 11–5:30.*

Daniel Gehrs Tasting Room. Heather Cottage, built in the early 1900s as a doctor's office, houses winemaker Gehrs's tasting room, where you can sample Chenin Blanc, Pinot Gris, Pinot Noir, and other small-lot wines. ✉ *2939 Grand Ave.* ☎ *805/693–9686* ⊕ *www.danielgehrswines.com* ☞ *Tasting $10* ⊙ *Sun.–Thurs. 11–5, Fri. and Sat. 11–6.*

Firestone Vineyard. Heirs to the Firestone tire fortune developed (but no longer own) this winery known for Chardonnay, Gewürztraminer, Merlot, Riesling, and Syrah—and for the fantastic valley views from its tasting room and picnic area. The tour here is highly informative. ✉ *5000 Zaca Station Rd., off U.S. 101* ☎ *805/688–3940* ⊕ *www.firestonewine.com* ☞ *Tastings $10–$15* ⊙ *Daily 10–5; tours 11:15, 1:15, and 3:15.*

5

WHERE TO EAT AND STAY

For expanded hotel reviews, visit Fodors.com.

$$ ✕ **Los Olivos Cafe.** Part wine store and part social hub, this café that
AMERICAN appeared in the film *Sideways* focuses on wine-friendly fish, pasta, and
meat dishes, plus salads, pizzas, and burgers. Don't miss the home-
made muffuletta and olive tapenade spreads. Other house favorites
include an artisanal cheese plate, baked Brie with honey-roasted hazel-
nuts, and braised short ribs with smashed potatoes. ⑤ *Average main:
$21* ⊠ *2879 Grand Ave.* ☎ *805/688–7265, 888/946–3748* ⊕ *www.
losolivoscafe.com.*

$$$ ✕ **Sides Hardware & Shoes: A Brothers Restaurant.** After renovating a his-
AMERICAN toric Los Olivos storefront, brothers Matt and Jeff Nichols shuttered
their highly popular Brothers restaurant and began serving comfort
food prepared with their inimitable panache. Popular breakfast dishes
include cooked-to-order beignets and eggs Benedict with house-made
bacon steak. The Kobe-style burgers make a great lunch, and the dinner
favorites include fried chicken and lamb sirloin with herbed gnocchi.
⑤ *Average main: $24* ⊠ *2375 Alamo Pintado Ave.* ☎ *805/688–4820*
⊕ *www.brothersrestaurant.com* ☉ *No breakfast Mon.–Thurs.*

$$$ ☷ **The Ballard Inn & Restaurant.** Set among orchards and vineyards in
B&B/INN the tiny town of Ballard, 2 miles south of Los Olivos, this inn makes
an elegant Wine Country escape. **Pros:** exceptional food; attentive
staff; secluded. **Cons:** some baths could use updating. ⑤ *Rooms from:
$245* ⊠ *2436 Baseline Ave., Ballard* ☎ *805/688–7770, 800/638–2466*
⊕ *www.ballardinn.com* ⇝ *15 rooms* ❖*Breakfast.*

$$$$ ☷ **Fess Parker's Wine Country Inn and Spa.** This luxury inn includes an
B&B/INN elegant, tree-shaded French country–style main building and an equally
attractive annex across the street with a pool and day spa. **Pros:** conve-
nient wine-touring base; walking distance from restaurants and galler-
ies; well-appointed rooms. **Cons:** pricey; staff attention is inconsistent.
⑤ *Rooms from: $345* ⊠ *2860 Grand Ave.* ☎ *805/688–7788, 800/446–
2455* ⊕ *www.fessparker.com* ⇝ *15 rooms, 4 suites* ❖*Breakfast.*

SOLVANG

5 miles south of Los Olivos.

You'll know you've reached the town of Solvang when the architecture
suddenly changes to half-timber buildings and windmills. The town
was settled in 1911 by Danish educators—the flatlands and rolling
green hills reminded them of home—and even today, more than half
the residents are of Danish descent. Although Solvang has attracted
tourists for decades, it's lately become more sophisticated, with gal-
leries, upscale restaurants, and wine-tasting rooms. To get your bear-
ings, park your car in one of the free public lots and stroll the town.
The visitor center on Copenhagen Drive has walking-tour maps (also
available online). The "Sweet Treats" tour covers the town's bakeries,
confectionary stores, and ice-cream parlors, all well worth investigating.

GETTING HERE AND AROUND

Highway 246 West (Mission Drive) traverses Solvang, connecting with U.S. 101 to the west and Highway 154 to the east. Alamo Pintado Road connects Solvang with Ballard and Los Olivos to the north. Santa Ynez Valley Transit shuttle buses run between Solvang and nearby towns.

TOURS

Segway Tours of Solvang. After a brief training session, tool around Solvang on a guided tour via electric-powered personal balancing transporters. This company also offers off-road wine tours, twilight adventures, and trips high up Figueroa Mountain. ☎ *805/688–8899* ⊕ *www. advoutwest.com* ✉ *$85* ⊙ *Nov.–Mar.: tours at 11, 1, and 3. Apr.–Oct.: tours at 9, 11, 1, 3, and 5.*

ESSENTIALS

Visitor Information Solvang Conference & Visitors Bureau ⊠ *1639 Copenhagen Dr., at 2nd St.* ☎ *805/688-6144* ⊕ *www.solvangusa.com.*

EXPLORING

Lafond Winery and Vineyards. A rich, concentrated Pinot Noir is the main attention-getter at this winery that also produces noteworthy Chardonnays and Syrahs. Bottles with Lafond's SRH (Santa Rita Hills) label are an especially good value. ⊠ *6855 Santa Rosa Rd., west off U.S. 101 Exit 139, Buellton* ☎ *805/688–7921* ⊕ *www.lafondwinery.com* ✉ *Tasting $5 weekdays, $10 weekends (includes logo glass)* ⊙ *Daily 10–5.*

Mission Santa Inés. The mission holds an impressive collection of paintings, statuary, vestments, and Chumash and Spanish artifacts in a serene bluff-top setting. Take a self-guided tour through the museum, sanctuary, and gardens. ⊠ *1760 Mission Dr., at Alisal Rd.* ☎ *805/688–4815* ⊕ *www.missionsantaines.org* ✉ *$5* ⊙ *Daily 9–4:30.*

Rideau Vineyard. This winery celebrates its locale's rich history—the King of Spain himself once owned this land, and the tasting room occupies a former guest ranch inn—but fully embraces the area's wine-making present. The Rhone varietals Marsanne, Mourvèdre, Roussanne, Syrah, and Viognier are the specialty. ⊠ *1562 Alamo Pintado Rd., 2 miles north of Hwy. 246* ☎ *805/688–0717* ⊕ *www.rideauvineyard.com* ✉ *Tasting $12* ⊙ *Sun.–Fri. 11–4:30, Sat. 11–5.*

WHERE TO EAT

$$
SCANDINAVIAN
✕ **Bit O' Denmark.** Perhaps the most authentic Danish eatery in Solvang, this restaurant occupies an old-beam building that was a church until 1929. Two specialties of the house are the *Frikadeller* (meatballs with pickled red cabbage, potatoes, and thick brown gravy) and the *Medisterpølse* (Danish beef and pork sausage with cabbage). ⑤ *Average main: $18* ⊠ *473 Alisal Rd., at Park Way* ☎ *805/688-5426* ⊕ *www. bitodenmark.com.*

$$$
AMERICAN
✕ **The Hitching Post II.** You'll find everything from grilled artichokes to quail at this casual eatery just outside Solvang, but most people come for the wonderful smoky Santa Maria–style barbecue. Be sure to try a glass of owner-chef-winemaker Frank Ostini's signature Highliner Pinot Noir, a star in the film *Sideways.* ⑤ *Average main: $29* ⊠ *406 E. Hwy. 246, off U.S. 101* ☎ *805/688-0676* ⊕ *www.hitchingpost2.com* ⊙ *No lunch.*

$$$
AMERICAN
Fodor's Choice
★

✕ **Root 246.** The chefs at this chic restaurant tap local purveyors and shop for organic ingredients at farmers' markets before deciding on the day's menu. Depending on the season, you might feast on local squid with sweet baby prawns, rib-eye steak grilled over an oak fire and served with root vegetable gratin, or rhubarb and polenta upside-down cake. The well-informed wait staff can recommend regional wines from the restaurant's 1,800-bottle selection. Root 246's gorgeous design incorporates wood, stone, tempered glass, and leather elements in several distinct areas, including a slick 47-seat dining room, a more casual bar with sofas and chairs, and a hip lounge. $ *Average main: $26* ⊠ *Hotel Corque, 420 Alisal Rd., at Molle Way* ☎ *805/686–8681* ⊕ *www.root-246.com* ☾ *No lunch. Closed Mon. and Tues.*

WHERE TO STAY

For expanded hotel reviews, visit Fodors.com.

$$$$
RESORT

⛺ **Alisal Guest Ranch and Resort.** Since 1946 this 10,000-acre ranch has been popular with celebrities and plain folk alike. **Pros:** Old West atmosphere; tons of activities; ultraprivate. **Cons:** isolated; cut off from high-tech world; some units aging. $ *Rooms from: $515* ⊠ *1054 Alisal Rd.* ☎ *805/688–6411, 800/425–4725* ⊕ *www.alisal.com* ⟿ *36 rooms, 37 suites* ⫶◎⫶ *Some meals.*

$$$
HOTEL

⛺ **Hotel Corque.** Sleek, stunning Hotel Corque—the Santa Ynez Valley's largest hotel—provides a full slate of upscale amenities. **Pros:** front desk staff are trained concierges; short walk to shops, tasting rooms and restaurants; smoke-free. **Cons:** no kitchenettes or laundry facilities; pricey. $ *Rooms from: $239* ⊠ *400 Alisal Rd.* ☎ *805/688–8000, 800/624–5572* ⊕ *www.hotelcorque.com* ⟿ *122 rooms, 10 suites* ⫶◎⫶ *No meals.*

$$
B&B/INN

⛺ **Petersen Village Inn.** The canopy beds here are plush, the bathrooms small but sparkling, and the rates include a European buffet breakfast. **Pros:** in the heart of Solvang; easy parking; comfy beds. **Cons:** on highway; some find atmosphere too traditional. $ *Rooms from: $150* ⊠ *1576 Mission Dr.* ☎ *805/688–3121, 800/321–8985* ⊕ *www. peterseninn.com* ⟿ *37 rooms, 1 suite* ⫶◎⫶ *Breakfast.*

$
B&B/INN

⛺ **Solvang Gardens Lodge.** The lush gardens with fountains and waterfalls and the cheery English-country-theme rooms make for a peaceful retreat just a few blocks—but worlds away—from Solvang's main tourist area. **Pros:** homey; family-friendly; colorful gardens. **Cons:** some rooms tiny; some need upgrades. $ *Rooms from: $119* ⊠ *293 Alisal Rd.* ☎ *805/688–4404, 888/688–4404* ⊕ *www.solvanggardens.com* ⟿ *16 rooms, 8 suites* ⫶◎⫶ *Breakfast.*

LOMPOC

20 miles west of Solvang.

Known as the flower-seed capital of the world, Lompoc is blanketed with vast fields of brightly colored flowers that bloom from May through August.

GETTING HERE AND AROUND

Driving is the easiest way to get to Lompoc. From Santa Barbara, follow U.S. 101 north to Highway 1 exit off Gaviota Pass, or Highway 246 west at Buellton.

ESSENTIALS

Visitor Information Lompoc Valley Chamber of Commerce & Visitors Bureau ⊠ *111 S. I St., at Hwy. 246* ☎ *805/736–4567, 800/240–0999* ⊕ *www.lompoc.com.*

EXPLORING

FAMILY **La Purisima Mission State Historic Park.** The state's most fully restored mission, founded in 1787, stands in a stark and still remote location that powerfully evokes the lives and isolation of California's Spanish settlers. Docents lead tours every afternoon, and vivid displays illustrate the secular and religious activities that formed mission life. Special events include crafts demonstrations by costumed docents. ⊠ *2295 Purisima Rd., off Hwy. 246* ☎ *805/733–3713* ⊕ *www.lapurisimamission.org* ☒ *$6 per vehicle* ⊙ *Daily 9–5; tour daily at 1.*

Lompoc Wine Ghetto. Nearly 20 laid-back tasting rooms with premium wines from the surrounding Santa Rita Hills appellation—among them Loring Wine Company and Longoria (both known for stellar Pinot Noirs)—cluster in a downtown industrial park. ⊠ *Take 7th St. north from Hwy. 1/246 and turn east (right), 200 N. 9th St.* ☎ *805/735–8937* ⊕ *www.lompocghetto.com* ☒ *Tasting fee varies, some free* ⊙ *Most rooms open Thurs.–Sun., 11 or noon until 4 or 5; some also Mon. and by appointment* ⊙ *Closed Tues. and Wed.*

EN ROUTE

Guadalupe-Nipomo Dunes Preserve. This spectacular preserve straddles the coast for 18 miles between Santa Barbara and San Luis Obispo counties. California's largest and most ecologically diverse dune system, this habitat shelters more than 200 species of birds as well as sea otters, black bears, bobcats, coyotes, and deer. The 1,500-foot Mussel Rock is the highest beach dune in the western states. About two dozen movies have been filmed here, including Cecil B. DeMille's 1923 silent epic *The Ten Commandments.* At the **Dunes Center** (⊠ *1065 Guadalupe Street*) in downtown Guadalupe, you can get nature information and view an exhibit about DeMille's movie set. ⊠ *Hwy. 166/Main St., west 5 miles from Hwy. 1, Guadalupe* ☎ *805/343–2455* ⊕ *www.dunescenter. org* ☒ *Free* ⊙ *Dunes daily sunrise–sunset; center weekends 10–4, weekdays by appointment.*

SAN LUIS OBISPO COUNTY

San Luis Obispo County's pristine landscapes and abundant wildlife areas, especially those around Morro Bay and Montaña de Oro State Park, have long attracted nature lovers. In the south, Pismo Beach and other coastal towns have great sand and surf; inland, a booming wine region stretches from the Edna, Arroyo Grande, and Avila valleys and Nipomo in the south to Paso Robles in the north. With historical attractions, a photogenic downtown, and busy shops and restaurants, the college town of San Luis Obispo is at the heart of the county.

GETTING HERE AND AROUND

San Luis Obispo Regional Transit Authority operates buses in San Luis Obispo and serves Paso Robles as well as Pismo Beach and other coastal towns.

ESSENTIALS

Transportation Contact San Luis Obispo Regional Transit Authority
☎ 805/541–2228 ⊕ www.slorta.org.

Visitor Information Visit San Luis Obispo County ⊠ 811 El Capitan Way, Suite 200, San Luis Obispo ☎ 805/541–8000, 800/634–1414 ⊕ www.visitsanluisobispocounty.com. **WineCoastCountry** ⊠ San Luis Obispo ⊕ winecoastcountry.com.

PISMO BEACH

40 miles north of Lompoc.

About 20 miles of sandy shoreline—nicknamed the Bakersfield Riviera for the throngs of vacationers who come here from the Central Valley—begins at the town of Pismo Beach. The southern end of town runs along sand dunes, some of which are open to cars and off-road vehicles. Sheltered by the dunes, a grove of eucalyptus trees attracts thousands of migrating monarch butterflies from November through February. A long, broad beach fronts the center of town, where a municipal pier extends into the sea at the foot of shop-lined Pomeroy Street. To the north, hotels and homes perch atop chalky oceanfront cliffs. Fewer than 10,000 people live in this quintessential surfer haven, but Pismo Beach has a slew of hotels and restaurants with great views of the Pacific Ocean.

GETTING HERE AND AROUND

Pismo Beach straddles both sides of U.S. 101. If you're coming from the south and have time for a scenic drive, exit U.S. 101 in Santa Maria and take Highway 166 west for 8 miles to Guadalupe and follow Highway 1 north 16 miles to Pismo Beach. South County Area Transit (SCAT; ⊕ *www.slorta.org*) buses run throughout San Luis Obispo and connect the city with nearby towns. On summer weekends, the free Avila Trolley extends service to Pismo Beach.

ESSENTIALS

Visitor Information California Welcome Center ⊠ 333 Five Cities Dr. ☎ 805/773–7924. **Pismo Beach Visitors Information Center** ⊠ Dolliver St./ Hwy. 1, at Hinds Ave. ☎ 800/443–7778 visitor center, 805/773–7034 visitor information ⊕ classiccalifornia.com ☉ Weekdays 9–5, Sat. 11–4.

BEACHES

Fodor's Choice ★ **Oceano Dunes State Vehicular Recreation Area.** Part of ⇨ *Guadalupe-Nipomo Dunes*, the largest and most ecologically diverse dunes complex in California, this popular state park offers a huge array of activities in a 3,600-acre coastal playground. This is one of the only places in California where you can drive or ride off-highway vehicles on the beach and sand dunes (1,500 acres are open to OHVs.) Hike, ride horses, kiteboard, join a Hummer tour, or rent an ATV or a dune buggy and cruise up the white-sand peaks for spectacular views. At **Oso Flaco Lake Nature Area**—3 miles west of Highway 1 on Oso Flaco Road—a 1½-mile boardwalk over the lake leads to a platform with views up and down the coast. Leashed dogs are allowed in much of the park except Oso Flaco and Pismo Dunes Natural Reserve. **Amenities:** food and drink; lifeguards (seasonal); parking (fee); showers; toilets; water sports. **Best for:** sunset; surfing; swimming; walking. ⊠ *West end of Pier Ave., off Hwy. 1, Oceano* ☎ *805/473–7220* ⊕ *www.parks.ca.gov* ⌦ *$5 per vehicle* ☉ *Daily 6 am–11 pm; Oso Flaco Lake sunrise to sunset.*

> **VOLCANOES?**
>
> Those funny looking, sawed-off peaks along the drive from Pismo Beach to Morro Bay are the Seven Sisters—a series of ancient volcanic plugs. Morro Rock, the northernmost sibling and a state historic monument, is the most famous and photographed of the clan.

Pismo State Beach. One of the busiest state beaches in the county, Pismo offers a slew of activities along the 17-mile western edges of Oceano, Grover Beach, and Pismo Beach. Hike, surf, golf, ride horses, swim, fish in a lagoon or off the pier, and dig for Pismo clams. From November through late February, one of the nation's largest colonies of monarch butterflies rests in a grove of eucalyptus and Monterey pine trees (Hwy. 1, 3 miles north of Pier Ave.). Entrances to day use parking areas are off Hwy. 1 (milepost 8) and at Pier Ave. in the south. **Facilities:** food and drink; lifeguards (seasonal); parking (fee); showers; toilets; water sports. **Best for:** sunset; surfing; swimming; walking. ⊠ *555 Pier Ave., Oceano* ☎ *805/489–1869* ⊕ *www.parks.ca.gov* ⌦ *Day use $5 per vehicle if parking at the beach* ☉ *Day use 6 am–11 pm.*

WHERE TO EAT

$$$ ✕ **Cracked Crab.** This traditional New England–style crab shack imports
SEAFOOD fresh seafood daily from Australia, Alaska, and the East Coast. Fish is line-caught, much of the produce is organic, and everything is made from scratch. For a real treat, don a bib and sample a bucket of steamed shellfish with Cajun sausage, potatoes, and corn on the cob, all dumped right onto your table. ⑤ *Average main: $24* ⊠ *751 Price St., near Main St.* ☎ *805/773–2722* ⊕ *www.crackedcrab.com* ⌦ *Reservations not accepted.*

$$ ✕ **Giuseppe's Cucina Italiana.** The classic flavors of southern Italy are
ITALIAN highlighted at this lively downtown spot. Most recipes originate from Bari, a seaport on the Adriatic; the menu includes breads and pizzas baked in the wood-burning oven, hearty dishes such as osso buco and lamb, and homemade pastas. The wait for a table can be long at peak dinner hours, but sometimes an accordion player gets the crowd singing. ⑤ *Average main: $22* ⊠ *891 Price St., at Pismo Ave.* ☎ *805/773–2870* ⊕ *www.giuseppesrestaurant.com* ⌦ *Reservations not accepted* ☉ *No lunch weekends.*

$ ✕ **Splash Café.** Folks stand in line down the block for clam chowder
SEAFOOD served in a sourdough bread bowl at this wildly popular seafood stand. You can also order beach food such as fresh steamed clams, burgers, and fried calamari at the counter (no table service). The grimy, cramped,

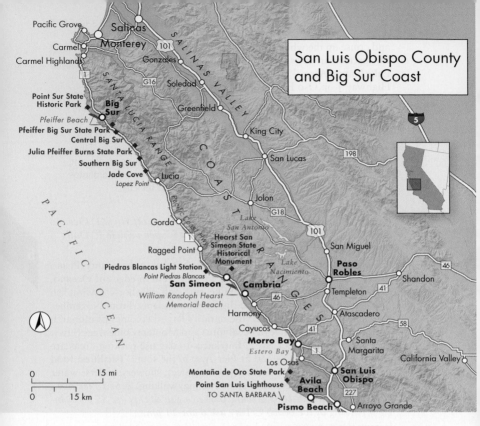

but cheery hole-in-the-wall is open daily for lunch and dinner (plus a rock-bottom basic breakfast), but closes early on weekday evenings during low season. $ *Average main: $8* ⊠ *197 Pomeroy St., at Cypress St.* ☎ *805/773–4653* ⊕ *www.splashcafe.com.*

WHERE TO STAY

For expanded hotel reviews, visit Fodors.com.

$$$ 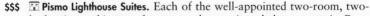 **The Cliffs Resort.** Perched dramatically on an oceanfront cliff, this
RESORT full-service resort is surrounded by lawns and palm trees; the pool, with a cascading fountain, overlooks the sea. **Pros:** beach access via short downhill path; oceanfront restaurant and lounge; blufftop walking trail. **Cons:** not close to downtown; rooms near service areas and elevator can be noisy. $ *Rooms from: $189* ⊠ *2757 Shell Beach Rd.* ☎ *805/773–5000, 800/826–7827* ⊕ *www.cliffsresort.com* ⤴ *160 rooms* ⦿*No meals.*

$$$ **Pismo Lighthouse Suites.** Each of the well-appointed two-room, two-
HOTEL bath suites at this oceanfront resort has a private balcony or patio. **Pros:** lots of space for families and groups; nice pool area. **Cons:** not easy to walk to main attractions; some units are next to busy road. $ *Rooms from: $239* ⊠ *2411 Price St.* ☎ *805/773–2411, 800/245–2411* ⊕ *www. pismolighthousesuites.com* ⤴ *70 suites* ⦿*Breakfast.*

$$$ **☎ Sea Venture Resort.** The bright, homey rooms at this hotel all have
HOTEL fireplaces and featherbeds; most have balconies with private hot tubs,
and some have beautiful ocean views. **Pros:** on the beach; excellent
food; romantic rooms. **Cons:** touristy area; some rooms and facilities
are beginning to age; dark hallways. ⑤ *Rooms from: $179 ⊠ 100 Ocean
View Ave.* ☎ *805/773–4994, 800/662–5545* ⊕ *www.seaventure.com*
⤳ *50 rooms* ⦿| *No meals.*

$ **☎ Shell Beach Inn.** Just 2½ blocks from the beach, this basic but cozy
HOTEL motor court is a great bargain for the area. **Pros:** walking distance from
the beach; clean rooms; friendly and dependable service. **Cons:** sits on
a busy road; small rooms; tiny pool. ⑤ *Rooms from: $100 ⊠ 653 Shell
Beach Rd.* ☎ *805/773–4373, 800/549–4727* ⊕ *www.shellbeachinn.com*
⤳ *10 rooms* ⦿| *No meals.*

AVILA BEACH

4 miles north of Pismo Beach.

FAMILY Because the village of Avila Beach and the sandy, cove-front shoreline
for which it's named face south into the Pacific Ocean, they get more
sun and less fog than any other stretch of coast in the area. With its
fortuitous climate and protected waters, Avila's public beach draws sun-
bathers and families; weekends are very busy. Downtown Avila Beach
has a lively seaside promenade and some shops and hotels, but for real
local color, head to the far end of the cove and watch the commercial
fishers offload their catch on the old Port San Luis wharf. A few sea-
food shacks and fish markets do business on the pier while sea lions
congregate below. On Friday from mid-April through mid-September,
a fish and farmers' market livens up the beach area with music, fresh
local produce and seafood, and children's activities.

GETTING HERE AND AROUND
Exit U.S. 101 at Avila Beach Drive and head 3 miles west to reach the
beach. The free Avila Trolley operates weekends year-round, plus Friday
afternoon/evenings from April to September. The minibuses connect
Avila Beach and Port San Luis to Shell Beach, with multiple stops along
the way. Service extends to Pismo Beach in summer.

ESSENTIALS
Visitor Information Avila Beach Tourism Alliance ⊕ *visitavilabeach.com.*

EXPLORING
Avila Beach Sea Life Center. You'll learn all about local marine plants
and animals from the hands-on exhibits at this science center next
to the main beach. ⊠ *50 San Juan St., at 1st St., off Avila Beach Dr.*
☎ *805/595–7280* ⊕ *www.sealifecenter.org* ⧉ *$5* ⊘ *Weekends 10–4.*

Avila Valley Barn. An old-fashioned, family-friendly country store jam-
packed with local fruits and veggies, prepared foods and gift items,
Avila Valley Barn also gives visitors a chance to experience rural Ameri-
can traditions. Pet farm animals, savor home-made ice cream and pies;
on weekends, ride a hay wagon out to the fields to pick your own farm-
fresh produce. ⊠ *560 Avila Beach Dr., San Luis Obispo* ☎ *805/595–
2810, 805/595–2816* ⊕ *avilavalleybarn.com* ⊘ *Daily 9–5.*

5

DID YOU KNOW?

You can unwind in a private lagoon fed by a hot mineral springs waterfall at Avila Beach's Sycamore Mineral Springs Resort.

FAMILY **Point San Luis Lighthouse.** Docents lead guided hikes along scenic Pecho Coast Trail (3½ miles round-trip) to see the historic 1890 lighthouse and its rare Fresnel lens. If you'd prefer a lift out to the lighthouse, join a trolley tour. Both tours require reservations. ✉ *Point San Luis, 1¾ miles west of Harford Pier, Port San Luis* ☎ *805/540–5771* ⊕ *www.sanluislighthouse.org* ✉ *Trolley tours $20; hikes free ($5 to enter lighthouse)* ⊙ *Trolley tours Sat. noon, 1, and 2; hikes Wed. and Sat. at 9.*

BEACHES

FAMILY **Avila State Beach.** At the edge of a sunny cove next to downtown shops and restaurants, Avila's ½-mile stretch of white sand lures scores of beachgoers on weekends year-round and daily in summer. It's especially family-friendly, with a playground, barbecue and picnic tables, volleyball and basketball courts, and lifeguards on watch in summer and on many holiday weekends. Limited free beachfront parking is available but fills up fast; otherwise park in a nearby pay lot ($5 for the day, $1 after 4 pm). Dogs are not allowed on the beach from 10 to 5. **Facilities:** food and drink; lifeguards (seasonal); parking; showers; toilets; water sports. **Best for:** sunset; surfing; swimming; walking. ✉ *Avila Beach Dr., at 1st St.* ⊕ *www.visitavilabeach.com* ✉ *Free* ⊙ *6 am–10 pm.*

WHERE TO STAY

For expanded hotel reviews, visit Fodors.com.

$$$$ ⭱ **Avila La Fonda.** Modeled after a village in early California's Mexican HOTEL period, Avila La Fonda surrounds guests with rich jewel tones, fountains, and upscale comfort. **Pros:** one-of-a-kind theme and artwork; flexible room combinations; a block from the beach. **Cons:** pricey; most rooms don't have an ocean view. ⑤ *Rooms from: $300* ✉ *101 San Miguel St.* ☎ *805/595–1700* ⊕ *www.avilalafondahotel.com* ⌁ *28 rooms, 1 suite* ⍥ *No meals.*

$$$$ ⭱ **Avila Lighthouse Suites.** Families, honeymooners, and business travel-HOTEL ers all find respite at this two-story, all-suite luxury hotel. **Pros:** directly across from sand; easy walk to restaurants and shops; free underground parking. **Cons:** noise from passersby can be heard in room; some ocean-view rooms have limited vistas. ⑤ *Rooms from: $289* ✉ *550 Front St.* ☎ *805/627–1900, 800/372–8452* ☒ *805/627–1909* ⊕ *www. avilalighthousesuites.com* ⌁ *54 suites* ⍥ *Breakfast.*

$$ ⭱ **Sycamore Mineral Springs Resort.** This wellness resort's hot mineral RESORT springs bubble up into private outdoor tubs on an oak-and-sycamore-forest hillside. **Pros:** great place to rejuvenate; nice hiking; incredible spa services. **Cons:** rooms vary in quality; 2½ miles from the beach. ⑤ *Rooms from: $169* ✉ *1215 Avila Beach Dr., San Luis Obispo* ☎ *805/595–7302, 800/234–5831* ⊕ *www.sycamoresprings.com* ⌁ *26 rooms, 50 suites* ⍥ *No meals.*

SAN LUIS OBISPO

8 miles north of Avila Beach.

About halfway between San Francisco and Los Angeles, San Luis Obispo—nicknamed SLO—spreads out below gentle hills and rocky extinct volcanoes. Its main appeal lies in its architecturally diverse, pedestrian-friendly downtown, which bustles with shoppers, restaurant goers, and students from California Polytechnic State University, known as Cal Poly. On Thursday evenings from 6 to 9 a farmers' market fills Higuera Street with local produce, entertainment, and food stalls. A Saturday-morning market in the Cost Plus World Market parking lot includes organic meats and wine tasting.

The wineries of the Edna Valley and Arroyo Grande Valley wine regions lie just south of the city off Highway 227, the parallel (to the east) Orcutt Road, and connecting roads. Wine-touring maps are available around town.

GETTING HERE AND AROUND

U.S. 101/Highway 1 traverses the city for several miles. From the north, Highway 1 merges with U.S. 101 when it reaches the city limits. SLO City Transit buses operate daily; Regional Transit Authority (SLORTA) buses connect with north county towns. The Downtown Trolley provides evening service to the city's hub every Thursday, on Fridays from June to early September, and on Saturdays from April through October.

ESSENTIALS

Visitor Information San Luis Obispo Chamber of Commerce ⊠ *895 Monterey St.* ☎ *805/781-2777* ⊕ *www.visitslo.com.* **San Luis Obispo City Visitor Information** ⊕ *www.sanluisobispovacations.com.* **San Luis Obispo Vintners Association** ☎ *805/541-5868* ⊕ *www.slowine.com.*

EXPLORING

TOP ATTRACTIONS

FAMILY **History Center of San Luis Obispo County.** Across the street from the old Spanish mission, the center presents exhibits that survey topics such as Native American life in the county, the California ranchos, and the impact of railroads. On the center's website are links to free downloadable video-podcast walking tours of historic San Luis Obispo. ⊠ *696 Monterey St., at Broad St.* ☎ *805/543-0638* ⊕ *historycenterslo.org* ⊠ *Free* ⊙ *Daily 10–4.*

Mission San Luis Obispo de Tolosa. Sun-dappled Mission Plaza fronts the fifth mission established in 1772 by Franciscan friars. A small museum exhibits artifacts of the Chumash Indians and early Spanish settlers. ⊠ *751 Palm St., at Chorro St.* ☎ *805/543-6850* ⊕ *www.missionsanluisobispo.org* ⊠ *$3* ⊙ *Early Mar.–early Nov. daily 9–5, early Nov.–early Mar. daily 9–4.*

San Luis Obispo Museum of Art. The permanent collection here focuses on the artistic legacy of the Central Coast. Temporary exhibits include traditional and cutting-edge arts and crafts by Central Coast, national, and international artists. ⊠ *Mission Plaza, 1010 Broad St., at Monterey St.* ☎ *805/543-8562* ⊕ *www.sloma.org* ⊙ *Early Sept.–early July, Wed.–Mon. 11–5; early July–early Sept., daily 11–5.*

WORTH NOTING

Baileyana Winery. A refurbished 1909 schoolhouse serves as tasting room for this winery that produces mostly Chardonnays, Pinot Noirs, and Syrahs. Four sister wineries share the facility. ✉ *5828 Orcutt Rd., at Righetti Rd.* ☎ *805/269–8200* ⊕ *www. baileyana.com* 🍷 *Tasting $8–$12* ⊙ *Daily 10–5.*

DEEP ROOTS

Way back in the 1700s, the Spanish padres who accompanied Father Junípero Serra planted grapevines from Mexico along California's Central Coast, and began using European wine-making techniques to turn the grapes into delectable vintages.

Claiborne & Churchill. An eco-friendly winery built from straw bales, C&C makes small lots of exceptional Alsatian-style wines such as dry Riesling and Gewürztraminer, plus Pinot Noir and Chardonnay. ✉ *2649 Carpenter Canyon Rd., at Price Canyon Rd.* ☎ *805/544–4066* ⊕ *www.claibornechurchill. com* 🍷 *Tasting $10* ⊙ *Daily 11–5.*

Edna Valley Vineyard. For sweeping valley views and crisp Sauvignon Blancs and Chardonnays, head to the modern tasting bar here. The reserve tasting ($15) is the best option. ✉ *2585 Biddle Ranch Rd., off Edna Rd.* ☎ *805/544–5855* ⊕ *www.ednavalleyvineyard.com* 🍷 *Tastings $10–$15* ⊙ *Daily 10–5.*

Old Edna. This peaceful, 2-acre site once *was* the town of Edna. Browse local art and antiques, peek at the vintage 1897 and 1908 farmhouse cottages, taste wines, pick up sandwiches at the gourmet deli, and stroll along Old Edna Lane. ✉ *1655 Old Price Canyon Rd., at Hwy. 227* ☎ *805/544–8062* ⊕ *www.oldedna.com.*

FAMILY **San Luis Obispo Children's Museum.** Activities at this delightful facility geared to kids under age eight include an "imagination-powered" elevator that transports visitors to a series of underground caverns. Elsewhere, simulated lava and steam sputter from an active volcano. Kids can pick rubber fruit at a farmers' market and race in a fire engine to fight a fire. ✉ *1010 Nipomo St., at Monterey St.* ☎ *805/545–5874* ⊕ *www.slocm.org* 🍷 *$8* ⊙ *May–Aug.: Mon.–Wed. 10–3, Thurs.–Sat. 10–5, Sun. and some holidays 11–5; Sept.–Apr.: Tues. and Wed. 10–3, Thurs.–Sat. 10–5, Sun. and some holidays 1–5.*

Fodor's Choice ★ **Talley Vineyards.** Acres of Chardonnay and Pinot Noir, plus smaller lots of Sauvignon Blanc, Syrah, and other varietals blanket Talley's mountain-ringed dell in the Arroyo Grande Valley. The estate tour, worth a splurge, includes wine and cheese, a visit to an 1860s adobe, and barrel-room tastings of upcoming releases. ✉ *3031 Lopez Dr., off Orcutt Rd., Arroyo Grande* ☎ *805/489–0446* ⊕ *www.talleyvineyards.com* 🍷 *Tastings $8–$12; basic tour $15, estate tour $25 or $35 (includes tasting)* ⊙ *Daily 10:30–4:30; tour by appointment.*

WHERE TO EAT

$$ ✕ **Big Sky Café.** Family-friendly Big Sky turns local and organically ECLECTIC grown ingredients into global dishes, starting with breakfast. Just pick your continent: Brazilian churrasco chicken breast, Thai catfish, North African vegetable stew, Maryland crab cakes. Vegetarians have

ample choices. ⑤ *Average main: $17* ✉ *1121 Broad St., at Higuera St.* ☎ *805/545-5401* ⊕ *www.bigskycafe.com* ⌖ *Reservations not accepted.*

$$
ITALIAN
✕ **Buona Tavola.** Homemade pasta with river shrimp in a creamy tomato sauce and porcini-mushroom risotto are among the northern Italian dishes served at this casual spot. Daily fresh fish and salad specials and an impressive wine list attract a steady stream of regulars. In good weather you can dine on the flower-filled patio. The Paso Robles branch is equally enjoyable. ⑤ *Average main: $22* ✉ *1037 Monterey St., near Osos St.* ☎ *805/545-8000* ⊕ *www.btslo.com* ⊘ *No lunch weekends.*

$$
NORTHERN
ITALIAN
✕ **Café Roma.** Authentic northern Italian cuisine is the specialty at this Railroad Square restaurant. Beneath a mural of Tuscany or out on the covered patio, you can dine on squash-filled ravioli with a sage-and-butter sauce or filet mignon glistening with porcini butter and a Pinot Noir reduction. ⑤ *Average main: $19* ✉ *1020 Railroad Ave., at Osos St.* ☎ *805/541-6800* ⊕ *www.caferomaslo.com* ⊘ *No lunch weekends.*

$$$
INTERNATIONAL
✕ **Luna Red.** A spacious, contemporary space with a festive outdoor patio, this restaurant near Mission Plaza serves creative tapas and cocktails. The small plates include wild-boar spare ribs, prawns adobo, skillet cornbread with honey-masala butter, and potstickers filled with red cabbage and carrot and served with a coconut-curry sauce. Among the large plates are saffron-onion shellfish stew and roasted chicken with dried summer fruit. ⑤ *Average main: $25* ✉ *1023 Chorro St., Monterey St.* ☎ *805/540-5243* ⊕ *www.lunaredslo.com.*

$
SOUTHERN
✕ **Mo's Smokehouse BBQ.** Barbecue joints abound on the Central Coast, but this one excels. Various Southern-style sauces season tender hickory-smoked ribs and shredded-meat sandwiches. Sides such as baked beans, coleslaw, homemade potato chips, and garlic bread extend the pleasure. ⑤ *Average main: $11* ✉ *1005 Monterey St., at Osos St.* ☎ *805/544-6193* ⊕ *www.smokinmosbbq.com.*

$$
ECLECTIC
✕ **Novo Restaurant & Lounge.** In the colorful dining room or on the large creek-side deck, this animated downtown eatery will take you on a culinary world tour. The salads, small plates, and entrées come from nearly every continent. The wine and beer list also covers the globe and includes local favorites. ⑤ *Average main: $19* ✉ *726 Higuera St., at Broad St.* ☎ *805/543-3986* ⊕ *www.novorestaurant.com.*

$$
MODERN
AMERICAN
✕ **Sidecar.** This hip eatery serves farm-fresh meals and small plates along with classic cocktails and 16 mostly local beers on tap. Burger patties made from grass-fed beef, free-range chicken, or housemade veggies are served on a brioche bun with inventive sauces such as bacon-maple ketchup. The menu includes many vegetarian and vegan options, among them the raw "green zebra" lasagna, made of basil-pistachio pesto, tomato sauce, and pine-nut "ricotta." Happy hour (daily from 4 to 6) and Sunday brunch (live jazz, five types of eggs Benedict) are very popular here. ⑤ *Average main: $16* ✉ *1127 Broad St., at Marsh St.* ☎ *805/540-5340* ⊕ *sidecarslo.com.*

WHERE TO STAY

For expanded hotel reviews, visit Fodors.com.

$$$ ⛭ **Apple Farm.** Decorated to the hilt with floral bedspreads and water-
HOTEL colors by local artists, this Wine Country–theme hotel is highly popu-
lar. **Pros:** flowers everywhere; convenient to Cal Poly and U.S. 101;
creek-side setting. **Cons:** hordes of tourists during the day; too floral
for some people's tastes. ⑤ *Rooms from: $219* ✉ *2015 Monterey St.*
☎ *800/255–2040, 805/544-2040* ⊕ *www.applefarm.com* ⇆ *104 rooms*
†⊙⫶*No meals.*

$$$ ⛭ **Garden Street Inn.** From this fully restored 1887 Italianate Queen Anne
B&B/INN downtown, you can walk to many restaurants and attractions. **Pros:**
classic B&B; convenient location; wine-and-cheese reception. **Cons:** city
noise filters into some rooms; not great for families. ⑤ *Rooms from:*
$182 ✉ *1212 Garden St.* ☎ *805/545–9802, 800/488–2045* ⊕ *www.*
gardenstreetinn.com ⇆ *9 rooms, 4 suites* †⊙⫶*Breakfast.*

$$$ ⛭ **Madonna Inn.** From its rococo bathrooms to its pink-on-pink frou-
HOTEL frou steak house, the Madonna Inn is fabulous or tacky, depending
on your taste. **Pros:** fun, one-of-a-kind experience. **Cons:** rooms vary
widely; must appreciate kitsch. ⑤ *Rooms from: $189* ✉ *100 Madonna*
Rd. ☎ *805/543–3000, 800/543–9666* 🖶 *805/543–1800* ⊕ *www.*
madonnainn.com ⇆ *106 rooms, 4 suites* †⊙⫶*No meals.*

$ ⛭ **Peach Tree Inn.** Extra touches such as rose gardens, a porch with
HOTEL rockers, and flower-filled vases turn this modest, family-run motel into
a relaxing creek-side haven. **Pros:** bargain rates; cozy rooms; decent
breakfast. **Cons:** near a busy intersection; basic amenities. ⑤ *Rooms*
from: $99 ✉ *2001 Monterey St.* ☎ *805/543–3170, 800/227–6396*
⊕ *www.peachtreeinn.com* ⇆ *37 rooms* †⊙⫶*Breakfast.*

$$ ⛭ **Petit Soleil.** A cobblestone courtyard, country-French custom furnish-
B&B/INN ings, and Gallic music piped through the halls evoke a Provençal mood
at this cheery inn on upper Monterey Street's motel row. **Pros:** French
details throughout; scrumptious breakfasts; cozy rooms. **Cons:** sits on a
busy avenue; cramped parking. ⑤ *Rooms from: $169* ✉ *1473 Monterey*
St. ☎ *805/549–0321, 800/676–1588* ⊕ *www.psslo.com* ⇆ *15 rooms,*
1 suite †⊙⫶*Breakfast.*

NIGHTLIFE AND THE ARTS
NIGHTLIFE
SLO's club scene is centered on Higuera Street off Monterey Street.

Koberl at Blue. A trendy crowd hangs out at this upscale restaurant's slick
bar to sip on exotic martinis and the many local and imported beers
and wines. ✉ *998 Monterey St., at Osos St.* ☎ *805/783–1135* ⊕ *www.*
epkoberl.com.

Linnaea's Cafe. A mellow java joint, Linnaea's sometimes hosts poetry
readings, as well as blues, jazz, and folk music performances. ✉ *1110*
Garden St., at Higuera St. ☎ *805/541–5888* ⊕ *linnaeas.com.*

MoTav. Chicago-style MoTav draws crowds with good pub food and
live entertainment in a turn-of-the-20th-century setting (complete with
antique U.S. flags and a wall-mounted moose head). ✉ *725 Higuera St.,*
at Broad St. ☎ *805/541–8733* ⊕ *www.motherstavern.com.*

SLO Brew. Handcrafted microbrews, live music most nights, and a rooftop patio make for a winning combination at this downtown watering hole and restaurant. ⊠ *736 Higuera St.* ☎ *805/543–1843* ⊕ *www. slobrewingco.com.*

THE ARTS

Performing Arts Center, San Luis Obispo. The center hosts live theater, dance, and music performances by artists from around the world. ⊠ *Cal Poly, 1 Grand Ave., off U.S. 101* ☎ *805/756–7222, 805/756–2787 box office, 888/233–2787 toll-free* ⊕ *www.pacslo.org.*

OFF THE BEATEN PATH

Montaña de Oro State Park. West of San Luis Obispo, Los Osos Valley Road winds past farms and ranches to this state park whose miles of nature trails traverse rocky shoreline, wild beaches, and hills overlooking dramatic scenery. Check out the tide pools, watch the waves roll into the bluffs, and picnic in the eucalyptus groves. From Montaña de Oro you can reach Morro Bay by following the coastline along South Bay Boulevard 8 miles through the quaint residential villages of Los Osos and Baywood Park. ⊠ *West about 13 miles from downtown San Luis Obispo on Madonna Rd., to Los Osos Valley Rd., to Pecho Valley Rd.; to continue on to Morro Bay, backtrack east to Los Osos Valley Rd., then head north on S. Bay Blvd., and west on State Park Rd.* ☎ *805/528–0513, 805/772–7434* ⊕ *www.parks.ca.gov.*

MORRO BAY

14 miles north of San Luis Obispo.

Commercial fishermen slog around Morro Bay in galoshes, and beat-up fishing boats bob in the bay's protected waters. Nature-oriented activities take center stage here: kayaking, hiking, biking, fishing, and wildlife watching around the bay and national marine estuary and along the state beach.

GETTING HERE AND AROUND

From U.S. 101 south or north, exit at Highway 1 in San Luis Obispo and head west. Scenic Highway 1 passes through the eastern edge of town. From Atascadero, two-lane Highway 41 West treks over the mountains to Morro Bay. San Luis Obispo RTA Route 12 buses travel year-round between Morro Bay, San Luis Obispo, Cayucos, Cambria, San Simeon, and Hearst Castle. The Morro Bay Shuttle picks up riders throughout the town from Friday through Monday in summer ($1.25 one-way, $3 day pass).

ESSENTIALS

Visitor Information Morro Bay Visitors Center ⊠ *255 Morro Bay Blvd., at Morro Ave.* ☎ *805/225–1633, 800/231–0592* ⊕ *www.morrobay.org* ☉ *Daily 9–5.*

EXPLORING

Embarcadero. The center of the action on land is the Embarcadero, where vacationers pour in and out of souvenir shops and seafood restaurants and stroll or bike along the scenic half-mile Harborwalk to Morro Rock. From here, you can get out on the bay in a kayak or tour boat. ⊠ *On waterfront from Beach St. to Tidelands Park.*

FAMILY **Morro Bay State Park Museum of Natural History.** Entertaining interactive exhibits at this spiffy museum explain the natural environment and how to preserve it—in the bay and estuary and on the rest of the planet. ⊠ *State Park Rd., south of downtown* 🕾 *805/772–2694* ⊕ *www.ccnha. org/morrobay* ⊠ *$3* ⊙ *Daily 10–5.*

Morro Rock. At the mouth of Morro Bay stands 576-foot-high Morro Rock, one of nine small volcanic peaks, or morros, in the area. A short walk leads to a breakwater, with the harbor on one side and crashing ocean waves on the other. You may not climb the rock, where endangered falcons and other birds nest. Sea lions and otters often play in the water below the rock. ⊠ *Northern end of Embarcadero.*

WHERE TO EAT

$$ **✕ Dorn's Original Breakers Cafe.** This restaurant overlooking the harbor has
SEAFOOD satisfied local appetites since 1948. In addition to straight-ahead dishes such as cod or shrimp fish-and-chips or calamari steaks sautéed in butter and wine, Dorn's serves breakfast. ⑤ *Average main: $22* ⊠ *801 Market Ave., at Morro Bay Blvd.* 🕾 *805/772–4415* ⊕ *www.dornscafe.com.*

$ **✕ Taco Temple.** This family-run diner serves some of the freshest food
SOUTHWESTERN around. The seafood-heavy menu includes salmon burritos, superb fish tacos with mango salsa, and other dishes hailing from somewhere between California and Mexico. This gem is in a supermarket parking lot on the frontage road parallel to Highway 1, just north of the Highway 41 junction. ⑤ *Average main: $14* ⊠ *2680 Main St., at Elena St.* 🕾 *805/772–4965* ⚠ *Reservations not accepted* ▭ *No credit cards* ⊙ *Closed Tues.*

$$$ **✕ Windows on the Water.** Diners at this second-floor restaurant view the
SEAFOOD sunset through giant picture windows. Meanwhile, fresh fish and other dishes based on local ingredients emerge from the wood-fired oven in the open kitchen, and oysters on the half shell beckon from the raw bar. The California-centric wine list includes about 20 selections poured by the glass. ⑤ *Average main: $28* ⊠ *699 Embarcadero, at Pacific St.* 🕾 *805/772–0677* ⊕ *www.windowsmb.com* ⊙ *No lunch.*

WHERE TO STAY

For expanded hotel reviews, visit Fodors.com.

$$$ **🛏 Anderson Inn.** Friendly, personalized service and an oceanfront set-
B&B/INN ting keep loyal patrons returning to this Embarcadero inn. **Pros:** walk
Fodor's Choice to restaurants and sights; nice rooms; attentive service. **Cons:** not low-
★ budget; waterfront area can get crowded. ⑤ *Rooms from: $239* ⊠ *897 Embarcadero* 🕾 *805/772–3434, 866/950–3434 toll-free reservations* ⊕ *www.andersoninnmorrobay.com* ⇆ *8 rooms* ⦿ *No meals.*

$$$ **🛏 Cass House.** In tiny Cayucos, 4 miles north of Morro Bay, a ship-
B&B/INN ping pioneer's 1867 home is now a luxurious B&B surrounded by rose
Fodor's Choice and other gardens. **Pros:** historic property; some ocean views; excellent
★ meals. **Cons:** away from nightlife and attractions; not good for families. ⑤ *Rooms from: $200* ⊠ *222 N. Ocean Ave., Cayucos* 🕾 *805/995–3669* ⊕ *casshouseinn.com* ⇆ *5 rooms* ⦿ *Breakfast.*

$$ **🛏 Embarcadero Inn.** The rooms at this waterfront hotel are cheery
HOTEL and welcoming, and many have fireplaces. **Pros:** right across from the waterfront. **Cons:** tiny lobby; no pool. ⑤ *Rooms from: $145*

5

✉ *456 Embarcadero* ☎ *805/772–2700, 800/292–7625* ⊕ *www. embarcaderoinn.com* ⇔ *29 rooms, 4 suites* ℉⟨ *Breakfast.*

$$ ⌃ **The Inn at Morro Bay.** Surrounded by eucalyptus trees, this inn abuts
RESORT a heron rookery and Morro Bay State Park. **Pros:** great for wildlife
enthusiasts; stellar views from restaurant and some rooms. **Cons:** some
rooms on the small side; birds and seals can wake you early. ⑤ *Rooms
from: $169* ✉ *60 State Park Rd.* ☎ *805/772–5651, 800/321–9566* ⊕ *in-
natmorrobay.com* ⇔ *97 rooms, 1 cottage* ℉⟨ *No meals.*

SPORTS AND THE OUTDOORS

Kayak Horizons. This outfit rents kayaks and gives lessons and guided
tours. ✉ *551 Embarcadero, near Marina St.* ☎ *805/772–6444* ⊕ *www.
kayakhorizons.com.*

Sub-Sea Tours. You can view sea life aboard this outfit's glass-bottom
boat, watch whales from its catamaran, or rent a kayak or canoe. ✉ *699
Embarcadero* ☎ *805/772–9463* ⊕ *subseatours.com.*

Virg's Landing. Virg's conducts deep-sea-fishing and whale-watching
trips. ✉ *1215 Embarcadero* ☎ *805/772–1222* ⊕ *www.virgs.com.*

PASO ROBLES

30 miles north of San Luis Obispo; 25 miles northwest of Morro Bay.

In the 1860s tourists began flocking to this dusty ranching outpost to
"take the cure" in a luxurious bathhouse fed by underground mineral
hot springs. An Old West town, complete with opera house, emerged,
and grand Victorian homes went up, followed in the 20th century by
Craftsman bungalows. A 2003 earthquake demolished or weakened
several beloved downtown buildings, but historically faithful recon-
struction has helped the district retain its character.

More than 200 wineries pepper the wooded hills of Paso Robles west
of U.S. 101 and blanket the flatter, more open land on the east side. The
region's brutally hot summer days and cool nights yield stellar grapes
that produce robust Cabernet Sauvignon, Merlot, Syrah, and Zinfandel.
Pinot Noir does well in some of the cooler, more fog-heavy western sec-
tions. Chardonnay, Sauvignon Blanc, and Viognier are among stellar
white-wine grapes grown here. Small-town friendliness prevails at most
wineries, especially smaller ones. Pick up a regional wine-touring map
at lodgings, wineries, and attractions around town. Many lodgings pass
out coupons good for discount tastings. Most tasting rooms close at 5
pm; many charge a small fee.

But more attracts people to the Paso Robles area than fine wine and
fancy tasting rooms. Golfers play the four local courses and spandex-clad
bicyclists race along the winding back roads. Down-home and upmarket
restaurants, bars, antiques stores, and little shops fill the streets around
oak-shaded City Park, where special events of all kinds—custom car
shows, an olive festival, Friday-night summer concerts—take place on
many weekends. Despite its increasing sophistication, Paso (as the locals
call it) more or less remains cowboy country. Each year in late July and
early August, the city throws the two-week California Mid-State Fair,
complete with livestock auctions, carnival rides, and corn dogs.

GETTING HERE AND AROUND

U.S. 101 runs through the city of Paso Robles. Highway 46 West links Paso Robles to Highway 1 and Cambria on the coast. Highway 46 East connects Paso Robles with Interstate 5 and the San Joaquin Valley. Public transit is not convenient for wine touring and sightseeing.

ESSENTIALS

Visitor Information Travel Paso Robles Alliance ✉ *1225 Park St., near 12th St.* ☎ *888/988–7276, 805/238–0506* ⊕ *www.travelpaso.com.* **Paso Robles Wine Country Alliance** ☎ *805/239–8463* ⊕ *www.pasowine.com.*

EXPLORING

TOP ATTRACTIONS

Eberle Winery. Even if you don't drink wine, stop at Eberle for a fascinating tour of the huge wine caves beneath the vineyards here. Gary Eberle, one of Paso wine's founding fathers, is obsessed with Cabernet Sauvignon. ✉ *3810 Hwy. 46 E, 3½ miles east of U.S. 101* ☎ *805/238–9607* ⊕ *www.eberlewinery.com* 🍷 *Tasting and tour free* ☉ *Apr.–Sept. daily 10–6, Oct.–Mar. daily 10–5.*

FAMILY **Estrella Warbirds Museum.** An entertaining homage to fighter planes, flyboys, and flygirls, this museum maintains indoor exhibits about wartime aviation and displays retired specimens (of planes) outdoors and in repair shops. Bonus attraction: a huge building with spruced-up autos, drag racers, and "funny cars." ✉ *4251 Dry Creek Rd., off Airport Rd., north off Hwy. 46E* ☎ *805/227–0440* ⊕ *www.ewarbirds.org* 🍷 *$10* ☉ *Thurs.–Sun. 10–4 and Mon. legal holidays.*

Firestone Walker Brewing Company. At this working craft brewery you can sample medal winners such as the Double Barrel Ale and learn about the beer-making process on 30-minute guided tours of the brew house and cellar. ✉ *1400 Ramada Dr., east side of U.S. 101; exit at Hwy. 46 W/Cambria, but head east* ☎ *805/225–5591* ⊕ *www.firestonebeer. com* 🍷 *Tasting $1.50–$3 per sample, tour free* ☉ *Daily 10–5; tours on the half hour Fri.–Sun. 10:30–3:30 and Mon.–Thurs. by appointment.*

Justin Vineyards & Winery. Swank Justin built its reputation—and, claim some, the Paso Robles wine region's as well—on Isosceles, a hearty Bordeaux blend, usually of Cabernet Sauvignon, Cabernet Franc, and Merlot. Justin's Cabernet Sauvignon is also well regarded. Tastings here take place in an elegant room; outside are gardens with flowers and grapevines of major varietals. ✉ *11680 Chimney Rock Rd., 15 miles west of U.S. 101's Hwy 46 E exit; take 24th St. west and follow road (name changes along the way) to Chimney Rock Rd.* ☎ *805/238–6932, 800/726–0049* ⊕ *www.justinwine.com* 🍷 *Tasting $10, tour $10, tour and tasting $15* ☉ *Daily 10–4:30.*

Fodor's Choice ★ **Pasolivo.** While touring the idyllic west side of Paso Robles, take a break from wine by stopping at Pasolivo. Find out how the artisans here make their Tuscan-style olive oils on a high-tech Italian press, and taste the acclaimed results. ✉ *8530 Vineyard Dr., west off U.S. 101 (Exit 224) or Hwy. 46 W (Exit 228)* ☎ *805/227–0186* ⊕ *www.pasolivo.com* 🍷 *Free* ☉ *Daily 11–5.*

5

River Oaks Hot Springs & Spa. The lakeside spa, on 240 hilly acres near the intersection of U.S. 101 and Highway 46 E, is a great place to relax after wine tasting or festival going. Soak in a private indoor or outdoor hot tub fed by natural mineral springs, or indulge in a massage or facial. ✉ *800 Clubhouse Dr., off River Oaks Dr.* ☎ *805/238-4600* ⊕ *www. riveroakshotsprings.com* ✆ *$20–$24 per hr* ⊙ *Tues.–Sun. 9–9.*

Tablas Creek Vineyard. Tucked in the far-west hills of Paso Robles, Tablas Creek Vineyard makes some of the area's finest wine by blending organically grown, hand-harvested Rhône varietals such as Syrah, Grenache, Roussanne, and Viognier. Tours include a chance to graft your own grapevine; call to reserve space. There's a fine picnic area here. ✉ *9339 Adelaida Rd., west of Vineyard Dr.* ☎ *805/237-1231* ⊕ *www. tablascreek.com* ✆ *Tasting $10* ⊙ *Daily 10–5.*

WORTH NOTING

Paso Robles Pioneer Museum. The museum's one-room schoolhouse and its displays of ranching paraphernalia, horse-drawn vehicles, hot-springs artifacts, and photos evoke Paso's rural heritage. ✉ *2010 Riverside Ave., at 21st St.* ☎ *805/239-4556* ⊕ *www.pasoroblespioneermuseum. org* ✆ *Free* ⊙ *Sep.–May Thurs.–Sun. 1–4; Jun.–Aug. Thurs., Fri. and Sun. 1–4, Sat. 10–4.*

Paso Wine Centre. Four dozen local wines are available for tasting via enomatic dispensers at this downtown space that's furnished with comfy sofas and hand-hewn oak tables. ✉ *1240 Park St., at 13th St.* ☎ *805/239-9156* ⊕ *www.pasowinecentre.com.*

WHERE TO EAT

$$$
AMERICAN
✕ **Artisan.** Innovative variations on traditional American comfort foods, well-chosen regional wines, and a sophisticated urban vibe have made this family-run American bistro such a hit with winemakers, locals, and tourists that it recently relocated to larger quarters. Chef Chris Kobayashi, a James Beard–award nominee, uses local, organic, wild-caught ingredients to put a superfresh spin on dishes such as wild boar tenderloin and pig cheek, which he serves with fennel risotto, and scallops with shrimp, mussels, clams, Spanish chorizo, and saffron. Save room for chef's home-style desserts: sundaes, puddings, cakes, cookies, and other sweet delights. ⑤ *Average main: $28* ✉ *843 12th St., at Pine St.* ☎ *805/237-8084* ⊕ *www.artisanpasorobles.com.*

$$$
FRENCH
✕ **Bistro Laurent.** Owner-chef Laurent Grangien's handsome, welcoming French bistro occupies an 1890s brick building across from City Park. He focuses on traditional dishes such as duck confit, rack of lamb, and onion soup, but always prepares a few au courant daily specials as well. The wines, sourced from the adjacent wine shop, come from around the world. ⑤ *Average main: $28* ✉ *1202 Pine St., at 12th St.* ☎ *805/226-8191* ⊕ *www.bistrolaurent.com* ⊙ *Closed Sun. and Mon.*

$$$
AMERICAN
✕ **McPhee's Grill.** Just south of Paso Robles in tiny Templeton, this casual chophouse in an 1860s wood-frame storefront serves sophisticated, contemporary versions of traditional Western fare such as oak-grilled filet mignon and cedar-planked salmon. The house-label wines, made especially for the restaurant, are quite good. ⑤ *Average main: $25* ✉ *416*

S. Main St., at 5th St., Templeton ☎ 805/434–3204 ⊕ mcpheesgrill. com ⊘ No lunch Sun.

$ ✗**Panolivo Family Bistro.** Scrump-
FRENCH tious, affordable French fare draws patrons to this cheery café just north of the town square. For breakfast, try a fresh pastry or quiche, or build your own omelet. Lunch and dinner choices include sandwiches, salads, and fresh pastas—including can-nelloni stuffed with vegetables or house-made beef—along with tra-ditional dishes like snails baked in garlic-butter sauce or beef bourgui-gnon. ⓢ *Average main: $15* ⊠ *1344 Park St., at 14th St.* ☎ *805/239–3366* ⊕ *www.panolivo.com.*

$$ ✗**Thomas Hill Organics Market Bis-**
MODERN **tro & Wine Bar.** Off a tiny alley, Joe
AMERICAN and Debbie Thomas serve inven-tive locavore cuisine. Much of the produce comes from their nearby

10-acre organic farm, and the meats and fish—even the olive oil, cheeses, not to mention the wines—come mostly from local providers as well. ■TIP→ When the weather's fine, ask for a table in the outdoor courtyard. ⓢ *Average main: $16* ⊠ *1305 Park St., at 13th St., Temple-ton* ☎ *805/226–5888* ⊕ *thomashillorganics.com* ⊘ *Closed Tues.*

$$$ ✗**Villa Creek.** With a firm nod to the Rancho and Mission cuisine of
SOUTHWESTERN California's early settlers, chef Tom Fundero conjures distinctly modern magic with local, organic ingredients. The seasonal menu has included butternut-squash enchiladas, braised lamb shank with pumpkin risotto, fennel-crusted salmon, and duck breast with sweet-potato latkes. Cen-tral Coast selections dominate the wine list. All brick and bare wood, the dining room can get loud, but the atmosphere is always festive. For lighter appetites or wallets, the bar serves smaller plates—and killer margaritas. ⓢ *Average main: $26* ⊠ *1144 Pine St., at 12th St.* ☎ *805/238–3000* ⊕ *www.villacreek.com* ⊘ *No lunch.*

WHERE TO STAY
For expanded hotel reviews, visit Fodors.com.

$ 🏨 **Adelaide Inn.** Family-owned and -managed, this clean, friendly oasis
HOTEL with meticulous landscaping offers spacious rooms and everything you need: coffeemaker, iron, hair dryer, and peace and quiet. **Pros:** great bargain; attractive pool area; ideal for families. **Cons:** not a romantic retreat; near a busy intersection. ⓢ *Rooms from: $99* ⊠ *1215 Ysabel Ave.* ☎ *805/238–2770, 800/549–7276* ⊕ *www.adelaideinn.com* ⌁ *108 rooms* ⓧ *Breakfast.*

$$$$ 🏨 **Hotel Cheval.** Equestrian themes surface throughout this intimate,
HOTEL European-style inn a half-block from the main square and near some of Paso's best restaurants. **Pros:** near downtown restaurants; sophisticated;

personal service. **Cons:** views aren't great; no pool or hot tub. $ *Rooms from: $330* ✉ *1021 Pine St.* ☎ *805/226–9995, 866/522–6999* ⊕ *www. hotelcheval.com* ⇨ *16 rooms* ⏐⊙⏐ *Breakfast.*

$$
HOTEL
⌂ **La Bellasera Hotel & Suites.** The swankest full-service hotel for miles around, La Bellasera caters to those looking for high-tech amenities and easy access to major Central Coast roadways. **Pros:** new property; tons of amenities. **Cons:** far from downtown; at a major intersection. $ *Rooms from: $169* ✉ *206 Alexa Court* ☎ *805/238–2834, 866/782–9669* ⊕ *www.labellasera.com* ⇨ *35 rooms, 25 suites* ⏐⊙⏐ *No meals.*

$$$
HOTEL
⌂ **Paso Robles Inn.** On the site of an old spa hotel of the same name, the inn is built around a lush, shady garden with a pool. **Pros:** private spring-fed hot tubs; historic property; across from town square. **Cons:** fronts a busy street; rooms vary in size and quality. $ *Rooms from: $183* ✉ *1103 Spring St.* ☎ *805/238–2660, 800/676–1713* ⊕ *www. pasoroblesinn.com* ⇨ *92 rooms, 6 suites* ⏐⊙⏐ *No meals.*

THE ARTS

Vina Robles Ampitheatre. At this 3,300-seat, Mission-style venue that opened in summer 2013, you can wine, dine, and listen to acclaimed musicians in concert. ✉ *Vina Robles winery, 3800 Mill Rd., off Hwy. 46* ☎ *805/227–4812* ⊕ *www.vinarobles.com* ⊙ *May–Nov.*

CAMBRIA

28 miles west of Paso Robles; 20 miles north of Morro Bay.

Cambria, set on piney hills above the sea, was settled by Welsh miners in the 1890s. In the 1970s, the gorgeous, isolated setting attracted artists and other independent types; the town now caters to tourists, but it still bears the imprint of its bohemian past. Both of Cambria's downtowns, the original East Village and the newer West Village, are packed with art and crafts galleries, antiques shops, cafés, restaurants, and B&Bs. Late-Victorian homes stand alongside streets, and the hills are filled with redwood-and-glass residences. If you're driving north up Highway 1 from Morro Bay, make a quick stop 7 miles south of Cambria at the cute former dairy town of Harmony, population 18, to visit its glassworks, pottery, and other enterprises.

GETTING HERE AND AROUND

Highway 1 leads to Cambria from the north and south. Highway 246 West curves from U.S. 101 through the mountains to Cambria. San Luis Obispo RTA Route 12 buses stop in Cambria (and Hearst Castle).

ESSENTIALS

Visitor Information Cambria Chamber of Commerce ☎ *805/927–3624* ⊕ *www.cambriachamber.org.*

EXPLORING

Fiscalini Ranch Preserve. Walk along a mile-long coastal bluff trail to spot migrating whales, otters, and shore birds at this 450-acre public open space. Miles of additional scenic trails crisscross the protected habitats of rare and endangered species of flora and fauna, including a Monterey pine forest, western pond turtles, monarch butterflies, and burrowing owls. Dogs are permitted on-leash everywhere and off-leash on all trails except the bluff. ⊠ *Hwy. 1, between Cambria Rd. and Main St. to the north, and Burton Dr. and Warren Rd. to the south; access either end of bluff trail off Windsor Blvd.* ☎ *805/927–2856* ⊕ *www.ffrpcambria.org.*

Leffingwell's Landing. A state picnic ground, the landing is a good place for examining tidal pools and watching otters as they frolic in the surf. ⊠ *North end of Moonstone Beach Dr.* ☎ *805/927–2070.*

Moonstone Beach Drive. The drive runs along a bluff above the ocean, paralleled by a 3-mile boardwalk that winds along the beach. On this fine walk—a great photo op—you might glimpse sea lions and sea otters, and perhaps a gray whale during winter and spring. Year-round, birds aplenty fly about, and tiny creatures scurry amid the tidepools. ⊠ *Off Hwy. 1.*

Nitt-Witt Ridge. Arthur Beal (aka Captain Nitt-Witt, Der Tinkerpaw) spent 51 years building a home out of all kinds of collected junk: beer cans, rocks, abalone shells, car parts, TV antennas—you name it. The site, above Cambria's West Village, is a state landmark. You can drive by and peek in—from the 700 block of Main Street, head southeast on Cornwall Street and east on Hillcrest Drive. Better yet, schedule a guided tour. ⊠ *881 Hillcrest Dr.* ☎ *805/927–2690* ⊠ *$10* ⊙ *Tour daily by appointment.*

WHERE TO EAT

$$$
AMERICAN

✕ **Black Cat Bistro.** Jazz wafts through the several small rooms of this intimate East Village bistro where stylish cushions line the banquettes. Start with an order of the fried olives stuffed with Gorgonzola, accompanied by a glass of local or imported wine. Mains on offer might include chipotle linguini (vegetarian or with shrimp) or breast of pheasant stuffed with caramelized apples. ⑤ *Average main: $24* ⊠ *1602 Main St.* ☎ *805/927–1600* ⊕ *www.blackcatbistro.com* ⩜ *Reservations essential* ⊙ *Closed Tues. and Wed. No lunch.*

$
CAFÉ

✕ **French Corner Bakery.** Place your order at the counter and then sit outside to watch the passing East Village scene. The rich aroma of coffee and fresh breakfast pastries makes mouths water in the morning; for lunch, try a quiche with flaky crust or a sandwich on house-baked bread. ⑤ *Average main: $8* ⊠ *2214 Main St.* ☎ *805/927–8227* ⩜ *Reservations not accepted* ⊙ *No dinner.*

$$
AMERICAN
FAMILY

✕ **Linn's Restaurant.** Homemade olallieberry pies, soups, potpies, and other farmhouse comfort foods share the menu with fancier dishes such as free-range chicken cordon bleu at this spacious East Village restaurant. Also on-site are a bakery, a café serving more casual fare (take-out available), and a gift shop that sells gourmet foods. ⑤ *Average main: $18* ⊠ *2277 Main St.* ☎ *805/927–0371* ⊕ *www.linnsfruitbin.com.*

$$
ECLECTIC

✕ **Robin's.** A multiethnic, vegetarian-friendly dining experience awaits you at this cozy East Village cottage. At dinner, choose from lobster enchiladas, five-spice duck breast, Thai green-curry chicken, and more. Lunchtime's extensive salad and sandwich menu embraces burgers and tofu alike. ■TIP→ Unless it's raining, ask for a table on the secluded (heated) garden patio. ⑤ *Average main: $22* ⊠ *4095 Burton Dr., at Center St.* ☎ *805/927–5007* ⊕ *www.robinsrestaurant.com.*

$$$ ✕**Sea Chest Oyster Bar and Restaurant.** Cambria's best place for seafood
SEAFOOD   fills up soon after it opens at 5:30. Those in the know grab seats at the
oyster bar and take in spectacular sunsets while watching the chefs broil
fresh halibut, steam garlicky clams, and fry crispy calamari steaks. If
you arrive to a wait, play cribbage or checkers in the game room. $ *Average main: $26* ✉ *6216 Moonstone Beach Dr., near Weymouth St.*
☎ *805/927–4514* ⊕ *www.seachestrestaurant.com* ☖ *Reservations not
accepted* ▭ *No credit cards* ⊘ *Closed Tues. mid-Sept.–May. No lunch.*

WHERE TO STAY

For expanded hotel reviews, visit Fodors.com.

$ ⊞**Bluebird Inn.** This sweet motel in Cambria's East Village sits amid
HOTEL   beautiful gardens along Santa Rosa Creek. **Pros:** excellent value; well-
kept gardens; friendly staff. **Cons:** few frills; basic rooms; on Cam-
bria's main drag; not on beach. $ *Rooms from: $78* ✉ *1880 Main St.*
☎ *805/927–4634, 800/552–5434* ⊕ *bluebirdmotel.com* ⤴ *37 rooms*
|◎| No meals.

$$ ⊞**Cambria Pines Lodge.** This 25-acre retreat up the hill from the East
RESORT   Village is a good choice for families. **Pros:** short walk from down-
town; many recreational facilities; verdant gardens; spacious grounds.
Cons: service and housekeeping not always top-quality; some units
need updating. $ *Rooms from: $169* ✉ *2905 Burton Dr.* ☎ *805/927–
4200, 800/966–6490* ⊕ *www.cambriapineslodge.com* ⤴ *77 rooms,
75 suites* |◎| *Breakfast.*

$$ ⊞**J. Patrick House.** Monterey pines and flower gardens surround this
B&B/INN   Irish-theme inn, which sits on a hilltop above Cambria's East Village.
Pros: fantastic breakfasts; friendly innkeepers; quiet neighborhood.
Cons: few rooms; fills up quickly. $ *Rooms from: $165* ✉ *2990 Bur-
ton Dr.* ☎ *805/927–3812, 800/341–5258* ⊕ *www.jpatrickhouse.com*
⤴ *8 rooms* |◎| *Breakfast.*

$$ ⊞**Moonstone Landing.** Friendly staff, lots of amenities, and reasonable
HOTEL   rates make this up-to-date motel a top pick of readers who like to stay
right on Moonstone Beach. **Pros:** sleek furnishings; across from the
beach; cheery lounge. **Cons:** narrow property; some rooms overlook
a parking lot. $ *Rooms from: $125* ✉ *6240 Moonstone Beach Dr.*
☎ *805/927–0012, 800/830–4540* ⊕ *www.moonstonelanding.com* ⤴ *29
rooms* |◎| *Breakfast.*

SAN SIMEON

9 miles north of Cambria; 65 miles south of Big Sur.

Whalers founded San Simeon in the 1850s but had virtually abandoned
the town by the time Senator George Hearst reestablished it 20 years
later. Hearst bought up most of the surrounding ranch land, built a
1,000-foot wharf, and turned San Simeon into a bustling port. His
son, William Randolph Hearst, further developed the area during the
construction of Hearst Castle. Today the town, 4 miles south of the
entrance to Hearst San Simeon State Historical Monument, is basically
a strip of gift shops and mediocre motels along Highway 1.

GETTING HERE AND AROUND

Highway 1 is the only way to reach San Simeon. Connect with the highway off U.S. 101 directly or via rural routes such as Highway 41 West (Atascadero to Morro Bay) and Highway 46 West (Paso Robles to Cambria).

EXPLORING

Hearst Castle. Officially known as "Hearst San Simeon State Historical Monument," Hearst Castle sits in solitary splendor atop La Cuesta Encantada (the Enchanted Hill). Its buildings and gardens spread over 127 acres that were the heart of newspaper magnate William Randolph Hearst's 250,000-acre ranch. Hearst devoted nearly 30 years and about $10 million to building this elaborate estate. He commissioned renowned California architect Julia Morgan, but he was very much involved with the final product, a blend of Italian, Spanish, and Moorish styles. The 115-room main building and three huge "cottages" are connected by terraces and staircases and surrounded by pools, gardens, and statuary. In its heyday the castle was a playground for Hearst and his guests—Hollywood celebrities, political leaders, scientists, and other well-known figures. Construction began in 1919 and was never officially completed. Work was halted in 1947 when Hearst had to leave San Simeon because of failing health. The Hearst family donated the property to the State of California in 1958.

Access to the castle is through the visitor center at the foot of the hill, which contains a collection of Hearst memorabilia and a giant-screen theater that shows a 40-minute film giving an overview of Hearst's life and of the castle's construction. Buses from the visitor center zigzag up to the neoclassical extravaganza, where guides conduct three different daytime tours of parts of the estate: grand rooms, upstairs suites, and cottages and kitchen. Daytime tours take about two hours and include the movie and time at the end to explore the castle exteriors. In spring and fall, docents in period costume portray Hearst's guests and staff for the slightly longer evening tour, which begins at sunset. Reservations are recommended for all the tours, which include a ½-mile walk and between 150 and 400 stairs. ⊠ *San Simeon State Park, 750 Hearst Castle Rd.* ☎ *800/444–4445* ⊕ *www.hearstcastle.com* ✑ *Daytime tours $25, evening tours $36* ⊙ *Tours daily 9–3:20, later in summer; additional tours take place most Fri. and Sat. evenings Mar.–May and Sept.–Dec.*

Old San Simeon. Turn west from Highway 1 across from the Hearst Castle entrance to see Old San Simeon, an 1850s whaling village that morphed into an outpost for Hearst employees. There's a one-room schoolhouse and Spanish-style buildings; don't miss Sebastian's General Store in an 1852 building. Now a state historic landmark, Sebastian's houses a store, a wine-tasting room, and a café that serves excellent sandwiches and salads. ⊠ *West of Hwy. 1, across from Hearst Castle entrance.*

FAMILY **Piedras Blancas Elephant Seal Rookery.** A large colony of elephant seals (at last count 15,000 members) gathers every year at Piedras Blancas Elephant Seal Rookery, on the beaches near Piedras Blancas Lighthouse. The huge males with their pendulous, trunklike noses typically start appearing on shore in late November, and the females begin to arrive

5

in December to give birth—most babies are born in the last two weeks of January. The newborn pups spend about four weeks nursing before their mothers head out to sea, leaving them on their own; the "weaners" leave the rookery when they are about 3½ months old. The seals return in the spring and summer months to molt or rest, but not en masse as in winter. You can watch them from a boardwalk along the bluffs just a few feet above the beach; do not attempt to approach them, as they are wild animals. The nonprofit Friends of the Elephant Seal runs a small visitor center and gift shop at 250 San Simeon Avenue in San Simeon. ⊠ *Off Hwy. 1, 4½ miles north of Hearst Castle, just south of Piedras Blancas Lighthouse* ☎ *805/924–1628* ⊕ *www.elephantseal.org.*

Piedras Blancas Light Station. If you think traversing craggy, twisting Highway 1 is tough, imagine trying to navigate a boat up the rocky coastline (piedras blancas means "white rocks" in Spanish) near San Simeon before lighthouses were built. Captains must have cheered wildly when the beam began to shine here in 1875. Try to time a visit to include a morning tour (reservations not required). ■**TIP→ Do not meet at the gate to the lighthouse—you'll miss the tour. Meet your guide instead at the former Piedras Blancas Motel, a mile and a half north of the light station.** ☎ *805/927–7361* ⊕ *piedrasblancas.org* 🔳 *$10* ⊗ *Tours at 9:45, mid-June–Aug. Mon–Sat.; Sept.–mid-June Tues., Thurs., and Sat.; no tours on national holidays* ⌕ *No pets allowed.*

BEACHES

William Randolph Hearst Memorial Beach. A popular destination on weekends and sunny summer days, this wide, sandy beach edges a protected cove on both sides of San Simeon Pier. Fish from the pier or from a charter boat, picnic and barbecue on the bluffs, or boogie board or body surf on relatively gentle waves. In summer, you can rent a kayak and paddle out into the bay for close encounters with marine life and sea caves. The Coastal Discovery Center here offers guided walks and special programs. **Amenities:** food and drink; parking; toilets; water sports. **Best for:** sunset; swimming; walking. ⊠ *750 Hearst Castle Rd., off Hwy. 1 directly west of the Hearst Castle entrance* ☎ *805/927–2020* ⊕ *slostateparks.com* 🔳 *Free* ⊗ *Daily sunrise–sunset.*

WHERE TO STAY

For expanded hotel reviews, visit Fodors.com.

$$ 🏨 **Best Western Cavalier Oceanfront Resort.** Reasonable rates, an ocean-
HOTEL   front location, evening bonfires, and well-equipped rooms—some with wood-burning fireplaces and private patios—make this motel a great choice. **Pros:** on the bluffs; fantastic views; close to Hearst Castle. **Cons:** room amenities and sizes vary; pools are small and sometimes crowded. ⑤ *Rooms from: $169* ⊠ *9415 Hearst Dr.* ☎ *805/927–4688, 800/826–8168* ⊕ *www.cavalierresort.com* ⤵ *90 rooms* ⦿ *No meals.*

$$ 🏨 **The Morgan San Simeon.** On Highway 1's ocean side, the Morgan
HOTEL   offers motel-style rooming options in two Asian-inspired buildings. **Pros:** fascinating artwork; easy access to Hearst Castle; some ocean views. **Cons:** not right on beach; no fitness room or laundry facilities. ⑤ *Rooms from: $149* ⊠ *9135 Hearst Dr.* ☎ *805/927–3878, 800/451–9900* ⊕ *www.hotel-morgan.com* ⤵ *54 rooms, 1 suite* ⦿ *Breakfast.*

BIG SUR COASTLINE

Long a retreat of artists and writers, Big Sur is a place of ancient forests and rugged shoreline, stretching 90 miles from San Simeon to Carmel. Residents have protected it from overdevelopment, and much of the region lies within several state parks and the more than 165,000-acre Ventana Wilderness, itself part of the Los Padres National Forest.

ESSENTIALS

Visitor Information Big Sur Chamber of Commerce ☎ *831/667–2100* ⊕ *www.bigsurcalifornia.org.*

SOUTHERN BIG SUR

Hwy. 1 from San Simeon to Julia Pfeiffer Burns State Park.

This especially rugged stretch of oceanfront is a rocky world of mountains, cliffs, and beaches.

GETTING HERE AND AROUND

Highway 1 is the only major access route from north or south. From the south, access Highway 1 from U.S. 101 in San Luis Obispo. From the north, take rural route Highway 46 West (Paso Robles to Cambria) or Highway 41 West (Atascadero to Morro Bay). Nacimiento-Fergusson Road snakes through mountains and forest from U.S. 101 at Jolon about 25 miles to Highway 1 at Kirk Creek, about 4 miles south of Lucia; this curving, at times precipitous road is a motorcyclist favorite, not recommended for the faint of heart or during inclement weather.

EXPLORING

Fodor'sChoice
★

Highway 1. One of California's most spectacular drives, Highway 1 snakes up the coast north of San Simeon. Numerous pullouts along the way offer tremendous views and photo ops. On some of the beaches, huge elephant seals lounge nonchalantly, seemingly oblivious to the attention of rubberneckers. Heavy rain sometimes causes mudslides that block the highway north and south of Big Sur. ☎ *888/836–0866 for Hwy. 1 conditions between Cambria and Carmel* ⊕ *www.dot.ca.gov.*

Jade Cove. In Los Padres National Forest just north of the town of Gorda is Jade Cove, a well-known jade-hunting spot. Rock hunting is allowed on the beach, but you may not remove anything from the walls of the cliffs. ⊠ *Hwy. 1, 34 miles north of San Simeon.*

Julia Pfeiffer Burns State Park. The park provides fine hiking, from an easy ½-mile stroll with marvelous coastal views to a strenuous 6-mile trek through redwoods. The big draw here, an 80-foot waterfall that drops into the ocean, gets crowded in summer; still, it's an astounding place to contemplate nature. Migrating whales, harbor seals, and sea lions can sometimes be spotted just offshore. ⊠ *Hwy. 1, 15 miles north of Lucia* ☎ *831/667–2315* ⊕ *www.parks.ca.gov* 🎫 *$10* ☉ *Daily sunrise–sunset.*

WHERE TO STAY

For expanded hotel reviews, visit Fodors.com.

$$ ☷ **Ragged Point Inn.** At this cliff-top resort—the only inn and restaurant
HOTEL for miles around—glass walls in most rooms open to awesome ocean
views. **Pros:** on the cliffs; great food; idyllic views. **Cons:** busy road
stop during the day; often booked for weekend weddings. $ *Rooms
from: $169* ✉ *19019 Hwy. 1, 20 miles north of San Simeon, Ragged
Point* ☎ *805/927–4502, 805/927–5708 restaurant* ⊕ *raggedpointinn.
com* ➣ *39 rooms* ⦿ *No meals.*

$$$ ☷ **Treebones Resort.** Perched on a hilltop, surrounded by national for-
RESORT est and stunning, unobstructed ocean views, this yurt resort provides
a stellar back-to-nature experience along with creature comforts. **Pros:**
360-degree views; spacious pool area; comfortable beds. **Cons:** steep
paths; no private bathrooms; not good for families with young children. $ *Rooms from: $199* ✉ *71895 Hwy. 1, Willow Creek Rd., 32
miles north of San Simeon, 1 mile north of Gorda* ☎ *805/927–2390,
877/424–4787* ⊕ *www.treebonesresort.com* ➣ *16 yurts, 5 campsites, 1
human nest w/campsite* ⦿ *Breakfast* ➣ *Two-night minimum on weekends and Apr.–Oct.*

CENTRAL BIG SUR

Hwy. 1, from Partington Cove to Bixby Bridge.

The countercultural spirit of Big Sur—which instead of a conventional
town is a loose string of coast-hugging properties along Highway 1—
is alive and well today. Its few residents include the very wealthy, the
enthusiastically outdoorsy, and the thoroughly evolved: since the 1960s
the Esalen Institute, a center for alternative education and East–West
philosophical study, has attracted seekers of higher consciousness and
devotees of the property's hot springs. Today, posh and rustic resorts
hidden among the redwoods cater to visitors drawn from near and far
by the extraordinary scenery and serene isolation.

GETTING HERE AND AROUND

From the north, follow Highway 1 south from Carmel. From the south,
continue the drive north from Julia Pfeiffer Burns State Park *(above)* on
Highway 1. Monterey-Salinas Transit operates the Line 22 Big Sur bus
from Monterey and Carmel to Central Big Sur (the last top is Nepenthe), daily from late May to early September and weekends only the
rest of the year.

Bus Contact Monterey-Salinas Transit ☎ *888/678–2871* ⊕ *www.mst.org.*

EXPLORING

Bixby Creek Bridge. The graceful arc of Bixby Creek Bridge is a photographer's dream. Built in 1932, the bridge spans a deep canyon, more
than 100 feet wide at the bottom. From the north-side parking area
you can admire the view or walk the 550-foot structure. ✉ *Hwy. 1, 6
miles north of Point Sur State Historic Park, 13 miles south of Carmel.*

Pfeiffer Big Sur State Park. Among the many hiking trails at Pfeiffer Big
Sur, a short route through a redwood-filled valley leads to a waterfall.
You can double back or continue on the more difficult trail along the

valley wall for views over miles of treetops to the sea. ✉ *47225 Hwy. 1* ☎ *831/667-2315* ⊕ *www.parks.ca.gov* 🄳 *$10 per vehicle* 🄯 *Daily sunrise–sunset.*

Point Sur State Historic Park. An 1889 lighthouse still stands watch from atop a large volcanic rock at this state park. Four lighthouse keepers lived here with their families until 1974, when the light station became automated. Their homes and working spaces are open to the public only on 2½- to 3-hour ranger-led tours. Considerable walking, including up two stairways, is involved. Strollers are not allowed. ✉ *Hwy. 1, 7 miles north of Pfeiffer Big Sur State Park* ☎ *831/625-4419* ⊕ *www.pointsur. org* 🄳 *$12* 🄯 *Tours generally Nov.–Mar., weekends at 10, Wed. at 1; Apr.–Oct., Sat. and Wed. at 10 and 2, Sun. at 10; call to confirm.*

BEACHES
Pfeiffer Beach. Through a hole in one of the gigantic boulders at secluded Pfeiffer Beach, you can watch the waves break first on the sea side and then on the beach side. Keep a sharp eye out for the unsigned, ungated road to the beach: it branches west of Highway 1 between the post office and Pfeiffer Big Sur State Park. The 2-mile, one-lane road descends sharply. **Amenities:** parking (fee); toilets. **Best for:** solitude; sunset. ✉ *Off Hwy. 1, 1 mile south of Pfeiffer Big Sur State Park* 🄳 *$5 per vehicle* 🄯 *Daily 9–8.*

WHERE TO EAT

$$$
AMERICAN
✕ **Deetjen's Big Sur Inn.** The candle-lighted, creaky-floor restaurant in the main house at the historic inn of the same name is a Big Sur institution. It serves spicy seafood paella, steak, and rack of lamb for dinner and wonderfully flavorful eggs Benedict for breakfast. The chef sources most ingredients from purveyors known for sustainable practices. 🅢 *Average main: $30* ✉ *Hwy. 1, 3½ mile south of Pfeiffer Big Sur State Park* ☎ *831/667-2377* ⊕ *www.deetjens.com* 🄯 *No lunch.*

$$$
AMERICAN
✕ **Nepenthe.** It may be that no other restaurant between San Francisco and Los Angeles has a better coastal view than this one. The food and drink are overpriced but good; there are burgers, sandwiches, and salads for lunch, and fresh fish and hormone-free steaks for dinner. For the real show, settle on the terraced deck in the late afternoon, order a glass from the extensive wine list, and watch the sun slip into the Pacific Ocean. The less expensive, outdoor Café Kevah serves brunch and lunch. 🅢 *Average main: $30* ✉ *Hwy. 1, 2½ miles south of Big Sur Station* ☎ *831/667-2345* ⊕ *www.nepenthebigsur.com.*

$$$$
AMERICAN
✕ **The Restaurant at Ventana.** The redwood, copper, and cedar elements at the Ventana Inn's restaurant pay tribute to the historic natural setting, while gleaming fixtures and dining accoutrements place the facility firmly in the 21st century. Chef Truman Jones's seasonal menu showcases meat, fish, and produce—such as rabbit loin, California white sea bass, artichokes, and abalone—grown or caught in California. A full slate of regional and international wines complements his dishes. The restaurant is also open for lunch. ∎**TIP**→ If the day is sunny, ask for a table on the outdoor terrace and take in the ocean views. 🅢 *Average main: $36* ✉ *Hwy. 1, 1½ miles south of Pfeiffer Big Sur State Park* ☎ *831/667-2242* ⊕ *www.ventanainn.com* 🄳 *Reservations essential.*

$$$$
AMERICAN

✕ **Sierra Mar.** Ocean-view dining doesn't get much better than this. At cliff's edge 1,200 feet above the Pacific at the ultra-chic Post Ranch Inn, Sierra Mar serves cutting-edge American food made from mostly organic, seasonal ingredients. The four-course prix-fixe option always shines. The nine-course Taste of Big Sur menu centers around ingredients grown and foraged on the property or sourced locally. The restaurant's wine list is among the nation's most extensive. $ *Average main: $50* ✉ *Hwy. 1, 1½ miles south of Pfeiffer Big Sur State Park* ☎ *831/667–2800* ⊕ *www. postranchinn.com/dining* ⚑ *Reservations essential.*

WHERE TO STAY
For expanded hotel reviews, visit Fodors.com.

$$$
HOTEL

⚏ **Big Sur Lodge.** Modern motel-style cottages with Mission-style furnishings and vaulted ceilings sit in a meadow, surrounded by trees and flowering shrubbery. **Pros:** near trailheads; good camping alternative. **Cons:** basic rooms; walk to main lodge. $ *Rooms from: $204* ✉ *Pfeiffer Big Sur State Park, 47225 Hwy. 1* ☎ *831/667–3100, 800/424–4787* ⊕ *www.bigsurlodge.com* ⇝ *61 rooms* ⦿| *No meals.*

$$
B&B/INN

⚏ **Deetjen's Big Sur Inn.** This historic 1930s Norwegian-style property is endearingly rustic, especially if you're willing to go with a camplike flow. **Pros:** tons of character; wooded grounds. **Cons:** thin walls; some rooms don't have private baths. $ *Rooms from: $160* ✉ *Hwy. 1, 3½ miles south of Pfeiffer Big Sur State Park* ☎ *831/667–2377* ⊕ *www. deetjens.com* ⇝ *20 rooms, 15 with bath* ⦿| *No meals.*

$$$$
HOTEL

⚏ **Glen Oaks Big Sur.** At this rustic-modern cluster of adobe-and-redwood buildings, you can choose between motel-style rooms, cabins, and cottages in the woods. **Pros:** in the heart of town; walking distance of restaurants. **Cons:** near busy road and parking lot; no TVs. $ *Rooms from: $275* ✉ *Hwy. 1, 1 mile north of Pfeiffer Big Sur State Park* ☎ *831/667–2105* ⊕ *www.glenoaksbigsur.com* ⇝ *16 rooms, 2 cottages, 7 cabins* ⦿| *No meals.*

$$$$
RESORT
Fodor's Choice
★

⚏ **Post Ranch Inn.** This luxurious retreat, designed exclusively for adult getaways, has remarkably environmentally conscious architecture. **Pros:** world-class resort; spectacular views; gorgeous property with hiking trails. **Cons:** expensive; austere design; not a good choice if heights scare you. $ *Rooms from: $675* ✉ *Hwy. 1, 1½ miles south of Pfeiffer Big Sur State Park* ☎ *831/667–2200, 888/524–4787* ⊕ *www.postranchinn.com* ⇝ *39 units* ⦿| *Breakfast.*

$$$$
HOTEL
Fodor's Choice
★

⚏ **Ventana.** Hundreds of celebrities, from Oprah Winfrey to Sir Anthony Hopkins, have escaped to Ventana, a romantic resort on 243 tranquil acres 1,200 feet above the Pacific. **Pros:** nature trails everywhere; great food; secluded. **Cons:** simple breakfast; some rooms have no ocean view. $ *Rooms from: $650* ✉ *Hwy. 1, almost 1 mile south of Pfeiffer Big Sur State Park* ☎ *831/667–2331, 800/628–6500* ⊕ *www.ventanainn.com* ⇝ *25 rooms, 31 suites* ⦿| *Breakfast.*

CHANNEL ISLANDS
NATIONAL PARK

WELCOME TO CHANNEL ISLANDS NATIONAL PARK

TOP REASONS TO GO

★ **Rare flora and fauna:** The Channel Islands are home to 145 species of terrestrial plants and animals found nowhere else on Earth.

★ **Time travel:** With no cars, phones, or services, these undeveloped islands provide a glimpse of what California was like hundreds of years ago, away from hectic modern life.

★ **Underwater adventures:** The incredibly healthy channel waters rank among the top 10 diving destinations on the planet—but you can also visit the kelp forest virtually via an underwater video program.

★ **Marvelous marine mammals:** More than 30 species of seals, sea lions, whales, and other marine mammals ply the park's waters at various times of year.

★ **Sea-cave kayaking:** Paddle around otherwise inaccessible portions of the park's 175 miles of gorgeous coastline—including one of the world's largest sea caves.

1 Anacapa National Park. Tiny Anacapa is a 5-mile stretch of three islets, with towering cliffs, caves, natural bridges, and rich kelp forests.

2 San Miguel. Isolated, windswept San Miguel, the park's westernmost island, has an ancient caliche forest and hundreds of archaeological sites chronicling the Chumash Indians' 11,000-year history on the island. More than 100,000 pinnipeds (seals and sea lions) hang out on the island's beaches during certain times of year.

3 Santa Barbara. More than 5 miles of scenic trails crisscross this tiny island, known for its excellent wildlife viewing and native plants. It's a favorite destination for diving, snorkeling, and kayaking.

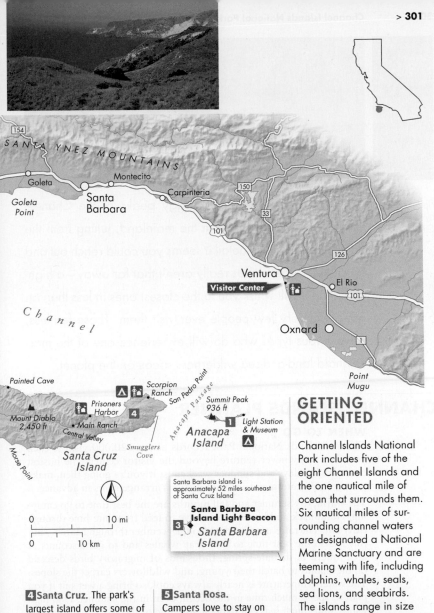

6

GETTING ORIENTED

Channel Islands National Park includes five of the eight Channel Islands and the one nautical mile of ocean that surrounds them. Six nautical miles of surrounding channel waters are designated a National Marine Sanctuary and are teeming with life, including dolphins, whales, seals, sea lions, and seabirds. The islands range in size from 1-square-mile Santa Barbara to 96-square-mile Santa Cruz. Together they form a magnificent nature preserve with 145 endemic or unique species of plants and animals.

4 Santa Cruz. The park's largest island offers some of the best hikes and kayaking opportunities, one of the world's largest and deepest sea caves, and more species of flora and fauna than any other park island.

5 Santa Rosa. Campers love to stay on Santa Rosa, with its myriad hiking opportunities, stunning white-sand beaches, and rare grove of Torrey pines. It's also the only island accessible by plane.

Updated
by Cheryl
Crabtree

On crystal clear days the craggy peaks of the Channel Islands are easy to see from the mainland, jutting from the Pacific in such sharp detail it seems you could reach out and touch them. The islands really aren't that far away—a high-speed boat will whisk you to the closest ones in less than an hour—yet very few people ever visit them. Those fearless, adventurous types who do will experience one of the most splendid land-and-sea wilderness areas on the planet.

CHANNEL ISLANDS PLANNER

WHEN TO GO

Channel Islands National Park records about 620,000 visitors each year, but many never venture beyond the visitor center. The busiest times are holidays and summer weekends; if you're going then, make your transportation and accommodations arrangements in advance.

The warm, dry summer and fall months are the best time to go camping. Humpback and blue whales arrive to feed from late June through early fall. The rains usually come from December through March—but this is also the best time to spot gray whales and to get discounts at area hotels. In the late spring, thousands of migratory birds descend on the islands to hatch their young, and wildflowers carpet the slopes. The water temperature is nearly always cool, so bring a wet suit if you plan to spend much time in the ocean, even in the summer. Fog, high winds, and rough seas can happen any time of the year.

GETTING HERE AND AROUND

AIR TRAVEL

Channel Islands Aviation flies solely to Santa Rosa Island. You can catch a flight to Santa Rosa Island from the Camarillo Airport, south of Ventura, and the Santa Barbara Airport.

Channel Islands Aviation. Channel Islands Aviation provides day excursions, surf fishing, and camper transportation year-round, flying from Camarillo Airport, about 10 miles southeast of Ventura, to an airstrip on Santa Rosa (25-minute flight). The operator will also pick up groups of six or more at Santa Barbara Airport. ⊠ *305 Durley Ave., Camarillo* ☏ *805/987–1301* ⊕ *www.flycia.com* ✉ *$160 per person half-day, $220 per person full-day, $300 per person if camping.*

BOAT TRAVEL

The visitor center for Channel Islands National Park is on California's mainland, in the town of Ventura, off U.S. 101. From the harbors at Ventura, Santa Barbara, and Oxnard you can board a boat to one of the islands. If you have your own boat, you can land at any of the islands without a permit, but you should visit the park website for instructions and information on restricted areas. A permit is required to land on the Nature Conservancy property on Santa Cruz Island. Boaters landing at San Miguel must contact the park ranger beforehand.

Island Packers. Sailing on high-speed catamarans from Ventura or a mono-hull vessel from Oxnard, Island Packers goes to Santa Cruz Island daily most of the year, weather permitting. The boats also go to Anacapa several days a week, and to the outer islands from late April through early November. They also cruise along Anacapa's north shore on three-hour wildlife tours (non-landing) several times a week. ⊠ *3550 S. Harbor Blvd., Oxnard* ☏ *805/642–1393* ⊕ *www.islandpackers.com* ⊠ *1691 Spinnaker Dr., Ventura* ☏ *805/642–1393* ⊕ *www.islandpackers.com* ✉ *$36–$147.*

CAR TRAVEL

To reach the Ventura harbor, exit U.S. 101 in Ventura at Seaward Boulevard or Victoria Avenue and follow the signs to Ventura Harbor/Spinnaker Drive. To access Channel Islands Harbor in Oxnard, exit U.S. 101 at Victoria Avenue and head south approximately 7 miles to Channel Islands Boulevard. To access dive and whale-watching boats in Santa Barbara, exit U.S. 101 at Castillo Street and head south to Cabrillo Boulevard, then turn right for the harbor entrance. Private vehicles are not permitted on the islands. Pets are also not allowed in the park.

PARK ESSENTIALS
PARK FEES AND PERMITS

There is no fee to enter Channel Islands National Park, but unless you have your own boat, you will pay $36 or more per person for a ride with a boat operator. The cost of taking a boat to the park varies depending on the island you visit. Also, there is a $15-per-day fee for staying in one of the islands' campgrounds.

If you take your own boat, landing permits are not required to visit islands administered by the National Park Service. However, boaters who want to land on the Nature Conservancy preserve on Santa Cruz Island must have a permit. Visit ⊕ *www.nature.org/cruzpermit* for permit information; allow 10 business days to process and return your permit application. If you anchor in a nearby cove at any island, at least one person should remain aboard the boat at all times. To hike beyond the ranger station on San Miguel you need a reservation and permit; call ☎ *805/658–5711* to be matched up with a ranger, who must accompany you. Anglers must have a state fishing license; for details, call the California Department of Fish and Game at ☎ *916/653–7664* or visit ⊕ *www.dfg.ca.gov.* Thirteen Marine Protected Areas (MPAs) with special resource protection regulations surround the islands, so read the guidelines carefully before you depart.

PARK HOURS

The islands are open every day of the year. Channel Islands National Park Visitor Center in Ventura is closed on Thanksgiving and Christmas. Channel Islands National Park is located in the Pacific time zone.

VISITOR INFORMATION

PARK CONTACT INFORMATION

Channel Islands National Park Visitor Center ⊠ *1901 Spinnaker Dr., Ventura* ☎ *805/658–5730* ⊕ *www.nps.gov/chis.*

VISITOR CENTERS

Channel Islands National Park Robert J. Lagomarsino Visitor Center. The park's main visitor center has a museum, a bookstore, a three-story observation tower with telescopes, and exhibits about the islands. There's also a marine life exhibit where you can see sea stars clinging to rocks, anemones waving their colorful, spiny tentacles, and a brilliant orange Garibaldi darting around. The center also has full-size reproductions of a male northern elephant seal and the pygmy mammoth skeleton unearthed on Santa Rosa Island in 1994. *Treasure in the Sea,* a 24-minute film narrated by Kevin Costner, shows throughout the day and gives an overview of the islands. Rangers lead various free public programs describing park resources on weekends and holidays at 11 and 3; they can also give you a detailed map and trip-planning packet if you're interested in visiting the actual islands. In summer you can watch live ranger broadcasts of underwater dives and hikes on Anacapa Island, shown at the center Wednesday through Saturday (hike at 11, dive at 2). ⊠ *1901 Spinnaker Dr., Ventura* ☎ *805/658–5730* ⊕ *www. nps.gov/chis* ⊗ *Daily 8:30–5.*

EXPLORING

THE ISLANDS

Anacapa Island. Although most people think of it as an island, Anacapa Island is actually comprised of three narrow islets. The tips of these volcanic formations nearly touch but are inaccessible from one another except by boat. All three islets have towering cliffs, isolated sea caves, and natural bridges; Arch Rock, on East Anacapa, is one of the best-known symbols of Channel Islands National Park. Wildlife viewing is the reason most people come to East Anacapa—particularly in summer when seagull chicks are newly hatched and sea lions and seals lounge on the beaches. Trips to Middle Anacapa Island require a ranger escort.

The compact **museum** on East Anacapa tells the history of the island and houses, among other things, the original lead-crystal Fresnel lens from the island's 1932 lighthouse.

Depending on the season and the number of desirable species lurking about there, a limited number of boats travel to **Frenchy's Cove** at West Anacapa, where there are pristine tide pools in which you might see anemones, limpets, barnacles, mussel beds, and colorful marine algae. The rest of West Anacapa is closed to protect nesting brown pelicans.

San Miguel Island. The westernmost of the Channel Islands, San Miguel Island is frequently battered by storms sweeping across the North Pacific. The 15-square-mile island's wild, windswept landscape is lush with vegetation. Point Bennett, at the western tip, offers one of the world's most spectacular wildlife displays when more than 100,000 pinnipeds hit its beach. Explorer Juan Rodríguez Cabrillo was the first European to visit this island; he claimed it for Spain in 1542. Legend holds that Cabrillo died on one of the Channel Islands—no one knows where he's buried, but there's a memorial to him on a bluff above Cuyler Harbor.

Santa Barbara Island. At about 1 square mile, Santa Barbara Island is the smallest of the Channel Islands and nearly 35 miles south of the others. Triangular in shape, Santa Barbara's steep cliffs—which offer a perfect nesting spot for the Scripps's murrelet, a rare seabird—are topped by twin peaks. In spring, you can enjoy a brilliant display of yellow coreopsis. Learn about the wildlife on and around the islands at the island's small museum.

Santa Cruz Island. Five miles west of Anacapa, 96-square-mile Santa Cruz Island is the largest of the Channel Islands. The National Park Service manages the easternmost 24% of the island; the rest is owned by the Nature Conservancy, which requires a permit to land. When your boat drops you off on the 70 miles of craggy coastline, you see two rugged mountain ranges with peaks soaring to 2,500 feet and deep canyons traversed by streams. This landscape is the habitat of a remarkable variety of flora and fauna—more than 600 types of plants, 140 kinds of land birds, 11 mammal species, five varieties of reptiles, and three amphibian species live here. Bird-watchers may want to look for the endemic island scrub jay, which is found nowhere else in the world.

One of the largest and deepest sea caves in the world, **Painted Cave**, lies along the northwest coast of Santa Cruz. Named for the colorful lichen and algae that cover its walls, Painted Cave is nearly ¼ mile long and 100 feet wide. In spring a waterfall cascades over the entrance. Kayakers may encounter seals or sea lions cruising alongside their boats inside the cave. The Channel Islands hold some of the richest archeological resources in North America; all artifacts are protected within the park. Remnants of a dozen Chumash villages can be seen on the island. The largest of these villages, at the eastern end of the island, occupied the area now called **Scorpion Ranch.** The Chumash mined extensive chert deposits on the island for tools to produce shell-bead money, which they traded with people on the mainland. You can learn about Chumash history and view artifacts, tools, and exhibits on native plant and wildlife at the interpretive visitor center near the landing dock. Visitors can also explore remnants of the early-1900s ranching era in the restored historic adobe and outbuildings.

Santa Rosa Island. Set between Santa Cruz and San Miguel, Santa Rosa Island is the second largest of the Channel Islands and has a relatively low profile, broken by a central mountain range rising to 1,589 feet. The coastal areas range from broad sandy beaches to sheer cliffs. The island is home to about 500 species of plants, including the rare Torrey pine. Three unusual mammals—the endemic island fox, spotted skunk, and deer mouse—are among those that make their home here. They hardly compare to the mammoths that once roamed the island; a nearly complete skeleton of a 6-foot-tall pygmy mammoth was unearthed here in 1994.

The island was once home to the **Vail & Vickers Ranch,** where sheep and cattle were raised from 1901 to 1998. You can catch a glimpse of what the operation was like when you walk from the landing dock to the campground; the route passes by the historic ranch buildings, barns, equipment, and the wooden pier where cattle were brought onto the island.

SPORTS AND THE OUTDOORS

DIVING

Some of the best snorkeling and diving in the world can be found in the cool waters surrounding the Channel Islands. The best time to scuba dive is in the summer and fall, when the water is often clear up to a 100-foot depth.

KAYAKING

The most remote parts of the Channel Islands are accessible only by a sea kayak. Some of the best kayaking in the park can be found on Anacapa, Santa Barbara, and the eastern tip of Santa Cruz. It's too far to kayak from the mainland out to the islands, but outfitters have tours that take you to the islands. Tours are offered year-round, but high seas may cause trip cancellations between December and March. ⚠ Channel waters can be unpredictable and challenging; guided trips are highly recommended.

WHALE-WATCHING

About a third of the world's cetacean species (27 to be exact) can be seen in the Santa Barbara Channel. In July and August, humpback and blue whales feed off the north shore of Santa Rosa. From late December through March, up to 10,000 gray whales pass through the Santa Barbara Channel on their way from Alaska to Mexico and back again, and on a whale-watching trip during this time frame, you should see one or more of them. Other types of whales, but fewer in number, swim the channel June through August.

THE MONTEREY BAY AREA

From Carmel to Santa Cruz

WELCOME TO THE MONTEREY BAY AREA

TOP REASONS TO GO

★ **Marine life:** Monterey Bay is the location of the world's third-largest marine sanctuary, home to whales, otters, and other underwater creatures.

★ **Getaway central:** For more than a century, urbanites have come to the Monterey Bay area to unwind, relax, and have fun. It's a great place to browse unique shops and galleries, ride a giant roller coaster, or play a round of golf on a world-class course.

★ **Nature preserves:** More than the sea is protected here—the region boasts nearly 30 state parks, beaches, and preserves, fantastic places for walking, jogging, hiking, and biking.

★ **Wine and dine:** The area's rich agricultural bounty translates to abundant fresh produce, great wines, and fabulous dining. It's no wonder more than 300 culinary events take place here every year.

★ **Small-town vibes:** Even the cities here are friendly, walkable places where you'll feel like a local.

1 Carmel and Pacific Grove. Exclusive Carmel-by-the-Sea and Carmel Valley Village burst with historic charm, fine dining, and unusual boutiques that cater to celebrity residents and well-heeled visitors. Nearby 17-Mile Drive—quite possibly the prettiest stretch of road you'll ever travel—runs between Carmel-by-the-Sea and Victorian-studded Pacific Grove, home to thousands of migrating monarch butterflies between October and February.

2 Monterey. A former Spanish military outpost, Monterey's well-preserved historic district is a hands-on history lesson. Cannery Row, the former center of Monterey's once-thriving sardine industry, has been reborn as a tourist attraction with shops, restaurants, hotels, and the Monterey Bay Aquarium.

3 Around Monterey Bay. Much of California's lettuce, berries, artichokes, and Brussels sprouts come from Salinas and Watsonville. Salinas is also home of the National Steinbeck Center, and Moss Landing and Watsonville encompass pristine wildlife wetlands. Aptos, Capitola, and Soquel are former lumber towns that became popular seaside resorts more than a century ago. Today they're filled with antiques shops, restaurants, and wine-tasting rooms; you'll also find some of the bay's best beaches along the shore here.

4 Santa Cruz. Santa Cruz shows its colors along an old-time beach boardwalk and municipal wharf. A University of California campus imbues the town with arts and culture and a liberal mind-set.

0   5 mi
0   5 km

Santa Cruz

17
9
1
4

Map Labels

The Forest of Nisene Marks State Park

Soquel
Aptos
Capitola
Rio del Mar
Soquel Cove
Freedom
Watsonville
Pajaro
Las Lomas
3
Moss Landing
Prunedale
Castroville
Marina
Salinas
Point Pinos
Pacific Grove
Seaside
Sand City
Spreckels
1
Pebble Beach
Monterey **2**
Del Rey Oaks
Cypress Point
Carmel Bay
Point Lobos
Carmel
Carmel Highlands
Carmel Valley
Carmel Valley Rd.
Carmel River
Salinas R.
SALINAS VALLEY
SIERRA DE SALINAS
Spanish Bay
17-Mile Dr.

M O N T E R E Y   B A Y

GETTING ORIENTED

North of Big Sur the coastline softens into lower bluffs, windswept dunes, pristine estuaries, and long, sandy beaches, bordering one of the world's most amazing marine environments—the Monterey Bay. On the Monterey Peninsula, at the southern end of the bay, are Carmel-by-the-Sea, Pacific Grove, and Monterey; Santa Cruz sits at the northern tip of the crescent. In between, Highway 1 cruises along the coastline, passing windswept beaches piled high with sand dunes. Along the route are wetlands, artichoke and strawberry fields, and workaday towns such as Castroville and Watsonville.

7

Updated
by Cheryl
Crabtree

Natural beauty is at the heart of this region's enormous appeal—you sense it everywhere, whether you're exploring one of Monterey Bay's attractive coast-side towns, relaxing at a luxurious resort, or touring the coast on the lookout for marine life.

It's been this way for a long time: an abiding current of plenty runs through the region's history. Military buffs see it in centuries' worth of battles for control of the rich territory. John Steinbeck saw it in the success of a community built on the elbow grease of farm laborers in the Salinas Valley and fishermen along Cannery Row. Biologists see it in the ocean's potential as a more sustainable source of food.

Downtown Carmel-by-the-Sea and Monterey are walks through history. The bay itself is protected by the Monterey Bay National Marine Sanctuary, the nation's largest undersea canyon—bigger and deeper than the Grand Canyon. And of course, the backdrop of natural beauty is still everywhere to be seen.

PLANNING

WHEN TO GO

Summer is peak season; mild weather brings in big crowds. In this coastal region, a cool breeze generally blows and fog often rolls in from offshore; you will frequently need a sweater or windbreaker. Off-season, from November through April, fewer people visit and the mood is mellower. Rainfall is heaviest in January and February, but autumn through spring days are crystal clear more often than in summer.

GETTING HERE AND AROUND

AIR TRAVEL

Monterey Regional Airport, 3 miles east of downtown Monterey off Highway 68, is served by Alaska, Allegiant, American Eagle, and United. Taxi service to downtown runs about $15 to $17; to Carmel the fare is $23 to $32. To and from San Jose International Airport and San Francisco International Airport, Monterey Airbus starts at $40 and the Early Bird Airport Shuttle runs $75 to $190.

Airport Contacts Monterey Regional Airport ⊠ *200 Fred Kane Dr., at Olmsted Rd., off Hwy. 68, Monterey* ☎ *831/648-7000* ⊕ *www.montereyairport.com.*

Ground Transportation Central Coast Cab Company ☎ *831/626-3333.* Early Bird Airport Shuttle ☎ *831/462-3933* ⊕ *www.earlybirdairportshuttle.com.* Monterey Airbus ☎ *831/373-7777* ⊕ *www.montereyairbus.com.* Yellow Cab ☎ *831/333-1234.*

BUS TRAVEL

Greyhound serves Santa Cruz and Salinas from San Francisco and San Jose. The trips take about 3 and 4½ hours, respectively. Monterey-Salinas Transit (MST) provides frequent service in Monterey County (fares $1.50 to $3.50; day pass $10), and Santa Cruz METRO ($2; day pass $6 to $10) buses operate throughout Santa Cruz County. You can switch between the two lines in Watsonville, in southern Santa Cruz County.

Bus Contacts Greyhound ☎ *800/231-2222* ⊕ *www.greyhound.com.* Monterey-Salinas Transit ☎ *888/678-2871* ⊕ *www.mst.org.*

CAR TRAVEL

Highway 1 runs south–north along the coast, linking the towns of Carmel-by-the-Sea, Monterey, and Santa Cruz; some sections have only two lanes. The freeway, U.S. 101, lies to the east, roughly parallel to Highway 1. The two roads are connected by Highway 68 from Pacific Grove to Salinas; Highway 156 from Castroville to Prunedale; Highway 152 from Watsonville to Gilroy; and Highway 17 from Santa Cruz to San Jose. ⚠ Traffic near Santa Cruz can crawl to a standstill during commuter hours. In the morning, avoid traveling between 7 and 9; in the afternoon avoid traveling between 4 and 7.

The drive south from San Francisco to Monterey can be made comfortably in three hours or less. The most scenic way is to follow Highway 1 down the coast past flower, pumpkin, and artichoke fields and small seaside communities. Unless you drive on sunny weekends when locals are heading for the beach, the two-lane coast highway may take no longer than the freeway. A sometimes-faster route is Interstate 280 south from San Francisco to Highway 17, north of San Jose.

From Los Angeles the drive to Monterey can be made in five to six hours by heading north on U.S. 101 to Salinas and then west on Highway 68. You can also follow Highway 1 all or part of the way north from Southern California.

TRAIN TRAVEL

Amtrak's *Coast Starlight* runs between Los Angeles, Oakland, and Seattle. From the train station in Salinas, you can connect with buses serving Carmel, Monterey, and Santa Cruz.

Train Contacts Amtrak ☎ *800/872-7245* ⊕ *www.amtrak.com.*

RESTAURANTS

The Monterey Bay area is a culinary paradise. The surrounding waters are full of fish, wild game roams the foothills, and the inland valleys are some of the most fertile in the country—local chefs draw on this bounty for their fresh, truly Californian cuisine. Except at beachside stands and inexpensive eateries, where anything goes, casual but neat

7

dress is the norm. *Prices in the restaurant reviews are the average cost of a main course at dinner or, if dinner is not served, at lunch (excluding sales tax).*

HOTELS

Accommodations in the Monterey area range from no-frills motels to luxurious hotels. Pacific Grove, amply endowed with ornate Victorian houses, is the region's B&B capital; Carmel also has charming inns. Lavish resorts cluster in exclusive Pebble Beach and pastoral Carmel Valley.

High season runs from April through October. Rates in winter, especially at the larger hotels, may drop by 50% or more, and B&Bs often offer midweek specials. Whatever the month, some properties require a two-night stay on weekends. *Prices in the hotel reviews are the lowest cost of a standard double room in high season. For expanded reviews, facilities, and current deals, visit Fodors.com.* ⚠ Many of the fancier accommodations aren't suitable for children; if you're traveling with kids, ask before you book.

Lodging Contact Bed and Breakfast Inns of Santa Cruz County. This association of innkeepers can help you find a bed-and-breakfast. ⊕ *www.santacruzbnb.com.*

TOUR OPTIONS

California Parlor Car Tours operates motor-coach tours from San Francisco that include one or two days in Monterey and Carmel. Ag Venture Tours runs wine-tasting, sightseeing, and agricultural tours to several towns.

Tour Contacts Ag Venture Tours ☎ 831/761–8463 ⊕ *www.agventuretours.com.* **California Parlor Car Tours** ☎ 415/474–7500, 800/227–4250 ⊕ *www.calpartours.com.*

VISITOR INFORMATION

Contacts Monterey County Convention & Visitors Bureau ☎ 877/666–8373 ⊕ *www.seemonterey.com.* **Monterey County Vintners and Growers Association** ☎ 831/375–9400 ⊕ *www.montereywines.org.* **Santa Cruz County Conference and Visitors Council** ✉ 303 Water St., #100, Santa Cruz ☎ 831/425–1234, 800/833–3494 ⊕ *www.santacruz.org.* **Santa Cruz Mountain Winegrowers Association** ✉ 725 Front St., #112, Santa Cruz ☎ 831/685–8463 ⊕ *www.scmwa.com.*

CARMEL AND PACIFIC GROVE

As Highway 1 swings inland about 30 miles north of Big Sur, historic Carmel-by-the Sea anchors the southern entry to the Monterey Peninsula—a gorgeous promontory at the southern tip of Monterey Bay. Just north of Carmel along the coast, the legendary 17-Mile Drive wends its way through private Pebble Beach and the town of Pacific Grove. Highway 1 skirts the peninsula to the east with more direct access to Pebble Beach and Pacific Grove.

CARMEL-BY-THE-SEA

26 miles north of Big Sur on Hwy. 1.

Although the community has grown quickly through the years and its population quadruples with tourists on weekends and in summer, Carmel-by-the-Sea, commonly referred to as Carmel, retains its identity as a quaint village. Self-consciously charming, the town is populated by many celebrities, major and minor, and has its share of quirky ordinances. For instance, women wearing high heels do not have the right to pursue legal action if they trip and fall on the cobblestone streets, and drivers who hit a tree and leave the scene are charged with hit-and-run.

Buildings have no street numbers (street names are written on discreet white posts) and consequently no mail delivery (if you want to see the locals, go to the post office). Artists started this community, and their legacy is evident in the numerous galleries.

GETTING HERE AND AROUND

From north or south follow Highway 1 to Carmel. Head west at Ocean Avenue to reach the main village hub. In summer the MST Carmel-by-the-Sea Trolley loops around town to the beach and mission every 30 minutes or so.

TOURS

For insight into Carmel's history and culture, join a guided two-hour Carmel Walks tour through hidden courtyards, gardens, and pathways. Tours ($25) depart from the Pine Inn courtyard on Lincoln Street. Call to reserve a spot.

ESSENTIALS

Tour Contacts Carmel Walks ⊠ *Lincoln St. at 6th Ave.* ☎ *831/642–2700* ⊕ *www.carmelwalks.com* ⊙ *Tues.–Fri. at 10, Sat. at 10 and 2.*

Visitor Information Carmel Chamber of Commerce ⊠ *Visitor Center, San Carlos, between 5th and 6th* ☎ *831/624–2522, 800/550–4333* ⊕ *www.carmelcalifornia.org* ⊙ *Daily 10–5.*

EXPLORING
TOP ATTRACTIONS

Carmel Mission. Long before it became a shopping and browsing destination, Carmel was an important religious center during the establishment of Spanish California. That heritage is preserved in the Mission San Carlos Borroméo del Rio Carmelo, more commonly known as the Carmel Mission. Founded in 1771, it served as headquarters for the mission system in California under Father Junípero Serra. Adjoining the stone church is a tranquil garden planted with California poppies. Museum rooms at the mission include an early kitchen, Serra's spartan sleeping quarters, and the first college library in California. ⊠ *3080 Rio Rd., at Lasuen Dr.* ☎ *831/624–1271* ⊕ *www.carmelmission.org* ☞ *$6.50* ⊙ *Museum: Mon.–Sun. 9:30–4:45, store open until 5.*

Fodor's Choice
★ **Point Lobos State Reserve.** A 350-acre headland harboring a wealth of marine life, this reserve lies a few miles south of Carmel. The best way to explore here is to walk along one of the many trails. The Cypress Grove

Monterey Bay Area

Santa Cruz Mountains
The Forest of Nisene Marks State Park
Gilroy

Santa Cruz
Soquel
Capitola
Aptos
Natural Bridges State Beach
Twin Lakes State Beach
Soquel Cove
Rio del Mar
La Selva Beach
Corralitos
Freedom
Watsonville
Pajaro
Las Lomas
Pajaro River
San Juan Bautista
Elkhorn Slough
Moss Landing
Dolan Rd.
Prunedale
Castroville
Gabilan Range
Marina
Salinas
Monterey see detail map
Seaside
Sand City
Asilomar State Beach
Point Pinos
Pacific Grove
Spanish Bay
17-Mile Drive
Cypress Point
Carmel Beach
Pebble Beach
Del Rey Oaks
Spreckels
Salinas Valley
Sierra de Salinas
Salinas River
Carmel-by-the-Sea
Carmel River State Beach
Carmel Bay
Carmel Valley Rd.
Refuge
Point Lobos State Reserve
Carmel Highlands
Yankee Point
Earthbound Farm
Garland Ranch Regional Park
Carmel Valley
TO PINNACLES NATIONAL PARK
Monterey Bay

0   5 mi
0   5 km

Trail leads through a forest of Monterey cypress (one of only two natural groves remaining), which clings to the rocks above an emerald green cove. Sea Lion Point Trail is a good place to view sea lions. From those and other trails you may also spot otters, harbor seals, and (in winter and spring) migrating whales. An additional 750 acres of the reserve is an undersea marine park open to qualified scuba divers. ■TIP➔ Arrive early (or in late afternoon) to avoid crowds; the parking lots fill up. No pets are allowed. Only California state park annual passes are accepted. ⊠ *Hwy. 1* 🕿 *831/624–4909, 831/624–8413 for scuba-diving reservations* ⊕ *www.pointlobos.org* 🖃 *$10 per vehicle* ⊙ *Daily 8 am–½ hr after sunset in winter, 8 am–7 pm spring–fall.*

WORTH NOTING

Carmel Plaza. In the east end of the village proper, Carmel Plaza holds nearly 50 shops and restaurants. ⊠ *Ocean Ave. and Mission St.* 🕿 *831/624–1385 concierge, 831/624–0137 shopping line* ⊕ *www. carmelplaza.com.*

Carmel Wine Walk By-the-Sea. Park the car and sample local wines at tasting rooms and shops in downtown Carmel, all within a few blocks of each other. Purchase a Wine Walk Passport, good for flights in seven tasting rooms and free corkage at local restaurants. There's no expiration date—participating venues will stamp it each time you visit. ⊠ *Carmel*

Chamber of Commerce Visitor Center, San Carlos St., between 5th and 6th Aves. ☎ *831/624–2522, 800/550–4333* ⊕ *www. carmelcalifornia.org* ⊠ *$50.*

Ocean Avenue. Downtown Carmel's chief lure is shopping, especially along its main street, Ocean Avenue, between Junipero Avenue and Camino Real. The architecture here is a mishmash of ersatz Tudor, Mediterranean, and other styles.

WORD OF MOUTH

"The beauty of Point Lobos State Reserve was so stunning, I could not believe it. Here you have a mix of tall cliffs, crashing waves, gorgeous wildflowers, abundant wild life (seals, sea otters, deer), and sheltered emerald green coves with white sandy beaches."

—Birder

Tor House. Scattered throughout the pines in Carmel-by-the-Sea are houses and cottages originally built for the writers, artists, and photographers who discovered the area decades ago. Among the most impressive dwellings is Tor House, a stone cottage built in 1919 by poet Robinson Jeffers on a craggy knoll overlooking the sea. Portraits, books, and unusual art objects fill the low-ceiling rooms. The highlight of the small estate is Hawk Tower, a detached edifice set with stones from the Carmel coastline—as well as one from the Great Wall of China. The docents who lead tours (six people maximum) are well informed about the poet's work and life. Reservations for tours, via e-mail at ✎ *thf@torhouse.org*, are recommended. ⊠ *26304 Ocean View Ave.* ☎ *831/624–1813, 831/624–1840 direct docent office line, available Fri. and Sat. only* ⊕ *www.torhouse.org* ⊠ *$10* ⊙ *Hourly tours Fri. and Sat. 10–3* ☞ *No children under 12.*

BEACHES

Carmel Beach. Carmel-by-the-Sea's greatest attraction is its rugged coastline, with pine and cypress forests and countless inlets. Carmel Beach, an easy walk from downtown shops, has sparkling white sands and magnificent sunsets. ■**TIP**→ Dogs are allowed to romp off-leash here. **Amenities:** parking (no fee); toilets. **Best for:** sunset; surfing; walking. ⊠ *End of Ocean Ave.*

Carmel River State Beach. This sugar-white beach, stretching 106 acres along Carmel Bay, is adjacent to a bird sanctuary, where you might spot pelicans, kingfishers, hawks, and sandpipers. **Amenities:** none. **Best for:** sunrise; sunset; walking. ⊠ *Off Scenic Rd., south of Carmel Beach* ☎ *831/624–4909, 831/649–2836* ⊕ *www.parks.ca.gov* ⊠ *Free* ⊙ *Daily 8 am–½ hr after sunset in winter; 8 am–7 pm spring–fall.*

WHERE TO EAT

$$$
FRENCH
✕**Andre's Bouchée.** The food here presents an innovative bistro-style take on local ingredients. A Monterey Bay sea scallop reduction adorns pan-seared veal tenderloin; grilled rib-eye steaks are topped with a shallot–Cabernet Sauvignon sauce. With its copper wine bar, the dining room feels more urban than most of Carmel; perhaps that's why this is the "cool" place in town to dine. The stellar wine list sources the selection at the in-house wine shop. ⑤ *Average main: $28* ⊠ *Mission St., between Ocean and 7th Aves.* ☎ *831/626–7880* ⊕ *www.andresbouchee. com* ⚘ *Reservations essential* ⊙ *No lunch Mon. and Tues.*

7

$$$
EUROPEAN

✗ **Anton and Michel.** Carefully prepared European cuisine is the draw at this airy restaurant. The rack of lamb is carved at the table, the grilled Halloumi cheese and tomatoes are meticulously stacked and served with basil and kalamata olive tapenade, and the desserts are set aflame before your eyes. ⑤ *Average main: $30* ✉ *Mission St. and 7th Ave.* ☏ *831/624–2406* ⊕ *www.antonandmichel.com* ⚐ *Reservations essential.*

$$$
MEDITERRANEAN

✗ **Casanova.** This cozy restaurant inspires European-style celebration and romance—accordions hang from the walls, and tiny party lights dance along the low ceilings. The food consists of delectable seasonal dishes from southern France and northern Italy. Private dining and a special menu are offered at Van Gogh's Table, a special table imported from France's Auberge Ravoux, the artist's final residence. ⑤ *Average main: $30* ✉ *5th Ave., between San Carlos and Mission Sts.* ☏ *831/625–0501* ⊕ *www.casanovarestaurant.com* ⚐ *Reservations essential.*

$
AMERICAN

✗ **The Cottage Restaurant.** This family-friendly spot serves sandwiches, pizzas, and homemade soups at lunch and simple entreés at dinner, but the best meal is breakfast (good thing it's served all day). The menu offers six variations on eggs Benedict, and all kinds of sweet and savory crepes. ⑤ *Average main: $14* ✉ *Lincoln St., between Ocean and 7th Aves.* ☏ *831/625–6260* ⊕ *www.cottagerestaurant.com* ⊙ *No dinner Sun.–Wed.*

$$$
SEAFOOD

✗ **Flying Fish Grill.** Simple in appearance yet bold with its flavors, this Japanese–California seafood restaurant is one of Carmel's most inventive eateries. Among the best entrées is the almond-crusted sea bass served with Chinese cabbage and rock shrimp stir-fry. The warm, wood-lined dining room is broken up into very private booths. ⑤ *Average main: $26* ✉ *Carmel Plaza, Mission St., between Ocean and 7th Aves.* ☏ *831/625–1962* ⊕ *www.flyingfishgrill.com* ⊙ *No lunch.*

$$$
AMERICAN

✗ **Grasing's Coastal Cuisine.** Chef Kurt Grasing draws from fresh Carmel Coast and Central Valley ingredients to whip up contemporary adaptations of European-provincial and American cooking. Longtime menu favorites include artichoke lasagna in a roasted tomato sauce, duck with fresh cherries and green peppercorns in a red wine sauce, a savory paella, and grilled steaks and chops. ⑤ *Average main: $30* ✉ *6th Ave. and Mission St.* ☏ *831/624–6562* ⊕ *www.grasings.com* ⚐ *Reservations essential.*

$
AMERICAN

✗ **Jack London's.** This pub-like local hangout is one of the only Carmel restaurants to serve food late at night, often until 11 pm or midnight. The menu includes everything from nachos to steaks. ⑤ *Average main: $15* ✉ *Su Vecino Court, Dolores St., between 5th and 6th Aves.* ☏ *831/624–2336* ⊕ *www.jacklondons.com.*

$$$
FRENCH

✗ **L'Escargot.** Chef-owner Kericos Loutas personally sees to each plate of food served at this romantic, unpretentious French restaurant. Order the pan-roasted duck breast or the cassoulet de Toulouse; or, if you can't decide, choose the three-course prix-fixe dinner. ⑤ *Average main: $30* ✉ *Mission and 4th Ave.* ☏ *831/620–1942* ⊕ *www.escargot-carmel.com* ⚐ *Reservations essential* ⊙ *No lunch.*

$$
TAPAS

✗ **Mundaka.** Traditional Spanish-style tapas made with fresh local ingredients, a full bar, and live music seven nights a week attract legions of locals to this cozy downtown eatery. The menu changes weekly,

Point Lobos Reserve State Park is home to one of the only two natural stands of Monterey Cypress in the world.

but longtime favorites include the Angus beef slider with Spanish blue cheese and truffle fries, the authentic Valencian paella, and a platter of housemade charcuterie. Come early in the evening for a more intimate experience—music starts at 9:30 pm on weekends, while mellower music entertains diners starting at 7:30 other nights. The breakfast menu includes Spanish tortillas, plus Belgian waffles and homemade baked goods; for lunch, choose among sandwiches, panini, and salads. $ *Average main: $21* ⊠ *San Carlos St., between Ocean and 7th Aves.* ☎ *831/624–7400* ⊕ *www.mundakacarmel.com.*

$ ✕ **Tuck Box.** This bright little restaurant is in a cottage right out of a fairy

AMERICAN tale, complete with stone fireplace. Handmade scones, good for breakfast or afternoon tea, are the specialty. $ *Average main: $12* ⊠ *Dolores St., between Ocean and 7th Aves.* ☎ *831/624–6365* ⊕ *www.tuckbox. com* ⌕ *Reservations not accepted* ⊟ *No credit cards* ⊘ *No dinner.*

$$$ ✕ **Vesuvio.** Chef and restaurateur Rich Pèpe heats up the night with

ITALIAN his latest venture, a lively trattoria downstairs and a swinging rooftop terrace, Starlight Lounge 65°. Pèpe's elegant take on traditional Italian cuisine yields dishes such as wild-boar Bolognese pappardelle, lobster ravioli, and velvety limoncello mousse cake. Pizzas and small plates are served in the restaurant and two bars. Upstairs, relax in comfy chairs by fire pits and enjoy bird's-eye views of the village and, most nights in summer, take in live music. $ *Average main: $24* ⊠ *6th and Junipero Aves.* ☎ *831/625–1766 ext. 2* ⊕ *www.vesuviocarmel.com* ⊘ *No lunch.*

WHERE TO STAY

For expanded hotel reviews, visit Fodors.com.

$$$
B&B/INN
Cypress Inn. A top-to-bottom redecorating project in 2013 gave this luxurious inn a fresh Mediterranean air with Moroccan touches. **Pros:** luxury without snobbery; popular lounge; traditional British-style afternoon tea. **Cons:** not for the pet-phobic. $ *Rooms from: $235* ⊠ *Lincoln St. and 7th Ave.* ☎ *831/624–3871, 800/443–7443* ⊕ *www.cypress-inn. com* ⇆ *39 rooms, 5 suites* ❘O❘ *Breakfast.*

$$$$
HOTEL
Hyatt Carmel Highlands. High on a hill overlooking the Pacific, this place has superb views; accommodations include king rooms with fireplaces, suites with personal Jacuzzis, and full town houses with all the perks. **Pros:** killer views; romantic getaway; great food. **Cons:** thin walls; must drive to Carmel. $ *Rooms from: $369* ⊠ *120 Highlands Dr.* ☎ *831/620–1234, 800/233–1234* ⊕ *carmelhighlands.hyatt.com* ⇆ *46 rooms, 2 suites.*

$$$$
B&B/INN
Fodor'sChoice
★
L'Auberge Carmel. Stepping through the doors of this elegant inn is like being transported to a little European village. **Pros:** in town but off the main drag; four blocks from the beach; full-service luxury. **Cons:** touristy area; not a good choice for families. $ *Rooms from: $425* ⊠ *Monte Verde, at 7th Ave.* ☎ *831/624–8578* ⊕ *www.laubergecarmel. com* ⇆ *20 rooms* ❘O❘ *Breakfast.*

$$$$
HOTEL
La Playa Hotel. A historic complex of lush gardens and Mediterranean-style buildings, La Playa reopened in 2012 after a $3.5 million renovation. **Pros:** residential neighborhood; manicured gardens; two blocks from the beach. **Cons:** four stories (no elevator); busy lobby; some rooms are on the small side. $ *Rooms from: $279* ⊠ *Camino Real, at 8th Ave.* ☎ *831/293–6100, 800/582–8900* ⊕ *www.laplayahotel.com* ⇆ *75 rooms* ❘O❘ *Breakfast.*

$$
HOTEL
Mission Ranch. Movie star Clint Eastwood owns this sprawling property whose accommodations include rooms in a converted barn, and several cottages, some with fireplaces. **Pros:** farm setting; pastoral views; great for tennis buffs. **Cons:** busy parking lot; must drive to the heart of town. $ *Rooms from: $140* ⊠ *26270 Dolores St.* ☎ *831/624–6436, 800/538–8221, 831/625–9040 restaurant* ⊕ *www.missionranchcarmel. com* ⇆ *31 rooms* ❘O❘ *Breakfast.*

$$$
B&B/INN
Sea View Inn. In a residential area a few hundred feet from the beach, this restored 1905 home has a double parlor with two fireplaces, oriental rugs, canopy beds, and a spacious front porch. **Pros:** quiet; private; close to the beach. **Cons:** small building; uphill trek to the heart of town. $ *Rooms from: $200* ⊠ *Camino Real, between 11th and 12th Aves.* ☎ *831/624–8778* ⊕ *www.seaviewinncarmel.com* ⇆ *8 rooms, 6 with private bath* ❘O❘ *Breakfast.*

$$$$
B&B/INN
Tickle Pink Inn. Atop a towering cliff, this inn has views of the Big Sur coastline, which you can contemplate from your private balcony. **Pros:** close to great hiking; intimate; dramatic views. **Cons:** close to a big hotel; lots of traffic during the day. $ *Rooms from: $289* ⊠ *155 Highland Dr.* ☎ *831/624–1244, 800/635–4774* ⊕ *www.ticklepink.com* ⇆ *23 rooms, 10 suites, 1 cottage* ❘O❘ *Breakfast.*

$$$
B&B/INN
Tradewinds Carmel. This converted motel with sleek decor inspired by the South Seas encircles a courtyard with waterfalls, a meditation

garden, and a fire pit. **Pros:** serene; within walking distance of restaurants; friendly service. **Cons:** no pool; long walk to the beach. $ *Rooms from: $250* ✉ *Mission St., at 3rd Ave.* ☎ *831/624–2776* ⊕ *www. tradewindscarmel.com* ↝ *26 rooms, 2 suites* ⦿ *Breakfast.*

SHOPPING

ART GALLERIES

Carmel Art Association. The association exhibits the original paintings and sculptures of local artists. ✉ *Dolores St., between 5th and 6th Aves.* ☎ *831/624–6176* ⊕ *www.carmelart.org.*

Galerie Plein Aire. The gallery showcases the oil paintings of a group of local artists. ✉ *Dolores St., between 5th and 6th Aves.* ☎ *831/625–5686* ⊕ *www.galeriepleinaire.com.*

Gallery Sur. Fine art photography of the Big Sur Coast and the Monterey Peninsula, including scenic shots and golf images, is the focus here. ✉ *6th Ave., between Dolores and Lincoln Sts.* ☎ *831/626–2615* ⊕ *www.gallerysur.com.*

Richard MacDonald/Dawson Cole Fine Art. Amazing images of dancers, athletes, and other humans in motion come to life in this gallery that is devoted to the artworks of Monterey Bay resident Richard MacDonald, one of the most famed figurative sculptors of our time. ✉ *Lincoln St., at 6th Ave.* ☎ *800/972–5528* ⊕ *www.dawsoncolefineart.com* ⊘ *Mon.–Sat. 10–6, Sun. 10–5:30.*

Weston Gallery. Run by the family of the late Edward Weston, this is hands down the best photography gallery around, with contemporary color photography complemented by classic black-and-whites. ✉ *6th Ave., between Dolores and Lincoln Sts.* ☎ *831/624–4453* ⊕ *www. westongallery.com.*

SPECIALTY SHOPS

Avant Garden & Home. An eclectic array of art, jewelry, home furnishings, garden accents, and handmade gift items from around the world are on display at this small, family-run shop. ✉ *San Carlos St., at 7th Ave.* ☎ *831/626–9899* ⊕ *www.avantgardenandhome.com.*

Bittner. The shop carries a fine selection of collectible and vintage pens from around the world. ✉ *Ocean Ave., between Mission and San Carlos Sts.* ☎ *831/626–8828* ⊕ *www.bittner.com.*

Intima. Find European lingerie here that ranges from lacy to racy. ✉ *San Carlos St., between Ocean and 6th Aves.* ☎ *831/625–0599* ⊕ *www. intimacarmel.com.*

Jan de Luz. This shop monograms and embroiders fine linens (including bathrobes) while you wait. ✉ *Dolores St., between Ocean and 7th Aves.* ☎ *831/622–7621* ⊕ *www.jandeluz.com.*

Madrigal. Sportswear, sweaters, and accessories for women are the specialties here. ✉ *Carmel Plaza and Mission St.* ☎ *831/624–3477.*

7

CARMEL VALLEY

10 miles east of Carmel, Hwy. 1 to Carmel Valley Rd.

Carmel Valley Road, which heads inland from Highway 1 south of Carmel, is the main thoroughfare through this valley, a secluded enclave of horse ranchers and other well-heeled residents who prefer the area's sunny climate to coastal fog and wind. Once thick with dairy farms, the valley has evolved into an esteemed wine appellation. Carmel Valley Village has crafts shops, art galleries, and the tasting rooms of numerous local wineries.

GETTING HERE AND AROUND

From U.S. 101 north or south, exit at Highway 68 and head west toward the coast. Scenic, two-lane Laureles Grade winds west over the mountains to Carmel Valley Road north of the village.

TOURS

The Carmel Valley Grapevine Express, aka MST's Line 24 bus, travels between downtown Monterey and Carmel Valley Village, with stops near wineries, restaurants, and shopping centers. At $10 for a ride-all-day pass, it's an incredible bargain.

Bus Contact Carmel Valley Grapevine Express ☎ 888/678-2871 ⊕ www.mst.org.

EXPLORING

Bernardus Tasting Room. At this tasting room you can sample many of Bernardus Winery's offerings, including older vintages and reserve wines. ✉ 5 W. Carmel Valley Rd., at El Caminito Rd. ☎ 831/298-8021, 800/223-2533 ⊕ www.bernardus.com ☉ Daily 11-5.

Château Julien. The expansive winery, recognized internationally for its Chardonnays and Merlots, offers tours by appointment only, but the tasting room is open daily. ✉ 8940 Carmel Valley Rd., at Schetter Rd. ☎ 831/624-2600 ⊕ www.chateaujulien.com ☉ Mon.–Fri. 8-5, Sat.–Sun. 11-5; tours Mon.–Fri. at 10:30 and 2:30, Sat.–Sun. at 12:30 and 2:30, by appointment.

Cowgirl Winery. Taste Chardonnay, Cabernet Sauvignon, Rosé, and blends in a hip, cowgirl-chic main building or at outdoor tables amid chickens, a tractor, and a rustic flatbed truck. Order woodfired pizzas from sister business Corkscrew Café down the block for delivery to your tasting table. ✉ 25 Pilot Rd. ☎ 831/298-7030 ☉ Apr.–Oct., Sun.–Fri. 11:30-5, Sat. 11:30-6. Nov.–Mar., Wed.–Fri. 11:30-5, Sat. 11:30-6.

Earthbound Farm. Pick up fresh veggies, ready-to-eat meals, gourmet groceries, flowers, and gifts at Earthbound Farm, the world's largest grower of organic produce. You can also take a romp in the kid's garden, cut your own herbs, and stroll through the chamomile aromatherapy labyrinth. Special events, on Saturdays from April through December, include bug walks and garlic-braiding workshops. ✉ 7250 Carmel Valley Rd. ☎ 831/625-6219 ⊕ www.ebfarm.com ✆ Free ☉ Mon.–Sat. 8-6:30, Sun. 9-6.

Garland Ranch Regional Park. Hiking trails stretch across much of this park's 4,500 acres of meadows, forested hillsides, and creeks. ✉ Carmel Valley Rd., 9 miles east of Carmel-by-the-Sea ☎ 831/659-4488 ⊕ www.mprpd.org.

WHERE TO EAT

$$
EUROPEAN
✕ **Café Rustica.** European country cooking is the focus at this lively roadhouse. Specialties include roasted meats, seafood, pastas, and thin-crust pizzas from the wood-fired oven. It can get noisy inside; for a quieter meal, request a table outside. ⑤ *Average main: $20* ⊠ *10 Delfino Pl., at Pilot Rd., off Carmel Valley Rd.* ☎ *831/659–4444* ⊕ *www. caferusticavillage.com* ⚖ *Reservations essential* ⊙ *Closed Mon.*

$$
MODERN
AMERICAN
✕ **Corkscrew Café.** Take a break from wine touring and fill up on farm-fresh wine-country food at this casual, Old Monterey-style bistro. Herbs and seasonal produce come from their own organic gardens; fish comes from local waters, meats are hormone-free. Popular dishes include the homemade chicken salad, fish tacos, and woodfired pizzas with classic toppings and more unusual combinations (Meyer lemon and prosciutto). Dine indoors near the open kitchen or in the garden patio, and check out the collection of corkscrews from their beginnings in 17th-century Europe to the present. ⑤ *Average main: $22* ⊠ *55 W. Carmel Valley Rd., at Pilot Rd.* ☎ *831/659–8888* ⊕ *www.corkscrewcafe.com.*

$
AMERICAN
✕ **Wagon Wheel Coffee Shop.** This local hangout decorated with wagon wheels, cowboy hats, and lassos serves terrific hearty breakfasts, including oatmeal and banana pancakes, eggs Benedict, and biscuits and gravy. The lunch menu includes a dozen different burgers and other sandwiches. ⑤ *Average main: $11* ⊠ *Valley Hill Center, 7156 Carmel Valley Rd., next to Quail Lodge* ☎ *831/624–8878* ▭ *No credit cards* ⊙ *No dinner.*

$$$
AMERICAN
✕ **Will's Fargo.** Around since the 1920s, this restaurant calls itself a "dressed-up saloon." Steer horns and gilt-frame paintings adorn the walls of the Victorian-style dining room; you can also eat on the patios. The menu is mainly seafood and steaks, including a 20-ounce porterhouse. ⑤ *Average main: $28* ⊠ *16 E. Carmel Valley Rd.* ☎ *831/659–2774* ⊕ *www.bernardus.com* ⊙ *No lunch.*

WHERE TO STAY

For expanded hotel reviews, visit Fodors.com.

$$$$
RESORT
Fodor'sChoice
★
🏨 **Bernardus Lodge.** The spacious guest rooms at this luxury spa resort have vaulted ceilings, featherbeds, fireplaces, patios, and bathtubs for two. **Pros:** exceptional personal service; outstanding food and wine. **Cons:** pricey; some guests can seem snooty. ⑤ *Rooms from: $455* ⊠ *415 W. Carmel Valley Rd.* ☎ *831/658–3400, 888/648–9463* ⊕ *www. bernardus.com* ⤳ *56 rooms, 1 suite.*

$$$$
RESORT
🏨 **Carmel Valley Ranch.** Hotel scion John Pritzker bought this 500-acre all-suites resort in 2009 and committed more than $30 million to transform the property into an upscale experiential getaway. **Pros:** stunning natural setting; tons of activities; state-of-the-art amenities. **Cons:** must drive several miles to shops and nightlife; pricey. ⑤ *Rooms from: $375* ⊠ *1 Old Ranch Rd.* ☎ *831/625–9500* ⊕ *www.carmelvalleyranch.com* ⤳ *139 suites.*

$$$
HOTEL
FAMILY
🏨 **Quail Lodge & Golf Club.** A sprawling collection of California ranch-style buildings on 850 acres of lush meadows, fairways, and lakes, Quail Lodge offers luxury rooms and outdoor activities at surprisingly affordable rates. **Pros:** on the golf course; two on-site restaurants;

7

Land Rover Driving School on property. **Cons:** extra fees for athletic club passes and some services; 5 miles from the beach and Carmel Valley Village. ⑤ *Rooms from: $225* ✉ *8205 Valley Greens Dr.* 📠 *831/624–2888* ☎ *866/675–1101* ⊕ *www.quaillodge.com* ⌑ *77 rooms, 16 suites* ⦿| *Breakfast.*

$$$$
RESORT
Fodor'sChoice
★

⊡ Stonepine Estate Resort. Set on 330 pastoral acres, this former estate of the Crocker banking family has been converted to a luxurious inn. **Pros:** supremely exclusive. **Cons:** difficult to get a reservation; far from the coast. ⑤ *Rooms from: $300* ✉ *150 E. Carmel Valley Rd.* ☎ *831/659–2245* ⊕ *www.stonepineestate.com* ⌑ *10 rooms, 2 suites, 3 cottages.*

SPAS

Refuge. Relax and recharge in a coed, European-style relaxation center on 2 serene acres—without breaking the bank. Heat up in the eucalyptus steam room or cedar sauna, plunge into cold pools, and relax indoors in zero-gravity chairs or outdoors in Adirondack chairs around fire pits. Repeat the cycle a few times, then lounge around the thermal waterfall pools. Talk is not allowed, and bathing suits are required. Optional 50-minute massages ($60) are available. ✉ *27300 Rancho San Carlos Rd., south off Carmel Valley Rd.* ☎ *831/620–7360* ⊕ *www. refuge.com* ▨ *$39* ⊙ *Daily 10–10.*

SPORTS AND THE OUTDOORS
GOLF

Quail Lodge & Golf Club. The championship course here incorporates several lakes into its design. ✉ *8000 Valley Greens Dr.* ☎ *831/620–8808 golf shop, 831/620–8866 club concierge* ⊕ *www.quaillodge.com* ⅄ *18 holes. 5,478 yds. Par 71. Greens fees: $125/$150* ☞ *Driving range, putting green, pitching area, golf carts, pull carts, rental clubs, pro shop, golf academy, lessons, restaurant, bar.*

Rancho Cañada Golf Club. Some of the holes at this public course with 36 holes overlook the Carmel River. ✉ *4860 Carmel Valley Rd., 1 mile east of Hwy. 1* ☎ *831/624–0111, 800/536–9459* ⊕ *www.ranchocanada. com* ⅄ *East Course: 18 holes. 6,125 yds. Par 71. Greens fee: $70. West Course: 18 holes. 6,357 yds. Par 71. Greens fee: $70* ☞ *Driving range, putting green, pitching area, golf carts, pull carts, rental clubs, pro shop, golf lessons, restaurant, bar.*

PEBBLE BEACH

Off North San Antonio Rd. in Carmel-by-the-Sea or off Sunset Dr. in Pacific Grove.

Fodor'sChoice
★

In 1919 the Pacific Improvement Company acquired 18,000 acres of prime land on the Monterey Peninsula, including the entire Pebble Beach coastal region and much of Pacific Grove. Pebble Beach Golf Links and the Lodge at Pebble Beach opened the same year, and the private enclave evolved into a world-class golf destination with three posh lodges, five golf courses, and some of the West Coast's ritziest homes.

GETTING HERE AND AROUND

If you drive south from Monterey on Highway 1, exit at 17-Mile-Drive/ Sunset Drive in Pacific Grove to find the northern entrance gate. Coming from Carmel, exit at Ocean Avenue and follow the road almost to the beach; turn right on North San Antonio Road to the Carmel Gate. You can also enter through the Highway 1 Gate at Scenic Drive/Sunridge Road. Monterey–Salinas Transit buses provide regular service in and around Pebble Beach.

EXPLORING

17-Mile Drive. Primordial nature resides in quiet harmony with palatial estates along 17-Mile Drive, which winds through an 8,400-acre microcosm of the Pebble Beach coastal landscape. Dotting the drive are rare Monterey cypress, trees so gnarled and twisted that Robert Louis Stevenson described them as "ghosts fleeing before the wind." Some sightseers balk at the $9.75-per-car collected at the gates to drive on the private roads, but most find the drive well worth the price. An alternative is to grab a bike; cyclists tour for free. ■TIP→ Visitors who spend at least $25 on dining or shopping in Pebble Beach receive a fee refund if they show a receipt at the exit gate.

Bird Rock. Bird Rock, the largest of several islands at the southern end of the Monterey Peninsula Country Club's golf course, teems with harbor seals, sea lions, cormorants, and pelicans.

Crocker Marble Palace. Many of the stately homes along 17-Mile Drive reflect the classic Monterey or Spanish Mission style typical of the region. A standout is the Crocker Marble Palace, about a mile south of the Lone Cypress (⇨ *below*). It's a private waterfront estate inspired by a Byzantine castle, easily identifiable by its dozens of marble arches.

The Lone Cypress. The most-photographed tree along 17-Mile Drive is the weather-sculpted Lone Cypress, which grows out of a precipitous outcropping above the waves about 1½ miles up the road from Pebble Beach Golf Links. You can't walk out to the tree, but you can stop for a view of the Lone Cypress at a small parking area off the road.

Seal Rock. Sea creatures and birds—as well as some very friendly ground squirrels—make use of Seal Rock, the largest of a group of islands about 2 miles north of Lone Cypress.

WHERE TO STAY

For expanded hotel reviews, visit Fodors.com.

$$$$
RESORT
Fodor's Choice
★

🖼 **Casa Palmero.** This exclusive boutique hotel evokes a stately Mediterranean villa, where rooms are decorated with sumptuous fabrics and fine art and each has a wood-burning fireplace and heated floor; some have private outdoor patios with in-ground whirlpools. **Pros:** ultimate in pampering; more private than sister resorts; right on the golf course. **Cons:** pricey; may be *too* posh for some. $ *Rooms from: $885* ✉ *1518 Cypress Dr.* ☎ *831/622–6650, 800/654–9300* ⊕ *www.pebblebeach.com* 🛏 *20 rooms, 4 suites.*

$$$$
RESORT

🖼 **The Inn at Spanish Bay.** This resort sprawls across a breathtaking stretch of shoreline and has lush, 600-square-foot rooms. **Pros:** attentive service; tons of amenities; spectacular views. **Cons:** huge hotel; 4 miles from other Pebble Beach Resorts facilities. $ *Rooms from:*

7

$625 ⊠ 2700 17-Mile Dr. ☎ 831/647–7500, 800/654–9300 ⊕ www. pebblebeach.com ⇌ 252 rooms, 17 suites.

$$$$
RESORT

⛯ **Lodge at Pebble Beach.** All rooms have fireplaces and many have wonderful ocean views at this circa-1919 resort. **Pros:** world-class golf; borders the ocean and fairways; fabulous facilities. **Cons:** some rooms are on the small side; very pricey. ⑤ *Rooms from: $725 ⊠ 1700 17-Mile Dr. ☎ 831/624–3811, 800/654–9300 ⊕ www.pebblebeach.com ⇌ 142 rooms, 19 suites.*

SPORTS AND THE OUTDOORS

GOLF

Links at Spanish Bay. This course, which hugs a choice stretch of shoreline, is designed in the rugged manner of a traditional Scottish course, with sand dunes and coastal marshes interspersed among the greens. Nonguests can reserve tee times up to two months in advance. ⊠ *17-Mile Dr., north end ☎ 800/654–9300 ⊕ www.pebblebeach.com ⅄ 18 holes. 6,821 yds. Par 72. Greens fee: $265 ⟿ Putting green, pitching area, golf carts, caddies, rental clubs, pro shop, golf academy, lessons, restaurant, bar.*

Fodor'sChoice
★

Pebble Beach Golf Links. This club attracts golfers from around the world. The ocean plays a major role in the 18th hole of the famed links. Each February the course is the main site of the AT&T Pebble Beach Pro-Am, where show-business celebrities and golf pros team up for one of the nation's most glamorous tournaments. Tee times are available to guests who book a minimum two-night stay. Nonguests can reserve a tee time only one day in advance on a space-available basis (up to a year for groups); resort guests can reserve up to 18 months in advance. ⊠ *17-Mile Dr., near Lodge at Pebble Beach ☎ 800/654–9300 ⊕ www.pebblebeach.com ⅄ 18 holes. 6,828 yds. Par 72. Greens fee: $495 ⟿ Driving range, putting green, pitching area, golf carts, caddies, rental clubs, pro shop, golf academy, lessons, restaurant, bar.*

Peter Hay. This 9-hole, par-3 course has attracted golfers of all skill levels since 1957. ⊠ *17-Mile Dr. ☎ 831/622–8723 ⊕ www.pebblebeach.com ⅄ 9 holes. 725 yds. Par 27. Greens fee: $30 ⟿ Rental clubs, pro shop, golf academy, lessons, restaurant, bar.*

Spyglass Hill. This course is among the most challenging Pebble Beach courses. With the first five holes bordering on the Pacific and the other 13 reaching deep into the Del Monte Forest, the course is tricky, but oh, the views! Reservations are essential and may be made up to one month in advance (18 months for resort guests). ⊠ *Stevenson Dr. and Spyglass Hill Rd. ☎ 800/654–9300 ⊕ www.pebblebeach.com ⅄ 18 holes. 6,960 yds. Par 72. Greens fee: $370 ⟿ Driving range, putting green, pitching area, golf carts, caddies, rental clubs, pro shop, golf academy, lessons, restaurant, bar.*

7

PACIFIC GROVE

3 miles north of Carmel-by-the-Sea on Hwy. 68.

This picturesque town, which began as a summer retreat for church groups more than a century ago, recalls its prim and proper Victorian heritage in its host of tiny board-and-batten cottages and stately mansions. However, long before the church groups flocked here the area received thousands of annual pilgrims—in the form of bright orange-and-black monarch butterflies. They still come, migrating south from Canada and the Pacific Northwest to take residence in pine and eucalyptus groves from October through March. In Butterfly Town USA, as Pacific Grove is known, the sight of a mass of butterflies hanging from the branches like a long, fluttering veil is unforgettable.

A prime way to enjoy Pacific Grove is to walk or bicycle the 3 miles of city-owned shoreline along Ocean View Boulevard, a cliff-top area landscaped with native plants and dotted with benches meant for sitting and gazing at the sea. You can spot many types of birds here, including the web-footed cormorants that crowd the massive rocks rising out of the surf. Two Victorians of note along Ocean View are the Queen Anne–style Green Gables, at No. 301—erected in 1888, it's now a B&B—and the 1909 Pryor House, at No. 429, a massive, shingled, private residence with a leaded- and beveled-glass doorway.

GETTING HERE AND AROUND

Reach Pacific Grove via Highway 68 off Highway 1, just south of Monterey. From Cannery Row in Monterey, head north until the road merges with Ocean Boulevard and follow it along the coast. MST buses travel within Pacific Grove and surrounding towns.

EXPLORING

FAMILY **Lovers Point Park.** The coastal views are gorgeous from this waterfront park whose sheltered beach has a children's pool and a picnic area. The main lawn has a volleyball court and a snack bar. ⊠ *Ocean View Blvd. northwest of Forest Ave.* ☎ *831/648–5730.*

FAMILY **Monarch Grove Sanctuary.** This sanctuary is a fairly reliable spot for viewing the butterflies between October and February. ⊠ *1073 Lighthouse Ave., at Ridge Rd.* ⊕ *www.pgmuseum.org.*

Pacific Grove Museum of Natural History. Contact the museum for the latest information about the butterfly population. Year-round, you can view the well-crafted butterfly tree exhibit here. ⊠ *165 Forest Ave., at Central Ave.* ☎ *831/648–5716* ⊕ *www.pgmuseum.org* ⊠ *$3 suggested donation; $5 per family* ⊗ *Tues.–Sun. 10–5.*

FAMILY **Point Pinos Lighthouse.** At this 1855-vintage lighthouse, the oldest continuously operating lighthouse on the West Coast, you can learn about the lighting and foghorn operations and wander through a small museum containing U.S. Coast Guard memorabilia. ⊠ *Asilomar Ave., between Lighthouse Ave. and Del Monte Blvd.* ☎ *831/648–3176* ⊕ *www. pointpinos.org* ⊠ *$2 suggested donation* ⊗ *Thur.–Mon. 1–4.*

BEACHES

Asilomar State Beach. A beautiful coastal area, Asilomar State Beach stretches between Point Pinos and the Del Monte Forest. The 100 acres of dunes, tidal pools, and pocket-size beaches form one of the region's richest areas for marine life—including surfers, who migrate here most winter mornings. Leashed dogs are allowed on the beach. **Amenities:** none. **Best for:** sunrise; sunset; surfing; walking. ⊠ *Sunset Dr. and Asilomar Ave.* ☎ *831/646–6440* ⊕ *www.parks.ca.gov.*

WHERE TO EAT

$$$
MEDITERRANEAN
✗ **Fandango.** The menu here is mostly Mediterranean and southern French, with such dishes as calves' liver and onions and paella served in a skillet. The decor follows suit: stone walls and country furniture give the restaurant the earthy feel of a European farmhouse. This is where locals come when they want to have a big dinner with friends, drink wine, have fun, and generally feel at home. ⑤ *Average main: $26* ⊠ *223 17th St., south of Lighthouse Ave.* ☎ *831/372–3456* ⊕ *www.fandangorestaurant.com.*

$$
SEAFOOD
✗ **Fishwife.** Fresh fish with a Latin accent makes this spot a favorite of locals for lunch or a casual dinner. Standards are the sea garden salads topped with your choice of fish and the fried seafood plates with fresh veggies. Diners with large appetites appreciate the fisherman's bowls— fresh fish served with rice, black beans, spicy cabbage, salsa, vegetables, and crispy tortilla strips. ⑤ *Average main: $22* ⊠ *1996½ Sunset Dr., at Asilomar Blvd.* ☎ *831/375–7107* ⊕ *www.fishwife.com.*

$$$
ITALIAN
✗ **Joe Rombi's La Mia Cucina.** Pasta, fish, steaks, and chops are the specialties at this modern trattoria, which is the best in town for Italian food. The look is spare and clean, with colorful antique wine posters decorating the white walls. Next door, Joe Rombi's La Piccola Casa Pizzeria & Coffee House serves breakfast (baked goods) and lunch daily, plus early dinner Wednesday through Sunday. ⑤ *Average main: $23* ⊠ *208 17th St., at Lighthouse Ave.* ☎ *831/373–2416* ⊕ *www.joerombi.com* ☺ *Closed Mon. and Tues. No lunch.*

$$$
MODERN
AMERICAN
✗ **Passionfish.** South American artwork and artifacts decorate the walls, and Latin and Asian flavors infuse the dishes. Chef Ted Walter shops at local farmers' markets several times a week to find the best produce, fish, and meat available, then pairs them with creative sauces. The menu might include sea scallops with tomato-truffle butter and savory rice pudding. ⑤ *Average main: $23* ⊠ *701 Lighthouse Ave., at Congress Ave.* ☎ *831/655–3311* ⊕ *www.passionfish.net* ☺ *No lunch.*

$
MEXICAN
✗ **Peppers Mexicali Cafe.** This cheerful white-walled storefront serves traditional dishes from Mexico and Latin America, with an emphasis on fresh seafood. Excellent red and green salsas are made throughout the day, and there's a large selection of beers, along with fresh lime margaritas. ⑤ *Average main: $15* ⊠ *170 Forest Ave., between Lighthouse and Central Aves.* ☎ *831/373–6892* ⊕ *www.peppersmexicalicafe.com* ☺ *Closed Tues. No lunch Sun.*

$$
AMERICAN
✗ **Red House Café.** When it's nice out, sun pours through the big windows of this cozy restaurant and across tables on the porch; when fog rolls in, the fireplace is lighted. The American menu changes with the seasons but typically includes grilled lamb fillets atop mashed potatoes for dinner and Dungeness crab cakes over salad for lunch. Breakfast on weekends

7

is a local favorite. ⑤ *Average main: $20* ⊠ *662 Lighthouse Ave., at 19th St.* ☎ *831/643–1060* ⊕ *www.redhousecafe.com* ⊙ *Closed Mon.*

$$
AMERICAN
✕ **Taste Café and Bistro.** Grilled marinated rabbit, roasted half chicken, filet mignon, and other meats are the focus at this café, which serves hearty European-inspired food in a casual, open-kitchen setting. ⑤ *Average main: $20* ⊠ *1199 Forest Ave.* ☎ *831/655–0324* ⊕ *www. tastecafebistro.com* ⊙ *Closed Sun.–Mon.*

WHERE TO STAY

For expanded hotel reviews, visit Fodors.com.

$$
B&B/INN
⚏ **Green Gables Inn.** Stained-glass windows and ornate interior details compete with spectacular ocean views at this Queen Anne–style mansion, built by a businessman for his mistress in 1888. **Pros:** exceptional views; impeccable attention to historic detail. **Cons:** some rooms are small; thin walls. ⑤ *Rooms from: $145* ⊠ *301 Ocean View Blvd.* ☎ *831/375–2095, 800/722–1774* ⊕ *www.greengablesinnpg.com* ⇨ *10 rooms, 7 with bath; 1 suite* ⦶ *Breakfast.*

$$
HOTEL
⚏ **Lighthouse Lodge and Cottages.** Near the tip of the peninsula, this basic complex straddles Lighthouse Avenue—the lodge is on one side, the all-suites facility on the other. **Pros:** near lighthouse and 17-Mile Drive; friendly reception; many room options. **Cons:** next to a cemetery; lodge rooms are basic. ⑤ *Rooms from: $139* ⊠ *1150 and 1249 Lighthouse Ave.* ☎ *831/655–2111, 800/858–1249* ⊕ *www.lighthouselodgecottages. com* ⇨ *64 rooms, 31 suites* ⦶ *Breakfast.*

$$$
B&B/INN
⚏ **Martine Inn.** The glassed-in parlor and many guest rooms at this 1899 Mediterranean-style villa have stunning ocean views, and thoughtful details such as robes and rocking chairs create an ambience of luxuriant comfort. **Pros:** romantic; fancy breakfast; ocean views. **Cons:** not child-friendly; sits on a busy thoroughfare. ⑤ *Rooms from: $199* ⊠ *255 Ocean View Blvd.* ☎ *831/373–3388, 800/852–5588* ⊕ *www. martineinn.com* ⇨ *25 rooms* ⦶ *Breakfast.*

MONTEREY

2 miles southeast of Pacific Grove via Lighthouse Ave.; 2 miles north of Carmel-by-the-Sea via Hwy. 1.

Early in the 20th century Carmel Martin, the first mayor of the city of Monterey, saw a bright future for his town: "Monterey Bay is the one place where people can live without being disturbed by manufacturing and big factories. I am certain that the day is coming when this will be the most desirable place in the whole state of California." His Honor was not far off the mark.

GETTING HERE AND AROUND

From San Jose or San Francisco, take U.S. 101 south to Highway 156 West at Prunedale. Head west about 8 miles to Highway 1 and follow it about 15 miles south. From San Luis Obispo, take U.S. 101 north to Salinas and drive west on Highway 68 about 20 miles.

Many MST bus lines connect at the Monterey Transit Center, at Pearl Street and Munras Avenue. In summer (daily from 10 until at least 7), the free

MST Monterey Trolley travels from downtown Monterey along Cannery Row to the Aquarium and back.

TOURS

Monterey Movie Tours. Board a customized motorcoach and relax while a film-savvy local takes you on a scenic tour of the Monterey Peninsula enhanced by film clips shown on overhead monitors. More than 200 movies have been shot in the area, and scenes with Marilyn Monroe, Clint Eastwood, Tom Hanks, and other stars play when the tour passes through the exact film locations. The three-hour adventure travels a 32-mile loop through Monterey, Pacific Grove, and Carmel, with stops along 17-Mile Drive and at Pebble Beach Lodge. The tour departs from the Monterey Conference Center; free pickup and return is available at some hotels. ☎ *831/372–6278, 800/343–6437* ⊕ *www.montereymovietours. com* ✉ *$55* ⏱ *Daily at 1 pm.*

Old Monterey Walking Tour. Learn all about Monterey's storied past by joining a guided walking tour through the historic district. Tours begin at Custom House Plaza, across from Fisherman's Wharf. ✉ *$5, includes admission to Custom House and Pacific House* ⏱ *Fri.–Sun. at 10:30, noon, and 2.*

ESSENTIALS

Visitor Information Monterey County Convention & Visitors Bureau ☎ *877/666–8373* ⊕ *www.seemonterey.com.*

JOHN STEINBECK'S CANNERY ROW

"Cannery Row in Monterey in California is a poem, a stink, a grating noise, a quality of light, a tone, a habit, a nostalgia, a dream. Cannery Row is the gathered and scattered, tin and iron and rust and splintered wood, chipped pavement and weedy lots and junk heaps, sardine canneries of corrugated iron, honky tonks, restaurants and whore houses, and little crowded groceries, and laboratories and flophouses."
—John Steinbeck, *Cannery Row*

EXPLORING

TOP ATTRACTIONS

Cannery Row. When John Steinbeck published the novel *Cannery Row* in 1945, he immortalized a place of rough-edged working people. The waterfront street, edging a mile of gorgeous coastline, once was crowded with sardine canneries processing, at their peak, nearly 200,000 tons of the smelly silver fish a year. During the mid-1940s, however, the sardines disappeared from the bay, causing the canneries to close. Through the years the old tin-roof canneries have been converted into restaurants, art galleries, and malls with shops selling T-shirts, fudge, and plastic sea otters. Recent tourist development along the row has been more tasteful, however, and includes several stylish inns and hotels, wine tasting rooms, and upscale specialty shops. ⊠ *Cannery Row, between Reeside and David Aves.* ⊕ *www.canneryrow.com.*

Colton Hall. A convention of delegates met here in 1849 to draft the first state constitution. The stone building, which has served as a school, a

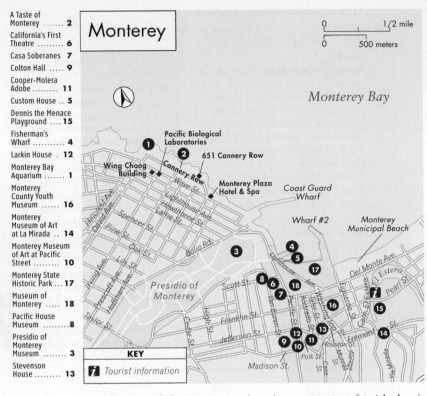

courthouse, and the county seat, is a city-run museum furnished as it was during the constitutional convention. The extensive grounds outside the hall surround the Old Monterey Jail. ⊠ *570 Pacific St., between Madison and Jefferson Sts.* ☎ *831/646–5640* ⊕ *www.monterey.org/museums* ☞ *Free* ⊙ *Daily 10–4; Tues. and Sun. noon–3 in winter.*

Cooper-Molera Adobe. The restored 2-acre complex includes a house dating from the 1820s, a gift shop, and a large garden enclosed by a high adobe wall. The mostly Victorian-era antiques and memorabilia that fill the house provide a glimpse into the life of a prosperous sea merchant's family. If the house is closed, you can still stop by the Cooper Store and pick up walking-tour maps and stroll the grounds. ⊠ *Monterey State Historic Park, Polk and Munras Sts.* ☎ *831/649–7111* ⊕ *www.parks.ca.gov/mshp* ☞ *$5* ⊙ *Store, daily 10–4; gardens, daily 9–4; tours, Fri.–Sun 10:30 and 1:30.*

Custom House. Built by the Mexican government in 1827 and now California's oldest standing public building, the Custom House was the first stop for sea traders whose goods were subject to duties. In 1846, Commodore John Sloat raised the American flag over this adobe structure and claimed California for the United States. The lower floor displays cargo from a 19th-century trading ship. If the house is closed, you can visit the cactus gardens and stroll the plaza. ⊠ *Monterey State*

Historic Park, 1 Custom House Plaza, across from Fisherman's Wharf 📞 *831/649–7118* 🌐 *www.parks.ca.gov/mshp* 💲*$3 (also includes admission to Pacific House)* 🕐 *Fri.–Mon. 10–4.*

FAMILY **Fisherman's Wharf.** The mournful barking of sea lions provides a steady soundtrack all along Monterey's waterfront, but the best way to actually view the whiskered marine mammals is to walk along one of the two piers across from Custom House Plaza. Lined with souvenir shops, the wharf is undeniably touristy, but it's lively and entertaining. At Wharf No. 2, a working municipal pier, you can see the day's catch being unloaded from fishing boats on one side and fishermen casting their lines into the water on the other. The pier has a couple of low-key restaurants, from whose seats lucky customers may spot otters and harbor seals. ✉ *At end of Calle Principal* 🌐 *www.montereywharf.com.*

FAMILY
Fodor's Choice
★
Monterey Bay Aquarium. The minute you hand over your ticket at this extraordinary aquarium you're surrounded by sea creatures; right at the entrance, you can see dozens of them swimming in a three-story-tall, sunlit kelp forest tank. The beauty of the exhibits here is that they are all designed to give a sense of what it's like to be in the water with the animals—sardines swim around your head in a circular tank, and jellyfish drift in and out of view in dramatically lighted spaces that suggest the ocean depths. A petting pool gives you a hands-on experience with bat rays, and the million-gallon Open Seas tank shows the vast variety of creatures (from sharks to placid-looking turtles) that live in the eastern Pacific. At the Splash Zone, which has 45 interactive bilingual exhibits, kids (and kids at heart) can commune with sea dragons, potbellied seahorses, and other fascinating creatures. The only drawback to the experience is that it must be shared with the throngs of people that crowd the place daily; most think it's worth it. ■TIP➜ **To avoid the crowds, arrive as soon as the aquarium opens or visit after 2 pm.** Weekend evenings in summer, the aquarium stays open later and is usually less crowded during the extended hours. ■TIP➜ **Reserve a lunch table at the aquarium's restaurant, perched on the ocean's edge. Otters and other sea creatures often frolic just outside the floor-to-ceiling windows.** ✉ *886 Cannery Row, at David Ave.* 📞 *831/648–4800 info, 866/963–9645 for advance tickets* 🌐 *www.montereybayaquarium. org* 💲*$35* 🕐 *Daily 10–6. Summer/holidays 9:30–6; summer weekends 9:30–8; winter daily 10–5.*

Monterey State Historic Park. You can glimpse Monterey's early history in the well-preserved adobe buildings scattered along several city blocks. Far from being a hermetic period museum, the park facilities are an integral part of the day-to-day business life of the town—within some of the buildings are a store, a theater, and government offices. At some of the historic houses, the gardens (open daily 10 to 5 in summer, 10 to 4 the rest of the year) are worthy sights themselves. ■TIP➜ **At this writing, some buildings are closed and tours are on hiatus due to state park budget cuts. Private tours of some adobes are available by reservation. Cell phone tours are available 24/7—dial (831) 998–9498, followed by a stop number (401–410). Visit the park's website for up-to-date information.** ✉ *20 Custom House Plaza* 📞 *831/649–7118* 🌐 *www.parks. ca.gov/mshp* 💲 *Free* 🕐 *Call for hrs.*

Trained "seals" that perform in circuses are actually California sea lions—intelligent, social animals that live (and sleep) close together in groups.

Museum of Monterey. The former Monterey Maritime Museum still displays maritime artifacts but has expanded its focus to include art, photography, and costumes from Monterey's earliest days to the present. The jewel in the museum's crown remains the enormous Fresnel lens from the Point Sur Light Station. ⊠ *Stanton Center, 5 Custom House Plaza* ☎ *831/372-2608* ⊕ *www.museumofmonterey.org* ✉ *$5. Free first Wed. of month 1–5* ☉ *May–Aug. Tues.–Sat. 10–7, Sun. noon–5; Sept.– Apr. Wed.–Sat. 10–5, Sun. noon–5.*

WORTH NOTING

A Taste of Monterey. Without driving the back roads, you can taste the wines of more than 90 area vintners while taking in fantastic bay views. Purchase a few bottles and pick up a map and guide to the county's wineries and vineyards. ⊠ *700 Cannery Row, Suite KK* ☎ *831/646-5446, 888/646-5446* ⊕ *www.atasteofmonterey.com* ✉ *Wine tastings $8–$15* ☉ *Sun.–Wed. 11–6, Thurs.–Sat. 11–7.*

California's First Theatre. This adobe began its life in 1846 as a saloon and lodging house for sailors. Four years later stage curtains were fashioned from army blankets, and some U.S. officers staged plays to the light of whale oil lamps. As of this writing, the building is open only for private tours, but you can stroll in the garden. ⊠ *Monterey State Historic Park, Scott and Pacific Sts.* ☎ *831/649-7118* ⊕ *www.parks. ca.gov/mshp* ✉ *Free* ☉ *Call for hrs.*

Casa Soberanes. A classic low-ceiling adobe structure built in 1842, this was once a Custom House guard's residence. Exhibits at the house survey life in Monterey from the era of Mexican rule to the present. The building is open only for private tour requests, but you can visit the peaceful rear garden and its rose-covered arbor. ✉ *Monterey State Historic Park, 336 Pacific St., at Del Monte Ave.* ☎ *831/649–7118* ⊕ *www.parks. ca.gov/mshp* ☜ *Free.*

FAMILY **Dennis the Menace Playground.** This play area was designed by the late cartoonist Hank Ketcham. The equipment is on a grand scale and made for Dennis-like daredevils: there's a roller slide, a clanking suspension bridge, and a real Southern Pacific steam locomotive.

> **FORMER CAPITAL OF CALIFORNIA**
>
> In 1602 Spanish explorer Sebastián Vizcaíno stepped ashore on a remote California peninsula. He named it after the viceroy of New Spain—Count de Monte Rey. Soon the Spanish built a military outpost, and the site was the capital of California until the state came under American rule.

You can rent a rowboat or a paddleboat for cruising around U-shaped Lake El Estero, populated with an assortment of ducks, mud hens, and geese. ✉ *El Estero Park, Pearl St. and Camino El Estero* ☎ *831/646–3866* ⊕ *www.monterey.org/Departments/MontereyRecreation/Parks andBeaches/ElEsteroParkComplex.aspx* ◔ *Daily 10–dusk in summer* ◔ *Closed Tues., Sept.–May.*

Larkin House. A veranda encircles the second floor of this 1835 adobe, whose design bears witness to the Mexican and New England influences on the Monterey style. Many of the antiques inside were brought from New Hampshire by the building's namesake, Thomas O. Larkin, an early California statesman. The building is open only for special tour requests, but you can peek in the windows and stroll the gardens. ✉ *Monterey State Historic Park, 464 Calle Principal, between Jefferson and Pacific Sts.* ☎ *831/649–7118* ⊕ *www.parks.ca.gov/mshp.*

FAMILY **Monterey County Youth Museum (MY Museum).** Monterey Bay comes to life from a child's perspective in this fun-filled, interactive indoor exploration center. The seven exhibit galleries showcase the science and nature of the Big Sur coast, theater arts, Pebble Beach golf, and beaches. There's also a live performance theater, a creation station, a hospital emergency room, and an agriculture corner where kids follow artichokes, strawberries, and other fruits and veggies on their evolution from sprout to harvest to farmers' markets. ✉ *425 Washington St., between E. Franklin St. and Bonifacio Pl.* ☎ *831/649–6444* ⊕ *www.mymuseum.org* ☜ *$7* ◔ *Tues.–Sat. 10–5, Sun. noon–5.*

Monterey Museum of Art at La Mirada. Asian and European antiques fill this 19th-century adobe house. A newer 10,000-square-foot gallery space, designed by Charles Moore, houses Asian and California regional art. Outdoors are magnificent rose and rhododendron gardens. ✉ *720 Via Mirada, at Fremont St.* ☎ *831/372–3689* ⊕ *www.montereyart. org* ☜ *$10, also good for admission to museum's Pacific Street facility* ◔ *Wed.–Sat. 11–5, Sun. 1–4.*

Monterey Museum of Art at Pacific Street. Photographs by Ansel Adams and Edward Weston, as well as works by other artists who have spent time on the peninsula, are on display here, along with international folk art, from Kentucky hearth brooms to Tibetan prayer wheels. ✉ *559 Pacific*

7

St., across from Colton Hall ☎ *831/372-5477* ⊕ *www.montereyart. org* ➾ *$10, also good for admission to museum's La Mirada facility* ⊗ *Wed.-Sat. 11-5, Sun. 1-4.*

Pacific House Museum. Once a hotel and saloon, this visitor center and museum now commemorates early-California life with gold-rush relics and photographs of old Monterey. The upper floor displays Native American artifacts, including gorgeous baskets and pottery. ⊠ *Monterey State Historic Park, 10 Custom House Plaza* ☎ *831/649-7118* ⊕ *www.parks.ca.gov/mshp* ➾ *$3 (includes admission to Custom House)* ⊗ *Fri.-Sun. 10-4.*

Presidio of Monterey Museum. This spot has been significant for centuries. Its first incarnation was as a Native American village for the Rumsien tribe. The Spanish explorer Sebastián Vizcaíno landed here in 1602, and Father Junípero Serra arrived in 1770. Notable battles fought here include the 1818 skirmish in which the corsair Hipólito Bruchard conquered the Spanish garrison that stood on this site and claimed part of California for Argentina. The indoor museum tells the stories; plaques mark the outdoor sites. ⊠ *Presidio of Monterey, Corporal Ewing Rd., off Lighthouse Ave.* ☎ *831/646-3456* ⊕ *www.monterey.org/museums* ➾ *Free* ⊗ *Mon. 10-1, Thurs.-Sat. 10-4, Sun. 1-4.*

Stevenson House. This house was named in honor of author Robert Louis Stevenson, who boarded here briefly in a tiny upstairs room. Items from his family's estate furnish Stevenson's room; period-decorated chambers elsewhere in the house include a gallery of memorabilia and a children's nursery stocked with Victorian toys and games. The house is open only for special tour requests, but you can stroll around the gardens. ⊠ *Monterey State Historic Park, 530 Houston St., near Pearl St.* ☎ *831/649-7118* ⊕ *www.parks.ca.gov/mshp* ⊗ *Daily 9-5, gardens only.*

WHERE TO EAT

$$
SEAFOOD

✗ **Monterey Fish House.** Casual yet stylish and always packed, this seafood restaurant is removed from the hubbub of the wharf. If the dining room is full, you can wait at the bar and savor deliciously plump oysters on the half shell. The bartenders and waitstaff will gladly advise you on the perfect wine to go with your poached, blackened, or oak-grilled seafood. ⑤ *Average main: $21* ⊠ *2114 Del Monte Ave., at Dela Vina Ave.* ☎ *831/373-4647* ⚹ *Reservations essential* ⊗ *No lunch Sat.-Sun.*

$$$
AMERICAN
Fodor's Choice
★

✗ **Montrio Bistro.** This quirky, converted firehouse, with its rawhide walls and iron indoor trellises, has a wonderfully sophisticated menu. Chef Tony Baker uses organic produce and meats and sustainably sourced seafood to create imaginative dishes that reflect local agriculture, such as baby artichoke risotto fritters, and pesto-rubbed prime sirloin with marinated prawns, spinach, and a red wine–veal reduction sauce. The wine list also draws primarily on California—Monterey-area wineries are well represented—and signature cocktails are infused with local fruits, herbs, and veggies. ⑤ *Average main: $24* ⊠ *414 Calle Principal, at W. Franklin St.* ☎ *831/648-8880* ⊕ *www.montrio.com* ⚹ *Reservations essential* ⊗ *No lunch.*

CLOSE UP

The Underwater Kingdom

Although Monterey's coastal landscapes are stunning, their beauty is more than equaled by the wonders that lie offshore. The huge Monterey Bay National Marine Sanctuary—which stretches 276 miles, from north of San Francisco almost all the way down to Santa Barbara—teems with abundant life, and has topography as diverse as that aboveground.

The preserve's 5,322 square miles include vast submarine canyons, which reach down 10,663 feet at their deepest point. They also encompass dense forests of giant kelp—a kind of seaweed that can grow more than a hundred feet from its roots on the ocean floor. These kelp forests are especially robust off Monterey.

The sanctuary was established in 1992 to protect the habitat of the many species that thrive in the bay. Some animals can be seen quite easily from land. In summer and winter you might glimpse the offshore spray of gray whales as

they migrate between their summer feeding grounds in Alaska and their breeding grounds in Baja. Clouds of marine birds—including white-faced ibis, three types of albatross, and more than 15 types of gull—skim the waves, or roost in the rock islands along 17-Mile Drive. Sea otters dart and gambol in the calmer waters of the bay; and of course, you can watch the sea lions—and hear their round-the-clock barking—on the wharves in Santa Cruz and Monterey.

The sanctuary supports many other creatures, however, that remain unseen by most on-land visitors. Some of these are enormous, such as the giant blue whales that arrive to feed on plankton in summer; others, like the more than 22 species of red algae in these waters, are microscopic. So whether you choose to visit the Monterey Bay Aquarium, take a whale-watch trip, or look out to sea with your binoculars, remember you're seeing just a small part of a vibrant underwater kingdom.

7

$$$
SEAFOOD
✕ **Old Fisherman's Grotto.** Watch otters and seals frolic in the water while savoring seafood, steak, and pasta at this family-owned and operated eatery, established in 1950 in the midsection of Fisherman's Wharf. The founder's son and current owner, Chris Shake, has updated the decor and menu while retaining the classic 1950s nautical style. Famed for its creamy clam chowder, the restaurant also serves a huge range of dishes, from seafood paella and sand dabs to filet mignon and teriyaki chicken. ■**TIP➜ Reserve a windowside table for the best views.** ⑤ *Average main: $25* ✉ *39 Fisherman's Wharf* ☎ *831/375–4604* ⊕ *www. oldfishersmansgrotto.com.*

$
AMERICAN
✕ **Old Monterey Café.** Breakfast here gets constant local raves. The café's fame rests on familiar favorites: a dozen kinds of omelets, and pancakes from blueberry to cinnamon-raisin-pecan. For lunch are good soups, salads, and sandwiches. This is a fine place to relax with an afternoon cappuccino. ⑤ *Average main: $12* ✉ *489 Alvarado St., at Munras Ave.* ☎ *831/646–1021* ⚲ *Reservations not accepted* ☽ *No dinner.*

$$$$
MODERN
AMERICAN
Fodor's Choice
★
✕ **Restaurant 1833.** Housed in the historic Stokes Adobe, built in 1833, this überpopular restaurant and bar showcases the region's colorful history and local bounty in one of the most unusual settings anywhere. The two-story structure, a national heritage site, was once the home of the mayor of Monterey. Today it includes seven distinct dining rooms; each honors an era and characters from the adobe's storied past. Sit in a leather booth on the Founder's Balcony for a bird's-eye view of the rocking bar scene below, or outdoors by the fire pits in the courtyard, near giant oak, redwood, palm, and magnolia trees. The casual menu changes daily and centers around seasonal local ingredients. Regular stars include bacon-cheddar biscuits with maple-chili butter and soy-glazed quail, pan-roasted mahi mahi, and bacon-wrapped pork loin. The cocktail menu pays tribute to the adobe's 1840s-era apothecary business with four categories: Pain Killers, Stress Relievers, Elixirs, and Aphrodisiacs, which, along with the extensive wine list, fuel a lively atmosphere indoors and out, especially on weekend nights. $ *Average main: $32* ✉ *500 Hartnell St.* ☎ *831/643–1833* ⊕ *www.restaurant1833.com* ☾ *No lunch.*

$$
AMERICAN
✕ **Tarpy's Roadhouse.** Fun, dressed-up American favorites—a little something for everyone—are served in this renovated early-1900s stone farmhouse several miles east of town. The kitchen cranks out everything from Cajun-spiced prawns to meat loaf with marsala-mushroom gravy to grilled ribs and steaks. Eat indoors by a fireplace or outdoors in the courtyard. $ *Average main: $22* ✉ *2999 Monterey–Salinas Hwy., Hwy. 68* ☎ *831/647–1444* ⊕ *www.tarpys.com.*

WHERE TO STAY

For expanded hotel reviews, visit Fodors.com.

$$$
RESORT
🛏 **Best Western Beach Resort Monterey.** With a great waterfront location about 2 miles north of Monterey—with views of the bay and the city skyline—and a surprising array of amenities, this hotel is one of the area's best values. **Pros:** on the beach; great value; family-friendly. **Cons:** several miles from major attractions; big-box mall neighborhood. $ *Rooms from: $189* ✉ *2600 Sand Dunes Dr.* ☎ *831/394–3321, 800/242–8627* ⊕ *www.montereybeachresort.com* ⇆ *196 rooms.*

$$
HOTEL
🛏 **Hotel Abrego.** In central Monterey just a half-block from the transit center and a 15-minute walk to Fisherman's Wharf, this full-service hotel offers six different room types in four Mission-style buildings. **Pros:** central location; near public transit; range of room options. **Cons:** not on waterfront; pool and exercise room on the small side; some rooms near busy street. $ *Rooms from: $139* ✉ *755 Abrego St., at Fremont St.* ☎ *831/372–7551, 800/982–1986 reservations* 🖷 *831/324–4625* ⊕ *www.hotelabrego.com* ⇆ *93 rooms* ❍| *No meals.*

$$$
HOTEL
FAMILY
🛏 **InterContinental The Clement Monterey.** Spectacular bay views, assiduous service, a slew of upscale amenities, and a superb waterfront location next to the aquarium propelled this full-service luxury hotel to immediate stardom. **Pros:** a block from the aquarium; fantastic views from some rooms; great for families. **Cons:** a tad formal; not budget-friendly. $ *Rooms from: $195* ✉ *750 Cannery Row* ☎ *831/375–4500, 866/781–2406 toll free* ⊕ *www.ictheclementmonterey.com* ⇆ *192 rooms, 16 suites.*

$$ **Monterey Bay Lodge.** Location
HOTEL (on the edge of Monterey's El
Estero Park) and superior ameni-
ties give this cheerful facility an
edge over other motels in town.
Pros: within walking distance of
beach and playground; quiet at
night; good family choice. Cons:
near busy boulevard. ⑤ *Rooms
from: $130* ✉ *55 Camino Aguajito*
☎ *831/372–8057, 800/558–1900*
⊕ *www.montereybaylodge.com*
⚲ *43 rooms, 3 suites.*

> ### THE FIRST ARTICHOKE QUEEN
>
> Castroville, a tiny town off High-
> way 1 between Monterey and
> Watsonville, produces about 95%
> of U.S. artichokes. Back in 1948,
> the town chose its first queen to
> preside during its Artichoke Fes-
> tival—a beautiful young woman
> named Norma Jean Mortenson,
> who later changed her name to
> Marilyn Monroe.

$$$$ **Monterey Plaza Hotel & Spa.** This
HOTEL hotel commands a waterfront loca-
tion on Cannery Row, where you can see frolicking sea otters from
the wide outdoor patio and many room balconies. Pros: on the ocean;
lots of amenities; attentive service. Cons: touristy area; heavy traffic.
⑤ *Rooms from: $269* ✉ *400 Cannery Row* ☎ *831/646–1700, 800/334–
3999* ⊕ *www.montereyplazahotel.com* ⚲ *280 rooms, 10 suites.*

$$$$ **Old Monterey Inn.** This three-story manor house was the home of Mon-
B&B/INN terey's first mayor, and today it remains a private enclave within walk-
Fodor'sChoice ing distance of downtown, set off by lush gardens shaded by huge old
★ trees and bordered by a creek. Pros: gorgeous gardens; refined luxury;
serene. Cons: must drive to attractions and sights; fills quickly. ⑤ *Rooms
from: $289* ✉ *500 Martin St.* ☎ *831/375–8284, 800/350–2344* ⊕ *www.
oldmontereyinn.com* ⚲ *6 rooms, 3 suites, 1 cottage* ⑪ *Breakfast.*

$$$ **Spindrift Inn.** This boutique hotel on Cannery Row has beach access
HOTEL and a rooftop garden that overlooks the water. Pros: close to aquarium;
steps from the beach; friendly staff. Cons: throngs of visitors outside;
can be noisy; not good for families. ⑤ *Rooms from: $209* ✉ *652 Can-
nery Row* ☎ *831/646–8900, 800/841–1879* ⊕ *www.spindriftinn.com*
⚲ *45 rooms* ⑪ *Breakfast.*

NIGHTLIFE

Cibo. An Italian restaurant with a big bar area, Cibo brings live jazz,
Latin, soul, and more to downtown Tuesday through Sunday. ✉ *301
Alvarado St., at Del Monte Ave.* ☎ *831/649–8151* ⊕ *www.cibo.com.*

Bruce Ariss Wharf Theater (*The New Wharf Theatre*). American musicals
past and present are the focus here, with dramas and comedies also in
the mix. ✉ *One Fisherman's Wharf* ☎ *831/649–2332.*

Dixieland Monterey. Traditional jazz bands play at waterfront venues
during this festival, held on the first full weekend of March. ☎ *831/675–
0298, 888/349–6879* ⊕ *www.dixieland-monterey.com.*

Monterey Jazz Festival. The world's oldest jazz festival attracts top-name
performers to the Monterey Fairgrounds on the third full weekend
of September. ☎ *888/248–6499 ticket office, 831/373–3366* ⊕ *www.
montereyjazzfestival.org.*

SPORTS AND THE OUTDOORS

Throughout most of the year, the Monterey Bay area is a haven for those who love tennis, golf, surfing, fishing, biking, hiking, scuba diving, and kayaking. In the rainy winter months, when the waves grow larger, adventurous surfers flock to the water.

BICYCLING

Adventures by the Sea, Inc. You can rent surreys plus tandem and standard bicycles from Adventures by the Sea, which also offers bike tours. ✉ *299 Cannery Row* ☎ *831/372–1807* ⊕ *www.adventuresbythesea.com* ✉ *210 Alvarado Mall* ✉ *Stillwater Cove, 17-Mile Drive, Pebble Beach* ✉ *Beach at Lovers Point, Pacific Grove.*

Bay Bikes. For bicycle and surrey rentals and tours, visit Bay Bikes' main location or its second shop at 486 Washington St. ✉ *585 Cannery Row* ☎ *831/655–2453* ⊕ *www.baybikes.com.*

FISHING

Randy's Fishing and Whale Watching Trips. Family-run Randy's has been in business since 1949. ✉ *66 Fisherman's Wharf* ☎ *831/372–7440, 800/251–7440* ⊕ *www.randysfishingtrips.com.*

SCUBA DIVING

Monterey Bay waters never warm to the temperatures of their Southern California counterparts (the warmest they get is the low 60s), but that's one reason why the marine life here is among the world's most diverse.

Aquarius Dive Shop. Staffers at Aquarius give diving lessons and tours, and rent equipment. The diving-conditions information line is updated daily. ✉ *2040 Del Monte Ave.* ☎ *831/375–1933, 831/657–1020 diving conditions* ⊕ *www.aquariusdivers.com.*

Monterey Bay National Marine Sanctuary. The sanctuary, home to mammals, seabirds, fishes, invertebrates, and plants, encompasses a 276-mile shoreline and 5,322 square miles of ocean. Ringed by beaches and campgrounds, it's a place for kayaking, whale-watching, scuba diving, and other water sports. ☎ *831/647–4201* ⊕ *www.montereybay.noaa.gov.*

WALKING

Monterey Bay Coastal Trail. From Custom House Plaza, you can walk along the coast in either direction on this 29-mile-long trail for spectacular views of the sea. The trail runs from north of Monterey to Pacific Grove, with sections continuing around Pebble Beach. ☎ *831/372–3196* ⊕ *www.mtycounty.com/pgs-parks/bike-path.html.*

WHALE-WATCHING

Thousands of gray whales pass close by the Monterey Coast on their annual migration between the Bering Sea and Baja California. The gigantic creatures are sometimes visible through binoculars from shore, but a whale-watching cruise is the best way to get a close look at these magnificent mammals. The migration south takes place from December through March; January is prime viewing time. The whales migrate north from March through June. In addition, some 2,000 blue whales and 600 humpbacks pass the coast and are easily spotted in late summer and early fall.

Monterey Bay Whale Watch. The marine biologists here lead three- to five-hour whale-watching tours. ⊠ *84 Fisherman's Wharf* ☎ *831/375–4658* ⊕ *www.montereybaywhalewatch.com.*

Princess Monterey Whale Watching. Tours are offered daily on a 150-passenger high-speed cruiser and a large 75-foot boat. ⊠ *96 Fisherman's Wharf #1* ☎ *831/372–2203, 831/205–2370 reservations, 888/223–9153 international reservations* ⊕ *www.montereywhalewatching.com.*

AROUND MONTEREY BAY

As Highway 1 follows the curve of the bay between Monterey and Santa Cruz, it passes through a rich agricultural zone. Opening right onto the bay, where the Salinas and Pajaro rivers drain into the Pacific, a broad valley brings together fertile soil, an ideal climate, and a good water supply to create optimum growing conditions for crops such as strawberries, artichokes, Brussels sprouts, and broccoli. Several beautiful beaches line this part of the coast. Salinas and Moss Landing are in Monterey County; the other cities and towns covered here are in Santa Cruz County.

GETTING HERE AND AROUND
All the towns in this area are on or just off Highway 1. MST buses serve Monterey County destinations, connecting in Watsonville with Santa Cruz METRO buses, which operate throughout Santa Cruz County.

7

SALINAS

17 miles east of Monterey on Hwy. 68.

Salinas, a hard-working city surrounded by vineyards and fruit and vegetable fields, honors the memory and literary legacy of John Steinbeck, its most famous native, with the National Steinbeck Center. The facility spurred the revival of Old Town Salinas, where renovated turn-of-the-20th-century stone buildings house shops and restaurants. Stop at the California Welcome Center, newly opened in 2012, for visitor information on the Salinas Valley and Monterey Bay region.

ESSENTIALS
Transportation Information Salinas Amtrak Station ⊠ *11 Station Place, Salinas* ☎ *800/872–7245.*

Visitor Information California Welcome Center ⊠ *1213 N. Davis Rd., west of Hwy. 101 exit #330, Salinas* ☎ *831/757–8687* ⊕ *www.visitcwc.com/Salinas* ⊙ *Open daily 9–5.*

EXPLORING
National Steinbeck Center. The center's exhibits document the life of Pulitzer- and Nobel-prize winner John Steinbeck and the history of the nearby communities that inspired novels such as *East of Eden*. Highlights include reproductions of the green pickup-camper from *Travels with Charley* and of the bunkroom from *Of Mice and Men*. **Steinbeck House,** the author's Victorian birthplace, at 132 Central Avenue, is two blocks from the center in a so-so neighborhood. Now a decent

lunch spot, it displays memorabilia. ⊠ *1 Main St., at Central Ave., Salinas* ☎ *831/775–4721* ⊕ *www.steinbeck.org* 🖾 *$15* ⊗ *Daily 10–5.*

FAMILY **Pinnacles National Park.** California's newest national park has many unusual attractions, including talus caves, 30 miles of hiking trails, and hundreds of rock climbing routes. A mosaic of diverse habitats supports an amazing number of wildlife species: 149 birds, 49 mammals, 69 butterflies, and nearly 400 bees. The park is also home to 32 of the world's remaining 405 condors in captivity and release areas. Fourteen of Calfornia's 34 bat species live in caves in the park. President Theodore Roosevelt declared this remarkable 26,000-acre geologic and wildlife preserve a national monument in 1908. President Barack Obama officially designated it a national park in January 2013. It's believed to have been created when two of the Earth's major tectonic plates heaved and lurched at their meeting points, spawning extensive volcanic activity in what's now called the Gabilan Mountains, southeast of Salinas and Monterey. The volcano eventually dried up and began to erode, leaving a rugged landscape with rocky spires and crags, or pinnacles, at the plates' intersection. Boulders fell into canyons and valleys, creating talus caves and a paradise for modern-day rock climbers. Spring is the most popular time to visit, when colorful wildflowers blanket the meadows; summer heat can be brutal. The park has two entrances—east and west—but they are not connected (there's no way to build a road over the spires). The Pinnacles Visitor Center, Bear Gulch Nature Center, Park Headquarters, the Pinnacles Campground, and the Bear Gulch Cave and Reservoir are on the east side. The Chaparral Ranger Station is on the west side, where you can feast on fantastic views of the Pinnacles High Peaks from the parking area. Dogs are not allowed on hiking trails. The east entrance is 32 miles southeast of Hollister via Highway 25. The west entrance is about 12 miles east of Soledad via Highway 146. ⊠ *5000 Hwy. 146, Paicines* ☎ *831/389–4485, 831/389–4427 Westside* ⊕ *www.nps.gov/pinn* 🖾 *$5 per vehicle day use, $3 per visitor if biking or walking* ⊗ *West entrance, daily 7:30 am–8 pm; West Pinnacles Visitor Center, daily 9–5. East entrance, daily 24 hrs; Pinnacles Visitor Center, daily 9:30–5.*

FAMILY **Monterey Zoo.** More than a hundred exotic animals—many of them retired from film, television, and live-production work, or rescued from less-than-ideal environments—find sanctuary at the Monterey Zoo (formerly called Wild Things) at Vision Quest Ranch. Visit tigers, lions, bears, elephants, and primates on guided hourlong walking tours with professional trainers and handlers. For an in-depth experience, stay in a safari bungalow at Vision Quest Safari B&B where, in the morning, breakfast from a basket is delivered by a resident elephant. ⊠ *400 River Rd., off Hwy. 68, Salinas* ☎ *831/455–1901, 800/228–7382* ⊕ *www. montereyzoo.com* 🖾 *Tours $10, optional post-tour elephant feeding $5* ⊗ *Tours daily at 1 pm; a second tour at 3 pm Jun.–Aug.*

MOSS LANDING

17 miles north of Monterey on Hwy. 1; 12 miles north of Salinas on Highway 183.

Moss Landing is not much more than a couple of blocks of cafés and restaurants, art galleries, and studios, plus a busy fishing port, but therein lies its charm. It's a fine place to overnight or stop for a meal and get a dose of nature.

GETTING HERE AND AROUND

From Highway 1 north or south, exit at Moss Landing Road on the ocean side. MST buses serve Moss Landing via Watsonville.

ESSENTIALS

Tour Contacts Elkhorn Slough Safari Nature Boat Tours. This outfit's naturalists lead two-hour tours of Elkhorn Sough aboard a 27-foot pontoon boat. Reservations are required. ⊠ *Moss Landing Harbor* ☎ *831/633–5555* ⊕ *www.elkhornslough.com* ⊡ *$35.*

Visitor Information Moss Landing Chamber of Commerce ☎ *831/633–4501* ⊕ *www.mosslandingchamber.com.*

EXPLORING

Elkhorn Slough National Estuarine Research Reserve. In the Elkhorn Slough National Estuarine Research Reserve, 1,400 acres of tidal flats and salt marshes form a complex environment that supports some 300 species of birds. A walk along the meandering waterways and wetlands can reveal hawks, white-tailed kites, owls, herons, and egrets. Also living or visiting here are sea otters, sharks, rays, and many other animals. On weekends, guided walks from the visitor center to the heron rookery begin at 10 and 1. ⊠ *1700 Elkhorn Rd., Watsonville* ☎ *831/728–2822* ⊕ *www.elkhornslough.org* ⊡ *$4 day use fee* ☉ *Wed.–Sun. 9–5.*

WHERE TO EAT AND STAY

For expanded hotel reviews, visit Fodors.com.

$$
SEAFOOD
✕ **Phil's Fish Market & Eatery.** Exquisitely fresh, simply prepared seafood (try the cioppino) is on the menu at this warehouse-like restaurant on the harbor; all kinds of glistening fish are for sale at the market in the front. ■**TIP→** Phil's Snack Shack, a tiny sandwich-and-smoothie joint, serves quicker meals at the north end of town. ⑤ *Average main: $17* ⊠ *7600 Sandholdt Rd.* ☎ *831/633–2152* ⊕ *www.philsfishmarket.com.*

$$
B&B/INN
⊡ **Captain's Inn.** Commune with nature and pamper yourself with upscale creature comforts at this green-certified getaway in the heart of town. **Pros:** walk to restaurants and shops; tranquil natural setting; homey atmosphere. **Cons:** rooms in historic building don't have water views; far from urban amenities; not appropriate for young children. ⑤ *Rooms from: $165* ⊠ *8122 Moss Landing Rd.* ☎ *831/633–5550* ⊕ *www.captainsinn.com* ↩ *10 rooms* ⦿l *Breakfast.*

SPORTS AND THE OUTDOORS

Monterey Bay Kayaks. Rent a kayak to paddle out into Elkhorn Slough for up-close wildlife encounters. ⊠ *2390 Hwy. 1, at North Harbor* ☎ *831/373–5357, 800/649–5357 toll free* ⊕ *www.montereybay kayaks.com.*

WATSONVILLE

7 miles north of Moss Landing on Hwy. 1.

If ever a city was built on berries, Watsonville is it. Produce has long driven the economy here, and this is where the Santa Cruz County Fair takes place each September.

GETTING HERE AND AROUND

From Santa Cruz or Monterey, follow Highway 1 to Watsonville. From U.S. 101, take Highway 152 West from Gilroy (a curving but scenic road over the mountains) or Highway 129 West from just north of San Juan Bautista. MST and Santa Cruz METRO buses connect at the Watsonville Transit Center, at Rodriguez Street and West Lake Avenue.

EXPLORING

FAMILY **Agricultural History Project.** One feature of the Santa Cruz County Fairgrounds is this project, which preserves the history of farming in the Pajaro Valley. In the Codiga Center and Museum, you can examine antique tractors and milking machines, peruse an exhibit on the era when Watsonville was the "frozen food capital of the West," and watch experts restore farm implements and vehicles. ⊠ *2601 E. Lake Ave., Hwy. 152, at Carlton Rd.* ☎ *831/724–5898* ⊕ *www.aghistoryproject. org* ⊠ *$2 suggested donation* ◷ *Thurs.–Sun. noon–4.*

FAMILY **Watsonville Fly-in & Air Show.** Every Labor Day weekend, aerial performers execute elaborate aerobatics at this air show. More than 300 classic, experimental, and military aircraft are on display; concerts and other events fill three days. ⊠ *Watsonville Municipal Airport, 100 Aviation Way* ☎ *831/763–5600* ⊕ *www.watsonvilleairshow.org* ⊠ *$15 plus $5 parking.*

APTOS

7 miles north of Watsonville on Hwy. 1.

Backed by a redwood forest and facing the sea, downtown Aptos—known as Aptos Village—is a place of wooden walkways and false-fronted shops. Antiques dealers cluster along Trout Gulch Road, off Soquel Drive east of Highway 1.

GETTING HERE AND AROUND

Use Highway 1 to reach Aptos from Santa Cruz or Monterey. Exit at State Park Drive to reach the main shopping hub and Aptos Village. You can also exit at Freedom Boulevard or Rio del Mar. Soquel Drive is the main artery through town.

ESSENTIALS

Visitor Information Aptos Chamber of Commerce ⊠ *7605-A Old Dominion Ct.* ☎ *831/688–1467* ⊕ *www.aptoschamber.com.*

BEACHES

Seacliff State Beach. Sandstone bluffs tower above popular Seacliff State Beach. You can fish off the pier, which leads out to a sunken World War I tanker ship built of concrete. Leashed dogs are allowed on the beach. **Amenities:** food and drink; lifeguards; parking (fee); showers; toilets. **Best for:** sunset; swimming; walking. ⊠ *201 State Park Dr., off Hwy. 1* ☎ *831/685–6442* ⊕ *www.parks.ca.gov* ⊠ *$10 per vehicle.*

SAN JUAN BAUTISTA

About as close to early-19th-century California as you can get, San Juan Bautista (15 miles east of Watsonville on Highway 156) has been protected from development since 1933, when much of it became a state park. Small antiques shops and restaurants occupy the Old West and art deco buildings that line 3rd Street.

The wide green plaza of San Juan Bautista State Historic Park is ringed by 18th- and 19th-century buildings, many of them open to the public.

The cemetery of the long, low, colonnaded mission church contains the unmarked graves of more than 4,300 Native American converts. Nearby is an adobe home furnished with Spanish-colonial antiques, a hotel frozen in the 1860s, a blacksmith shop, a stable, a pioneer cabin, and a jailhouse.

The first Saturday of each month, costumed volunteers engage in quilting bees, tortilla making, and other frontier activities. ⊕ www.san-juan-bautista.ca.us.

WHERE TO EAT AND STAY

For expanded hotel reviews, visit Fodors.com.

$$$
MEDITERRANEAN

✗ **Bittersweet Bistro.** A large old tavern with cathedral ceilings houses this popular bistro, where chef-owner Thomas Vinolus draws culinary inspiration from the Mediterranean. The menu changes seasonally, but regular highlights include paella, seafood puttanesca, and maple-soy marinated skirt steak. The decadent chocolate desserts are not to be missed. Breakfast and lunch are available in the casual Bittersweet Café. Pets are welcome on the outdoor patio. ⑤ *Average main: $25* ⊠ *787 Rio Del Mar Blvd., off Hwy. 1* ☎ *831/662–9799* ⊕ *www.bittersweetbistro.com.*

$$$
HOTEL
FAMILY

☷ **Best Western Seacliff Inn.** Families and business travelers like this 6-acre property near Seacliff State Beach that's more resort than hotel. **Pros:** walking distance to the beach; family-friendly; hot breakfast buffet. **Cons:** close to freeway; occasional nighttime bar noise. ⑤ *Rooms from: $180* ⊠ *7500 Old Dominion Ct.* ☎ *831/688–7300, 800/367–2003* ⊕ *www.seacliffinn.com* ⊷ *139 rooms, 10 suites* ⑩ *Breakfast.*

$$$
B&B/INN

☷ **Flora Vista.** Multicolor fields of flowers, strawberries, and veggies unfold in every direction at this luxury neo-Georgian inn set on two serene acres just south of Aptos, where innkeepers Deanna and Ed Boos transformed an 1867 home, a replica of Abe Lincoln's Springfield farmhouse, adding modern conveniences like Wi-Fi and spa tubs while retaining the house's original redwood floors and country charm. **Pros:** superprivate; near Sand Dollar Beach; flowers everywhere. **Cons:** no restaurants or nightlife within walking distance; not a good place for kids. ⑤ *Rooms from: $195* ⊠ *1258 San Andreas Rd., La Selva Beach* ☎ *831/724–8663, 877/753–5672* ⊕ *www.floravistainn.com* ⊷ *5 rooms* ⑩ *Breakfast.*

$$$$
RESORT
FAMILY

☷ **Seascape Beach Resort.** On a bluff overlooking Monterey Bay, Seascape is a full-fledged resort that makes it easy to unwind. **Pros:** time-share-style apartments; access to miles of beachfront; superb views. **Cons:** far from city life; most bathrooms are small. ⑤ *Rooms from: $300* ⊠ *1 Seascape Resort Dr.* ☎ *831/688–6800, 800/929–7727* ⊕ *www.seascaperesort.com* ⊷ *285 suites.*

7

CAPITOLA AND SOQUEL

4 miles northwest of Aptos on Hwy. 1.

On the National Register of Historic places as California's first sea-side resort town, the village of Capitola has been in a holiday mood since the late 1800s. Casual eateries, surf shops, and ice-cream parlors pack its walkable downtown. Inland, across Highway 1, antiques shops line Soquel Drive in the town of Soquel. Wineries dot the Santa Cruz Mountains beyond.

GETTING HERE AND AROUND

From Santa Cruz or Monterey, follow Highway 1 to the Capitola/Soquel (Bay Avenue) exit about 7 miles south of Santa Cruz and head west to reach Capitola and east to access Soquel Village. On summer weekends, park for free in the lot behind the Crossroads Center, a block west of the freeway, and hop aboard the free Capitola Shuttle to the village.

ESSENTIALS

Visitor Information Capitola-Soquel Chamber of Commerce
✉ *716-G Capitola Ave.* ☎ *831/475–6522* ⊕ *www.capitolachamber.com.*

BEACHES

New Brighton State Beach. New Brighton State Beach, once the site of a Chinese fishing village, is now a popular surfing and camping spot. Its Pacific Migrations Visitor Center traces the history of the Chinese and other peoples who settled around Monterey Bay, as well as the migratory patterns of the area's wildlife, such as monarch butterflies and gray whales. Leashed dogs are allowed in the park. ■**TIP→ New Brighton Beach connects with Seacliff Beach, and at low tide you can walk or run along this scenic stretch of sand for nearly 16 miles south (you might have to wade through a few creeks). The 1½-mile stroll from New Brighton to Seacliff's cement ship is a local favorite.** **Amenities:** parking (fee); showers; toilets. **Best for:** sunset; swimming; walking. ✉ *1500 State Park Dr., off Hwy. 1* ☎ *831/464–6330* ⊕ *www.parks. ca.gov* 🚗 *$10 per vehicle.*

WHERE TO EAT

$ ✗**Carpo's.** Locals love this casual counter. Seafood predominates, but
SEAFOOD Carpo's also serves burgers, salads, and steaks. Favorites include the
FAMILY baskets of fresh battered snapper, calamari and prawns, seafood kebabs, and homemade olallieberry pie. Many items cost less than $10. Go early to beat the crowds. ⑤ *Average main: $10* ✉ *2400 Porter St., at Hwy. 1* ☎ *831/476–6260* ⊕ *www.carposrestaurant.com/default1.html.*

$ ✗**Gayle's Bakery & Rosticceria.** Whether you're in the mood for an
CAFÉ orange-olallieberry muffin, a wild rice and chicken salad, or tri-tip
FAMILY on garlic toast, this bakery-cum-deli's varied menu is likely to satisfy. Munch your chocolate macaroon on the shady patio or dig into the daily blue-plate dinner amid the whirl of activity inside. ⑤ *Average main: $12* ✉ *504 Bay Ave., at Capitola Ave.* ☎ *831/462–1200* ⊕ *www. gaylesbakery.com.*

$$ ✗**Michael's on Main.** Creative variations on classic comfort food draw
AMERICAN lively crowds to this upscale-but-casual creek-side eatery. Chef Michael

Clark's menu changes seasonally, but you can always count on finding such home-style dishes as pork osso bucco in red-wine tomato-citrus sauce, as well as unusual entrées like pistachio-crusted salmon with mint vinaigrette. For a quiet conversation spot, ask for a table on the romantic patio overlooking the creek. The busy bar area hosts live music Tuesday through Saturday. $ *Average main: $22* ✉ *2591 Main St., at Porter St.* ☎ *831/479–9777* ⊕ *www.michaelsonmain.net* ⊗ *Closed Mon.*

$$$$
EUROPEAN
✕ **Shadowbrook.** To get to this romantic spot overlooking Soquel Creek, you can take a cable car or walk the stairs down a steep, fern-lined bank beside a running waterfall. Dining room options include the rooftop Redwood Room, the wood-paneled Wine Cellar, and the airy, glass-enclosed Garden Room. Prime rib and grilled seafood are the stars of the simple menu. A cheaper menu of light entrées is available in the lounge. $ *Average main: $32* ✉ *1750 Wharf Rd., at Lincoln Ave.* ☎ *831/475–1511, 888/475–1222 toll free* ⊕ *www.shadowbrook-capitola.com* ⊗ *No lunch.*

CALIFORNIA'S OLDEST RESORT TOWN

As far as anyone knows for certain, Capitola is the oldest seaside resort town on the Pacific Coast. In 1856 a pioneer acquired Soquel Landing, the picturesque lagoon and beach where Soquel Creek empties into the bay, and built a wharf. Another man opened a campground along the shore, and his daughter named it Capitola after a heroine in a novel series. After the train came to town in the 1870s, thousands of vacationers began arriving to bask in the sun on the glorious beach.

WHERE TO STAY

For expanded hotel reviews, visit Fodors.com.

$$$$
B&B/INN
🏨 **Inn at Depot Hill.** This inventively designed B&B in a former rail depot sees itself as a link to the era of luxury train travel. **Pros:** short walk to beach and village; historic charm; excellent service. **Cons:** fills quickly; hot tub conversation on the patio may irk second-floor guests. $ *Rooms from: $259* ✉ *250 Monterey Ave.* ☎ *831/462–3376, 800/572–2632* ⊕ *www.innatdepothill.com* 🛏 *12 rooms* ⦿ *Breakfast.*

SANTA CRUZ

5 miles west of Capitola on Hwy. 1; 48 miles north of Monterey on Hwy. 1.

The big city on this stretch of the California coast, Santa Cruz (pop. 57,500) is less manicured than Carmel or Monterey. Long known for its surfing and its amusement-filled beach boardwalk, the town is a mix of grand Victorian-era homes and rinky-dink motels. The opening of the University of California campus in the 1960s swung the town sharply to the left politically, and the counterculture more or less lives on here. At the same time, the revitalized downtown and an insane real-estate market reflect the city's proximity to Silicon Valley and to a growing wine country in the surrounding mountains.

GETTING HERE AND AROUND

From the San Francisco Bay Area, take Highway 17 south over the mountains to Santa Cruz, where it merges with Highway 1. Use Highway 1 to get around the area. The Santa Cruz Transit Center is at 920 Pacific Avenue, at Front Street, a short walk from the Wharf and Boardwalk, with connections to public transit throughout the Monterey Bay and San Francisco Bay areas. You can purchase Santa Cruz METRO bus day passes here.

ESSENTIALS

Transportation Information Santa Cruz METRO ☎ *831/425–8600* ⊕ *www.scmtd.com.*

Visitor Information Santa Cruz County Conference and Visitors Council ⊠ *303 Water St., #100* ☎ *831/425–1234, 800/833–3494* ⊕ *www.santacruz.org.*

EXPLORING

TOP ATTRACTIONS

Pacific Avenue. When you've had your fill of the city's beaches and waters, take a stroll in downtown Santa Cruz, especially on Pacific Avenue between Laurel and Water streets. Vintage boutiques and mountain sports stores, sushi bars and Mexican restaurants, day spas, and nightclubs keep the main drag and the surrounding streets hopping midmorning until late evening.

FAMILY **Santa Cruz Beach Boardwalk.** Santa Cruz has been a seaside resort since the mid-19th century. Along one end of the broad, south-facing beach, the boardwalk has entertained holidaymakers for more than a century. Its Looff carousel and classic wooden Giant Dipper roller coaster, both dating from the early 1900s, are surrounded by high-tech thrill rides and easygoing kiddie rides with ocean views. Video and arcade games, a mini-golf course, and a laser-tag arena pack one gigantic building, which is open daily even if the rides aren't running. You have to pay to play, but you can wander the entire boardwalk for free while sampling delicacies such as corn dogs and garlic fries. ⊠ *Along Beach St.* ☎ *831/423–5590 info line* ⊕ *www.beachboardwalk.com* ⌚ *$32 day pass for unlimited rides, or pay per ride* ⊙ *Apr.–early Sept., daily; early Sept.–late May, weekends, weather permitting; call for hrs.*

FAMILY **Santa Cruz Municipal Wharf.** Jutting half a mile into the ocean near one end of the boardwalk, the century-old Municipal Wharf is lined with seafood restaurants, a wine bar, souvenir shops, and outfitters offering bay cruises, fishing trips, and boat rentals. A salty soundtrack drifts up from under the wharf, where barking sea lions lounge in heaps on crossbeams. Docents from the Seymour Marine Discovery Center lead free, guided 30-minute tours Saturday and Sunday at 1 and 3; meet at the stage on the west side of the wharf between Olita's restaurant and Marini's candies. ⊠ *Beach St., at Pacific Ave.* ☎ *831/420–6025 wharf administration, 831/459–3800 tour information* ⊕ *www.santacruzwharf.com.*

Santa Cruz Surfing Museum. This museum inside the Mark Abbott Memorial Lighthouse chronicles local surfing history. Photographs show old-time surfers, and a display of boards includes rarities such as a heavy redwood plank predating the fiberglass era and the remains of a modern board chomped by a great white shark. On-site surfer-docents talk about the good old days. ⊠ *Lighthouse Point Park, 701 W. Cliff Dr., near Pelton Ave.* ☎ *831/420–6289* ⊕ *www.santacruzsurfingmuseum. org* ⊠ *$2 suggested donation* ⊙ *Sept.–June, Thurs.–Mon. noon–4; July–Aug., Wed.–Mon. 10–5.*

West Cliff Drive. The road that winds along an oceanfront bluff from the municipal wharf to Natural Bridges State Beach makes for a spectacular drive, but it's even more fun to walk, blade, or bike the paved path that parallels the road. Surfers bob and swoosh in Monterey Bay at several points near the foot of the bluff, especially at a break known as Steamer Lane. Named for a surfer who died here in 1965, the nearby Mark Abbott Memorial Lighthouse stands at Point Santa Cruz, the cliff's major promontory. From here you can watch pinnipeds hang out, sunbathe, and frolic on Seal Rock.

WORTH NOTING

FAMILY **Monterey Bay National Marine Sanctuary Exploration Center.** Learn all about the treasures in the nation's largest marine sanctuary via interactive and multimedia exhibits in this fascinating interpretive center. The two-story building, right across the street from the main beach and municipal wharf, was completed in summer 2012. Exhibits educate about watersheds, underwater canyons, kelp forests, and intertidal zones. In the minitheater, follow migratory species (whales, dolphins, sea turtles) as they travel through the open ocean. Head out to the second-floor deck for stellar ocean views, and to get real-time weather, surf, and buoy reports at an interactive station. The center also provides extensive information on the sanctuary's many activities. ⊠ *35 Pacific Ave.* ☎ *831/421–9993* ⊕ *montereybay.noaa.gov/vc/sec* ⊠ *Free* ⊙ *Wed.–Sun. 10–5.*

Mystery Spot. Hokey tourist trap or genuine scientific enigma? Since 1940, curious throngs baffled by the Mystery Spot have made it one of the most visited attractions in Santa Cruz. The laws of gravity and physics don't appear to apply in this tiny patch of redwood forest, where balls roll uphill and people stand on a slant. Advance online tickets ($6) are recommended for weekend and holiday visits. ⊠ *465 Mystery Spot Rd., off Branciforte Dr. (north off Hwy. 1)* ☎ *831/423–8897* ⊕ *www.mysteryspot.com* ⊠ *$5 on-site, $6 in advance, parking $5* ⊙ *Late May–early Sept., daily 10–7; early Sept.–late May, weekdays 10–4, weekends 10–5.*

Santa Cruz Mission State Historic Park. On the northern fringes of downtown is the site of California's 12th Spanish mission, built in the 1790s and destroyed by an earthquake in 1857. A museum in a restored 1791 adobe and a half-scale replica of the mission church are part of the complex. ⊠ *144 School St., at Adobe St.* ☎ *831/425–5849* ⊕ *www.parks. ca.gov/?page_id=548* ⊠ *Free* ⊙ *Thurs.–Sat. 10–4 (call park to confirm).*

University of California at Santa Cruz. The 2,000-acre UC Santa Cruz campus nestles in the forested hills above town. Its sylvan setting, sweeping ocean vistas, and redwood architecture make the university worth a visit. Wander about on your own (maps available at the office of admissions) or on a guided tour (reservations required). Either way, the free campus shuttles can help you get around. ⊠ *Main entrance at Bay and High Sts.* ☏ *831/459–0111* ⊕ *www.ucsc.edu/visit.*

Surf City Vintners. A dozen limited-production winery tasting rooms cluster in renovated warehouse spaces in Swift Street Courtyard, on the westside near UC Santa Cruz. Other green-minded businesses here include Santa Cruz Mountain Brewing Company, a bakery/deli, and a popular shop with homemade organic sausages. ⊠ *334 Ingalls St. at Swift St., off Hwy. 1 (Mission St.)* ⊕ *www.surfcityvintners.com.*

Vinocruz. A slick, contemporary tasting room in downtown's Abbott Square, Vinocruz pours vintages from more than 60 wineries in the Santa Cruz Mountains AVA, including small operations that don't have their own tasting rooms. It's part of a historic building that was once part of an old jail. ⊠ *725 Front St., enter in Abbott Square off Cooper St.* ☏ *831/426–8466* ⊕ *www.vinocruz.com* ☼ *Tues.–Thurs. noon–7, Fri. and Sat. noon–8, Sun. 1–6.*

OFF THE BEATEN PATH

Santa Cruz Mountains wineries. Highway 9 heads northeast from Santa Cruz into hills densely timbered with massive coastal redwoods. The road winds through the lush San Lorenzo Valley, past hamlets consisting of a few cafés, antiques shops, and old-style tourist cabins. Residents of the hunting-and-fishing persuasion coexist with hardcore flower-power survivors and wannabes, and a new generation has joined the pioneers who opened wineries decades ago. Mountain grapes produce some superb Chardonnays, Pinot Noirs, and Cabernet Sauvignons, among other wines. To sample some, you can start a **winery tour** in downtown Santa Cruz at Storrs Winery, at 303 Potrero Street—a block off River Street, which, heading north from here becomes Highway 9. Drive north to Felton to visit Hallcrest Vineyards and Organic Wine Works, just west of Highway 9 on Felton Empire Road downtown. Continue north on Highway 9 and east on Bear Creek Road to the classy Byington and David Bruce wineries, both in Los Gatos. ■TIP→ The Santa Cruz Mountains Winegrowers Association (⊕ www.scmwa.com) distributes a wine-touring map at member wineries and many lodgings and attractions around Santa Cruz.

BEACHES

FAMILY **Natural Bridges State Beach.** At the end of West Cliff Drive lies Natural Bridges State Beach, a stretch of soft sand edged with tide pools and sea-sculpted rock bridges. ■TIP→ From October to early March a colony of monarch butterflies roosts in a eucalyptus grove. **Amenities:** lifeguards; parking (fee); toilets. **Best for:** sunrise; sunset; surfing; swimming. ⊠ *2531 W. Cliff Dr.* ☏ *831/423–4609* ⊕ *www.parks.ca.gov* ☒ *Beach free, parking $10* ☼ *Beach: daily 8 am–sunset. Visitor center: Oct.–Feb., daily 10–4; Mar.–Sept., weekends 10–4.*

Twin Lakes State Beach. Stretching a half mile along the coast on both sides of the small-craft harbor jetties, Twin Lakes is one of the sunniest beaches on the bay. It encompasses Seabright State Beach (with access in a residential neighborhood on the upcoast side) and Black's Beach on the downcoast side. Families often come here to sunbathe, picnic, and hike the nature trail around adjacent Schwann Lake. Limited parking is available next to the main access down from the harbor—arrive early in the day to nab a space (free during the week, permits required on weekends from April through September). You can also park in the pay lot in the harbor. Leashed dogs are allowed. **Amenities:** food and drink; lifeguards (seasonal); parking; showers; toilets; water sports (seasonal). **Best for:** sunset; surfing; swimming; walking. ⊠ *7th Ave., at East Cliff Dr.* ☎ *831/427–4868* ⊕ *www.parks.ca.gov/?page_id=547.*

WHERE TO EAT

$$
SEAFOOD
✘ **Crow's Nest.** This classic California beachside eatery sits right on the water in Santa Cruz Harbor. Vintage surfboards and local surf photography line the walls in the main dining room; nearly every table overlooks the sand and surf. Seafood and steaks, served with local veggies, dominate the menu; favorite appetizers include the chilled shrimp-stuffed artichoke and crispy tempura prawns, served with rice pilaf. No need to pile high on your first trip to the endless salad bar—you can return as often as you like. For sweeping ocean views and more casual fare (think fish tacos and burgers), head upstairs to the Breakwater Bar & Grill. Live entertainment several days a week makes for a dynamic atmosphere year-round. ⑤ *Average main: $20* ⊠ *2218 E. Cliff Dr., west of 7th Ave.* ☎ *831/476–4560* ⊕ *www.crowsnest-santacruz.com.*

$$
ITALIAN
✘ **Gabriella Café.** The work of local artists hangs on the walls of this petite, romantic café in a tile-roof cottage. Featuring organic produce from area farms, the seasonal Italian menu has included wild-mushroom risotto; bouillabaisse; marinated chicken with apricots, currants, and olives; and roasted beet salad with arugula, goat cheese, and pistachios. ⑤ *Average main: $22* ⊠ *910 Cedar St., at Church St.* ☎ *831/457–1677* ⊕ *www.gabriellacafe.com.*

$$
AFGHAN
✘ **Laili Restaurant.** Exotic Mediterranean flavors with an Afghan twist take center stage in this artsy, stylish space with soaring ceilings across from Cooper Square. The chef uses authentic herbs and spices and fresh, healthy ingredients sourced from local purveyors. Traditional dishes range from Moroccan beet salad and grilled chicken flatbread to pomegranate eggplant and *maush-awa* soup with lentils, beans, and lamb, topped with yogurt. The menus also include housemade pastas and numerous vegetarian options; fresh *naan* and delectable chutneys and dips accompany every meal. Evenings are especially lively, when locals come to relax over wine and soft jazz at the blue-concrete bar, the heated patio with twinkly lights, or at a communal table near the stainless-steel open kitchen. ⑤ *Average main: $18* ⊠ *101–B Cooper St.* ☎ *831/423–4545* ⊕ *www.lailirestaurant.com.*

$$
ITALIAN
✘ **La Posta.** Authentic Italian fare made with fresh local produce lures diners into cozy, modern-rustic La Posta. Nearly everything is housemade, from the pizzas and breads baked in the brick oven to the pasta and the vanilla-bean gelato. The seasonal menu includes flavorful dishes such as fried artichokes, ravioli filled with crab, chicken with Brussels sprouts, or sautéed fish from local waters. ⑤ *Average main: $22* ⊠ *538 Seabright Ave., at Logan St.* ☎ *831/457–2782* ⊕ *www.lapostarestaurant.com* ☺ *Closed Mon. No lunch.*

7

$$$ ✕**Oswald.** Sophisticated yet unpretentious European-inspired Califor-
EUROPEAN   nia cooking is the order of the day at this intimate and stylish bistro.
The menu changes seasonally but might include such items as perfectly
prepared seafood stew or roasted rack of lamb. Sit at the slick marble
bar and order a creative concoction like whiskey mixed with apple and
lemon juices and bitters, or tequila with celery juice and lime. ⑤ *Average
main: $25* ✉ *121 Soquel Ave., at Front St.* ☎ *831/423-7427* ⊕ *www.
oswaldrestaurant.com* ☉ *Closed Mon. Lunch Fri. only.*

$ ✕**Seabright Brewery.** Great burgers, big salads, and stellar microbrews
AMERICAN   make this a favorite hangout in the youthful Seabright neighborhood
east of downtown. Sit outside on the patio or inside at a comfort-
able, spacious booth; both are popular with families. ⑤ *Average main:
$13* ✉ *519 Seabright Ave., at Murray St.* ☎ *831/426-2739* ⊕ *www.
seabrightbrewery.com.*

$$ ✕**Soif.** Wine reigns at this sleek bistro and wine shop that takes its name
MEDITERRANEAN   from the French word for thirst. The lengthy list includes selections
from near and far, many of which you can order by the taste or glass.
Infused with the tastes of the Mediterranean, small plates and mains
are served at the copper-top bar, the big communal table, and private
tables. A jazz combo or solo pianist plays some evenings. ⑤ *Average
main: $22* ✉ *105 Walnut Ave., at Pacific Ave.* ☎ *831/423-2020* ⊕ *www.
soifwine.com* ☉ *No lunch.*

$ ✕**Zachary's.** This noisy café filled with students and families defines
AMERICAN   the funky essence of Santa Cruz. It also dishes up great breakfasts: stay
simple with sourdough pancakes, or go for Mike's Mess—eggs scram-
bled with bacon, mushrooms, and home fries, then topped with sour
cream, melted cheese, and fresh tomatoes. ∎TIP➔ If you arrive after 9
am, expect a long wait for a table; lunch is a shade calmer (closing time
is 2:30 pm). ⑤ *Average main: $12* ✉ *819 Pacific Ave.* ☎ *831/427-0646*
⌂ *Reservations not accepted* ☉ *Closed Mon. No dinner.*

WHERE TO STAY

For expanded hotel reviews, visit Fodors.com.

$$$ ⊡ **Babbling Brook Inn.** Though it's smack in the middle of Santa Cruz,
B&B/INN   this B&B has lush gardens, a running stream, and tall trees that make
you feel as if you're in a secluded wood. **Pros:** close to UCSC; within
walking distance of downtown shops; woodsy feel. **Cons:** near a high
school; some rooms close to a busy street. ⑤ *Rooms from: $185* ✉ *1025
Laurel St.* ☎ *831/427-2437, 800/866-1131* ⊕ *www.babblingbrookinn.
com* ⤴ *13 rooms* ⎮◎⎮ *Breakfast.*

$$$ ⊡ **Chaminade Resort & Spa.** A full-on renovation of the entire property,
RESORT   completed in 2009, sharpened this hilltop resort's look, enhanced
its amenities, and qualified it for regional green certification. **Pros:**
far from city life; spectacular property; ideal spot for romance and
rejuvenation. **Cons:** must drive to attractions and sights; near major
hospital. ⑤ *Rooms from: $249* ✉ *1 Chaminade La.* ☎ *800/283-6569
reservations, 831/475-5600* ⊕ *www.chaminade.com* ⤴ *112 rooms,
44 suites.*

$ ⊡ **Harbor Inn.** Family-run, friendly, and funky, this basic but sparkling-
B&B/INN   clean lodge offers exceptional value just a few blocks from Santa Cruz

Harbor and Twin Lakes Beach. **Pros:** affordable; free Wi-Fi; park your car and walk to the beach. **Cons:** not fancy; not near downtown. $ *Rooms from: $89* ✉ *645 7th Ave.* ☎ *831/479–9731* ⊕ *www. harborinnsantacruz.com* ⇆ *17 rooms, 2 suites.*

$$$
HOTEL

⚎ **Hotel Paradox.** Less than two miles from the wharf and boardwalk and a short walk to Pacific Avenue, this new stylish, forest-themed complex is among the few full-service hotels in town. **Pros:** close to downtown and main beach; good alternative to beach-oriented lodgings; new property. **Cons:** pool area can get crowded on warm-weather days; some rooms on the small side. $ *Rooms from: $215* ✉ *611 Ocean St.* ☎ *831/425–7100, 855/425–7200* ⊕ *www.thehotelparadox.com* ⇆ *164 rooms, 6 suites* ⦿ *No meals.*

$$$
B&B/INN

⚎ **Pacific Blue Inn.** Green themes reign in this three-story, eco-friendly B&B, built from scratch in 2009 on a sliver of prime property downtown. **Pros:** free bicycles; five-minute walk to boardwalk and wharf; right in downtown. **Cons:** tiny property; not suitable for children. $ *Rooms from: $189* ✉ *636 Pacific Ave.* ☎ *831/600–8880* ⊕ *www. pacificblueinn.com* ⇆ *9 rooms* ⦿ *Breakfast.*

$$$$
HOTEL

⚎ **Santa Cruz Dream Inn.** Just a short stroll from the boardwalk and wharf, this full-service luxury hotel is the only lodging in Santa Cruz directly on the beach. **Pros:** directly on the beach; easy parking; walk to boardwalk and downtown. **Cons:** expensive; area gets congested on busy weekends. $ *Rooms from: $309* ✉ *175 W. Cliff Dr.* ☎ *831/426–4330, 866/774–7735 reservations* 🖷 *831/427–2025* ⊕ *www.dreaminnsantacruz.com* ⇆ *149 rooms, 16 suites.*

$$$
B&B/INN

⚎ **West Cliff Inn.** Perched on the bluffs across from Cowell Beach, this posh nautical-theme inn commands sweeping views of the boardwalk and Monterey Bay. **Pros:** killer views; walking distance of the beach; close to downtown. **Cons:** boardwalk noise; street traffic. $ *Rooms from: $185* ✉ *174 West Cliff Dr.* ☎ *800/979–0910 toll free, 831/457–2200* ⊕ *www. westcliffinn.com* ⇆ *7 rooms, 2 suites, 1 cottage* ⦿ *Breakfast.*

NIGHTLIFE AND THE ARTS

NIGHTLIFE

Catalyst. Dance with the crowds at this huge, grimy club that regularly features bands ranging from punk groups like Dropkick Murphys to death-metal bands like Decapitated. ✉ *1011 Pacific Ave.* ☎ *831/423–1338* ⊕ *www.catalystclub.com.*

Kuumbwa Jazz Center. The renowned center draws top performers such as the Brubeck Brothers Quartet, Ladysmith Black Mambazo, and Chick Corea; the café serves meals an hour before most shows. ✉ *320–2 Cedar St.* ☎ *831/427–2227* ⊕ *www.kuumbwajazz.org.*

Moe's Alley. Blues, salsa, reggae, funk: Moe's has it all (and more), six nights a week. ✉ *1535 Commercial Way* ☎ *831/479–1854* ⊕ *www. moesalley.com.*

THE ARTS

Cabrillo Festival of Contemporary Music. Each August, this music festival brings some of the world's finest artists to the Santa Cruz Civic Auditorium to play groundbreaking symphonic music, including major world premieres. ☎ *831/426–6966, 831/420–5260 box office* ⊕ *www. cabrillomusic.org.*

Santa Cruz Baroque Festival. Using period and reproduction instruments, the festival presents classical music at various venues. As the name suggests, the focus is on 17th- and 18th-century composers such as Bach and Handel. ☎ *831/457–9693* ⊕ *www.scbaroque.org.*

Shakespeare Santa Cruz. This six-week festival in July and August occasionally includes a modern dramatic performance. Most performances are outdoors under the redwoods. A holiday program takes place in December. ✉ *SSC/UCSC Theater Arts Center, 1156 High St.* ☎ *831/459–2121 administration, 831/459–2159 tickets* ⊕ *www. shakespearesantacruz.org.*

Tannery Arts Center. The grounds of a former leather tannery were transformed into a major arts complex, with a performing arts center, galleries, workshops, retail stores, and cafés opening in stages in 2013–14. ✉ *1050 River St., at intersection of Hwys. 1 and 9* ☎ *831/621–6226* ⊕ *www.tanneryartscenter.org.*

SPORTS AND THE OUTDOORS

ADVENTURE TOURS

Mount Hermon Adventures. Zipline through the redwoods, climb a giant live oak tree, and hunt for edibles in the Santa Cruz Mountains at this adventure center near Felton, 9 miles north of downtown Santa Cruz. On the two-hour Redwood Canopy Tour, follow a guide along a series of six ziplines and two suspension bridges in the redwood canopy. You can also join an ECO tour, where you harness up and ascend a live oak tree using a double-rope system, then go on an ecology walk to forage for sustainable edibles or learn about sand hill habitat restoration (four hours total). On select summer weekends, you can sign up for an aerial adventure course with a set of obstacles and challenges in the redwoods. You must be at least 10 years old and weigh between 75 and 250 pounds to join a tour. Reservations are essential. ✉ *17 Conference Drive, Mount Hermon* ☎ *831/430–4357* ⊕ *www. mounthermonadventures.com* 🎟 *Redwood canopy tours $80, tree climbing tours $50* ☺ *Redwood Canopy Tour: Apr.–Oct., daily 8–6. Nov.–Mar., Thurs.–Mon., 11–4. ECO Tours: weekdays at 9 and 1:30.*

BICYCLING

Another Bike Shop. Mountain bikers should head here for tips on the best area trails and to browse cutting-edge gear made and tested locally. ✉ *2361 Mission St., at King St.* ☎ *831/427–2232* ⊕ *www. anotherbikeshop.com.*

BOATS AND CHARTERS

Chardonnay Sailing Charters. The 70-foot *Chardonnay II* departs year-round from Santa Cruz yacht harbor on whale-watching, sunset, and other cruises around Monterey Bay. Most regularly scheduled excursions cost $50; food and drink are served on many of them. Reservations are essential. ☎ *831/423–1213* ⊕ *www.chardonnay.com.*

Stagnaro Sport Fishing, Charters, & Whale Watching Cruises. Stagnaro operates salmon, albacore, and rock-cod fishing expeditions; the fees ($55 to $80) include bait. The company also runs whale-watching, dolphin, and sea-life cruises ($46) year-round. ⊠ *June–Aug., Santa Cruz Municipal Wharf; Sept.–May, Santa Cruz West Harbor* ☎ *831/427–2334, 800/979–3370 tickets, 212/209–3370 international tickets* ⊕ *www.stagnaros.com.*

GOLF

Pasatiempo Golf Club. Designed by famed golf architect Dr. Alister MacKenzie in 1929, this semiprivate course, set amid undulating hills just above the city, is among the nation's top championship courses. Golfers rave about the spectacular views and challenging terrain. ⊠ *20 Clubhouse Rd.* ☎ *831/459–9155* ⊕ *www.pasatiempo.com* 🏌 *18 holes. 6,125 yds. Par 72. Greens fees: $220/$250* ☞ *Driving range, putting green, pitching area, golf carts, pull carts, caddies, rental clubs, pro shop, golf lessons, restaurant, bar.*

KAYAKING

Kayak Connection. In March, April, and May, participants on this outfit's tours mingle with gray whales and their calves on their northward journey to Alaska. Throughout the year, the company rents kayaks and paddle boards and conducts tours of Natural Bridges State Beach, Capitola, and Elkhorn Slough. Most regularly scheduled tours cost $55. ⊠ *Santa Cruz Harbor, 413 Lake Ave. #3* ☎ *831/479–1121* ⊕ *www.kayakconnection.com.*

Venture Quest Kayaking. Explore hidden coves and kelp forests on guided nature tours that depart from Santa Cruz Wharf or Harbor, depending on the season. A two-hour kayak nature tour and introductory lesson costs $58. A three-hour kayak rental is $30 and includes wet suit and gear. Venture Quest also arranges tours at other Monterey Bay destinations, including Capitola and Elkhorn Slough. ⊠ *#2 Santa Cruz Wharf* ☎ *831/427–2267 kayak hotline, 831/425–8445 rental office* ⊕ *www.kayaksantacruz.com.*

SURFING

Pleasure Point. Surfers gather for the spectacular waves and sunsets here. ⊠ *E. Cliff and Pleasure Point Drs.*

Steamer Lane. This area near the lighthouse on West Cliff Drive has a decent break. Steamer Lane hosts several competitions in summer.

EQUIPMENT AND LESSONS

Club-Ed Surf School and Camps. Find out what all the fun is about at Club-Ed. Your first private or group lesson ($85 and up) includes all equipment. ⊠ *Cowell Beach, at Santa Cruz Dream Inn* ☎ *831/464–0177* ⊕ *www.club-ed.com.*

Cowell's Beach Surf Shop. This shop sells gear, clothing, and swimwear; rents surfboards, standup paddle boards, and wet suits; and offers lessons. ⊠ *30 Front St.* ☎ *831/427–2355* ⊕ *www.cowellssurfshop.com.*

7

SHOPPING

Annieglass. The works of famed Santa Cruz glass artist Annie Morhauser are on display at the Smithsonian and New York's MOMA—but at the gallery in Cooper Square you can collect your own luxury Annieglass tableware, decorative accessories, and jewelry, all designed and hand-made in Santa Cruz County. The store also sells discounted studio seconds with barely perceptible flaws and gift items made by other artists. ⊠ *110 Cooper St.* ☎ *800/347–6133* ⊕ *www.annieglass.com.*

Bookshop Santa Cruz. The town's best and most beloved independent bookstore has been sating readers' thirst for new, used, and discount books since 1966. The children's section is especially comprehensive, and the shop's special events calendar is packed with readings, social mixers, booksignings, and discussions. ⊠ *1520 Pacific Ave.* ☎ *831/423–0900* ⊕ *www.bookshopsantacruz.com.*

O'Neill Surf Shop. O'Neill operates two flagship stores, this one in downtown Santa Cruz and one at 1115 41st Avenue, Capitola, close to Jack O'Neill's home on Pleasure Point. There's also a smaller outlet on the Santa Cruz Wharf at 400 Beach Street. Sporting stores all over town also carry the line (it's everywhere). ⊠ *110 Cooper St.* ☎ *831/469–4377* ⊕ *www.oneill.com.*

The True Olive Connection. Taste your way through boutique extra-virgin olive oils and balsamic vinegars from around the world at this family-run shop just off Pacific Avenue. You can also pick up gourmet food products and olive-oil-based gift items. ⊠ *106 Lincoln St.* ☎ *831/458–6457* ⊕ *www.trueoliveconnection.com.*

THE INLAND EMPIRE

East of Los Angeles to the
San Jacinto Mountains

WELCOME TO THE INLAND EMPIRE

TOP REASONS TO GO

★ **Wine Country:** The Temecula Valley is a mélange of rolling hills, faint ocean breezes, beautiful and funky wineries, lovely lodging options, and gourmet restaurants.

★ **The Mission Inn:** One of the most unique hotels in America, Riverside's rambling, eclectic Mission Inn feels like an urban Hearst Castle.

★ **Apple country:** Oak Glen is one of Southern California's largest apple-growing regions. Attend an old-fashioned hoedown, take a wagon ride, and sample Mile High apple pies and homemade ciders.

★ **Soothing spas:** The lushly landscaped grounds, bubbling hot springs, and playful mud baths of Glen Ivy are ideal spots to unwind, while Kelly's Spa at the historic Mission Inn provides a cozy Tuscan-style retreat.

★ **Alpine escapes:** Breathe in the clean mountain air or cozy up in a rustic cabin at one of the Inland Empire's great mountain hideaways: Lake Arrowhead, Big Bear, and Idyllwild.

1 The Western Inland Empire. At the foot of 10,000-foot-high Mt. Baldy in the San Gabriel Mountains, the tree-lined communities of Pomona and Claremont are known for their prestigious colleges: California State Polytechnic University–Pomona and the seven-school Claremont Colleges complex. Pomona is urban and industrial, but Claremont is a classic tree-shaded, lively, sophisticated college town that more resembles trendy sections of Los Angeles than the laid-back Inland Empire.

2 Riverside Area. In the late 1700s, Mexican settlers called this now-suburban region Valle de Paraiso. Citrus-growing here began in 1873, when homesteader Eliza Tibbets planted two navel-orange trees in her yard. The area's biggest draws are the majestic Mission Inn, with its fine restaurants and unique history and architecture, and Glen Ivy Hot Springs in nearby Corona.

GETTING ORIENTED

Several freeways provide access to the Inland Empire from Los Angeles and San Diego. Ontario, Corona, and Temecula line up along Interstates 10 and 215; and Corona, Riverside, and San Bernardino lie along Highway 91. As a Los Angeles bedroom community, the area sees nasty freeway congestion on Highway 60 and Interstates 10 and 15, so try to avoid driving during rush hour, usually from 6 to 9 am and 4 to 7 pm.

8

3 San Bernardino Mountains. Lake Arrowhead and always-sunny Big Bear are the recreational centers of this area. Though the two are geographically close, they're distinct in appeal. Lake Arrowhead, with its cool mountain air, trail-threaded woods,

and brilliant lake, draws a summertime crowd—a well-heeled one, if the prices in its shops and restaurants are any indication. Big Bear's ski and snowboarding slopes, cross-country trails, and cheerful lodges come alive in winter. Even if you're not interested in visiting the resorts themselves, the Rim of the World Scenic Byway (Highway 18), which connects Big Bear Lake and Lake Arrowhead at an elevation up to 8,000 feet, is a magnificent drive. On a clear day, you'll feel like you can see forever.

4 The Southern Inland Empire. Life is quieter in the southern portion of the Inland Empire than it is to the north. In this corner of Riverside County, towns such as Idyllwild and Temecula are oases of the good life for locals and visitors alike.

Updated by
Bobbi Zane
The Inland Empire, an area often overlooked by visitors because of its tangled freeways and suburban sprawl, has its charms. No more than a couple of hours' drive from metropolitan Los Angeles, you can ski a 7,000-foot mountain overlooking a crystal blue lake or go wine tasting at a vineyard cooled by ocean breezes.

At the heart of this desert and mountain region is Riverside, the birthplace of California's multimillion-dollar navel-orange industry—the tree that started it all still flourishes on Magnolia Avenue—and home of the University of California at Riverside. The downtown streets buzz with people on their way to shop for antiques, dine in interesting restaurants, and listen to live jazz.

The scene is completely different northeast of Riverside, in the San Bernardino Mountains. There Big Bear Lake and Lake Arrowhead are set like bowls surrounded by wooded mountain peaks. To the south, in the San Jacinto Mountains west of Palm Springs, Idyllwild is a year-round getaway with romantic cottages, impressive art galleries, and cozy restaurants. In the southernmost reaches of the Inland Empire, on the way from Riverside to San Diego, is what's come to be known as the Southern California Wine Country around Temecula. This is prime territory for hot-air ballooning, golfing, fine dining, and—of course—vineyard tours and wine tasting.

PLANNING

WHEN TO GO
The climate varies greatly depending on what part of the Inland Empire you're visiting. Summer temperatures in the mountains and in Temecula, 20 miles from the coast, usually hover around 80°F, though it's not uncommon for Riverside to reach temperatures of 100°F or higher. From September to March this area is subject to increasingly high Santa Ana winds, sometimes strong enough to overturn trucks on the freeway. In winter, temperatures in the mountains and in Temecula usually

range from 30°F to 55°F, and in the Riverside area from 40°F to 60°F. Most of the ski areas open when the first natural snow falls (usually in November) and close in mid-March.

GETTING HERE AND AROUND

AIR TRAVEL
LA/Ontario International Airport (ONT) is the local airport. Aeromexico, Alaska, American, Delta, Southwest, and United fly here.

Airport Contacts LA/Ontario International Airport ⊠ *Airport Dr., Archibald Ave. exit off I-10, Ontario* ☎ *909/937–2700* ⊕ *www.lawa.org.*

BUS TRAVEL
Greyhound serves Riverside, San Bernardino, and Temecula.

Bus Contact Greyhound ☎ *800/231–2222* ⊕ *www.greyhound.com.*

CAR TRAVEL
Avoid Highway 91 if possible; it's almost always backed up from Corona through Orange County. Check with Caltrans for information about highway conditions, or dial 511 or log on to the IE511 website, which also has bus-train trip planners.

Contacts Caltrans ☎ *800/427–7623* ⊕ *www.dot.ca.gov.*
IE511 ⊕ *www.ie511.org.*

TRAIN TRAVEL
■ **TIP→ Many locals get around on Metrolink, which is clean and quick, and generally a much nicer way to travel than by bus.** Metrolink trains stop at several stations on the Inter-County, San Bernardino, and Riverside lines. You can buy tickets and passes at station vending machines, or by telephone. The IE511 website *(⇨ Car Travel, above)* has bus-train trip planners; dial 511 for recorded train-schedule information.

Train Contact Metrolink ☎ *800/371–5465* ⊕ *www.metrolinktrains.com.*

HEALTH AND SAFETY
In an emergency dial 911.

Emergency Services Big Bear Lake Sheriff ☎ *909/866–0100.*

RESTAURANTS
Downtown Riverside is home to a few ambitious restaurants, along with the familiar chains. The college towns of Claremont and Redlands have creative contemporary and ethnic fare. Innovative cuisine has become the norm in Temecula, especially at the wineries, many of which showcase their products alongside fine dining. The options are more limited in the smaller mountain communities; typically each town supports a single upscale restaurant, along with fast-food outlets, steak-and-potatoes family spots, and perhaps an Italian or Mexican eatery. Universally, dining out is casual. *Prices in the reviews are the average cost of a main course at dinner or, if dinner is not served, at lunch.*

HOTELS
In the San Bernardino Mountains, many accommodations are bed-and-breakfasts or rustic cabins, though Lake Arrowhead and Big Bear offer more luxurious resort lodging. Rates for Big Bear lodgings fluctuate widely, depending on the season. When winter snow brings droves of

8

Angelenos to the mountains for skiing, expect to pay sky-high prices for any kind of room. Most establishments require a two-night stay on weekends. In Riverside, the landmark Mission Inn is the marquee accommodation. In the Wine Country, lodgings can be found at wineries, golf resorts, and chain hotels. *Prices in the reviews are the lowest cost of a standard double room in high season. For expanded reviews, facilities, and current deals, visit Fodors.com.*

THE WESTERN INLAND EMPIRE

Straddling the line between Los Angeles and San Bernardino counties, the western section of the Inland Empire is home to some of California's oldest vineyards and original citrus orchards. Now a busy suburban community, it holds the closest ski slopes to metro Los Angeles. Fairplex, where the L.A. County Fair is held each year, is here, as is Claremont, home to a collection of high-ranking colleges.

GETTING HERE AND AROUND

To reach this area from Los Angeles, take Interstate 10, which bisects the Western Inland Empire west to east; from Pasadena, take Interstate 210, which runs parallel to the north. Take Highway 57 from Anaheim. Some areas are quite walkable, especially the Claremont Colleges, where you can stroll through parks from one school building to another.

The Foothill Transit Bus Line serves Pomona, Claremont, and Montclair, with stops at Cal Poly and the Fairplex. Metrolink serves the area from Los Angeles and elsewhere.

Bus Contact Foothill Transit ☎ *800/743–3463, 909/621–2126* ⊕ *www.foothilltransit.org.*

POMONA

23 miles north of Anaheim, 27 miles east of Pasadena.

The green hills of Pomona, dotted with horses and houses, are perhaps best known as the site of the Los Angeles County Fair and of California State Polytechnic University–Pomona. Named for the Roman goddess of fruit, the city has a rich citrus-growing heritage.

GETTING HERE AND AROUND

The most direct routes from Los Angeles to Pomona are the Pomona Freeway (Highway 60) and Interstate 10. It pays to check traffic reports before starting out. Mission Boulevard (west–east) and Garey Avenue (north–south) are the main surface streets through downtown.

ESSENTIALS

Visitor Information Pomona Chamber of Commerce ⊠ *101 W. Mission Blvd., #223* ☎ *909/622-8484* ⊕ *www.pomonachamber.org* ⊟ *No credit cards.*

EXPLORING

California Polytechnic University at Pomona. The university occupies 1,438 rolling acres of the Kellogg Ranch, originally the winter home of cereal magnate W.K. Kellogg. Cal Poly specializes in teaching agriculture, and you can find rose gardens, avocado groves, many farm animals, and a working Arabian horse ranch. The Farm Store (✉ *4102 University Dr. S.* ☎ *909/869–4906, open daily 10–6*) sells locally grown meat, produce, and cheeses, along with plants grown in the university nursery. ✉ *3801 W. Temple Ave.* ☎ *909/869–7659* ⊕ *www.csupomona.edu.*

Fairplex. The site of the Los Angeles County Fair (North America's largest county fair), the Fairplex exposition center hosts open-air markets, antiques shows, roadster shows, historical train and model train exhibits, horse shows and racing, dog shows, and the annual International Wine and Spirits competition. Also here is the **Wally Parks NHRA Motorsports Museum** (⊕ *www.museum.nhra.com*), which pays tribute to the rich history of American motor sports with exhibits of vintage racing vehicles and has an amusing collection of tricked-out drag-racing cars. ✉ *1101 W. McKinley Ave.* ☎ *909/623–3111, 909/622–2133 museum* ⊕ *www.fairplex.com* ⛺ *Museum $8* ☉ *Museum Wed.–Sun. 10–5.*

W.K. Kellogg Arabian Horse Shows. The classic shows, started by cereal maker Kellogg in 1926, remain a tradition on the CSU–Pomona campus. Many purebreds live at the ranch, and the university presents exhibitions of the equines in English and Western tack the first Sunday of the month at 2 pm from October through May. Stable tours and pony rides take place after the show. ✉ *3801 W. Temple Ave.* ☎ *909/869–2224* ⊕ *www.csupomona.edu/~equine* ⛺ *$4.*

WHERE TO EAT AND STAY

For expanded hotel reviews, visit Fodors.com.

$$$
AMERICAN

✕ **Pomona Valley Mining Company.** Atop a hill near an old mining site, this rustic steak-and-seafood restaurant provides great city views at night. Though somewhat dated, the decor reflects the local mining heritage. Authentic gold-rush pieces and 1800s memorabilia hang on the walls, and old lanterns adorn the tables. The food—heavy on steak and prime rib—is well prepared; save space for dessert that includes mud pie or bourbon bread pudding. ⑤ *Average main: $26* ✉ *1777 Gillette Rd.* ☎ *909/623–3515* ⊕ *www.pomonavalleyminingco.com* ⚓ *Reservations essential* ☉ *Closed Mon. No lunch Tues.–Sat.*

$
HOTEL

⛾ **Sheraton Suites Fairplex.** County-fair murals and whimsical carousel animals welcome you to this all-suites hotel at the entrance to Pomona's Fairplex. **Pros:** adjacent to convention center; clean rooms; comfortable beds. **Cons:** parts feel dated; not close to many restaurants. ⑤ *Rooms from: $119* ✉ *601 W. McKinley Ave.* ☎ *800/325–3535, 909/622–2220* ⊕ *www.sheraton.com* ⤳ *247 suites* ⎧⎨⎩ *No meals.*

CLAREMONT

4 miles north of Pomona.

The seven Claremont Colleges are among the most prestigious in the nation. The campuses are all laid out cheek-by-jowl; as you wander from one leafy street to the next, you won't be able to tell where one college ends and the next begins.

Claremont was originally the home of the Sunkist citrus growers cooperative movement. Today, Claremont Village, home to descendants of those early farmers, is bright and lively. The business district village, with streets named for prestigious eastern colleges, is walkable and appealing with a collection of boutiques, fancy food emporiums, cafés, and lounges. The downtown district is a beautiful place to visit, with Victorian, Craftsman, and Spanish-colonial buildings.

CLAREMONT WEATHER

Be prepared for hot and smoggy conditions in summer; the town is not gifted with SoCal's best climate.

GETTING HERE AND AROUND

If you're driving, exit Interstate 10 at Indian Hill Boulevard, and drive north to Claremont. Parking can be difficult, although there are metered spots. Overnight parking is prohibited within the village; however there is a parking structure adjacent to the College Heights Packing House Fairplex that is also north of the freeway; exit Garey and drive toward the mountains. You can reach this area by public transportation, but you'll need a car to get around unless you plan to spend all your time in the Claremont Village.

ESSENTIALS

Visitor Information Claremont Chamber of Commerce ⊠ *205 Yale Ave.* ☎ *909/624–1681* ⊕ *www.claremontchamber.org.*

EXPLORING

Claremont Heritage. College walking tours, a downtown tour, and historic home tours are conducted throughout the year by Claremont Heritage. On the first Saturday of each month the organization gives guided walking tours ($5) of the village. The website has self-guided tour maps. ⊠ *840 N. Indian Hill Blvd.* ☎ *909/621–0848* ⊕ *www. claremontheritage.org* ⊡ *$5.*

Pomona College Museum of Art. This small museum on the campus of Pomona College exhibits significant contemporary art, works by old masters, and examples of Native American arts and artifacts. Highlights include the first mural painted by the Mexican artist Jose Clemente Orozco in North America, first-edition etchings by Goya, and the Kress collection of 15th- and 16th-century Italian panel paintings. The fun Art After Hours events on Thursday nights often include local bands and music. ⊠ *333 N. College Ave.* ☎ *909/621–8283* ⊕ *www.pomona. edu/museum* ⊡ *Free* ☉ *Tues.–Sun. 12–5, Thurs. until 11.*

QUICK BITES

Bert & Rocky's Cream Company. The sinfully innovative concoctions at this popular ice-cream store include the Elvis special with bananas and peanut butter and the Tuscany marble, chocolate-raspberry swirl, and blueberry-cheesecake ice creams. The vanilla's delightful, too. ⊠ *242 Yale Ave.* ☎ *909/625–1852.*

Fodor's Choice ★ **Rancho Santa Ana Botanic Garden.** Founded in 1927 by Susanna Bixby Bryant, a wealthy landowner and conservationist, the garden is a living museum and research center dedicated to the conservation of native-California plant species. You can meander here for hours enjoying the shade of an oak tree canopy or take a guided tour of the grounds, whose 86 acres of ponds and greenery shelter such specimens as California wild lilacs (*ceanothus*), big berry manzanita, and four-needled piñon. Countless birds also make their homes here. ⊠ *1500 N. College Ave.* ☎ *909/625–8767* ⊕ *www.rsabg.org* ⊡ *$8* ⊘ *Daily 8–5.*

WHERE TO EAT

$$
ITALIAN
✕ **La Parolaccia.** Locals line up on weekends to get a table at this busy spot where waiters zip through a series of small rooms delivering fresh and beautifully seasoned items from an extensive Italian menu. Popular dishes include pasta with fresh salmon and capers, and risotto with seafood, white wine, and tomato sauce. Topping the dessert list is bread pudding made with ciabatta bread and crème anglaise. ⑤ *Average main: $19* ⊠ *201 N. Indian Hill Blvd.* ☎ *909/624–1516* ⊕ *www.laparolacciausa.com.*

$$$$
ITALIAN
✕ **Tutti Mangia Italian Grill.** College students get their visiting parents to take them to this storefront dining room that has a warm and cozy feel. Top menu choices include roasted double pork chops, veal shank, and pan-roasted salmon with blood-orange sauce. The small plates entice. ⑤ *Average main: $40* ⊠ *102 Harvard Ave.* ☎ *909/625–4669* ⊕ *www.tuttimangia.com* ⌕ *Reservations essential* ⊘ *No lunch weekends.*

$$
ECLECTIC
✕ **Walter's Restaurant.** With a menu that roams the globe from France to Italy to Afghanistan, Walter's is where locals gather to dine, sip wine, and chat. You can eat outside on the sidewalk, on the lively patio, or in a cozy setting inside. Wherever you sit, the owner, Nangy, will stroll by to make sure you're happy with your meal. He'll urge you to try the puffy Afghan fries with hot sauce, tabouleh salad, or lamb stew. Breakfast possibilities include omelets, sausage and eggs, and burritos; for lunch are salads, soups, pastas, kebabs, and vegetarian items. ⑤ *Average main: $21* ⊠ *310 N. Yale Ave.* ☎ *909/624–4914* ⊕ *waltersrestaurant. biz* ⌕ *Reservations essential.*

WHERE TO STAY

For expanded hotel reviews, visit Fodors.com.

$$$
B&B/INN
Fodor'sChoice
★
⚏ **Casa 425.** This boutique inn on a corner opposite the College Heights Lemon Packing House entertainment and shopping complex is the most attractive lodging option in Claremont Village. **Pros:** bicycles available; walking distance to attractions and restaurants; considerate service; small plates served in the evening. **Cons:** occasional noise. ⑤ *Rooms from: $195* ⊠ *425 W. 1st St.* ☎ *866/450–0425* ⊕ *www.foursisters.com* ⇆ *28 rooms* ⦿ *Some meals.*

$$
HOTEL
FAMILY
⚏ **DoubleTree by Hilton Hotel Claremont.** The hotel of choice for parents visiting children attending local colleges has spacious rooms clustered in three Spanish-style buildings that surround a flower-decked central courtyard. **Pros:** convenient to colleges; family-friendly; free-form swimming pool. **Cons:** small bathrooms. ⑤ *Rooms from: $126* ⊠ *555 W. Foothill Blvd.* ☎ *909/626–2411* ⊕ *www.doubletreeclaremont.com* ⇆ *190 rooms* ⦿ *No meals.*

NIGHTLIFE

Being a college town, Claremont has many bars and cafés, some of which showcase bands.

Flappers Comedy Club. A typical stand-up venue, Flappers is a branch of a Burbank club. Headliners such as Hal Sparks and Titus perform, as do up-and-coming comedians. Snacks and beverages are available. ⊠ *532*

W. 1st St. ☎ 818/845–9721 ⊕ www.flapperscomedy.com ⊠ $10–$20, some shows free ⊙ Closed Mon.–Wed.

SPORTS AND THE OUTDOORS

SKIING

Mt. Baldy Ski Resort. The 10,064-foot mountain's real name is Mt. San Antonio, but Mt. Baldy Ski Resort—the oldest ski area in Southern California—takes its name from the treeless slopes. The Mt. Baldy base lies at 6,500 feet, and four chairlifts ascend to 8,600 feet. The resort is known for its steep triple-diamond runs; the longest of the 26 runs here is 2,100 vertical feet. Backcountry skiing is available via shuttle in the spring, and there's a school on weekends for kids ages 5 to 12. Winter or summer, you can take a scenic chairlift ride ($25) to the Top of the Notch restaurant and hiking and mountain-biking trails. ⊠ 8401 Mt. Baldy Rd., Mt. Baldy ☎ 909/982–0800 ⊕ www.mtbaldyskilifts.com ⊠ Full day $69, half day $49 ⊙ Snow season Nov.–Apr., weekdays 8–4:30, weekends 7:30–4:30; summer season May–Oct., weekends 7–sunset.

ONTARIO

6 miles east of Pomona.

Ontario has a rich agricultural and industrial heritage. The valley's warm climate once supported vineyards that produced grape varietals such as Grenache, Mourvèdre, and Zinfandel. Today, housing tracts and shopping malls have replaced most of the vineyards. But the airport is here, so you may well find yourself passing through.

GETTING HERE AND AROUND

Ontario lies between Interstate 10 to the north and Highway 60 (Pomona Freeway) to the south. Metrolink connects the L.A. area to the airport and other destinations, but driving is the best way to get around the area.

ESSENTIALS

Visitor Information Ontario Convention & Visitors Bureau ⊠ 2000 E. Convention Center Way ☎ 909/937–3000 ⊕ www.ontariocc.com.

EXPLORING

Graber Olive House. Ontario's oldest business opened in 1894, when C.C. Graber bottled his meaty, tree-ripened olives and started selling them. They're still sold throughout the United States. Stop by the gourmet shop for a jar, then have a picnic on the shaded grounds. Tours are conducted year-round; in fall you can watch workers grade, cure, and can the olives. ⊠ 315 E. 4th St. ☎ 800/996–5483 ⊕ www.graberolives. com ⊠ Free ⊙ Daily 9–5:30.

WHERE TO STAY

For expanded hotel reviews, visit Fodors.com.

$ 🖼 **DoubleTree by Hilton Ontario Airport.** A beautifully landscaped court-
HOTEL   yard greets you at Ontario's only full-service hotel. **Pros:** clean, large
FAMILY   rooms; free shuttle to airport and Ontario Mills Mall; chocolate chip
cookies. **Cons:** airport and freeway noise; Internet charge; dated

rooms. ⑤ *Rooms from: $99* ⊠ *222 N. Vineyard Ave.* ☎ *909/937–0900, 800/222–8733* ⊕ *www.doubletree.com* ↩ *482 rooms* ⏏ *Breakfast.*

SHOPPING

FAMILY **Ontario Mills Mall.** The gargantuan mall packs in more than 200 outlet stores including Nordstrom Rack and Sax Fifth Avenue Off 5th. Also here are Carleton Day Spa, a 30-screen movie theater, the Improv Comedy Club and Dinner Theater, and two entertainment complexes. Dining options include a food court, Chipotle Mexican Grill, and the kid-friendly Rainforest Cafe. ⊠ *1 Mills Circle, off 4th St. and I-15* ☎ *909/484–8300* ⊕ *www.ontariomills.com* ☉ *Mon.–Sat. 10–9, Sun. 11–8.*

RANCHO CUCAMONGA

5 miles north of Ontario.

Once a thriving wine-making area with more than 50,000 acres of wine grapes, Rancho Cucamonga—the oldest wine district in California—lost most of its pastoral charm after real-estate developers bought up the land for a megamall and affordable housing. Most of it is now a squeaky-clean planned community, but the wine-making tradition still thrives at the Joseph Filippi Winery.

GETTING HERE AND AROUND

Historic Route 66 (Foothill Boulevard) cuts east–west across Rancho Cucamonga. The community is best reached via Interstate 10.

EXPLORING

Joseph Filippi Winery. J.P. and Jared Filippi continue the family tradition that was started in 1922 at Joseph Filippi, crafting wines from Cabernet, Sangiovese, and Zinfandel grapes, among other varietals. A small museum chronicles the history of Rancho Cucamonga wine making. ⊠ *12467 Base Line Rd.* ☎ *909/899–5755* ⊕ *www.josephfilippiwinery. com* ⓣ *Tasting $5* ☉ *Mon. 12–5, Tues.–Thurs. and Sun., 12–6, Fri. and Sat. 11–7; tour Wed.–Sun. at 1.*

FAMILY **Victoria Gardens.** With its vintage signs, antique lampposts, and relaxing 1920s-style Town Square—complete with old-fashioned trolley—this family-oriented shopping, dining, and entertainment complex feels a lot like Disneyland. Amid 12 blocks you'll find Macy's, A&F, Williams-Sonoma, an AMC movie multiplex, and a Ben & Jerry's ice-cream shop. Restaurants include the Cheesecake Factory and Lucille's Smokehouse Bar-B-Que. The Victoria Gardens Cultural Center houses a 540-seat performing-arts center. ⊠ *12505 N. Mainstreet* ☎ *909/463–2830 info, 909/477–2775 Cultural Center* ⊕ *www.victoriagardensie.com* ⓣ *Free* ☉ *Mon.–Thurs. 10–9, Fri. and Sat. 10–10, Sun. 11–7.*

WHERE TO EAT

$$$$ ✕ **The Sycamore Inn.** Flickering gas lamps and a glowing fireplace greet
STEAKHOUSE you at this rustic restaurant. Built in 1921, the Sycamore Inn occupies the site of a stagecoach stop on Historic Route 66. The specialty here is USDA prime steak—portion sizes range from 8 to 22 ounces—but also on the menu are ahi tuna, Australian lobster tail, and Colorado rack of lamb. The impressive wine list includes selections from the best Napa and Sonoma wineries, and France, New Zealand, Australia, and

South America are also well represented. $ *Average main: $34* ⊠ *8318 Foothill Blvd.* ☎ *909/982–1104* ⊕ *www.thesycamoreinn.com* ⚲ *Reservations essential* ⊘ *No lunch.*

RIVERSIDE AREA

Historic Riverside lies at the heart of the Inland Empire. Major highways linking it to other regional destinations spoke out from this city to the north, south, and east.

GETTING HERE AND AROUND

The most direct route from Los Angeles to Riverside is by Highway 60 (Pomona Freeway). From San Diego take Interstate 15 northeast to the junction with Highway 60. From North Orange County, Highway 91 is the best route.

Bus Contacts Omnitrans ☎ *800/966–6428* ⊕ *www.omnitrans.org.*
Riverside Transit Authority ☎ *951/562–5002* ⊕ *www.riversidetransit.com.*

CORONA

13 miles south of Ontario.

Corona's Temescal Canyon is named for the dome-shaped mud saunas that the Luiseño Indians built around the area's artesian hot springs in the early 19th century. Starting in 1860, weary Overland Stage Company passengers stopped here to relax in the soothing mineral springs. In 1890 Mr. and Mrs. W.G. Steers turned the springs into Glen Ivy Hot Springs, whose popularity has yet to fade.

GETTING HERE AND AROUND

Primarily a bedroom community, Corona lies at the intersection of Interstate 15 and Highway 91. The many roadside malls make it a convenient stop for food or gas.

EXPLORING

FAMILY **Tom's Farms.** Opened as a produce stand along I–15 in 1974, Tom's Farms has grown to include a locally popular hamburger stand, a furniture showroom, and a sweets shop. You can still buy produce here, but the big draw is various weekend attractions for the kiddies: tractor driving, Tom's mining company, a petting zoo, a children's train, a pony ride, free magic shows, face painting, and an old-style carousel. Most cost a modest fee. Of interest for adults is the wine-and-cheese shop, which has more than 600 varieties of wine, including some from the nearby Temecula Valley. ⊠ *23900 Temescal Canyon Rd.* ☎ *951/277–4422* ⊕ *www.tomsfarms.com* ▣ *Free, attraction fees vary; wine tasting $5* ⊘ *Daily 7 am–8 pm; wine tasting 11–5.*

SHOPPING

SPAS

Glen Ivy Hot Springs Spa. Presidents Herbert Hoover and Ronald Reagan are among the guests who have soaked their toes at this beautiful, relaxing spa. Colorful bougainvillea and birds-of-paradise surround the secluded Glen Ivy, which offers a full range of facials, manicures,

It's okay to get a little dirty at Glen Ivy Hot Springs, which offers a wide variety of treatments at its famous spa—including the red clay pool at Club Mud.

pedicures, body wraps, and massages. Some treatments are performed in underground granite chambers (highly recommended by readers) known collectively as the Grotto. The Under the Oaks treatment center holds eight open-air massage rooms surrounded by waterfalls and ancient oak trees. Don't bring your best bikini if you plan to dive into the red clay (brought in daily from a local mine) of Club Mud. Paying the admission fee entitles you to lounge here all day. Make reservations for treatments, which cost extra. ⊠ *25000 Glen Ivy Rd.* ☎ *888/453-6489* ⊕ *www.glenivy.com* ✉ *Admission Mon.–Thurs. $46, Fri.–Sun. $64; treatments $25–$183* ⊙ *Daily 9–5, closes later in warm weather.*

RIVERSIDE

14 miles northeast of Corona, 34 miles northeast of Anaheim.

By 1882 Riverside was home to more than half of California's citrus groves, making it the state's wealthiest city per capita in 1895. The prosperity produced a downtown area of opulent architecture, which is well preserved today. Main Street's pedestrian strip is lined with antiques and gift stores, art galleries, salons, and the UCR/California Museum of Photography.

GETTING HERE AND AROUND

Downtown Riverside lies north of Highway 91 at the University Avenue exit. The Mission Inn is at the corner of Mission Inn Avenue and Orange Street, and key museums, shops, and restaurants are near by. You can park around here and walk to them.

Navel Oranges in California: Good as Gold

In 1873 a woman named Eliza Tibbets changed the course of California history when she planted two Brazilian navel-orange trees in her Riverside garden.

The trees (which were called Washington Navels in honor of America's first president) flourished in the area's warm climate and rich soil—and before long, Tibbett's garden was producing the sweetest seedless oranges anyone had ever tasted. After winning awards at several major exhibitions, Tibbets realized she could make a profit from her trees. She sold buds to the increasing droves of citrus farmers flocking to the Inland Empire, and by 1882, almost 250,000 citrus trees had been planted in Riverside alone. California's citrus industry had been born.

Today, Riverside still celebrates its citrus-growing heritage. The downtown Marketplace district contains several restored packing houses, and the Riverside Metropolitan Museum is home to a permanent exhibit of historic tools and machinery once used in the industry. The University of California at Riverside still remains at the forefront of citrus research; its Citrus Variety Collection includes specimens of 1,000 different fruit trees from around the world.

EXPLORING

Mission Inn Museum. The crown jewel of Riverside is the Mission Inn, a Spanish-revival hotel whose elaborate turrets, clock tower, mission bells, and flying buttresses rise above downtown. Docent-led tours of the hotel are offered by the Mission Inn Foundation, which also operates an expansive museum with displays depicting the building's illustrious history. The inn was designed in 1902 by Arthur B. Benton and Myron Hunt; the team took its cues from the Spanish missions in San Gabriel and Carmel. You can climb to the top of the Rotunda Wing's five-story spiral stairway, or linger a while in the Courtyard of the Birds, where a tinkling fountain and shady trees invite meditation. You can also peek inside the St. Francis Chapel, where celebrities such as Bette Davis, Humphrey Bogart, and Richard and Pat Nixon tied the knot before the Mexican cedar altar. The Presidential Lounge, a bright, wood-panel bar, has been patronized by eight U.S. presidents. ⊠ 3696 Main St. ☎ 951/788–9556 ⊕ www.missioninnmuseum.com ⊠ Admission $2, tour $13 ☉ Daily 9:30–4:30.

Riverside Art Museum. Hearst Castle architect Julia Morgan designed this museum that houses a fine collection of paintings by Southern California landscape artists, including William Keith, Robert Wood, and Ralph Love. Major temporary exhibitions are mounted year-round. ⊠ 3425 Mission Inn Ave. ☎ 951/684–7111 ⊕ www.riversideartmuseum.org ⊠ $5; free 1st Thurs. of month 6–9 ☉ Tues.–Sat. 10–4, Sun. noon–4.

Fodor's Choice ★ **UCR/California Museum of Photography.** With an impressive collection that includes thousands of Kodak Brownie and Zeiss Ikon cameras, this museum surveys the history of photography *and* the devices that produced it. Exhibitions—some of contemporary images, others historically oriented—are always top-notch and often incorporate photographs from the permanent collection. When not on display, works by Ansel Adams, Olindo Ceccarini, and other greats can be viewed by appointment. ⊠ *3824 Main St.* ☎ *951/827–4787* ⊕ *artsblock. ucr.edu/exhibitions* ⊠ *$3* ⊘ *Tues.–Sat. 12–5.*

WHERE TO EAT AND STAY
For expanded hotel reviews, visit Fodors.com.

$$$$
ITALIAN

✕ **Mario's Place.** The clientele is as beautiful as the food at this intimate jazz and supper club across the street from the Mission Inn. The northern Italian cuisine is first-rate, as are the jazz bands that perform Friday and Saturday at 10 pm. Try the pear-and-Gorgonzola wood-fired pizza, followed by the star anise panna cotta for dessert. Jazz groups play weekend nights in the Lounge. $ *Average main: $36* ⊠ *3646 Mission Inn Ave.* ☎ *951/684–7755* ⊕ *www.mariosplace.com* ⚐ *Reservations essential* ⊘ *Closed Sun. No lunch Mon.–Wed.*

$
AMERICAN

✕ **Simple Simon's.** Expect to wait in line at this little sandwich shop on the pedestrian-only shopping strip outside the Mission Inn. Salads, soups, and sandwiches on house-baked breads are served; standouts include the chicken-apple sausage sandwich and the roast lamb sandwich topped with grilled eggplant, red peppers, and tomato-fennel-olive sauce. $ *Average main: $10* ⊠ *3636 Main St.* ☎ *951/369–6030* ⚐ *Reservations not accepted* ⊘ *Closed Sun. No dinner.*

$$$
HOTEL
Fodor'sChoice
★
FAMILY

🏨 **Mission Inn and Spa.** One of California's most historic hotels, the inn grew from a modest adobe lodge in 1876 to the grand Spanish-Revival hotel it is today. **Pros:** fascinating historical site; luxurious rooms; great restaurants; family-friendly. **Cons:** train noise can be deafening at night. $ *Rooms from: $190* ⊠ *3649 Mission Inn Ave.* ☎ *951/784–0300, 800/843–7755* ⊕ *www.missioninn.com* ⮌ *238 rooms, 29 suites* ⦿ *No meals.*

NIGHTLIFE
Sevilla Nightclub. Patrons dance to live music on most nights at this combination restaurant and nightclub that serves tapas in both small-plate and entrée-size portions. Expect Latin-Euro Top 40 dancing on weekends. ⊠ *3252 Mission Inn Ave.* ☎ *951/778–0611* ⊕ *www. sevillanightclub.com* ⊠ *$5 cover weekends.*

REDLANDS

15 miles northeast of Riverside.

Redlands lies at the center of what once was the largest navel-orange-producing region in the world. Orange groves are still plentiful throughout the area. Populated in the late 1800s by wealthy citrus farmers, the town holds a colorful collection of Victorian homes.

GETTING HERE AND AROUND
Redlands straddles Interstate 10 north and south of the freeway at its intersection with Highway 210, one of the main roads into the San Bernardino Mountains.

ESSENTIALS
Visitor Information Redlands Chamber of Commerce ⊠ *1 E. Redlands Blvd.* ☎ *909/793-2546* ⊕ *www.redlandschamber.org.*

8

EXPLORING

Asistencia Mission de San Gabriel. Franciscan Fathers built the mission in 1819, but it functioned as one for only a few years. In 1834 it became part of a rancho and later served as a school and a factory. The current mission is a replica. The landscaped courtyard contains an old Spanish mission bell, and one building holds a small museum. ⊠ *26930 Barton Rd.* ☎ *909/793–5402* ⊕ *www.sbcounty.gov/museum/branches/asist.htm* ⊠ *$2* ⊗ *Tues.–Sat. 10–3.*

Kimberly Crest House and Gardens. In 1897 Cornelia A. Hill built what's now Kimberly Crest House and Gardens to mimic the châteaux of France's Loire Valley. Surrounded by orange groves, lily ponds, and terraced Italian gardens, the mansion has a French-revival parlor, a mahogany staircase, a glass-mosaic fireplace, and a bubbling fountain in the form of Venus rising from the sea. Alfred and Helen Kimberly, founders of the Kimberly-Clark Paper Company, purchased the estate in 1905, and their daughter, Mary, lived here until 1979. Most of the 22 rooms are in original condition. ⊠ *1325 Prospect Dr.* ☎ *909/792–2111* ⊕ *www.kimberlycrest.org* ⊠ *$10* ⊗ *Thurs., Fri., and Sun. 1–3:30* ⊗ *Closed Aug. and major holidays.*

Lincoln Memorial Shrine. The shrine houses the largest collection of Abraham Lincoln artifacts on the West Coast. You can view a marble bust of Lincoln by sculptor George Grey Barnard, along with more than a dozen letters and rare pamphlets. The gift shop sells many books, toys, and reproductions pertaining to the Civil War. ⊠ *125 W. Vine St.* ☎ *909/798–7636, 909/798–7632* ⊕ *www.lincolnshrine.org* ⊠ *Free* ⊗ *Tues.–Sun. 1–5.*

FAMILY **San Bernardino County Museum.** To learn more about Southern California's shaky history, head to this museum where you can watch a working seismometer or check out a display about the San Andreas Fault. Specializing in the natural and regional history of Southern California, the museum is big on birds, eggs, dinosaurs, and mammals. ⊠ *2024 Orange Tree La.* ☎ *909/307–2669* ⊕ *www.sbcounty.gov/museum* ⊠ *$8* ⊗ *Tues.–Sun., holiday Mon. 9–5.*

OAK GLEN

17 miles east of Redlands.

More than 60 varieties of apples are grown in Oak Glen. This rustic village, tucked in the foothills above Yucaipa, is home to acres of farms, produce stands, country shops, and homey cafés. The town really comes alive during the fall harvest (from September through December), which is celebrated with piglet races, live entertainment, and other events. Many farms also grow berries and stone fruit, which are available in summer. Most of the apple farms lie along Oak Glen Road.

GETTING HERE AND AROUND

Oak Glen is tucked into a mountainside about halfway up the San Bernardinos. Exit Interstate 10 at Yucaipa Boulevard, heading east to the intersection with Oak Glen Road, a 5-mile loop along which you'll find most of the shops, cafés, and apple orchards.

ESSENTIALS

Visitor Information **Oak Glen Apple Growers Association** ✉ *39600 Oak Glen Rd., Yucaipa* ☎ *909/797–6833* ⊕ *www.oakglen.net.*

EXPLORING

Mom's Country Orchards. Oak Glen's informal information center is at Mom's, where you can belly up to the bar and learn about the nuances of apple tasting, or warm up with a hot cider heated on an antique stove. Organic produce, local honey, apple butter, and salsa are also specialties here. ✉ *38695 Oak Glen Rd.* ☎ *909/797–4249* ⊕ *www. momscountryorchards.com* ⊗ *Daily 10–3.*

FAMILY **Oak Tree Village.** This 14-acre children's park has miniature train rides, trout fishing, gold panning, exotic animal exhibits, and a petting zoo and several eateries. ✉ *38480 Oak Glen Rd.* ☎ *909/797–4020* ⊕ *www. oaktreevillageoakglen.net* ✉ *$5* ⊗ *Daily 10–5.*

FAMILY **Riley's Farm.** Employees dress in period costumes at Riley's Farm, one of the most interactive and kid-friendly ranches in apple country. The farm hosts school groups from September to June. Individuals can join the groups by reservation. You can hop on a hayride, take part in a barn dance, pick your own apples, press some cider, or throw a tomahawk while enjoying living-history performances throughout the orchard. The farm is also home to Colonial Chesterfield, a replica New England–style estate where costumed 18th-century reenactors offer lessons in cider pressing, candle dipping, and colonial games, and etiquette. The four-hour Revolutionary War Adventures are especially popular. Afterward, head to the Public House for a bite of colonial specialties. The warm apple pies are unforgettable. ✉ *12261 S. Oak Glen Rd.* ☎ *909/797–7534* ⊕ *www.rileysfarm.com* ✉ *Free to visit ranch, $14 for school tour, fees vary for activities* ⊗ *Mon.-Sat. 9–4.*

Rileys at Los Rios Rancho. This farm, with 50 acres of apple trees, has a fantastic country store where you can stock up on jams, cookbooks, syrups, and candied apples. Head into the bakery for a hot tri-tip sandwich before going outside to the picnic grounds for lunch. During the fall, you can pick your own apples and pumpkins, take a hayride, or enjoy live bluegrass music. On the rancho grounds, the **Wildlands Conservancy** preserves 400 acres of nature trails, open weekends from 8:30 to 4:30. From April through December, guided night walks take place on the third Saturday of the month. ✉ *39611 S. Oak Glen Rd.* ☎ *909/797–1005* ⊕ *www. losriosrancho.com* ⊗ *Oct.–Nov., daily 9–5; Dec.–Sept., Wed.–Sun. 10–5.*

WHERE TO EAT

$ ✕ **Apple Annie's Restaurant and Bakery.** You won't leave hungry from this
AMERICAN country-western diner, known for its 5-pound apple pies and family-style seven-course dinners. The decor is comfortable and rustic; old guns and handcuffs hang on the walls alongside pictures of cowboys, trail wagons, and outlaws. Standout dishes include the tuna melt and

---

BEFORE YOU GO PICKING

Be sure to call before visiting the farms, most of which are family run. Unpasteurized cider—sold at some farms—should not be consumed by children, the elderly, or those with weakened immune systems.

8

the Annie deluxe burger. $ *Average main: $12* ⊠ *38480 Oak Glen Rd.* ☎ *909/797–7311* ☉ *Daily 8–7.*

$ ✕ **Law's Oak Glen Coffee Shop.** Since 1953, this old-fashioned coffee shop

AMERICAN has been serving up hot java, hearty breakfasts and lunches, and famous apple pies. Menu stalwarts include meat loaf, country-fried steak, and Reuben sandwiches. Law's stays open until 7 pm on Fridays and weekends and closes at 3 the rest of the week. $ *Average main: $8* ⊠ *38392 Oak Glen Rd.* ☎ *909/797–1642* ☉ *No dinner Mon.–Thurs.*

SAN BERNARDINO MOUNTAINS

One of three transverse mountain ranges that lie in the Inland Empire, the San Bernardino range holds the tallest peak in Southern California, San Gorgonio Mountain, at 11,503 feet. It's frequently snowcapped in winter, providing the region's only challenging ski slopes. In summer the forested hillsides and lakes provide a cool retreat from the city for many locals.

LAKE ARROWHEAD

37 miles northeast of Riverside.

Lake Arrowhead Village is an alpine community with lodgings, shops, outlet stores, and eateries that descend a hill to the lake. Outside the village, access to the lake and its beaches is limited to area residents and their guests.

GETTING HERE AND AROUND

Access Lake Arrowhead by driving north from Interstate 10 at Redlands on Highway 210 and continuing north on Highway 330 to the town of Running Springs, where you'll turn west onto Highway 18. Also called the Rim of the World, Highway 18 straddles a mountainside ledge at elevation 5,000 feet, revealing fabulous views. At the Lake Arrowhead turnoff, you'll descend into a wooded bowl surrounding the lake. The village itself is walkable, but hilly. Scenic Highway 173 winding along the east side of the lake offers scenic blue water views through the forest. In winter, check for chain control along this route.

ESSENTIALS

Visitor Information Lake Arrowhead Chamber ⊠ *28200 Hwy. 189, Lake Arrowhead* ☎ *909/337–3715* ⊕ *lakearrowhead.net.*

EXPLORING

Lake Arrowhead Queen. One of the few ways visitors can access Lake Arrowhead is on a 50-minute *Lake Arrowhead Queen* cruise, operated daily from the Lake Arrowhead Village marina. ⊠ *28200 Hwy. 189, Building C-100* ☎ *909/336–6992* ⊕ *lakearrowheadqueen.com* 🖵 *$16.*

WHERE TO EAT AND STAY

For expanded hotel reviews, visit Fodors.com.

$ ✕ **Belgian Waffle Works.** This dockside eatery, just steps from the

CAFÉ *Lake Arrowhead Queen,* is quaint and homey, with country decor

FAMILY and beautiful lake views. All day you can dive into a mud-pie Belgian waffle with chocolate fudge sauce or try a Belgian S'more with a marshmallow-and-chocolate sauce. For lunch there are delicious burgers, tuna melts, chili, meat loaf, chicken dishes, and salads. Weekends at lunchtime can get crowded. ⑤ *Average main: $9* ✉ *28200 Hwy. 189, Suite #150* ☎ *909/337–5222* ⊕ *belgianwaffle.com* ⚲ *Reservations not accepted* ⊘ *No dinner.*

$$$$
AMERICAN
✗ **Casual Elegance.** Owner-chef Kathleen Kirk charms diners with her inventive cuisine. The specialties include rack of lamb prepared with an herb crust, crispy breast of duck, and Alaskan halibut. Dine by the fireplace for a particularly cozy experience. ⑤ *Average main: $38* ✉ *26848 Hwy. 189, Blue Jay* ☎ *909/337–8932* ⊕ *www.casualelegancerestaurant.com* ⚲ *Reservations essential* ⊘ *Closed Mon. and Tues. No lunch.*

$$$$
RESORT
Fodor's Choice
★
🏨 **Lake Arrowhead Resort and Spa.** This lakeside lodge is warm and comfy with fireplaces everywhere. **Pros:** beautiful lake views; delicious on-site dining. **Cons:** some rooms have thin walls; resort amenity fee $17 per night. ⑤ *Rooms from: $289* ✉ *27984 Hwy. 189* ☎ *909/336–1511, 800/800–6792* ⊕ *www.lakearrowheadresort.com* ⟳ *162 rooms, 11 suites* ⑩ *No meals.*

SPORTS AND THE OUTDOORS
WATERSKIING
McKenzie Waterski School. Summer ski-boat rides and waterskiing and wakeboarding lessons are available through this school in summer. ✉ *28200 Hwy. 189* ☎ *909/337–3814* ⊕ *www.mckenziewaterskischool.com.*

BIG BEAR LAKE

24 miles east of Lake Arrowhead.

When Angelenos say they're going to the mountains, they usually mean Big Bear, where Alpine-style villages surround the 7-mile-long lake. The south shore has ski slopes, the Big Bear Zoo, water-sports opportunities, restaurants, and lodgings that include the gorgeous Windy Point Inn. The more serene north shore offers easy to moderate hiking and biking trails and splendid alpine scenery.

GETTING HERE AND AROUND
Driving is the best way to get to and explore the Big Bear area. But there are alternatives. The Mountain Area Regional Transit Authority (MARTA) provides bus service to and in San Bernardino Mountain communities and connects with Metrolink, Omnitrans, and Greyhound.

ESSENTIALS
Bus Contact MARTA ☎ *909/878–5200* ⊕ *www.marta.cc.*

Visitor Information Big Bear Lake Resort Association ✉ *630 Bartlett Rd.* ☎ *909/866–7000, 800/424–4232* ⊕ *www.bigbearinfo.com.*

EXPLORING
FAMILY
Alpine Slide at Magic Mountain. Take a ride down a twisting bobsled course in winter, or beat the summer heat on a dual waterslide at Alpine Slide, which also has an 18-hole miniature golf course and go-carts. ✉ *800 Wildrose La.* ☎ *909/866–4626* ⊕ *www.alpineslidebigbear.com* 🎫 *$5 single rides, $20 5-ride pass, $25 all-day snow-play pass* ⊘ *Daily 10–4.*

8

FAMILY
Fodor's Choice
★

Big Bear Discovery Center. At this nature center you can sign up for a canoe ride through Grout Bay or a naturalist-led tour of the Baldwin Lake Ecological Reserve or the Holcomb Valley, where a small gold rush took place more than a century ago. Exhibits here explain the area's flora and fauna, and staffers provide maps and camping and hiking information. ✉ *40971 North Shore Dr. (Hwy. 38), 2½ miles east of Fawnskin, Fawnskin* 🕾 *909/382-2790* 🌐 *www.bigbeardiscoverycenter. com* ✉ *Free* ☉ *Thurs.–Mon. 8:30–4:30.*

Big Bear Marina. The paddle wheeler *Big Bear Queen* departs from the marina for 90-minute lake tours. The marina also rents fishing boats, jet skis, kayaks, and canoes. ✉ *500 Paine Ct.* 🕾 *909/866–3218* 🌐 *www. bigbearmarina.com* ✉ *$18* ☉ *Tours May–early Sept., daily noon, 2, and 4; call to confirm.*

FAMILY

Big Bear Alpine Zoo. This rescue and rehabilitation center specializes in animals native to the San Bernardino Mountains. Among its residents are black and (nonnative) grizzly bears, bald eagles, coyotes, beavers, mountain lions, grey wolves, and bobcats. An animal presentation takes place daily at noon and a feeding tour daily (except Wednesday) at 3. The facility has plans to move by late 2014, so check before visiting. ✉ *43285 Goldmine Dr.* 🕾 *909/878–4200* 🌐 *www.bigbearzoo.com* ✉ *$9* ☉ *June–early Sept., daily 10–5; early Sept.–May, weekdays 10–4, weekends 10–5.*

FAMILY

Time Bandit Pirate Ship. Featured in the 1981 movie *Time Bandits*, this small-scale replica of a 17th-century English galleon cruises Big Bear Lake daily from roughly April through October. The ship travels along the southern lakeshore to 6743-foot-high Big Bear Dam; along the way you'll pass big bayfront mansions, some owned by celebrities. A sightseeing excursion with the crew dressed up like pirates, the cruise is popular with kids and adults. There's a bar, but no dining onboard. ✉ *Holloway's Marina and RV Park, 398 Edgemoor Rd.* 🕾 *909/878–4040* 🌐 *www.bigbearboating.com/pirateship* ✉ *$19* ☉ *Confirmed tours daily at 2 in warm weather; call for additional times.*

WHERE TO EAT

$
NEPALESE
FAMILY

✕ **Himalayan Restaurant.** It's best to order family style at this no-frills storefront restaurant so that everyone gets a taste of the many Nepalese and Indian delicacies offered. Customer favorites include the spicy mo-mo (potstickers), daal (green lentils), lamb and shrimp-curry vindaloo, fish and chicken masala, and clay-oven-roasted tandoori meats and seafood. The aromatic teas and lemonades provide a perky contrast to your meal's savory flavors. ⑤ *Average main: $15* ✉ *672 Pine Knot Ave., Ste. 2* 🕾 *909/866–2907* 🌐 *www.himalayanbigbear.com* ⚑ *Reservations essential* ☉ *Closed Wed.*

$$$$
FRENCH

✕ **Madlon's Restaurant.** A triple threat that also serves breakfast (many types of waffles) and lunch (burgers and other standards), this restaurant in a cozy, gingerbread-style cottage shines brightest at dinner with sophisticated French-inspired dishes. As might be expected, escargots, rack of lamb, and dry-aged filet mignon are on the menu, along with diversions like the chicken breast served with dried cherries and a Gorgonzola-sherry sauce. Midweek prix-fixe three-course specials include wine. $ *Average main: $39* ⊠ *829 W. Big Bear Blvd., Big Bear City* ☎ *909/585–3762* ⊕ *www.madlonsrestaurant.com* ⚲ *Reservations essential* ☉ *Closed Tues.*

WHERE TO STAY

For expanded hotel reviews, visit Fodors.com.

$$$
B&B/INN
⛺ **Apples Bed & Breakfast Inn.** Despite its location on a busy road to the ski lifts, the inn feels remote and peaceful, thanks to the surrounding pines. **Pros:** large rooms; clean; free snacks and movies; delicious big breakfast. **Cons:** some traffic noise; fussy decor; sometimes feels busy. $ *Rooms from: $198* ⊠ *42430 Moonridge Rd.* ☎ *909/866–0903* ⊕ *www.applesbigbear.com* ➳ *19 rooms* ⏹ *Some meals.*

$$
B&B/INN
Fodor's Choice
★
⛺ **Gold Mountain Manor.** Each room at this restored 1928 log mansion has its own theme based on a rich Hollywood history: the Clark Gable room, for example, contains the Franklin stove that once warmed the honeymoon suite Gable and actress Carole Lombard shared. **Pros:** gracious hosts; snowshoes and kayaks available; congenial ambiance. **Cons:** somewhat thin walls; 10-minute drive to the village; many stairs; narrow corridors. $ *Rooms from: $149* ⊠ *1117 Anita Ave., Big Bear City* ☎ *909/585–6997, 800/509–2604* ⊕ *www.goldmountainmanor. com* ➳ *4 rooms, 3 suites* ⏹ *Multiple meal plans.*

$
HOTEL
⛺ **Northwoods Resort.** A giant log cabin with the amenities of a resort, Northwoods has a lobby that resembles a 1930s hunting lodge: canoes, antlers, and fishing poles decorate the walls, and there's a grand stone fireplace. **Pros:** pool heated in winter; ski packages available; beautiful grounds. **Cons:** parts of hotel showing their age; noise at night in some rooms; rate increases when it snows. $ *Rooms from: $102* ⊠ *40650 Village Dr.* ☎ *909/866–3121, 800/866–3121* ⊕ *www.northwoodsresort. com* ➳ *140 rooms, 7 suites* ⏹ *No meals.*

$$
B&B/INN
⛺ **Windy Point Inn.** Surrounded on three sides by water, Windy Point offers the best views and the most luxurious accommodations in the Big Bear area. **Pros:** secure parking; gracious hosts; privacy; views. **Cons:** remote from lake activities; windy at times. $ *Rooms from: $155* ⊠ *31094 North Shore Dr., Fawnskin* ☎ *909/866–2746* ⊕ *windypointinn.com* ➳ *5 rooms* ⏹ *Breakfast.*

SPORTS AND THE OUTDOORS

BOATS AND CHARTERS

Pine Knot Landing Marina. This full-service marina rents fishing boats, pontoon boats, and kayaks and sells bait, ice, and snacks. On weekends, the paddle wheeler *Miss Liberty* leaves from the landing for a 90-minute tour ($20; times vary) of Big Bear Lake from late April through September. Refreshments are available on board. ⊠ *439 Pine Knot Blvd.* ☎ *909/866–8129* ⊕ *pineknotmarina.com.*

HORSEBACK RIDING

Baldwin Lake Stables. Explore the forested mountain on horseback on a group or private guided trail ride (one hour to a half day) arranged by this outfit. Reservations are required for private rides and suggested for all. ⊠ *46475 Pioneertown Rd., Fawnskin* ☎ *909/585–6482* ⊕ *www. baldwinlakestables.com* ▤ *$40 and up per person per hr.*

8

SKIING

Big Bear Mountain Resorts. Two distinct resorts, Bear Mountain and Snow Summit, comprise Southern California's largest winter playground, one of the few that challenge skilled skiers. The complex offers 438 skiable acres, 55 runs, and 26 chairlifts, including four high-speed quads. The vibe is youthful at Bear, which has beginner slopes (training available) and the after-ski hangout The Scene. Snow Summit holds challenging runs and is open for night skiing. On weekends and holidays, it's best to reserve tickets for either mountain. Bear rents skis and boards.

The resorts are open in summer for mountain biking, hiking, golfing, and some special events. The Snow Summit Scenic Sky Chair zips to the mountain's 8,200-foot peak, where View Haus ($), a casual outdoor restaurant, has breathtaking views of the lake and San Gorgonio Mountain. ⊠ *Big Bear, 880 Summit Blvd., off Moonridge Rd.* ☏ *909/866–5766* ⊕ *www.bigbearmountainresorts.com* ⊠ *$59–$72.*

THE SOUTHERN INLAND EMPIRE

The southern end of the Inland Empire is devoted to the good life. Mile-high Idyllwild atop Mt. San Jacinto holds a renowned arts academy, charming restaurants, and galleries. It's also a good place to hike, mountain climb, and test high-altitude biking skills. Temecula, lying at the base of the mountain, is a popular wine region where you'll find vineyards, tasting rooms, fine dining, and cozy lodgings.

IDYLLWILD

44 miles east of Riverside.

Set in a valley halfway up Mt. San Jacinto, Idyllwild has been a serene forested getaway for San Diegans and Angelenos for nearly a century. The town's simple, quiet lifestyle attracts artists and performers as well as outdoor types who enjoy hiking, biking, and serious rock climbing.

GETTING HERE AND AROUND

Two routes from the interstates lead to Idyllwild; both are slow and winding but provide memorable mountain views. From Interstate 10 in Banning, take scenic Highway 243 south to Idyllwild. From Interstate 15 near Lake Elsinore, drive east on Highway 74 to Highway 243 and turn north. Once in Idyllwild, you can walk nearly everywhere in the village, though you'll need to drive to trailheads, fishing holes, and rock-climbing locations.

ESSENTIALS

Visitor Information Idyllwild Chamber of Commerce ⊠ *54325 N. Circle Dr., Box 304* ☏ *951/659–3259, 888/659–3259* ⊕ *www.idyllwildchamber.com.*

EXPLORING

FAMILY **Idyllwild Nature Center.** At the center, you can learn about the area's Native American history, try your hand at astronomy, and listen to traditional storytellers. Outside are 3 miles of hiking trails, plus biking and equestrian trails and picnic areas. The park is pet-friendly. ⊠ *25225 Hwy. 243* ☎ *951/659–3850* ⊕ *www.rivcoparks.org/parks* ⊠ *$3* ⊘ *Tues.–Sun. 9–4:30* ⊘ *Closed Mon.*

WHERE TO EAT

$$$$ ✕ **Restaurant Gastrognome.** Elegant and dimly lighted, with wood paneling,
FRENCH lace curtains, and an oft-glowing fireplace, "The Gnome" is where locals go for a romantic dinner. The overall feel is French, but the menu goes beyond the Gallic, with entrées such as calamari almandine, sausage pasta, and lobster tacos. The French onion soup always satisfies, and the roast duck with orange sauce and the Southwest-style grilled pork are excellent entrées. The crème brûlée makes for a sweet finale. For lighter dinner fare, check out the bar menu. ⑤ *Average main: $39* ⊠ *54381 Ridgeview Dr.* ☎ *951/659–5055* ⊕ *www.gastrognome.com* ⚐ *Reservations essential.*

THE ARTS

Idyllwild Arts Academy. The Idyllwild Arts Academy is a summer camp offering more than 60 workshops in dance, music, Native American arts, theater, visual arts, and writing. There are free summer concerts and theater productions featuring students and professional performers. ⊠ *52500 Temecula Rd.* ☎ *951/659–2171* ⊕ *www.idyllwildarts.org.*

SPORTS AND THE OUTDOORS

FISHING

Lake Fulmor. The lake is stocked with rainbow trout, largemouth bass, catfish, and bluegill. To fish, you'll need a California fishing license and a National Forest Adventure Pass ($5 per vehicle per day). ⊠ *Hwy. 243, 10 miles north of Idyllwild* ☎ *951/659–2117* ⊕ *www.fs.usda.gov/sbnf.*

HIKING

Humber Park Trailhead. Two great hikes begin at this site, the 2.5-mile Devils Slide Trail and the 2.6-mile Ernie Maxwell Scenic Trail. Permits ($5) are needed for both. ⊠ *At top of Fern Valley Rd.* ☎ *951/659–2117* ⊕ *www.fs.usda.gov/recarea/sbnf/recarea/?recid=26483.*

Pacific Crest Trail. Access the trail at Highway 74, 1 mile east of Highway 371; or via the Fuller Ridge Trail at Black Mountain Road, 15 miles north of Idyllwild. Permits ($5 per day), required for camping and day hikes in the San Jacinto Wilderness, are available online or at the Idyllwild Ranger Station (⊠ *Pine Crest Ave., off Hwy. 243* ☎ *951/659–2117*). ⊕ *www.fs.usda.gov/sbnf.*

8

TEMECULA

43 miles south of Riverside, 60 miles north of San Diego, 90 miles southeast of Los Angeles.

Fodor's Choice Temecula, with its rolling green vineyards, country inns, and first-rate
★ restaurants, bills itself as "Southern California Wine Country." The region is home to more than three-dozen wineries, several of which offer spas, fine dining, or luxury lodging and shopping. The name Temecula comes from a Luiseño Indian word meaning "where the sun shines through the mist"—ideal conditions for growing wine grapes. Intense afternoon sun and cool nighttime temperatures, complemented by ocean breezes that flow through the Rainbow and Santa Margarita

DID YOU KNOW?

Many water sport options—including waterskiing, jet skiing, fishing, and boating—are available at Big Bear Lake.

gaps in the coastal range, help grapevines flourish in the area's granite soil. Best known for Chardonnay, Temecula Valley winemakers are moving in new directions, producing Viognier, Syrah, and other Rhône-style blended reds and whites. Most wineries charge a small fee ($10 to $15) for a tasting that includes several wines.

The oldest wineries are strung out along Rancho California Road, east of Interstate 15; a few newer ones lie along the eastern portion of De Portola Road. On its website the Temecula Valley Winegrowers Association offers suggestions for self-guided winery tours and has coupons good for tasting discounts.

GETTING HERE AND AROUND

Interstate 15 cuts right through Temecula. The wineries lie on the east side of the freeway along Rancho California Road. Old Town Temecula lies west of the freeway along Front Street.

TOURS

Destination Temecula runs full-day winery tours, with pickups in Old Town Temecula (starting at $89 round-trip) and at San Diego hotels ($97). Tours include stops at three wineries, a picnic lunch, and time to explore Old Town. The Grapeline Wine Country Shuttle also has pickups in Temecula and at San Diego hotels. Its Vineyard Picnic Tour ($98, $118 on Saturday) includes transportation, a winemaking demonstration, tastings at four wineries, and a gourmet picnic lunch.

ESSENTIALS

Tour Contacts Destination Temecula ☎ 951/695–1232 ⊕ www.destem.com. **Grapeline Wine Country Shuttle** ☎ 951/693–5755, 888/894–6379 ⊕ www.gogrape.com.

Visitor Information Temecula Valley Convention and Visitors Bureau ✉ 28690 Mercedes St. ☎ 951/491–6085, 888/363–2852 ⊕ www.temeculacvb. com. **Temecula Valley Winegrowers Association** ☎ 951/699–3626 ⊕ www.temeculawines.org.

EXPLORING

TOP ATTRACTIONS

Fodor's Choice ★ **Hart Family Winery.** A perennial crowd-pleaser, this winery specializes in well-crafted red wines made by father-son winemakers Joe and Jim Hart. Joe, who started the winery in the 1970s with his wife, Nancy, focuses on growing grapes suited to the Temecula region's singular climate and soils—Zinfandel, Cabernet Sauvignon, and Sangiovese as might be expected, but also little known varietals such as Aleatico, used in the winery's marvelous dessert wine. The reds are the stars, though, along with the amiable Hart family members themselves. ✉ *41300 Avenida Biona* ☎ *951/676–6300* ⊕ *www.hartfamilywinery.com* 🍷 *Tasting $10 (includes logo glass)* ☉ *Daily 9–4:30.*

Old Town Temecula. Temecula is more than just vineyards and tasting rooms. For a bit of old-fashioned fun, head to Old Town Temecula, a turn-of-the-20th-century-style cluster of storefronts and boardwalks that holds more than 640 antiques stores, boutiques, a performing-arts center and jazz club, and art galleries. ✉ *Front St., between Rancho California Rd. and Hwy. 79* ☎ *888/363–2852* ⊕ *www.temeculacvb.com.*

FAMILY   **Pennypickle's Workshop—Temecula Children's Museum.** If you have the kids along, check out the fictional 7,500-square-foot workshop of Professor Phineas T. Pennypickle, PhD. This elaborately decorated children's museum is filled with secret passageways, machines, wacky contraptions, and time-travel inventions. ⊠ *42081 Main St.* ☎ *951/308-6370* ⊕ *www.pennypickles.org* ▨ *$5* ⊘ *Tues.–Sat. 10–5, Sun. 12:30–5.*

Ponte Family Estates. Lush gardens and more than 300 acres of vineyards provide a rustic, elegant setting at Ponte, whose small-lot wines range from sparklers and light whites to potent Super Tuscan–style offerings. In the airy, light-filled tasting room you can sample the aptly named Super T, a blend of Cabernet Sauvignon and Sangiovese grapes, and other vintages crafted by winemaker Mark Schabel; ceramics, specialty foods, and gift baskets are for sale at the adjacent marketplace. The shaded, outdoor Restaurant at Ponte serves salads, sandwiches, wood-fired pizzas, and seafood daily for lunch and on weekends for dinner. ⊠ *35053 Rancho California Rd.* ☎ *951/694-8855* ⊕ *www.pontewinery. com* ▨ *Tasting $12 weekdays, $20 weekends* ⊘ *Winery daily 10–5; restaurant Mon.–Thurs. 11–3, Fri. and Sat. 11–8, Sun. 11–5.*

Thornton Winery. In a French Mediterranean–style stone building, you can taste winemaker David Vergari's Blanc de Noirs or Cuvée Rouge sparkling wines at a table in the lounge, or over lunch or dinner at Café Champagne. The Syrah and Cabernet Franc stand out among the reds here. On weekends, take a free 20-minute tour of the grounds and the wine cave. The winemaker dinners ($80) and the summer Champagne Jazz Series concerts ($55–$95), featuring performers such as George Benson and David Benoit, make this a fun place to spend an afternoon or evening. ⊠ *32575 Rancho California Rd.* ☎ *951/699-0099* ⊕ *www. thorntonwine.com* ▨ *Tastings $12–$17* ⊘ *Daily 10–8; tours Sat. 11–4 on the hr, Sun. 11, 12:30, 2, and 4.*

WORTH NOTING
Callaway Vineyard and Winery. One of the oldest wineries in Temecula is centered on a stunning steel-and-glass cube with vineyard views all around. You can draw your own wine from tap stations placed around the room. Callaway made its reputation with Chardonnay but has moved on to Italian-style varietals such as Sangiovese, Nebbiolo, and Dolcetto. The Meritage Restaurant, open for lunch daily and dinner on weekends, specializes in tapas, salads, and sandwiches. ⊠ *32720 Rancho California Rd.* ☎ *951/676-4001* ⊕ *www.callawaywinery.com* ▨ *Tasting $10; tour free with tasting or $5* ⊘ *Daily 10–5; tour weekdays at 11, 1, and 3, on the hr Sat. 11–1 and Sun. 11–2.*

Europa Village. Though all of this luxury wine resort's dining, lodging, winery, and other components won't be completed for a few years, a pleasant tasting room here serves wines made from French, Spanish, and Italian varietals. The selections range from light whites like Sauvignon Blanc and Albariño to heavy reds like a complex Syrah and a powerful Primitivo. Winemaker dinners take place in the village, which also presents live music on some weekend nights. ⊠ *33475 La Serena Way* ☎ *951/216-3380* ⊕ *www.europavillage.com* ▨ *Tasting $15* ⊘ *Daily 10–5.*

Leoness Cellars. Rhone- and Tuscan-style blends—along with killer views—are the specialties of this mountaintop facility. Winemaker Tim Kramer and his staff produce about a dozen and a half wines each year, of which you can select six. If you like reds, be sure to try the Syrahs, which are almost always winners. Winery tours take in the vineyards and the wine-making areas. The tours require a reservation, as do wine-and-food pairing sessions that might include fruits and cheeses or, in the case of dessert wines, some chocolates. ⊠ *38311 DePortola Rd.* ☎ *951/302–7601* ⊕ *www.leonesscellars.com* ⊡ *Tasting $14, tours $16–$85* ⊙ *Daily 11–5.*

Miramonte Winery. At Temecula's hippest winery, perched on a hilltop, listen to Spanish-guitar recordings while sampling the Opulente Meritage, a supple Sauvignon Blanc, or the sultry Syrah. Owner Cane Vanderhoof's wines have earned dozens of awards. While you're enjoying your wine on the deck, order an artisan cheese plate. On Friday and Saturday nights from 7 to 10, the winery turns into a local hot spot with tastings of signature wines ($6–$10) and beer, live music, and dancing that spills out into the vineyards. ⊠ *33410 Rancho California Rd.* ☎ *951/506–5500* ⊕ *www. miramontewinery.com* ⊡ *Tastings $12–15, tours $20–$25 (reservations required)* ⊙ *Sun.–Thurs. 11–6, Fri. and Sat. 11–10.*

Mount Palomar Winery. One of the original Temecula Valley wineries, opened in 1969, Mount Palomar introduced Sangiovese grapes, a varietal that has proven perfectly suited to the region's soil and climate. New owners have transformed the homey winery into a grand Mediterranean villa with acres of gardens and trees. Some of the wines are made from grapes brought from Italy nearly 50 years ago. Try the dry Sangiovese or Bordeaux-style Meritage. Shorty's Bistro, open for lunch daily and for dinner on Fridays and weekends, presents live entertainment on Friday nights. ⊠ *33820 Rancho California Rd.* ☎ *951/676–5047* ⊕ *www.mountpalomar.com* ⊡ *Winery free, tasting $12 Mon.–Thurs., $15 Fri.– Sun.* ⊙ *Mon.–Thurs. 10:30–5, Fri.–Sun. 10:30–6.*

Wiens Family Cellars. Up-and-coming Wiens promotes its "Big Reds"— among them the Reserve Primitivo and an intriguing Tempranillo–Petite Sirah blend—but many visitors often wind up taking home a bottle of the perky-fruity Amour De L'Orange sparkling wine. Other wines of note include the Ruby Port and the Dulce Maria, made from Chardonnay and Muscat Canelli grapes. The ambience at Wiens is informal, but the cordial tasting-room staffers are well informed about the wines they enthusiastically pour. ⊠ *35055 Via Del Ponte* ☎ *951/694–9892* ⊕ *www. wienscellars.com* ⊡ *Tasting $15* ⊙ *Daily 10–5.*

Wilson Creek Winery & Vineyards. One of Temecula's busiest tasting rooms sits amid inviting, parklike grounds. Wilson is known for its Almond Champagne, but the winery also produces appealing still wines. The Viognier, Reserve Syrah, Reserve Zinfandel, and late-harvest Zinfandel all merit a taste. The on-site Creekside Grill Restaurant serves sandwiches, salads, and entrées such as Mexican white sea bass and gluten-free vegetable potpie. Dine inside or select a picnic spot and the servers will deliver your meal to you. ⊠ *35960 Rancho California Rd.* ☎ *951/699–9463* ⊕ *www.wilsoncreekwinery.com* ⊡ *Tasting $12 weekdays, $15 weekends* ⊙ *Daily 10–5, restaurant daily 11–5.*

8

WHERE TO EAT AND STAY

For expanded hotel reviews, visit Fodors.com.

$$$ ✗ **Baily's Fine Dining and Front Street Bar & Grill.** Locals swoon over the
AMERICAN cuisine served upstairs (dinner only) at Baily's Fine Dining. The menu
varies according to the chef's creative whims and might include chicken
schnitzel drizzled with lemon-caper-wine sauce or salmon Wellington.
Temecula Valley wines are well represented on the extensive list here.
Downstairs at Front Street the fare is more casual—fish prepared sev-
eral ways, burgers, pastas, soups, and salads. ⑤ *Average main: $26*
⊠ *28699 Old Town Front St.* ☎ *951/676–9567* ⊕ *www.oldtowndining.
com* ⌕ *Reservations essential.*

$$$ ✗ **Café Champagne.** The spacious patio, with its bubbling fountain, flow-
ECLECTIC ering trellises, and vineyard views, is the perfect place to lunch on a
sunny day. Inside, the dining room is decked out in French country style,
and the open kitchen turns out such dishes as braised beef short ribs and
cioppino. The reasonably priced wines served here include the signature
Thornton Winery sparklers. ⑤ *Average main: $29* ⊠ *Thornton Winery,
32575 Rancho California Rd.* ☎ *951/699–0088* ⊕ *www.thorntonwine.
com* ⌕ *Reservations essential.*

$$$ ⊞ **Ponte Vineyard Inn.** Slow down in old Californio Rancho style at this
HOTEL delightful hotel that opened in 2012 on the grounds of the Ponte Family
Estate winery. **Pros:** huge rooms; lounges everywhere; excellent winery
on-site; gracious service. **Cons:** weddings; very, very quiet. ⑤ *Rooms
from: $199* ⊠ *35001 Rancho California Rd.* ☎ *951/587–6688* ⊕ *www.
pontevineyardinn.com* ⟿ *60 rooms* ⦶ *No meals.*

$$ ⊞ **Temecula Creek Inn.** Each room at this inn has a private patio or
RESORT balcony overlooking the championship golf course and is decorated
in soothing earth tones with a Southwestern theme. **Pros:** beautiful
grounds; top golf course; spacious; great views. **Cons:** simple furnishings; shows its age; location away from Old Town and wineries.
⑤ *Rooms from: $126* ⊠ *44501 Rainbow Canyon Rd.* ☎ *951/694–1000,
877/517–1823* ⊕ *www.temeculacreekinn.com* ⟿ *130 rooms, 1 guest-
house* ⦶ *No meals.*

NIGHTLIFE

Pechanga Resort and Casino. Casino gambling is the main attraction here,
and there are several entertainment venues. Headliners such as Paul
Anka, B.B. King, and Jerry Seinfeld have appeared at the Showroom
Theater, while the intimate Comedy Club books up-and-coming talent.
HBO and Fox Sports championship boxing matches draw thousands
of fans. ⊠ *45000 Pechanga Pkwy.* ☎ *877/711–2946, 951/770–1819*
⊕ *www.pechanga.com.*

SHOPPING

Rancho Fruit Market. This cheerful little shop sells Valencia oranges, avo-
cadoes, grapefruit, and other locally sourced produce. Much of it is
organic, and the prices are reasonable. ⊠ *28670 Old Town Front St.*
☎ *951/676–5519* ⊙ *Daily 9–6.*

Temecula Lavender Co. Owner Jan Schneider offers an inspiring collection of the herb that fosters peace, purification, sleep, and longevity. Bath salts, hand soaps, essential oil—she's got it all, even

There's no more relaxing way to enjoy Temecula's Wine Country than by taking a peaceful hot-air balloon ride over the vineyards.

dryer bags to freshen up the laundry. ✉ *28561 Old Town Front St.* ☎ *951/676–1931* ⊕ *www.temeculalavenderco.com* ☉ *Mon.–Thurs. 11–5, Fri.–Sat. 10–6.*

Temecula Olive Oil Company. While you're shopping in Old Town, stop by the cool tasting room here for a sample of extra-virgin olive oils, bath products, and Mission, Ascalano, and Italian olives. ✉ *28653 Old Town Front St., Suite H* ☎ *951/693–0607* ⊕ *www.temeculaoliveoil.com* ☉ *Sun.–Thurs. 9:30–6, Fri.–Sat. 9:30–7.*

SPORTS AND THE OUTDOORS
GOLF
Temecula has several championship golf courses cooled by the valley's ocean breezes.

Redhawk Golf Club. Ron Fream designed the public club's championship golf course. ✉ *45100 Redhawk Pkwy.* ☎ *951/302–3850* ⊕ *www. redhawkgolfcourse.com* ⛳ *18 holes. 7,110 yds. Par 72. Greens fees: $70/$90* ⚑ *Driving range, putting green, pitching area, golf carts, lessons, restaurant, bar.*

Temeku Golf Club. The tiered greens, five lakes, and many blind spots make for challenging rounds at this club's Ted Robinson-designed championship course. ✉ *41687 Temeku Dr.* ☎ *951/694–9998* ⊕ *www. temekuhillsgolfcourse.com* ⛳ *18 holes. 6,636 yds. Par 72. Greens fees: $25/65* ⚑ *Driving range, putting green, pitching area, golf carts, rental clubs, restaurant, bar.*

HOT-AIR BALLOONING

California Dreamin'. Float serenely above Temecula's vineyards and country estates on an early-morning balloon adventure. The ride includes champagne, coffee, a pastry breakfast, and a souvenir photo. ⊠ *Flights depart from La Vindemia Vineyard, 33133 Vista Del Monte Rd.* ☎ *800/373–3359* ⊕ *www.californiadreamin.com* ✉ *$140–$178.*

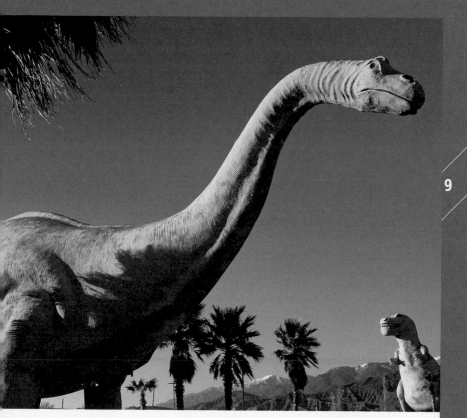

PALM SPRINGS

and the Desert Resorts

WELCOME TO PALM SPRINGS

TOP REASONS TO GO

★ **Fun in the sun:**
The Palm Springs area has 350 days of sun each year, and the weather's usually perfect for playing one of the area's more than 100 golf courses.

★ **Spa under the stars:**
Many resorts and small hotels now offer after-dark spa services, including outdoor soaks and treatments you can savor while sipping wine under the clear, starry sky.

★ **Personal pampering:**
The resorts here have it all: beautifully appointed rooms packed with amenities, professional staffs, sublime spas, and delicious dining options.

★ **Divine desert scenery:**
You'll probably spend a lot of time taking in the gorgeous 360-degree natural panorama, a flat desert floor surrounded by 10,000-foot mountains rising into a brilliant blue sky.

★ **The Hollywood connection:** The Palm Springs area has more celebrity ties than any other resort community. So keep your eyes open for your favorite star.

1 The Desert Resorts.
Around the desert resorts, privacy is the watchword. Celebrities flock to the desert from Los Angeles, and many communities are walled and guarded. Still, you might spot Hollywood stars, sports personalities, politicians, and other high-profile types in restaurants, out on the town, at the weekly Villagefest, or on a golf course. For the most part, the desert's social, sports, shopping, and entertainment scenes center on Palm Springs, Palm Desert, and La Quinta.

2 Along Twentynine Palms Highway. The towns of Yucca Valley, Joshua Tree, and Twentynine Palms punctuate Twentynine Palms Highway (Highway 62)—the northern highway from the desert resorts to Joshua Tree National Park (⇨ see Chapter 10)—and provide visitor information, lodging, and other services to park visitors.

3 Anza-Borrego Desert.
If you're looking for a break from the action, you'll find sublime solitude in this 600,000-acre desert landscape.

4 Joshua Tree National Park. This is desert scenery at its best and most abundant. Tiptoe through fields of wildflowers in spring, scramble on and around giant boulders, and check out the park's bizarre namesake trees (⇨ see Chapter 10).

29 Palms Hwy.

Joshua Tree

Twentynine Palms

Oasis Visitor Center

HILLS

GOLDFIELD MOUNTAINS

Pinto Basin Rd.

Joshua Tree National Park

PINTO BASIN

MOUNTAINS
HILLS

COACHELLA VALLEY

Cottonwood Visitor Center

Indio

Coachella

La Quinta

Thermal

Mecca

Salton Sea State Recreation Area

Salton Sea

Sonny Bono Wildlife Refuge

Split Mountain

Anza-Borrego Desert State Park

0   10 mi
0   10 km

TO SAN DIEGO

El Centro

GETTING ORIENTED

The Palm Springs resort area lies within the Colorado Desert, on the western edge of the Coachella Valley. The area holds seven cities that are strung out along Highway 111, with Palm Springs at the northwestern end of this strip and Indio at the southeastern end. North of Palm Springs, between Interstate 10 and Highway 62, is Desert Hot Springs. Northeast of Palm Springs, the towns of the Morongo Valley lie along Twentynine Palms Highway (Highway 62), which leads to Joshua Tree National Park (⇨ see Chapter 10). Head south on Highway 86 from Indio to reach Anza-Borrego State Park and the Salton Sea. All of the area's attractions are easy day trips from Palm Springs.

9

Updated by
Bobbi Zane

Many millions of years ago, the Southern Desert was the bottom of a vast sea. By 10 million years ago, the waters had receded and the climate was hospitable to prehistoric mastodons, zebras, and camels. The first human inhabitants of record were the Agua Caliente, part of the Cahuilla people, who settled in and around the Coachella Valley about 1,000 years ago.

Lake Cahuilla dried up about 300 years ago, but by then the Agua Caliente had discovered the area's hot springs and were making use of their healing properties during winter visits to the desert. The springs became a tourist attraction in 1871, when the tribe built a bathhouse (on a site near the current Spa Resort Casino in Palm Springs) to serve passengers on a pioneer stage highway. The Agua Caliente still own about 32,000 acres of desert, 6,700 of which lie within the city limits of Palm Springs.

In the last half of the 19th century, farmers established a date-growing industry at the southern end of the Coachella Valley. By 1900 word had spread about the health benefits of the area's dry climate, inspiring the gentry of the northern United States to winter under the warm desert sun. Growth hit the Coachella Valley in the 1970s, when developers began to construct the fabulous golf courses, country clubs, and residential communities that would draw celebrities, tycoons, and politicians. Communities sprang up south and east of what is now Palm Springs, creating a sprawl of tract houses and strip malls and forcing nature lovers to push farther south into the sparsely settled Anza-Borrego Desert.

PLANNING

WHEN TO GO

Desert weather is best between January and April, the height of the visitor season. The fall months are nearly as lovely, but less crowded and less expensive (although autumn draws a lot of conventions and business travelers). In summer, an increasingly popular time for European visitors, daytime temperatures may rise above 110°F (though evenings cool to the mid-70s); some attractions and restaurants close or reduce their hours during this time.

GETTING HERE AND AROUND

AIR TRAVEL

Palm Springs International Airport serves California's desert communities. Alaska, Allegiant, American, Delta, Frontier, Sun Country, United, Virgin America, and WestJet all fly to Palm Springs, some only seasonally. Yellow Cab of the Desert serves the airport, which is about 3 miles from downtown. The fare is $2.80 to enter the cab and about $3.12 per mile.

Airport Information Palm Springs International Airport ⊠ *3200 E. Tahquitz Canyon Way, Palm Springs* ☎ *760/323–8299* ⊕ *www.palmspringsairport.com.*

Airport Transfers Yellow Cab of the Desert ⊠ *75150 St. Charles Place, Palm Desert* ☎ *760/340–8294* ⊕ *www.yellowcabofthedesert.com.*

BUS TRAVEL

Greyhound provides service to Palm Springs from many cities. SunBus, operated by the SunLine Transit Agency, serves the entire Coachella Valley, from Desert Hot Springs to Mecca.

Bus Contacts Greyhound ⊠ *3700 Vista Chino Rd., Suite D, Palm Desert* ☎ *800/231–2222* ⊕ *www.greyhound.com.* **SunLine Transit Agency** ⊠ *32-505 Harry Oliver Tr., Thousand Palms* ☎ *800/347–8628* ⊕ *www.sunline.org.*

CAR TRAVEL

The desert resort communities occupy a 20-mile stretch between Interstate 10, to the east, and Palm Canyon Drive (Highway 111), to the west. The region is about a two-hour drive east of the Los Angeles area and a three-hour drive northeast of San Diego. It can take twice as long to make the trip from Los Angeles to the desert on winter and spring weekends because of heavy traffic. From Los Angeles take the San Bernardino Freeway (Interstate 10) east to Highway 111. From San Diego, Interstate 15 heading north connects with the Pomona Freeway (Highway 60), leading to the San Bernardino Freeway east.

To reach Borrego Springs from Los Angeles, take Interstate 10 east past the desert resorts area to Highway 86 south to the Borrego Salton Seaway (Highway S22) west. You can reach the Borrego area from San Diego via Interstate 8 to Highway 79 through Cuyamaca State Park. This will take you to Highway 78 in Julian, which you follow east to Yaqui Pass Road (S3) into Borrego Springs.

TAXI TRAVEL

Yellow Cab of the Desert serves the entire Coachella Valley. The fare is $2.80 to enter a cab and about $3 per mile.

TRAIN TRAVEL

The Amtrak Sunset Limited, which runs between Florida and Los Angeles, stops in Palm Springs.

Train Contact Amtrak ☎ *800/872-7245* ⊕ *www.amtrakcalifornia.com.*

HEALTH AND SAFETY

Never travel alone in the desert. Let someone know your trip route, destination, and estimated time and date of return. Before setting out, make sure your vehicle is in good condition. Carry a jack, tools, towrope or chain, and a cell phone, even though service can be spotty. Fill up your tank whenever you see a gas pump. Stay on main roads, and watch out for horses and range cattle.

Drink at least a gallon of water a day (three gallons if you're hiking or otherwise exerting yourself). Dress in layered clothing and wear comfortable, sturdy shoes and a hat. Keep snacks, sunscreen, and a first-aid kit on hand. If you suddenly have a headache or feel dizzy or nauseous, you could be suffering from dehydration. Get out of the sun immediately and drink plenty of water. Dampen your clothing to lower your body temperature.

Do not enter mine tunnels or shafts. Avoid canyons during rainstorms. Never place your hands or feet where you can't see them: Rattlesnakes, scorpions, and black widow spiders may be hiding there.

Emergency Services Borrego Medical Center ⊠ *4343 Yaqui Pass Rd., Borrego Springs* ☎ *760/767-5051* ⊕ *www.borregomedical.org.* **Desert Regional Medical Center** ⊠ *1150 N. Indian Canyon Dr., Palm Springs* ☎ *760/323-6511* ⊕ *www.desertmedctr.com.*

TOUR OPTIONS

Desert Adventures conducts two- to four-hour red jeep tours ($25 to $200) on private land along the canyons and palm oases, and inside the San Andreas earthquake fault. Other public tours include Painted Canyon/Mecca Hills and Joshua Tree National Park (⇨ *see Chapter 15*). Groups are small and guides are knowledgeable. Departures are from Palm Springs and La Quinta; hotel pickups are available.

Elite Land Tours offers two- to five-hour luxurious treks via Hummer and helicopter led by knowledgeable guides who take you to the San Andreas Fault, Joshua Tree, the Salton Sea, and other locations. Tours include hotel pickup, lunch, snacks, and beverages.

The city of Palm Desert offers four self-guided tours of its 150-piece Art in Public Places collection. Each tour is walkable or drivable. Maps are available at the Palm Desert Visitor Center and online (⊕ *www.palm-desert. org/arts-culture/public-art*). You can also take guided tours on the second Saturday of the month or by appointment for groups of four or more.

Tour Contacts Desert Adventures ⊠ *74-794 Lennon Pl., Suite B, Palm Desert* ☎ *760/324-5337* ⊕ *www.red-jeep.com.* **Elite Land Tours** ⊠ *540 S. Vella Rd., Palm Springs* ☎ *760/318-1200* ⊕ *www.elitelandtours.com.* **Palm Desert Visitor Center** ⊠ *73-470 El Paseo, Suite 7-F, Palm Desert* ☎ *760/568-1441* ⊕ *www.palm-desert.org.* **Palm Springs Hiking Guides** ⊠ *Palm Springs* ☎ *760/413-1575* ⊕ *www.palmspringshiking.com.* **Palm Springs Tours** ⊠ *Palm Springs* ☎ *800/409-3174* ⊕ *www.palmspringstours.net.*

The green revolution is proudly on display in many parts of the Palm Springs area.

RESTAURANTS

During the season, restaurants can be busy, as many locals and visitors dine out every night, and some for every meal. An influx of talented young chefs has expanded the dining possibilities of a formerly staid scene. The meat-and-potatoes crowd still has plenty of options, but you'll also find fresh seafood superbly prepared and contemporary Californian, Asian, Indian, and vegetarian cuisine; Mexican food abounds. Most restaurants have early-evening happy hours, with discounted drinks and small-plate menus. Restaurants that remain open in July and August frequently discount deeply; others close in July and August or offer limited service. *Prices in the reviews are the average cost of a main course at dinner or, if dinner is not served, at lunch.*

HOTELS

In general you can find the widest choice of lodgings in Palm Springs, ranging from tiny B&Bs and chain motels to business and resort hotels. All-inclusive resorts dominate in down-valley communities, such as Palm Desert and Rancho Mirage. You can stay in the desert for as little as $80 or spend more than $1,000 a night. Rates vary widely by season and expected occupancy—a $200 room midweek can jump in price to $450 by Saturday.

Hotel/resort prices are frequently 50% less in summer and fall than in winter and early spring. From January through May prices soar, and lodgings book up far in advance. You should book well ahead for stays during events such as Modernism Week or the Coachella and Stagecoach music festivals.

Most resort hotels charge a resort fee of up to $35 (charged daily) that is not included in the room rate; be sure to ask about extra fees when you book. Many hotels are pet friendly and offer special services. Small boutique hotels and bed-and-breakfasts have historic character and offer good value; discounts are sometimes given for extended stays. Casino hotels can also offer good deals on lodging; check their ads before you book. Take care when considering budget lodgings; other than reliable chains, they may not be up to par. *Prices in the reviews are the lowest cost of a standard double room in high season. For expanded hotel reviews, visit Fodors.com.Prices do not include taxes (as high as 14%, depending on the city).*

NIGHTLIFE

Desert nightlife is concentrated and abundant in Palm Springs, where there are many straight and gay bars and clubs. The Fabulous Palm Springs Follies—a vaudeville-style revue starring retired professional performers—is a must-see. Arts festivals occur on a regular basis, especially in winter and spring. *Palm Springs Life* magazine (⊕ *www. palmspringslife.com*), available at hotels and visitor centers, has nightlife listings, as does the *Desert Sun* newspaper (⊕ *www.mydesert.com*). The *Gay Guide to Palm Springs* (⊕ *palmspringsgayinfo.com*) covers the lesbian and gay scenes.

THE DESERT RESORTS

The term *desert resorts* refers to the communities along or just off Highway 111—Palm Springs, Cathedral City, Rancho Mirage, Palm Desert, Indian Wells, Indio, and La Quinta—along with Desert Hot Springs, which is north of Palm Springs off Highway 62 and Interstate 10.

PALM SPRINGS

90 miles southeast of Los Angeles on I-10.

A tourist destination since the late 19th century, Palm Springs evolved into an ideal hideaway for early Hollywood celebrities. They could slip into town, play some tennis, lounge around the pool, attend a party or two, and, unless things got out of hand, remain beyond the reach of gossip columnists. But the place really blossomed in the 1930s after actors Charlie Farrell and Ralph Bellamy bought 200 acres of land for $30 an acre and opened the Palm Springs Racquet Club, which soon listed Ginger Rogers, Humphrey Bogart, and Clark Gable among its members.

During its slow, steady growth period from the 1930s to 1970s, the Palm Springs area drew some of the world's most famous architects to design homes for the rich and famous. The collected works, inspired by the mountains and desert sands and notable for the use of glass and indoor–outdoor space, became known as Palm Springs Modernism. The city lost some of its luster in the 1970s as the wealthy moved to newer down-valley, golf-oriented communities. But Palm Springs reinvented itself starting in the 1990s, restoring the bright and airy old midcentury modern houses and hotels, and cultivating a welcoming atmosphere for gay visitors.

The Desert Resorts

You'll find reminders of the city's glamorous past in its unique architecture and renovated hotels—for an overview, pick up a copy of *Palm Springs: Brief History and Architectural Guide* at the Palm Springs Visitor Center—and you'll see change and progress in the trendy restaurants and upscale shops. Formerly exclusive Palm Canyon Drive is now a lively avenue filled with coffeehouses, outdoor cafés, and bars.

GETTING HERE AND AROUND
Most visitors arrive in the Palm Springs area by car from the Los Angeles or San Diego area via Interstate 10, which intersects with Highway 111 just north of Palm Springs. ■TIP→ Tahquitz Canyon Way marks the division between north and south on major streets (e.g., North and South Palm Canyon Drive).

ESSENTIALS
Visitor Information Greater Palm Springs Convention and Visitors Bureau ⊠ *Visitor Center, 70-100 Hwy. 111, at Via Florencia, Rancho Mirage* ☎ *760/770–9000, 800/967–3767* ⊕ *www.palmspringsoasis.com* ⊗ *Weekdays 8:30–5.* **Palm Springs Visitor Information Center** ⊠ *2901 N. Palm Canyon Dr., Palm Springs* ☎ *760/778–8418, 800/347–7746* ⊕ *www.palm-springs.org* ⊗ *Daily 9–5.*

EXPLORING

FAMILY **Indian Canyons.** The Indian Canyons are the ancestral home of the Agua Caliente, part of the Cahuilla people. You can see remnants of their ancient life, including rock art, house pits and foundations, irrigation ditches, bedrock mortars, pictographs, and stone houses and shelters atop cliff walls. Short, easy walks through the canyons reveal palm oases, waterfalls, and spring wildflowers. Tree-shaded picnic areas are abundant. The attraction includes three canyons open for touring: Palm Canyon, noted for its stand of Washingtonia palms; Murray Canyon, home of Peninsula bighorn sheep and a herd of wild ponies; and Andreas Canyon, where a stand of fan palms contrast with sharp rock formations. Ranger-led hikes to Palm and Andreas canyons are offered daily for an additional charge. The trading post at the entrance to Palm Canyon has hiking maps and refreshments, as well as Native American art, jewelry, and weavings. ⊠ *38520 S. Palm Canyon Dr., south of Acanto Dr.* ☎ *760/323–6018* ⊕ *www.indian-canyons.com* ☞ *$9, ranger hikes $3* ⊙ *Oct.–June, daily 8–5; July–Sept., Fri.–Sun. 8–5.*

WORD OF MOUTH

"My husband loved the Palm Springs Air Museum, which focuses on WWII. We enjoyed going up the Aerial Tramway and doing the Desert View and Discovery Trails at the top. They are both easy. Indian Canyons is a great place to hike and Andreas Canyon is the easiest of the three and very lovely. We also did the Palm Canyon hike which wasn't very difficult and well worth it."

—Sam_A

FAMILY **Palm Springs Aerial Tramway.** A trip on the Palm Springs Aerial Tramway provides a 360-degree view of the desert through the picture windows of rotating tramcars. The 2½-mile ascent through Chino Canyon, the steepest vertical cable ride in the United States, brings you to an elevation of 8,516 feet in less than 20 minutes. On clear days, which are common, the view stretches 75 miles—from the peak of Mt. San Gorgonio in the north, to the Salton Sea in the southeast. Stepping out into the snow at the summit is a winter treat. At the top, a bit below the summit of Mt. San Jacinto, are several diversions. Mountain Station has an observation deck, two restaurants, a cocktail lounge, apparel and gift shops, picnic facilities, a small wildlife exhibit, and a theater that screens movies on the history of the tramway and the state park. Take advantage of free guided and self-guided nature walks through the adjacent Mount San Jacinto State Park and Wilderness, or if there's snow on the ground, rent skis, snowshoes, or snow tubes (inner tubes or similar contraptions for sliding down hills). The tramway generally closes for maintenance in mid-September. ■TIP➜ Ride-and-dine packages are available in late afternoon. The tram is a popular attraction; to avoid a two-hour or longer wait, arrive before the first car leaves in the morning. ⊠ *1 Tramway Rd., off N. Palm Canyon Dr. (Hwy. 111)* ☎ *888/515–8726* ⊕ *www.pstramway.com* ☞ *$23.95, ride-and-dine package $36* ⊙ *Tramcars depart at least every 30 mins. from 10 am weekdays and 8 am weekends; last car up leaves at 8 pm, last car down leaves Mountain Station at 9:45 pm.*

ELVIS IN PALM SPRINGS

Elvis's Honeymoon Hideaway—where the King and Priscilla lived during the first year of their marriage—is perched on a hilltop right up against the mountains in Palm Springs. The house, which is opened for tours, is a stunning example of Palm Springs Midcentury Modern; it's rich in Elvis lore, photos, and furnishings. Docents describe the fabulous parties, celebrities, and some local legends. You can see some home movies of the loving couple, sit on the King's sofa, and strum one of his guitars.

The house, built in 1962 by one of Palm Spring's largest developers, Robert Alexander, consists of four perfect circles, each set on a different level. At the time, *Look* magazine described it as the "house of tomorrow." (And indeed many features, like the huge kitchen with circular island, are standard in today's homes.) Tours are offered daily by appointment only; they're $30, $35 weekends and holidays. Call ☎ *760/322–1192* or visit ⊕ *www.elvishoneymoon.com* for reservations.

Fodor's Choice
★
FAMILY

Palm Springs Air Museum. This museum's impressive collection of World War II aircraft includes a B-17 Flying Fortress bomber, a P-51 Mustang, a Lockheed P-38, and a Grumman TBF Avenger. Among the cool exhibits are model warships, a Pearl Harbor diorama, and a Grumman Goose into which kids can crawl. Photos, artifacts, memorabilia, and uniforms are also on display, and educational programs take place on Saturdays. Flight demonstrations are scheduled regularly. Biplane rides are offered on Saturday. ⊠ *745 N. Gene Autry Trail* ☎ *760/778–6262* ⊕ *palmspringsairmuseum.org* ✉ *$15* ⊙ *Daily 10–5.*

Palm Springs Art Museum. This world-class art museum focuses on photography, modern architecture, and the traditional arts of the Americas. Galleries are bright and open. The permanent collection includes a shimmering exhibition of contemporary studio glass, highlighted by works by Dale Chihuly, Ginny Ruffner, and William Morris. You'll also find handcrafted furniture by the late actor George Montgomery, a collection of midcentury modern architectural photos by Julius Shulman, an array of enormous Native American baskets, and works by artists like Allen Houser, Arlo Namingha, and Fritz Scholder. The museum also displays significant works of 20th-century sculpture by Henry Moore, Marino Marina, Deborah Butterfield, and Mark Di Suvero. The Annenberg Theater presents plays, concerts, lectures, operas, and other cultural events. ⊠ *101 Museum Dr., off W. Tahquitz Canyon Dr.* ☎ *760/322–4800* ⊕ *www.psmuseum.org* ✉ *$12.50, free Thurs. 4–8 during Villagefest* ⊙ *Tues.–Sun. 10–5* ⊙ *Closed Mon.*

Palm Springs Walk of Stars. Along the walk, more than 300 bronze stars are embedded in the sidewalk (à la Hollywood Walk of Fame) to honor celebrities with a Palm Springs connection. Frank, Elvis, Marilyn, Dinah, Lucy, Ginger, Liz, and Liberace have all received their due. Those still around to walk the Walk and see their stars include Nancy Sinatra, Kathy Griffin, and Adam West. ⊠ *Palm Canyon Dr., around Tahquitz Canyon Way, and Tahquitz Canyon Way, between Palm Canyon and Indian Canyon Drs.* ☎ *760/320-3129* ⊕ *www.palmsprings.com/stars.*

9

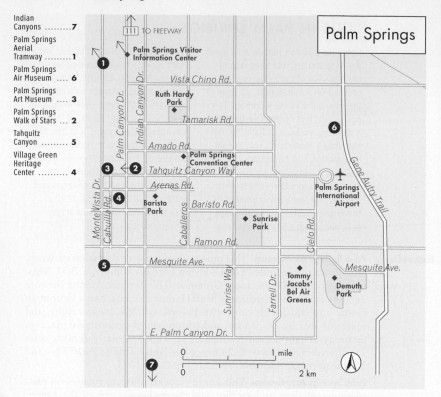

Tahquitz Canyon. On ranger-led tours of this secluded canyon on the Agua Caliente Reservation, you can view a spectacular 60-foot waterfall, rock art, ancient irrigation systems, and native wildlife and plants. Tours are conducted several times daily; participants must be able to navigate 100 steep rock steps. (You can also take a self-guided tour of the 1.8-mile trail.) A visitor center at the canyon entrance screens a video, displays artifacts, and sells maps. ⊠ *500 W. Mesquite Ave., west of S. Palm Canyon Dr.* ☎ *760/416–7044* ⊕ *www.tahquitzcanyon.com* ☞ *$12.50* ⊙ *Oct.–June, daily 7:30–5; July–Sept., Fri.–Sun. 7:30–5.*

Village Green Heritage Center. Three small museums at the Village Green Heritage Center illustrate early life in Palm Springs. The **Agua Caliente Cultural Museum,** the centerpiece, traces the culture and history of the Cahuilla tribe with several exhibits. The **McCallum Adobe** holds the collection of the Palm Springs Historical Society. **Rudy's General Store Museum** is a re-creation of a 1930s general store. ⊠ *219–221 S. Palm Canyon Dr.* ☎ *760/323-8297* ☞ *Agua Caliente free, McCallum $2, Rudy's $1* ⊙ *Agua Caliente Sept.–May, Wed.–Sat. 10–5; Sun. noon–5, call for others.*

WHERE TO EAT

$$$ ✕ **Copley's on Palm Canyon.** Chef Manion Copley prepares innovative
MODERN cuisine in a setting that's straight out of Hollywood—a hacienda once
AMERICAN owned by Cary Grant. Dine in the clubby house or under the stars in
the garden. Start with appetizers such as roasted beet and warm goat
cheese salad or one of the Hawaiian ahi tacos. Oh My Lobster Pot Pie
is the biggest hit on an entrée menu that also includes sesame seared
tofu. Save room for Copley's sweet and savory herb ice creams. Ⓢ *Average main: $26* ⊠ *621 N. Palm Canyon Dr., at E. Granvia Valmonte*
☎ *760/327–9555* ⊕ *www.copleyspalmsprings.com* ✍ *Reservations
essential* ◔ *No lunch.*

$$ ✕ **El Mirasol.** Chef Felipe Castañeda opened his second Mexican res-
MODERN taurant at the north end of Palm Springs in 2011—he's been serving
MEXICAN overflow crowds for years at a simple café at the other end of town.
His latest venture, within the Los Arboles Hotel, which he owns, is
outside on a charming patio set amid flower gardens and shaded by red
umbrellas. Castañeda prepares classic combinations of tacos, tamales,
and enchiladas, along with specialties such as double-cooked pork and
chicharrones (fried pork rinds) with tomatillo salsa. Vegetarian offerings include delightfully delicate spinach enchiladas. Ⓢ *Average main:
$18* ⊠ *140 E. Palm Canyon Dr., at E. Avenida Olancha* ☎ *760/459–
3605* ⊕ *www.elmirasolrestaurants.com.*

$$$$ ✕ **The Falls.** A mile-long martini menu lures a chic, moneyed crowd to
STEAKHOUSE this hot spot overlooking Palm Canyon Drive. Reserve well in advance
for one of the outdoor balcony tables to get the best view. The restaurant specializes in dry aged beef, but you can also get seafood and
chops, and there are vegetarian choices. Steaks and chops are prepared
your way with a selection of sides that includes mac and cheese, roasted
potatoes, and steamed asparagus with hollandaise sauce. Go early for
the nightly happy hour (between 4 and 6:30), when items on the bar
menu are half price—or hang around late to catch the action at the
Martini Dome bar. Ⓢ *Average main: $38* ⊠ *155 S. Palm Canyon Dr.,
near W. Arenas Rd.* ☎ *760/416–8664* ⊕ *thefallsprimesteakhouse.com*
✍ *Reservations essential* ◔ *No lunch.*

$$$$ ✕ **Le Vallauris.** A longtime favorite that occupies the historic Roberson
FRENCH House, Le Vallauris is popular with ladies who lunch, all of whom get a
hug from the maître d'. The menu changes daily, and each day it's hand-
written on a white board. Lunch entrées might include perfectly rare
tuna niçoise salad, or grilled whitefish with Dijon mustard sauce. Dinner might bring a sublime smoked salmon, sautéed calves' liver, roasted
quail with orange sauce, or rack of lamb. There are also weekly prix-fixe
menus, with and without wine, for lunch and dinner. The restaurant
has a lovely tree-shaded garden. On cool winter evenings, request a
table by the fireplace. Ⓢ *Average main: $35* ⊠ *385 W. Tahquitz Canyon
Way, west of Palm Canyon Dr.* ☎ *760/325–5059* ⊕ *www.levallauris.
com* ✍ *Reservations essential* ◔ *Closed July and Aug.*

$$$ ✕ **Matchbox Vintage Pizza Bistro.** The name says pizza, but this bistro also
ITALIAN serves interesting salads topped with grilled tuna, and a selection of sand-
wiches like crabcakes on a toasted brioche. Main courses include bacon-
wrapped scallops, macaroni and cheese, and fish-and-chips. The pizzas

9

are made just about any way you'd like, including vegetarian. On the second-floor overlooking the action on Palm Canyon Drive, this is a great place to go for cocktails and small plates. ⑤ *Average main: $28* ✉ *155 S. Palm Canyon Dr., near W. Arenas Rd.* ☎ *760/778–6000* ⊕ *www.matchboxpalmsprings.com* ◷ *No lunch Mon. and Tues.*

$$$$
MODERN
AMERICAN

✗ **Purple Palm.** The hottest tables in Palm Springs are those that surround the pool at the Colony Palms Hotel, where the hip and elite pay homage to Purple Gang mobster Al Wertheimer, who reportedly built the hotel in the mid-1930s. Now it's a casual, convivial place where you can dine alfresco surrounded by a tropical garden. The dinner menu is heavy on seafood, such as bouillabaisse and roasted barrammundi; you can also shuck oysters,

> **TRIBAL WEALTH**
>
> The Agua Caliente band of Cahuilla Indians owns nearly half the land in the Palm Springs area. Wanting to encourage the railroad to bring their trains through the desert, Congress granted half the land to the railroad and the other half to the Native Americans. The Cahuilla were granted all the even-numbered one-square-mile sections—but they were unable to develop the land for years due to litigation. The resulting patchwork of developed and vacant land can still be seen today (though the Cahuilla are making up for lost time by opening new hotels and casinos).

crab legs, and prawns. The impressive wine list roams the globe. The restaurant is also open for breakfast, lunch, and dinner. ■TIP→ The ladies room features a fabulous black-and-white image of a very young Paul Newman. ⑤ *Average main: $31* ✉ *572 N. Indian Canyon Dr., at E. Granvia Valmonte* ☎ *800/557–2187* ⊕ *www.colonypalmshotel.com* ⚿ *Reservations essential.*

$$$$
BASQUE
Fodor's Choice
★

✗ **Tinto.** The talented Jose Garces, a Food Channel Iron Chefs winner and the recipient of a James Beard Award, takes small plates to a new level at Tinto, his Spanish Basque wine bar in the Saguaro Hotel. Garces concocts such delightfully exotic items as bleu de Basque cheese, marinated white anchovies with pine nuts, succulent pork belly, and a mini short-rib sandwich with celery aioli. Order two or three plates per person and share, or select the chef's tasting menu, available with wine pairing. This is a fun place where tables are closely spaced, so dinner becomes a party. The extensive wine list showcases Spanish vintages. ⑤ *Average main: $55* ✉ *1800 E. Palm Canyon Dr., at S. Sunshine Way* ☎ *760/323-1711* ⊕ *www.jdvhotels.com/dining/riverside/tinto* ⚿ *Reservations essential.*

$$
MODERN
AMERICAN

✗ **Trios.** The owners of this high-energy restaurant in the Uptown Design District claim that it's "where Palm Springs eats." It certainly seems so most nights, when the lines run deep near the front door. The interesting menu has a wide range of both home-style staples such as Yankee pot roast and trendy dishes like crawfish pie. Vegetarian and gluten-free items are available. You can dine outside or inside, where the walls display works by local artists. ⑤ *Average main: $20* ✉ *707 N. Palm Canyon Dr.* ☎ *760/864-8746* ⊕ *www.TrioPalmSprings.com* ⚿ *Reservations essential.*

$$$ ✕ **The Tropicale.** Tucked onto a side-street corner, the Tropicale is a mid-
INTERNATIONAL century–style watering hole with a contemporary vibe. The bar and
main dining room hold cozy leather booths while flowers and water
features brighten the outdoor area. The menu spans the globe with
small and large plates, from the miso-glazed salmon rice bowl, to the
grilled Idaho trout with aioli sauce, to prime filet mignon with Zinfandel
sauce. ⑤ *Average main: $28* ✉ *330 E. Amado Rd., at N. Calle Encilia*
☎ *760/866–1952* ⊕ *www.thetropicale.com* ⚲ *Reservations essential*
☽ *No lunch.*

$$ ✕ **Alicante.** One of the best people-watching spots in Palm Springs, this
MEDITERRANEAN sidewalk café is a fine choice before or after seeing the Follies. The lunch
and dinner menus feature a wide selection of small plates in addition to
hearty items such as pasta, pizza, *pollo alla diavolo* (macadamia-crusted
chicken breast), and veal scaloppini. On a separate tapas menu you
can find some surprises: spicy chickpeas with Mediterranean chicken
sausage, chorizo-stuffed calamari, pine nuts with honey topped with
blue cheese, or spicy lime-drizzled shrimp. ⑤ *Average main: $20* ✉ *140
S. Palm Canyon Dr., at La Plaza* ☎ *760/325–9464* ⊕ *www.alicanteps.
com* ⚲ *Reservations essential.*

WHERE TO STAY

For expanded hotel reviews, visit Fodors.com.

$$ ⛽ **Ace Hotel and Swim Club.** Take a trip back to the 1960s at the Ace:
RESORT With the hotel's vintage feel and hippie-chic decor, it would be no sur-
prise to find the Grateful Dead playing in the bar. **Pros:** Amigo Room
has late-night dining; poolside stargazing deck; Sunday DJ scene at
the pool. **Cons:** party atmosphere not for everyone; limited amenities;
casual staff and service. ⑤ *Rooms from: $169* ✉ *701 E. Palm Canyon
Dr.* ☎ *760/325–9900* ⊕ *www.acehotel.com/palmsprings* ☌ *180 rooms,
8 suites* �‖ *No meals.*

$ ⛽ **Alcazar Palm Springs.** Amid an area known as the Movie Colony, Alca-
HOTEL zar embodies the desert's popular midcentury-modern design style; the
ample, blazing-white guestrooms here wrap around a sparkling pool.
Pros: walking distance of downtown; parking on site; bikes available.
Cons: limited service; wall air-conditioners. ⑤ *Rooms from: $119* ✉ *622
N. Indian Canyon Dr.* ☎ *760/318–9850* ⊕ *www.alcazarpalmsprings.
com* ☌ *34* �‖ *Breakfast.*

$ ⛽ **Casa Cody.** The service is personal and gracious at this historic B&B
B&B/INN near the Palm Springs Art Museum; spacious studios and one- and two-
bedroom suites hold Santa Fe–style rustic furnishings. **Pros:** family-size
digs; friendly ambience; good value. **Cons:** old buildings; limited ame-
nities. ⑤ *Rooms from: $99* ✉ *175 S. Cahuilla Rd.* ☎ *760/320–9346,
800/231–2639* ⊕ *www.casacody.com* ☌ *16 rooms, 7 suites, 2 cottages*
�‖ *Breakfast.*

$$$ ⛽ **Colony Palms Hotel.** This hotel has been a hip place to stay since the
HOTEL 1930s, when gangster Al Wertheimer built it to front his casino, bar,
and brothel. **Pros:** glam with a swagger; attentive staff; all that history.
Cons: high noise level outside; not for families with young children.
⑤ *Rooms from: $179* ✉ *572 N. Indian Canyon Dr.* ☎ *760/969–1800,
800/577–2187* ⊕ *www.colonypalmshotel.com* ☌ *43 rooms, 3 suites,
8 casitas* �‖ *No meals.*

9

$$
B&B/INN
⊡ **East Canyon Hotel & Spa.** Serving a primarily gay clientele, this classy resort is the only one in the desert with an in-house, full-service spa exclusively for men. **Pros:** elegant laid-back feel; attentive service; complimentary poolside cocktails. **Cons:** spa is for men only. ⑤ *Rooms from: $149* ⊠ *288 E. Camino Monte Vista* ☎ *760/320–1928, 877/324–6835* ⊕ *www.eastcanyonps.com* ⟿ *15 rooms, 1 suite* ⍩ *Breakfast.*

$$
HOTEL
⊡ **Hyatt Regency Suites Palm Springs.** The best-situated downtown hotel in Palm Springs, the Hyatt has rooms where you can watch the sun rise over the city or set behind the mountains from your bedroom's balcony. **Pros:** underground parking; hypoallergenic rooms. **Cons:** lots of business travelers; some street noise. ⑤ *Rooms from: $174* ⊠ *285 N. Palm Canyon Dr.* ☎ *760/322–9000, 800/633–7313* ⊕ *www.palmsprings. hyatt.com* ⟿ *197 suites* ⍩ *No meals.*

$$
B&B/INN
⊡ **La Maison.** Offering all the comforts of home, this small bed-and-breakfast features large guest rooms with European-style furnishings that surround the pool area, where you can spend quiet time soaking up the sun or taking a dip. **Pros:** restaurants nearby; quiet; genial innkeepers. **Cons:** on busy Hwy. 111; rooms open directly onto pool deck. ⑤ *Rooms from: $169* ⊠ *1600 E. Palm Canyon Dr.* ☎ *760/325–1600* ⊕ *www.lamaisonpalmsprings.com* ⍩ *Breakfast.*

$$
B&B/INN
⊡ **Movie Colony Hotel.** Designed in 1935 by Albert Frey, this intimate hotel evokes midcentury minimalist ambience; its gleaming white, two-story buildings, flanked with balconies and porthole windows, evoke the image of a luxury yacht. **Pros:** architectural icon; happy hour; cruiser bikes. **Cons:** close quarters; off the beaten path; staff not available 24 hours. ⑤ *Rooms from: $124* ⊠ *726 N. Indian Canyon Dr.* ☎ *760/320–6340, 888/953–5700* ⊕ *www.moviecolonyhotel.com* ⟿ *13 rooms, 3 suites* ⍩ *Breakfast.*

$$
B&B/INN
⊡ **Orbit In Hotel.** Step back to 1957 at this hip inn, located on a quiet backstreet downtown. **Pros:** saltwater pool; in-room spa services; Orbitini cocktail hour. **Cons:** best for couples; style not to everyone's taste; staff not available 24 hours. ⑤ *Rooms from: $149* ⊠ *562 W. Arenas Rd.* ☎ *760/323–3585, 877/996–7248* ⊕ *www.orbitin.com* ⟿ *9 rooms* ⍩ *Breakfast.*

$$$$
RESORT
⊡ **The Parker Palm Springs.** A cacophony of color and over-the-top contemporary art assembled by New York designer Jonathan Adler, this hip hotel appeals to a stylish, L.A.-based clientele. **Pros:** fun in the sun; celebrity clientele; high jinks at the Palm Springs Yacht Club Spa. **Cons:** pricey drinks and wine; long walks in the hot sun to get anywhere. ⑤ *Rooms from: $369* ⊠ *4200 E. Palm Canyon Dr.* ☎ *760/770–5000, 800/543–4300* ⊕ *www.theparkerpalmsprings.com* ⟿ *131 rooms, 13 suites* ⍩ *No meals.*

$$$
RESORT
⊡ **Riviera Resort & Spa.** A party place built in 1958 and renovated in 2008, the Riviera attracts young, well-heeled, bikini-clad guests who hang out around the pool by day and the Bikini Bar by night. **Pros:** personal beachy fire pits throughout the property; hip vibe; sublime spa. **Cons:** high noise level outdoors; party atmosphere; location at north end of Palm Springs. ⑤ *Rooms from: $179* ⊠ *1600 N. Indian Canyon Dr.* ☎ *760/327–8311* ⊕ *www.psriviera.com* ⟿ *406 rooms, 43 suites* ⍩ *No meals.*

$$$$
ALL-INCLUSIVE
FAMILY

⊡ **Smoke Tree Ranch.** A world apart from Palm Springs' pulsating urban village, the area's most exclusive resort occupies 400 pristine desert acres, surrounded by mountains and unspoiled vistas. **Pros:** priceless privacy; simple luxury; many recreation choices include horseback riding, lawn bowling, hiking, and jogging. **Cons:** no glitz or glamour; limited entertainment options; family atmosphere not for everyone. ⑤ *Rooms from: $330* ✉ *1850 Smoke Tree La.* ☎ *760/327–1221, 800/787–3922* ⊕ *www.smoketreeranch.com* ⌁ *49 cottages, includes 18 suites* ⊘ *Closed Apr.–late Oct.* ⦿ *Multiple meal plans.*

$
HOTEL

⊡ **Vagabond Inn.** Rooms are smallish at this centrally located motel, but they're clean, comfortable, and a good value. **Pros:** quiet; kids stay free. **Cons:** limited amenities, facilities, and service. ⑤ *Rooms from: $69* ✉ *1699 S. Palm Canyon Dr.* ☎ *760/325–7211, 800/522–1555* ⊕ *www.vagabondinn.com* ⌁ *117 rooms* ⦿ *Breakfast.*

$$$$
RESORT

⊡ **The Viceroy Palm Springs.** Stepping into the Viceroy you're greeted with a bright, sunny white-and-yellow ambience, reminiscent of a sun-filled desert day. **Pros:** poolside cabanas; complimentary fitness classes; celebrity clientele. **Cons:** uneven service; popular wedding site. ⑤ *Rooms from: $290* ✉ *415 S. Belardo Rd.* ☎ *760/320–4117, 800/327–3687* ⊕ *www.viceroypalmsprings.com* ⌁ *67 rooms, 12 villas.*

$$$$
B&B/INN

⊡ **Willows Historic Palm Springs Inn.** An opulent Mediterranean-style mansion built in the 1920s to host the rich and famous, this luxurious hillside B&B has gleaming hardwood and slate floors, stone fireplaces, frescoed ceilings, hand-painted tiles, iron balconies, antiques throughout, and a 50-foot waterfall that splashes into a pool outside the dining room. **Pros:** ultra luxurious; sublime service. **Cons:** closed June–Sept.; pricey. ⑤ *Rooms from: $325* ✉ *412 W. Tahquitz Canyon Way* ☎ *760/320–0771, 800/966–9597* ⊕ *www.thewillowspalmsprings. com* ⌁ *8 rooms* ⦿ *Breakfast.*

NIGHTLIFE AND THE ARTS
NIGHTLIFE

Ace Hotel and Swim Club. Events are held here nearly every night, including film screenings, live concerts, DJs with dancing, parties, and seasonal entertainment. Many are free, and quite a few are family friendly. ✉ *701 E. Palm Canyon Dr., at Calle Palo Fierro* ☎ *760/325–9900* ⊕ *www.acehotel.com.*

Casino Morongo. A 20-minute drive west of Palm Springs, this casino has 2,000 slot machines, video games, the Vibe nightclub, plus Vegas-style shows. ✉ *49500 Seminole Dr., off I–10, Cabazon* ☎ *800/252–4499, 951/849–3080* ⊕ *www.morongocasinoresort.com.*

Hair of the Dog English Pub. Drawing a young crowd that likes to tip back English ales and ciders, this bar is lively and popular. ✉ *238 N. Palm Canyon Dr., near E. Amado Rd.* ☎ *760/323–9890* ⊕ *www. thehairofthedog.net.*

Spa Resort Casino. This resort holds 1,000 slot machines, blackjack tables, a high-limit room, four restaurants, two bars, and the Cascade Lounge for entertainment. ✉ *401 E. Amado Rd., at N. Calle Encilia* ☎ *888/999–1995.*

9

Palm Springs is a golfer's paradise: the area is home to more than 125 courses.

Village Pub. With live entertainment, DJs, and friendly service, this popular bar caters to a young crowd. ✉ *266 S. Palm Canyon Dr., at Baristo Rd.* ☎ *760/323–3265* ⊕ *www.palmspringsvillagepub.com.*

Zelda's Nightclub. A Palm Springs institution, Zelda's moved south in 2010, but the high-energy DJs, dancing, and drinking are still going strong and the dance floor is still thumping with Latin, hip-hop, and sounds from the '60s, '70s, and '80s. The club offers bottle service in the VIP Sky Box. ✉ *611 S. Palm Canyon Dr., at E. Camino Parocela* ☎ *760/325–2375* ⊕ *www.zeldasnightclub.com* ☉ *Tues.–Sat. 9 pm–2 am.*

GAY AND LESBIAN

The Dinah. In late March, when the world's finest female golfers hit the links for the Annual LPGA Kraft Nabisco Championship in Rancho Mirage, thousands of lesbians converge on Palm Springs for a four-day party popularly known as The Dinah. ⇨ *Kraft Nabisco Championship in Rancho Mirage.* ☎ *888/923–4624* ⊕ *www.clubskirts.com.*

Hunter's Video Bar. Drawing a young gay and straight crowd, Hunter's is a club-scene mainstay. ✉ *302 E. Arenas Rd., at Calle Encilia* ☎ *760/323–0700* ⊕ *huntersnightclubs.com* ☉ *Daily 10 am–2 am.*

Toucans Tiki Lounge. A friendly place with a tropical jungle in a rain-forest setting, Toucans Tiki Lounge serves festive drinks and has live entertainment and theme nights. ✉ *2100 N. Palm Canyon Dr., at W. Via Escuela* ☎ *760/416–7584* ⊕ *www.toucanstikilounge.com.*

White Party Palm Springs. Held during spring break, the White Party draws tens of thousands of gay men from around the country to the

Palm Springs area for four days of parties and events. ⊠ *Palm Springs* ⊕ *jeffreysanker.com.*

THE ARTS

Annenberg Theater. Broadway shows, opera, lectures, Sunday-afternoon chamber concerts, and other events take place here. ⊠ *Palm Springs Art Museum, 101 N. Museum Dr., at W. Tahquitz Canyon Way* ☎ *760/325–4490* ⊕ *www.psmuseum.org.*

Fabulous Palm Springs Follies. For years the hottest ticket in the desert, the Follies sells out 10 weekly performances from November through May. The vaudeville-style revue, about half of which focuses on midcentury nostalgia, stars extravagantly costumed, retired (but very fit) show-girls, comedians, singers, and dancers. ⊠ *Plaza Theatre, 128 S. Palm Canyon Dr., at La Plaza* ☎ *760/327–0225* ⊕ *www.palmspringsfollies. com* 💲 *$50–$93.*

Modernism Week. Each February, the desert communities celebrate the work of the architects and designers who created the Palm Springs "look" in the 1940s, 1950s, and 1960s. Described these days as mid-century modern (you'll also see the term "desert modernism" used), these structures were created by Albert Frey, Richard Neutra, William F. Cody, John Lautner, and other notables. The 11-day event features lectures, a modernism show, films, vintage car and trailer shows, galas, and home and garden tours. ⊠ *Palm Springs* ☎ *760/322–2502* ⊕ *www. modernismweek.com.*

Palm Springs International Film Festival. In mid-January this festival brings stars and more than 150 feature films from 25 countries, plus panel discussions, short films, and documentaries, to the Annenberg Theater and other venues. ⊠ *1700 E. Tahquitz Canyon Way, Ste. 3* ☎ *760/322–2930, 800/898–7256* ⊕ *www.psfilmfest.org.*

Plaza Theatre. The Spanish-style Plaza Theatre opened in 1936 with a glittering premiere of the MGM film *Camille.* In the '40s and '50s, it presented some of Hollywood's biggest stars, including Bob Hope and Bing Crosby. Now home of the Fabulous Palm Springs Follies, it is favored by fans of old-time radio even in the off-season. ⊠ *128 S. Palm Canyon Dr., at La Plaza* ☎ *760/327–0225* ⊕ *www.psfollies.com.*

SPORTS AND THE OUTDOORS

BICYCLING

Many hotels and resorts have bicycles available for guest use.

Big Wheel Tours. Rent cruisers, performance road bikes, and mountain bikes from this agency that also offers road tours to La Quinta Loop, Joshua Tree National Park, and the San Andreas fault. Off-road tours are available, too. The company has no retail outlet but will pick up and deliver bikes to your hotel and supply you with area maps. ⊠ *Palm Springs* ☎ *760/779–1837* ⊕ *www.bwbtours.com.*

Palm Springs Recreation Division. This organization can provide you with maps of city bike trails. Printable versions of several routes are available on the website. ⊠ *401 S. Pavilion Way* ☎ *760/323–8272* ⊕ *www. palmspringsca.gov/index.aspx?page=752* ☉ *Weekdays 7:30–6.*

9

GOLF

Affordable Palm Springs TeeTimes. This service matches golfers with courses and arranges tee times. If you know which course you want to play, you can book online up to 60 days in advance via telephone or email. ☏ *760/324–5012* ⊕ *www.palmspringsteetimes.com.*

Indian Canyons Golf Resort. Operated by the Aqua Caliente tribe, this spot at the base of the mountains includes two 18-hole courses designed by Casey O'Callaghan, Amy Alcott, and William P. Bell. The North Course is adjacent to property once owned by Walt Disney and contains several midcentury modern houses. In the 1960s it was the go-to golf course for celebrities visiting the desert, including presidents Dwight Eisenhower, Lyndon Johnson, and Ronald Reagan. ✉ *1097 E. Murray Canyon Dr., at Kings Rd. E* ☏ *760/833–8700* ⊕ *www.indiancanyonsgolf. com* ⚑ *North Course: 18 holes. 6,943 yds. Par 72. Slope 118–127. Greens fees: $40–$115. South Course: 18 holes. 6,582 yds. Par 72. Slope 108–118. Greens fees: $40–$115.* ☞ *Facilities: Driving range, club rentals, lessons, two restaurants, bar.*

Palm Springs Desert Resorts Convention and Visitors Bureau. Palm Springs hosts more than 100 golf tournaments annually; the bureau's website posts listings. ⊕ *www.palmspringsusa.com.*

Tahquitz Creek Golf Resort. Conveniently located in Palm Springs near Cathedral City, Tahquitz Golf Resort has two popular courses. Golfers have been walking the Legend course for more than 50 years. The newer Resort course, designed by Ted Robinson, offers sweeping mountain views and scenic waterscapes. ✉ *1885 Golf Club Dr., at 34th Ave.* ☏ *760/328–1005* ⊕ *www.tahquitzgolfresort.com* ⚑ *Legend Course: 18 holes. 4 configurations. 6,815 yds. Par 71. Slope 117–123. Greens fees: $20–$100. Resort Course: 18 holes. 3 configurations. 6,705 yds. Par 72. Slope 123–139. Greens fees: $20–$100.* ☞ *Facilities: Driving range, putting greens, golf carts, lessons, restaurant, bar.*

Tommy Jacobs' Bel Air Greens Country Club. This small executive course is a good choice if you want to walk. Although it's only 9 holes, you can configure your route to 18 or more. ✉ *1001 S. El Cielo Rd., at E. Mesquite Ave.* ☏ *760/322–6062* ⚑ *9 holes. 1,675 yds. Par 32. Slope 92. Greens fees: $15–$30.*

SHOPPING

SPECIALTY STORES

Desert Hills Premium Outlets. About 20 miles west of Palm Springs in Cabazon lies this outlet center with more than 130 brand-name discount fashion shops, including J. Crew, Giorgio Armani, Gucci, and Prada. ✉ *48400 Seminole Rd., off I–10, Cabazon* ☏ *951/849–6641* ⊕ *www.premiumoutlets.com.*

Uptown Heritage Galleries & Antiques District. A loose-knit collection of consignment and secondhand shops, galleries, and lively restaurants extends north of Palm Springs' main shopping area. The theme here is decidedly retro. Many businesses sell midcentury modern furniture and decorator items, and others carry clothing and estate jewelry. ✉ *N. Palm Canyon Dr., between Amado Rd. and Vista Chino* ⊕ *www. palmcanyondrive.org.*

SPAS

Estrella Spa at the Viceroy Palm Springs. This spa earns top honors each year for the indoor/outdoor experience it offers with a touch of Old Hollywood ambience. You can enjoy your massage in one of four outdoor treatment canopies in a garden, experience a Vichy shower massage, get a facial or pedicure fireside, or receive a full-body treatment with lemon crystals in the spa's Ice Haus. Whatever the treatment, you can use the spa's private pool, take a break for lunch, and order a drink from the hotel's bar. ⊠ *415 S. Belardo Rd.* ☎ *760/320–4117* ⊕ *www. viceroypalmsprings.com* ☞ *Services: body wrap, facials, specialty massages, prenatal massages, outdoor treatments, salon, wellness classes. $135 60-minute massage, $370 spa package.*

Feel Good Spa at the Ace Hotel. Despite its funkiness, this 21st-century hippie hangout takes its services very seriously. The estheticians use local clay, mud, and sea algae, and you can make your own scrub from organic botanicals such as lotions and essential oils. There are a variety of settings where you can get a rubdown, but the most relaxing is poolside. ⊠ *701 E. Palm Canyon Dr.* ☎ *760/866–6188* ⊕ *www.acehotel. com/palmsprings* ☞ *Services: wraps and scrubs, massage, facials, paraffin, manicures, pedicures, in-room treatments, fully equipped gym, wellness classes, yoga, water aerobics. $125 60-min massage, $149 spa package.*

Palm Springs Yacht Club. It's all about fun at the Palm Springs Yacht Club in the Parker Palm Springs hotel. Guests receive a complimentary shot of whiskey, vodka, or the Commodore Special while lounging in a poolside tent. Before your treatments, you can play video games, use an iPod Touch, or select a book from the spa's library. When you're ready to crash, wander over to the outdoor café for a burger and Pimm's. ⊠ *4200 E. Palm Canyon Dr.* ☎ *760/321–4606* ⊕ *www.theparkerpalmsprings. com/spa* ☞ *Sauna, steam room, indoor pool, library. Services: scrubs and wraps, massage, facials, manicures, pedicures, waxing, salon, fitness center with Cybex equipment, dining and cocktails. $150 60-min massage, $285 spa package.*

Spa Resort Casino. Taking the waters at this resort is an indulgent pleasure. You can spend a full day enjoying a five-step, wet-and-dry treatment that includes a mineral bath with water from the original spring, steam, sauna, and eucalyptus inhalation. The program allows you to take fitness classes and use the gym and, for an extra charge, add massage or body treatments. Bring a swimsuit for sunbathing and swimming in the pool. ⊠ *100 N. Indian Canyon Dr., at E. Tahquitz Canyon Way* ☎ *760/778–1772* ⊕ *www.sparesortcasino.com* ☞ *Hair and nail salon, sauna, steam room, hot tubs, relaxation room, lounge. Gym with: cardiovascular equipment, free weights, circuit machines. Services: body wraps and scrubs, facials, massage, waxing, salon services. $115 50-min massage, $285 spa package.*

9

CATHEDRAL CITY

2 miles southeast of Palm Springs on Hwy. 111.

One of the fastest-growing communities in the desert, Cathedral City is more residential than tourist-oriented. However, the city has a number of good restaurants and entertainment venues with moderate prices.

GETTING HERE AND AROUND

Cathedral City lies due east of the Palm Springs International Airport. Much of the city is suburban/residential community with large and small malls everywhere. Main streets north and south are Landau and Date Palm; west to east are Ramon Road, Dinah Shore, and Highway 111.

EXPLORING

FAMILY **Boomers Palm Springs.** At this theme park you can play miniature golf, drive bumper boats, climb a rock wall, drive a go-kart, swing in the batting cages, test your skills in an arcade, and play video games. ⊠ *67-700 E. Palm Canyon Dr., at Cree Rd.* ☎ *760/770–7522* ⊕ *www. boomerspark.com* ⊠ *$6–$8 per activity, $25 day passes* ☉ *Mon.–Thurs. 12–9, Fri. 12–11, Sat. 11–11, Sun. 11–8.*

Pickford Salon. This small museum inside a multiplex celebrates silent film star Mary Pickford. Items on display include her 1976 Oscar for contributions to the film industry, a gown she wore in the 1927 film *Dorothy Vernon of Haddon Hall,* and dinnerware from Pickfair, the Beverly Hills mansion she shared with actor Douglas Fairbanks. Pickford herself produced one of the film bios the Salon screens. ⊠ *Mary Pickford Theatre, 36-850 Pickfair St., at Buddy Rogers Ave.* ☎ *760/328-7100* ⊠ *Free* ☉ *Daily 10:30 am–midnight.*

WHERE TO EAT

$$$ ✕ **Cello's.** A favorite of locals and critics, this art-laden café in a strip
BISTRO mall serves modern twists on classics such as the crab Napoleon or onion soup fondue for starters, and liver and onions, chicken caprese, and eggplant Parmesan for main courses. The owner, Bonnie Barley, is as friendly as they come. ⑤ *Average main: $23* ⊠ *35-943 Date Palm Dr., at Gerald Ford Dr.* ☎ *760/328–5353* ⊕ *www.cellosbistro.com* ⚘ *Reservations essential.*

$$$ ✕ **Trilussa.** Locals gather at this San Francisco–style storefront restau-
ITALIAN rant for delicious food, big drinks, and a friendly welcome. The congenial bar is busy during happy hour, after which diners drift to their nicely spaced tables indoors and out. The long menu changes daily, but staples include antipasti, homemade pasta, pizza, risotto, veal, and fish. All come with an Italian accent. ⑤ *Average main: $27* ⊠ *68718 E. Palm Canyon Dr., at Monty Hall Dr.* ☎ *760/328–2300* ⚘ *Reservations essential.*

DESERT HOT SPRINGS

9 miles north of Palm Springs on Gene Autry Trail.

Desert Hot Springs's famous hot mineral waters, thought by some to have curative powers, bubble up at temperatures of 90°F to 148°F and flow into the wells of more than 40 hotel spas.

GETTING HERE AND AROUND
Desert Hot Springs lies due north of Palm Springs. Take Gene Autry Trail north to Interstate 10, where the street name changes to Palm. Continue north to Pierson Boulevard, the town's center.

EXPLORING
Cabot's Pueblo Museum. Cabot Yerxa, the man who found the spring that made Desert Hot Springs famous, built a quirky four-story, 35-room pueblo between 1939 and his death in 1965. Now a museum run by the city of Desert Hot Springs—Yerxa was the town's first mayor—the Hopi-inspired adobe structure is filled with memorabilia of his time as a homesteader; his encounters with Hollywood celebrities at the nearby Bar-H Ranch; his expedition to the Alaskan gold rush; and many other events. The home, much of it crafted out of materials Yerxa recycled from the desert, can only be seen on hour-long tours. Outside, you can walk the beautiful grounds to a lookout with amazing desert views. ⊠ *67-616 E. Desert View Ave., at Eliseo Rd.* ☎ *760/329–7610* ⊕ *www.cabotsmuseum.org* ⊠ *$11* ☉ *Tues.–Sun. 9–4, tours 9:30, 10:30, 11:30, 1:30, 2:30.*

SHOPPING
SPAS
Fodor'sChoice **The Spring.** Designed for those who want to detox, lose weight, or take
★ special spa treatments, The Spring caters to guests seeking quiet and personal service. Primarily a day spa, The Spring also holds a collection of simply furnished rooms for those who want to enjoy the spa's tranquility for more than one day. In addition to the typical wraps, scrubs, and massages, the spa menu offers packages that include one or two nights' accommodations, Continental breakfast, and up to four hours of treatment. ⊠ *12699 Reposo Way* ☎ *760/251–6700, 877/200–2110* ⊕ *www.the-spring.com* ☞ *Mineral pools, Finnish sauna. Services: scrubs and wraps, massage, facials, gentleman's packages, 5-day detoxifying retreats. $110 60-min massage, $265 spa packages.*

RANCHO MIRAGE

4 miles southeast of Cathedral City on Hwy. 111.

The rich and famous of Rancho Mirage live in beautiful estates and patronize elegant resorts and expensive restaurants. Although many mansions here are concealed behind the walls of gated communities and country clubs, the grandest of them all, Sunnylands, the Annenberg residence, is open to the public as a museum and public garden.

The city's golf courses host many high-profile tournaments. You'll find some of the swankiest resorts in the desert in Rancho Mirage—plus great golf, and plenty of peace and quiet. For those truly needing to take things down a notch further, the Betty Ford Center, the famous drug-and-alcohol rehab center, is also here.

GETTING HERE AND AROUND
Due east of Cathedral City, Rancho Mirage stretches from Ramon Road on the north to the hills south of Highway 111. The western border is Da Vall Drive, the eastern one Monterey Avenue. Major east–west

cross streets are Frank Sinatra Drive and Country Club Drive. Most shopping and dining spots are on Highway 111.

EXPLORING

The Annenberg Retreat at Sunnylands. The stunning 25,000-square-foot winter home and retreat of the late Ambassador Walter H. and Leonore Annenberg opened to the public in 2012. You can spend a whole day enjoying the 9 glorious acres of gardens, or take a guided 90-minute tour of the residence (reservations essential), a striking midcentury modern edifice designed by A. Quincy Jones. Floor-to-ceiling windows frame views of the gardens and Mount San Jacinto, and the expansive rooms hold furnishings from the 1960s and later, along with impressionist art (some original, some replicas). The history made here is as captivating as the surroundings. Seven U.S. presidents—from Dwight Eisenhower to Bill Clinton—and their First Ladies visited Sunnylands; Ronald and Nancy Reagan were frequent guests. Britain's Queen Elizabeth and Prince Philip also relaxed here, as did Princess Grace of Monaco and Japanese Prime Minister Toshiki Kaifu. Photos, art, letters, journals, and mementos provide insight into some of the history that unfolded here. ⊠ *37-977 Bob Hope Dr., south of Gerald Ford Dr.* ☎ *760/202–2260* ⊕ *www.sunnylands.org* ✉ *Tours $35, tickets available online 2 wks in advance; visitor center and gardens free* ۝ *Thurs.–Sun. 9-4* ۝ *Closed July–Aug. and during retreats.*

FAMILY **Children's Discovery Museum of the Desert.** With instructive hands-on exhibits, this museum contains a miniature rock-climbing area, a magnetic sculpture wall, make-it-and-take-it-apart projects, a rope maze, and an area for toddlers. Kids can paint a VW Bug, work as chefs in the museum's pizza parlor, and build pies out of arts and crafts supplies. Newer exhibits include a race track for which kids can assemble their own cars. ⊠ *71-701 Gerald Ford Dr., at Bob Hope Dr.* ☎ *760/321–0602* ⊕ *www.cdmod.org* ✉ *$8* ۝ *Jan.–Apr., daily 10–5; May–Dec., Tues.–Sun. 10–5.*

WHERE TO EAT AND STAY

For expanded hotel reviews, visit Fodors.com.

$$ ✕ **Las Casuelas Nuevas.** Hundreds of artifacts from Guadalajara, Mexico,
MEXICAN   lend festive charm to this casual restaurant, which has an expansive
FAMILY   garden patio. Tamales and shellfish dishes are among the specialties. The tequila menu lists dozens of aged and reserve selections, served by the shot or folded into a margarita. There's live entertainment on weekends. ⑤ *Average main: $19* ⊠ *70-050 Hwy. 111* ☎ *760/328–8844* ⊕ *www.lascasuelasnuevas.com* ⚖ *Reservations essential.*

$$$ ✕ **Catalan.** Beautifully prepared and presented Mediterranean cuisine
MEDITERRANEAN   stands out in this inventive restaurant, where you can dine inside or under the stars in the atrium. The service is attentive, and the menu roams the Riviera and beyond. Entrées include fabulous seared scallops with wild mushrooms, pan-roasted rainbow trout, and paella with clams, calamari chorizo, and Laughing Bird shrimp. ⑤ *Average main: $30* ⊠ *70026 Hwy. 111, Rancho Mirage* ☎ *760/770–9508* ⊕ *www. catalanrestaurant.com* ⚖ *Reservations essential.*

$ ⌦ **Agua Caliente Casino, Resort & Spa.** As in Las Vegas, the Agua Caliente
RESORT casino is in the lobby, but once you get into the spacious, beautifully
appointed rooms of the resort, all of the cacophony at the entrance
is forgotten. **Pros:** gorgeous; access to high rollers room offered for
$25; value priced. **Cons:** casino ambience; not appropriate for kids.
$ *Rooms from: $109* ✉ *32-250 Bob Hope Dr.* ☎ *888/999–1995*
⊕ *www.hotwatercasino.com* ⇆ *340 rooms, 26 suites* ⦿⊘ *No meals.*

$$$ ⌦ **Rancho Las Palmas Resort & Spa.** The most family-friendly resort in the
RESORT desert, this large venue holds Splashtopia, a huge water play-zone. **Pros:**
FAMILY family friendly; trails for hiking and jogging; nightly entertainment.
Cons: second-floor rooms accessed by very steep stairs; golf course
surrounds rooms; resort hosts conventions. $ *Rooms from: $199*
✉ *41-000 Bob Hope Dr.* ☎ *760/568–2727, 866/423–1195* ⊕ *www.*
rancholaspalmas.com ⇆ *422 rooms, 22 suites.*

$$ ⌦ **Westin Mission Hills Resort and Spa.** A sprawling resort on 360 acres,
RESORT the Westin is surrounded by fairways, putting greens, and time-share
FAMILY accommodations; rooms, in two-story buildings amid patios and fountains, have a stylish Arts and Crafts look with sleek mahogany furnishings accented with sand-color upholstery and crisp white linens. **Pros:**
gorgeous grounds; first-class golf facilities; daily activity program for
kids. **Cons:** rooms are spread out. $ *Rooms from: $169* ✉ *71333 Dinah*
Shore Dr. ☎ *760/328–5955, 800/937–8461* ⊕ *www.westinmissionhills.*
com ⇆ *512 rooms, 40 suites* ⦿⊘ *No meals.*

NIGHTLIFE
Agua Caliente Casino. This elegant and surprisingly quiet casino contains 1,400 slot machines, 39 table games, an 18-table poker room,
a high-limit room, a no-smoking area, and six restaurants. The Show,
the resort's concert theater, presents acts such as Joel McHale, Music
of ABBA, and Crosby, Stills and Nash, as well as live sporting events.
✉ *32-250 Bob Hope Dr., at E. Ramon Rd.* ☎ *760/321–2000* ⊕ *www.*
hotwatercasino.com.

SPORTS AND THE OUTDOORS
GOLF
Kraft Nabisco Championship. The best female golfers in the world compete
in this championship held in late March or early April. ✉ *Mission Hills*
Country Club ☎ *760/324–4546* ⊕ *www.kncgolf.com.*

Westin Mission Hills Resort Golf Club. Of the two golf courses in the Westin
Mission Hills Resort campus, the Pete Dye course is especially noteworthy. The club is a member of the Troon Golf Institute, and has several teaching facilities, including the Westin Mission Hills Resort Golf
Academy and the *Golf Digest* Golf School. ✉ *71333 Dinah Shore Dr.*
☎ *760/328–3198* ⊕ *www.playmissionhills.com* ⛳ *Pete Dye Resort: 18*
holes. 4 configurations. 5,525 yds. Par 72. Slope 115–131. Greens fees:
$99/$109. Gary Player Signature: 18 holes. 4 configurations. 5,327 yds.
Par 70, Slope 116–131. Greens fees: $99/$109 ⌕ *Facilities: Golf carts,*
Golf Academy, restaurants, bars in hotel.

9

SHOPPING

SPECIALTY STORES

River at Rancho Mirage. This shopping-dining-entertainment complex holds 20 high-end shops, including Hats Unlimited, Robann's Fine Jewelers, Forever 21, and Tulip Hill Winery tasting room, all fronting a faux river with cascading waterfalls. Also here are a 12-screen cinema, an outdoor amphitheater, and eight restaurants, among them Aqua Pazza, the place to see and be seen at lunchtime. Others include Flemings Prime Steakhouse, Babe's Bar-B-Que and Brewery, and P.F. Chang's. ⊠ *71-800 Hwy. 111, at Bob Hope Dr.* ☎ *760/341–2711* ⊕ *www.theriveratranchomirage.com.*

SPAS

The Spa at Mission Hills. The theme at the Spa at Mission Hills is comfort rather than glitz and glamour. Tucked into a quiet corner, this spa is nicely secluded from the hustle and bustle of the Weston Mission Hills Resort. Therapists are attentive to your needs and comfort. Some treatments use botanicals like coconut milk, lemon balm, mint, thyme, red algae, and hydrating honey. ⊠ *71333 Dinah Shore Dr.* ☎ *760/770–2134* ⊕ *www.spaatmissionhills.com* ☞ *Steam room. Gym with: machines, cardio, pool. Services: rubs and scrubs, massage, facials, nail services. $140 50-min massage.*

PALM DESERT

2 miles southeast of Rancho Mirage on Hwy. 111.

Palm Desert is a thriving retail and business community with popular restaurants, private and public golf courses, and premium shopping. Its stellar sight to see is the Living Desert complex.

GETTING HERE AND AROUND

Palm Desert stretches from north of Interstate 10 to the hills south of Highway 111. West–east cross streets north to south are Frank Sinatra Drive, Country Club Drive (lined on both sides with gated golfing communities), and Fred Waring Drive. Monterey Avenue marks the western boundary, and Washington Street forms the eastern edge.

EXPLORING

El Paseo. West of and parallel to Highway 111, this mile-long Mediterranean-style avenue is lined with fountains and courtyards, French and Italian fashion boutiques, plus Tommy Bahama's Emporium, Saks Fifth Avenue, and Gucci. You'll find shoe salons, jewelry stores, children's shops, 23 restaurants, and nearly 20 art galleries. The strip is a pleasant place to stroll, window-shop, people-watch, and exercise your credit cards. During the season a free city-operated bright-yellow shuttle can take you from shop to shop or to your car in the parking lot. ⊠ *Between Monterey and Portola Aves.* ☎ *877/735–7273* ⊕ *www.elpaseo.com.*

Fodor's Choice
★
FAMILY

Living Desert. Come eyeball-to-eyeball with wolves, coyotes, mountain lions, cheetahs, bighorn sheep, golden eagles, warthogs, and owls at the 1,800-acre Living Desert. Easy-to-challenging scenic trails traverse desert terrain populated with plants of the Mojave, Colorado, and Sonoran deserts in numerous habitats. In recent years, the park has expanded its vision to include Africa. At the 3-acre African WaTuTu village, you'll find a traditional marketplace as well as camels, leopards, hyenas, and other African animals. Children can pet African domesticated animals, including goats and guinea fowl, in a "petting kraal." Gecko Gulch is a children's playground with crawl-through underground tunnels, climb-on snake sculptures, a carousel, and a Discovery Center that holds ancient Pleistocene animal bones. Elsewhere, a small enclosure contains butterflies and hummingbirds, and a cool model train travels through miniatures of historic California towns. ■TIP➔ A garden center sells native desert flora, much of which is unavailable elsewhere. ✉ *47900 Portola Ave., south from Hwy. 111* ☎ *760/346–5694* ⊕ *www.livingdesert.org* 🎟 *$17.25* ☉ *June–Sept., daily 8–1:30; Oct.–May, daily 9–5.*

> ### GREEN PALM DESERT
>
> The City of Palm Desert's ambitious plan to reduce energy consumption includes incentives to install efficient pool pumps, air-conditioners, refrigeration, and lighting. The city has banned drive-through restaurants and made golf carts legal on city streets.

Palm Desert Golf Cart Parade. Each October, this parade launches "the season" with a procession of 80 golf carts decked out as floats buzzing up and down El Paseo. ✉ *72559 Highway 111* ☎ *760/346–6111* ⊕ *www.golfcartparade.com.*

Palm Springs Art Museum in Palm Desert. An outpost of the larger Palm Springs Art Museum, this museum tucked into a desert garden at the west entrance to El Paseo offers a splendid peek at cutting-edge works by contemporary sculptors and painters. Shows at this gorgeous open white space change on a regular basis. ✉ *72567 Hwy. 111* ☎ *760/346-5600* ⊕ *www.psmuseum.org* ☉ *Tues., Wed., Fri.–Sun. 10–5, Thurs. noon–8.*

Santa Rosa and San Jacinto Mountains National Monument. Administered by the U. S. Bureau of Land Management, this monument protects Peninsula bighorn sheep and other wildlife on 280,000 acres of desert habitat. Stop by the visitor center for an introduction to the site and information about the natural history of the desert. A landscaped garden displays native plants and frames a sweeping view. The well-informed staffers can recommend hiking trails that show off the beauties of the desert. Free guided hikes are offered on Thursdays and Saturdays. ✉ *51-500 Hwy. 74* ☎ *760/862–9984* ⊕ *www.ca.blm.gov/palmsprings* 🎟 *Free* ☉ *Daily 9–4.*

WHERE TO EAT AND STAY

For expanded hotel reviews, visit Fodors.com.

$$$$
SEAFOOD
✕ **Pacifica Seafood.** Sublime seafood, rooftop dining, and reduced prices at sunset draw locals to this busy restaurant on the second floor of the Gardens of El Paseo. Seafood that shines in dishes such as butter-poached Maine lobster tail, grilled Pacific swordfish, and barbecued sugar-spiced salmon arrives daily from San Diego; the menu also includes chicken, steaks, and meal-size salads. Preparations feature sauces such as orange-cumin glaze, Szechuan peppercorn butter, and green curry-coconut. The restaurant bar boasts a 130-bottle collection of vodka. ■TIP➔ Arrive between 3 and 5:30 to select from the

lower-price sunset menu. Ⓢ *Average main: $36* ✉ *73505 El Paseo* ☏ *760/674–8666* ⊕ *www.pacificaseafoodrestaurant.com* ⌚ *Reservations essential* ◷ *No lunch June–Aug.*

$$$ ⊡ **Desert Springs J. W. Marriott Resort and Spa.** With a dramatic U-shape
RESORT design, this sprawling convention-oriented hotel is set on 450 land-
FAMILY scaped acres and wraps around the desert's largest private lake. **Pros:**
gondola rides to restaurants; Kids Club daily activities; lobby bar is a
popular watering hole. **Cons:** crowded in season; $27 resort fee; extra
charges; business-traveler vibe. Ⓢ *Rooms from: $246* ✉ *74-855 Country
Club Dr.* ☏ *760/341–2211, 888/538–9459* ⊕ *www.desertspringsresort.
com* ⤳ *833 rooms, 51 suites* ☉ *No meals.*

THE ARTS

McCallum Theatre. The principal cultural venue in the desert, this theater
stages productions from fall through spring. *Fiddler on the Roof* has
played here; Lily Tomlin and Michael Feinstein have performed, and
Joffrey Ballet dancers have pirouetted across the stage. ✉ *73-000 Fred
Waring Dr.* ☏ *760/340–2787* ⊕ *www.mccallumtheatre.com.*

SPORTS AND THE OUTDOORS

BALLOONING

Fantasy Balloon Flights. Operating sunrise excursions over the southern
end of the Coachella Valley, Fantasy offers flights ($185 per person)
that run from an hour to an hour and a half, followed by a traditional
Champagne toast. ✉ *74-181 Parosella St.* ☏ *760/568–0997* ⊕ *www.
fantasyballoonflight.com.*

BICYCLING

Big Wheel Bike Tours. Palm Desert-based Big Wheel delivers rental
mountain, three-speed, and tandem bikes to area hotels. The company
also conducts full- and half-day escorted on- and off-road bike tours
throughout the area, starting at about $95 per person. ☏ *760/779–1837*
⊕ *www.bwbtours.com.*

GOLF

Desert Willow Golf Resort. Praised for its environmentally smart design,
this golf resort features pesticide-free and water-thrifty turf grasses. A
public course, managed by the City of Palm Desert, this is one of the
top-rated golf courses in the country. Mountain View has four configu-
rations; Firecliff is tournament quality with five configurations. ✉ *38-
995 Desert Willow Dr.* ☏ *760/346-0015* ⊕ *www.desertwillow.com*
🏌 *Mountain View: 18 holes. 7,079 yds. Par 72. Slope 116–128. Greens
fees: $99–$185. Firecliff: 18 holes. 7,056 yds. Par 72. Slope 117–138.
Greens fees: $99–$185* ☞ *Facilities: Driving range, putting green, golf
carts, golf academy, restaurant, bars, golf shop, group facilities.*

INDIAN WELLS

5 miles east of Palm Desert on Hwy. 111.

For the most part a quiet residential community, Indian Wells is the site
of golf and tennis tournaments throughout the year, including the BNP
Paribus Open tennis tournament. The city has three hotels that share
access to city-owned championship golf and tennis facilities.

GETTING HERE AND AROUND

Indian Wells lies between Palm Desert and La Quinta with most of its hotels, restaurants, and shopping set back from Highway 111. Private country clubs and gated residential communities are tucked along back roads.

WHERE TO EAT AND STAY

For expanded hotel reviews, visit Fodors.com.

FROM DATES TO DOLLARS

Originally several communities of humble date farmers, 15-square-mile Indian Wells has evolved into one of the country's wealthiest cities. The average family here has a six-figure annual income.

$$$
AMERICAN

✕ **IW Club at the Indian Wells Golf Resort.** This not-so-private restaurant at the Indian Wells Golf Resort offers a glimpse of how the country club set lives. The service is impeccable, and the outdoor tables offer lovely views of mountain peaks that seem close enough to touch. The menus play it safe by offering cheeseburgers, Cobb salad, and buffalo wings for lunch and scallops, Maine lobster, and beef short ribs for dinner. ⑤ *Average main: $29* ⊠ *44-500 Indian Wells Lane* ☎ *760/834–3800* ⊕ *www.iwclub.com* ⌕ *Reservations essential.*

$$$
RESORT

⌗ **Hyatt Grand Regency Indian Wells Resort.** This stark-white resort, set adjacent to the Golf Resort at Indian Wells, is one of the grandest in the desert. **Pros:** spacious rooms; excellent business services; butler service in some rooms. **Cons:** big and impersonal; spread out over 45 acres; noisy public areas. ⑤ *Rooms from: $239* ⊠ *44-600 Indian Wells La.* ☎ *760/341–1000, 800/552–4386* ⊕ *www.grandchampions.hyatt.com* ⌒ *454 rooms, 26 suites, 40 villas* ⦾ *No meals.*

$$$
RESORT

⌗ **Miramonte Resort & Spa.** A warm bit of Tuscany against a backdrop of the Santa Rosa Mountains characterizes the smallest, most intimate, and most opulent of the Indian Wells hotels. **Pros:** romantic intimacy; gorgeous gardens; daily wellness classes. **Cons:** adult-oriented; limited resort facilities on-site. ⑤ *Rooms from: $229* ⊠ *45000 Indian Wells Lane* ☎ *760/341–2200* ⊕ *www.miramonteresort.com* ⌒ *215 rooms* ⦾ *Some meals.*

$$$$
RESORT
FAMILY

⌗ **Renaissance Esmeralda Resort and Spa.** The centerpiece of this luxurious resort, adjacent to the Golf Resort at Indian Wells, is an eight-story atrium lobby, onto which most rooms open. **Pros:** balcony views; adjacent to golf-tennis complex; kids club; bicycles available. **Cons:** higher noise level in rooms surrounding pool; somewhat impersonal ambience. ⑤ *Rooms from: $269* ⊠ *44-400 Indian Wells La.* ☎ *760/773–4444* ⊕ *www.renaissanceesmeralda.com* ⌒ *538 rooms, 22 suites* ⦾ *No meals.*

SPORTS AND THE OUTDOORS

GOLF

Golf Resort at Indian Wells. Adjacent to the Hyatt Regency Indian Wells, this complex includes the Celebrity Course, designed by Clive Clark, and the Players Course, designed by John Fought. Both courses consistently rank among the best public courses in California according to golfing magazines and websites. Since this is a public facility, it pays to reserve well in advance, up to 60 days. ⊠ *44-500 Indian Wells La.* ☎ *760/346–4653* ⊕ *www.indianwellsgolfresort.com* ⛳ *Celebrity*

9

Course: 18 holes, 5 configurations. 7,050 yds. Par 72. Slope 69.9–75.6. Greens fees: $25–$139/$25–$160. Players Course: 18 holes, 5 configurations. 7,376 yds. Par 72. Slope 67.7–75.3. Greens fees: $25–$139/$25–$160 ☞ *Facilities: Callaway Performance Center, instruction, group lessons, golf clinic, club repair, restaurant, bar, gift shop.*

TENNIS

BNP Paribas Open. Drawing 200 of the world's top players, this tennis tournament takes place at Indian Wells Tennis Garden for two weeks in March. Various ticket plans are available, with some packages including stays at the adjoining Hyatt Regency Indian Wells or Renaissance Esmeralda resorts. ✉ *78200 Miles Ave.* ☎ *800/999–1585* ⊕ *www.bnpparibasopen.com* 💲 *$40 per day.*

LA QUINTA

4 miles south of Indian Wells, Washington St. off Hwy 111.

The desert became a Hollywood hideout in the 1920s, when La Quinta Hotel (now La Quinta Resort and Club) opened, introducing the Coachella Valley's first golf course. Old Town La Quinta is a popular attraction; the area holds dining spots, shops, and galleries.

GETTING HERE AND AROUND

Most of La Quinta lies south of Highway 111. The main drag through town is Washington Street.

WHERE TO EAT AND STAY

$$$$
AMERICAN

✗ **Arnold Palmer's.** From the photos on the walls to the trophy-filled display cases to the putting green for diners awaiting a table, Arnie's essence infuses this restaurant. It's a big, clubby place where families gather for birthdays and Sunday dinners, and the service is always attentive. Among the well-crafted main courses are Arnie's homemade meatloaf, double-cut pork chops with potatoes fondant, and the popular mac and cheese. The wine list is top-notch, and there's entertainment most nights. At Arnie's Pub, the more limited menu focuses on comfort food. 💲 *Average main: $31* ✉ *78164 Ave. 52* ☎ *760/771–4653* ⊕ *www.arnoldpalmersrestaurant.com* 🍴 *Reservations essential.*

$$$$
BISTRO
Fodor'sChoice
★

✗ **Lavender Bistro.** This romantic bistro gives diners the impression that they've been transported to southern France. The spacious outdoor atrium is decked out with flowers, fountains, and twinkling lights. Choices on the large menu include a take-home portion of steamed mussels, rack of lamb with olive tapenade, and crispy roasted duck with orange sauce. For dessert you can't go wrong with the baked apple tart with frangipane or the banana walnut brioche bread pudding. Dessert wines and cognacs are also available. 💲 *Average main: $34* ✉ *78073 Calle Barcelona* ☎ *760/327–8311* ⊕ *www.lavenderbistro.com* 🍴 *Reservations essential.*

$$$
AMERICAN

✗ **Hog's Breath Inn La Quinta.** Clint Eastwood watches over this replica of his Hog's Breath restaurant in Carmel; his presence is felt in the larger-than-life photos that fill the walls of its bright dining room. The large selection of American comfort food ranges from Guinness braised short ribs to sole stuffed with crab. The signature dish is the Dirty Harry dinner: chopped sirloin with capers, garlic mashed potatoes, and red cabbage, served with horseradish mushroom sauce. $ *Average main: $27* ✉ *78-065 Main St., 2nd floor* ☎ *760/564–5556, 866/464–7888* ⌕ *Reservations essential.*

$$$
RESORT
FAMILY
⌕ **La Quinta Resort and Club.** Opened in 1926 and now a member of the Waldorf-Astoria Collection, the desert's oldest resort is a lush green oasis set on 45 acres. **Pros:** individual swimming pools; gorgeous gardens; pet and family friendly. **Cons:** a party atmosphere sometimes prevails; spotty housekeeping/maintenance. $ *Rooms from: $239* ✉ *49499 Eisenhower Dr.* ☎ *760/564–4111, 800/598–3828* ⊕ *www. laquintaresort.com* ⌕ *562 rooms, 24 suites, 210 villas.*

THE ARTS

La Quinta Arts Festival. More than 200 artists participate each March in a four-day juried show that's considered one of the best in the West. The event, held at La Quinta Civic Center, includes sculptures, paintings, watercolors, fiber art, and ceramics. Proceeds benefit arts programs in area schools. ✉ *78495 Calle Tampico* ☎ *760/564–1244* ⊕ *www.lqaf. com* ⌕ *$12.*

SPORTS AND THE OUTDOORS

GOLF

PGA West. A world-class golf destination where Phil Mickelson and Jack Nicklaus play, this private/public facility includes five courses and facilities open to guests of La Quinta Resort & Club, and three courses open to the public. ✉ *49-499 Eisenhower Dr.* ☎ *760/564–5729 for tee times* ⊕ *www.pgawest.com* ⌕ *Mountain Course: 18 holes. 6,732 yds. Par 72. Slope 135. Greens fees: $69–$225. Dunes: 18 holes. 6,712 yds. Par 72. Slope 134. Greens fees: $49–$185. Greg Norman: 18 holes. 7,156 yds. Par 72. Slope 139. Greens fees: $69–$225. TPC Stadium: 18 holes. 7,300 yds. Par 72. Slope 150. Greens fees: $79–$225. Jack Nicklaus Tournament: 18 holes. 7,204 yds. Par 72. Slope 143. Greens fees: $69–$225* ⊙ *Facilities: Driving range, putting green, golf cart rentals, caddies, rental clubs, pro shop, PGA West Golf Academy, restaurant, bar.*

SHOPPING

SPAS

Spa La Quinta. The gorgeous Spa La Quinta may be the grandest in the entire desert. At this huge stand-alone facility you'll find everything from massages to facials to salon services, plus a beautiful garden setting with a large fountain, flowers galore, and plenty of nooks where you can hide out and enjoy the sanctuary. There are four outdoor treatment spaces, showers, secluded soaking tubs, and a Jacuzzi with a waterfall. The spa uses organic products including SpaRitual and Davines hair-care line. ■**TIP➔** Spa La Quinta has a Canine Suite where your dog can enjoy a world-class animal massage. The canine services are also offered in-room. ✉ *49499 Eisenhower Dr.* ☎ *760/777–4800* ⊕ *www. laquintaresort.com* ⌕ *Fitness center with: cardio and weight training machines. Services: aromatherapy, body wraps and scrubs, massage, skin care, waxing, salon services, water therapies. $165 50-min massage; $250 30-min HydraFacial; $105 45-min junior spa; $36 10-min celestial shower; $50 20-min garden bath.*

INDIO

5 miles east of Indian Wells on Hwy. 111.

Indio is the home of the date shake, which is exactly what it sounds like: an extremely thick milk shake made with dates. The city and surrounding countryside generate 95% of the dates grown and harvested in the United States. If you take a hot-air balloon ride, you will likely drift over the tops of date palm trees.

GETTING HERE AND AROUND

Indio is east of Indian Wells and north of La Quinta. Highway 111 runs right through Indio, and Interstate 10 skirts it to the north.

EXPLORING

FAMILY **Coachella Valley History Museum.** Make a date to learn about dates at this museum inside a former farmhouse. The exhibits here provide an intriguing glimpse into irrigation, harvesting, and other farming practices; a timeline and other displays chronicle how the industry emerged in the desert a century ago. ⊠ *82-616 Miles Ave.* ☎ *760/342–6651* ⊕ *www.coachellavalleymuseum.org* ᗑ *$10* ☉ *Oct.–May, Thurs.–Sat. 10–4, Sun. 1–4.*

FAMILY **National Date Festival and Riverside County Fair.** Indio celebrates its raison d'être each February at this festival and county fair. The midmonth festivities include an Arabian Nights pageant, camel and ostrich races, and exhibits of local dates, plus monster truck shows, a demolition derby, a nightly musical pageant, and a rodeo. Admission includes camel rides. ⊠ *Riverside County Fairgrounds, 82-503 Hwy. 111* ☎ *800/811–3247, 760/863-8247* ⊕ *www.datefest.org* ᗑ *$9.*

Shields Date Garden and Café. You can sample, select, and take home some of Shields's locally grown dates. Ten varieties are available, including the giant super-sweet royal medjools, along with specialty date products such as date crystals, stuffed dates, confections, and local honey. At the Shields Date Garden Café, you can try an iconic date shake, dig into date pancakes, or go exotic with a date tamale. Breakfast and lunch are served daily. ⊠ *80-225 Hwy. 111* ☎ *760/347–0996* ⊕ *www. shieldsdategarden.com* ☉ *Store 9–5, café 7–2:30* ☉ *No dinner.*

WHERE TO EAT AND STAY

For expanded hotel reviews, visit Fodors.com.

$$ ✕ **Ciro's Ristorante and Pizzeria.** Serving pizza and pasta since the 1960s,
SICILIAN this popular casual restaurant has a few unusual pies on the menu, including cashew with three cheeses. The decor is classic pizza joint, with checkered tablecloths and bentwood chairs. Daily pasta specials vary but might include red- or white-clam sauce or scallops with parsley and red wine. ⑤ *Average main: $17* ⊠ *81-963 Hwy. 111* ☎ *760/347–6503* ⊕ *www.cirospasta.com* ☉ *No lunch Sun.*

$$$ ✕ **Jackalope Ranch.** It's worth the drive to Indio to sample flavors of
AMERICAN the Old West here, 21st-century style. Inside a rambling 21,000 foot building, holding a clutch of indoor/outdoor dining spaces, you may be seated near an open kitchen, a bar, fountains, fireplaces, or waterworks (both inside and out). Jackalope can be a busy, noisy place; ask for a quiet corner if that's your pleasure. The large menu roams the west,

featuring grilled and barbecued items of all sorts, spicy and savory sauces, flavorful vegetables, and sumptuous desserts. Locals like the place, especially the bar; but some reviews complain that the quality of the food doesn't match the setting. ⑤ *Average main: $24* ✉ *80-400 Hwy. 111* ☎ *760/342-1999* ⊕ *www.thejackaloperanch.com* ⚠ *Reservations essential.*

$$ **Fantasy Springs Resort Casino.**
HOTEL   Operated by the Cabazon Band of
FAMILY   Mission Indians, this family-oriented resort casino stands out in the Coachella Valley, affording mountain views from most rooms and the rooftop wine bar. **Pros:** headliner entertainment; great views from the rooftop bar; bowling alley; golf course. **Cons:** in the middle of nowhere; average staff service. ⑤ *Rooms from: $169* ✉ *84-245 Indio Springs Pkwy.* ☎ *760/342-5000, 800/827-2946* ⊕ *www.fantasyspringsresort. com* ⤶ *240 rooms, 11 suites.*

EN
ROUTE   **Coachella Valley Preserve.** For a glimpse of how the desert appeared before development, head northeast from Palm Springs to this preserve. It has a system of sand dunes and several palm oases that were formed because the San Andreas Fault lines here allow water flowing underground to rise to the surface. A mile-long walk along Thousand Palms Oasis reveals pools supporting the tiny endangered desert pupfish and more than 183 bird species. The preserve has a visitor center, nature and equestrian trails, restrooms, and picnic facilities. Guided hikes are offered. Note that it is exceptionally hot in summer here. ✉ *29200 Thousand Palms Canyon Rd., Thousand Palms* ☎ *760/343-2733* ⊕ *www.coachellavalleypreserve.org* ⤶ *Free* ☼ *Visitor Center Sept. 1–Oct. 14, daily 8–noon; Oct. 15–Apr. 14, daily 8–4; Apr. 15–May 31, daily 8–noon. Closed June–Aug.*

ROCKIN' AT COACHELLA

The Coachella Valley Music and Arts Festival, one of the biggest parties in SoCal, draws hundreds of thousands of rock music fans to Indio for two weekends of live concerts and dancing each April. Hundreds of bands show up, including headliners such as Jack Johnson, the Raconteurs, Portishead, Roger Waters, and My Morning Jacket. Everybody camps at the polo grounds. Visit ⊕ *www.coachella.com* for details and tickets, which sell out months in advance.

ALONG TWENTYNINE PALMS HIGHWAY

Designated a California Scenic Highway, the Twentynine Palms Highway not only connects two of the three entrances to Joshua Tree National Park (⇨ *see Chapter 10*), it also offers a gorgeous view of the high desert, especially in winter and spring when you may be driving beneath snowcapped peaks or through a field of wildflowers. Park entrances are located at Joshua Tree and Twentynine Palms. Yucca Valley and Twentynine Palms have lodging, dining options, and other services. If you see any strange artworks along the way, they might be created by artists associated with the avant-garde High Desert Test Sites (⊕ *www.highdeserttestsites.com*).

YUCCA VALLEY

30 miles northeast of Palm Springs on Hwy. 62/Twentynine Palms Hwy.

One of the high desert's fastest-growing cities, Yucca Valley is emerging as a bedroom community for people who work as far away as Ontario, 85 miles to the west. In this sprawling suburb you can shop for necessities, get your car serviced, and chow down at the fast-food outlets.

GETTING HERE AND AROUND

The drive to Yucca Valley on Highway 62/Twentynine Palms Highway passes through the Painted Hills and drops down into a valley. Yucca Valley is the first town you come to. Take Pioneertown Road north to the Old West outpost.

EXPLORING

FAMILY   **Hi-Desert Nature Museum.** Creatures that make their homes in Joshua Tree National Park are the focus here. A small live-animal display includes scorpions, snakes, ground squirrels, and chuckwallas (a type of lizard). You'll also find rocks, minerals, and fossils from the Paleozoic era and Native American artifacts, and there's a children's room. ⊠ *Yucca Valley Community Center, 57116 Twentynine Palms Hwy.* ☎ *760/369–7212* ⊕ *hidesertnaturemuseum.org* ⊠ *Free* ☉ *Tues.–Sat. 10–5.*

Pioneertown. In 1946 Roy Rogers, Gene Autry, the Sons of the Pioneers (the music group for whom the town is named), and Russ Hayden built Pioneertown, an 1880s-style Wild West movie set complete with hitching posts, saloon, and an OK Corral. You can stroll past wooden and adobe storefronts and feel like you're back in the Old West. Or not: Pappy and Harriet's Pioneertown Palace, now the town's top draw, has evolved into a hip venue for indie and other bands. ⊠ *53688 Pioneertown Rd., 4 miles north of Yucca Valley, Pioneertown* ⊕ *pappyandharriets.com.*

WHERE TO EAT AND STAY

For expanded hotel reviews, visit Fodors.com.

$$$ ✕ **Pappy & Harriet's Pioneertown Palace.** Smack in the middle of a Western-
AMERICAN   movie-set town is this Western-movie-set saloon where you can have dinner, relax over a drink at the bar, or check out some great indie and other bands—Leon Russell, Sonic Youth, the Get Up Kids, and Robert Plant have all played here, as have many Cali groups. The food ranges from Tex-Mex to Santa Maria–style barbecue to steak and burgers. No surprises but plenty of fun. ■ **TIP→ Pappy & Harriet's may be in the middle of nowhere, but you'll need reservations for dinner on weekends.** ⑤ *Average main: $24* ⊠ *53688 Pioneertown Rd., Pioneertown* ☎ *760/365–5956* ⊕ *www.pappyandharriets.com* ⚶ *Reservations essential* ☉ *Closed Tues. and Wed.*

$ 🏨 **Best Western Joshua Tree Hotel & Suites.** Opened in 2008, this hotel is a
HOTEL   welcome addition to the slim pickings near Joshua Tree National Park; rooms are spacious, nicely appointed, and decorated in soft desert colors. **Pros:** convenient to Joshua Tree NP; pleasant lounge. **Cons:** location on busy highway; limited service. ⑤ *Rooms from: $108* ⊠ *56525 Twentynine Palms Hwy.* ☎ *760/365–3555* ⊕ *www.bestwestern.com* ⇘ *95 rooms* ⦿❘ *Breakfast.*

TWENTYNINE PALMS

24 miles east of Yucca Valley on Hwy. 62, Twentynine Palms Hwy.

The main gateway town to Joshua Tree National Park (⇨ *see Chapter 15*), Twentynine Palms is also the location of the U.S. Marine Air Ground Task Force Training Center. You can find services, supplies, and lodging in town.

GETTING HERE AND AROUND

Highway 62 is the main route to and through Twentynine Palms. Most businesses here center around Highway 62 and Utah Trail, 3 miles north of Joshua Tree's entrance.

ESSENTIALS

Visitor Information Twentynine Palms Chamber of Commerce and Visitor Center ⊠ *73484 Twentynine Palms Hwy.* ☎ *760/367–6197* ⊕ *www.visit29.org* ⊘ *Visitor Center Mon.–Fri. 9–5, Sat.–Sun. 10–4.*

EXPLORING

Oasis of Murals. The history and current life of Twentynine Palms is depicted in this collection of 20 murals painted on the sides of buildings. If you drive around town, you can't miss the murals, but you can also pick up a free map from the Twentynine Palms Chamber of Commerce.

29 Palms Art Gallery. This gallery features work by local painters, sculptors, and jewelry makers who find inspiration in the desert landscape. ⊠ *74055 Cottonwood Dr.* ☎ *760/367–7819* ⊕ *www.29palmsartgallery. com* ⊘ *Wed.–Sun. noon–3.*

WHERE TO STAY

For expanded hotel reviews, visit Fodors.com.

$$
B&B/INN

29 Palms Inn. The closest lodging to the entrance to Joshua Tree National Park, the funky 29 Palms Inn scatters a collection of adobe and wood-frame cottages, some dating back to the 1920s and 1930s, over 70 acres of grounds that are popular with birds and bird-watchers year-round. **Pros:** gracious hospitality; exceptional bird-watching; popular with artists. **Cons:** rustic accommodations; limited amenities. ⑤ *Rooms from: $145* ⊠ *73950 Inn Ave.* ☎ *760/367–3505* ⊕ *www.29palmsinn. com* ⊅ *18 rooms, 5 suites* |◯| *Multiple meal plans.*

$$
B&B/INN

Roughley Manor. To the wealthy pioneer who erected the stone mansion now occupied by this B&B, expense was no object, which is evident in the 50-foot-long planked maple floor in great room, the intricate carpentry on the walls, and the huge stone fireplaces that warm the house on the rare cold night. **Pros:** elegant rooms and public spaces; good stargazing in the gazebo; great horned owls on property. **Cons:** somewhat isolated location; three-story main building doesn't have an elevator. ⑤ *Rooms from: $135* ⊠ *74744 Joe Davis Rd.* ☎ *760/367–3238* ⊕ *www. roughleymanor.com* ⊅ *2 suites, 7 cottages* |◯| *Multiple meal plans.*

9

ANZA-BORREGO DESERT

Largely uninhabited, the Anza-Borrego Desert is popular with those who love solitude, silence, space, starry nights, light, and sweeping mountain vistas. This desert lies south of the Palm Springs area, stretching along the western shore of the Salton Sea down toward Interstate 8 along the Mexican border. Isolated from the rest of California by mile-high mountains to the north and west, most of this desert falls within the borders of Anza-Borrego Desert State Park, which at more than 600,000 acres is the largest state park in the contiguous United States. This is a place where you can escape the cares of the human world.

For thousands of years Native Americans of the Cahuilla and Kumeyaay people inhabited this area, spending their winters on the warm desert floor and their summers in the mountains. The first Europeans—a party led by the Spanish explorer Juan Baptiste de Anza—crossed this desert in 1776. Anza, for whom the desert is named, made the trip through here twice. Roadside signs along Highways 86, 78, and S2 mark the route of the Anza expedition, which spent Christmas Eve 1776 in what is now Anza-Borrego Desert State Park. Seventy-five years later thousands of immigrants on their way to the goldfields up north crossed the desert on the Southern Immigrant Trail, remnants of which remain along Highway S2. Permanent settlers arrived early in the 20th century, and by the 1930s the first adobe resort cottage had been built.

BORREGO SPRINGS

59 miles south of Indio via Hwys. 86 and S22.

The permanent population of Borrego Springs, set squarely in the middle of Anza-Borrego Desert State Park, hovers around 2,500. Long a quiet town, it's emerging as a laid-back destination for desert lovers. From September through June, when temperatures stay in the 80s and 90s, you can engage in outdoor activities such as hiking, nature study, golf, tennis, horseback riding, and mountain biking. If winter rains cooperate, Borrego Springs puts on some of the best wildflower displays in the low desert. In some years the desert floor is carpeted with color: yellow dandelions and sunflowers, pink primrose, purple sand verbena, and blue wild heliotrope. The bloom generally runs from late February through April. For current information on wildflowers around Borrego Springs, call Anza-Borrego Desert State Park's wildflower hotline (☎ 760/767–4684).

GETTING HERE AND AROUND

You can reach the Anza Borrego Desert from the Palm Springs area by taking the Highway 86 exit from Interstate 10, south of Indio. Highway 86, mostly not freeway, passes through Coachella and along the western shore of the Salton Sea. Turn west on Highway S22 at Salton City and follow it to Peg Leg Road, where you turn south until you reach Palm Canyon Drive. Turn west and the road leads to the center of Borrego Springs, Christmas Circle, where most major roads come together. Well-marked roads radiating from the circle will take you to the most popular sites in the park. If you are coming from the San Diego area, you'll need to drive east on Interstate 8 to the Cuyamaca Mountains, exit at Highway 79 and enjoy a lovely 23-mile drive through the mountains until you reach Julian; head east on Highway 78 and follow well-marked signs to Borrego Springs.

ESSENTIALS
Visitor Information Borrego Springs Chamber of Commerce
✉ *786 Palm Canyon Dr.* ☎ *760/767–5555, 800/559–5524*
⊕ *www.borregospringschamber.com.*

EXPLORING
Anza-Borrego Desert State Park. One of the richest living natural-history museums in the nation, this state park is a vast, nearly uninhabited wilderness where you can step through a field of wildflowers, cool off in a palm-shaded oasis, count zillions of stars in the black night sky, and listen to coyotes howl at dusk. The landscape, largely undisturbed by humans, reveals a rich natural history. There's evidence of a vast inland sea in the piles of oyster beds near Split Mountain and of the power of natural forces such as earthquakes and flash floods. In addition, recent scientific work has confirmed that the Borrego Badlands, with more than 6,000 meters of exposed fossil-bearing sediments, is likely the richest such deposit in North America, telling the story of 7 million years of climate change, upheaval, and prehistoric animals. They've found evidence of sabertooth cats, flamingos, zebras, and the largest flying bird in the northern hemisphere beneath the now-parched sand. Today the desert's most treasured inhabitants are the herds of elusive and endangered native bighorn sheep, or borrego, for which the park is named. Among the strange desert plants you may observe are the gnarly elephant trees. As these are endangered, rangers don't encourage visitors to seek out the secluded grove at Fish Creek, but there are a few examples at the visitor center garden. After a wet winter you can see a short-lived but stunning display of cacti, succulents, and desert wildflowers in bloom.

The park is unusually accessible to visitors. Admission to the park is free, and few areas are off-limits. There are two developed campgrounds, but you can camp anywhere; just follow the trails and pitch a tent wherever you like. There are more than 500 miles of dirt roads, two huge wilderness areas, and 110 miles of riding and hiking trails. Many sites can be seen from paved roads, but some require driving on dirt roads, for which rangers recommend you use a four-wheel-drive vehicle. When you do leave the pavement, carry the appropriate supplies: a cell phone (which may be unreliable in some areas), a shovel and other tools, flares, blankets, and plenty of water. The canyons are susceptible to flash flooding, so inquire about weather conditions (even on sunny days) before entering. ■ TIP→ Borrego resorts, restaurants, and the state park have Wi-Fi, but the service is spotty at best. If you need to talk to someone in the area, it's best to find a phone with a landline.

The sites and hikes listed below are arranged by region of the park and distance from the Visitor Center: in the valley and hills surrounding Borrego Springs, near Tamarisk Campground, along Highway S2, south of Scissors Crossing, and south of Ocotillo Wells.

If you think the desert is just a sandy wasteland, the colorful beauty of the Anza-Borrego Desert will be a pleasant surprise.

Stop by the **Visitor Center** to get oriented, to pick up a park map, and to learn about weather, road, and wildlife conditions. Designed to keep cool during the desert's blazing hot summers, the center is built underground, beneath a demonstration desert garden containing examples of most of the native flora and a little pupfish pond. Displays inside the center illustrate the natural history of the area. Picnic tables are scattered throughout, making this a good place to linger and enjoy the view.

A 1½-mile trail leads to **Borrego Palm Canyon,** one of the few native palm groves in North America. The canyon, about 1 mile west of the Visitor Center, holds a grove of more than 1,000 native fan palms, a stream, and a waterfall. Wildlife is abundant along this route. This moderate hike is the most popular in the park.

With a year-round stream and lush plant life, **Coyote Canyon,** approximately 4½ miles north of Borrego Springs, is one of the best places to see and photograph spring wildflowers. Portions of the canyon road follow a section of the old Anza Trail. This area is closed between June 15 and September 15 to allow native bighorn sheep undisturbed use of the water. The dirt road that gives access to the canyon may be sandy enough to require a four-wheel-drive vehicle.

The late-afternoon vista of the Borrego badlands from **Font's Point,** 13 miles east of Borrego Springs, is one of the most breathtaking views in the desert, especially when the setting sun casts a golden glow in high relief on the eroded mountain slopes. The road from the Font's Point turnoff can be rough enough to make using a four-wheel-drive vehicle advisable; inquire about road conditions at the Visitor Center before starting out. Even if you can't make it out on the paved road, you can see some of the view from the highway.

East of Tamarisk Grove campground (13 miles south of Borrego Springs), the **Narrows Earth Trail** is a short walk off the road. Along the way you can see evidence of the many geologic processes involved in forming the canyons of the desert, such as a contact zone between two earthquake faults, and sedimentary layers of metamorphic and igneous rock.

The 1.6-mile round trip **Yaqui Well Nature Trail** takes you along a path to a desert water hole where birds and wildlife are abundant. It's also a good place to look for wildflowers in spring. Pick up a self-guided brochure at the trailhead across from Tamarisk Campground.

Traversing a boulder-strewn trail is the easy, mostly flat **Pictograph/ Smuggler's Canyon Trail.** At the end is a collection of rocks covered with muted red and yellow pictographs painted within the last hundred years or so by Native Americans. Walk about ½ mile beyond the pictures to reach Smuggler's Canyon, where an overlook provides views of the Vallecito Valley. The hike is 2 to 3 miles round-trip and begins in Blair Valley, 6 miles southeast of Highway 78, off Highway S2, at the Scissors Crossing intersection.

Just a few steps off the paved road, **Carrizo Badlands Overlook** offers a view of eroded and twisted sedimentary rock that obscures the fossils of the mastodons, saber-tooths, zebras, and camels that roamed this region a million years ago. The route to the overlook through Earthquake Valley and Blair Valley parallels the Southern Emigrant Trail. It's off Highway S2, 40 miles south of Scissors Crossing.

Geology students from all over the world visit the Fish Creek area of Anza-Borrego to explore the canyon through Split Mountain. The narrow gorge with 600-foot walls was formed by an ancient stream. Fossils in this area indicate that a sea once covered the desert floor. From Highway 78 at Ocotillo Wells, take Split Mountain Road south 9 miles. ⊠ *Visitor Center, 200 Palm Canyon Dr., Hwy. S22* ☎ *760/767–5311, 800/444–7275 campground reservations only, 760/767–4684 wildflower hotline* ⊕ *www.parks.ca.gov* ▨ *Free* ☯ *Park daily dawn–dusk. Visitor Center Oct.–May 1, daily 9–5.*

Galleta Meadows. Flowers aren't the only things popping up from the earth in Borrego Springs. At Galleta Meadows camels, llamas, saber-toothed tigers, tortoises, and monumental gomphotherium (a sort of ancient elephant) appear to roam the earth again. These life-size bronze figures are of prehistoric animals whose fossils can be found in the Borrego Badlands. The collection, more than 50 sets of animals, was the project of Dennis Avery, a wealthy resident who installed the works of art on property he owned for the entertainment of locals and visitors. Maps are available from Borrego Springs Chamber of Commerce. ⊠ *Borrego Springs Rd. from Christmas Circle to Henderson Canyon* ☎ *760/767–5555* ⊕ *www.galletameadows.com* ▨ *Free.*

WHERE TO EAT

$$ ✕ **The Arches.** On the edge of the Borrego Springs Resort Golf Course,
MODERN   set beneath a canopy of grapefruit trees, the Arches is a pleasant place
AMERICAN   to eat. For breakfast you'll find burritos alongside standard fare such
as pancakes and biscuits and gravy. At lunch, best enjoyed on the patio,
sandwiches and salads are the main options. Dinner selections include
chicken pot pie, bourbon-spiced pork, and grilled carne asada. ⑤ *Average main: $19* ✉ *1112 Tilting T Dr.* ☎ *760/767–5700* ⏱ *Summer hrs vary; call ahead.*

$$$ ✕ **Carlee's Place.** Sooner or later most visitors to Borrego Springs wind
AMERICAN   up at Carlee's Place for a drink and a bite to eat. It's an all-American
type of establishment, where your server might call you "honey" while
setting a huge steak in front of you. An extra-large menu has everything:
burgers, salads, seafood, sandwiches, and prime rib. At the bar, ask for
a lemon-drop martini. ⑤ *Average main: $23* ✉ *660 Palm Canyon Dr.* ☎ *760/767–3262.*

$ ✕ **Carmelita's Mexican Grill and Cantina.** A friendly, family-run eatery
MEXICAN   tucked into a back corner of what is called "The Mall," Carmelita's
draws locals and visitors all day, whether it's for a hearty breakfast, a
cooked-to-order enchilada or burrito, or to tip back a brew at the bar.
The menu lists typical combination plates (enchiladas, burritos, tamales,
and tacos). Salsas have a bit of zing, and the *masas* (corn dough used to
make tortillas and tamales) are tasty and tender. ⑤ *Average main: $12* ✉ *575 Palm Canyon Dr.* ☎ *760/767–5666.*

$$$ ✕ **Coyote Steak House/Red Ocotillo.** The owners of the Palms at Indian
MODERN   Head operate these two restaurants together. Red Ocotillo serves break-
AMERICAN   fast (all the usual suspects) and lunch—burgers, Caesar salads, fish and
chips, and the like. The more fancy Coyote Steak House serves rack of
lamb, filet mignon, and other hearty standbys for dinner. What you eat
is less important than the lovely 1950s-modern setting and the casual
atmosphere. Dog lovers will appreciate the canine menu, whose treats
include house-made peanut-butter dog cookies. ⑤ *Average main: $23* ✉ *2220 Hoberg Rd.* ☎ *760/767–7400* ⚑ *Reservations essential* ⏱ *Coyote Steak House: no breakfast or lunch. Red Ocotillo: no breakfast or lunch July and Aug.*

WHERE TO STAY

For expanded hotel reviews, visit Fodors.com.

$$ ⌂ **Borrego Springs Resort & Spa.** At this quiet resort, the large, smartly
RESORT   refurbished rooms all surround a swimming pool and come with either
a shaded balcony or a patio with pleasant desert views. **Pros:** golf and
tennis on-site; most rooms have good desert views; pink grapefruit
bathroom products. **Cons:** limited amenities; average service. ⑤ *Rooms from: $160* ✉ *1112 Tilting T Dr.* ☎ *760/767–5700, 888/826–7734* ⊕ *www.borregospringsresort.com* ⇆ *66 rooms, 34 suites* ❙❀❙ *No meals.*

$$$ ⌂ **Borrego Valley Inn.** Desert gardens of mesquite, ocotillo, and creo-
B&B/INN   sote surround the adobe Southwestern-style buildings here that house
spacious rooms with plenty of natural light, original art, pine beds,
and double futons facing corner fireplaces. **Pros:** swim under the
stars in the clothing-optional pool; exquisite desert gardens. **Cons:**
potential street noise in season; not a good choice for families with

young children or pets. ⑤ *Rooms from: $200* ⊠ *405 Palm Canyon Dr.* ☎ *760/767–0311, 800/333–5810* ⊕ *www.borregovalleyinn.com* ➱ *15 rooms, 1 suite* ⓘ⃝*Breakfast.*

SPORTS AND THE OUTDOORS
GOLF
Borrego Springs Resort & Spa Country Club. The 27 holes of golf at this resort and country club are open to the public. Three 9-hole courses, with natural desert landscaping and mature date palms, can be played individually or in any combination. Greens fees are $40 to $65, depending on the course and the day of the week, and include a cart and range balls. ⊠ *1112 Tilting T Dr.* ☎ *760/767–5700* ⊕ *www. borregospringsresort.com* 🏌 *Black Course: 9 holes, 3 courses. 3,237 yds. Slope 123. Greens fees: $40–65* ☞ *Facilities: Driving range, putting green, club rentals, lessons, restaurant, bar.*

Roadrunner Club. Adjacent to the Springs at Borrego course with some shared facilities, this club has an 18-hole course par-3 golf course. The terrain is mostly flat. ⊠ *1010 Palm Canyon Dr.* ☎ *760/767–5373* ⊕ *www.roadrunnerclub.com* 🏌 *18 holes. 2,451 yds. Par 54. Greens fee: $35* ☞ *Facilities: Putting green, golf cart rentals, club rentals, pro shop, lessons.*

The Springs at Borrego. Part of a luxurious RV park complex, The Springs at Borrego has a public golf course with 9 holes that can be configured to play as 18. ⊠ *2255 DiGiorgio Rd.* ☎ *760/767–0004* ⊕ *www. springsatborrego.com* 🏌 *9 holes. 3,000 yds. Par 36. Slope 111. Greens fee: $45 for 18 holes* ☞ *Facilities: Driving range, putting green, golf carts, rental clubs, lessons, pro shop.*

TENNIS
Anza Borrego Tennis Center. A busy tennis club that's also open for public play, this center holds four hard surface courts, a swimming pool, and club house. You can play all day for $5; it's $10 to use all the facilities. ⊠ *286 Palm Canyon Dr.* ☎ *760/767–0577* ⊙ *Closed May–Sept.*

SHOPPING
Anza-Borrego State Park Store. You can find guidebooks and maps, clothing, desert art, and gifts for kids here, and the staff organizes hikes, naturalist talks, classes, research programs, and nature walks. Or they can help you organize your own visit. Proceeds from sales benefit preservation of the park and its resources. ⊠ *587 Palm Canyon Dr., #110* ☎ *760/767–4063* ⊕ *www.theabf.org* ⊙ *Oct.–May 14, daily 10-4; May 15–Sept., weekdays 11–3.*

Borrego Outfitters. This contemporary general store stocks high-end outdoor gear from Kelty and Columbia, personal care items from Burt's Bees, footwear from Teva and Acorn, Speedo and Fresh Produce swimsuits, and tabletop and home-decor items. You can browse through racks of clothing and piles of hats, all suited to the desert climate. The off season brings some great bargains. ⊠ *579 Palm Canyon Dr.* ☎ *760/767–3502* ⊕ *www.borregooutfitters.com.*

9

SALTON SEA

30 miles southeast of Indio via Hwy. 86S on western shore and via Hwy. 111 on eastern shore; 29 miles east of Borrego Springs via Hwy. S22.

The Salton Sea, one of the largest inland seas on Earth, is the product of both natural and artificial forces. The sea occupies the Salton Basin, a remnant of prehistoric Lake Cahuilla. Over the centuries the Colorado River flooded the basin and the water drained into the Gulf of California. In 1905 a flood once again filled the Salton Basin, but the exit to the gulf was blocked by sediment. The floodwaters remained in the basin, creating a saline lake 228 feet below sea level, about 35 miles long and 15 miles wide, with a surface area of nearly 380 square miles. The sea, which lies along the Pacific Flyway, supports 400 species of birds. Fishing for tilapia, boating, camping, and bird-watching are popular activities year-round.

GETTING HERE AND AROUND

Salton Sea State Recreation Area includes about 14 miles of coastline on the northeastern shore of the sea, about 30 miles south of Indio via Highway 111. The Sonny Bono Salton Sea National Wildlife Refuge fills the southernmost tip of the sea's shore. To reach it from the recreation area, continue south about 60 miles to Niland; continue south to Sinclair Road, and turn west following the road to the Refuge Headquarters.

EXPLORING

FAMILY **Salton Sea State Recreation Area.** This huge recreation area on the sea's north shore draws thousands each year to its playgrounds, hiking trails, fishing spots, and boat launches. Ranger-guided bird walks take place on Saturdays; you'll see migrating and native birds including Canada geese, pelicans, and shorebirds. On Sundays there are free kayak tours. ✉ *100-225 State Park Rd., North Shore* ☎ *760/393-3052* ⊕ *www. parks.ca.gov* ⊠ *$5* ☾ *Park daily 8–sunset.*

Sonny Bono Salton Sea National Wildlife Refuge. The 2,200-acre wildlife refuge here, on the Pacific Flyway, is a wonderful spot for viewing migratory birds. There's an observation deck where you can watch migrating Canada geese. Along the trails you might view eared grebes, burrowing owls, great blue herons, ospreys, or yellow-footed gulls. ✉ *906 W. Sinclair Rd., Calipatria* ☎ *760/348-5278* ⊕ *www.fws.gov/saltonsea* ⊠ *Free* ☾ *Park Oct.–Feb., daily sunrise–sunset. Visitor center Oct.–Feb., weekdays 7–3:, weekends 8–4:15; Mar.–Sept., closed weekends.*

JOSHUA TREE
NATIONAL PARK

WELCOME TO JOSHUA TREE NATIONAL PARK

TOP REASONS TO GO

★ **Rock climbing:** Joshua Tree is a world-class site with challenges for climbers of just about every skill level.

★ **Peace and quiet:** Savor the solitude of one of the last great wildernesses in America.

★ **Stargazing:** You'll be mesmerized by the Milky Way flowing across the summer sky. For spectacular natural fireworks, visit in mid-August during the Perseid meteor shower and watch shooting stars streak overhead.

★ **Wildflowers:** In spring, the hillsides explode in a patchwork of yellow, blue, pink, and white.

★ **Sunsets:** Twilight is a magical time here, especially during the winter, when the setting sun casts a golden glow on the mountains.

1 Keys View. This is the most dramatic overlook in the park—on clear days you can see Signal Mountain in Mexico.

2 Hidden Valley. Crawl between the big rocks and you'll understand why this boulder-strewn area was once a cattle rustlers' hideout.

3 Cholla Cactus Garden. Come here in the late afternoon, when the spiky stalks of the bigelow (jumping) cholla cactus are backlit against an intense blue sky.

4 Oasis of Mara. Walk the nature trail around this desert oasis, which the first settlers, the Serrano, dubbed "the place of little springs and much grass."

Utah Trail Rd.

Amboy Rd.

62

62

CALIFORNIA

0   5 mi

0   5 km

PINTO MOUNTAINS

COXCOMB MOUNTAINS

3

PINTO BASIN

Cholla
Cactus Garden

Pinto Basin Rd.

HEXIE
MOUNTAINS

NT

Kaiser Road

EAGLE MOUNTAINS

177

Visitor Center

Cottonwood Spring

Bajada Nature Trail

COTTONWOOD MTS.

Desert Center

Lost Palms Oasis

10

Chiriaco
Summit

← TO
MECCA

10

GETTING
ORIENTED

Daggerlike tufts grace
the branches of the
namesake of Joshua Tree
National Park in south-
eastern California, where
the arid Mojave Desert
meets the sparsely veg-
etated Colorado Desert
(part of the Sonoran
Desert, which lies within
California, Arizona, and

Northern Mexico).
Passenger cars are fine
for paved areas, but you'll
need four-wheel drive
for many of the rugged
backcountry roadways.
At the park's most popular
sites, parking is limited.
Joshua Tree does not have
public transportation.

Updated by
Bobbi Zane

Ruggedly beautiful desert scenery attracts nearly 2 million visitors each year to Joshua Tree National Park, one of the last great wildernesses in the continental United States. Its mountains support mounds of enormous boulders and jagged rock; natural cactus gardens and lush oases shaded by tall fan palms mark the meeting place of the Mojave (high) and Sonora (low) deserts. Extensive stands of Joshua trees gave the park its name; the plants (members of the yucca family of shrubs) reminded Mormon pioneers of the biblical Joshua, with their thick, stubby branches representing the prophet raising his arms toward heaven.

JOSHUA TREE PLANNER

WHEN TO GO

October through May, when the desert is cooler, is when most visitors arrive. Daytime temperatures range from the mid-70s in December and January to mid-90s in October and May. Lows can dip to near freezing in midwinter, and you may even encounter snow at the higher elevations. Summers can be torrid, with daytime temperatures reaching 110°F.

PLANNING YOUR TIME

JOSHUA TREE IN ONE DAY

One day is enough time to visit the most interesting sites of Joshua Tree National Park, enjoy a picnic lunch, and be back in Palm Springs for dinner. Try a loop tour that starts in the town of Joshua Tree at the West Entrance Visitor Center—right off Twentynine Palms Highway. Here you can get maps and information on ranger programs and hikes before you start. Take a leisurely drive along Park Boulevard, stopping to explore Hidden Valley. Detour to Keyes View for a sweeping view of the valley amid 10,000-foot-high peaks. Return to Park Boulevard and then head east for Queen Valley, where you can learn about pioneer life on a 90-minute guided tour of Keys Ranch. While here take a few minutes to check out Barker Dam and possibly spot some wildlife. Return to Park Boulevard and continue east to Jumbo Rocks campground, which has nice picnic tables. Beyond Jumbo Rocks, follow Park Boulevard past the North Entrance Station to the Oasis of Mara, where you can take a nature walk and explore the Visitor Center. The adjacent rustic 29 Palms Inn has a popular restaurant that is open for lunch and dinner.

GETTING HERE AND AROUND
CAR TRAVEL
An isolated island of pristine wilderness—a rarity these days—Joshua Tree National Park is within a short drive of 11 million Southern California residents. Most visitors, in fact, make the two-hour drive from the Los Angeles area to enjoy a weekend of solitude in 792,726 acres of untouched desert. The urban sprawl of Palm Springs (home to the nearest airport) is 45 miles away, but gateway towns Joshua Tree, Yucca Valley, and Twentynine Palms are just north of the park. If you're staying in the Palm Springs area, you can enjoy the highlights of the park in one day, including a stop for a picnic at a scenic spot.

■TIP➜ If you'd prefer not to drive, most Palm Springs area hotels can arrange a half- or full-day tour that hits the highlights of Joshua Tree National Park. But you'll need to spend two or three days camping here to truly experience the quiet beauty of the desert.

PARK ESSENTIALS
PARK FEES AND PERMITS
Park admission is $15 per car, $5 per person on foot, bicycle, motorcycle, or horse. The Joshua Tree Pass, good for one year, is $30. Free permits—available at all visitor centers—are required for rock climbing.

PARK HOURS
The park is open every day, around the clock. The park is in the Pacific time zone.

VISITOR INFORMATION
PARK CONTACT INFORMATION
Joshua Tree National Park. Joshua Tree National Park ⊠ *74485 National Park Dr., Twentynine Palms* ☎ *760/367–5500* ⊕ *www.nps.gov/jotr.*

VISITOR CENTERS
Joshua Tree Visitor Center. This visitor center has interesting exhibits illustrating park geology, cultural and historic sites, and hiking and rock-climbing activities. There's also a small bookstore. Restrooms with flush toilets are on the premises, and showers are nearby. ⊠ *6554 Park Blvd., Joshua Tree* ☎ *760/366–1855* ⊕ *www.nps.gov/jotr* ☞ *$15 entrance fee* ⊙ *Daily 8–5.*

Oasis Visitor Center. Exhibits here illustrate how Joshua Tree was formed, reveal the differences between the park's two types of desert, and demonstrate how plants and animals eke out an existence in this arid climate. Take the 0.5-mile nature walk through the nearby

Oasis of Mara, which is alive with cottonwood trees, palm trees, and mesquite shrubs. Facilities include picnic tables, restrooms, and a bookstore. ⊠ *74485 National Park Dr., Twentynine Palms* ☎ *760/367–5500* ⊕ *www.nps.gov/jotr* ⊠ *$15* ⊘ *Daily 8–5.*

EXPLORING

SCENIC DRIVES

Fodor's Choice **Park Boulevard.** If you have time only for a short visit, driving Park Bou-
★ levard is your best choice. Traversing the most scenic portions of Joshua
Tree, this well-paved road connects the north and west entrances in
the park's high desert section. Along with some sweeping desert views,
you'll see jumbles of splendid boulder formations, stands of Joshua
trees, and Hidden Valley and Barker Dam, remnants of the area's wild
and woolly past. From the Oasis Visitor Center, drive south. After about
5 miles, the road forks; turn right and head west toward Jumbo Rocks
(clearly marked with a road sign).

Pinto Basin Road. This paved road takes you from high Mojave desert to
low Colorado desert. A long, slow drive, the route runs from the main
part of the park to I–10; it can add as much as an hour to and from Palm
Springs (round-trip), but the views and roadside exhibits make it worth
the extra time. From the Oasis Visitor Center, drive south. After about 5
miles, the road forks; take a left and continue another 9 miles to the Cholla
Cactus Garden, where the sun fills the cactus needles with light. Past that
is the Ocotillo Patch, filled with spindly plants bearing razor-sharp thorns
and brilliant red flowers. Side trips from this route require a 4X4.

HISTORIC SITES

FAMILY **Hidden Valley.** This legendary cattle-rustlers hideout is set among big boulders, which kids love to scramble over and around. There are shaded
picnic tables here. ⊠ *Park Blvd., 14 miles south of West Entrance.*

Fodor's Choice **Keys Ranch.** This 150-acre ranch, which once belonged to William and
★ Frances Keys and is now on the National Historic Register, illustrates
one of the area's most successful attempts at homesteading. The couple raised five children under extreme desert conditions. Most of the
original buildings, including the house, school, store, and workshop,
have been restored to the way they were when William died in 1969.
The only way to see the ranch is on one of the 90-minute walking
tours offered daily October to May. ⊠ *2 miles north of Barker Dam
Rd.* ☎ *760/367–5555* ⊕ *www.nps.gov* ⊠ *$5, available at visitor centers*
⊘ *Oct.–May, daily at 10 and 1.*

SCENIC STOPS

Barker Dam. Built around 1900 by ranchers and miners to hold water for
cattle and mining operations, the dam now collects rainwater and is a
good place to spot wildlife such as the elusive bighorn sheep. ⊠ *Barker
Dam Rd., off Park Blvd., 14 miles south of West Entrance.*

Cholla Cactus Garden. This stand of bigelow cholla (sometimes called jumping cholla, since its hooked spines seem to jump at you) is best seen and photographed in late afternoon, when the backlit spiky stalks stand out against a colorful sky. ⊠ *Pinto Basin Rd., 20 miles north of Cottonwood Visitor Center.*

Cottonwood Spring. Home to the native Cahuilla people for centuries, this spring provided water for travelers and early prospectors. The area, which supports a large stand of fan palms, is a stop for migrating birds and a winter water source for bighorn sheep. A number of gold mines were located here, and the area still has some remains, including an *arrastra* (gold-mining tool) and concrete pillars. You can access the site via a 1-mile paved trail that begins at sites 13A and 13B of the Cottonwood Campground. ⊠ *Cottonwood Visitor Center.*

> ## PLANTS AND WILDLIFE IN JOSHUA TREE
>
> Joshua Tree will shatter your notions of the desert as a wasteland. Life flourishes here, as flora and fauna have adapted to heat and drought. In most areas you'll be walking among native Joshua trees, ocotillos, and yuccas. One of the best spring desert wildflower displays in Southern California blooms here. You'll see plenty of animals—reptiles such as nocturnal sidewinders, birds like golden eagles or burrowing owls, and occasionally mammals like coyotes and bobcats.

Fortynine Palms Oasis. A short drive off Highway 62, this site is a bit of a preview of what the park's interior has to offer: stands of fan palms, interesting petroglyphs, and evidence of fires built by early American Indians. Since animals frequent this area, you may spot a coyote, bobcat, or roadrunner. ⊠ *End of Canyon Rd., 4 miles west of Twentynine Palms.*

Fodor's Choice
★

Keys View. At 5,185 feet, this point affords a sweeping view of the Santa Rosa Mountains and Coachella Valley, the San Andreas Fault, the peak of 11,500-foot Mount San Gorgonio, the shimmering surface of Salton Sea, and—on a rare clear day—Signal Mountain in Mexico. Sunrise and sunset are magical times, when the light throws rocks and trees into high relief before bathing the hills in brilliant shades of red, orange, and gold. ⊠ *Keys View Rd., 21 miles south of park's west entrance.*

Lost Palms Oasis. More than 100 fan palms comprise the largest group of the exotic plants in the park. A spring bubbles from between the rocks, but disappears into the sandy, boulder-strewn canyon. If you hike along the 4-mile trail, you might spot bighorn sheep. ⊠ *Cottonwood Visitor Center.*

10

SPORTS AND THE OUTDOORS

HIKING

There are more than 191 miles of hiking trails in Joshua Tree, ranging from quarter-of-a-mile nature trails to 35-mile treks. Some connect with each other, so you can design your own desert maze. Remember that drinking water is hard to come by—you won't find water in the park except at the entrances. Bring along at least a gallon per person for all but the shortest hikes, more if the weather is hot. Before striking out on a hike or apparent nature trail, check out the signage. Roadside signage identifies hiking- and rock-climbing routes.

EASY

Cap Rock. This ½-mile wheelchair-accessible loop—named after a boulder that sits atop a huge rock formation like a cap—winds through fascinating rock formations and has signs that explain the geology of the Mojave Desert. *Easy.* ⊠ *Trailhead at junction of Park Blvd. and Keys View Rd.*

> ## BEST CAMPGROUNDS IN JOSHUA TREE
>
> Camping is the best way to experience the stark, exquisite beauty of Joshua Tree. You'll also have a rare opportunity to sleep outside in a semi-wilderness setting. The campgrounds, set at elevations from 3,000 to 4,500 feet, have only primitive facilities; few have drinking water. Black Rock and Indian Cove campgrounds, on the northern edge of the park, accept reservations up to six months in advance. Campsites elsewhere are on a first-come, first-served basis.

MODERATE

Fodor's Choice ★ Ryan Mountain Trail. The payoff for hiking to the top of 5,461-foot Ryan Mountain is one of the best panoramic views of Joshua Tree. From here you can see Mt. San Jacinto, Mt. San Gorgonio, Lost Horse Valley, and the Pinto Basin. You'll need two to three hours to complete the 3-mile round-trip. *Moderate.* ⊠ *Trailhead at Ryan Mountain parking area, 16 miles southeast of park's west entrance or Sheep Pass, 16 miles southwest of Oasis Visitor Center.*

DIFFICULT

Mastodon Peak Trail. Some boulder scrambling is required on this 3-mile hike up 3,371-foot Mastodon Peak, but the journey rewards you with stunning views of the Salton Sea. The trail passes through a region where gold was mined from 1919 to 1932, so be on the lookout for open mines. The peak draws its name from a large rock formation that early miners believed looked like the head of a prehistoric behemoth. *Difficult.* ⊠ *Trailhead at Cottonwood Spring Oasis.*

ROCK CLIMBING

Fodor's Choice ★ With an abundance of weathered igneous boulder outcroppings, Joshua Tree is a world-class climbing destination. There are more than 4,500 established routes offering a full menu of climbing experiences—from bouldering for beginners in the Wonderland of Rocks to multiple-pitch climbs at Echo Rock and Saddle Rock. The best-known climb in the park is Hidden Valley's Sports Challenge Rock. A map inside the *Joshua Tree Guide* shows locations of selected wilderness and nonwilderness climbs.

THE MOJAVE DESERT

With Owens Valley

WELCOME TO THE MOJAVE DESERT

TOP REASONS TO GO

★ **Nostalgia:** Old neon signs, historic motels, and restored (or neglected but still striking) Harvey House rail stations abound across this desert landscape. Don't miss the classic eateries along the way, including Bagdad Cafe in Newberry Springs and Emma Jean's Holland Burger Cafe in Victorville.

★ **Death Valley wonders:** Visit this distinctive landscape to tour some of the most varied desert terrain in the world (⇨ Chapter 12, Death Valley National Park).

★ **Great ghost towns:** California's gold rush brought miners to the Mojave, and the towns they left behind have their own unique charms.

★ **Cool down in Sierra country:** Head up gorgeous U.S. 395 toward Bishop to visit the High Sierra, home to majestic Mt. Whitney.

★ **Explore ancient history:** The Mojave Desert is replete with rare petroglyphs, some dating back almost 16,000 years.

1 The Western Mojave. Stretching from the town of Ridgecrest to the base of the San Gabriel Mountains, the western Mojave is a varied landscape of ancient Native American petroglyphs, tufa towers, and hillsides covered in bright orange poppies.

2 The Eastern Mojave. Joshua trees and cacti dot a predominantly flat landscape that is interrupted by dramatic, rock-strewn mountains. The area is largely uninhabited, so be cautious when driving the back roads, where towns and services are scarce.

3 Owens Valley. Lying in the shadow of the Eastern Sierra Nevada, the Owens Valley stretches along U.S. 395 from the Mono–Inyo county line, in the north, to the town of Olancha, in the south. Tiny towns punctuate the highway, and the scenery is quietly powerful. If you're traveling between Yosemite National Park and Death Valley National Park or are headed from Lake Tahoe or Mammoth to the desert, U.S. 395 is your north–south corridor.

11

4 **Death Valley National Park.** This arid desert landscape is one of the hottest, lowest, and driest places in North America. From the surrounding mountains, you look down on its vast beauty. Among the beautiful canyons and wide-open spaces, you'll find quirky bits of Americana, including the elaborate Scotty's Castle and eclectic Amargosa Opera House (⇨ *Chapter 12, Death Valley National Park.*).

GETTING ORIENTED

The Mojave Desert, once part of an ancient inland sea, is one of the largest swaths of open land in Southern California. Its boundaries include the San Gabriel and San Bernardino mountain ranges to the south; the areas of Palmdale and Ridgecrest to the west; Death Valley to the north; and Needles and Lake Havasu in Arizona and Primm, Nevada, to the east. The area is distinguishable by its wide-open sandy spaces, peppered with creosote bushes, Joshua trees, cacti, and abandoned homesteads. You can access the Mojave via interstates 40 and 15, highways 14 and 95, and U.S. 395.

Updated by
Reed Parsell

Dust and desolation, tumbleweeds and rattlesnakes, barren landscapes—these are the bleak images that come to mind when most people hear the word *desert*. But east of the Sierra Nevada, where the land flattens and rain seldom falls, the desert is anything but a wasteland.

The topography here is extreme; while Death Valley drops to almost 300 feet below sea level and contains the lowest (and hottest) spot in the Western Hemisphere, the Mojave Desert, which lies to the south, has elevations ranging from 3,000 to 5,000 feet. These remote regions (which are known, respectively, as low desert and high desert) possess a singular beauty, the vast open spaces populated with spiky Joshua trees, undulating sand dunes, faulted mountains, and dramatic rock formations. Owens Valley is where the desert meets the mountains; its 80-mile width separates the depths of Death Valley from Mt. Whitney, the highest mountain in the contiguous United States. Note: You may spot fossils at archaeological sites in the desert. If you do, leave them where they are; it's against the law to remove them.

PLANNING

WHEN TO GO
Spring and fall are the best seasons to tour the desert and Owens Valley. Winters are generally mild, but summers can be cruel. If you're on a budget, keep in mind that room rates drop as the temperatures rise.

GETTING HERE AND AROUND
AIR TRAVEL
Inyokern Airport, near Ridgecrest, is served by United Express from Los Angeles. Needles Airport serves small, private planes.

Contacts Inyokern Airport ✉ *1669 Airport Rd., off Hwy. 178, 9 miles west of Ridgecrest, Inyokern* ☎ *760/377–5844* ⊕ *www.inyokernairport.com.* **McCarran International Airport** ✉ *5757 Wayne Newton Blvd., Las Vegas, Nevada* ☎ *702/261–5211* ⊕ *www.mccarran.com.* **Needles Airport** ✉ *711 Airport Rd., Needles* ☎ *760/326–5263.*

11

BUS TRAVEL

Greyhound provides bus service to Barstow, Victorville, Palmdale, and Needles; check with the chambers of commerce about local bus service, which is generally more useful to residents than to tourists.

Contact Greyhound ☎ 800/231-2222 ⊕ www.greyhound.com.

CAR TRAVEL

Much of the desert can be seen from the comfort of an air-conditioned car. Most visitors approach Death Valley (⇨ Chapter 17) from the west or the southeast. Whether you've come south from Bishop or north from Ridgecrest, head east from U.S. 395 on Highway 190 or 178. To enter Death Valley from the southeast, take Highway 127 north from Interstate 15 in Baker and link up with Highway 178, which travels west into the valley and then cuts north toward Highway 190 at Furnace Creek.

The major north–south route through the western Mojave is U.S. 395, which intersects with Interstate 15 between Cajon Pass and Victorville. U.S. 395 travels north into the Owens Valley, passing such relatively remote outposts as Lone Pine, Independence, Big Pine, and Bishop. Farther west, Highway 14 runs north–south between Inyokern (near Ridgecrest) and Palmdale. Two major east–west routes travel through the Mojave: to the north, Interstate 15 to Las Vegas, Nevada; to the south, Interstate 40 to Needles. At the intersection of the two interstates, in Barstow, Interstate 15 veers south toward Victorville and Los Angeles, and Interstate 40 gives way to Highway 58 west toward Bakersfield.

■TIP➔ For the latest Mojave traffic and weather, tune in to the Highway Stations (98.1 FM near Barstow, 98.9 FM near Essex, and 99.7 FM near Baker). Traffic can be especially troublesome Friday through Sunday, when thousands of Angelenos head to Las Vegas for a bit of R&R.

Contacts Caltrans Current Highway Conditions ☎ 800/427-7623 ⊕ www.dot.ca.gov.

TRAIN TRAVEL

Amtrak trains traveling east and west stop in Victorville, Barstow, and Needles, but the stations aren't staffed, so you'll have to purchase tickets in advance and handle your own baggage. The Barstow station is served daily by Amtrak California motor coaches that travel among Los Angeles, Bakersfield, and Las Vegas.

Contact Amtrak ☎ 800/872-7245 ⊕ www.amtrak.com.

HEALTH AND SAFETY

In an emergency dial 911.

Let someone know your trip route, destination, and estimated time of return. Before setting out, make sure your vehicle is in good condition. Carry water, a jack, tools, and towrope or chain. Keep an eye on your gas gauge and try to keep the needle above half. Stay on main roads, and watch out for wildlife, horses, and cattle.

Drink at least a gallon of water a day (three gallons if you're hiking or otherwise exerting yourself). Dress in layered clothing and wear comfortable, sturdy shoes and a hat. Keep snacks, sunscreen, and a first-aid kit on hand. If you have a headache or feel dizzy or nauseous, you could be suffering from dehydration. Get out of the sun immediately and drink plenty of water. Dampen your clothing to lower your body temperature. Do not enter abandoned mine tunnels or shafts, of which there are hundreds in the Mojave Desert. The structures may be unstable, and there may be hidden dangers such as pockets of bad air. Avoid canyons during rainstorms. Floodwaters can quickly fill up dry riverbeds and cover or wash away roads. Never place your hands or feet where you can't see them: rattlesnakes, scorpions, and black widow spiders may be hiding there.

HIKING IN THE MOJAVE DESERT

Hiking trails are abundant throughout the desert and along the eastern base of the Sierra, meandering toward sights that you can't see from the road. Some of the best trails are unmarked; ask locals for directions. Among the prime hiking spots is the John Muir Trail, which starts near Mt. Whitney. Whether you're exploring the high or low desert, wear sunscreen, protective clothing, and a hat. Watch for tarantulas, black widows, scorpions, snakes, and other creatures.

Contacts BLM Rangers ☎ 760/326–7000 ⊕ www.blm.gov/ca. **Barstow Community Hospital** ✉ 820 E. Mountain View St., Barstow ☎ 760/256–1761 ⊕ www.barstowhospital.com. **San Bernardino County Sheriff** ☎ 760/256–1796 in Barstow, 760/733–4448 in Baker.

HOURS OF OPERATION

Early morning is the best time to visit sights and avoid crowds, but some museums and visitor centers don't open until 10. If you schedule your town arrivals for late afternoon, you can drop by the visitor centers just before closing hours to line up an itinerary for the next day.

RESTAURANTS

Throughout the desert and the Eastern Sierra, dining is a fairly simple affair. Owens Valley is home to many mom-and-pop eateries, as well as a few fast-food chains. There are chain establishments in Ridgecrest, Victorville, and Barstow, as well as some ethnic eateries. *Prices in the reviews are the average cost of a main course at dinner or, if dinner is not served, at lunch.*

HOTELS

Hotel chains and roadside motels are the desert's primary lodging options. The tourist season runs from late May through September. Reservations are rarely a problem, but it's still wise to make them. *Prices in the reviews are the lowest cost of a standard double room in high season. For expanded hotel reviews, visit Fodors.com.*

TOUR OPTIONS

The Mojave Group of the Sierra Club regularly organizes field trips to interesting spots, and the San Gorgonio Sierra Club chapter also conducts desert excursions.

Contact **Sierra Club** ☎ *213/387–4287, 951/684–6203 for San Gorgonio chapter* ⊕ *www.sierraclub.com.*

VISITOR INFORMATION

Contacts **Bureau of Land Management** ✉ *California Desert District Office, 22835 Calle San Juan De Los Lagos, Moreno Valley* ☎ *909/697–5200* ⊕ *www.blm.gov/ca.* **Barstow Welcome Center** ✉ *2796 Tanger Way, Barstow* ☎ *760/253–4782* ⊕ *www.visitcwc.com/Barstow.* **Death Valley Chamber of Commerce** ✉ *860 Tecopa Hot Springs Rd., Tecopa* ☎ *760/852–4420* ⊕ *www.deathvalleychamber.com.* **San Bernardino County Regional Parks Department** ✉ *777 E. Rialto Ave., San Bernardino* ☎ *909/387–2757* ⊕ *cms.sbcounty.gov/parks.*

THE WESTERN MOJAVE

This vast area is especially beautiful along U.S. 395. From January through March, wildflowers are in bloom and temperatures are manageable. Year-round, snowcapped mountain peaks are irresistible sights.

PALMDALE

60 miles north of Los Angeles on Hwy. 14.

Before proclaiming itself the aerospace capital of the world, the town of Palmdale was an agricultural community. Settlers of Swiss and German descent, moving west from Illinois and Nebraska, populated the area in 1886, and most residents made their living as farmers, growing alfalfa, pears, and apples. After World War II, with the creation of Edwards Air Force Base and U.S. Air Force Plant 42, the region evolved into a center for aerospace and defense activities, with contractors such as McDonnell Douglas, Rockwell, Northrop, and Lockheed establishing factories here. Until the housing crisis and recent recession struck, Palmdale was one of Southern California's fastest-growing cities.

GETTING HERE AND AROUND

From the Los Angeles basin take Highway 14 to get to Palmdale. From the east, arrive via the Pearblossom Highway (Highway 18/138). Regional Metrolink trains serve the area from Los Angeles. Palmdale attractions are most easily seen by car, but you can see some of the town via local transit.

ESSENTIALS

Bus and Train Information Antelope Valley Transit Authority ☎ *661/945–9445* ⊕ *www.avta.com.* **Metrolink** ☎ *800/371–5465* ⊕ *www.metrolinktrains.com.*

Visitor Information Palmdale Chamber of Commerce ✉ *817 East Ave., Ste. Q-9* ☎ *661/273-3232* ⊕ *www.palmdalechamber.org.*

EXPLORING

Devil's Punchbowl Natural Area. A mile from the San Andreas Fault, the namesake of this attraction is a natural bowl-shaped depression in the earth, framed by 300-foot rock walls. At the bottom is a stream, which you can reach via a moderately strenuous 1-mile hike. You also can veer off on a short nature trail; at the top an interpretive center has displays of native flora and fauna, including live animals such as snakes, lizards, and birds of prey. ✉ *28000 Devil's Punchbowl Rd., south of Hwy. 138, Pearblossom* ☎ *661/944-2743* 🖂 *Free* ☉ *Park daily sunrise–sunset; center daily 8–4.*

St. Andrew's Abbey. This Benedictine monastery occupies 760 acres made lush by natural springs. The Abbey Ceramics studio, established here in 1969, sells handmade tile saints, angels, and plaques designed by Father Maur van Doorslaer, a Belgian monk whose work U.S. and Canadian collectors favor. The entertainment at the abbey's fall festival includes singing nuns and dancing monks. ✉ *31101 N. Valyermo Rd., south of Hwy. 138, Valyermo* ☎ *888/454-5411, 661/944-1047 ceramics studio* ⊕ *www.saintsandangels.org* 🖂 *Free* ☉ *Weekdays 9–12:30 and 1:30–4:30, weekends 9–11:45 and 12:30–4:30.*

Shambala Preserve. An 80-acre wildlife operation run by Hitchcock actress Tippi Hedren (*The Birds*), the sanctuary conducts safaris one weekend a month that bring participants as close as a foot away from the dozens of rescued exotic felines sheltered here. ✉ *6867 Soledad Canyon Rd., off Hwy. 14, Acton* ☎ *661/268-0380* ⊕ *www.shambala.org* 🖂 *$50 minimum donation (tax-deductible)* ☉ *noon–3 once a month.*

WHERE TO STAY

For expanded hotel reviews, visit Fodors.com.

$ 🏨 **Best Western John Jay Inn & Suites.** All rooms at this modern hotel
HOTEL have large desks and ergonomic chairs; suites have balconies, fireplaces, wet bars, and Jacuzzis. **Pros:** clean; good rates; spacious rooms. **Cons:** no on-site restaurant; ambulance noise from the hospital next door. 💲 *Rooms from: $90* ✉ *600 W. Palmdale Blvd.* ☎ *661/575-9322* ⊕ *www.bestwestern.com* 📶 *54 rooms, 13 suites* ⊺⊙⊺ *Breakfast.*

$$ 🏨 **Residence Inn Palmdale.** Accommodations here range from studios to
HOTEL one-bedroom suites, all with full kitchens, sitting areas, and sleeper sofas. **Pros:** spacious rooms; close to town. **Cons:** no room service. 💲 *Rooms from: $149* ✉ *514 W. Ave. P* ☎ *661/947-4204, 800/331-3131* ⊕ *www.marriott.com* 📶 *90 suites* ⊺⊙⊺ *Breakfast.*

SPORTS AND THE OUTDOORS
AERIAL TOURS

Brian Ranch Airport. The school here offers introductory flights that allow you to pilot (with an instructor) two-seater ultralight aircraft across the Mojave. The airport's annual World's Smallest Air Show, held on Memorial Day weekend, draws aviation enthusiasts from around the country. ✉ *34180 Largo Vista Rd., off Hwy. 138, Llano* ☎ *661/261-3216* ⊕ *www.brianranch.com* 🖂 *$40, 15-min. flight; $75, 30 min.; $130, 1 hr.*

SKYDIVING

Southern California Soaring Academy. The academy operates sailplane rides (no engines!) over the scenic San Gabriel mountain pines, across the jagged San Andreas Fault, and over the sandy soil of El Mirage Dry Lake. Accompanied by a certified instructor, you'll learn the basics before handling the craft on your own. Reservations are required. ✉ *32810 165th St. E, off Hwy 138, Llano* ☎ *661/944-1090* ⊕ *www.soaringacademy.org* 🖂 *$109–$250* ☉ *Fri.–Mon. 9–sunset Tues.–Thurs. by appointment.*

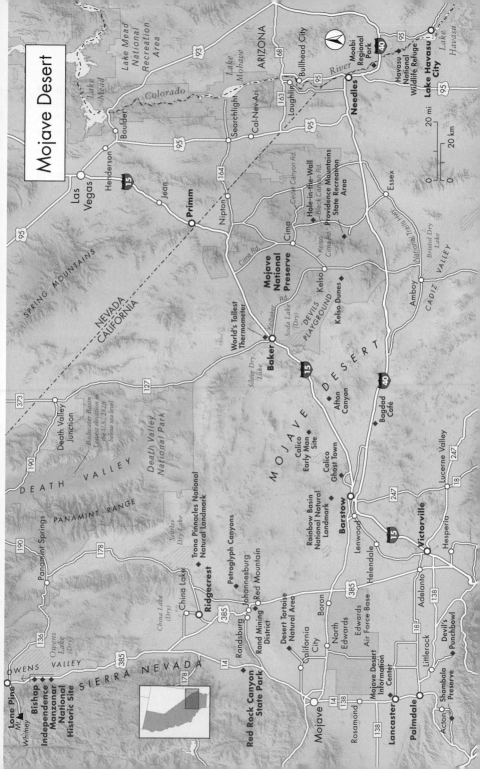

LANCASTER

8 miles north of Palmdale via Hwy. 14.

Lancaster was founded in 1876, when the Southern Pacific Railroad arrived. Before that, several Native American tribes, some of whose descendants still live in the surrounding mountains, inhabited it. Points of interest around Lancaster are far from the downtown area, and some are in neighboring communities.

GETTING HERE AND AROUND

From the Los Angeles basin take Highway 14, which proceeds north to Mojave and Highway 58, a link between Bakersfield and Barstow. Regional Metrolink trains serve Lancaster from the Los Angeles area. Local transit exists, but a car is the best way to experience this area.

ESSENTIALS

Transportation Contacts Antelope Valley Transit Authority ☎ *661/945–9445* ⊕ *www.avta.com.* **Metrolink** ☎ *800/371-5465* ⊕ *www.metrolinktrains.com.*

Visitor Information Destination Lancaster ✉ *44933 Fern Ave., at W. Lancaster Blvd.* ☎ *661/723-6110* ⊕ *www.destinationlancasterca.org.*

EXPLORING

Air Flight Test Center Museum at Edwards Air Force Base. The museum at what many consider to be the birthplace of supersonic flight chronicles the rich history of flight testing. A dozen airplanes are on exhibit, from the first F-16B to the giant B-52D bomber. To visit, you must pass a security screening by providing your full name, Social Security number or driver's license number, and date and place of birth at least one week in advance. The 90-minute walking tours are open to the public on two Fridays of each month. ✉ *405 S. Rosamond Blvd., off Yeager Blvd., Edwards* ☎ *661/277-3517* ⊕ *www.afftcmuseum.org* ☜ *Free* ☉ *Two Fridays of each month, tours every 90 mins 9:30–3.*

Antelope Valley Indian Museum. Notable for its one-of-a-kind artifacts from California, Southwest, and Great Basin native tribes, the museum occupies an unusual Swiss chalet–style building that clings to the rocky hillside of Piute Butte. To get here, exit north off Highway 138 at 165th Street East and follow the signs. ✉ *15701 E. Ave. M* ☎ *661/946–3045* ⊕ *www.avim.parks.ca.gov* ☜ *$3* ☉ *Mid-Sept.–mid-June, weekends 11–4.*

Antelope Valley Poppy Reserve. The California poppy, the state flower, can be spotted throughout the state, but this quiet park holds the densest concentration. Seven miles of trails—parts of which are paved, though inclines are too steep for wheelchairs—wind through 1,745 acres of hills carpeted with poppies and other wildflowers. ■TIP→ Peak blooming time is usually March through May. On a clear day at any time of year, you'll be treated to sweeping views of Antelope Valley. ✉ *15101 Lancaster Rd., west off Hwy. 14, Ave. I Exit* ☎ *661/724–1180, 661/942–0662* ⊕ *www.parks.ca.gov/?page_id=627* ☜ *$8 per vehicle* ☉ *Visitor center mid-Mar.–mid-May daily 9–5.*

Antelope Valley Winery and Buffalo Company. Desert vineyards? Industry scoffing hasn't deterred Cecil W. McLester, a graduate of UC Davis's renowned wine-making and viticulture program, from crafting decent

wines—yes, from grapes grown on-site—including an award-winning Tempranillo and Paloma Blanca, a Riesling-style blend. The winery is also home to the Antelope Valley Buffalo Company, a producer of meat products made from its roaming herd in the Leona Valley. ⊠ *42041 20th St. W, at Ave. M* ☎ *661/722–0145, 888/282–8332* ⊕ *www.avwinery. com* ⊠ *Winery free, tasting $6* ⊙ *Wed.–Sun. 11–6.*

OFF THE
BEATEN
PATH

Desert Tortoise Natural Area. Between mid-March and mid-June, this natural habitat of the elusive desert tortoise blazes with desert candles, primroses, lupine, and other wildflowers. Arrive bright and early to spot the state reptile, while it grazes on fresh flowers and grass shoots. It's also a great spot to see desert kit fox, red-tailed hawks, cactus wrens, and Mojave rattlesnakes. ⊠ *8 miles northeast of California City via Randsburg Mojave Rd.* ☎ *951/683–3872* ⊕ *www.tortoise-tracks.org* ⊠ *Free* ⊙ *Daily.*

Exotic Feline Breeding Compound's Feline Conservation Center. About a dozen species of wild cats, from the weasel-size jaguarundi to leopards, tigers, and jaguars, inhabit this small, orderly facility. You can see the cats (behind barrier fences) in the parklike public zoo and research center. The on-site museum's taxidermied cats all reportedly died of old age. ⊠ *Rhyolite Ave. off Mojave-Tropico Rd., Rosamond* ☎ *661/256–3793* ⊕ *www.cathouse-fcc.org* ⊠ *$7* ⊙ *Thurs.–Tues. 10–4.*

RED ROCK CANYON STATE PARK

48 miles north of Lancaster via Hwy. 14; 17 miles west of U.S. 395 via Red Rock–Randsburg Rd.

GETTING HERE AND AROUND
The only practical way to get here is by car, taking Highway 14 north from Los Angeles and the Palmdale/Lancaster area or south from Ridgecrest.

Red Rock Canyon State Park. A geological feast for the eyes with its layers of pink, white, red, and brown rock, this remote canyon is also a region of fascinating biological diversity—the ecosystems of the Sierra Nevada, the Mojave Desert, and the Basin Range all converge here. Entering the park from the south just beyond Red Rock–Randsburg Road, you pass through a steep-walled gorge to a wide bowl tinted pink by volcanic ash. Native Americans known as the Old People lived here some 20,000 years ago; later, Mojave Indians roamed the land for centuries. Gold-rush fever hit the region in the mid-1800s, and you can still see remains of mining operations in the park. In the 20th century, Hollywood invaded the canyon, shooting westerns, TV shows, commercials, music videos, and movies such as *Jurassic Park* here. Be sure to check out the Red Cliffs Preserve on Highway 14, across from the entrance to the Red Rock campground. ⊠ *Ranger station, Abbott Dr., off Hwy. 14* ☎ *661/946–6092* ⊕ *www.parks.ca.gov* ⊠ *$6 per vehicle* ⊙ *Daily sunrise–sunset visitor center open mid-March–early June and early Sept.–Nov., Fri.–Sun.*

RIDGECREST

11

28 miles northeast of Red Rock Canyon State Park via Hwy. 14; 77 miles south of Lone Pine via U.S. 395.

A military town that serves the U.S. Naval Weapons Center to its north, Ridgecrest has scores of stores, restaurants, and hotels. With about 25,000 residents, it's the last city of any significant size you'll encounter as you head northeast toward Death Valley National Park.

GETTING HERE AND AROUND

Come here by car so you can see regional attractions such as the Trona Pinnacles. Arrive via U.S. 395 or, from the Los Angeles area, Highway 14. The local bus service is of limited use to tourists.

ESSENTIALS

Transportation Contacts City Transit ☎ *760/499–5040* ⊕ *ci.ridgecrest.ca.us/transit.*

Visitor Information Ridgecrest Area Convention and Visitors Bureau ✉ *139 Balsam St., at Panamint Ave.* ☎ *760/375–8202, 800/847–4830* ⊕ *www.visitdeserts.com.*

EXPLORING

Fodor'sChoice
★
Petroglyph Canyons. The two canyons, commonly called Big Petroglyph and Little Petroglyph, are in the Coso Mountain range on the million-acre U.S. Naval Weapons Center at China Lake. Each of the canyons holds a superlative concentration of ancient rock art, the largest of its kind in the Northern Hemisphere. Thousands of well-preserved images of animals and humans are scratched or pecked into dark basaltic rocks. The military requires everyone to produce a valid driver's license, Social Security number, passport, and vehicle registration before the trip (non-drivers must provide a birth certificate). ⊕ *www.maturango.org* ⊠ *$40; tours booked through Maturango Museum.*

Maturango Museum. The only way to see the amazing Petroglyph Canyons is on a guided tour conducted by the Maturango Museum. Tours ($40) depart from the museum February–June, and September or October–early December; call for tour times. Children under 10 are not allowed on the tour. The museum's interesting exhibits survey the area's art, history, and geology. ⊠ *100 E. Las Flores Ave., at Hwy. 178* ☎ *760/375–6900* ⊕ *www.maturango.org* ⊠ *$5* ☉ *Daily 10–5. Tours Feb.–June and Sept. or Oct.–early Dec.; call for tour times.*

Rand Mining District. The towns of Randsburg, Red Mountain, and Johannesburg make up the Rand Mining District, which first boomed with the discovery of gold in the Rand Mountains in 1895. Rich tungsten ore, used in World War I to make steel alloy, was discovered in 1907, and silver was found in 1919. The boom has gone bust, but the area still has some residents, a few antiques shops, and plenty of character. An archetypal Old West cemetery perched on a hillside looms over Johannesburg. ⊠ *U.S. 395, 20 miles south of Ridgecrest, Randsburg.*

Trona Pinnacles National Natural Landmark. Fantastic-looking formations of calcium carbonate, known as tufa, were formed underwater along fault lines in the bed of what is now Searles Dry Lake. Some of the more than 500 spires stand as tall as 140 feet, creating a landscape so surreal that it doubled for outer-space terrain in the film *Star Trek V.*

An easy-to-walk ½-mile trail allows you to see the tufa up close, but wear sturdy shoes—tufa cuts like coral. The best road to the area can be impassable after a rainstorm. ⊠ *Pinnacle Rd., 5 miles south of Hwy. 178, 18 miles east of Ridgecrest, Death Valley* ☎ *760/384–5400 Ridgecrest BLM office* ⊕ *www.blm.gov/ca/st/en/fo/ridgecrest/trona.3.html.*

White House Saloon. Randsburg's tiny city jail is among the original buildings still standing; its White House Saloon is one of the Wild West's few surviving saloons, swinging wooden doors and all. Step in and order food if you're adventuresome and not too picky. ⊠ *168 Butte Ave., Randsburg* ☎ *760/374–2464.*

Desert Museum. The small Desert Museum exhibits mining paraphernalia and historic photos. It's open weekends 10–5, or by appointment. ⊠ *161 Butte Ave., Randsburg* ☎ *760/374–2359.*

General Store. Built as Randsburg's Drug Store in 1896, the General Store is one of the area's few surviving ghost-town buildings with an original tin ceiling, light fixtures, and 1906-era marble-and-stained-glass soda fountain. You can still enjoy a phosphate soda from that same fountain, or lunch on chili dogs, burgers, and barbecue-beef sandwiches. ⊠ *35 Butte Ave., Randsburg* ☎ *760/374–2143* ⊕ *www. randsburggeneralstore.com* ⊙ *Mon. –Fri. 9–4; Sat. 9–5; Sun. 10–5.*

OFF THE BEATEN PATH

Indian Wells Brewing Company. After driving through the hot desert, you'll surely appreciate a cold one at Indian Wells Brewing Company, where master brewer Rick Lovett lovingly crafts his Lobotomy Bock, Amnesia I.P.A., and Death Valley Pale Ale, among others. If you have the kids along, grab a six-pack of his specialty root beer, black cherry, orange, or cream soda. ⊠ *2565 N. Hwy. 14, 2 miles west of U.S. 395, Inyokern* ☎ *760/377–5989* ⊕ *www.mojavered.com* ⊴ *$5 beer tasting* ⊙ *Daily 9:30–5.*

WHERE TO STAY

For expanded hotel reviews, visit Fodors.com.

$$
HOTEL

Hampton Inn & Suites Ridgecrest. Clean and reliable, the Hampton Inn & Suites Ridgecrest features a well-equipped exercise room, spotless Internet service, and a welcoming breakfast area that help keep guests in shape, in touch, and invigorated. **Pros:** attentive, friendly service; good breakfast; big rooms. **Cons:** a rather strong chain vibe. ⑤ *Rooms from: $129* ⊠ *104 East Sydnor Ave., Ridgecrest* ☎ *855/271–3622, 760/446–1968* ⊕ *hamptoninn3.hilton.com/en/hotels/california/hampton-inn-and-suites-ridgecrest-RCTCAHX/index.html* ❑ *Breakfast.*

$
HOTEL

SpringHill Suites Ridgecrest. The bar might not be set that high, but SpringHill Suites Ridgecrest is the best hotel in town. **Pros:** clean; good breakfast; helpful staff. **Cons:** some guests complain of a bleach smell. ⑤ *Rooms from: $119* ⊠ *113 E Sydnor Ave.* ☎ *888/236–2427, 760/446–1630* ⊕ *www.marriott.com/hotels/travel/iyksh-springhill-suites-ridgecrest* ❑ *Breakfast.*

THE EASTERN MOJAVE

11

Majestic, wide-open spaces define this region, with the Mojave National Preserve being one of the state's most remote but rewarding destinations.

VICTORVILLE

87 miles south of Ridgecrest on U.S. 395 off Bear Valley Rd.

At the southwest corner of the Mojave is the sprawling town of Victorville, a town rich in Route 66 heritage. Victorville was named for Santa Fe Railroad pioneer Jacob Nash Victor, who drove the first locomotive through the Cajon Pass here in 1885. Once home to Native Americans, the town later became a rest stop for Mormons and missionaries. In 1941, George Air Force Base (now an airport and storage area) brought scores of military families to the area, many of which have stayed on to raise families of their own. February, when the city holds its annual Adelanto Grand Prix, the largest motorcycle and quad off-road event in the country, is a great time to visit.

GETTING HERE AND AROUND

Drive here on Interstate 15 from Los Angeles or Las Vegas, or from the north via U.S. 395. Amtrak and Greyhound also serve the town. There are local buses, but touring by car is more practical.

ESSENTIALS

Transportation Information The Victor Valley Transit Authority ☎ *760/948–3030* ⊕ *www.vvta.org.*

Visitor Information Victor Valley Chamber of Commerce ✉ *14174 Green Tree Blvd., at St. Andrews Dr.* ☎ *760/245–6506* ⊕ *www.vvchamber.com.*

EXPLORING

California Route 66 Museum. Fans of the Mother Road (as John Steinbeck dubbed Route 66) will love this museum whose exhibits chronicle the famous highway's history. A book sold here contains a self-guided tour of 11 miles of the old Sagebrush Route from just north of Victorville in Oro Grande to Helendale. The tour passes by icons such as Potapov's Gas and Service Station and the once-rowdy Sagebrush Inn, now a private residence. ✉ *16825 D St., between 5th and 6th Sts.* ☎ *760/951–0436* ⊕ *www.califrt66museum.org* ✉ *Free* ⊙ *Mon. and Thurs.–Sat. 10–4, Sun. 11–3.*

FAMILY **Mojave Narrows Regional Park.** In one of the few spots where the Mojave River flows aboveground, this park has two lakes surrounded by cottonwoods and cattails. You'll find fishing, rowboat rentals, a bait shop, equestrian paths, and a wheelchair-accessible trail. ✉ *18000 Yates Rd., north on Ridgecrest Rd. off Bear Valley Rd.* ☎ *760/245–2226* ⊕ *cms.sbcounty.gov/parks* ✉ *$8 weekdays, $10 weekends and holidays.*

Silverwood Lake State Recreation Area. One of the desert's most popular boating and fishing areas, 1,000-acre Silverwood Lake also has campgrounds and a beach with a lifeguard. You can rent boats; fish for trout, largemouth bass, crappie, and catfish; and hike and bike the trails. In winter, bald eagles nest in the tall Jeffrey pines by the shore. ✉ *14651*

Cedar Cir., at Cleghorn Rd., off Hwy. 138, Hesperia ☎ *760/389–2303* ⊕ *www.parks.ca.gov/?page_id=650* ☎ *$10 per car, $8 per boat* ☉ *May–Sept. daily 7–9, Oct.–Apr. daily 7–5.*

WHERE TO EAT AND STAY

For expanded hotel reviews, visit Fodors.com.

$ ✕ **Emma Jean's Holland Burger Cafe.** This circa-1940s diner sits right on
AMERICAN   U.S. Historic Route 66 and is favored by locals for its generous portions and old-fashioned home cooking. Try the biscuits and gravy, chicken-fried steak, or the famous Trucker's Sandwich, stuffed with roast beef, bacon, chilies, and cheese. The Brian Burger also elicits consistent praise. ⑤ *Average main: $12* ⊠ *17143 N. D St., at Water Power Housing Dr.* ☎ *760/243–9938* ☉ *Closed Sun. No dinner.*

$ ✕ **Summit Inn.** Elvis Presley is one of many famous customers who passed
AMERICAN   through this kitschy diner perched atop the Cajon Pass. Open since 1952, the restaurant is filled with Route 66 novelty items, a gift shop, and vintage jukebox, which plays oldies from the 1960s. The food tends to generates positive reviews, and the funky decor and historic significance make it worth a stop. ⑤ *Average main: $12* ⊠ *5970 Mariposa Rd., exit I–15 at Oak Hills, Oak Hills* ☎ *760/949–8688.*

$ ☲ **La Quinta Inn and Suites Victorville.** If you're looking for a clean, com-
HOTEL   fortable, and non-smoking hotel with reasonable prices, this is a good choice. **Pros:** near shopping mall; clean rooms; hot breakfast. **Cons:** near a busy freeway. ⑤ *Rooms from: $94* ⊠ *12000 Mariposa Rd., Hesperia* ☎ *760/949–9900* ⊕ *www.lq.com* ⇆ *53 rooms, 22 suites* ⏀ *Breakfast.*

BARSTOW

32 miles northeast of Victorville on I–15.

Barstow was born in 1886, when a subsidiary of the Atchison, Topeka, and Santa Fe Railway began construction of a depot and hotel here. Outlet stores, chain restaurants, and motels define today's landscape, though old-time neon signs light up the town's main street.

GETTING HERE AND AROUND

Driving here on Interstate 15 from Los Angeles or Las Vegas is the best option, although you can reach Barstow via Amtrak or Greyhound. The local bus service is helpful for sights downtown.

ESSENTIALS

Transportation Information Barstow Area Transit ☎ *760/256–0311*
⊕ *www.transitunlimited.org/Barstow_Area_Transit.*

Visitor Information Barstow Area Chamber of Commerce and Visitors Bureau ⊠ *681 N. 1st Ave., near Riverside Dr.* ☎ *760/256–8617*
⊕ *www.barstowchamber.com.* **California Welcome Center** ⊠ *2796 Tanger Way, off Lenwood Rd.* ☎ *760/253–4782* ⊕ *www.visitcwc.com* ☉ *Daily 9–6.*

EXPLORING

TOP ATTRACTIONS

Calico Early Man Site. The earliest-known Americans fashioned the arti-facts buried in the walls and floors of the pits here. Nearly 12,000 stone tools—used for scraping, cutting, and gouging—have been

Many of the buildings in the popular Calico Ghost Town are authentic.

excavated here. The apparent age of some of these items (said to be as much as 200,000 years old) contradicts the dominant archaeological theory that humans populated North America only 13,000 years ago. Noted archaeologist Louis Leakey was so impressed with the Calico site that he became its director in 1963 and served in that capacity until his death in 1972. His old camp is now a visitor center and museum. The only way into the site is by guided tour (call ahead, as scheduled tours sometimes don't take place). ⊠ *Off I–15, Minneola Rd. exit, 15 miles northeast of Barstow* ☎ *760/254-2248* ⊕ *www. blm.gov/ca/st/en/fo/barstow/calico.html* ✉ *$5* ☉ *Visitor center Wed. 12:30–4:30, Thurs.–Sun. 9–4:30; tours Wed. 1:30 and 3:30, Thurs.– Sun. 9:30, 11:30, 1:30, and 3:30.*

FAMILY **Calico Ghost Town.** Once a wild and wealthy mining town, Calico took off in 1881 when prospectors found a rich deposit of silver in the area, and by 1886 more than $85 million worth of silver, gold, and other precious metals had been harvested from the surrounding hills. Many buildings here are authentic, but the restoration has created a sanitized version of the 1880s. You can stroll the wooden sidewalks of Main Street, browse shops filled with Western goods, roam the tunnels of Maggie's Mine ($1), and take an enjoyable ride on the Calico-Odessa Railroad ($3). Calico is a fun and mildly educational place for families to stretch their legs on the drive between Los Angeles and Las Vegas. Festivals in March, May, October, and November celebrate Calico's Wild West theme. ⊠ *Ghost Town Rd., 3 miles north of I–15, 5 miles east of Barstow* ☎ *760/254-2122* ⊕ *www.calicotown.com* ✉ *$6* ☉ *Daily 9–5.*

Casa Del Desierto Harvey House. This distinctive two-story structure—its Spanish name means "house of the desert"—was one of many hotel and restaurant depots opened by Santa Fe Railroad guru Fred Harvey in the early 20th century. In its heyday the building starred in Judy Garland's film *The Harvey Girls;* now, it houses the Route 66 Mother Road Museum and the Western Railroad Museum. ⊠ *681 N. 1st Ave., near Riverside Dr.* ☎ *760/255–1890* ⊕ *www.route66museum.org* ⊠ *Free* ☉ *Fri.–Sun. 10–4. Guided tours by appointment.*

Fodor's Choice   **Goldstone Deep Space Communications Complex.** Friendly and enthusi-
★   astic staffers conduct guided tours of this 53-square-mile complex.
FAMILY   Tours start at the Goldstone Museum, where exhibits detail past and present space missions and Deep Space Network history. From there, you'll drive out to see the massive concave antennas, starting with those used for early manned space flights and culminating with the 11-story-tall "listening" device and its always-staffed mission control room used to track spacecraft that have drifted beyond our solar system. Appointments are required; contact the complex to reserve a slot. ⊠ *Ft. Irwin Military Base, Ft. Irwin Rd. off I–15, 35 miles north of Barstow* ☎ *760/255–8688* ⊕ *deepspace.jpl.nasa.gov/dsn/features/ goldstonetours.html* ⊠ *Free* ☉ *Guided tours by appointment only.*

Rainbow Basin National Natural Landmark. Many science-fiction movies set on Mars have been filmed at this landmark 8 miles north of Barstow. Huge slabs of red, orange, white, and green stone tilt at crazy angles like ships about to capsize. Hike the washes, and you might see the fossilized remains of mastodons and bear-dogs, which roamed the basin up to 16 million years ago. At times, only 4-wheel-drive vehicles are permitted. If you have the time, park and hike. ⊠ *Fossil Bed Rd., 3 miles west of Fort Irwin Rd. (head north from (I-15)* ☎ *760/252–6000* ⊕ *www.blm. gov/ca/barstow/basin.html.*

WORTH NOTING

Afton Canyon. Because of its colorful, steep walls, Afton Canyon is often called the Grand Canyon of the Mojave. It was carved over thousands of years by the rushing waters of the Mojave River, which makes one of its few aboveground appearances here. The dirt road that leads to the canyon is ungraded in spots, so it is best to explore it in an all-terrain vehicle. ⊠ *Off Afton Rd., 36 miles northeast of Barstow via I–15* ⊕ *www.blm.gov/ca/st/en/fo/barstow/afton.html.*

FAMILY   **Desert Discovery Center.** The center's main attraction is Old Woman Meteorite, the second-largest such celestial object ever found in the United States. It was discovered in 1976 about 50 miles from Barstow. The center also has exhibits of fossils, plants, and local animals. ⊠ *831 Barstow Rd., at E. Virginia Way* ☎ *760/252–6060* ⊕ *www.desertdiscoverycenter. com* ⊠ *Free* ☉ *Tues.–Sat. 11–4.*

Inscription Canyon. One of the world's largest natural Native American art galleries, this canyon is 42 miles northwest of Barstow in the Black Mountains, and has nearly 10,000 petroglyphs and pictographs of bighorn sheep and other Mojave wildlife. ⊠ *EF373, off Copper City Rd., 10 miles west of Fort Irwin Rd.* ☎ *760/252–6000* ☉ *Weekdays 7:45–4:30.*

Mojave River Valley Museum. Two blocks from the Desert Discovery Center, this complementary museum is crowded with exhibits that include American Indian pottery, mammoth bones, and elephant tracks. Worth a look outside are the iron-strap jail and rare Santa Fe Railroad drover's car. ⊠ *270 E. Virginia Way, at Belinda St.* ☎ *760/256–5452* ⊕ *www. mojaverivervalleymuseum.org* ⊠ *Free* ☉ *Daily 11–4.*

Skyline Drive-In Theatre. When the sun sets in the Mojave, check out a bit of surviving Americana at this dusty drive-in, where you can watch the latest Hollywood flicks among the Joshua trees and starry night sky in good old-fashioned stereo FM sound. ⊠ *31175 Old Hwy. 58* ☎ *760/256–3333* ⊠ *$6* ☉ *Shows Wed.–Sun. at 7:30; closed Mon. and Tues.*

FAMILY **Western American Rail Museum.** For a truly nostalgic experience, check out the old locomotives and cabooses at this museum that houses memorabilia from Barstow's early railroad days, as well as interactive and historic displays on railroad history. ⊠ *Casa Del Desierto, 685 N. 1st St., near Riverside Dr.* ☎ *760/256–9276* ⊕ *www.barstowrailmuseum. org* ⊠ *Free* ☉ *Fri.–Sun. 11–4.*

WHERE TO EAT AND STAY
For expanded hotel reviews, visit Fodors.com.

$ ✕ **Bagdad Café.** Tourists from all over the world flock to the Route 66
AMERICAN eatery where the 1988 film of the same name was shot. Built in the 1940s, the Bagdad Café serves burgers, chicken-fried steak, and seafood. The walls are crammed with memorabilia donated by visitors famous and otherwise. ⑤ *Average main: $12* ⊠ *46548 National Trails Hwy., at Nopal La., Newberry Springs* ☎ *760/257–3101.*

$$$ ✕ **Idle Spurs Steakhouse.** Since the 1950s this roadside ranch has been a
AMERICAN Barstow dining staple, and it's still beloved by locals. Covered in cacti outside and Christmas lights inside, it's a colorful, cheerful place with a big wooden bar. The menu features prime cuts of meat, ribs, and lobster, and there's a great microbrew list. ⑤ *Average main: $24* ⊠ *690 Hwy. 58, at Camarillo Ave.* ☎ *760/256–8888* ⊕ *www.idlespurssteakhouse. com* ☉ *Closed Mon.; no lunch weekends.*

$ ✕ **Slash X Ranch Cafe.** Burgers, cold beer, and chili-cheese fries in hearty
SOUTHERN portions lure visitors and locals to this rowdy Wild West-esque watering hole named for the cattle ranch that preceded it. Shuffleboard tables and horseshoe pits add to the fun, provided it's not too sizzling hot outside. ⑤ *Average main: $13* ⊠ *28040 Barstow Rd., at Powerline Rd.* ☎ *760/252–1197* ☉ *Closed weekdays.*

$$ ⊡ **Country Inn & Suites By Carlson.** A friendly and attentive staff make this
HOTEL chain hotel stand out in a town that has a sea of them. **Pros:** very clean rooms, engaged management; entirely non-smoking. **Cons:** pricey for Barstow; nearest nightlife is two hours away. ⑤ *Rooms from: $129* ⊠ *2812 Lenwood Rd.* ☎ *760/307–3121* ⊕ *www.countryinns.com* ⟿ *121.*

BAKER

63 miles northeast of Barstow on I–15; 84 miles south of Death Valley Junction via Hwy. 127.

Death Valley's gateway to the central and western Mojave, the pit-stop town of Baker has several gas stations, some fast-food outlets, a few motels, and a general store that claims to sell the most winning Lotto tickets in California.

GETTING HERE AND AROUND

Baker sits at the intersection of I–15 and Highway 127. The only practical way to get here is by car.

EXPLORING

Thermometer. Baker's 134-foot-tall thermometer, the world's tallest such instrument, pays homage to the record U.S. temperature, 134°F, recorded in Death Valley on July 10, 1913. Note: As of 2013, the thermometer is no longer working, and is currently up for sale. ⊠ *72157 Baker Blvd., near Death Valley Rd.*

PRIMM, NV

52 miles northeast of Baker, via I–15; 118 miles east of Death Valley, via Hwy. 160 and I–15; 114 miles north of Barstow, via I–15.

Amid the rugged beauty of the Mojave's landscapes, three casinos clustered on the Nevada side of Interstate 15 attract low rollers and travelers unable to hold off gambling until they arrive in Las Vegas.

GETTING HERE AND AROUND

Shuttles from the Las Vegas airport serve Primm; driving is another option. The three casinos are within walking distance of each other.

EXPLORING

Shopping the outlets and hitting the amusement park at Buffalo Bill's or the casinos' video arcades are among the non-gambling diversions Primm offers.

WHERE TO STAY

For expanded hotel reviews, visit Fodors.com.

$
RESORT
Buffalo Bill's Resort and Casino. Decorated in the style of a Western frontier town, this hotel is the biggest and most popular in Primm. **Pros:** swimming pool and large amusement park; on-site restaurants and shops; comparatively exciting atmosphere. **Cons:** roller coaster noise at night; basic rooms seem a little worn. $ *Rooms from: $90* ⊠ *31700 Las Vegas Blvd. S* ☎ *702/386–7867, 800/386–7867* ⊕ *www. primmvalleyresorts.com* ↻ *1,193 rooms, 49 suites.*

SPORTS AND THE OUTDOORS

GOLF

Primm Valley Golf Club. Hotel guests have privileges at the Primm Valley Golf Club, which has two 18-hole courses (Lakes and Desert) designed by Tom Fazio that rank among the top 100 in the nation. Expect to pay more than $100 a round in high season (spring and fall). ⊠ *1 Yates Well Rd., 4 miles south of Primm Valley Resort, Nipton, California* ☎ *702/679–5509* ⊕ *www.primmvalleygolf.com.*

MOJAVE NATIONAL PRESERVE

Between I–15 and I–40, roughly east of Baker and Ludlow to the California/Nevada border.

The 1.4 million acres of the Mojave National Preserve hold a surprising abundance of plant and animal life—especially considering their elevation (nearly 8,000 feet in some areas). There are traces of human history here as well, including abandoned army posts and vestiges of mining and ranching towns. The town of Cima still has a small functioning store.

GETTING HERE AND AROUND

The best way to see the preserve is by car. The fully paved Kelbaker Road bisects the park north–south; northbound Essex Road gets you to Hole-in-the-Wall on pavement but is graveled beyond there.

EXPLORING

Hole-in-the-Wall. Created millions of years ago by volcanic activity, Hole-in-the-Wall formed when gases were trapped between layers of deposited ash, rock, and lava; the gas bubbles left holes in the solidified material. A member of the Butch Cassidy gang gave the area its name because it reminded him of his former hideout in Wyoming. You will encounter one of California's most distinctive hiking experiences here. Proceeding clockwise from a small visitor center, you walk gently down and around a craggy hill, past cacti and fading petroglyphs to Banshee Canyon, whose pockmarked walls resemble Swiss cheese. From there you head back out of the canyon, supporting yourself with widely spaced iron rings (some of which wiggle precariously from their rock moorings) as you ascend a 200-foot incline that deposits you back near the visitor center. The 90-minute adventure is mildly dangerous but wholly entertaining. ⊠ *From I–40, take Essex Rd. exit, drive north 10 miles to Black Canyon Rd., and continue north another 10 miles* ☎ *760/928–2572* ⊕ *www.nps.gov/ moja* ☉ *Fri.–Sun. 9–4.*

Fodor's Choice
★ **Kelso Dunes.** As you enter the preserve from the south, you'll pass miles of open scrub brush, Joshua trees, and beautiful red-black cinder cones before encountering the Kelso Dunes. These golden, fine-sand slopes cover 70 square miles, reaching heights of 600 feet. You can reach them via a ½-mile walk from the main parking area, but be prepared for a serious workout. When you reach the top of a dune, kick a little bit of sand down the lee side and listen to the sand "sing." North of the dunes, in the town of Kelso, is the Mission revival–style **Kelso Depot Visitor Center.** The striking building, which dates to 1923, was extensively renovated last decade and contains several rooms of desert- and train-themed exhibits. The Depot's restaurant, The Beanery, has an early- to mid-20th-century diner look that will have you reaching for your camera. ⊠ *For Kelso Depot Visitor Center, take Kelbaker Rd. exit from I–15 (head south 34 miles) or I–40 (head north 22 miles)* ☎ *760/928–2572, 760/252–6100* ⊕ *www.nps.gov/moja.*

Providence Mountains State Recreation Area. Budget cuts have resulted in the closure of this distinctive state park "until further notice," but you can still drive around the area and marvel at the desert vistas. The visitor center has been closed for a few years, as has the nearby **Mitchell Caverns.** ⊠ *Essex Rd., 16 miles north of I–40* 🕾 *760/928–2586* ⊕ *www.parks.ca.gov/?page_id=26732.*

NEEDLES

I–40, 150 miles east of Barstow.

Along Route 66 and the Colorado River, Needles is a decent base for exploring Mojave National Preserve and other desert attractions. Founded in 1883, the town, named for the jagged mountain peaks that overlook the city, served as a stop along the Santa Fe railroad line.

GETTING HERE AND AROUND

Greyhound and Amtrak both pass through town daily, though most travelers arrive by car, either via Interstate 40 (east–west) or Highway 95 (north–south). Needles Area Transit is the local bus service.

ESSENTIALS

Bus Information Needles Area Transit 🕾 *760/326–2113* ⊕ *www.transitunlimited.org/Needles_Area_Transit.*

Visitor Information Needles Chamber of Commerce ⊠ *100 G St., at Front St.* 🕾 *760/326–2050* ⊕ *www.needleschamber.com.*

EXPLORING

El Garces Harvey House Train Depot. Stop and gawk at the crumbling 1908 train depot, one of the many restaurant–boardinghouses built by the Fred Harvey company, and imagine how magnificent this skeletal structure would look in the unlikely event it were restored. The shady city park out front has inviting benches. ⊠ *900 Front St., at F. St.* 🕾 *760/326–5678.*

Fodor'sChoice ★ FAMILY **Havasu National Wildlife Refuge.** In 1941, after the construction of Parker Dam, President Franklin D. Roosevelt set aside Havasu National Wildlife Refuge, a 24-mile stretch of land along the Colorado River between Needles and Lake Havasu City. Best seen by boat, this beautiful waterway is punctuated with isolated coves, sandy beaches, and Topock Marsh, a favorite nesting site of herons, egrets, and other waterbirds. You can see wonderful petroglyphs on the rocky red canyon cliffs of Topock Gorge. The park has 11 boat-access points; there's camping below Castle Rock. ∎TIP➜ Springtime is by far the best time to visit, as the river is more likely to be robust and wildflowers aflame. ⊠ *Off I–40, 13 miles southeast of Needles* 🕾 *760/326–3853* ⊕ *www.fws.gov/ southwest/refuges/arizona/havasu.*

Moabi Regional Park. This park on the banks of the Colorado River is a good place for swimming, boating, picnicking, horseback riding, and fishing. Bass, bluegill, and trout are plentiful in the river. The 600 campsites have full amenities. ⊠ *Park Moabi Rd., off I–40, 11 miles southeast of Needles* 🕾 *760/326–3831* ⊕ *cms.sbcounty.gov/parks* 🖾 *Day use $10, camping $15–$40.*

WHERE TO EAT AND STAY

For expanded hotel reviews, visit Fodors.com.

$ ✗ **River City Pizza.** Good grub is hard to find in Needles, but this inex-
PIZZA pensive pizza place off Interstate 40 is a local favorite. Try the Vegetarian Deluxe pizza with a mug of cold lager or a glass of wine out on
the small patio. ⑤ *Average main: $8* ⊠ *1901 Needles Hwy., at P St.*
☎ *760/326-9191* ⊕ *www.rivercitypizzaco.com.*

$ ⊡ **Best Western Colorado River Inn.** The spartan country western–style
HOTEL rooms here are decorated in rich colors; expect the standard Best Western amenities. **Pros:** good rates; clean rooms; nice pool. **Cons:** town's
dead at night (and not much livelier during the day!); occasional train
noise. ⑤ *Rooms from: $80* ⊠ *2371 Needles Hwy.* ☎ *760/326-4552,*
800/780-7234 ⊕ *www.bestwestern.com* ⊸ *63 rooms* ⏀ *Breakfast.*

$ ⊡ **Fender's River Road Resort.** On a calm section of the Colorado River,
RESORT this funky little 1960s-era motel-resort—off the beaten path in a town
FAMILY that's in the proverbial middle of nowhere—caters to families with
shade trees and an area with grills and picnic tables. **Pros:** on the river;
clean rooms; peaceful; camping is $28–$40 a night. **Cons:** several minutes from the freeway; rooms could use some refreshing. ⑤ *Rooms*
from: $69 ⊠ *3396 Needles Hwy.* ☎ *760/326-3423* ⊸ *10 rooms, 27*
campsites with full hookups.

LAKE HAVASU CITY, AZ

Arizona Hwy. 95, 43 miles southeast of Needles in Arizona.

This wide spot in the Colorado River, created in the 1930s by Parker
Dam, is accessed from its eastern shore in Arizona. Here you can swim;
zip around on a Jet Ski; paddle a kayak; fish for trout, bass, or bluegill;
or boat beneath the London Bridge, one of the desert's oddest sights.
During sunset the views are breathtaking. Just be wary of coming here
during March, when spring-breaking students definitely change the vibe.

GETTING HERE AND AROUND

Shuttles operate between here and Las Vegas, but as with other desert
sites, traveling by car is the only practical way to go. Havasu Area
Transit is the local bus service.

ESSENTIALS

Transportation Contacts Havasu Area Transit ☎ *928/453-7600*
⊕ *www.lhcaz.gov/operations/transit.html.*

EXPLORING

London Bridge. What really put Lake Havasu City on the map was
the piece-by-piece reconstruction in 1971 of London Bridge by town
founder, Robert P. McCulloch. Today, the circa-1831 bridge, designed
by John Rennie, connects the city to a small island. Riverbanks on both
sides have numerous restaurants, hotels, and RV parks. There's also
a reconstructed English village whose quiet streets suggest that it has
lost some of its luster. ☎ *928/855-4115* ⊕ *www.havasuchamber.com*
⊡ *Free* ☉ *Daily 24 hrs.*

WHERE TO EAT

$$$ ✕ **Shugrue's.** This lakefront restaurant serves up beautiful views of Lon-
AMERICAN don Bridge and the English Village, along with fresh seafood, steak,
and specialties such as Bombay chicken and shrimp, served with spicy
yogurt sauce and mango chutney. ⑤ *Average main: $24* ✉ *1425 N.
McCulloch Blvd.* ☎ *928/453–1400* ⊕ *www.shugrues.com/lhc.*

SPORTS AND THE OUTDOORS

FAMILY **Lake Havasu Dixie Bell.** The two-story, old-fashioned paddle-wheel
boat, with air-conditioning and a cocktail lounge, takes its passengers
on a one-hour narrated tour around the island. ✉ *1477 Queens Bay*
☎ *928/453–6776* ⊕ *www.londonbridgeresort.com* ✆ *$20* ☉ *Tours daily
at noon and 1:30.*

London Bridge Watercraft Tours & Rentals. Right on the beach, this outfitter
rents personal watercraft such as Jet Skis and Sea-Doos. ✉ *Crazy Horse
Campground, 1534 Beachcomber Blvd.* ☎ *928/453–8883* ⊕ *www.
londonbridgewatercraft.com.*

OWENS VALLEY

Along U.S. 395 east of the Sierra Nevada.

In this undervisited region, the snowcapped Sierra Nevada range
abruptly and majestically rises to the west, and the high desert whistles
to the east.

LONE PINE

30 miles west of Panamint Valley via Hwy. 190.

Mt. Whitney towers majestically over this tiny community, which sup-
plied nearby gold- and silver-mining outposts in the 1860s, and for the
past century—especially from the 1920s through the 50s—the town
has been touched by Hollywood glamour: several hundred movies, TV
episodes, and commercials have been filmed here.

GETTING HERE AND AROUND

Arrive by car via U.S. 395 from the north or south, or Highway 190
from Death Valley National Park. No train or regularly scheduled bus
service is available.

ESSENTIALS

Visitor Information Lone Pine Chamber of Commerce ✉ *126 S. Main St., at
Whitney Portal Rd.* ☎ *760/876–4444, 877/253–8981* ⊕ *www.lonepinechamber.org.*

EXPLORING

Alabama Hills. Drop by the Lone Pine Visitor Center for a map of the
Alabama Hills and take a drive up Whitney Portal Road (turn west at
the light) to this wonderland of granite boulders. Erosion has worn the
rocks smooth; some have been chiseled to leave arches and other for-
mations. The hills have become a popular location for rock climbing.
There are three campgrounds among the rocks, each with a stream for
fishing. ✉ *Whitney Portal Rd., 4½ miles west of Lone Pine.*

Beverly and Jim Rogers Museum of Lone Pine Film History. Hopalong Cassidy, Barbara Stanwyck, Roy Rogers, John Wayne—even Robert Downey Jr.—are among the stars who have starred in westerns and other films shot in the Alabama Hills and surrounding dusty terrain. The marquee-embellished museum relates this Hollywood-in-the-desert tale via exhibits and a rollicking 20-minute documentary. ⊠ *701 S. Main St., U.S. 395* ☎ *760/876–9909* ⊕ *www.lonepinefilmhistorymuseum.org* ▣ *$5* ⊙ *Mon.–Sat. 10–5, Sun. 10–4.*

Mt. Whitney. Straddling the border of Sequoia National Park and Inyo National Forest–John Muir Wilderness, Mt. Whitney (14,496 feet) is the highest mountain in the contiguous United States. A favorite game for travelers passing through Lone Pine is trying to guess which peak is Mt. Whitney. Almost no one gets it right because Mt. Whitney is hidden behind other mountains. There is no road that ascends the peak, but you can catch a glimpse of the mountain by driving curvy Whitney Portal Road west from Lone Pine into the mountains. The pavement ends at the trailhead to the top of the mountain, which is also the start of the 211-mile John Muir Trail from Mt. Whitney to Yosemite National Park. At the portal, a restaurant (known for its pancakes) and a small store mostly cater to hikers and campers staying at Whitney Portal Campground. You can see a waterfall from the parking lot and go fishing in a small trout pond. The portal area is closed from mid-October to early May; the road closes when snow conditions require. ⊠ *Whitney Portal Rd., west of Lone Pine* ⊕ *www.fs.usda.gov/attmain/inyo.*

WHERE TO EAT AND STAY

For expanded hotel reviews, visit Fodors.com.

$ ✕**Alabama Hills Café & Bakery.** The extensive breakfast and lunch menus
AMERICAN at this eatery just off the main drag include many vegetarian items. Portions are huge. ⑤ *Average main: $10* ⊠ *111 W. Post St., at S. Main St.* ☎ *760/876–4675.*

$ ▦ **Dow Villa Motel and Hotel.** Built in 1923 to cater to the film indus-
HOTEL try, Dow Villa is in the center of Lone Pine. **Pros:** clean rooms; great mountain views; in-room whirlpool tubs. **Cons:** somewhat dated decor; some rooms share bathrooms. ⑤ *Rooms from: $105* ⊠ *310 S. Main St., Lone Pine* ☎ *760/876–5521, 800/824–9317* ⊕ *www.dowvillamotel.com* ↴ *91 rooms* ⦿*No meals.*

MANZANAR NATIONAL HISTORIC SITE

U.S. 395, 11 miles north of Lone Pine.

GETTING HERE AND AROUND

There's no public transportation here; virtually everyone arrives by car.

EXPLORING

Manzanar National Historic Site. A reminder of an ugly episode in U.S. history, the former Manzanar War Relocation Center is where some 10,000 Japanese-Americans were confined behind barbed-wire fences between 1942 and 1945. Today not much remains of Manzanar but a guard post, the auditorium, and some concrete foundations. But you can drive the one-way dirt road past the ruins to a small cemetery, where a monument stands. Signs mark where the barracks, a hospital, a school, and the fire station once stood. An outstanding 8,000-square-foot interpretive center has exhibits and screens a short film. ■TIP➔ This place has great bathrooms. ⊠ *U.S. 395, 11 miles north of Lone Pine* ☎ *760/878-2932* ⊕ *www.nps.gov/manz* ⊠ *Free* ☉ *Park daily dawn-dusk. Center Apr.-Nov., daily 9-5:30; Nov.-Apr., daily 9-4:30.*

INDEPENDENCE

U.S. 395, 5 miles north of Manzanar National Historic Site.

Named for a military outpost that was established near here in 1862, Independence is small and sleepy. But the town has some wonderful historic buildings and is certainly worth a stop on your way from the Sierra Nevada to Death Valley (➪ *Chapter 12*).

GETTING HERE AND AROUND

Greyhound passes through town, but most travelers arrive by car on U.S. 395.

ESSENTIALS

Visitor Information Independence Chamber of Commerce ⊠ *139 N. Edwards. St., U.S. 395* ☎ *760/878-0084* ⊕ *www.independence-ca.com.*

EXPLORING

Eastern California Museum. The highlights at this glimpse into Inyo County's history include the Paiute and Shoshone Indian basketry, the exhibit about the Manzanar internment camp, and the yard full of implements used by early area miners and farmers. ⊠ *155 N. Grant St., at W. Center St.* ☎ *760/878-0258* ⊕ *www.inyocounty.us/ecmuseum* ⊠ *Donations accepted* ☉ *Daily 10-5.*

Mt. Whitney Fish Hatchery. Here's a delightful place for a family picnic. Bring some change for the fish-food machines; the lakes are full of hefty, always-hungry breeder trout. Built in 1915, the hatchery was one of the first trout farms in California, and today it produces fish that stock lakes throughout the state. ⊠ *Fish Hatchery Rd., 2 miles north of town* ☎ *760/876-4128* ⊕ *mtwhitneyfishhatchery.org* ⊠ *Free* ☉ *Thurs.-Mon. 9-4.*

■ EN ROUTE — **Ancient Bristlecone Pine Forest.** About an hour's drive from Bishop you can view some of the oldest living trees on earth, some of which date back more than 40 centuries. The world's largest bristlecone pine can be found in Patriarch Grove. ⊠ *Schulman Grove Visitor Center, White Mountain Rd. (from U.S. 395, turn east onto Hwy. 168 and follow signs for 23 miles), Bishop* ⊠ *$3* ☉ *Mid-May-Nov., shorter or longer as weather permits.*

A memorial honors the 10,000 Japanese-Americans who were held at the Manzanar War Relocation Center during World War II.

BISHOP

U.S. 395, 43 miles north of Independence.

One of the biggest towns along U.S. 395, Bishop has views of the Sierra Nevada and the White and Inyo mountains. First settled by the Northern Paiute Indians, the area was named in 1861 for cattle rancher Samuel Bishop, who established a camp here. Paiute and Shoshone people reside on four reservations in the area.

GETTING HERE AND AROUND

To fully enjoy the many surrounding attractions, you must get here by car. Arrive and depart via U.S. 395 or, from Nevada, U.S. 6. Local transit provides limited service to nearby tourist sites.

ESSENTIALS

Bus Information Eastern Sierra Transit Authority ☎ *800/922–1930* ⊕ *estransit.com.*

Visitor Information Bishop Chamber of Commerce ✉ *690 N. Main St., at Park St.* ☎ *760/873–8405, 888/395–3952* ⊕ *www.bishopvisitor.com.*

EXPLORING

FAMILY **Laws Railroad Museum.** The laid-back and wholly nostalgic Laws Railroad Museum celebrates the Carson and Colorado Railroad Company, which set up a narrow-gauge railroad yard here in 1883. Among the exhibits are a self-propelled car from the Death Valley Railroad and a full village of rescued buildings, including a post office, the original 1883 train depot, and a restored 1900 ranch house. Many of the buildings are chock-full of "modern amenities" of days gone by. ✉ *200 Silver Canyon Rd., off U.S. 6, 4.5 miles north of town* ☎ *760/873–5950* ⊕ *www.lawsmuseum.org* ✉ *$5 suggested donation* ☉ *Daily 10–4.*

WHERE TO EAT AND STAY

For expanded hotel reviews, visit Fodors.com.

$ ✕ **Erick Schat's Bakkery.** A bustling stop for motorists traveling to and
BAKERY from Mammoth Lakes, this shop is crammed with delicious pastries, cookies, rolls, and other baked goods. The biggest draw, though, is the sheepherder bread, a hand-shaped and stone hearth–baked sourdough that was introduced during the gold rush by immigrant Basque sheepherders in 1907. That bread and others baked here are sliced to make the mammoth sandwiches the shop is also famous for. ⑤ *Average main: $8* ✉ *763 N. Main St., near Park St.* ☎ *760/873–7156* ⊕ *www. erickschatsbakery.com.*

$$ ✕ **Whiskey Creek.** Since 1924, this Wild West–style saloon, restaurant,
AMERICAN and gift shop has been serving salads, warm soups, and barbecued steaks to locals and tourists. Sit on the shaded deck and enjoy one of the many available microbrews. ⑤ *Average main: $20* ✉ *524 N. Main St., at Grove St.* ☎ *760/873–7174* ⊕ *www.whiskeycreekbishop.com.*

$$ ⌨ **Bishop Creekside Inn.** The nicest spot to stay in Bishop, this clean
B&B/INN and comfortable mountain-style hotel is a good base from which to explore the town or go skiing and trout fishing nearby. **Pros:** nice pool; spacious and modern rooms. **Cons:** pets not allowed. ⑤ *Rooms from: $150* ✉ *725 N. Main St.* ☎ *760/872–3044, 800/273–3550* ⊕ *www. bishopcreeksideinn.com* ⇆ *89 rooms* ⏻ *Breakfast.*

DEATH VALLEY
NATIONAL PARK

WELCOME TO DEATH VALLEY NATIONAL PARK

TOP REASONS TO GO

★ **Roving rocks:**
Death Valley's Racetrack is home to moving boulders, an unexplained phenomenon that has scientists baffled.

★ **Lowest spot on the continent:** Stand on the lowest spot on the continent at Badwater, 282 feet below sea level.

★ **Wildflower explosion:**
During the spring, this desert landscape is ablaze with greenery and colorful flowers, especially between Badwater and Ashford Mill.

★ **Ghost towns:**
Death Valley is renowned for its Wild West heritage and is home to dozens of crumbling settlements including Ballarat, Cerro Gordo, Chloride City, Greenwater, Harrisburg, Keeler, Leadfield, Panamint City, Rhyolite, and Skidoo.

★ **Naturally amazing:**
From canyons to sand dunes to salt flats and dry lake beds, Death Valley serves up plenty of geological treasures.

NEVADA
CALIFORNIA

Visitor Center
Scotty's Castle 267
Ubehebe Crater Grapevine
Mesquite Spring
2 △

The Racetrack

P A N A M I N T   R A N G E

← TO LONE PINE

Panamint Dunes
Father Crowley Point 190
Panamint Springs
TO HWY. 395

Darwin Falls 4
Wildrose Canyon Rd.
Darwin

TO RIDGECREST
178

0 ————— 10 mi
0 ————— 10 km

1 Central Death Valley.
Furnace Creek sits in the heart of Death Valley—if you have only a short time in the park, head here. You can visit gorgeous Golden Canyon, Zabriskie Point, the Salt Creek Interpretive Trail, and Artist's Drive, among other popular points of interest.

2 Northern Death Valley.
This region is uphill from Furnace Creek, which means marginally cooler temperatures. Be sure to stop by Rhyolite Ghost Town on Highway 374 before entering the park and exploring Moorish Scotty's Castle, colorful Titus Canyon, and jaw-dropping Ubehebe Crater.

3 Southern Death Valley.
This is a desolate area, but there are plenty of sights that help convey Death Valley's rich history. Don't miss the Dublin Gulch Caves.

CALIFORNIA

12

4 Western Death Valley. Panamint Springs Resort is a nice place to grab a meal and get your bearings before moving on to quaint Darwin Falls, smooth rolling sand dunes, beehive-shaped Wildrose Charcoal Kilns, and historic Stovepipe Wells Village.

GETTING ORIENTED

Death Valley National Park covers 5,310 square miles, ranges from 6 to 60 miles wide, and measures 140 miles north to south. Within the park, the Panamint Range parallels Death Valley to the west, the Amargosa Range to the east. Nearly the entire park lies in southeastern California, with a small eastern portion crossing over into Nevada.

Updated by
Reed Parsell

The desert is no Disneyland. With its scorching summer heat and vast, sparsely populated tracts of land, it's not often at the top of the list when most people plan their California vacations. But the natural riches of Death Valley—the largest national park outside Alaska—are overwhelming: rolling waves of sand dunes, black cinder cones thrusting up hundreds of feet from a blistered desert floor, riotous sheets of wildflowers, bizarrely shaped Joshua trees basking in the orange glow of a sunset, tiny pupfish that enthrall youngsters, and a silence that is both dramatic and startling.

DEATH VALLEY PLANNER

WHEN TO GO

Most of the park's 1 million annual visitors still come between late fall and early spring, taking advantage of moderate temperatures and the lack of rainfall. During these cooler months you will need to book a room in advance, but don't worry: the park never feels crowded. If you visit during summer, believe everything you've ever heard about desert heat—it can be brutal, with temperatures often topping 120°F. The dry air wicks moisture from the body without causing a sweat, so drink plenty of water. Bring sunglasses, a hat, and sufficient clothing to block the sun's rays and the wind. Flash floods are fairly common; sections of roadway can be flooded or washed away. The wettest month is February, when the park receives an average of 0.3 inch of rain.

GETTING HERE AND AROUND
CAR TRAVEL
It can take more than three hours to cross from one side of the park to another, so it's important to choose an entrance point that makes sense for what you want to see. If you're driving from Los Angeles, enter through the western portion along Highway 395; if you're coming from Las Vegas, enter from the north at Beatty, Nevada, or via the central entrance at Death Valley Junction. Travelers from Orange County, San Diego, and the Inland Empire should access the park via Interstate 15 North at Baker.

Distances can be deceiving within the park: what seems close can be very far away. Much of the park can be viewed on regularly scheduled bus tours, but these often don't allow time for hikes to sites not seen from the road, such as Salt Creek, Golden Canyon, and Natural Bridge. The best option is to drive to a number of the sites, get out of the car, and walk.

When driving in Death Valley, reliable maps are important, as signage is often limited or, in a few places, nonexistent. Other important accessories include a compass, a mobile phone (though these don't always work in remote areas), and extra food and water (3 gallons per person per day is recommended, plus additional radiator water). If you're able to take a four-wheel-drive vehicle, bring it: many of Death Valley's most spectacular canyons are otherwise inaccessible. Be aware of possible winter closures or driving restrictions due to snow.

Driving Information California State Department of Transportation Hotline. Call this hotline for updates on Death Valley road conditions. ☎ 800/427–7623 ⊕ www.dot.ca.gov. **California Highway Patrol.** The California Highway Patrol offers the latest traffic incident information. ☎ 800/427–7623 recorded info, 760/872–5900 live dispatcher ⊕ cad.chp.ca.gov.

PARK ESSENTIALS
PARK FEES AND PERMITS
The entrance fee is $20 per vehicle and $10 for those entering on foot, bus, bike, or motorcycle. The payment, valid for seven consecutive days, is collected at the park's entrance stations and at the visitor center at Furnace Creek. (If you enter the park on Highway 190, you won't find an entrance station; remember to stop by the visitor center to pay the fee.) Annual park passes, valid only at Death Valley, are $40.

A permit is not required for groups of 14 or fewer, but if you're planning an overnight visit to the backcountry, complete a registration form at the Furnace Creek Visitor Center. Backcountry camping is allowed in areas that are at least 2 miles from maintained campgrounds and the main paved or unpaved roads and ¼ mile from water sources. Most abandoned mining areas are restricted to day use.

PARK HOURS
Most facilities within the park remain open year-round, daily 8–6.

12

TOURS

Death Valley & Scotty's Castle Adventure Tour. These 11-hour luxury motor-coach tours of the park pass through its most famous landmarks. Tours include lunch and hotel pickup from designated Las Vegas–area hotels. Tours depart Tuesday and Saturday at 7 am and cost $199 per person. ☎ *800/719–3768 Death Valley Tours, 800/566–5868, 702/233–1627 Look Tours.*

Furnace Creek Visitor Center tours. This center has the most tour options, including a weekly 2-mile Harmony Borax Walk and guided hikes to Mosaic Canyon and Golden Canyon. Less strenuous options include wildflower, birding, and geology walks, and a Furnace Creek Inn historical tour. The visitor center also offers orientation programs every half hour daily from 8 to 5. ⊠ *Furnace Creek Visitor Center, Rte. 190, 30 miles northwest of Death Valley Junction* ☎ *760/786–2331.*

Pink Jeep Tours Las Vegas. Hop aboard a distinctive, pink four-wheel-drive vehicle with Pink Jeep Tours Las Vegas to visit places—the Charcola Kilns, the Racetrack, and Titus Canyon among them—that your own vehicle might not be able to handle. Pink Jeep tours last 9 to 10 hours from Las Vegas (you also can board at Furnace Creek) and cost up to $239. ⊠ *3629 West Hacienda Ave., Las Vegas, Nevada* ☎ *888/900–4480 ⊕ www.pinkjeep.com.*

VISITOR INFORMATION

PARK CONTACT INFORMATION

Death Valley National Park ☎ *760/786–3200 ⊕ www.nps.gov/deva.*

VISITOR CENTERS

Furnace Creek Visitor Center and Museum. The exhibits and artifacts here provide a broad overview of how Death Valley formed; you can pick up maps at the bookstore run by the Death Valley Natural History Association. This is also the place to sign up for ranger-led walks (available November through April) or check out a live presentation about the valley's cultural and natural history. The helpful center offers 12-minute slide shows about the park every 30 minutes. Your children are likely to receive plenty of individual attention from the enthusiastic rangers. Ongoing renovations to the center and museum are improving the displays and level of hands-on interactivity. ⊠ *Hwy. 190, 30 miles northwest of Death Valley Junction* ☎ *760/786–3200 ⊕ www.nps.gov/ deva ☉ Daily 8–5.*

Scotty's Castle Visitor Center and Museum. If you visit Death Valley, make sure you make the hour's drive north from Furnace Creek to Scotty's Castle. In addition to living-history tours, you'll find a nice display of exhibits, books, self-guided tour pamphlets, and displays about the castle's creators, Death Valley Scotty and Albert M. Johnson. Fuel up with sandwiches or souvenirs (there's no gasoline sold here anymore) before heading back out to the park. ⊠ *Rte. 267, 53 miles northwest of Furnace Creek and 45 miles northwest of Stovepipe Wells Village* ☎ *760/786–2392 ⊕ www.nps.gov/deva ☉ Daily 9–4:15 (hours vary seasonally).*

EXPLORING

SCENIC DRIVE

Artist's Drive. This 9-mile, one-way route skirts the foothills of the Black Mountains and provides intimate views of the changing landscape. Once inside the palette, the huge expanses of the valley are replaced by the small-scale natural beauty of pigments created by volcanic deposits. It's a quiet, lonely drive, and shouldn't be rushed. Reach Artist's Palette by heading north off Badwater Road. ⊠ *Death Valley National Park.*

12

HISTORIC SITES

FAMILY **Scotty's Castle.** This Moorish-style mansion, begun in 1924 and never completed, takes its name from Walter Scott, better known as Death Valley Scotty. An ex-cowboy, prospector, and performer in Buffalo Bill's Wild West Show, Scotty always told people the castle was his, financed by gold from a secret mine. In reality, there was no mine, and the house belonged to a Chicago millionaire named Albert Johnson, whom Scott had finagled into investing in the fictitious mine. Despite the con, Johnson and Scott became great friends. The house functioned for a while as a hotel and still contains works of art, imported carpets, handmade European furniture, and a tremendous pipe organ. Costumed rangers, with varying degrees of enthusiasm, re-create life at the castle circa 1939. Check out the Underground Tour, which takes you through a ¼-mile tunnel in the castle basement. ⊠ *Scotty's Castle Rd. (Hwy. 267), 53 miles north of Salt Creek Interpretive Trail* ☎ 760/786–2392 ⊕ *www.nps.gov/ deva* ☞ *$15* ⊙ *Daily 8:30–4:15, tours daily 9–4 (hours vary seasonally).*

SCENIC STOPS

Artist's Palette. So called for the contrasting colors of its volcanic deposits, this is one of signature sights of Death Valley. Artist's Drive, the approach to the area, is one way heading north off Badwater Road, so if you're visiting Badwater from Furnace Creek, come here on the way back. The drive winds through foothills of sedimentary and volcanic rocks. About 4 miles into the drive, a short side road veers right to a parking lot that's a few hundred feet before the "palette," whose natural colors include shades of green, gold, and pink. ⊠ *off Badwater Rd., 11 miles south of Furnace Creek.*

Badwater. At 282 feet below sea level, Badwater is the lowest spot on land in the Western Hemisphere—and also one of the hottest. Stairs and wheelchair ramps descend from the parking lot to a wooden platform that overlooks a sodium chloride pool, a small but remarkably persistent reminder that the valley floor used to contain a lake. You can continue past the platform on a broad, white path that peters out after a half-mile or so. Badwater is one of the most popular and easily accessible sites within the park. From this lowest point, be sure to look across to Telescope Peak, which towers more than 2 miles above the valley floor. ⊠ *Badwater Rd., 19 miles south of Furnace Creek.*

DID YOU KNOW?

One of the best ways to experience Artist's Palate—a beautiful landscape of colorful mineral deposits—is by following Artist's Drive, a 9-mile one-way road through the area.

Dante's View. This lookout is more than 5,000 feet up in the Black Mountains. In the dry desert air you can see across most of 110-mile-long Death Valley. The view is astounding. Take a 10-minute, mildly strenuous walk from the parking lot toward a series of rocky overlooks, where with binoculars you can spot some of Death Valley's signature sites. A few interpretive signs point out the highlights below in the valley and across, in the Sierra. Getting here from Furnace Creek takes an hour—time well invested. ⊠ *Dante's View Rd., off Hwy. 190, 35 miles from Badwater, 20 miles south of Twenty Mule Team Canyon.*

Devil's Golf Course. Thousands of miniature salt pinnacles carved into surreal shapes by the desert wind dot this wildly varied landscape. The salt was pushed up to the earth's surface by pressure created as underground salt- and water-bearing gravel crystallized. Get out of your vehicle and take a closer look; you'll see perfectly round holes descending into the ground. ⊠ *Badwater Rd., 13 miles south of Furnace Creek. Turn right onto dirt road and drive 1 mi.*

Racetrack. Getting here involves a 28-mile journey over a rough dirt road, but the reward is well worth the trip. Where else in the world do rocks move on their own? This phenomenon has baffled scientists for years and is perhaps one of the last great natural mysteries. No one has actually seen the rocks in motion, but theory has it that when it rains, the hard-packed lake bed becomes slippery enough that gusty winds push the rocks along—sometimes for several hundred yards. When the mud dries, a telltale trail remains. The trek to the Racetrack can be made in a sedan, but sharp rocks can slash tires; a truck or SUV with thick tires, high clearance, and a spare tire are suggested. ⊠ *27 miles west of Ubehebe Crater via dirt road.*

Sand Dunes at Mesquite Flat. These dunes, made up of minute pieces of quartz and other rock, are ever-changing products of the wind-rippled hills, with curving crests and a sun-bleached hue. The dunes are the most photographed destination in the park, and you can see them at their best at sunrise and sunset. Keep your eyes open for animal tracks—you may even spot a coyote or fox. Bring plenty of water, and note where you parked your car: it's easy to become disoriented in this ocean of sand. If you lose your bearings, climb to the top of a dune and scan the horizon for the parking lot. ⊠ *19 miles north of Hwy. 190, northeast of Stovepipe Wells Village.*

Titus Canyon. This is a popular 27-mile drive from Beatty south along Scotty's Castle Road. Along the way you'll pass Leadville Ghost Town, petroglyphs at Klare Spring, and spectacular limestone and dolomite narrows at the end of the canyon. Toward the end, a two-section of gravel road will lead you into the mouth of the canyon. ⊠ *Access road off Scotty's Castle Rd., 33 miles northwest of Furnace Creek.*

Zabriskie Point. Although only about 710 feet in elevation, this is one of Death Valley National Park's most scenic spots, overlooking a striking panorama of wrinkled, multicolor hills. It's a great place to watch the sunrise, but it can be bustling any time of day. Pair it with a drive out to magnificent Dante's View. ⊠ *Hwy. 190, 5 miles south of Furnace Creek.*

SPORTS AND THE OUTDOORS

BIRD-WATCHING

Approximately 350 bird species have been identified in Death Valley. The best place to see the park's birds is along the Salt Creek Interpretive Trail, where you can spot ravens, common snipes, killdeer, spotted sandpipers, and great blue herons. Along the fairways at Furnace Creek Golf Club, you can see kingfishers, peregrine falcons, hawks, Canada geese, yellow warblers, and the occasional golden eagle. Scotty's Castle attracts wintering birds from around the globe that are attracted to its running water, shady trees, and shrubs. Other good spots to find birds are at Saratoga Springs, Mesquite Springs, Travertine Springs, and Grimshaw Lake near Tecopa. You can download a complete park bird checklist, divided by season, at ⊕ *www.nps.gov/deva/naturescience/ birds.htm.* Rangers at Furnace Creek Visitor Center often lead birding walks through Salt Creek between November and March.

FOUR-WHEELING

Maps and SUV guidebooks for four-wheel-drive and other backcountry roads (including the popular Cottonwood/Marble canyons, Racetrack, Eureka Dunes, Saratoga Springs, and Warm Springs Canyon) are offered at the Furnace Creek Visitor Center. Remember: Never travel alone and be sure to pack plenty of water and snacks. Driving off established roads is strictly prohibited in the park.

HIKING

Plan to hike before or after midday in the spring, summer, or fall, unless you're in the mood for a masochistic baking. Carry plenty of water, wear protective clothing, and keep an eye out for black widows, scorpions, snakes, and other potentially dangerous creatures. Some of the best trails are unmarked; if the opportunity arises, ask for directions.

EASY

Fodor's Choice ★

FAMILY

Darwin Falls. This lovely 2-mile round-trip hike rewards you with a refreshing waterfall surrounded by thick vegetation and a rocky gorge. No swimming or bathing is allowed, but it's a beautiful place for a picnic. Adventurous hikers can scramble higher toward more rewarding views of the falls. *Easy.* ⊠ *Access the 2-mile graded dirt road and parking area off Hwy. 190, 1 mile west of Panamint Springs Resort.*

FAMILY

Salt Creek Interpretive Trail. This trail, a ½-mile boardwalk circuit, loops through a spring-fed wash. The nearby hills are brown and gray, but the floor of the wash is alive with aquatic plants such as pickerelweed and salt grass. The stream and ponds here are among the few places in the park to see the rare pupfish, the only native fish species in Death Valley. Animals such as bobcats, fox, coyotes, and snakes visit the spring, and you may also see ravens, common snipes, killdeer, and great blue herons. *Easy.* ⊠ *Off Hwy. 190, 14 miles north of Furnace Creek.*

"I'd always wanted to photograph this remote location, and on my drive into Death Valley I was rewarded at Zabriskie Point with this amazing view." —photo by Rodney Ee, Fodors.com member

MODERATE

Fall Canyon. This is a 3-mile one-way hike from the Titus canyon parking area. First, walk ½ miles north along the base of the mountains to a large wash, then go 2½ miles up the canyon to a 35-foot dry fall. You can continue by climbing around to the falls on the south side. *Moderate.* ✉ *Access road off Scotty's Castle Rd., 33 miles northwest of Furnace Creek.*

FAMILY **Mosaic Canyon.** A gradual uphill trail (4 miles round-trip) winds through the smoothly polished walls of this narrow canyon. There are dry falls to climb at the upper end. *Moderate.* ✉ *Access road off Hwy. 190, ½ mile west of Stovepipe Wells Village.*

DIFFICULT

Fodor's Choice **Telescope Peak Trail.** The 14-mile round-trip begins at Mahogany Flat
★ Campground, which is accessible by a very rough dirt road. The steep and at some points treacherous trail winds through pinyon, juniper, and bristlecone pines, with excellent views of Death Valley and Panamint Valley. Ice axes and crampons may be necessary in winter—check at the Furnace Creek Visitor Center. It takes a minimum of six grueling hours to hike to the top of the 11,049-foot peak and then return. Getting to the peak is a strenuous endeavor; take plenty of water and only attempt it in fall unless you're an experienced hiker. *Difficult.* ✉ *Off Wildrose Rd., south of Charcoal Kilns.*

HORSEBACK AND CARRIAGE RIDES

TOURS AND OUTFITTERS

Furnace Creek Stables. Set off on a one- or two-hour guided horseback or carriage ride ($45–$70) from Furnace Creek Stables. The rides traverse trails with views of the surrounding mountains, where multicolor volcanic rock and alluvial fans form a background for date palms and other vegetation. Evening carriage rides take passengers around the golf course and Furnace Creek Ranch. Cocktail rides, with champagne, margaritas, and hot spiced wine, are available. The stables are open October–May only. ✉ *Hwy. 190, Furnace Creek* ☎ *760/614–1018* ⊕ *www.furnacecreekstables.net.*

12

WHERE TO EAT

Prices in the reviews are the average cost of a main course at dinner or, if dinner is not served, at lunch.

$$
CAFÉ
FAMILY

✗ **Forty-Niner Cafe.** This casual coffee shop serves typical American fare for breakfast (except in the summer), lunch, and dinner. It's done up in a rustic mining style with whitewashed pine walls, vintage map-covered tables, and prospector-branded chairs. Past menus and old photographs decorate the walls. ⑤ *Average main: $15* ✉ *Furnace Creek Ranch, Hwy. 190, Furnace Creek* ☎ *760/786–2345* ⊕ *www.furnacecreekresort.com.*

$$$
AMERICAN
Fodor's Choice
★

✗ **Furnace Creek Inn Dining Room.** Fireplaces, beamed ceilings, and spectacular views provide a visual feast to match the inn's ambitious menu. Dishes may include such desert-theme items as crispy cactus fritters, and simpler fare such as salmon and free-range chicken and filet mignon all pair well with the signature prickly-pear margarita. There's a seasonal menu of vegetarian dishes, too. There's a minimal evening dress code (no T-shirts or shorts). Lunch is served, too, and you can always have afternoon tea in the lobby, an inn tradition since 1927. Breakfast and Sunday brunch are also served. Reservations are essential for dinner only. ⑤ *Average main: $28* ✉ *Furnace Creek Inn Resort, Hwy. 190, Furnace Creek* ☎ *760/786–3385* ⊕ *www.furnacecreekresort.com* ⩲ *Reservations essential* ⊘ *Restaurant closed June–Sept.*

WHERE TO STAY

During the busy season (November through March) you should make reservations for lodgings within the park several months in advance. *Prices in the reviews are the lowest cost of a standard double room in high season. For expanded hotel reviews, visit Fodors.com.*

$$$$
HOTEL
Fodor's Choice
★

⛺ **Furnace Creek Inn.** This is Death Valley's most luxurious accommodations, going so far as to have valet parking. **Pros:** refined; comfortable; great views. **Cons:** a far cry from roughing it; expensive. ⑤ *Rooms from: $375* ✉ *Furnace Creek Village, near intersection of Hwy. 190 and Badwater Rd.* ☎ *760/786–2345* ⊕ *www.furnacecreekresort.com* ⇨ *66 rooms* ⊘ *Closed mid-May–mid-Oct.* ⫴◎⫽ *Breakfast.*

CLOSE UP

Plants and Wildlife in Death Valley

There's a general misconception that Death Valley National Park consists of mile upon endless mile of flat desert sands, scattered cacti, and an occasional cow skull. Many people don't realize that across the valley floor from Badwater—the lowest point in the Western Hemisphere—Telescope Peak towers at 11,049 feet above sea level. The extreme topography of Death Valley is a lesson in geology. Two hundred million years ago seas covered the area, depositing layers of sediment and fossils. Between 3.5 million and 5 million years ago faults in the Earth's crust and volcanic activity pushed and folded the ground, causing mountain ranges to rise and the valley floor to drop. The valley was then filled periodically by lakes, which eroded the surrounding rocks into fantastic formations and deposited the salts that now cover the floor of the basin.

Most animal life in Death Valley (51 mammal, 36 reptile, 307 bird, and 3 amphibian species) is found near the limited sources of water. The bighorn sheep spend most of their time in the secluded upper reaches of the park's rugged canyons and ridges. Coyotes often can be seen lazing in the shade next to the golf course and have been known to run onto the fairways to steal a golf ball. The only native fish in the park is the pupfish, which grows to slightly longer than 1 inch. In winter, when the water is cold, the fish lie dormant in the bottom mud, becoming active again in spring. Because they are wary of large moving shapes, you must stand quietly over a pool at Salt Creek to see them.

Botanists say there are more than 1,000 species of plants here (21 exist nowhere else in the world), though many annual plants lie dormant as seeds for all but a few months in spring, when rains trigger a bloom. The rest congregate around the few water sources. Most of the low-elevation vegetation grows around the oases at Furnace Creek and Scotty's Castle, where oleanders, palms, and salt cedar grow. At higher elevations you will find pinyon, juniper, and bristlecone pine.

$ · B&B/INN — 🏨 **Panamint Springs Resort.** Ten miles inside the west entrance of the park, this low-key resort overlooks the sand dunes and peculiar geological formations of the Panamint Valley. **Pros:** slow-paced; friendly; there's a glorious amount of peace and quiet after sundown. **Cons:** far from the park's main attractions. ⑤ *Rooms from: $79 ⊠ Hwy. 190, 28 miles west of Stovepipe Wells* ☎ *775/482–7680 ⊕ www.deathvalley.com/psr* ↪ *14 rooms, 1 cabin* ⎜⎮⎜⎮ *No meals.*

$$ · HOTEL — 🏨 **Stovepipe Wells Village.** If you prefer quiet nights and an unfettered view of the night sky and nearby sand dunes, this property is for you. **Pros:** intimate, relaxed; no big-time partying; authentic desert-community ambience. **Cons:** isolated; a bit dated. ⑤ *Rooms from: $120 ⊠ Hwy. 190, Stovepipe Wells* ☎ *760/786–2387 ⊕ www.escapetodeathvalley. com* ↪ *83 rooms* ⎜⎮⎜⎮ *No meals.*

THE CENTRAL VALLEY

Highway 99 from Bakersfield to Lodi

WELCOME TO THE CENTRAL VALLEY

TOP REASONS TO GO

★ **Down under:** Forestiere Underground Gardens is not the flashiest tourist attraction in California, but it is one of the strangest—and oddly inspirational.

★ **Grape escape:** In the past two decades, Lodi's wineries have grown sufficiently in stature for the charming little town to become a must-sip destination.

★ **Utopian spirit:** A century ago, a small but resourceful group of citizens established the state's first all–African American town. Colonel Allensworth State Historic Park celebrates their utopian spirit.

★ **Go with the flow:** White-water rafting will get your blood pumping, and maybe your clothes wet, on the Stanislaus River near Oakdale.

★ **Hee haw!:** Kick up your heels and break out your drawl at Buck Owens' Crystal Palace in Bakersfield, a city some believe is the heart of country music.

1 Southern Central Valley. When gold was discovered in Kern County in the 1860s, settlers flocked to the southern end of the Central Valley. Black gold—oil—is now the area's most valuable commodity; the county provides two-thirds of California's oil production. Kern is also among the country's five most productive agricultural counties. From the flat plains around Bakersfield, the landscape grows gently hilly and then graduates to mountains as it nears Kernville, which lies in the Kern River valley.

2 Mid-Central Valley. The Mid-Central Valley extends over three counties—Tulare, Kings, and Fresno. Historic Hanford and bustling Visalia are off the tourist-traffic radar but have their charms. From Visalia, Highway 198 winds east 35 miles to Generals Highway, which passes through Sequoia and Kings Canyon national parks (⇨ see Chapter 16). Highway 180 snakes east 55 miles to Sequoia and Kings Canyon. From Fresno, Highway 41 leads north 95 miles to Yosemite National Park (⇨ see Chapter 15).

3 North Central Valley. The northern section of the valley cuts through Merced, Madera, Stanislaus, and San Joaquin counties, from the flat, abundantly fertile terrain between Merced and Modesto north to the edges of the Sacramento River delta and the fringes of the Gold Country. If you're heading to Yosemite National Park (⇨ see Chapter 15) from Northern California, chances are you'll travel through (or near) one or more small gateway communities such as Oakdale.

Tree Ripened Fruit

13

GETTING ORIENTED

California has a diversity of delicious vacation possibilities. Among its many outstanding regions, however, the Central Valley is arguably the least inviting. This flat landscape, sometimes blistery hot and smelly, contains no famous attractions beyond its bountiful farmland, which few would regard as scenic except perhaps just before harvest. For many vacationers, it is a region to drive through as quickly as possible on the way to fabulous Sequoia, Kings Canyon, and Yosemite national parks (⇨ *see Chapters 15 and 16)*. For those who have an extra day or two, whose tourism tastes don't demand Disneyland-level excitement, it can represent a pleasant diversion and provide insights into an enormous agricultural region. The valley is the vast geographical center of California and, from a breadbasket perspective, its proverbial heart.

Updated by
Reed Parsell

Among the world's most fertile working lands, the 225-mile Central Valley is important due to the scale of its food production but, to be honest, for most people this is simply a place to pass through on the way to greater attractions in the north, south, east, or west. Those willing to explore California's heartland, however, find that a detour off the freeway provides unexpected delights.

The Central Valley cuts through Kern, Tulare, Kings, Fresno, Madera, Merced, Stanislaus, and San Joaquin counties. It's bounded on the east by the mighty Sierra Nevada and on the west by the smaller coastal ranges. The agriculturally rich area is home to a diversity of birds; many telephone posts are crowned by a hawk or kestrel hunting the land below. Vineyards, especially in the northern valley around Lodi, and almond orchards, whose white blossoms make February a brighter month, are pleasant sights out motorists' windows. In the towns, historical societies display artifacts of the valley's eccentric past, concert halls and restored theaters showcase samplings of contemporary culture, and museums provide a blend of both. Restaurants can be very good, both fancy and mom-and-pop, and roadside farm stands provide veritable bursts of flavor. Country-music enthusiasts will find a lot to appreciate on the radio and on stages, especially in the Bakersfield area. Summer nights spent at one of the valley's minor-league baseball parks—Bakersfield, Fresno, Modesto, Stockton, and Visalia have teams—can be a relaxing experience. Whether on back roads or main streets, people tend to be proud to help outsiders explore the Central Valley.

PLANNING

WHEN TO GO
Spring, when wildflowers are in bloom and the scent of fruit blossoms is in the air, and fall, when the air is brisk and leaves turn red and gold, are the best times to visit. Many of the valley's biggest festivals take place during these seasons. (If you suffer from allergies, though, beware

of spring, when stone-fruit trees blossom.) Summer, when temperatures often top 100°F, can be oppressive, though area water parks and lakes provide much-needed respite. Many attractions close in winter, when thick, ground-hugging tule fog is a common driving hazard.

GETTING HERE AND AROUND

AIR TRAVEL

The area's main airport is Fresno Yosemite International Airport (FYI), served by AeroMexico, Alaska/Horizon, Allegiant, American, Delta, United/United Express, US Airways, and Volaris. Bakersfield's Kern County Airport at Meadows Field (BFL), served by United Express and US Airways, is the southern air gateway to the Central Valley. United Express serves Modesto's airport (⇨ *see Modesto, below*).

Airport Contacts Fresno Yosemite International Airport ⊠ *5175 E. Clinton Way, Fresno* ☎ *559/621–4500, 800/244–2359 automated information* ⊕ *www.flyfresno.com.* **Kern County Airport at Meadows Field** ⊠ *1401 Skyway Dr., Bakersfield* ☎ *661/391–1800* ⊕ *www.meadowsfield.com.*

BUS TRAVEL

Greyhound provides bus service to several major cities, and Orange Belt Stages provides coach service (and some Amtrak connections) to Bakersfield, Visalia, Hanford, and other large towns.

Bus Contact Greyhound ☎ *800/231–2222* ⊕ *www.greyhound.com.* **KART** ☎ *559/584–0101* ⊕ *www.mykartbus.com.* **Orange Belt Stages** ☎ *800/266–7433* ⊕ *www.orangebelt.com.*

CAR TRAVEL

Highway 99 is the main route between the valley's major cities and towns. Interstate 5 runs roughly parallel to it to the west but misses the major population centers; its main use is for quick access to San Francisco or Los Angeles. Major roads that connect the interstate with Highway 99 are highways 58 (to Bakersfield), 198 (to Hanford and Visalia), 152 (to Chowchilla, via Los Banos), 140 (to Merced), 132 (to Modesto), and 120 (to Manteca).

Road Conditions Caltrans ☎ *800/427–7623* ⊕ *www.dot.ca.gov.*

TRAIN TRAVEL

Amtrak's daily *San Joaquin* travels to Bakersfield, Hanford, Fresno, Merced, Modesto, and Stockton.

Train Contact Amtrak ☎ *800/872–7245* ⊕ *www.amtrak.com.*

RESTAURANTS

Fast-food places and chain restaurants dominate valley highways, but away from the main drag, homegrown bistros and fine restaurants take advantage of the local produce and meats that are the cornerstone of California cuisine. Superb Mexican restaurants can be found here, and Chinese, Italian, Armenian, and Basque cuisines are amply represented. *Prices in the reviews are the average cost of a main course at dinner or, if dinner is not served, at lunch.*

HOTELS

Chain motels and hotels—utilitarian but clean and comfortable—predominate, but there are also upscale lodgings, small inns, and Victorian-style B&Bs. *Prices in the reviews are the lowest cost of a standard double room in high season. For expanded hotel reviews, visit Fodors.com.*

SOUTH CENTRAL VALLEY

BAKERSFIELD

110 miles north of Los Angeles; 110 miles west of Ridgecrest.

Bakersfield's founder, Colonel Thomas Baker, arrived with the discovery of gold in the nearby Kern River valley in 1851. Now Kern County's biggest city—its 352,000 residents include the largest Basque community in the United States—Bakersfield probably is best known as Nashville West, a country-music haven closely affiliated with performers Buck Owens (who died here in 2006) and Merle Haggard (who was born here in 1937). It also has two very fine museums.

GETTING HERE AND AROUND

Arrive here by car via Highway 99 from the north or south, or via Highway 58 from the east or west. Amtrak and Greyhound provide train and bus service. GETbus operates local buses.

ESSENTIALS

Bus Contact GETbus ☎ *661/869-2438* ⊕ *www.getbus.org.*

Visitor Information Greater Bakersfield Convention & Visitors Bureau ⊠ *515 Truxtun Ave.* ☎ *661/852-7282, 866/425-7353* ⊕ *www.visitbakersfield.com.* **Kern County Board of Trade** ⊠ *2101 Oak St.* ☎ *661/500-5376, 800/500-5376* ⊕ *www.visitkern.com.*

EXPLORING

FAMILY **California Living Museum.** At this combination zoo, botanical garden, and natural-history museum, the emphasis is on the zoo. All animal and plant species displayed are native to the state. Within the reptile house lives every species of rattlesnake found in California. The landscaped grounds—in the hills about a 20-minute drive northeast of Bakersfield—also shelter captive bald eagles, tortoises, coyotes, black bears, and foxes. ⊠ *10500 Alfred Harrell Hwy., Hwy. 178 east to Harrell Hwy. north* ☎ *661/872-2256* ⊕ *www.calmzoo.org* 🖼 *$9* ☉ *Mar.–Oct., daily 9–5; Nov.–Feb., daily 9–4.*

FAMILY **Kern County Museum and Lori Brock Children's Discovery Center.** This 16-acre site is one of the Central Valley's top museum complexes. The indoor-outdoor Kern County Museum is an open-air, walk-through historic village with more than 55 restored or re-created buildings dating from the 1860s to the 1940s. "Black Gold: The Oil Experience," a permanent exhibit, shows how oil is created, discovered, extracted, and transformed for various uses. The Lori Brock Children's Discovery Center, for ages eight and younger, has hands-on displays and an indoor playground. ⊠ *3801 Chester Ave., at 38th St.* ☎ *661/868-8400* ⊕ *www. kcmuseum.org* 🖼 *$10* ☉ *Tue.–Sat. 9–5, Sun. 12–5.*

The Central Valley

WHERE TO EAT

$ ✗ **Jake's Original Tex Mex Cafe.** Don't let the cafeteria-style service fool

MEXICAN you; this is probably the best lunch place in Bakersfield. The chicken burritos and the chili fries (with meaty chili ladled on top) are superb; the coleslaw is a favorite, too. Locals rave about the chocolate cake—with good reason. Jake's is open for dinner, too. ⑤ *Average main: $9* ✉ *1710 Oak St., near Truxtun Ave.* ☎ *661/322–6380* ⊕ *www. jakestexmex.com* ⚓ *Reservations not accepted* ⊘ *Closed Sun.*

$$ ✗ **Uricchio's Trattoria.** Everyone from office workers to oil barons heads

ITALIAN here for the tasty food and casual atmosphere. Panini (served at lunch only), pasta, and Italian-style chicken dishes dominate the menu; the chicken piccata outsells all other offerings. ⑤ *Average main: $16* ✉ *1400 17th St., at K St.* ☎ *661/326–8870* ⊕ *www.uricchios-trattoria. com* ⊘ *Closed Sun. No lunch Sat.*

WHERE TO STAY

For expanded hotel reviews, visit Fodors.com.

$ 🏨 **Four Points by Sheraton.** Fountains, lush lawns, and exotic plants pro-

HOTEL vide a spectacular setting for this hotel. **Pros:** clean; good neighborhood. **Cons:** somewhat impersonal; far from main attractions. ⑤ *Rooms from: $99* ✉ *5101 California Ave.* ☎ *661/325–9700, 800/368–7764* ⊕ *www. starwoodhotels.com/fourpoints* 🛏 *198 rooms* 🍽 *Breakfast.*

NIGHTLIFE AND THE ARTS

Buck Owens' Crystal Palace. Buck Owens is Bakersfield's local boy made good, and this venue is a combination nightclub, restaurant, souvenir store, and showcase of country-music memorabilia. Country-and-western singers perform here, as Owens did countless times before his death in 2006. A dance floor beckons customers who can still twirl after sampling the menu of steaks, burgers, nachos, and gooey desserts. Expect a cover charge some weeknights and most weekends. ✉ *2800 Buck Owens Blvd., off Hwy. 178* ☎ *661/328–7500* ⊕ *www.buckowens. com* ⊘ *Closed Mon.*

KERNVILLE

50 miles northeast of Bakersfield.

The wild Kern River, which flows through Kernville en route from Mt. Whitney to Bakersfield, delivers some of the most exciting white-water rafting in the state. Kernville (population 1,700) rests in a mountain valley on both banks of the river and at the northern tip of Lake Isabella, a dammed portion of the river used as a reservoir and for recreation. By far the most scenic town in this region, Kernville has lodgings, restaurants, and antiques shops. Old West–style buildings line the main streets, reflecting Kernville's heritage as a rough-and-tumble gold-mining town once known as Whiskey Flat. Present-day Kernville dates from the 1950s, when it was moved upriver to make room for Lake Isabella. The road from Bakersfield includes stretches where the rushing river is on one side and granite cliffs are on the other.

GETTING HERE AND AROUND
Highway 178 connects Kernville and Bakersfield; take Highway 155 if coming from Delano. There's no train line or scheduled bus service.

ESSENTIALS
Visitor Information VisitKern.com ☏ *661/500–5376, 800/500–5376* ⊕ *www.visitkern.com.*

WHERE TO EAT AND STAY
For expanded hotel reviews, visit Fodors.com.

$ ✕ **That's Italian.** For northern Italian cuisine in a typical trattoria, this
ITALIAN is the spot. Try the braised lamb shanks in a Chianti wine sauce or the linguine with clams, mussels, calamari, and shrimp in a white-wine clam sauce. ⑤ *Average main: $14* ⊠ *9 Big Blue Rd., at Kernville Rd.* ☏ *760/376–6020.*

$$$ ⊡ **Whispering Pines Lodge Bed & Breakfast.** On the banks of the Kern
B&B/INN River, this 8-acre property has units that are motel-style or in duplex bungalows; all have fireplaces, coffeemakers, and king-size beds. **Pros:** rustic setting; big breakfasts; great views; very clean. **Cons:** bungalows are pricey; town is remote. ⑤ *Rooms from: $189* ⊠ *13745 Sierra Way* ☏ *760/376–3733, 877/241–4100* ⊕ *www.kernvalley.com/ whisperingpines* ⇨ *17 rooms* ⦿⊢ *Breakfast.*

SPORTS AND THE OUTDOORS
BOATING AND WINDSURFING
The Lower Kern River, which extends from Lake Isabella to Bakersfield and beyond, is open for fishing year-round. Catches include rainbow trout, catfish, smallmouth bass, crappie, and bluegill. Lake Isabella is popular with anglers, water-skiers, sailors, and windsurfers. Its shoreline marinas have boats for rent, bait and tackle, and moorings.

French Gulch Marina. This marina is near the dam on Lake Isabella's west shore. ☏ *760/379–8774* ⊕ *www.frenchgulchmarina.com.*

North Fork Marina. North Fork is in Wofford Heights, on the lake's north shore. ☏ *760/376–1812* ⊕ *www.northforkmarina.com.*

WHITE-WATER RAFTING
The three sections of the Kern River—known as the Lower Kern, Upper Kern, and the Forks—add up to nearly 50 miles of white water, ranging from Class I (easy) to Class V (expert). The Lower and Upper Kern are the most popular and accessible sections. Organized trips can last from one hour (for as little as $35) to more than two days. Rafting season usually runs from late spring until the end of summer.

Kern River Tours. This outfit leads several rafting tours, from half-day (from $105) to three-day ($868) trips navigating Class V rapids, and also arranges for mountain-bike trips. ☏ *800/844–7238* ⊕ *www.kern rivertours.com.*

Mountain & River Adventures. This outfit conducts calm-water kayaking tours as well as white-water rafting trips, leads mountain-bike excursions, and has a campground. In the wintertime, M&R rents snowshoes, cross-country skis, and other snow gear. ☏ *760/376–6553, 800/861–6553* ⊕ *www.mtnriver.com.*

13

Sierra South. Half-day Class II and III white-water rafting trips (starting at $74) are emphasized at Sierra South, which also offers kayaking classes and calm-water excursions. ☎ *760/376–3745, 800/457–2082* ⊕ *www.sierrasouth.com.*

MID-CENTRAL VALLEY

COLONEL ALLENSWORTH STATE HISTORIC PARK

45 miles north of Bakersfield.

GETTING HERE AND AROUND
The easiest way to get here is by car. The park is off Highway 43, a 15-minute drive west of Highway 99.

Fodor's Choice **Colonel Allensworth State Historic Park.** It's worth the slight detour off
★ Highway 99 to learn about and pay homage to the dream of Allen Allensworth and other black pioneers who in 1908 founded Allensworth, the only California town settled, governed, and financed by African Americans. At its height, the town prospered as a key railroad transfer point, but after cars and trucks reduced railroad traffic and water was diverted for Central Valley agriculture, the town declined and was eventually deserted. Today, the restored and rebuilt schoolhouse, library, and other structures commemorate Allensworth's heyday, as do festivities that take place each October. The parking lot is open only on Fridays and weekends, but daily you can park nearby, walk over to the buildings, and peek in. ✉ *4129 Palmer Ave., off Hwy. 43; from Hwy. 99 at Delano, take Garces Hwy. west to Hwy. 43 north; from Earlimart, take County Rd. J22 west to Hwy. 43 south* ☎ *661/849–3433* ⊕ *www. parks.ca.gov* ✑ *$6 per car* ☉ *Daily sunrise–sunset; visitor center Fri.– Sun. 10–4; buildings open by appointment.*

VISALIA

75 miles north of Bakersfield.

Visalia's combination of a reliable agricultural economy and civic pride has yielded the Central Valley's most vibrant downtown. If you're into Victorian and other old houses, drop by the city's visitor center and pick up a free map of them. A clear day's view of the Sierra from Main Street is spectacular, if sadly rare due to smog and dust, and even Sunday night can find the streets bustling with pedestrians.

GETTING HERE AND AROUND
Highway 198, just east of its exit from Highway 99, cuts through town (and proceeds up the hill to Sequoia National Park). Greyhound stops here, but not Amtrak. KART buses serve the locals.

ESSENTIALS
Visitor Information Visalia Visitor Center ✉ *303 E. Acequia Ave., at S. Bridge St.* ☎ *559/334–0141* ⊕ *www.visitvisalia.org* ☉ *Mon. 10–5, Tues.–Fri. 8:30–5.*

Each spring the fruit orchards along the Blossom Trail, near Fresno, burst into bloom.

EXPLORING

Kaweah Oaks Preserve. Trails at this 322-acre wildlife sanctuary off the main road to Sequoia National Park *(⇨ see Chapter 16)* lead past majestic valley oak, sycamore, cottonwood, and willow trees. Among the 134 bird species you might spot are hawks, hummingbirds, and great blue herons. Lizards, coyotes, and cottontails also live here. ⊠ *Follow Hwy. 198 for 7 miles east of Visalia, turn north on Rd. 182, and proceed ½ mile to gate on left side* ☎ *559/738–0211* ⊕ *www.sequoiariverlands.org* ⊡ *Free* ⊘ *Daily sunrise–sunset.*

FAMILY **Mooney Grove Park.** Amid shady oaks you can picnic alongside duck ponds, rent a boat for a ride around the lagoon, and view a replica of the famous *End of the Trail* statue. The original, designed by James Earl Fraser for the 1915 Panama-Pacific International Exposition, is now in the Cowboy Hall of Fame in Oklahoma. ⊠ *27000 S. Mooney Blvd., Hwy. 63, 5 miles south of downtown* ⊡ *$7 per car, free in winter (dates vary)* ⊘ *Daily 8–sunset; sometimes closed Tues. and Wed.*

Tulare County Museum. This indoor-outdoor museum contains several re-created environments from the pioneer era. Also on display are Yokuts tribal artifacts (basketry, arrowheads, clamshell-necklace currency) as well as saddles, guns, dolls, quilts, and gowns. A separate wing chronicles farm history and labor. ⊠ *Mooney Grove Park, 27000 S. Mooney Blvd., Hwy. 63, 5 miles south of downtown* ☎ *559/733–6616* ⊕ *www.co.tulare.ca.us/government/parks/museum.asp* ⊡ *Free with park entrance fee of $7* ⊘ *Mon., Thu., and Fri. 10–4, weekends 12–3.*

WHERE TO EAT

$ ✕ **Henry Salazar's Fresh Mex Grill.** Traditional Mexican food with a con-
MEXICAN   temporary twist is served at this restaurant that uses fresh ingredients from local farms. Two signature dishes are the Burrito Fantastico—a large flour tortilla stuffed with your choice of meat, beans, and chili sauce, and smothered with melted Monterey Jack cheese—and grilled salmon with lemon-butter sauce. Colorfully painted walls, soft reflections from candles in wall niches, and color-coordinated tablecloths and napkins make the atmosphere cozy and restful. $ *Average main: $12* ⊠ *123 W. Main St.* ☎ *559/741–7060* ⊕ *www.henrysalazars.com.*

$$$ ✕ **The Vintage Press.** Built in 1966, this is the best restaurant in the
EUROPEAN   Central Valley. Cut-glass doors and bar fixtures decorate the artfully
Fodor'sChoice   designed rooms. The California–Continental cuisine includes dishes
★   such as crispy veal sweetbreads with a port-wine sauce, and a bacon-wrapped filet mignon stuffed with mushrooms. The chocolate Grand Marnier cake is a standout among the homemade desserts and ice creams. The wine list has more than 900 selections. $ *Average main: $30* ⊠ *216 N. Willis St.* ☎ *559/733–3033* ⊕ *www.thevintagepress.com.*

WHERE TO STAY

For expanded hotel reviews, visit Fodors.com.

$ 🏨 **The Spalding House.** This restored colonial-revival B&B is decked
B&B/INN   out with antiques, Oriental rugs, handcrafted woodwork, and glass doors. **Pros:** warm feel; old-time atmosphere; great place for a twilight stroll. **Cons:** only three rooms. $ *Rooms from: $95* ⊠ *631 N. Encina St.* ☎ *559/739–7877* ⊕ *www.thespaldinghouse.com* 🛏 *3 suites* ⍾ *Breakfast.*

HANFORD

20 miles west of Visalia.

Founded in 1877 as a Southern Pacific Railroad stop, Hanford had one of California's largest Chinatowns—the Chinese came to help build the railroads and stayed on to farm. If you arrive on a typically laid-back Hanford day, it might be hard to imagine the fatal skirmish that took place in 1880 between local settlers and railroad law agents over land titles. Known as the Mussel Slough Tragedy, the incident inspired Frank Norris's best-seller *The Octopus.*

You can take a self-guided walking tour of Hanford with the help of a free brochure from its visitor agency, which also books driving tours ($85 per hour) in a restored 1930 Studebaker fire truck. One tour explores the restored buildings of Courthouse Square, whose art-deco Hanford Auditorium is a visual standout; another heads to narrow China Alley.

GETTING HERE AND AROUND
Highway 198 serves Hanford east to west, Highway 41 north to south. Amtrak trains serve Hanford, as do KART buses.

ESSENTIALS
Visitor Information Hanford Conference and Visitor Agency ⊠ *113 Court St.* ☎ *559/582–5024* ⊕ *www.visithanford.com.*

EXPLORING

China Alley. Worth a brief look if you're in town—for the photo op, if nothing else—this frozen-in-time street holds the last remains of Hanford's once-bustling Chinatown. The centerpiece is the 1893 **Taoist Temple.** The alley's other buildings of note include the decaying L.T. Sue Herb building. ⊠ *Temple, 12 China Alley, off N. Green St.* ⊕ *www.chinaalley.com.*

Hanford Carnegie Museum. Fashions, furnishings, toys, and military artifacts at this living-history museum tell the region's story. The facility is inside the former Carnegie Library, a Romanesque building dating from 1905. ⊠ *108 E. 8th St., at N. Douty St.* ☎ *559/584–1367* ⊕ *www. hanfordcarnegiemuseum.org* ⊠ *$3* ☉ *Wed.–Sat. 11–4.*

13

WHERE TO EAT AND STAY

For expanded hotel reviews, visit Fodors.com.

$ | ✕ **La Fiesta.** Mexican-American families, farmworkers, and farmers all
MEXICAN | eat here, polishing off traditional Mexican dishes such as enchiladas and tacos. The Fiesta Special—for two or more—includes nachos, garlic shrimp, shrimp in a spicy red sauce, clams, and two pieces of top sirloin. ⑤ *Average main: $10* ⊠ *106 N. Green St.* ☎ *559/583–8775.*

$ | ✕ **Niklana's Cafe.** Truck company-bookkeepers Nichole Weed and
BAKERY | Dalana Church took the leap from passion to entrepreneurism when they opened their bustling breakfast and lunch spot. The duo's already deeply devoted patrons hail the crepes, cinnamon buns, soups, and sandwiches. ⑤ *Average main: $9* ⊠ *102 W. 7th St., at N. Douty St.* ☎ *559/410–8826* ☉ *Closed weekends. No dinner.*

$ | ⊞ **Comfort Inn Hanford.** Attentive service and generous breakfasts are
HOTEL | touted at this clean chain hotel on the fringes of historic downtown. **Pros:** Clean, friendly, convenient. **Cons:** Impersonal, no grounds to speak of. ⑤ *Rooms from: $90* ⊠ *10 N. Irwin St.* ☎ *559/584–9300* ⊕ *www.comfortinn.com* ⊅ *65* ⑪ *Breakfast.*

FRESNO

35 miles north of Hanford.

Sprawling Fresno, with half a million people, is the center of the richest agricultural county in the United States. Cotton, grapes, and tomatoes are among the major crops; poultry and milk are also important. About 75 ethnic groups, including Armenians, Laotians, and Indians, live here. The city has a relatively vibrant arts scene, several public parks, and many low-price restaurants. The Tower District—with its chic restaurants, coffeehouses, and boutiques—is the trendy spot, though like the rest of Fresno it can look drab on a cloudy day. The Pulitzer Prize–winning playwright and novelist William Saroyan (*The Time of Your Life, The Human Comedy*) was born here in 1908.

GETTING HERE AND AROUND

Highway 99 is the biggest road through Fresno. Highways 41 and 180 also bisect the city. Amtrak trains stop here daily (and often). Fresno Area Express (FAX) provides comprehensive local bus service.

Forestiere
Underground
Gardens 6

Fresno Art
Museum 4

Kearney
Mansion
Museum 7

Legion of
Valor
Museum 2

Meux Home
Museum 3

Roeding
Park 1

Woodward
Park 5

KEY

ℹ️ *Tourist information*

ESSENTIALS

Transportation Contacts FAX ☎ *559/621–7433* ⊕ *www.fresno.gov/ discoverfresno.*

Visitor Information Fresno / Clovis Convention & Visitors Bureau
✉ *1550 E. Shaw Ave.* ☎ *559/981–5500, 800/788–0836* ⊕ *playfresno.org.*

EXPLORING

TOP ATTRACTIONS

Fodor's Choice
★
FAMILY

Forestiere Underground Gardens. Sicilian immigrant Baldasare Forestiere spent four decades (1906–46) carving out an odd, subterranean realm of rooms, tunnels, grottoes, alcoves, and arched passageways that once extended for more than 10 acres between Highway 99 and busy, mall-pocked Shaw Avenue. Though not an engineer, Forestiere called on his memories of the ancient Roman structures he saw as a youth and on techniques he learned digging subways in New York and Boston. Only a fraction of his prodigious output is on view, but you can tour his underground living quarters, including bedrooms (one with a fireplace), the kitchen, living room, and bath, as well as a fishpond and auto tunnel. Skylights allow exotic full-grown fruit trees to flourish more than 20 feet belowground. ✉ *5021 W. Shaw Ave., 2 blocks east of Hwy. 99* ☎ *559/271–0734* ⊕ *www. undergroundgardens.com* 🎟 *$15* 🕙 *Tours June–Aug., Wed.–Sun. 10–4; call or check website for other tour times* 🕙 *Closed Dec.–Feb.*

Fresno Art Museum. The museum's key permanent collections include pre-Columbian Mesoamerican art, Andean pre-Columbian textiles and artifacts, Japanese prints, Berkeley School abstract expressionist paintings, and contemporary sculpture. Temporary exhibits include important traveling shows. ⊠ *Radio Park, 2233 N. 1st St., at E. Yale Ave.* ☎ *559/441–4221* ⊕ *www.fresnoartmuseum.org* ⊡ *$5; free Sun.* ☉ *Thur.–Sun. 11–5.*

Meux Home Museum. A restored 1889 Victorian, "the Meux" contains furnishings typical of an upper-class household in early Fresno. The house's namesake, Thomas Richard Meux, was a Confederate army doctor during the Civil War who became a family practitioner after moving to Fresno. The Meux can be viewed on guided tours only. ⊠ *1007 R St., at Tulare St.* ☎ *559/233–8007* ⊕ *www.meux.mus.ca.us* ⊡ *$5* ☉ *Fri.–Sun. noon–3:30.*

13

WORTH NOTING

Blossom Trail. The 62-mile self-guided Blossom Trail driving tour takes in Fresno-area orchards, citrus groves, and vineyards during spring blossom season. The trail passes through small towns and past rivers, lakes, and canals. The most colorful and aromatic time to go is from late February to mid-March, when almond, plum, apple, apricot, and peach blossoms shower the landscape with shades of white, pink, and red. ☎ *559/600–4271* ⊕ *www.goblossomtrail.com.*

Kearney Mansion Museum. The drive along palm-lined Kearney Boulevard is one of the best reasons to visit the museum, which stands in shaded 225-acre **Kearney Park.** The century-old home of M. Theo Kearney, Fresno's onetime "raisin king," is accessible only on guided 45-minute tours. ⊠ *7160 W. Kearney Blvd., 6 miles west of Fresno off Hwy. 180* ☎ *559/441–0862* ⊕ *www.valleyhistory.org* ⊡ *Museum $5; park entry $5 (waived for museum visitors)* ☉ *Park 7 am–10 pm; museum tours Fri.–Sun. at 1, 2, and 3.*

Legion of Valor Museum. Military-history buffs enjoy this museum whose collection includes German bayonets and daggers, a Japanese Namby pistol, a Gatling gun, and Japanese, German, and American uniforms. The staff is extremely enthusiastic. ⊠ *2425 Fresno St., between N and O Sts.* ☎ *559/498–0510* ⊕ *www.legionofvalor.com* ⊡ *Free* ☉ *Mon.–Sat. 10–3.*

FAMILY **Roeding Park.** Tree-shaded Roeding Park is a place of respite on hot summer days; it has picnic areas, playgrounds, tennis courts, horseshoe pits, and a zoo (⇨ *Fresno Chaffee Zoo*). A train, little race cars, paddleboats, a carousel, and other rides for kids are among the amusements at **Playland.** Children can explore attractions with fairy-tale themes at **Rotary Storyland.** ⊠ *890 W Belmont Ave., at Olive Ave.* ☎ *559/498–1551* ⊕ *storylandplayland.com* ⊡ *Roeding Park $5 per vehicle; Playland free (rides $1.50–$3); Storyland $5* ☉ *Park daily Apr.–Oct. 6 am–10 pm, Nov.–Mar. 6 am–7 pm; Playland weekends 10–6; Storyland weekends 10–4, plus some holidays.*

Fresno Chaffee Zoo. The zoo's most striking exhibit is its tropical rain forest, where you'll encounter exotic birds along paths and bridges. Elsewhere at the zoo live tigers, grizzly bears, sea lions, tule elk, camels, elephants, and siamang apes. The facility has a high-tech reptile house and there's a petting zoo. ⊠ *Roeding Park, 894 W. Belmont Ave.,* *east of Hwy. 99* ☎ *559/498–5910* ⊕ *www.fresnochaffeezoo.org* ⟁ *$7* ☉ *Apr.–Sept., daily 9–6; Oct.–Mar., daily 9–4.*

Woodward Park. The Central Valley's largest urban park, with 300 acres of jogging trails, picnic areas, and playgrounds in the city's northern reaches, is especially pretty in spring, when plum and cherry trees, magnolias, and camellias bloom. Outdoor concerts take place in summer. The **Shinzen Friendship Garden** has a teahouse, a koi pond, arched bridges, a waterfall, and Japanese art. ✉ *Audubon Dr. and Friant Rd.* ☎ *559/621–2900* ⟁ *$5 per car Feb.–Oct.; additional $3 for Shinzen Garden* ☉ *Apr.–Oct., daily 6 am–10 pm; Nov.–Mar., daily 6–7.*

OFF THE BEATEN PATH

Old Town Clovis. The restored brick buildings of a former lumber-industry district now hold antiques shops, art galleries, restaurants and saloons. At the visitor center (or online) you can access a walking-tour map. To get here from Fresno, head east on Herndon Avenue for about 10 miles to Clovis Avenue and drive south. Note that not much is open on Sunday. ✉ *Visitor Center, 399 Clovis Ave., at 4th St., Clovis* ⊕ *www.visitclovis.com.*

WHERE TO EAT AND STAY

For expanded hotel reviews, visit Fodors.com.

$$
STEAKHOUSE

✕ **Tahoe Joe's.** This restaurant is known for its steaks—rib eye, strip, or filet mignon. Other selections include the slow-roasted prime rib, center-cut pork chops, and chicken breast in a whiskey-peppercorn sauce. The baked potato that accompanies almost every dish is loaded tableside with your choice of butter, sour cream, chives, and bacon bits. Tahoe Joe's has two Fresno locations. ⑤ *Average main: $18* ✉ *7006 N. Cedar Ave., at E. Herndon Ave.* ☎ *559/299–9740* ⊕ *www.tahoejoes.com* ⌂ *Reservations not accepted* ☉ *No lunch* ⑤ *Average main: $18* ✉ *2700 W. Shaw Ave., at N. Marks Ave.* ☎ *559/277–8028* ⊕ *www.tahoejoes.com.*

$
HOTEL

⛺ **Piccadilly Inn Shaw.** This two-story property has 7½ attractively landscaped acres and a big swimming pool. **Pros:** big rooms; nice pool; town's best lodging option. **Cons:** some rooms show mild wear; neighborhood is somewhat sketchy. ⑤ *Rooms from: $99* ✉ *2305 W. Shaw Ave.* ☎ *559/348–5520, 888/286–2645* ⊕ *www.piccadillyinn.com/shaw* ⟁ *183 rooms, 5 suites.*

NIGHTLIFE AND THE ARTS

Roger Rocka's Dinner Theater. This Tower District venue stages Broadway-style musicals. ✉ *1226 N. Wishon Ave., at E. Olive Ave.* ☎ *559/266–9494, 800/371–4747* ⊕ *www.rogerrockas.com.*

Tower Theatre for the Performing Arts. The restored 1930s art-deco movie house, the anchor and namesake of the trendy Tower District of theaters, clubs, restaurants, and cafés, presents theater, ballet, concerts, and other cultural events. ✉ *815 E. Olive Ave., at N. Wishon Ave.* ☎ *559/485–9050* ⊕ *www.towertheatrefresno.com.*

SPORTS AND THE OUTDOORS
WATER PARKS

Wild Water Adventures. This 52-acre water park about 10 miles east of Fresno is open from late May to early September. ✉ *11413 E. Shaw Ave., off Hwy. 168, Clovis* ☎ *559/299–9453, 800/564–9453* ⊕ *www.wildwater.net* ⟁ *$28, $17 after 4 pm.*

WHITE-WATER RAFTING

Kings River Expeditions. This outfit arranges one- and two-day white-water rafting trips on the Kings River. ⊠ *1840 W. Shaw Ave., Clovis* ☏ *559/233–4881, 800/846–3674* ⊕ *www.kingsriver.com.*

NORTH CENTRAL VALLEY

MERCED

13

50 miles north of Fresno.

Thanks to a branch of the University of California opening in 2005 and an aggressive community redevelopment plan, the downtown section of county seat Merced is coming back to life. The transformation is not yet complete, but there are promising signs: a brewpub, several boutiques, a multiplex, the restoration of historic buildings, and foot traffic won back from outlying strip malls.

GETTING HERE AND AROUND

The most scenic approach to Yosemite National Park, at least from the west, is via Highway 140 as it rambles through and past Merced. Most people arrive by car via Highway 99, but Amtrak also stops several times daily. The Bus provides transit service except on Sundays.

ESSENTIALS

Bus Contact The Bus ☏ *209/725-3813* ⊕ *www.mercedthebus.com.*

Visitor Information Merced Visitor Services ⊠ *710 W. 16th St.* ☏ *209/724-8104, 800/446-5353* ⊕ *www.yosemite-gateway.org.*

EXPLORING

Merced County Courthouse Museum. Even if you don't go inside, be sure to swing by this three-story former courthouse. Built in 1875, it's a striking example of Victorian Italianate style. The upper two floors are a museum of early Merced history. Highlights include ornate restored courtrooms and an 1870 Chinese temple with carved redwood altars. ⊠ *621 W. 21st St., at N St.* ☏ *209/723-2401* ⊕ *www.mercedmuseum. org* ⊠ *Free* ⊙ *Wed.–Sun. 1–4.*

Merced Multicultural Arts Center. The center displays paintings, sculpture, and photography. The Big Valley Arts & Culture Festival, which celebrates the area's ethnic diversity and children's creativity, takes place here in the fall. ⊠ *645 W. Main St., at N St.* ☏ *209/388-1090* ⊕ *www. artsmerced.org* ⊠ *Free* ⊙ *Wed.–Thur. 11–7, Fri.–Sat. 10–5.*

WHERE TO EAT AND STAY

For expanded hotel reviews, visit Fodors.com.

$$
STEAKHOUSE
✕ **The Branding Iron.** Beef is what this restaurant is all about. It's the place where farmers and ranchers come to refuel as they travel through cattle country. Try the juicy cut of prime rib paired with potato and Parmesan-cheese bread. California cattle brands decorate the walls, and when the weather is nice, cooling breezes refresh diners on the outdoor patio. ⑤ *Average main: $21* ⊠ *640 W. 16th St., between M and N Sts.* ☏ *209/722-1822* ⊕ *www.thebrandingiron-merced.com* ⊙ *No lunch weekends.*

$$ ✕ **DeAngelo's.** This restaurant, about 2 miles from downtown, is one of
ITALIAN   the Central Valley's best. Chef Vincent DeAngelo, a graduate of the Culi-
nary Institute of America, brings his considerable skill to everything from
basic ravioli to calamari steak. Half the restaurant is occupied by Bellini's,
a bar-bistro with its own menu, which includes brick-oven pizza. ⑤ *Aver-
age main: $20* ⊠ *2000 E. Childs Ave., at Parsons Ave.* ☎ *209/383-3020*
⊕ *www.deangelosrestaurant.com* ⊘ *No lunch weekends.*

$$ ⚎ **Hooper House Bear Creek Inn.** This 1931 neocolonial home stands
B&B/INN   regally at the corner of M Street; rooms are appointed with well-chosen
antiques and big, soft beds. **Pros:** historic charm; friendly staff; good
breakfast. **Cons:** front rooms can be noisy. ⑤ *Rooms from: $129* ⊠ *575
W. N. Bear Creek Dr., at M St.* ☎ *209/723-3991* ⊕ *www.hooperhouse.
com* ⊲ *3 rooms, 2 cottages* ◎ *Breakfast.*

SPORTS AND THE OUTDOORS

Lake Yosemite Regional Park. At this park surrounding a 387-acre irrigation reservoir, you can boat, swim, windsurf, water-ski, and fish. Paddle
boat rentals and picnic areas are available. ⊠ *N. Lake Rd. off Yosemite
Ave., 5 miles northeast of Merced* ☎ *209/385-7426* ⊠ *$6 per car late
May–early Sept.*

▌ EN
  ROUTE

Castle Air Museum. You can stroll among dozens of restored military
aircraft at this outdoor facility. The vintage war birds include the B-25
Mitchell medium-range bomber—best known for the Jimmy Doolittle
raid on Tokyo after the attack on Pearl Harbor—and the speedy SR-71
Blackbird, used for reconnaissance over Vietnam and Libya. ⊠ *Castle
Airport, 5050 Santa Fe Dr., 6 miles north of Merced, Buhach Rd. exit
off Hwy. 99, Atwater* ☎ *209/723-2178* ⊕ *www.castleairmuseum.org*
⊠ *$10* ⊘ *Apr.–Sept., daily 9–5; Oct.–Mar., daily 10–4.*

MODESTO

38 miles north of Merced.

Modesto, a gateway to Yosemite *(➪ see Chapter 15)* and the southern
reaches of the Gold Country, was founded in 1870 to serve the Central
Pacific Railroad. The frontier town was originally to be named Ralston,
after a railroad baron, but as the story goes, he modestly declined—
thus the name Modesto. The Stanislaus County seat, a tree-lined city
of 203,000, is perhaps best known as the site of the annual Modesto
Invitational Track Meet and Relays and the birthplace of producer-
director George Lucas, creator of the *Star Wars* film series.

GETTING HERE AND AROUND

Highway 99 is the major traffic artery; Highway 132 heads east from
here toward Yosemite National Park. United serves the airport here,
and several Amtrak trains arrive daily. Modesto Area Express (MAX)
is the local bus service.

ESSENTIALS

Airport Contacts Modesto City-County Airport ⊠ *617 Airport Way,
of Mitchell Rd., south from Yosemite Blvd./Hwy 132* ☎ *209/577-5200*
⊕ *www.modairport.com.*

Bus Contacts MAX ☎ *209/521-1274* ⊕ *www.modestoareaexpress.com.*

The Central Valley is California's agricultural powerhouse.

Visitor Information Modesto Convention and Visitors Bureau ✉ *1150 9th St., Suite C* 🕾 *209/526-5588, 888/640-8467* ⊕ *www.visitmodesto.com.*

EXPLORING

Blue Diamond Growers Store. You can witness the everyday abundance of the Modesto area with a visit here; on offer are tasty samples, a film about almond growing, and many roasts and flavors of almonds, as well as other nuts. ✉ *4800 Sisk Rd., at Kiernan Ave., off Hwy. 99* 🕾 *209/545-6230.*

McHenry Mansion. A rancher and banker built the 1883 McHenry Mansion, the city's sole surviving original Victorian home. The Italianate mansion has been decorated to reflect Modesto life in the late 19th century. Its period-appropriate wallpaper is especially impressive. ✉ *15th and I Sts.* 🕾 *209/577-5341* ⊕ *www.mchenrymansion.org* 🎫 *Free* ⊙ *Tours Sun.–Thurs. 12:30–4.*

McHenry Museum. A repository of early Modesto and Stanislaus County memorabilia, the museum's displays include re-creations of an old-time dentist's office, a blacksmith's shop, a one-room schoolhouse, an extensive doll collection, and a general store stocked with period goods such as hair crimpers and corsets. ✉ *1402 I St., at 14th St.* 🕾 *209/577-5235* ⊕ *www.mchenrymuseum.org* 🎫 *Free* ⊙ *Tues.–Sun. noon–4.*

Modesto Arch. One of the broadest and most striking "welcome to downtown" signs you'll see, the Modesto Arch bears the city's motto: "Water, Wealth, Contentment, Health." ✉ *9th and I Sts.*

WHERE TO EAT AND STAY

For expanded hotel reviews, visit Fodors.com.

$ ✕ **Hero's Sports Lounge & Pizza Co.** Modesto's renowned microbrewery
AMERICAN   makes Hero's beers. The 20 or so on tap include the delicious Whistle
Stop pale ale and Red Sky ale. The casual restaurant serves a tasty beer-
sausage nibbler and corned-beef sandwiches loaded with sauerkraut.
⑤ *Average main: $12* ✉ *821 L St., at 9th St.* ☎ *209/524–2337* ⊕ *www.
herosmodesto.com* ☼ *Closed Sun.*

$$$ ✕ **Tresetti's World Caffé.** An intimate setting with white tablecloths and
AMERICAN   contemporary art draws diners to this eatery—part wineshop (with 500-
plus selections), part restaurant—with a seasonally changing menu. The
Cajun-style crab cakes, served for lunch year-round, are outstanding.
For a small fee, your waiter will uncork any wine you select from the
shop. ⑤ *Average main: $26* ✉ *927 11th St., at I St.* ☎ *209/572–2990*
⊕ *www.tresetti.com* ☼ *Closed Sun.*

$ ⊞ **Best Western Town House Lodge.** The downtown location is the pri-
HOTEL   mary draw for this hotel. **Pros:** perfect location; updated. **Cons:** staff's
limited knowledge of town. ⑤ *Rooms from: $69* ✉ *909 16th St.*
☎ *209/524–7261, 800/772–7261* ⊕ *www.bestwesterncalifornia.com*
⇨ *59 rooms* �ⓞ *Breakfast.*

OAKDALE

15 miles northeast of Modesto.

Oakdale was founded as an orchard community and, in a real stretch,
calls itself the Cowboy Capital of the World. Formerly the home of a
Hershey's chocolate factory, the city still holds the Oakdale Chocolate
Festival, on the third weekend in May. The main attraction of this sweet
event, which attracts more than 50,000 people, is Chocolate Avenue,
where vendors proffer cakes, cookies, ice cream, fudge, and cheesecake.
The Oakdale Chamber of Commerce can provide more details.

GETTING HERE AND AROUND

Reach Oakdale via Highway 108 from Modesto. Local transit is of
little use to tourists.

ESSENTIALS

Visitor Information Oakdale Chamber of Commerce ✉ *590 N. Yosemite
Ave., at E. A St.* ☎ *209/847–2244* ⊕ *www.oakdalechamber.com.*

EXPLORING

FAMILY   **Knights Ferry Recreation Area.** The featured attraction is the 355-foot-long
Knights Ferry covered bridge. The beautiful and haunting structure,
built in 1863, crosses the Stanislaus River near the ruins of an old
gristmill. The park has camping, picnic, and barbecue areas along the
riverbanks, as well as three campgrounds accessible only by boat. You
can hike, fish, canoe, and raft on 4 miles of rapids. ✉ *Corps of Engi-
neers Park, 17968 Covered Bridge Rd., Knights Ferry, 12 miles east of
Oakdale via Hwy. 108* ☎ *209/881–3517* ⊠ *Free* ☼ *Daily dawn–dusk.*

FAMILY   **Oakdale Cheese & Specialties.** You can sample the wares at this homey
factory complex, which has tastings (try the aged Gouda) and cheese-
making tours, a store, and a bakery. Outside are a picnic area and a

petting zoo. ⊠ *10040 Valley Home Rd., at River Rd.* ☎ *209/848–3139* ⊕ *www.oakdalecheese.com.*

SPORTS AND THE OUTDOORS

WHITE-WATER RAFTING

River Journey. Rafting on the Stanislaus River is a popular activity near Oakdale. River Journey will take you out for a few hours of fun. ⊠ *14842 Orange Blossom Rd., off Hwy. 120/108, 4 miles* ☎ *209/847–4671, 800/292–2938* ⊕ *www.riverjourney.com.*

Sunshine Rafting Adventures. To satisfy your white-water or flat-water cravings, contact Sunshine. ☎ *209/848–4800, 800/829–7238* ⊕ *www.raftadventure.com.*

STOCKTON

29 miles north of Modesto.

California's first inland port—connected since 1933 to San Francisco via a 60-mile-long deepwater channel—is wedged between Interstate 5 and Highway 99, on the eastern end of the Sacramento River delta. Stockton, founded during the gold rush as a way station for miners traveling from San Francisco to the Mother Lode and now a city of 296,000, is where many of the valley's agricultural products begin their journey to other parts of the world. The city has attempted to spruce up its riverfront area downtown, including building a spiffy minor-league baseball park for the Stockton Ports, but there remains much room for improvement.

GETTING HERE AND AROUND

Highway 99 (on the city's eastern side) and Interstate 5 (on the western side) are connected through downtown by Highway 4, so you can zip from place to place efficiently via freeways. Amtrak stops here, as does Greyhound. San Joaquin RTD (⊕ *www.sanjoaquinrtd.com*) provides local bus service.

ESSENTIALS

Visitor Information Stockton Visitors Bureau ⊠ *525 N. Center St.* ☎ *209/938–1555, 877/778–6258* ⊕ *www.visitstockton.org.*

EXPLORING

Haggin Museum. In pretty Victory Park, the Haggin has one of the Central Valley's finest art collections. Highlights include landscapes by Albert Bierstadt and Thomas Moran, a still life by Paul Gauguin, a Native American gallery, and an Egyptian mummy. ⊠ *1201 N. Pershing Ave., at Rose St.* ☎ *209/940–6300* ⊕ *www.hagginmuseum.org* ☞ *$8* ⊙ *Wed.–Fri. 1:30–5, weekends noon–5; open until 9 on 1st and 3rd Thurs.*

Stockton Asparagus Festival. If you're here in late April, don't miss the asparagus festival. The food booths are the highlight of this waterfront event, as the more than 500 vendors collectively try to prove that almost any dish can be made (and made better) with asparagus. ☎ *209/644–3740* ⊕ *asparagusfest.com.*

13

WHERE TO EAT

$$$ **✕ Le Bistro.** This upscale restaurant serves modern interpretations of
EUROPEAN classic French cuisine—steak tartare, Grand Marnier soufflé—and
warms hearts with a romantic atmosphere. ⑤ *Average main: $28* ✉ *Marina Center Mall, 3121 W. Benjamin Holt Dr., off I–5, behind Lyon's*
☎ *209/951–0885* ⊕ *www.lebistrostockton.com* ☉ *No lunch.*

LODI

13 miles north of Stockton, 34 miles south of Sacramento.

Founded on agriculture, Lodi was once the watermelon capital of the
country. Today it's surrounded by fields of asparagus, pumpkins, beans,
safflowers, sunflowers, kiwis, melons, squashes, peaches, and cherries.
It's also emerged as a wine-grape hub, producing Zinfandel, Merlot,
Cabernet Sauvignon, Chardonnay, and Sauvignon Blanc grapes. For
years California wineries have built their reputations on the juice of
grapes grown around Lodi. Now the area that includes Lodi, Lockeford, and Woodbridge is a wine destination in itself, boasting about
40 wineries, many offering tours and tastings. Lodi still retains an old
rural charm, despite its population of 63,000. You can stroll downtown
or visit a wildlife refuge, all the while benefiting from a Sacramento
River delta breeze that keeps this microclimate cooler in summer than
anyplace else in the area.

GETTING HERE AND AROUND

Most of Lodi lies to the west of Highway 99, several miles east of
Interstate 5. Buses and Amtrak trains stop here frequently. Although
the GrapeLine bus (☎ *209/333–6806*) can get you around town and to
many of the wineries, you are better off with your own vehicle.

ESSENTIALS

Visitor Information Lodi Conference and Visitors Bureau ✉ *25 N. School St.*
☎ *209/365–1195, 800/798–1810* ⊕ *www.visitlodi.com.*

EXPLORING

Berghold Vineyards & Winery. The tasting room at Berghold recalls an
earlier wine era with its vintage Victorian interior, including restored,
salvaged mantlepieces, leaded glass, and a 26-foot-long bar. The wines—
among them Viognier, Cabernet Sauvignon, Merlot, Syrah, and Zinfandel—pay homage to French winemaking styles. ✉ *17343 N. Cherry
Rd., off E. Victor Rd./Hwy. 12* ☎ *209/333–9291* ⊕ *bergholdvineyards.
com* ⌨ *Tasting $7* ☉ *Thurs.–Sun. 11–5.*

Jessie's Grove Winery. Shaded by ancient oak trees, a ramshackle 1870s
farm building house the tasting room of this winery whose vineyards
and horse ranch have been in the same family since 1863. In addition
to producing old-vine Zinfandels, it presents blues concerts on various
Saturdays from June through October. Jessie's also has a downtown
tasting room at 27 East Locust Street. ✉ *1973 W. Turner Rd., west of
Davis Rd.* ☎ *209/368–0880* ⊕ *www.jessiesgrovewinery.com* ⌨ *Tasting
$5* ☉ *Daily noon–5.*

Lodi Wine & Visitor Center. A fine place to sample Lodi wines (there's a
tasting bar), the center has exhibits that chronicle Lodi's viticultural

Lodi Lake Park is a great place to escape the Central Valley heat in summer.

history. You can also buy wine here and pick up a map of area wineries to explore. ⊠ *2545 W. Turner Rd., at Woodhaven La.* ☎ *209/365–0621* ⊕ *www.lodiwine.com* ⊗ *Daily 10–5.*

Lucas Winery. David Lucas was one of the first local producers to start making serious wine, and today his Zinfandels and other vintages are among Lodi's most sought-after vintages. In addition to fruity Zins, Lucas makes a light Chardonnay with subtle oaky flavors. The 90-minute tour and tasting ($55) will get you up to speed on the Lodi wine appellation. ⊠ *18196 N. Davis Rd., at W. Turner Rd.* ☎ *209/368–2006* ⊕ *www.lucaswinery.com* ⌷ *Tastings $10–$50, tour (includes tasting) $55* ⊗ *Thurs.–Sun. noon–4:30.*

FAMILY **Micke Grove Regional Park.** This 258-acre, oak-shaded park, about 5 miles south of downtown, has a Japanese tea garden, picnic areas, children's play areas, softball fields, an agricultural museum, a golf course, and a water-play feature. Most rides and attractions at **Fun Town at Micke Grove**, a family-oriented amusement park, are geared toward children. Geckos and frogs, black-and-white ruffed lemurs, and hissing cockroaches found only on Madagascar inhabit "An Island Lost in Time," an exhibit at the **Micke Grove Zoo.** California sea lions, Chinese alligators and a walk-through Mediterranean aviary are among the other highlights. (Micke Grove Golf Links, an 18-hole course, is next to the park.) ⊠ *11793 N. Micke Grove Rd., off Hwy. 99 Armstrong Rd. exit* ☎ *209/953–8800* ⌷ *Parking $5, Fun Town ride prices vary, zoo $4* ⊗ *Park daily 8–sunset; Fun Town daily 11–5, weekends and holidays Apr.–Sept. 11–6; zoo May–Sept. 10–6, Oct.–Apr. 10–5.*

Fodor'sChoice **Phillips Farms Fruit Stand/Michael David Winery.** Fifth-generation farmers
★ turned winery owners Michael and David Phillips operate their tasting
room at a rustic roadside fruit stand where they also sell their family's
gorgeous produce. Michael David is well known for its Zinfandels,
including the widely distributed 7 Deadly Zins, but the Rhône-style
wines labeled Incognito are especially worth a try. Breakfast or lunch at
the café here is a treat. ⊠ *4580 W. Hwy. 12, at N. Ray Rd.* ☎ *209/368–
7384* ⊕ *www.lodivineyards.com* ⊠ *Tastings $5–$10* ⊙ *Daily 10–5,
reserve tasting Fri.–Sun. only.*

WHERE TO EAT

$ ✕ **Habañero Hots.** If your mouth can handle the heat promised by the res-
MEXICAN taurant's name, try the tamales. If you want to take it easy on your taste
buds, stick with the rest of the menu. ⑤ *Average main: $10* ⊠ *1024 E.
Victor Rd., at N. Cluff Ave.* ☎ *209/369-3791* ⊕ *www.habanerohots.com.*

$$$ ✕ **Rosewood Bar & Grill.** Operated by the folks at Wine & Roses Hotel
AMERICAN and Restaurant, this low-key downtown spot serves American fare with
a twist, such as meat loaf wrapped in bacon, and daily seafood specials.
The bar has a full-service menu, and live music on Friday and Saturday.
⑤ *Average main: $29* ⊠ *28 S. School St., at W. Oak St.* ☎ *209/369–0470*
⊕ *www.rosewoodbarandgrill.com* ⊙ *No lunch.*

WHERE TO STAY
For expanded hotel reviews, visit Fodors.com.

$$ 🛏 **The Inn at Locke House.** Built in 1865, this B&B was a pioneer doctor's
B&B/INN family home and is on the National Register of Historic Places. **Pros:**
friendly; quiet; lovely. **Cons:** remote; can be hard to find. ⑤ *Rooms
from: $145* ⊠ *19960 Elliott Rd., Lockeford* ☎ *209/727-5715* ⊕ *www.
theinnatlockehouse.com* ⇗ *4 rooms, 1 suite* ⎸○⎹ *Breakfast.*

$$$ 🛏 **Wine & Roses Hotel and Restaurant.** Set on 7 acres amid a tapestry of
HOTEL informal gardens, this hotel has cultivated a sense of refinement typi-
cally associated with Napa or Carmel. **Pros:** luxurious; relaxing; quiet.
Cons: expensive; isolated; some guests mention that walls are thin.
⑤ *Rooms from: $229* ⊠ *2505 W. Turner Rd.* ☎ *209/334–6988* ⊕ *www.
winerose.com* ⇗ *47 rooms, 4 suites* ⎸○⎹ *Breakfast.*

SPORTS AND THE OUTDOORS
Lodi Lake Park. Even locals need respite from the heat of Central Valley
summers, and Lodi Lake Park is where they find it. The banks, shaded
by grand old elms and oaks, are much cooler than other spots in town.
Swimming, bird-watching, and picnicking are possibilities, as is renting
a kayak, canoe, or pedal boat. ⊠ *1101 W. Turner Rd., at Mills Ave.*
☎ *209/333–6742* ⊠ *$5.*

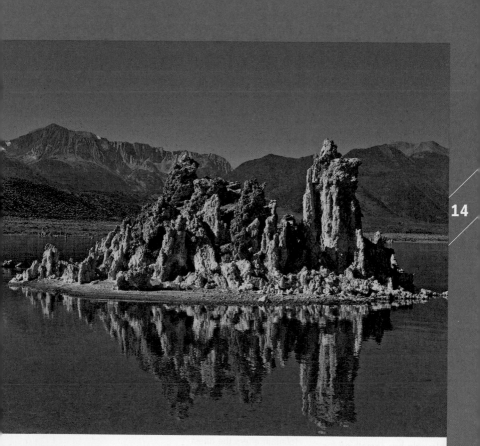

THE SOUTHERN SIERRA

Around Sequoia, Kings Canyon,
and Yosemite National Parks

WELCOME TO THE SOUTHERN SIERRA

TOP REASONS TO GO

★ **Strap 'em on:** Whether you walk the paved loops in the national parks (⇨ Chapter 15, Yosemite National Park, and Chapter 16, Sequoia and Kings Canyon National Parks) or head off the beaten path into the backcountry, a hike through groves and meadows or alongside streams and waterfalls will allow you to see, smell, and feel nature up close.

★ **Down you go:** Famous for its incredible snow-pack—some of the deepest in the North American continent—the Sierra Nevada has something for every winter-sports fan.

★ **Live it up:** Mammoth Lakes is eastern California's most exciting resort area.

★ **Pamper yourself:** Tucked in the hills south of Oakhurst, the elegant Château du Sureau will make you feel like you've stepped into a fairy tale.

★ **Go with the flow:** Three Rivers, the gateway to Sequoia National Park, is the launching pad for white-water trips down the Kaweah River.

1 South of Yosemite National Park. Several gateway towns to the south and west of Yosemite National Park (⇨ Chapter 15), most within an hour's drive of Yosemite Valley, have food, lodging, and other services.

2 Mammoth Lakes. A jewel in the vast Eastern Sierra Nevada, the Mammoth Lakes area lies just east of the Sierra crest, on the backside of Yosemite and the Ansel Adams Wilderness. It's a place of rugged beauty, where giant sawtooth mountains drop into the vast deserts of the Great Basin. In winter, 11,053-foot-high Mammoth Mountain offers the finest skiing and snowboarding in California—sometimes as late as June or even July. Once the snows melt, Mammoth transforms itself into a warm-weather playground, with fishing, mountain biking, golfing, hiking, and horseback riding. Nine deep-blue lakes are spread through the Mammoth Lakes Basin, and another 100 lakes dot the surrounding countryside.

3 East of Yosemite National Park. The area to the east of Yosemite National Park (⇨ Chapter 15) includes some ruggedly handsome, albeit desolate, terrain, most notably around Mono Lake. The area is best visited by car, as distances are great and public transportation is negligible. U.S. 395 is the main north–south road on the eastern side of the Sierra Nevada, at the western edge of the Great Basin. It's one of California's most beautiful highways; plan to snap pictures at roadside pullouts.

GETTING ORIENTED

The transition between the Central Valley and the rugged Southern Sierra may be the most dramatic in California sightseeing; as you head into the mountains, your temptation to stop the car and gawk will increase with every foot gained in elevation. Although you should spend most of your time here in the national parks (⇨ *Chapter 15, Yosemite National Park, and Chapter 16, Sequoia and Kings Canyon National Parks*), be sure to check out some of the mountain towns on the parks' fringes—in addition to being great places to stock up on supplies, they have worthy attractions, restaurants, and lodging options.

4 South of Sequoia and Kings Canyon: Three Rivers. Scenic Three Rivers is the main gateway for Sequoia and Kings Canyon National Parks (⇨ *Chapter 16*).

Updated by
Reed Parsell

Vast granite peaks and giant sequoias are among the Southern Sierra's mind-boggling natural wonders, many of which are protected in three national parks. Mother Nature goes so far over the top in this region that it might wow you even more than California's more famous urban attractions.

Outside the national parks (⇨ *Chapter 15, Yosemite National Park, and Chapter 16, Sequoia and Kings Canyon National Parks)*, pristine lakes, superb skiing, rolling hills, and small towns complete the picture of the Southern Sierra. Heading up U.S. 395 on the Sierra's eastern side, you'll be rewarded with outstanding vistas of dramatic mountain peaks, including Mt. Whitney, the highest point in the contiguous United States, and Mono Lake, a vast expanse of deep blue—one of the most-photographed natural attractions in California—that is struggling to survive.

PLANNING

GETTING HERE AND AROUND

AIR TRAVEL

Fresno Yosemite International Airport (FYI) is the nearest airport to the national parks; Reno–Tahoe is the closest major airport to Mammoth Lakes.

Airports Fresno Yosemite International Airport ⊠ *5175 E. Clinton Ave., Fresno* ☎ *559/621–4500, 800/244–2359* ⊕ *www.flyfresno.org.*
Reno–Tahoe International Airport ⊠ *U.S. 395, Exit 65B, Reno, Nevada* ☎ *775/328–6400* ⊕ *www.renoairport.com.*

CAR TRAVEL

From San Francisco, heading east on Interstate 80 to 580 to 205E is the most efficient connecting route to Interstate 5 and Highway 99, which straddle the western side of the Sierra Nevada. To best reach the eastern side from the Bay Area, take Interstate 80 to U.S. 395, then head south.

To get to Mammoth Lakes in summer and early fall (or whenever snows aren't blocking Tioga Road), you can travel via Highway 120 (to U.S. 395 south) through the Yosemite high country; the quickest route in winter is Interstate 80 to U.S. 50 to Highway 207 (also known as the Kingsbury Grade, just east of South Lake Tahoe) to U.S. 395 south; either route takes about seven hours. ■TIP➔ Watch your gas gauge. Gas stations are few and far between in the Sierra, so fill your tank when you can. If you're traveling between October and May, heavy snow may cover mountain roads. Carry tire chains, know how to put them on (on Interstate 80 and U.S. 50 you can pay a chain installer $35 to do it for you, but on other routes you'll have to do it yourself), and always check road conditions before you leave.

Travel Reports Caltrans Current Highway Conditions ☎ 800/427-7623 ⊕ www.dot.ca.gov.

14

BUS TRAVEL

Greyhound serves Fresno, Madera, and other Central Valley towns west of the Sierra. Madera County Connection buses travel between Madera and Oakhurst (and Bass Lake). Eastern Sierra Transit Authority buses serve Mammoth Lakes, Bishop *(➪ Chapter 16)*, and other eastern Sierra towns.

Bus Contacts Eastern Sierra Transit Authority ☎ 760/872-1901, 800/922-1930 ⊕ www.estransit.com. **Greyhound** ✉ Fresno ☎ 800/231-2222 ⊕ www.greyhound.com. **Madera County Connection** ✉ Madera ☎ 559/661-7433 ⊕ www.maderactc.com/pubtrans.html.

RESTAURANTS

Most small towns in the Sierra Nevada have at least one restaurant; with few exceptions, dress is casual. You'll most likely be spending a lot of time in the car while you're exploring the area, so pick up snacks and drinks to keep with you. With picnic supplies on hand, you'll be able to enjoy an impromptu meal under giant trees or in one of the eastern Sierra towns' municipal parks. *Prices in the reviews are the average cost of a main course at dinner or, if dinner is not served, at lunch.*

HOTELS

For visits to the Sierra Nevada's western side, book your hotel in advance—especially in summer—or you may wind up in the Central Valley, far from the action. Booking in advance is less crucial for travel to the Eastern Sierra. In either area, keep in mind that rural and rustic does not always mean inexpensive. *Prices in the reviews are the lowest cost of a standard double room in high season. For expanded hotel reviews, visit Fodors.com.*

Hotel Contacts Mammoth Lakes Visitors Bureau Lodging Referral ✉ Mammoth Lakes ☎ 760/934-2712, 888/466-2666 ⊕ www.visitmammoth.com. **Mammoth Reservations** ✉ Mammoth Lakes ☎ 800/223-3032 ⊕ www.mammothreservations.com.

SOUTH OF YOSEMITE NATIONAL PARK

People heading to Yosemite National Park, especially those interested in seeing the giant redwoods on the park's south side, pass through Oakhurst and Fish Camp on Highway 41.

OAKHURST

40 miles north of Fresno on Hwy. 41.

Motels, restaurants, gas stations, and small businesses line Highway 41 in Oakhurst, the last sizeable community before Yosemite *(⇨ Chapter 15)*—the south entrance is 23 miles north of town—and a good spot to find provisions. Continue north on Highway 41 to get to Yosemite. Three miles north of town on Highway 41, then 6 miles east, lies honky-tonk Bass Lake, a popular spot in summer with motorboaters, Jet Skiers, and families looking to cool off in the reservoir.

GETTING HERE AND AROUND

At the junction of highways 41 and 49, Oakhurst is a solid hour's drive north of Fresno. It's the southern gateway to Yosemite, so many people fly to Fresno and rent a car to get here and beyond. In town, there's no public transportation system of any consequence.

ESSENTIALS

Visitor Information Yosemite Sierra Visitors Bureau ☎ *559/683–4636* ⊕ *www.yosemitethisyear.com.*

WHERE TO EAT

$$$$
EUROPEAN
Fodor'sChoice
★

✕ **Erna's Elderberry House.** Erna Kubin-Clanin, the grande dame of Château du Sureau, created this culinary oasis, stunning for its understated elegance, gorgeous setting, and impeccable service. Red walls and wood beams accent the dining room's high ceilings, and arched windows reflect the glow of candles. The seasonal six-course prix-fixe dinner can be paired with superb wines, with every course delivered in perfect synchronicity by the elite waitstaff. A short bistro menu is served in the former wine cellar. $ *Average main: $95* ✉ *Château du Sureau, 48688 Victoria La., off Hwy. 41* ☎ *559/683–6800* ⊕ *www.elderberryhouse. com* ⚇ *Reservations essential* ☉ *No lunch Mon.–Sat.*

WHERE TO STAY

For expanded hotel reviews, visit Fodors.com.

$$
HOTEL
FAMILY

⌷ **Best Western Yosemite Gateway Inn.** Oakhurst's best motel has carefully tended landscaping and rooms with attractive colonial–style furniture and slightly kitschy hand-painted wall murals of Yosemite. **Pros:** reasonably close to Yosemite; clean; two pools, one heated; comfortable. **Cons:** chain property; getting to Yosemite Valley from here is a haul. $ *Rooms from: $144* ✉ *40530 Hwy. 41, Oakhurst* ☎ *800/545–5462, 559/683–2378* ⊕ *www.yosemitegatewayinn.com* ⌁ *121 rooms, 16 suites.*

$$$$
RESORT
Fodor'sChoice
★

⌷ **Château du Sureau.** You'll feel pampered from the moment you drive through the wrought-iron gates of this fairy-tale castle. **Pros:** luxurious; great views. **Cons:** expensive; if you're not really into spas, it might not be worth your while. $ *Rooms from: $385* ✉ *48688 Victoria La.,*

Oakhurst ☎ *559/683–6860* ⊕ *www.chateausureau.com* ⇝ *10 rooms, 1 villa* ⦿*Breakfast.*

$$ **⊡ Homestead Cottages.** Set on 160 acres of rolling hills that once held a
B&B/INN Miwok village, these cottages (the largest sleeps six) have gas fireplaces, fully equipped kitchens, and queen-size beds. **Pros:** remote location; quiet setting; friendly owners. **Cons:** might be a little *too* quiet for some. ⑤ *Rooms from: $155* ⊠ *41110 Rd. 600, 2½ miles off Hwy. 49, Ahwahnee* ☎ *559/683–0495, 800/483–0495* ⊕ *www.homesteadcottages.com* ⇝ *5 cottages, 1 loft.*

FISH CAMP

57 miles north of Fresno and 4 miles south of Yosemite National Park's south entrance.

14

As you climb in elevation along Highway 41 northbound, you see nothing but trees until you get to the small settlement of Fish Camp, where there's a post office and general store, but no gasoline (for gas, head 10 miles north to Wawona, in the park, or 17 miles south to Oakhurst).

GETTING HERE AND AROUND

Arrive here by car via Highway 41, from Yosemite National Park a few miles to the north, or from Oakhurst (and, farther down the road, Fresno) to the south. Unless you're on foot or a bicycle, a car is your only option.

EXPLORING

FAMILY **Yosemite Mountain Sugar Pine Railroad.** Travel back to a time when powerful steam locomotives hauled massive log trains through the Sierra. This 4-mile, narrow-gauge railroad excursion takes you near Yosemite's south gate; there's also a moonlight special, with dinner and entertainment ($48). Take Highway 41 south from Yosemite about 8 miles to the departure point. ⊠ *56001 Hwy. 41, Fish Camp* ☎ *559/683–7273* ⊕ *www.ymsprr.com* ⊡ *$19* ⊙ *Mar.–Oct., daily.*

WHERE TO STAY

For expanded hotel reviews, visit Fodors.com.

$$ **⊡ Narrow Gauge Inn.** The well-tended rooms at this family-owned
B&B/INN property have balconies with great views of the surrounding woods and mountains. **Pros:** close to Yosemite's south entrance; nicely appointed rooms; wonderful balconies. **Cons:** rooms can be a bit dark; dining options are limited, especially for vegetarians. ⑤ *Rooms from: $145* ⊠ *48571 Hwy. 41, Fish Camp* ☎ *559/683–7720, 888/644–9050* ⊕ *www.narrowgaugeinn.com* ⇝ *26 rooms, 1 suite* ⦿*Breakfast.*

$$$$ **⊡ Tenaya Lodge.** One of the region's largest hotels, Tenaya Lodge is
HOTEL ideal for people who enjoy wilderness treks by day but prefer creature comforts at night. **Pros:** rustic setting with modern comforts; good off-season deals; very close to Yosemite National Park. **Cons:** so big it can seem impersonal; pricey during summer; few dining options. ⑤ *Rooms from: $315* ⊠ *1122 Hwy. 41* ☎ *559/683–6555, 888/514–2167* ⊕ *www.tenayalodge.com* ⇝ *244 rooms, 6 suites.*

EL PORTAL

14 miles west of Yosemite Valley on Hwy. 140.

The market in town is a good place to pick up provisions before you get to Yosemite (⇨ *Chapter 15).* You'll find a post office and a gas station, but not much else.

GETTING HERE AND AROUND

The drive here on Highway 140 from Mariposa and, farther west, Merced, is the prettiest and gentlest (in terms of steep uphill and downhill portions) route to Yosemite National Park. Much of the road follows the Merced River in a rugged canyon. The Yosemite Area Regional Transportation System (YARTS ⊕ *www.yarts.com*) is a cheap and dependable way to go between Merced and Yosemite Valley; all buses stop in El Portal, where many park employees reside.

WHERE TO STAY

For expanded hotel reviews, visit Fodors.com.

$$$ **Evergreen Lodge at Yosemite.** Near Hetch Hetchy on Yosemite National
RESORT   Park's northwest side, this sprawling property set in the woods is perfect
FAMILY   for families: The 90-cabin complex includes a playground, an amphitheater, a movie room, a restaurant, a gift shop, and an activities desk. **Pros:** near the underrated Hetch Hetchy; family atmosphere; clean cabins. **Cons:** not cheap; about an hour's drive from Yosemite Valley. ⑤ *Rooms from: $220* ⊠ *33160 Evergreen Road* ☎ *209/379–2606, 888/935–6343* ⊕ *www.evergreenlodge.com* ⌁ *90 cabins.*

$$$ **Yosemite View Lodge.** Just 2 miles outside the park's Arch Rock
B&B/INN   entrance, this modern property is the most convenient place to spend the night if you are unable to secure lodgings in the Valley. **Pros:** great location; good views; lots of on-site amenities. **Cons:** somewhat pricey; due to demand, it can be a challenge to get the dates you want. ⑤ *Rooms from: $229* ⊠ *11136 Hwy. 140, El Portal* ☎ *209/379–2681, 888/742–4371* ⊕ *www.yosemite-motels.com* ⌁ *279 rooms.*

MAMMOTH LAKES

30 miles south of eastern edge of Yosemite National Park on U.S. 395.

International real-estate developers joined forces with Mammoth Mountain Ski Area to transform the once sleepy town of Mammoth Lakes (elevation 7,800 feet) into an upscale ski destination. The Village at Mammoth is the epicenter of the recent development. Much of the architecture here is of the faux-alpine variety, but you'll find relatively sophisticated dining and lodging options. Winter is high season; in summer, room rates drop.

GETTING HERE AND AROUND

The best way to get to Mammoth Lakes is by car. The town is a couple of miles west of U.S. 395. The Yosemite Area Regional Transportation System (YARTS ⊕ *www.yarts.com*) provides once-a-day service between here and Yosemite Valley. The shuttle buses of Eastern Sierra Transit Authority (☎ *800/922–1930* ⊕ *www.estransit.com*) serve Mammoth Lakes, Bishop, and nearby tourist sites.

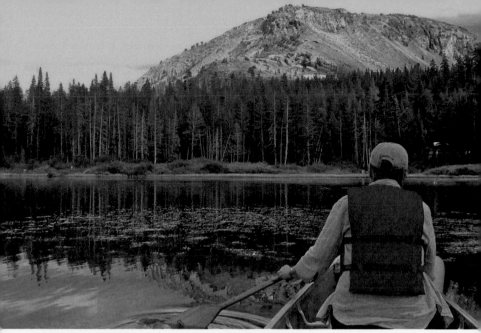
Twin Lakes, in the Mammoth Lakes region, is a great place to unwind.

Highway 203 heads west from U.S. 395, becoming Main Street as it passes through the town of Mammoth Lakes, and later Minaret Road (which makes a right turn) as it continues west to the Mammoth Mountain ski area and Devils Postpile National Monument.

ESSENTIALS

Visitor Information Mammoth Lakes Visitors Bureau ⊠ *Welcome Center, 2510 Main St., near Sawmill Cutoff Rd.* ☎ *760/934–2712* ⊕ *www.visitmammoth.com.*

EXPLORING

Mammoth Lakes Basin. The lakes, reached by Lake Mary Road off Highway 203 southwest of town, are popular for fishing and boating in summer. First comes Twin Lakes, at the far end of which is Twin Falls, where water cascades 300 feet over a shelf of volcanic rock. Also popular are Lake Mary, the largest lake in the basin; Lake Mamie; and Lake George. Horseshoe Lake is the only lake in which you can swim.

Minaret Vista. The glacier-carved sawtooth spires of the Minarets, the remains of an ancient lava flow, are best viewed from the Minaret Vista, off Highway 203 west of Mammoth Lakes.

Fodor's Choice **Panorama Gondola.** Even if you don't ski, ride the gondola to see Mammoth Mountain, the aptly named dormant volcano that gives Mammoth Lakes its name. Gondolas serve skiers in winter and mountain bikers and sightseers in summer. The high-speed, eight-passenger gondolas whisk you from the chalet to the summit, where you can read about the area's volcanic history and take in top-of-the-world views.

★

FAMILY

Standing high above the tree line, you can look west 150 miles across the state to the Coastal Range; to the east are the highest peaks of Nevada and the Great Basin beyond. You won't find a better view of the Sierra High Country without climbing. Remember, though, that the air is thin at the 11,053-foot summit; carry water, and don't overexert yourself. The boarding area is at the Main Lodge. ⊠ *Off Hwy. 203* ☎ *760/934–2571 information, 3850 gondola station* 🖃 *$24* ⊙ *July 4– Oct., daily 9–4:30; Nov.–July 3, daily 8:30–4.*

Village at Mammoth. This huge complex of shops, restaurants, and luxury accommodations is the town's tourist center. Parking can be tricky, even seemingly impossible. There's a parking lot across the street on Minaret Road; cross your fingers and pay attention to time limits.

WHERE TO EAT

$$$
STEAKHOUSE

✕ **The Mogul.** This longtime favorite is the place to go when you want a straightforward steak and salad bar. The only catch is that the waiters cook your steak—and the result depends on the waiter's experience. But generally you can't go wrong. And kids love it. The knotty-pine walls lend a woodsy touch and suggest Mammoth Mountain before all the development. 🖇 *Average main: $24* ⊠ *1528 Mammoth Tavern Rd., off Old Mammoth Rd.* ☎ *760/934–3039* ⊕ *www.themogul.com* ⊙ *No lunch.*

$$$
AMERICAN

✕ **Petra's Bistro & Wine Bar.** The ambience at Petra's—quiet, dark, and warm—complements the carefully prepared meat main dishes and seasonal sides, and the more than two dozen California wines from behind the bar. The service is top-notch. Downstairs, the Clocktower Cellar bar provides a late-night, rowdy alternative—or chaser. 🖇 *Average main: $28* ⊠ *6080 Minaret Rd.* ☎ *760/934–3500* ⊕ *www.petrasbistro.com* ⊛ *Reservations essential* ⊙ *Closed Mon.; no lunch.*

$$$$
AMERICAN

✕ **Restaurant at Convict Lake.** Tucked in a tiny valley ringed by mile-high peaks, Convict Lake is one of the most spectacular spots in the eastern Sierra. Thank heaven the food lives up to the view. The chef's specialties include beef Wellington, rack of lamb, and pan-seared local trout, all beautifully prepared. The woodsy room has a vaulted knotty-pine ceiling and a copper-chimney fireplace that roars on cold nights. Natural light abounds in the daytime, but if it's summer, opt for a table outdoors under the white-barked aspens. Service is exceptional, as is the wine list, with reasonably priced European and California varietals. 🖇 *Average main: $32* ⊠ *Convict Lake Rd. off U.S. 395, 4 miles south of Mammoth Lakes* ☎ *760/934–3803* ⊕ *www.convictlake.com* ⊛ *Reservations essential* ⊙ *No lunch early Sept.–July 4.*

$$
WINE BAR

✕ **Side Door Café.** Half wine bar, half café, this is a laid-back spot for an easy lunch or a long, lingering afternoon. The café serves grilled panini sandwiches, sweet and savory crepes, and espresso. At the wine bar, order cheese plates and charcuterie platters, designed to pair with the 25 wines (fewer in summertime) available by the glass. If you're lucky, a winemaker will show up and hold court at the bar. 🖇 *Average main: $18* ⊠ *Village at Mammoth, 1111 Forest Trail, Unit 229* ☎ *760/934–5200* ⊕ *www.sidedoormammoth.com.*

$$ ✗ **The Stove.** A longtime family favorite for down-to-earth, folksy cooking,
AMERICAN   this is the kind of place you take the family to fill up before a long car ride.
The omelets, pancakes, huevos rancheros, and meat loaf won't win any
awards, but they're tasty. The room is cozy, with gingham curtains and
dark-wood booths, and service is friendly. Breakfast and lunch are the best
bets here. $ *Average main: $16* ✉ *644 Old Mammoth Rd.* ☎ *760/934–
2821* ⚲ *Reservations not accepted* ⊘ *No dinner Mon. and Tues.*

WHERE TO STAY

For expanded hotel reviews, visit Fodors.com.

$ ⛱ **Alpenhof Lodge.** The owners of Alpenhof Lodge lucked out when
B&B/INN   developers built the fancy-schmancy Village at Mammoth across the
street from their mom-and-pop motel, which remains a simple lodging
offering basic comforts and a few niceties like attractive pine furniture.
Pros: convenient for skiers; good price. **Cons:** could use an update;
rooms above the pub can be noisy. $ *Rooms from: $124* ✉ *6080 Mina-
ret Rd.* ☎ *760/934–6330, 800/828–0371* ⊕ *www.alpenhof-lodge.com*
☞ *54 rooms, 3 cabins.*

$$ ⛱ **Cinnamon Bear Inn Bed and Breakfast.** In a business district off Main
B&B/INN   Street, this bed-and-breakfast feels more like a small motel, with nicely
decorated rooms, many with four-poster beds. **Pros:** comparatively
quiet; affordable; friendly. **Cons:** a bit tricky to find; limited parking.
$ *Rooms from: $149* ✉ *113 Center St.* ☎ *760/934–2873, 800/845–
2873* ⊕ *www.cinnamonbearinn.com* ☞ *22 rooms* ⦿ *Breakfast.*

$$$ ⛱ **Double Eagle Resort and Spa.** You won't find a better spa retreat in the
RESORT   eastern Sierra than the Double Eagle, which is in a spectacularly beautiful
spot under towering peaks and along a creek, near June Lake, 20 min-
utes north of Mammoth Lakes. **Pros:** pretty setting; generous breakfast;
spectacular indoor pool. **Cons:** expensive, remote. $ *Rooms from: $229*
✉ *5587 Hwy. 158* ☎ *760/648–7004, 877/648–7004* ⊕ *www.doubleeagle.
com* ☞ *16 2-bedroom cabins, 16 cabin suites, 1 3-bedroom cabin.*

$$ ⛱ **Juniper Springs Lodge.** Tops for slope-side comfort, these condomin-
RESORT   ium-style units have full kitchens and ski-in ski-out access to the moun-
tain. **Pros:** bargain during summer; direct access to the slopes; good
views. **Cons:** no nightlife within walking distance; no a/c. $ *Rooms
from: $159* ✉ *4000 Meridian Blvd.* ☎ *760/924–1102, 800/626–6684*
⊕ *www.mammothmountain.com* ☞ *10 studios, 99 1-bedrooms, 92
2-bedrooms, 3 3-bedrooms.*

$$ ⛱ **Mammoth Mountain Inn.** If you want to be within walking distance
RESORT   of the Mammoth Mountain Main Lodge, this is the place. **Pros:** great
location; big rooms; a traditional place to stay. **Cons:** can be crowded
in ski season; 9,000-feet elevation can affect sleep patterns. $ *Rooms
from: $134* ✉ *1 Minaret Rd.* ☎ *760/934–2581, 800/626–6684* ⊕ *www.
mammothmountain.com* ☞ *124 rooms, 91 condos.*

$$$ ⛱ **Tamarack Lodge Resort & Lakefront Restaurant.** Tucked away on the
RESORT   edge of the John Muir Wilderness Area, where cross-country ski trails
Fodor's Choice   loop through the woods, this original 1924 lodge looks like some-
★   thing out of a snow globe, and the lake it borders is serenely beautiful.
Pros: rustic but not run-down; plenty of eco-sensitivity; tons of nearby

14

outdoor activities. **Cons:** pricey; some main lodge rooms have shared bathrooms. ⑤ *Rooms from: $218 ⊠ Lake Mary Rd., off Hwy. 203* ☎ *760/934–2442, 800/626–6684* ⊕ *www.tamaracklodge.com* ⤚ *11 rooms, 35 cabins.*

$$$
RESORT

⛏ **The Village Lodge.** At the epicenter of Mammoth's dining and night-life scene, this cluster of four-story timber-and-stone condo buildings nods to Alpine style, with exposed timbers and peaked roofs. **Pros:** central location; clean; big rooms; lots of good restaurants nearby. **Cons:** comes with big price tag; can be noisy outside. ⑤ *Rooms from: $239 ⊠ 1111 Forest Trail* ☎ *760/934–1982, 800/626–6684* ⊕ *www.mammothmountain.com* ⤚ *277 units.*

SPORTS AND THE OUTDOORS

BICYCLING

Mammoth Mountain Bike Park. The park opens when the snow melts, usually by July, and has 70-plus miles of single-track trails—from mellow to super-challenging. Chairlifts and shuttles provide trail access, and rentals are available. Various shops around town also rent bikes and provide trail maps, if you don't want to ascend the mountain. ⊠ *Mammoth Mountain Ski Area* ☎ *760/934–0706* ⊕ *www.mammothmountain.com* ⛬ *$45 day pass.*

FISHING

The fishing season runs from the last Saturday in April until the end of October. Crowley Lake is the top trout-fishing spot in the area; Convict Lake, June Lake, and the lakes of the Mammoth Basin are other prime spots. One of the best trout rivers is the San Joaquin, near Devils Postpile. Hot Creek, a designated Wild Trout Stream, is renowned for fly-fishing (catch-and-release only).

Kittredge Sports. This outfit rents rods and reels and also conducts guided trips. ⊠ *3218 Main St., at Forest Trail* ☎ *760/934–7566* ⊕ *www.kittredgesports.com.*

Sierra Drifters Guide Service. To maximize your time on the water, get tips from local anglers, or better yet, book a guided fishing trip with this service. ☎ *760/935–4250* ⊕ *www.sierradrifters.com.*

HIKING

Hiking in Mammoth is stellar, especially along the trails that wind through the pristine alpine scenery around the Lakes Basin. Carry lots of water; and remember, the air is thin at 8,000 feet.

U.S. Forest Service Ranger Station and Welcome Center. Stop at the ranger station, just east of the town of Mammoth Lakes, for an area trail map and permits for backpacking in wilderness areas. ⊠ *2510 Main St., Hwy. 203* ☎ *760/924–5500* ⊕ *www.fs.usda.gov/main/inyo.*

HORSEBACK RIDING

Stables around Mammoth are typically open from June through September.

Mammoth Lakes Pack Outfit. This company runs day and overnight horseback trips, or will shuttle you to the high country. ⊠ *Lake Mary Rd., between Twin Lakes and Lake Mary* ☎ *888/475–8747* ⊕ *www.mammothpack.com.*

McGee Creek Pack Station. These folks customize pack trips or will shuttle you to camp alone. ☎ *760/935–4324 summer, 760/878–2207, 800/854–7407* ⊕ *www.mcgeecreekpackstation.com.*

SKIING

In winter, check the On the Snow website or call the Snow Report for information about Mammoth weather conditions.

June Mountain Ski Area. In their rush to Mammoth Mountain, most people overlook June Mountain, a compact, low-key resort 20 miles north of Mammoth. Snowboarders especially dig it. Two freestyle terrain areas are for both skiers and boarders, including a huge 16-foot-wall super pipe. Best of all, there's rarely a line for the lifts—if you want to avoid the crowds but must ski on a weekend, this is the place. And in a storm, June is better protected from wind and blowing snow than Mammoth Mountain. (If it starts to storm, you can use your Mammoth ticket at June.) Expect all the usual services, including a rental-and-repair shop, ski school, and sports shop, but the food quality is better at Mammoth. Lift tickets cost $72, with discounts for multiple days. ✉ *3819 Hwy. 158, off June Lake Loop, June Lake* ☎ *760/648–7733, 888/586–3686* ⊕ *www.junemountain.com* ☞ *35 trails on 500 acres, rated 35% beginner, 45% intermediate, 20% advanced. Longest run 2½ miles, base 7,510 feet, summit 10,174 feet. Lifts: 7.*

Fodor's Choice
★

Mammoth Mountain Ski Area. One of the West's largest and best ski areas, Mammoth has more than 3,500 acres of skiable terrain and a 3,100-foot vertical drop. The views from the 11,053-foot summit are some of the most stunning in the Sierra. Below, you'll find a 6½-mile-wide swath of groomed boulevards and canyons, as well as pockets of tree-skiing and a dozen vast bowls. Snowboarders are everywhere on the slopes; there are three outstanding freestyle terrain parks of varying technical difficulty, with jumps, rails, tabletops, and giant super pipes (this is the location of several international snowboarding and, in summer months, mountain-bike competitions). Mammoth's season begins in November and often lingers into May. Lift tickets start at $79. Lessons and equipment are available, and there's a children's ski and snowboard school. Mammoth runs free shuttle-bus routes around town and to the ski area, and the Village Gondola runs from the Village complex to Canyon Lodge. However, only overnight guests are allowed to park at the Village for more than a few hours. ⚠ The main lodge is dark and dated, unsuited in most every way for the crush of ski season. Within a decade, it's likely to be replaced. ✉ *Minaret Rd., west of Mammoth Lakes* ☎ *760/934–2571, 800/626–6684, 760/934–0687 shuttle* ⊕ *www.mammothmountain.com* ☞ *150 trails on 3,500 acres, rated 30% beginner, 40% intermediate, 30% advanced. Longest run 3 miles, base 7,953 feet, summit 11,053 feet. Lifts: 27, including 9 high-speed and 2 gondolas.*

Tamarack Cross Country Ski Center. Trails at the center, adjacent to Tamarack Lodge, meander around several lakes. Rentals are available. The all-day inclusive rate is $55. ✉ *Lake Mary Rd., off Hwy. 203* ☎ *760/934–5293, 760/934–2442* ⊕ *www.tamaracklodge.com.*

14

SKI RENTALS AND RESOURCES

Footloose. When the U.S. Ski Team visits Mammoth and needs boot adjustments, everyone heads to Footloose, the best place in town—and possibly all California—for ski-boot rentals and sales, as well as custom insoles. ✉ *3043 Main St., at Mammoth Rd.* ☎ *760/934–2400* ⊕ *www. footloosesports.com.*

Kittredge Sports. Advanced skiers should consider this outfit, which has been around since the 1960s. ✉ *3218 Main St.* ☎ *760/934–7566* ⊕ *www.kittredgesports.com.*

Mammoth Sporting Goods. This company rents good skis for intermediates and sells equipment, clothing, and accessories. ✉ *1 Sierra Center Mall, Old Mammoth Rd.* ☎ *760/934–3239* ⊕ *www.mammothoutdoorsports.com.*

OnTheSnow.com ⊕ *www.onthesnow.com/california/mammoth-mountain-ski-area/skireport.html.*

Snow Report. For information on winter conditions around Mammoth, call the Snow Report. ☎ *760/934–7669, 888/766–9778.*

EAST OF YOSEMITE NATIONAL PARK

Most people enter Yosemite National Park from the west, having driven out from the Bay Area or Los Angeles. The eastern entrance on Tioga Pass Road (Highway 120), however, provides stunning, sweeping views of the High Sierra. Gray rocks shine in the bright sun, with scattered, small vegetation sprinkled about the mountainside. To drive from Lee Vining to Tuolumne Meadows is an unforgettable experience, but keep in mind the road tends to be closed for at least seven months of the year.

LEE VINING

20 miles east of Tuolumne Meadows via Hwy. 120 to U.S. 395; 30 miles north of Mammoth Lakes on U.S. 395.

Tiny Lee Vining is known primarily as the eastern gateway to Yosemite National Park (summer only; ⇨ *Chapter 15*) and the location of vast and desolate Mono Lake. Pick up supplies at the general store year-round, or stop here for lunch or dinner before or after a drive through the high country. In winter the town is all but deserted, except for the ice climbers who come to scale frozen waterfalls. You can meet these hearty souls at Nicely's restaurant, where climbers congregate for breakfast around 8 on winter mornings. To try your hand at ice climbing, contact Doug Nidever (☎ *760/937–6922* ⊕ *www.themountainguide.com*), aka the Mountain Guide.

GETTING HERE AND AROUND

Lee Vining is on U.S. 395, just north of the road's intersection with Highway 120 and on the south side of Mono Lake. Yosemite Area Regional Transportation System (YARTS ⊕ *www.yarts.com*) can get you here from Yosemite Valley, but you'll need a car to explore the area.

ESSENTIALS

Visitor Information Lee Vining Chamber of Commerce ☎ *760/647–6629* ⊕ *www.leevining.com.* **Mono Lake** ☎ *760/647–6595* ⊕ *www.monolake.org.*

EXPLORING

Fodor's Choice
★

Mono Lake. Since the 1940s Los Angeles has diverted water from this lake, exposing striking towers of tufa, or calcium carbonate. Court victories by environmentalists have meant fewer diversions, and the lake is rising again. Although to see the lake from U.S. 395 is stunning, make time to walk about South Tufa, whose parking lot is 5 miles east of U.S. 395 off Highway 120. There during the summer you can join the naturalist-guided **South Tufa Walk,** which lasts about 1½ hours. The sensational **Scenic Area Visitor Center,** on U.S. 395, is open daily from June through September (Sunday to Thursday 8–5, Friday and Saturday 8–7); it's closed December through March and open weekends the rest of the year. The center's hilltop and sweeping views of Mono Lake, along with its interactive exhibits inside, make this one of California's best visitor centers. Rangers and naturalists lead walking tours of the tufa daily in summer and on weekends (sometimes on cross-country skis) in winter. In town at U.S. 395 and 3rd Street, the **Mono Lake Committee Information Center & Bookstore** has more information about this beautiful area. ⊠ *Hwy. 120, east of Lee Vining, Lee Vining* ☎ *760/647–3044.*

14

**EN
ROUTE**

June Lake Loop. Heading south from Lee Vining, U.S. 395 intersects the June Lake Loop. This gorgeous 17-mile drive follows an old glacial canyon past Grant, June, Gull, and other lakes before reconnecting with U.S. 395 on its way to Mammoth Lakes. The loop is especially colorful in fall. ⊠ *Hwy. 158 W.*

WHERE TO EAT AND STAY

For expanded hotel reviews, visit Fodors.com.

$
AMERICAN

✕ **Nicely's.** Artworks for sale decorate the walls of this vintage diner. The country cooking isn't fancy—think blueberry pancakes for breakfast and chicken-fried steak for dinner—but this is a good spot for families with kids and unfussy eaters looking for a square meal. It's the kind of place where the waitress walks up with a pot of coffee and asks, "Ya want a warm-up, hon?" ⑤ *Average main: $15* ⊠ *U.S. 395 and 4th St., Lee Vining* ☎ *760/647–6477* ⊘ *Closed Tues. and Wed. in winter.*

$
AMERICAN

✕ **Tioga Gas Mart & Whoa Nelli Deli.** This might be the only gas station in the United States that serves cocktails, but its appeal goes way beyond novelty. The mahimahi tacos are succulent, the gourmet pizzas tasty, and the herb-crusted pork loin with berry glaze elegant. Order at the counter and grab a seat inside or out. ⑤ *Average main: $14* ⊠ *Hwy. 120 and U.S. 395, Lee Vining* ☎ *760/647–1088* ⊕ *www.whoanelliedeli.com* ⊘ *Closed mid-Nov.–mid-Apr.*

$
B&B/INN

▦ **Lake View Lodge.** Enormous rooms and lovely landscaping, which includes several shaded sitting areas, set this motel apart from its competitors in town. **Pros:** attractive; clean; friendly staff. **Cons:** could use updating. ⑤ *Rooms from: $89* ⊠ *51285 U.S. 395* ☎ *760/647–6543, 800/990–6614* ⊕ *www.lakeviewlodgeyosemite.com* ⇆ *76 rooms, 12 cottages.*

BODIE STATE HISTORIC PARK

23 miles northeast of Lee Vining via U.S. 395 to Hwy. 270.

The historic town of Bridgeport is the gateway to Bodie State Historic Park, and the only supply center for miles around. The scenery is spectacular, with craggy, snowcapped peaks looming over vast prairies. Tiny and for tourist purposes worth nothing more than a place to sleep and eat, Bridgeport's claim to fame is that most of the 1947 film-noir classic *Out of the Past* was filmed here. In winter, much of Bridgeport shuts down.

GETTING HERE AND AROUND

You need to get here by private car. About 15 miles north of Lee Vining (7 miles south of Bridgeport), look for signs pointing you east toward the ghost town, another 13 miles via Highway 270. The last 3 miles are unpaved, and possibly treacherous depending on erosion and the weather. A snowmobile might be necessary in winter.

EXPLORING

Fodor'sChoice
★

Bodie Ghost Town. The mining village of Rattlesnake Gulch, abandoned mine shafts, and the remains of a small Chinatown are among the sights at this fascinating ghost town. The town boomed from about 1878 to 1881, but by the late 1940s all its residents had departed. A state park was established here in 1962, with a mandate to preserve everything in a state of "arrested decay." Evidence of Bodie's wild past survives at an excellent museum, and you can tour an old stamp mill where ore was crushed into fine powder to extract gold and silver. The town is 23 miles from Lee Vining, north on U.S. 395, then east on Highway 270; the last 3 miles are unpaved. Snow may close Highway 270 from late fall through early spring. No food, drink, or lodging is available in Bodie. ⊠ *Main and Green Sts., Bodie* 🕾 *760/647–6445* ⊕ *www.bodie. com* 🖃 *Park $5, museum free* 🕙 *Park: late May–early Sept., daily 8–7; early Sept.–late May, daily 8–4. Museum: late May–early Sept., daily 9–6; early Sept.–late May, hrs vary.*

SOUTH OF SEQUOIA AND KINGS CANYON: THREE RIVERS

200 miles north of Los Angeles via I–5 to Hwy. 99 to Hwy. 198; 8 miles south of Ash Mountain/Foothills entrance to Sequoia National Park on Hwy. 198.

In the foothills of the Sierra along the Kaweah River, the serpentine hamlet of Three Rivers serves as the main gateway town to Sequoia and Kings Canyon national parks (⇨ *Chapter 16, Sequoia and Kings Canyon National Parks*). Its livelihood depends largely on tourism from the parks, courtesy of two markets, a few service stations, banks, a post office, and several lodgings, which are good spots to find a room when park accommodations are full (or if you dislike camping and would like to save money).

14

GETTING HERE AND AROUND

From Memorial Day through Labor Day, you can ride the city of Visalia's Sequoia Shuttle (☎ 877/404–6473 ⊕ www.ci.visalia.ca.us) to and from Three Rivers, up to and down from Sequoia National Park. You probably should count on driving here yourself, however, via Highway 198. The town is slender and long, and to walk from your hotel to a restaurant might wear you out before you set foot in the national park.

WHERE TO EAT AND STAY

For expanded hotel reviews, visit Fodors.com.

$ ✕ **We Three Bakery.** This friendly, popular spot packs lunches for trips
ECLECTIC into the nearby national parks; it's also open for breakfast. Baked goods for the curvy road ahead, anyone? ⑤ *Average main: $10* ⊠ *43688 Sierra Dr.* ☎ *559/561–4761.*

$$ ⌂ **Buckeye Tree Lodge.** Every room at this two-story motel has a patio
B&B/INN facing a sun-dappled grassy lawn, right on the banks of the Kaweah River. **Pros:** near the park entrance; fantastic river views; friendly staff. **Cons:** can fill up quickly in the summer; could use a little updating. ⑤ *Rooms from: $123* ⊠ *46000 Sierra Dr., Hwy. 198, Three Rivers* ☎ *559/561–5900* ⊕ *www.buckeyetree.com* ↬ *11 rooms, 1 cottage* ⦿ *Breakfast.*

$ ⌂ **Sequoia Motel.** An old-fashioned single-story mom-and-pop motel,
B&B/INN the Sequoia stands out with such extra touches as country-style quilts and mismatched Americana furnishings that lend a retro charm to the rooms. **Pros:** clean; friendly; comparatively affordable. **Cons:** not especially modern; fills up quickly in the summer. ⑤ *Rooms from: $109* ⊠ *43000 Sierra Dr., Hwy. 198, Three Rivers* ☎ *559/561–4453* ⊕ *www.sequoiamotel.com* ↬ *11 rooms, 3 cottages.*

SPORTS AND THE OUTDOORS

TOUR OUTFITTERS

Sequoia Natural History Association. The association's highly regarded Sequoia Field Institute conducts single-day and mulitiday "edventure" tours that include backpacking hikes, natural-history walks, and kayaking excursions. ⊠ *47050 Generals Hwy. #10, Three Rivers* ☎ *559/565–3759* ⊕ *www.sequoiahistory.org.*

RAFTING

Kaweah White Water Adventures. From April through July, this outfit conducts two-hour and full-day rafting trips, with some Class III rapids. Longer trips may include some Class IV. ☎ *559/561–1000, 800/229–8658* ⊕ *www.kaweah-whitewater.com* ⊡ *$50 to $140 per person.*

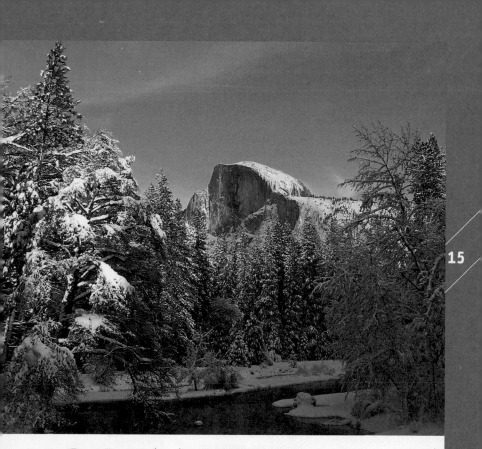

YOSEMITE
NATIONAL PARK

WELCOME TO YOSEMITE

TOP REASONS TO GO

★ **Wet and wild:** An easy stroll brings you to the base of Lower Yosemite Falls, where roaring springtime waters make for misty lens caps and lasting memories.

★ **Tunnel vision:** Approaching Yosemite Valley, Wawona Road passes through a mountainside and emerges before one of the park's most heart-stopping vistas.

★ **Inhale the beauty:** Pause to smell the light, pristine air as you travel about the High Sierra's Tiaga Pass and Tuolumne Meadows, where 10,000-foot granite peaks just might take your breath away.

★ **Walk away:** Leave the crowds behind—but do bring along a buddy—and take a hike somewhere along Yosemite's 800 miles of trails.

★ **Powder your nose:** Winter's hush floats into Yosemite on snowflakes. Lift your face to the sky and listen to the trees.

1 Yosemite Valley. At an elevation of 4,000 feet, in roughly the center of the park, beats Yosemite's heart. This is where you'll find the park's most famous sights and biggest crowds.

2 Wawona and Mariposa Grove. The park's southern tip holds Wawona, with its grand old hotel and pioneer history center, and the Mariposa Grove of Big Trees, filled with giant sequoias. These are closest to the South Entrance, 35 miles (a one-hour drive) south of Yosemite Village.

3 Tuolumne Meadows. The highlight of east-central Yosemite is this wildflower-strewn valley with hiking trails, nestled among sharp, rocky peaks. It's a two-hour drive northeast of Yosemite Valley along Tioga Road (closed mid-October to late May).

4 Hetch Hetchy. The most remote, least visited part of Yosemite accessible by automobile, this glacial valley is dominated by a reservoir and veined with wilderness trails. It's near the park's western boundary, about a half-hour drive north of the Big Oak Flat Entrance.

CALIFORNIA

GETTING ORIENTED

Yosemite is so large that you can think of it as five parks. Yosemite Valley, famous for waterfalls and cliffs, and Wawona, where the giant sequoias stand, are open all year. Hetch Hetchy, home of less-used backcountry trails, is most accessible from late spring through early fall. The subalpine high country, Tuolumne Meadows, is open for summer hiking and camping; in winter it's accessible via cross-country skis or snowshoes. Badger Pass Ski Area is open in winter only. Most visitors spend their time along the park's southwestern border, between Wawona and Big Oak Flat Entrance; a bit farther east in Yosemite Valley and Badger Pass Ski Area; and along the east–west corridor of Tioga Road, which spans the park north of Yosemite Valley and bisects Tuolumne Meadows.

15

Updated by
Reed Parsell

By merely standing in Yosemite Valley and turning in a circle, you can see more natural wonders in a minute than you could in a full day pretty much anywhere else. Half Dome, Yosemite Falls, El Capitan, Bridalveil Fall, Sentinel Dome, the Merced River, white-flowering dogwood trees, maybe even bears ripping into the bark of fallen trees or sticking their snouts into beehives—it's all in Yosemite Valley.

In the mid-1800s, when tourists were arriving to the area, the valley's special geologic qualities, and the giant sequoias of Mariposa Grove 30 miles to the south, so impressed a group of influential Californians that they persuaded President Abraham Lincoln to grant those two areas to the state for protection. On Oct. 1, 1890—thanks largely to lobbying efforts by naturalist John Muir and Robert Underwood Johnson, the editor of *Century Magazine*—Congress set aside 1,500 square miles for Yosemite National Park.

YOSEMITE PLANNER

WHEN TO GO

During extremely busy periods—such as the 4th of July—you will experience delays at the entrance gates. ■TIP➔ For smaller crowds, visit midweek. Or come mid-April through Memorial Day or mid-September through October, when the park is only a bit busy and the days usually are sunny and clear.

Summer rainfall is rare. In winter, heavy snows occasionally cause road closures, and tire chains or four-wheel drive may be required on the roads that remain open. The road to Glacier Point beyond the turnoff for Badger Pass is closed after the first major snowfall; Tioga Road is closed from late October through May or mid-June. Mariposa Grove Road is typically closed for a shorter period in winter.

GETTING HERE AND AROUND
BUS TRAVEL

Once you're in Yosemite you can take advantage of the free shuttle buses, which operate on low emissions, have 21 stops, and run every 10 minutes or so from 9 am to 6 pm year-round; a separate (but also free) summer-only shuttle runs out to El Capitan. Also during the summer, you can pay to take the morning "hikers' bus" from Yosemite Valley to Tuolumne or the bus up to Glacier Point. Bus service from Wawona is geared to people who are staying there and want to spend the day in Yosemite Valley. Free and frequent shuttles transport people between the Wawona Hotel and Mariposa Grove. During the snow season, buses run regularly between Yosemite Valley and Badger Pass Ski Area.

CAR TRAVEL

Roughly 200 miles from San Francisco, 300 miles from Los Angeles, and 500 miles from Las Vegas, Yosemite takes a while to reach—and its many sites and attractions merit much more time than what rangers say is the average visit: four hours. Most people arrive via automobile or tour bus, but public transportation (courtesy of Amtrak and the regional YARTS bus system) also can get you to the valley efficiently.

Of the park's four entrances, Arch Rock is the closest to Yosemite Valley. The road that goes through it, Route 140 from Merced and Mariposa, is a scenic western approach that snakes alongside the boulder-packed Merced River. Route 41, through Wawona, is the way to come from Los Angeles (or Fresno, if you've flown in and rented a car). Route 120, through Crane Flat, is the most direct route from San Francisco. The only way in from the east is Tioga Road, which may be the best route in terms of scenery—though due to snow accumulation it's open for a frustratingly short amount of time each year (typically early June through mid-October).

There are few gas stations within Yosemite (Crane Flat, Tuolumne Meadows, and Wawona; none in the valley), so fuel up before you reach the park. From late fall until early spring, the weather is especially unpredictable, and driving can be treacherous. You should carry chains.

PARK ESSENTIALS
PARK FEES AND PERMITS

The admission fee, valid for seven days, is $20 per vehicle or $10 per individual.

If you plan to camp in the backcountry or climb Half Dome, you must have a wilderness permit. Availability of permits, which are free, depends upon trailhead quotas. It's best to make a reservation, especially if you will be visiting May through September. You can reserve two days to 24 weeks in advance by phone (☎ 209/372–0740 or 209/372–0739); a $5-per-person processing fee is charged if and when your reservation is confirmed. Requests must include your name, address, daytime phone, the number of people in your party, trip date, alternative dates, starting and ending trailheads, and a brief itinerary. Without a reservation, you may still get a free permit on a first-come, first-served basis at wilderness permit offices at Big Oak Flat, Hetch Hetchy, Tuolumne, Wawona, the Wilderness Center in Yosemite Village, and Yosemite Valley in summer. From fall to spring, visit the Valley Visitor Center.

15

Plants and Wildlife in Yosemite

CLOSE UP

Dense stands of incense cedar and Douglas fir—as well as ponderosa, Jeffrey, lodgepole, and sugar pines—cover much of the park, but the stellar standout, quite literally, is the *Sequoia sempervirens,* the giant sequoia. Sequoias grow only along the west slope of the Sierra Nevada between 4,500 and 7,000 feet in elevation. Starting from a seed the size of a rolled-oat flake, each of these ancient monuments assumes remarkable proportions in adulthood; you can see them in the Mariposa Grove of Big Trees. In late May the valley's dogwood trees bloom with white, starlike flowers. Wildflowers, such as black-eyed Susan, bull thistle, cow parsnip, lupine, and meadow goldenrod, peak in June in the valley and in July at higher elevations.

The most visible animals in the park—aside from the omnipresent

western gray squirrel—are the mule deer. Though sightings of bighorn sheep are infrequent in the park itself, you can sometimes see them on the eastern side of the Sierra Crest, just off Route 120 in Lee Vining Canyon. You may also see the American black bear, which often has a brown, cinnamon, or blond coat. The Sierra Nevada is home to thousands of bears, and you should take all necessary precautions to keep yourself—and the bears—safe. For one, do not feed the bears. Bears that acquire a taste for human food can become very aggressive and destructive and often must be destroyed by rangers.

Watch for the blue Steller's jay along trails, near public buildings, and in campgrounds, and look for golden eagles soaring over Tioga Road.

PARK HOURS

The park is open 24/7 year-round. All entrances are open at all hours, except for the Hetch Hetchy Entrance, which is open roughly dawn to dusk. Yosemite is in the Pacific time zone.

TOURS

Ansel Adams Photo Walks. Photography enthusiasts shouldn't miss these 90-minute guided camera walks offered four mornings (Mon., Tue., Thu., and Sat.) each week by professional photographers. All are free, but participation is limited to 15 people. Meeting points vary, and advance reservations are essential. ☎ *209/372–4413, 800/568–7398* ⊕ *www.anseladams.com* ✉ *Free.*

FAMILY **Wee Wild Ones.** Designed for kids under seven, this 45-minute program includes animal-theme games, songs, stories, and crafts. The event is held outdoors before the regular Yosemite Lodge or Curry Village evening programs in summer and fall; it moves to the Ahwahnee's big fireplace in winter and spring. All children must be accompanied by an adult. ☎ *209/372–1240* ✉ *Free.*

VISITOR INFORMATION
PARK CONTACT INFORMATION
Yosemite National Park ☎ *209/372–0200* ⊕ *www.nps.gov/yose.*

VISITOR CENTERS

Le Conte Memorial Lodge. This small but striking National Historic Landmark, with its granite walls and steeply pitched shingle roof, is Yosemite's first permanent public information center. Step inside to see the cathedral-like interior, which contains a library and environmental exhibits. To find out about evening programs, check the kiosk out front. ⊠ *Southside Dr., about ½ mile west of Curry Village* ☉ *Memorial Day–Labor Day, Wed.–Sun. 10–4.*

Valley Visitor Center. Learn about Yosemite Valley's geology, vegetation, and human inhabitants at this visitor center. Don't leave without watching *Spirit of Yosemite*, a 23-minute introductory film that runs every half-hour in the theater behind the visitor center. Strangely, the film shows no animals other than one deer. ⊠ *Yosemite Village* ☎ *209/372–0299* ☉ *Late May–early Sept., daily 9–7:30; early Sept.–late May, daily 9–5.*

EXPLORING

15

HISTORIC SITES

Ahwahneechee Village. This solemn smattering of structures, accessed by a short loop trail behind the Yosemite Valley Visitor Center, is a look at what Native American life might have been like in the 1870s. One interpretive sign points out that the Miwok people referred to the 19th-century newcomers as "Yohemite" or "Yohometuk," which have been translated as meaning "some of them are killers." ⊠ *Northside Dr., Yosemite Village* ⊠ *Free* ☉ *Daily sunrise–sunset.*

Pioneer Yosemite History Center. Some of Yosemite's first structures—those not occupied by Native Americans, that is—were relocated here in the 1950s and 1960s. You can spend a pleasurable and informative half-hour walking about them and reading the signs, perhaps springing for a self-guided-tour pamphlet (50¢) to further enhance the history lesson. Weekends and some weekdays in the summer, costumed docents conduct free blacksmithing and "wet-plate" photography demonstrations, and for a small fee you can take a stagecoach ride. ⊠ *Rte. 41, Wawona* ☎ *209/375–9531, 209/379–2646* ⊠ *Free* ☉ *Building interiors are open mid-June–Labor Day, Wed. 2–5, Thurs.–Sun. 10–1 and 2–5.*

SCENIC STOPS

El Capitan. Rising 3,593 feet—more than 350 stories—above the Valley, El Capitan is the largest exposed-granite monolith in the world. Since 1958, people have been climbing its entire face, including the famous "nose." You can spot adventurers with your binoculars by scanning the smooth and nearly vertical cliff for specks of color. ⊠ *Off Northside Dr., about 4 miles west of the Valley Visitor Center.*

Fodor'sChoice
★ **Glacier Point.** If you lack the time, desire, or stamina to hike more than 3,200 feet up to Glacier Point from the Yosemite Valley floor, you can drive here—or take a bus from the Valley—for a bird's-eye view. You are likely to encounter a lot of day-trippers on the short, paved trail that leads

"This is us taking a break before conquering the top of Lembert Dome, while enjoying the beautiful view over Yosemite's high country." —photo by Rebalyn, Fodors.com member

from the parking lot to the main overlook. Take a moment to veer off a few yards to the Geology Hut, which succinctly explains and illustrates how the Valley looked like 10 million, 3 million, and 20,000 years ago. ✉ *Glacier Point Rd., 16 miles northeast of Rte. 41* ☎ *209/372–1240.*

Half Dome. Visitors' eyes are continually drawn to this remarkable granite formation that tops out at more than 4,700 feet above the valley floor. Despite its name, the dome is actually about three-quarters intact. You can hike to the top of Half Dome on an 8.5-mile (one-way) trail whose last 400 feet must be ascended while holding onto a steel cable. Permits are required (and checked on the trail), and there's a 300-person limit each day. Back down in the valley, see Half Dome reflected in the Merced River by heading to Sentinel Bridge just before sundown. The brilliant orange light on Half Dome is a stunning sight.

Hetch Hetchy Reservoir. When Congress approved the O'Shaughnessy Dam in 1913, pragmatism triumphed over aestheticism. Some 2.5 million residents of the San Francisco Bay Area continue to get their water from this 117-billion-gallon reservoir. Although spirited efforts are being made to restore the Hetch Hetchy Valley to its former, pristine glory, three-quarters of San Francisco voters in 2012 ultimately opposed a measure to possibly drain the reservoir. Eight miles long, the reservoir is Yosemite's largest body of water, and one that can be seen up close from several trails. ✉ *Hetch Hetchy Rd., about 15 miles north of the Big Oak Flat entrance station.*

Fodor's Choice ★ **Mariposa Grove of Big Trees.** Of Yosemite's three sequoia groves—the others being Merced and Tuolumne, both near Crane Flat well to the north—Mariposa is by far the largest and easiest to walk around.

Grizzly Giant, whose base measures 96 feet around, has been estimated to be one of the largest in the world. Perhaps more astoundingly, it's about 2,700 years old. Up the hill, you'll find many more sequoias, a small museum, and fewer people. Summer weekends are especially crowded here. Consider taking the free shuttle from Wawona. ⊠ *Rte. 41, 2 miles north of the South Entrance station.*

Tuolumne Meadows. The largest subalpine meadow in the Sierra (at 8,600 feet) is a popular way station for backpack trips along the Pacific Crest and John Muir trails. The setting is not as dramatic as Yosemite Valley, 56 miles away, but the almost perfectly flat basin, about 2½ miles long, is intriguing, and in July it's resplendent with wildflowers. The most popular day hike is up Lembert Dome, atop which you'll have breathtaking views of the basin below. Keep in mind that Tioga Road rarely opens before June and usually closes by mid-October. ⊠ *Tioga Rd. (Rte. 120), about 8 miles west of the Tioga Pass entrance station.*

15

WATERFALLS

Yosemite's waterfalls are at their most spectacular in May and June. When the snow starts to melt (usually peaking in May), streaming snow-melt spills down to meet the Merced River. By summer's end, some falls, including the mighty Yosemite Falls, trickle or dry up. Their flow increases in late fall, and in winter they may be hung dramatically with ice. Even in drier months, the waterfalls can be breathtaking. If you choose to hike any of the trails to or up the falls, be sure to wear shoes with no-slip soles; the rocks can be extremely slick. Stay on trails at all times.

■ **TIP→** Visit the park during a full moon and you can stroll in the valley without a flashlight and still make out the ribbons of falling water, as well as silhouettes of the giant granite monoliths.

Bridalveil Fall. This 620-foot waterfall is often diverted dozens of feet one way or the other by the breeze. It is the first marvelous site you will see up-close when you drive into Yosemite Valley. ⊠ *Yosemite Valley, access from parking area off Wawona Rd.*

Nevada Fall. Climb Mist Trail from Happy Isles for an up-close view of this 594-foot cascading beauty. If you don't want to hike (the trail's final approach is quite taxing), you can see it—albeit distantly—from Glacier Point. Stay safely on the trail, as people sometimes die when they climb over the railing and onto the slippery rocks. ⊠ *Yosemite Valley, access via Mist Trail from Nature Center at Happy Isles.*

Ribbon Fall. At 1,612 feet, this is the highest single fall in North America. It's also the first waterfall to dry up in summer; the rainwater and melted snow that create the slender fall evaporate quickly at this height. Look just west of El Capitan for the best view of the fall from the base of Bridalveil Fall. ⊠ *Yosemite Valley, west of El Capitan Meadow.*

Vernal Fall. Fern-covered black rocks frame this 317-foot fall, and rainbows play in the spray at its base. You can get a distant view from Glacier Point, or hike to see it close up. You'll get wet, but the view is worth it. ⊠ *Yosemite Valley, access via Mist Trail from Nature Center at Happy Isles.*

Yosemite's Valley Floor

KEY

- 👫 Ranger Station
- ⛺ Campground
- 🏕 Picnic Area
- 🍴 Restaurant
- 🏨 Lodge
- 🚶 Trailhead
- 🚻 Restrooms
- ⚑ Scenic Viewpoint
- --- Walking/Hiking Trails
- – – John Muir Trail
- ⋯ Bicycle Path
- Valley Floor

Half Dome 8,836 ft.

Liberty Cap

Mist Trail

Nevada Fall

Emerald Pools

Vernal Fall

Footbridge

John Muir Trail

Clark Point

Mist Trail

Panorama Cliff

Sierra Point

Grizzly Peak

John Muir Trail

Illilouette Gorge

Mirror Lake

Washington Column

Happy Isles Bridge

Road open only to bicycles and Shuttlebuses

bicycle path

Upper Pines

Clarks Bridge

North Pines

Royal Arches

Royal Arch Cascade

Nature Center at Happy Isles

Lower Pines

CURRY VILLAGE

Road open only to bicycles and Shuttlebuses

Glacier Point 7,214 ft.

Panorama Trail

The Ahwahnee Hotel

bicycle path

Curry Village Store

Staircase Falls

Glacier Point Road

Pohono Trail

Village Store

Auto Repair

Le Conte Memorial Lodge

Moran Point

Four Mile Trail

Medical Clinic

P.O.

YOSEMITE VILLAGE

Yosemite Museum

Ansel Adams Gallery

Ahwahneechee Village

Valley Visitor Center

Road open only to bicycles and Shuttlebuses

Chapel

Union Point

Sentinel Rock

Lower Yosemite Fall

Merced River

bicycle path

Yosemite Lodge

Four Mile Trail

Sentinel Fall

1/2 mi

1/2 km

GOOD READS

■ The Photographer's Guide to Yosemite, by Michael Frye, is an insider's guide to the park, with maps for shutterbugs looking to capture perfect images.

■ John Muir penned his observations of the park he long advocated for in The Yosemite.

■ Yosemite and the High Sierra, edited by Andrea G. Stillman and John Szarkowski, features beautiful reproductions of landmark photographs by Ansel Adams, accompanied by excerpts from the photographer's journals written when Adams traveled in Yosemite National Park in the early 20th century.

■ An insightful collection of essays accompanies the museum-quality artworks in Yosemite: Art of an American Icon by Amy Scott.

■ Perfect for beginning wildlife watchers, Sierra Nevada Wildflowers, by Karen Wiese, identifies more than 230 kinds of flora growing in the Sierra Nevada region.

15

Fodor's Choice **Yosemite Falls.** Actually three falls, they together constitute the highest waterfall in North America and the fifth highest in the world. The water from the top descends a total of 2,425 feet, and when the falls run hard, you can hear them thunder across the valley. If they dry up—that sometimes happens in late summer—the valley seems naked without the wavering tower of spray. ■ TIP➜ **If you hike the mile-long loop trail (partially paved) to the base of the Lower Falls in May, prepare to get wet.** You can get a good full-length view of the falls from the lawn of Yosemite Chapel, off Southside Drive. ⊠ *Yosemite Valley, access from Yosemite Lodge or trail parking area.*

EDUCATIONAL OFFERINGS

CLASSES AND SEMINARS

Art Classes. Professional artists conduct workshops in watercolor, etching, drawing, and other mediums. Bring your own materials or purchase the basics at the Art Activity Center, next to the Village Store. Children under 13 must be accompanied by an adult. ⊠ *Art Activity Center, Yosemite Village* ☎ *209/372–1442* ⊕ *www.yosemitepark.com* ✉ *Free* ⊙ *Early Apr.–early Oct., Mon.–Sat., 10 am–2 pm.*

Yosemite Outdoor Adventures. Naturalists, scientists, and park rangers lead multi-hour to multiday educational outings on topics from woodpeckers to fire management to pastel painting. Most sessions take place spring through fall, but a few focus on winter phenomena. ⊠ *Various locations* ☎ *209/379–2321* ⊕ *www.yosemitepark.com* ✉ *$82–$465.*

RANGER PROGRAMS

Junior Ranger Program. Children ages 3 to 13 can participate in the informal, self-guided Little Cub and Junior Ranger programs. A park activity handbook ($4) is available at the Valley Visitor Center or the Nature Center at Happy Isles. Once kids complete the book, rangers present them with a certificate and a badge. ⊠ *Valley Visitor Center or the Nature Center at Happy Isles* ☎ *209/372–0299.*

Ranger-Led Programs. Rangers lead entertaining walks and give informative talks several times a day from spring to fall. The schedule is more limited in winter, but most days you can find a program somewhere in the park. In the evenings at Yosemite Lodge and Curry Village, lectures, slide shows, and documentary films present unique perspectives on Yosemite. On summer weekends, Camp Curry and Tuolumne Meadows Campground host sing-along campfire programs. Schedules and locations are posted on bulletin boards throughout the park. ⊕ *www. yosemitepark.com.*

SPORTS AND THE OUTDOORS

BICYCLING

One enjoyable way to see Yosemite Valley is to ride a bike beneath its lofty granite monoliths. The eastern valley has 12 miles of paved, flat bicycle paths across meadows and through woods, with bike racks at convenient stopping points. For a greater challenge but at no small risk, you can ride on 196 miles of paved park roads; bicycles are not allowed on hiking trails or in the backcountry. Kids under 18 must wear a helmet.

TOURS AND OUTFITTERS
Yosemite bike rentals. You can arrange for rentals from Yosemite Lodge and Curry Village bike stands. Bikes with child trailers, baby-jogger strollers, and wheelchairs are also available. The cost is about $11 per hour, or $32 a day. ⊠ *Yosemite Lodge or Curry Village* ☎ *209/372–1208* ⊕ *www.yosemitepark.com* ☉ *Apr.–Oct.*

BIRD-WATCHING

Nearly 250 bird species have been spotted in the park, including the sage sparrow, pygmy owl, blue grouse, and mountain bluebird. Park rangers lead free bird-watching walks in Yosemite Valley one day each week in summer; check at a visitor center or information station for times and locations. Binoculars sometimes are available for loan.

HIKING

TOURS AND OUTFITTERS
Wilderness Center. This facility provides free wilderness permits, which are required for overnight camping (advance reservations are available for $5 and are highly recommended for popular trailheads in summer and on weekends). The staff here also provides maps and advice to hikers heading into the backcountry. ☎ *209/372–0308.*

Yosemite Mountaineering School and Guide Service. From April to November, Yosemite Mountaineering School and Guide Service leads two-hour to full-day treks, as well as backpacking and overnight excursions. Reservations are recommended. ⊠ *Yosemite Mountain Shop, Curry Village* ☎ *209/372–8344* ⊕ *www.yosemitepark.com/ Activities_RockClimbing.aspx.*

EASY

Yosemite Falls Trail. This is the highest waterfall in North America. The upper fall (1,430 feet), the middle cascades (675 feet), and the lower fall (320 feet) combine for a total of 2,425 feet and, when viewed from the valley, appear as a single waterfall. The ¼-mile trail leads from the parking lot to the base of the falls. Upper Yosemite Fall Trail, a strenuous 3½-mile climb rising 2,700 feet, takes you above the top of the falls. Lower trail: *Easy.* Upper trail: *Difficult.* ⊠ *Trailhead off Camp 4, north of Northside Dr.*

MODERATE

Mist Trail. Except for Lower Yosemite Falls, more visitors take this trail (or portions of it) than any other in the park. The trek up to and back from Vernal Fall is 3 miles. Add another 4 miles total by continuing up to 594-foot Nevada Fall; the trail becomes quite steep and slippery in its final stages. The elevation gain to Vernal Fall is 1,000 feet, and to Nevada Fall an additional 1,000 feet. Merced River tumbles down both falls on its way to a tranquil flow through the Valley. *Moderate.* ⊠ *Trailhead at Happy Isles.*

Panorama Trail. Few hikes come with the visual punch that this 8½-mile trail provides. The star attraction is Half Dome, visible from many intriguing angles, but you also see three waterfalls up close and walk through a manzanita grove. Before you begin, look down on Yosemite Valley from Glacier Point, a special experience in itself. ⚠ **If you start after taking the last bus from the valley floor to Glacier Point, you might run out of daylight before you finish.** *Moderate.* ⊠ *Trailhead at Glacier Point.*

DIFFICULT

Fodor's Choice
★

John Muir Trail to Half Dome. Ardent and courageous trekkers continue on from Nevada Fall to the top of Half Dome. Some hikers attempt this entire 10- to 12-hour, 16¾-mile round-trip trek in one day; if you're planning to do this, remember that the 4,800-foot elevation gain and the 8,842-foot altitude will cause shortness of breath. Another option is to hike to a campground in Little Yosemite Valley near the top of Nevada Fall the first day, then climb to the top of Half Dome and hike out the next day. Get your wilderness permit (required for a one-day hike to Half Dome, too) at least a month in advance. Be sure to wear hiking boots and bring gloves. The last pitch up the back of Half Dome is very steep—the only way to climb this sheer rock face is to pull yourself up using the steel cable handrails, which are in place only from late spring to early fall. Those who brave the ascent will be rewarded with an unbeatable view of Yosemite Valley below and the high country beyond. *Difficult.* ⚠ **Only 300 hikers per day are allowed atop Half Dome, and they all must have permits.** ⊠ *Trailhead at Happy Isles.*

HORSEBACK RIDING

Reservations for guided trail rides must be made in advance at the hotel tour desks or by phone. For overnight saddle trips, which use mules, call ☎ *209/372–8348* on or after September 15 to request a lottery application for the following year. Scenic trail rides range from two hours to a full day; six-day High Sierra saddle trips are also available.

TOURS AND OUTFITTERS

Tuolumne Meadows Stables. Tuolumne Meadows Stables runs two-, four-, and eight-hour trips that start at $64, as well as four- to six-day camping treks on mules that begin at $625. Reservations are mandatory. ⊠ *Off Tioga Rd., 2 miles east of Tuolumne Meadows Visitor Center* ☎ *209/372–8427* ⊕ *www.yosemitepark.com.*

Wawona Stables. Wawona Stables has two- and five-hour rides starting at $64. Reservations are recommended. ⊠ *Rte. 41, Wawona* ☎ *209/ 375–6502.*

Yosemite Valley Stables. You can tour the valley and the start of the high country on two-hour, four-hour, and daylong rides at Yosemite Valley Stables. Reservations are strongly recommended for the trips, which start at $64. ⊠ *At entrance to North Pines Campground, 100 yards northeast of Curry Village* ☎ *209/372–8348* ⊕ *www.yosemitepark.com.*

RAFTING

15

Rafting is permitted only on designated areas of the Middle and South forks of the Merced River. Check with the Valley Visitor Center for closures and other restrictions.

OUTFITTERS

Curry Village raft stand. The per-person rental fee ($28.50 adults, $23.50 children) at Curry Village raft stand covers the four- to six-person raft, two paddles, and life jackets, plus a shuttle to the launch point on Sentinel Beach. ⊠ *South side of Southside Dr., Curry Village* ☎ *209/372– 4386* ⊕ *www.yosemitepark.com* ⊠ *$28.50* ⊙ *Late May–July.*

ROCK CLIMBING

Fodor's Choice ★ The granite canyon walls of Yosemite Valley are world renowned for rock climbing. El Capitan, with its 3,593-foot vertical face, is the most famous, but there are many other options here for all skill levels.

TOURS AND OUTFITTERS

Yosemite Mountaineering School and Guide Service. The one-day basic lesson at Yosemite Mountaineering School and Guide Service includes some bouldering and rappelling, and three or four 60-foot climbs. Climbers must be at least 10 years old and in reasonably good physical condition. Intermediate and advanced classes include instruction in first aid, anchor building, multi-pitch climbing, summer snow climbing, and big-wall climbing. There's a nordic program in the winter. ⊠ *Yosemite Mountain Shop, Curry Village* ☎ *209/372–8344* ⊕ *www.yosemitepark. com* ⊠ *Starting at $148* ⊙ *Apr.–Nov.*

WINTER SPORTS

ICE-SKATING

Curry Village Ice Rink. Winter visitors have skated at this outdoor rink for decades, and there's no mystery why: it's a kick to glide across the ice while soaking up views of Half Dome and Glacier Point. ⊠ *South side of Southside Dr., Curry Village* ☎ *209/372–8319* ⊠ *$9.75 per session,*

$4 skate rental ☉ *Mid-Nov.–mid-Mar. afternoons and evenings daily, morning sessions weekends (hrs vary).*

SKIING AND SNOWSHOEING

Badger Pass Ski Area. California's first ski resort has five lifts and 10 downhill runs, as well as 90 miles of groomed cross-country trails. Free shuttle buses from Yosemite Valley operate between December and early April, weather permitting. Lift tickets are $47, downhill equipment rents for $36, and snowboard rental with boots is $37.50. ⊠ *Badger Pass Rd., off Glacier Point Rd., 18 miles from Yosemite Valley* ☎ *209/372–8430.*

Yosemite Ski School. The gentle slopes of Badger Pass make Yosemite Ski School an ideal spot for children and beginners to learn downhill skiing or snowboarding for as little as $45.50 for a group lesson. ☎ *209/372–8430* ⊕ *www.yosemitepark.com.*

Yosemite Mountaineering School. Yosemite Mountaineering School conducts snowshoeing, cross-country skiing, telemarking, and skate-skiing classes starting at $35.50. ⊠ *Badger Pass Ski Area* ☎ *209/372–8344* ⊕ *www.yosemitepark.com.*

Yosemite Cross-Country Ski School. The highlight of Yosemite's cross-country skiing center is a 21-mile loop from Badger Pass to Glacier Point. You can rent cross-country skis for $25 per day at the Cross-Country Ski School, which also rents snowshoes ($24 per day) and telemarking equipment ($29.50). ☎ *209/372–8444* ⊕ *www.yosemitepark.com.*

WHERE TO EAT

In addition to the dining options listed here, you'll find fast-food grills and cafeterias, plus hamburger stands, pizza joints, and temporary snack bars near park roads in summer. Many dining facilities in the park are open summer only. *Prices in the reviews are the average cost of a main course at dinner or, if dinner is not served, at lunch.*

$$$$
EUROPEAN
Fodor'sChoice
★

✕ **Ahwahnee Hotel Dining Room.** Rave reviews about the dining room's appearance are fully justified—it features towering windows, a 34-foot-high ceiling with interlaced sugar-pine beams, and massive chandeliers. Although many continue to applaud the food, others have reported that they sense a dip in the quality both in the service and what is being served. Diners must spend a lot of money here, so perhaps that inflates the expectations and amplifies the disappointments. In any event, the $43 Sunday brunch is consistently praised. Reservations are always advised, and the attire is "resort casual." ⑤ *Average main: $40* ⊠ *Ahwahnee Hotel, Ahwahnee Rd., about ¾ mile east of Yosemite Valley Visitor Center, Yosemite Village* ☎ *209/372–1489* ⚑ *Reservations essential.*

$$$
AMERICAN

✕ **Mountain Room.** Though good, the food becomes secondary when you see Yosemite Falls through this dining room's wall of windows—almost every table has a view. The chef makes a point of using locally sourced, organic ingredients, so you can be assured of fresh vegetables. Vegans are accommodated, too. The Mountain Room Lounge, a few steps away in the Yosemite Lodge complex, has a broad bar with about 10 beers on tap. ⑤ *Average main: $23* ⊠ *Yosemite Lodge, Northside Dr. about ¾ mile west of the visitor center, Yosemite Village* ☎ *209/372–1281* ☉ *No lunch.*

15

$ ✕ **Tuolumne Meadows Grill.** Serving continuously throughout the day until
FAST FOOD 5 or 6 pm, this fast-food eatery cooks up breakfast, lunch, and snacks.
It's possible that ice cream tastes better at this altitude. Stop in for a
quick meal before exploring the Meadows. $ *Average main: $8 ⊠ Tioga
Rd. (Rte. 120), 1½ mile east of Tuolumne Meadows Visitor Center
☎ 209/372–8426 ⊙ Closed Oct.–Memorial Day.*

$$ ✕ **Tuolumne Meadows Lodge.** At the back of a small building that contains
AMERICAN the lodge's front desk and small gift shop, this restaurant serves hearty
American fare at breakfast and dinner. The decor is ultra-woodsy, with
dark-wood walls and red-and-white-checkered tablecloths. Meals are
mostly of the meat-and-potato variety, but vegetarians' requests are
honored. If you have any dietary restrictions, let the front desk know
in advance and the cooks will not let you down. Order box lunches
from here for before hikes. $ *Average main: $18 ⊠ Tioga Rd. (Rte. 120)
☎ 209/372–8413 ⚱ Reservations essential ⊙ Closed late Sept.–Memo-
rial Day. No lunch.*

$$$ ✕ **Wawona Hotel Dining Room.** Watch deer graze on the meadow while you
AMERICAN dine in the romantic, candlelit dining room of the whitewashed Wawona
Hotel, which dates from the late 1800s. The American-style cuisine
favors fresh ingredients and flavors; trout is a menu staple. There's also
a Sunday brunch Easter through Thanksgiving, and a barbeque on the
lawn Saturday evenings in summer. A jacket is required at dinner. $ *Av-
erage main: $27 ⊠ Wawona Hotel, Rte. 41, Wawona ☎ 801/559–4935
⚱ Reservations essential ⊙ Closed Jan., Feb., and Mar.*

PICNIC AREAS

Considering how large the park is and how many visitors come here—
some 4 million people every year, most of them just for the day—it is
somewhat surprising that Yosemite has so few formal picnic areas,
though in many places you can find a smooth rock to sit on and enjoy
breathtaking views along with your lunch. The convenience stores all
sell picnic supplies, and prepackaged sandwiches and salads are widely
available. Those options can come in especially handy during the middle
of the day, when you might not want to spend precious daylight hours
in such a spectacular setting sitting in a restaurant for a formal meal.

WHERE TO STAY

*Prices in the reviews are the lowest cost of a standard double room in
high season. For expanded hotel reviews, visit Fodors.com.*

$$$$ ▦ **Ahwahnee Hotel.** A National Historic Landmark, the hotel is con-
HOTEL structed of sugar-pine logs and features Native American design
Fodor's Choice motifs; public spaces are enlivened with art-deco flourishes, oriental
★ rugs, and elaborate iron- and woodwork. **Pros:** best lodge in Yosemite; helpful concierge. **Cons:** expensive rates; some reports that service
has slipped in recent years. $ *Rooms from: $471 ⊠ Ahwahnee Rd.,
about ¾ miles east of Yosemite Valley Visitor Center, Yosemite Village ☎ 801/559–4884 ⊕ www.yosemitepark.com ⇗ 99 lodge rooms,
4 suites, 24 cottage rooms.*

CLOSE UP

Best Campgrounds in Yosemite

If you are going to concentrate solely on valley sites and activities, you should endeavor to stay in one of the "Pines" campgrounds, which are clustered near Curry Village and within an easy stroll from that busy complex's many facilities. For a more primitive and quiet experience, and to be near many backcountry hikes, try one of the Tioga Road campgrounds.

National Park Service Reservations Office. Reservations are required at most of Yosemite's campgrounds, especially in summer; while you can book a site up to five months in advance, those made more than 21 days in advance require prepayment. $ *Rooms from: $193* ☎ *800/436–7275* ⊕ *www.recreation. gov* ☉ *Daily 7–7.*

Bridalveil Creek. This campground sits among lodgepole pines at 7,200 feet, above the valley on Glacier Point Road. From here, you can easily drive to Glacier Point's magnificent valley views. ✉ *From Hwy. 41 in Wawona, go north to Glacier Point Rd. and turn right; entrance to campground is 25 miles ahead on right side.*

Camp 4. Formerly known as Sunnyside Walk-In, this is the only valley campground available on a first-come, first-served basis. ✉ *Base of Yosemite Falls Trail, just west of Yosemite Lodge on Northside Dr., Yosemite Village.*

Crane Flat. This camp on Yosemite's western boundary, south of Hodgdon Meadow, is just 17 miles from the valley but far from its bustle. ✉ *From Big Oak Flat entrance on Hwy. 120, drive 10 miles east to campground entrance on right.*

Housekeeping Camp. Composed of three walls (usually concrete) and covered with two layers of canvas, each unit has an open-ended fourth side that can be closed off with a heavy white canvas curtain. You rent "bedpacks," consisting of blankets, sheets, and other comforts. ✉ *Southside Dr., ½ mile west of Curry Village.*

Lower Pines. This moderate-size campground sits directly along the Merced River; it's a short walk to the trailheads for the Mirror Lake and Mist trails. ✉ *At east end of valley.*

Porcupine Flat. Sixteen miles west of Tuolumne Meadows, this campground sits at 8,100 feet. If you want to be in the high country, this is a good bet. ✉ *16 miles west of Tuolumne Meadows on Hwy. 120.*

Tuolumne Meadow. In a wooded area at 8,600 feet, just south of its namesake meadow, this is one of the most spectacular and sought-after campgrounds in Yosemite. ✉ *Hwy. 120, 46 miles east of Big Oak Flat entrance station.*

Upper Pines. This is the valley's largest campground and the closest one to the trailheads. Expect large crowds in the summer—and little privacy. ✉ *At east end of valley, near Curry Village.*

Wawona. Near the Mariposa Grove, just downstream from a popular fishing spot, this year-round campground has larger, less densely packed sites than campgrounds in the valley. ✉ *Hwy. 41, 1 mile north of Wawona.*

White Wolf. Set in the beautiful high country at 8,000 feet, this is a prime spot for hikers. ✉ *From Big Oak Flat entrance, go 15 miles east on Tioga Rd.*

15

$$ 🏨 **Curry Village.** Opened in 1899 as
HOTEL a place for budget-conscious travelers, Curry Village has plain accommodations: standard motel rooms, simple cabins, and tent cabins with private baths. **Pros:** close to many activities; family-friendly atmosphere. **Cons:** not that economical after a recent price surge; can be crowded; sometimes a bit noisy. ⑤ *Rooms from: $124* ✉ *South side of Southside Dr.* ☎ *801/559–4884* ⊕ *www.yosemitepark.com* ⌁ *18 rooms, 389 cabins* 🍽 *No meals.*

LODGING TIP

Reserve your room or cabin in Yosemite as far in advance as possible. You can make a reservation up to a year before your arrival (within minutes after the reservation office makes a date available, the Ahwahnee, Yosemite Lodge, and Wawona Hotel often sell out their weekends, holiday periods, and all days between May and September).

$$ 🏨 **Wawona Hotel.** This 1879
HOTEL National Historic Landmark at Yosemite's southern end is an old-fashioned New England–style estate, with whitewashed buildings, wraparound verandas, and pleasant, no-frills rooms decorated with period pieces. **Pros:** lovely building; peaceful atmosphere. **Cons:** few modern amenities; an hour's drive from Yosemite Valley. ⑤ *Rooms from: $160* ✉ *Hwy. 41, Wawona* ☎ *801/559–4884* ⊕ *www.yosemitepark.com* ⌁ *104 rooms, 50 with bath* ⊙ *Closed Jan. and Feb.*

$ 🏨 **White Wolf Lodge.** Set in a subalpine meadow, the rustic accommo-
HOTEL dations at White Wolf Lodge make it an excellent base camp for hiking the backcountry. **Pros:** quiet location; convenient for hikers; good restaurant. **Cons:** far from the Valley; not much to do here. ⑤ *Rooms from: $115* ✉ *Off Tioga Rd. (Rte. 120), 25 miles west of Tuolumne Meadows and 15 miles east of Crane Flat* ☎ *801/559–4884* ⌁ *24 tent cabins, 4 cabins* ⊙ *Closed mid-Sept.–mid-June.*

$$ 🏨 **Yosemite Lodge at the Falls.** This 1915 lodge near Yosemite Falls more
HOTEL closely resembles a 1960s resort with its numerous two-story structures tucked beneath the trees. **Pros:** centrally located; dependably clean rooms; lots of tours leave from out front. **Cons:** can feel impersonal; appearance is little dated; prices recently skyrocketed. ⑤ *Rooms from: $193* ✉ *Northside Dr. about ¾ mile west of the visitor center, Yosemite Village* ☎ *801/559–4884* ⊕ *www.yosemitepark.com* ⌁ *245 rooms.*

SEQUOIA AND KINGS CANYON NATIONAL PARKS

WELCOME TO SEQUOIA AND KINGS CANYON NATIONAL PARKS

TOP REASONS TO GO

★ **Gentle giants:** You'll feel small—in a good way—walking among some of the world's largest living things in Sequoia's Giant Forest and Kings Canyon's Grant Grove.

★ **Because it's there:** You can't even glimpse it from the main part of Sequoia, but the sight of majestic Mt. Whitney is worth the trek to the eastern face of the High Sierra.

★ **Underground explora-tion:** Far older even than the giant sequoias, the gleaming limestone for-mations in Crystal Cave will draw you along dark, marble passages.

★ **A grander-than-Grand Canyon:** Drive the twist-ing Kings Canyon Scenic Byway down into the jag-ged, granite Kings River Canyon, deeper in parts than the Grand Canyon.

★ **Regal solitude:** To spend a day or two hiking in a subalpine world of your own, pick one of the 11 trailheads at Mineral King.

1 Giant Forest–Lodge-pole Village. The most heavily visited area of Sequoia lies at the base of the "thumb" portion of Kings Canyon National Park and contains major sights such as Giant Forest, Gen-eral Sherman Tree, Crystal Cave, and Moro Rock.

2 Grant Grove Village–Redwood Canyon. The "thumb" of Kings Canyon National Park is its busiest section, where Grant Grove, General Grant Tree, Pan-oramic Point, and Big Stump are the main attractions.

3 Cedar Grove. Most visitors to the huge, high-country portion of Kings Canyon National Park don't go farther than Roads End, a few miles east of Cedar Grove on the canyon floor. Here, the river runs through Zumwalt Meadow, surrounded by magnificent granite formations.

4 Mineral King. In the southeast section of Sequoia, the highest road-accessible part of the park is a good place to hike, camp, and soak up the unspoiled grandeur of the Sierra Nevada.

5 Mount Whitney. The highest peak in the Lower 48 stands on the eastern edge of Sequoia; to get there from Giant Forest you must either backpack eight days through the mountains or drive nearly 300 miles around the park to its other side.

CALIFORNIA

GETTING ORIENTED

The two parks comprise 865,952 acres, mostly on the western flank of the Sierra. A map of the adjacent parks looks vaguely like a mitten, with the palm of Sequoia National Park south of the north-pointing, skinny thumb and long fingers of Kings Canyon National Park. Between the western thumb and eastern fingers, north of Sequoia, lies part of Sequoia National Forest, which includes Giant Sequoia National Monument.

16

Map labels:

LE CONTE DIVIDE
McClure Meadow
Le Conte Canyon
John Muir Trail
Bench Lake
MONARCH DIVIDE
Woods Creek Trail
Kings Canyon Scenic Byway
3 KINGS CANYON
Rae Lakes
Roads End Permit Station
Charlotte Lake
Roaring River
Visitor Center
KINGS-KERN DIVIDE
Highway
Table Mountain 13,630 ft.
Tyndall Creek
Whitney Portal
Stony Creek Village
Wuksachi Village
Visitor Center
Crystal Cave
1
5
Mount Whitney 14,491 ft.
Giant Forest Museum
General Sherman Tree
Bearpaw Meadow
Crabtree
John Muir Trail
Moro Rock
Mount Kaweah 13,802 ft.
Buckeye Flat
Potwisha
Mount Guyot 12,300 ft.
Rock Creek
Visitor Center
Little Five Lakes
Ash Mountain Entrance
Mineral King
4
Lookout Point Entrance
KERN CANYON
Cold Springs
Hockett Meadows
South Fork
Kern Canyon
Sheep Mountain 10,050 ft.

Updated by
Reed Parsell

Although *Sequoiadendron giganteum* is the formal name for the redwoods that grow here, everyone outside the classroom calls them sequoias, big trees, or Sierra redwoods. Their monstrously thick trunks and branches, remarkably shallow root systems, and neck-craning heights are almost impossible to believe, as is the fact they can live for more than 2,500 years. Many of these towering marvels are in the Giant Forest stretch of Generals Highway, which connects Sequoia and Kings Canyon national parks.

Next to or a few miles off the 43-mile road Generals Highway are most of Sequoia National Park's main attractions and Grant Grove Village, the orientation hub for Kings Canyon National Park. The two parks share a boundary that runs west–east, from the foothills of the Central Valley to the Sierra Nevada's dramatic eastern ridges. Kings Canyon has two portions: the smaller is shaped like a bent finger and encompasses Grant Grove Village and Redwood Mountain Grove (the two parks' largest concentration of sequoias), and the larger is home to stunning Kings River Canyon, whose vast, unspoiled peaks and valleys are a backpacker's dream. Sequoia is in one piece and includes Mt. Whitney, the highest point in the Lower 48 states (although it is impossible to see from the western part of the park and is a chore to ascend from either side).

SEQUOIA AND KINGS CANYON PLANNER

WHEN TO GO

The best times to visit are late spring and early fall, when temperatures are moderate and crowds thin. Summertime can draw hoards of tourists to see the giant sequoias, and the few, narrow roads mean congestion at peak holiday times. If you must visit in summer, go during the week. By contrast, in wintertime you may feel as though you have the parks all to yourself. But because of heavy snows, sections of the main park roads can be closed without warning, and low-hanging clouds can move in and obscure mountains and valleys for days. Check road and weather conditions before venturing out mid-November to late April.

GETTING HERE AND AROUND

CAR TRAVEL

Sequoia is 36 miles east of Visalia on Route 198; Kings Canyon is 53 miles east of Fresno on Route 180. There is no automobile entrance on the eastern side of the Sierra. Routes 180 and 198 are connected by Generals Highway, a paved two-lane road that sometimes sees delays at peak times due to ongoing improvements. The road is extremely narrow and steep from Route 198 to Giant Forest, so keep an eye on your engine temperature gauge, as the incline and congestion can cause vehicles to overheat; to avoid overheated brakes, use low gears on downgrades.

If you are traveling in an RV or with a trailer, study the restrictions on these vehicles. Do not travel beyond Potwisha Campground with an RV longer than 22 feet on Route 198; take straighter, easier Route 180 instead. Maximum vehicle length on Generals Highway is 40 feet, or 50 feet combined length for vehicles with trailers.

Generals Highway between Lodgepole and Grant Grove is sometimes closed by snow. The Mineral King Road from Route 198 into southern Sequoia National Park is closed 2 miles below Atwell Mill either on November 1 or after the first heavy snow. The Buckeye Flat–Middle Fork Trailhead Road is closed mid-October through mid-April when the Buckeye Flat Campground closes. The lower Crystal Cave Road is closed when the cave closes in November. Its upper 2 miles, as well as the Panoramic Point and Moro Rock–Crescent Meadow roads, are closed with the first heavy snow. Because of the danger of rockfall, the portion of Kings Canyon Scenic Byway east of Grant Grove closes in winter. For current conditions, call ☎ 559/565–3341 Ext. 4.

■TIP→ Snowstorms are common late October through April. Unless you have four-wheel drive with snow tires, you should carry chains and know how to apply them to the tires on the drive axle.

PARK ESSENTIALS

PARK FEES AND PERMITS

The admission fee is $20 per vehicle and $10 for those who enter by bus, on foot, bicycle, motorcycle, or horse; it is valid for seven days in both parks. U.S. residents over the age of 62 pay $10 for a lifetime pass, and permanently disabled U.S. residents are admitted free.

If you plan to camp in the backcountry, you need a permit, which costs $15 for hikers or $30 for stock users (e.g., horseback riders). One permit covers the group. Availability of permits depends upon trailhead quotas. Reservations are accepted by mail or fax for a $15 processing fee, beginning March 1 each year, and must be made at least 14 days in advance (☎ 559/565–3766). Without a reservation, you may still get a permit on a first-come, first-served basis starting at 1 pm the day before you plan to hike. For more information on backcountry camping or travel with pack animals (horses, mules, burros, or llamas), contact the Wilderness Permit Office (☎ 530/565–3761).

16

PARK HOURS

The parks are open 24/7 year-round. They are in the Pacific time zone.

VISITOR INFORMATION

PARK CONTACT INFORMATION

Sequoia and Kings Canyon National Parks ⊠ *47050 Generals Hwy.(Rte. 198), Three Rivers* 🕾 *559/565–3341, 559/565–3134* ⊕ *www.nps.gov/seki.*

SEQUOIA VISITOR CENTERS

Foothills Visitor Center. Exhibits focusing on the foothills and resource issues facing the parks are on display here. You can also pick up books, maps, and a list of ranger-led walks, and get wilderness permits. ⊠ *Generals Hwy. (Rte. 198), 1 mile north of the Ash Mountain entrance* 🕾 *559/565– 4212* ☉ *Oct.–mid-May, daily 8–4:30; mid-May–Sept., daily 8–5.*

Lodgepole Visitor Center. Along with exhibits on the area's geologic history, wildlife, and longtime American Indian inhabitants, this center screens an outstanding 22-minute film about bears. You can also buy books, maps, Wolverton barbecue, and cave tour tickets here. ⊠ *Generals Hwy. (Rte. 198), 21 miles north of Ash Mountain entrance* 🕾 *559/565–4436* ☉ *June–Oct., daily 7–6; Nov.–May, weekends 7–6.*

KINGS CANYON VISITOR CENTERS

Cedar Grove Visitor Center. Off the main road and behind the Sentinel Campground, this small ranger station has books and maps, plus information about hikes and other things to do in the area. ⊠ *Kings Canyon Scenic Byway, 30 miles east of park entrance* 🕾 *559/565–3793* ☉ *mid-May–late September, daily 9–5.*

Kings Canyon Visitor Center. Acquaint yourself with the varied charms of this two-section national park by watching a 15-minute film and perusing the center's exhibits on the canyon, sequoias, and human history. Books, maps, and free wilderness permits are available, as are updates on the parks' weather and air-quality conditions. ⊠ *Generals Hwy. (Rte. 198), 3 miles northeast of Rte. 180, Big Stump entrance* 🕾 *559/565– 4307* ☉ *Summer, daily 8–6; mid-May–late Sept., daily 9–4:30; winter, daily 9:30–4:30.*

SEQUOIA NATIONAL PARK

EXPLORING

SCENIC DRIVES

Generals Highway. One of the most scenic drives in a state replete with them is this 43-mile road, the main asphalt artery between Sequoia and Kings Canyon national parks. Named after the landmark Grant and Sherman trees that leave so many visitors awestruck, it runs from the Foothills Visitor Center north to Grant Grove Village. Along the way, it passes the turnoff to Crystal Cave, the Giant Forest Museum, Lodgepole Village, and Sequoia National Park's other most popular attractions. The lower portion, from Hospital Rock to the Giant Forest, is especially steep and windy. If your vehicle is 22 feet or longer, avoid that stretch by entering the parks via Route 180 (from Fresno) rather than Route 198

Western Sequoia and Kings Canyon National Park

Boyden Cave

Kings Canyon Scenic Byway
South Fork
Kings River

Hume Lake

Sheep Creek
Cedar Grove Visitor Center

KINGS CANYON NATIONAL PARK

General Grant Tree
Crystal Springs
Grant Grove Visitor Center
Sunset

180

Big Stump Entrance
Redwood Mountain Overlook

Eshom

Montecito Sequoia Lodge

REDWOOD CANYON

Generals Highway

Stony Creek

Stony Creek Village

SILLIMAN CREST

Dorst Creek

Twin Lakes Trail

Wuksachi Village

Lodgepole Visitor Center and Village

Wolverton

Crystal Cave

General Sherman Tree

Kaweah River

Yucca Creek

Giant Forest Museum

Tharps Log

High Sierra Trail

CRESCENT MEADOW

Colony Mill Trail

Tunnel Log
Moro Rock

North Fork

ASH PEAKS

Potwisha

Buckeye Flat

SEQUOIA NATIONAL PARK

Ash Mountain Entrance

Foothills Visitor Center

Generals Highway

0   3 mi
0   3 km

198

Kaweah River

Three Rivers

Atwell Mill

Lookout Point Entrance

Kaweah River

(from Visalia). And take your time on this road—there's a lot to see, and wildlife can scamper across at any time. ⚠ **Major roadwork between Foothills Visitor Center and Giant Forest Museum might not be completed by 2014, which could delay your drive up to an hour each way.**

SCENIC STOPS

Sequoia National Park is all about the trees, and to understand the scale of these giants you must walk among them. If you do nothing else, get out of the car for a short stroll through one of the groves. But there is much more to the park than the trees. Try to get up to one of the vista points that offer a panoramic view over the forested mountains. Whether you're driving south to north or north to south, Generals Highway (Route 198) will be your route to most of the park's sights. A few short spur roads lead off the highway to some sights, and Mineral King Road branches off Route 198 to enter the park at Lookout Point, winding east from there into the southernmost part of the park.

Crescent Meadow. John Muir called this the "gem of the Sierra." Walk around for an hour or two and you might decide that the Scotland-born naturalist was exaggerating a wee bit. Wildflowers bloom here throughout the summer. ⊠ *End of Moro Rock–Crescent Meadow Rd., 2.6 miles east off Generals Hwy.*

Crystal Cave. One of more than 200 caves in Sequoia and Kings Canyon national parks, Crystal Cave is unusual in that it's composed largely of marble, the result of limestone being hardened under heat and pressure. It contains several impressive formations that today are much easier to make out, thanks to an environmentally sensitive relighting project. Unfortunately, some of the cave's formations have been damaged or destroyed by early 20th-century dynamite blasting. The standard tour will give you 45 minutes inside the cave. ⊠ *Crystal Cave Rd., 6 miles west off Generals Hwy.* ☎ *559/565–3759* ⊕ *www.sequoiahistory.org* ⊠ *$15* ⊙ *Mid-May–mid-Oct., daily 10–4.*

Fodor's Choice **General Sherman Tree.** Neither the world's tallest nor oldest sequoia,
★ General Sherman is nevertheless tops in volume—and it is still putting on weight, adding the equivalent of a 60-foot-tall tree every year to its 2.7 million-pound mass. ⊠ *Generals Hwy. (Rte. 198), 2 miles south of Lodgepole Visitor Center.*

Mineral King. This subalpine valley sits at 7,800 feet at the end of a steep, winding road. The trip from the park's entrance can take up to two hours. This is the highest point to which you can drive in the park. ⊠ *End of Mineral King Rd., 25 miles east of Generals Hwy. (Rte. 198), east of Three Rivers.*

Fodor's Choice **Moro Rock.** Sequoia National Park's best non-tree attraction offers pan-
★ oramic views to those fit and determined enough to mount its 350-ish steps. In a case where the journey rivals the destination, Moro's stone stairway is so impressive in its twisty inventiveness that it's on the National Register of Historic Places. The rock's 6,725-foot summit overlooks the Middle Fork Canyon, sculpted by the Kaweah River and approaching the depth of Arizona's Grand Canyon, although smoggy, hazy air almost always compromises the view. ⊠ *Moro Rock–Crescent Meadow Rd., 2 miles east off Generals Hwy. (Rte. 198) to parking area.*

Tunnel Log. It's been almost 45 years since you could drive through a standing sequoia—and that was in Yosemite National Park's Mariposa Grove, not here. This 275-foot tree fell in 1937, and soon a 17-foot-wide, 8-foot-high hole was cut through it for vehicular passage that continues today. Large vehicles take the nearby bypass. ✉ *Moro Rock–Crescent Meadow Rd., 2 miles east of Generals Hwy. (Rte. 198).*

EDUCATIONAL OFFERINGS

CLASSES AND SEMINARS

Evening Programs. In summer, the park shows documentary films and slide shows, and has evening lectures. Locations and times vary; pick up a schedule at any visitor center or check bulletin boards near ranger stations. ☎ *559/565–3341.*

Seminars. Expert naturalists lead seminars on a range of topics, including birds, wildflowers, geology, botany, photography, park history, backpacking, and pathfinding. Some courses offer transferable credits. Reserve in advance.

Sequoia Natural History Association. For information and prices, pick up a course catalogue at any visitor center or contact the Sequoia Natural History Association. ☎ *559/565–3759* ⊕ *www.sequoiahistory.org.*

16

Sequoia Sightseeing Tours. The only licensed tour operator in either park offers daily interpretive sightseeing tours in a 10-passenger van with a friendly, knowledgeable guide. Reservations are essential. The company also offers private tours of Kings Canyon. ✉ *Three Rivers* ☎ *559/561–4489* ⊕ *www.sequoiatours.com* 🖿 *$65 half-day tour, $88 full-day tour.*

RANGER PROGRAMS

Free Nature Programs. Almost any summer day, half-hour to 1½-hour ranger talks and walks explore subjects such as the life of the sequoia, the geology of the park, and the habits of bears. Giant Forest, Lodgepole Visitor Center, Wuksachi Village, and Dorst Creek Campground are frequent starting points. Check bulletin boards throughout the park for the week's offerings.

SPORTS AND THE OUTDOORS

The best way to see Sequoia is to take a hike. Unless you do so, you'll miss out on the up-close grandeur of mist wafting among deeply scored, red-orange tree trunks bigger than you've ever seen. If it's winter, put on some snowshoes or cross-country skis and plunge into the snow-swaddled woodland. There are not too many other outdoor options: no off-road driving is allowed in the parks, and no special provisions have been made for bicycles. Boating, rafting, and snowmobiling also are prohibited.

BIRD-WATCHING

More than 200 species of birds inhabit Sequoia and Kings Canyon national parks. Not seen in most parts of the United States, the white-headed woodpecker and the pileated woodpecker are common in most mid-elevation areas here. There are also many hawks and owls, including the renowned spotted owl. Species are diverse in both parks due to the changes in elevation, and range from warblers, kingbirds, thrushes, and sparrows in the foothills to goshawk, blue grouse, red-breasted nuthatch, and brown creeper at the highest elevations. Ranger-led bird-watching tours are held on a sporadic basis. Call the park's main information number to find out more about these tours.

Sequoia Natural History Association. The association's highly regarded Sequoia Field Institute conducts single-day and multiday "edventure" tours that include backpacking hikes, natural-history walks, and kayaking excursions. ⊠ *47050 Generals Hwy. #10, Three Rivers* ☎ *559/565–3759* ⊕ *www.sequoiahistory.org.*

CROSS-COUNTRY SKIING

Wuksachi Lodge. Rent skis here. Depending on snowfall amounts, instruction may also be available. Reservations are recommended. Marked trails cut through Giant Forest, just 5 miles south of the lodge. ⊠ *Off Generals Hwy. (Rte. 198), 2 miles north of Lodgepole* ☎ *559/565–4070* ⊠ *$23–$30 ski rental* ☉ *Nov.–May (unless no snow), daily 9–4.*

HIKING

The best way to see the park is to hike it. The grandeur and majesty of the Sierra is best seen up close. Carry a hiking map—available at any visitor center—and plenty of water. Check with rangers for current trail conditions, and be aware of rapidly changing weather. As a rule of thumb, plan on trekking about a mile per hour.

EASY

Fodor's Choice ★ **Congress Trail.** This easy 2-mile trail, arguably the best hike in the parks in terms of natural beauty, is a paved loop that begins near General Sherman Tree and winds through the heart of the sequoia forest. You'll get close-up views of more big trees here than on any other Sequoia hike. Watch for the clusters known as the House and Senate. An easy offshoot leads to Crescent Meadow, where in summer you can catch free shuttles back to the Sherman parking lot. ■TIP→ **Be sure to stop and gawk at the President Tree, which supplanted the General Grant Tree in 2012 as the world's second largest in volume (behind the General Sherman Tree).** ⊠ *Trail begins off Generals Hwy. (Rte. 198), 2 miles north of Giant Forest.*

Crescent Meadow Trails. John Muir reportedly called Crescent Meadow the "gem of the Sierra." Brilliant wildflowers bloom here by midsummer, and a 1.8-mile trail loops around the meadow. A 1.6-mile trail begins at Crescent Meadow and leads to Tharp's Log, a cabin built from a fire-hollowed sequoia. ⊠ *Trail begins at the end of Moro Rock–Crescent Meadow Rd., 2.6 miles east off Generals Hwy. (Rte. 198).*

MODERATE

Tokopah Falls Trail. This moderate trail follows the Marble Fork of the Kaweah River for 1.75 miles one way and dead-ends below the impressive granite cliffs and cascading waterfall of Tokopah Canyon. It takes 2½ to 4 hours to make the 3.5-mile round-trip journey. The trail passes through a mixed-conifer forest. ⊠ *Trail begins off Generals Hwy. (Rte. 198), ¼ mile north of Lodgepole Campground.*

CLOSE UP

Plants and Wildlife in Sequoia and Kings Canyon

The parks can be divided into three distinct zones. In the west (1,500–5,000 feet) are the rolling, lower elevation foothills, covered with shrubby chaparral vegetation or golden grasslands dotted with oaks. Chamise, red-barked manzanita, and the occasional yucca plant grow here. Fields of white popcorn flower cover the hillsides in spring, and the yellow fiddleneck flourishes. In summer, intense heat and absence of rain cause the hills to turn golden brown. Wildlife includes the California ground squirrel, noisy blue-and-gray scrub jay, black bear, coyote, skunk, and gray fox.

At middle elevation (5,000–9,000 feet), where the giant sequoia belt resides, rock formations mix with meadows and huge stands of evergreens—red and white fir, incense cedar, and

ponderosa pines, to name a few. Wildflowers such as yellow blazing star and red Indian paintbrush bloom in spring and summer. The mule deer, golden-mantled ground squirrel, Steller's jay, and black bear (most active in fall) inhabit the area, as does the chickaree.

The high alpine section of the parks is extremely rugged, with a string of rocky peaks reaching above 13,000 feet to Mt. Whitney's 14,494 feet. Fierce weather and scarcity of soil make vegetation and wildlife sparse. Foxtail and whitebark pines have gnarled and twisted trunks, the result of high wind, heavy snowfall, and freezing temperatures. In summer you can see the yellow-bellied marmot, pika, weasel, mountain chickadee, and Clark's nutcracker.

DIFFICULT

Mineral King Trails. Many trails to the high country begin at Mineral King. The two most popular day hikes are Eagle Lake and Timber Gap, both of which are somewhat strenuous. At 7,800 feet, this is the highest point to which one can drive in either of the parks. Get a map and provisions, and check with rangers about conditions. ⊠ *Trailhead at end of Mineral King Rd., 25 miles east of Generals Hwy. (Rte. 198).*

HORSEBACK RIDING

Trips take you through redwood forests, flowering meadows, across the Sierra, or even up to Mt. Whitney. Costs per person range from $45 for a one-hour guided ride to around $275 per day for fully guided trips for which the packers do all the cooking and camp chores.

TOURS AND OUTFITTERS

Horse Corral Pack Station. Hourly, half-day, full-day, or overnight trips through Sequoia are available for beginning and advanced riders. ⊠ *Off Big Meadows Rd., 12 miles east of Generals Hwy. (Rte. 198) between Sequoia and Kings Canyon national parks* ☎ *559/565–3404 in summer, 559/564–6429 year-round* ⊠ *$35–$145 day trips* ☉ *May–Sept.*

SLEDDING AND SNOWSHOEING

The Wolverton area, on Route 198 near Giant Forest, is a popular sledding spot, where sleds, inner tubes, and platters are allowed. You can buy sleds and saucers, starting at $10, at the Wuksachi Lodge (☎ *559/565–4070*), 2 miles north of Lodgepole.

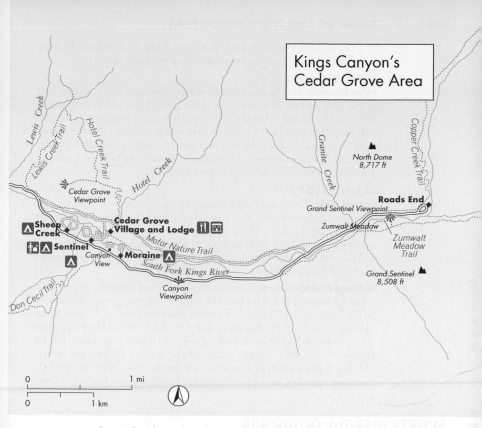

Kings Canyon's Cedar Grove Area

Lewis Creek

Lewis Creek Trail

Hotel Creek Trail

Hotel Creek

Granite Creek

Copper Creek Trail

North Dome
8,717 ft

Cedar Grove
Viewpoint

Grand Sentinel Viewpoint

Roads End

Sheep
Creek

Cedar Grove
Village and Lodge

Zumwalt Meadow

Zumwalt
Meadow
Trail

Sentinel

Motor Nature Trail

Canyon
View

Moraine

South Fork Kings River

Grand Sentinel
8,508 ft

Don Cecil Trail

Canyon
Viewpoint

0 ——— 1 mi

0 ——— 1 km

The Wuksachi Lodge also rents snowshoes for $18–$27. Naturalists lead snowshoe walks here and around Giant Forest, conditions permitting, on Saturdays and holidays. Snowshoes are provided for a $1 donation. Make reservations and check schedules at Giant Forest Museum (☎ 559/565–4480) or Wuksachi Lodge.

KINGS CANYON NATIONAL PARK

EXPLORING

SCENIC DRIVES

Kings Canyon Scenic Byway. About 10 miles east of Grant Grove Village is Jackson View, where you'll first see Kings River Canyon. Near Yucca Point, it's thousands of feet deeper than the much more famous Grand Canyon. Continuing through Sequoia National Forest past Boyden Cavern, you'll enter the larger portion of Kings Canyon National Park and, eventually, Cedar Grove Village. Past there, the U-shaped canyon becomes broader. Be sure to allow an hour to walk through Zumwalt Meadow. Also, be sure to park and take the less-than-five-minute walks to the base of Grizzly Falls and Roaring River Falls. The drive dead-ends at a big parking lot, the launch point for many backpackers. Driving the byway takes about one hour each way (without stops).

HISTORIC SITES

Fallen Monarch. This Sequoia's hollow base was used in the second half of the 19th century as a home for settlers, a saloon, and even to stable U.S. Cavalry horses. As you walk through it (assuming entry is permitted, which has not always been the case in recent years), check out how little the wood has decayed, and imagine yourself tucked safely inside, sheltered from a storm or protected from the searing heat. ⊠ *Trailhead 1 mile north of Grant Grove Visitor Center.*

SCENIC STOPS

Canyon View. There are many places along the scenic byway to pull over for sightseeing, but this special spot showcases evidence of the canyon's glacial history. Here, maybe more than anywhere else, you'll understand why John Muir compared Kings Canyon vistas with those in Yosemite. ⊠ *Kings Canyon Scenic Byway (Rte. 180), 1 mile east of the Cedar Grove turnoff.*

Redwood Mountain Grove. If you are serious about sequoias, you should consider visiting this, the world's largest big-tree grove. Within its 2,078 acres are 2,172 sequoias whose diameters exceed 10 feet. Your options range from the distant (pulling off the Generals Highway onto an overlook) to the intimate (taking a 6- to 10-mile hike down into its richest regions, which include two of the world's 25 heaviest trees). ⊠ *Drive 5 miles south of Grant Grove on Generals Hwy. (Rte. 198), then turn right at Quail Flat; follow it 1½ miles to the Redwood Canyon trailhead.*

SPORTS AND THE OUTDOORS

CROSS-COUNTRY SKIING

Roads to Grant Grove are accessible during heavy snowfall, making the trails here a good choice over Sequoia's Giant Forest when harsh weather hits.

HIKING

You can enjoy many of Kings Canyon's sights from your car, but the giant gorge of the Kings River Canyon and the sweeping vistas of some of the highest mountains in the United States are best seen on foot. Carry a hiking map—available at any visitor center—and plenty of water. Check with rangers for current trail conditions, and be aware of rapidly changing weather.

Road's End Permit Station. If you're planning to hike the backcountry, you can pick up a permit and information on the backcountry at Road's End Permit Station. You can also rent or buy bear canisters, a must for campers. When the station is closed, you can still complete a self-service permit form. ⊠ *6 miles east of Cedar Grove Visitor Center, at the end of Kings Canyon Scenic Byway* ☉ *Late May–late Sept., daily 7–3:30.*

Hiking in the Sierra Mountains is a thrilling experience, putting you amid some of the world's highest trees.

EASY

Fodor's Choice ★

Zumwalt Meadow Trail. Rangers say this is the best (and most popular) day hike in the Cedar Grove area. Just 1.5 miles long, it offers three visual treats: the South Fork of the Kings River, the lush meadow, and the high granite walls above, including those of Grand Sentinel and North Dome. ⊠ *Trailhead 4½ miles east of Cedar Grove Village turnoff from Kings Canyon Scenic Byway.*

MODERATE

Big Baldy. This hike climbs 600 feet and 2 miles up to the 8,209-feet summit of Big Baldy. Your reward is the view of Redwood Canyon. The round-trip hike is 4 miles. *Moderate.* ⊠ *Trailhead 8 miles south of Grant Grove on Generals Hwy. (Rte. 198).*

Redwood Canyon Trail. Avoid the hubbub of Giant Forest and its General Sherman Tree by hiking down to Redwood Canyon, the world's largest grove of sequoias. Opt for the trail toward Hart Tree, and you'll soon lose track of how many humongous trees you pass along the 6-mile loop. Count on spending four to six peaceful hours here—although some backpackers linger overnight (wilderness permit required). ⊠ *Trail begins off Quail Flat. Drive 5 miles south of Grant Grove on Generals Hwy. (Rte. 198), then turn right at Quail Flat; follow it 1½ miles to the Redwood Canyon trailhead.*

DIFFICULT

Hotel Creek Trail. For gorgeous canyon views, take this trail from the canyon floor at Cedar Grove up a series of switchbacks until it splits. Follow the route left through chaparral to the forested ridge and rocky outcrop known as Cedar Grove Overlook, where you can see the Kings

CLOSE UP

Mt. Whitney

At 14,494 feet, Mt. Whitney is the highest point in the contiguous United States and the crown jewel of Sequoia National Park's wild eastern side. The peak looms high above the tiny, high-mountain desert community of Lone Pine, where numerous Hollywood Westerns have been filmed. The high mountain ranges, arid landscape, and scrubby brush of the Eastern Sierra are beautiful in their vastness and austerity.

Despite the mountain's scale, you can't see it from the more traveled west side of the park because it is hidden behind the Great Western Divide. The only way to access Mt. Whitney from the main part of the park is to circumnavigate the Sierra Nevada via an eight-hour, nearly 300-mile drive outside the park. No road ascends the peak; the best vantage point from which to catch a glimpse of the mountain is at the end of Whitney Portal Road. The 13 miles of winding road leads from U.S. 395 at Lone Pine to the trailhead for the hiking route to the top of the mountain. Whitney Portal Road is closed in winter.

River Canyon stretching below. This strenuous 5-mile round-trip hike gains 1,200 feet and takes three to four hours to complete. For a longer hike, return via Lewis Creek Trail for an 8-mile loop. ⊠ *Trailhead at Cedar Grove pack station, 1 mile east of Cedar Grove Village.*

HORSEBACK RIDING

One-day destinations by horseback out of Cedar Grove include Mist Falls and Upper Bubb's Creek. In the backcountry, many equestrians head for Volcanic Lakes or Granite Basin, ascending trails that reach elevations of 10,000 feet. Costs per person range from $45 for a one-hour guided ride to around $275 per day for fully guided trips for which the packers do all the cooking and camp chores.

TOURS AND OUTFITTERS

Cedar Grove Pack Station. Take a day or overnight trip along the Kings River Canyon with Cedar Grove Pack Station. Popular routes include the Rae Lakes Loop and Monarch Divide. ⊠ *Kings Canyon Scenic Byway, 1 mile east of Cedar Grove Village* ☎ *559/565–3464 in summer, 559/337–2314 off-season* ☎ *Call for prices* ☉ *May–Oct.*

Grant Grove Stables. A one- or two-hour trip through Grant Grove leaving from Grant Grove Stables is a good way to get a taste of horseback riding in Kings Canyon. ⊠ *Rte. 180, ½ mile north of Grant Grove Visitor Center* ☎ *559/335–9292 mid-June–Sept., 559/594–9307 Oct.–mid-June* ☎ *$45–$70* ☉ *June–Labor Day, daily 8–6.*

SLEDDING AND SNOWSHOEING

In winter, Kings Canyon has a few great places to play in the snow. Sleds, inner tubes, and platters are allowed at both the Azalea Campground area on Grant Tree Road, ¼ mile north of Grant Grove Visitor Center, and at the Big Stump picnic area, 2 miles north of the lower Route 180 entrance to the park.

Snowshoeing is good around Grant Grove, where you can take naturalist-guided snowshoe walks on Saturdays and holidays mid-December through mid-March as conditions permit.

WHERE TO EAT

Prices in the reviews are the average cost of a main course at dinner or, if dinner is not served, at lunch.

SEQUOIA

$ ✕**Lodgepole Market and Snack Bar.** The choices here run the gamut from
CAFÉ simple to very simple, with the three counters only a few strides apart in a central eating complex. For hot food, venture into the snack bar. The deli sells prepackaged sandwiches along with ice cream scooped from tubs. You'll find other prepackaged foods and souvenirs in the market. ⑤ *Average main: $6 ⊠ Next to Lodgepole Visitor Center ☎ 559/565–3301 ⊙ Closed late Sept.–mid-Apr.*

$$$ ✕**Wolverton Barbecue.** Weather permitting, diners congregate on a
BARBECUE wooden porch that looks directly out onto a small but strikingly verdant meadow. In addition to the predictable meats such as ribs and chicken, the all-you-can-eat buffet has sides that include baked beans, corn on the cob, and potato salad. Following the meal, listen to a ranger talk and clear your throat for a campfire sing-along. Purchase tickets at Lodgepole Market, Wuksachi Lodge, or Wolverton Recreation Area's office. ⑤ *Average main: $24 ⊠ Wolverton Rd., 1½ miles northeast off Generals Hwy. (Rte. 198) ☎ 559/565–4070, 559/565–3301 ⊙ No lunch. Closed Mon.–Thurs. and early Sept.–mid-June.*

$$ ✕**Wuksachi Village Dining Room.** Huge windows run the length of the high-
AMERICAN ceilinged dining room, and a large fireplace on the far wall warms both the body and the soul. The diverse dinner menu—by far the best in the two parks—includes filet mignon, rainbow trout, and vegetarian pasta dishes, in addition to the ever-present burgers. The children's menu is economically priced. Breakfast and lunch also are served. ⑤ *Average main: $21 ⊠ Wuksachi Village ☎ 559/565–4070 ⬥ Reservations essential.*

KINGS CANYON

$ ✕**Cedar Grove Restaurant.** For a small operation, the menu here is sur-
AMERICAN prisingly extensive, with dinner entrées such as pasta, pork chops, and steak. For breakfast, try the biscuits and gravy, French toast, pancakes, or cold cereal. Burgers (including vegetarian patties) and hot dogs dominate the lunch choices. Outside, a patio dining area overlooks the Kings River. ⑤ *Average main: $13 ⊠ Cedar Grove Village ☎ 559/565–0100 ⊙ Closed Oct.–May.*

$$ ✕**Grant Grove Restaurant.** In a no-frills, open room, this restaurant offers
AMERICAN basic American fare such as pancakes for breakfast or hot sandwiches and chicken for later meals. Vegetarians and vegans will have to content themselves with a simple salad. Take-out service is available. ⑤ *Average main: $19 ⊠ Grant Grove Village ☎ 559/335–5500.*

16

WHERE TO STAY

Prices in the reviews are the lowest cost of a standard double room in high season. For expanded hotel reviews, visit Fodors.com.

SEQUOIA

$$$
HOTEL
Fodor'sChoice
★

⌂ Wuksachi Lodge. The striking cedar-and-stone main building here is a fine example of how a structure can blend effectively with lovely mountain scenery. **Pros:** best place to stay in the parks; lots of wildlife. **Cons:** rooms can be small; main lodge is a few minutes' walk from guest rooms. ⑤ *Rooms from: $185* ⊠ *64740 Wuksachi Way, Wuksachi Village* ☎ *559/565–4070, 888/252–5757* ⊕ *www.visitsequoia.com* ⮐ *102 rooms.*

KINGS CANYON

$$$
HOTEL

⌂ John Muir Lodge. This modern, timber-sided lodge is nestled in a wooded area in the hills above Grant Grove Village and offers year-round accommodations. **Pros:** common room stays warm; it's far enough from the main road to be quiet. **Cons:** check-in is down in the village. ⑤ *Rooms from: $195* ⊠ *Kings Canyon Scenic Byway, ¼ mile north of Grant Grove Village* ☎ *559/335–5500, 866/522–6966* ⊕ *www. sequoia-kingscanyon.com* ⮐ *24 rooms, 6 suites.*

TRAVEL SMART
SOUTHERN
CALIFORNIA

GETTING HERE AND AROUND

Wherever you plan to go in Southern California, getting there will likely involve driving, even if you fly. With the exception of San Diego, major airports are usually far from main attractions. For example, four airports serve the Los Angeles area—but three of them are outside the city limits. Southern California's major airport hubs is LAX in Los Angeles, but satellite airports can be found around most major cities. When booking flights, it pays to check these locations, as you may find more convenient times and a better location in relation to your hotel. Most small cities have their own commercial airports, with connecting flights to larger cities—but service may be extremely limited, and it may be cheaper to rent a car and drive from L.A.

FROM LOS ANGELES TO:	BY AIR	BY CAR
San Diego	55 mins	2 hrs
Death Valley		6 hrs
San Francisco	1 hr 30 mins	5 hrs 30 mins
Monterey	1 hr 10 mins	5 hrs 25 mins
Santa Barbara	45 mins	1 hr 45 mins
Big Sur		5 hrs 30 mins
Sacramento	1 hr 25 mins	5 hrs 30 mins

▌ AIR TRAVEL

Flying time to California is about 5½ hours from New York and 4 hours from Chicago. Travel from London to Los Angeles is 11 hours and from Sydney approximately 14½. Flying between San Francisco and Los Angeles takes about 90 minutes.

AIRPORTS

Southern California's gateways are Los Angeles International Airport (LAX) and San Diego International Airport (SAN). Other Los Angeles airports include Long Beach (LGB), Bob Hope Airport (BUR), LA/Ontario (ONT), and John Wayne Airport (SNA).

Airport Information Bob Hope Airport ✉ Burbank ☎ 818/840-8840 ⊕ www. burbankairport.com. **John Wayne Airport** ☎ 949/252-5200 ⊕ www.ocair.com. **LA/ Ontario International Airport** ☎ 909/937-2700 ⊕ www.flyontario.com. **Long Beach Airport** ☎ 562/570-2600 ⊕ www.lgb.org. **Los Angeles International Airport** ☎ 310/646-5252 ⊕ www.lawa.org/lax. **Oakland International Airport** ☎ 510/563-3300 ⊕ www. flyoakland.com. **Sacramento International Airport** ☎ 916/929-5411 ⊕ www.sacramento. aero/smf. **San Diego International Airport** ☎ 619/400-2404 ⊕ www.san.org.**San Francisco International Airport** ☎ 650/821-8211, 800/435-9736 ⊕ www.flysfo.com. **San Jose International Airport** ☎ 408/392-3600 ⊕ www.flysanjose.com.

FLIGHTS

United, with hubs in San Francisco and Los Angeles, has the greatest number of flights into and within California. But most national and many international airlines fly to the state. Southwest Airlines connects smaller cities within California, often from satellite airports near major cities.

Airline Contacts Air Canada ☎ 888/247-2262 ⊕ www.aircanada.com.**Alaska Airlines/ Horizon Air** ☎ 800/252-7522 ⊕ www. alaskaair.com. **American Airlines** ☎ 800/433-7300 ⊕ www.aa.com. **British Airways** ☎ 800/247-9297 ⊕ www.britishairways.com. **Cathay Pacific** ☎ 800/233-2742 ⊕ www. cathaypacific.com. **Delta Airlines** ☎ 800/221-1212 for U.S. reservations, 800/241-4141 for international reservations ⊕ www.delta.com. **Frontier Airlines** ☎ 800/432-1359 ⊕ www.flyfrontier.com. **Japan Air Lines**

800/525-3663 ⊕ www.jal.com. JetBlue
800/538-2583 ⊕ www.jetblue.com. Qantas
800/227-4500 ⊕ www.qantas.com.
au. **Southwest Airlines** 800/435-9792
⊕ www.southwest.com. **Spirit Airlines**
800/772-7117 ⊕ www.spirit.com. **United
Airlines** 800/864-8331 for U.S. reservations, 800/538-2929 for international
reservations ⊕ www.united.com. **US Airways**
800/428-4322 for U.S. and Canada reservations, 800/622-1015 for international reservations ⊕ www.usairways.com.

▮ BOAT TRAVEL

CRUISES

A number of major cruise lines offer trips
that begin or end in California. Most
voyages sail north along the Pacific Coast
to Alaska or south to Mexico. California cruise ports include Los Angeles, San
Diego, and San Francisco.

Cruise Lines Carnival Cruise Line
305/599-2600, 800/227-6482 ⊕ www.
carnival.com. **Celebrity Cruises** 800/647-
2251, 800/437-3111 ⊕ www.celebritycruises.
com. **Crystal Cruises** 310/785-9300,
800/446-6620 ⊕ www.crystalcruises.com.
Holland America Line 206/281-3535,
877/932-4259 ⊕ www.hollandamerica.com.
Norwegian Cruise Line 305/436-4000,
866/234-7350 ⊕ www.ncl.com. **Princess
Cruises** 661/753-0000, 800/774-6237
⊕ www.princess.com. **Regent Seven Seas
Cruises** 954/776-6123, 877/505-5370
⊕ www.rssc.com.**Royal Caribbean International** 305/539-6000, 866/562-7625
⊕ www.royalcaribbean.com. **Silversea Cruises**
954/522-4477, 877/276-6816 ⊕ www.
silversea.com.

▮ BUS TRAVEL

Greyhound is the major bus carrier in California. Regional bus service is available
in metropolitan areas.

Bus Information Greyhound 800/231-
2222 ⊕ www.greyhound.com.

▮ CAR TRAVEL

There are two basic north–south routes in
California: Interstate 5 runs inland most
of the way from the Oregon border to
the Mexican border; and U.S. 101 hugs
the coast for part of the route from Oregon to Mexico. A slower but much more
scenic option is to take California State
Route 1, also referred to as Highway 1
and the Pacific Coast Highway, which
winds along much of the California coast
and provides an occasionally hair-raising,
but breathtaking, ride.

From north to south, the state's east–
west interstates are Interstate 80, Interstate 15, Interstate 10, and Interstate 8.
Much of California is mountainous, and
you may encounter winding roads, frequently cliff-side, and steep mountain
grades. In winter, roads crossing the
Sierra from east to west may close at
any time due to weather. Also in winter,
Interstate 5 north of Los Angeles closes
during snowstorms.

The flying and driving times in the
accompanying charts represent best-case
scenario estimates, but know that the
infamous California traffic jam can occur
at any time.

GASOLINE

Gasoline prices in California vary widely,
depending on location, oil company, and
whether you buy it at a full-service or
self-serve pump. It's less expensive to
buy fuel in the southern part of the state
than in the north. If you're planning to
travel near Nevada, you can save a bit by
purchasing gas over the border. Gas stations are plentiful throughout the state.
Most stay open late (24 hours along
major highways and in big cities), except
in rural areas, where Sunday hours are
limited and where you may drive long
stretches without a chance to refuel.

ROAD CONDITIONS

Rainy weather can make driving along
the coast or in the mountains treacherous. Some of the smaller routes over
mountain ranges and in the deserts

are prone to flash flooding. When the rains are severe, coastal Highway 1 can quickly become a slippery nightmare, buffeted by strong winds and obstructed by falling debris from the cliffs above. When the weather is particularly bad, Highway 1 may be closed due to mud and rock slides.

Road Conditions Caltrans Current Highway Conditions ☎ 800/427-7623 ⊕ www.dot.ca.gov.

WEATHER CONDITIONS
National Weather Service ☎ 707/443-6484 *northernmost California, 831/656-1725 San Francisco Bay area and central California, 775/673-8100 Reno, Lake Tahoe, and northern Sierra, 805/988-6610 Los Angeles area, 858/675-8700 San Diego area* ⊕ *www.weather.gov.*

ROADSIDE EMERGENCIES
Dial 911 to report accidents on the road and to reach the police, the California Highway Patrol (CHP), or the fire department. On some rural highways and on most interstates, look for emergency phones on the side of the road. In Los Angeles, the Metro Freeway Service Patrol provides assistance to stranded motorists under nonemergency conditions. Call #399 on your cell phone to reach them 24 hours a day.

RULES OF THE ROAD
All passengers must wear seat belts at all times. It is illegal to leave a child six years of age or younger unattended in a motor vehicle. A child must be secured in a federally approved child passenger restraint system and ride in the back seat until at least eight years of age or until the child is at least 4 feet 9 inches tall. Children who are eight but don't meet the height requirement must ride in a booster seat or a car seat. Unless otherwise indicated, right turns are allowed at red lights after you've come to a full stop. Left turns between two one-way streets are allowed at red lights after you've come to a full stop.

Drivers with a blood-alcohol level higher than 0.08 who are stopped by police are subject to arrest, and those under 21 convicted of driving with a level of 0.01 or more can have their driving privileges revoked for a year. California's drunk-driving laws are extremely tough—violators may have their licenses immediately suspended, pay hefty fines, and spend the night in jail.

The speed limit on many interstate highways is 70 mph; unlimited-access roads are usually 55 mph. In cities, freeway speed limits are between 55 mph and 65 mph. Many city routes have commuter lanes during rush hour.

You must turn on your headlights whenever weather conditions require the use of windshield wipers.

Those 18 and older must use a hands-free device for their mobile phones while driving; those under 18 may not use mobile phones or wireless devices while driving. Texting on a wireless device is illegal for all drivers. Smoking in a vehicle where a minor is present is an infraction. For more information refer to the Department of Motor Vehicles driver's handbook at ⊕ *www.dmv.ca.gov.*

CAR RENTAL
When you reserve a car, ask about cancellation penalties, taxes, drop-off charges (if you're planning to pick up the car in one city and leave it in another), and surcharges (for being under or over a certain age, for additional drivers, or for driving across state or country borders or beyond a specific distance from your point of rental). All of these things can add substantially to your costs. Request car seats and extras such as GPS when you book.

Rates are sometimes—but not always—better if you book in advance or reserve through a rental agency's website. There are other reasons to book ahead, though: for popular destinations, during busy times of the year, or to ensure that you get certain types of cars (vans, SUVs, exotic sports cars).

■TIP→ Make sure that a confirmed reservation guarantees you a car. Agencies sometimes overbook, particularly for busy weekends and holiday periods.

A car is essential in most parts of California. In sprawling cities such as Los Angeles and San Diego you'll have to take the freeways to get just about anywhere.

Rates statewide for the least expensive vehicle begin as low as $30 a day, usually on weekends, and less than $200 a week (though they increase rapidly from here). This does not include additional fees or the tax on car rentals, which is 9.00% in Los Angeles, 8.75% in San Francisco, and 8.00% in San Diego.Be sure to shop around—you can get a decent deal by carefully shopping the major car rental companies' websites. Also, rates are sometimes lower in San Diego; compare prices by city before you book, and ask about "drop charges" if you plan to return the car in a city other than the one where you rented the vehicle. If you pick up at an airport, there may also be a facility charge of as much as $12 per rental; ask when you book.

In California, you must have a valid driver's license and be 21 to rent a car; rates may be higher if you're under 25. Some agencies will not rent to those under 25; check when you book. Non-U.S. residents must have a license with text that is in the Roman alphabet that is valid for the entire rental period. Though it need not be entirely written in English, it must have English letters that clearly identify it as a driver's license. In addition, most companies also require an international license; check in advance.

If you dream of driving down the coast with the top down, or you want to explore the desert landscape not visible from the road, consider renting a specialty vehicle. Agencies that specialize in convertibles and sport-utility vehicles will often arrange airport delivery in larger cities. Unlike most of the major agencies, the following companies guarantee the car class that you book.

Specialty Car Agencies Enterprise Exotic Car Rentals ☎ *800/400-8412, 866/458-9227 locations in San Francisco, Los Angeles, and other Southern California locations ⊕ exotic-cars.enterprise.com.* **Beverly Hills Rent a Car** ☎ *800/479-5996 San Francisco and several locations in Los Angeles, 310/274-6969* ⊕ *www.bhrentacar.com.* **Midway Car Rental** ☎ *866/717-6802 several locations in Los Angeles* ⊕ *www.midwaycarrental.com.*

Major Rental Agencies
Alamo ☎ *800/462-5266* ⊕ *www.alamo.com.* **Avis** ☎ *800/331-1212* ⊕ *www.avis.com.* **Budget** ☎ *800/527-0700* ⊕ *www.budget. com.* **Hertz** ☎ *800/654-3131* ⊕ *www.hertz. com.* **National Car Rental** ☎ *877/222-9058* ⊕ *www.nationalcar.com.*

■ TRAIN TRAVEL

One of the most beautiful train trips in the country, Amtrak's *Coast Starlight*, begins in Los Angeles and hugs the Pacific Coast to San Luis Obispo before it turns inland for the rest of its journey to Portland and Seattle. The *California Zephyr* travels from Chicago to Oakland via Denver; the *Pacific Surfliner* connects San Diego and San Luis Obispo via Los Angeles and Santa Barbara with multiple departures daily; and the *Sunset Limited* runs from Los Angeles to New Orleans via Arizona, New Mexico, and Texas.

Information Amtrak ☎ *800/872-7245* ⊕ *www.amtrak.com.*

ESSENTIALS

■ ACCOMMODATIONS

The lodgings we review are the top choices in each price category. ⇨ *For an expanded review of each property, please see ⊕ www.fodors.com.* We don't specify whether the facilities cost extra; when pricing accommodations, ask what's included and what costs extra.

Most hotels require you to give your credit-card details before they will confirm your reservation. If you don't feel comfortable emailing this information, ask if you can fax it (some places even prefer faxes). However you book, get confirmation in writing and have a copy of it handy when you check in.

Be sure you understand the hotel's cancellation policy. Some places allow you to cancel without any kind of penalty— even if you prepaid to secure a discounted rate—if you cancel at least 24 hours in advance. Others require you to cancel a week in advance or penalize you the cost of one night. Small inns and B&Bs are most likely to require you to cancel far in advance. Most hotels allow children under a certain age to stay in their parents' room at no extra charge, but others charge for them as extra adults; find out the cutoff age for discounts.

Many B&Bs are entirely nonsmoking, and hotels and motels are decreasing their inventory of smoking rooms; if you require one, ask when you book if any are available.

BED-AND-BREAKFASTS

California has more than 1,000 bed-and-breakfasts. You'll find everything from simple homestays to lavish luxury lodgings, many in historic hotels and homes. The California Association of Bed and Breakfast Inns has about 300 member properties that you can locate and book through its website.

Reservation Services Bed & Breakfast.com ☎ *512/322–2710, 800/462–2632* ⊕ *www. bedandbreakfast.com.* **Bed & Breakfast Inns Online** ☎ *800/215–7365* ⊕ *www.bbonline. com.* **BnB Finder.com** ☎ *212/480–0414, 888/547–8226* ⊕ *www.bnbfinder.com.* **California Association of Bed and Breakfast Inns** ☎ *800/373–9251* ⊕ *www.cabbi.com.*

■ COMMUNICATIONS

INTERNET

Internet access is widely available in urban areas, but it's usually more difficult to get online in the state's rural areas. Most hotels offer some kind of connection—usually broadband or Wi-Fi. Many hotels charge a daily fee (about $10) for Internet access. Cybercafés are located throughout California.

Cybercafés ⊕ *www.cybercafes.com.*

■ EATING OUT

California has led the pack in bringing natural and organic foods to the forefront of American cooking. Though rooted in European cuisine, California cooking sometimes has strong Asian and Latin influences. Wherever you go, you're likely to find that dishes are made with fresh produce and other local ingredients.

The restaurants we list are the cream of the crop in each price category. ⇨ *For price information, see the planner in each chapter.*

CUTTING COSTS

■TIP➜ If you're on a budget, take advantage of the "small plates" craze sweeping California by ordering several appetizer-size portions and having a glass of wine at the bar, rather than having a full meal. Also, the better grocery and specialty-food stores have grab-and-go sections, with prepared foods on par with restaurant cooking, perfect for picnicking (remember, it rarely rains between May and October). At resort areas in the off-season (such as San Diego in January), you can often find two-for-one dinner specials at upper-end restaurants; check coupon apps or local papers or with visitor bureaus.

RESERVATIONS AND DRESS

Regardless of where you are, it's a good idea to make a reservation if you can. We only mention reservations specifically when they are essential (there's no other way you'll ever get a table) or when they are not accepted. For popular restaurants, book as far ahead as you can (often 30 days), and reconfirm as soon as you arrive. (Large parties should always call ahead to check the reservations policy.) We mention dress only when men are required to wear a jacket or a jacket and tie.

Online reservation services make it easy to book a table before you even leave home. OpenTable covers many California cities.

Contacts OpenTable ⊕ *www.opentable.com.*

WINES, BEER, AND SPIRITS

Throughout the state, you can visit wineries, many of which have tasting rooms and offer tours. Microbreweries are an emerging trend in the state's cities and in some rural areas in northern California. The legal drinking age is 21.

▮ HEALTH

Do not fly within 24 hours of scuba diving. Smoking is illegal in all California bars and restaurants, including on outdoor dining patios in some cities. If you have an existing medical condition that may require emergency treatment, be aware that many rural and mountain communities have only daytime clinics, not hospitals with 24-hour emergency rooms.

▮ HOURS OF OPERATION

Banks in California are typically open weekdays from 9 to 6 and Saturday morning; most are closed on Sunday and most holidays. Smaller shops usually operate from 10 to 6, with larger stores remaining open until 8 or later. Hours vary for museums, historical sites, and state parks, and many are closed one or more days a week, or for extended periods during off-season months. It's a good idea to check before you visit a tourist site.

▌MONEY

Los Angeles, San Diego, and San Francisco tend to be expensive cities to visit, and rates at coastal and desert resorts are almost as high. A day's admission to a major theme park can run as much as $87 per person, though you may be able to get discounts by purchasing tickets in advance online. Hotel rates average $150 to $250 a night (though you can find cheaper places), and dinners at even moderately priced restaurants often cost $20 to $40 per person. Costs in the Gold Country, the Far North, and the Death Valley/Mojave Desert region are considerably less—many fine Gold Country bed-and-breakfasts charge around $100 a night, and some motels in the Far North and the Mojave charge $70 to $90.

CREDIT CARDS

It's a good idea to inform your credit-card company before you travel. Otherwise, the credit-card company might put a hold on your card owing to unusual activity—not a good thing halfway through your trip. Record all your credit-card numbers—as well as the phone numbers to call if your cards are lost or stolen—in a safe place, so you're prepared should something go wrong. Both MasterCard and Visa have general numbers you can call (collect if you're abroad) if your card is lost, but you're better off calling the number of your issuing bank, since MasterCard and Visa normally just transfer you to your bank; your bank's number is usually printed on your card.

Reporting Lost Cards American Express 🕾 800/992–3404 in U.S., 715/343–7977 collect from abroad ⊕ www.americanexpress.com. **Discover** 🕾 800/347–2683 in U.S., 801/902–3100 collect from abroad ⊕ www.discovercard.com. **Diners Club** 🕾 800/234–6377 in U.S., 514/877–1577 collect from abroad ⊕ www.dinersclub.com. **MasterCard** 🕾 800/627–8372 in U.S., 636/722–7111 collect from abroad ⊕ www.mastercard.com. **Visa** 🕾 800/847–2911 in U.S., 303/967–1096 collect from abroad ⊕ www.visa.com.

▌SAFETY

California is a safe place to visit, as long as you take the usual precautions. In large cities ask the concierge or desk clerk to point out areas on your map that you should avoid. Lock valuables in a hotel safe when you're not using them. (Some hotels have in-room safes large enough to hold a laptop computer.) Keep an eye on your handbag when you're out in public. Security is high (but mostly invisible) at theme parks and resorts.

▌TAXES

Sales tax in California varies from about 7.5% to 10% and applies to all purchases except for food purchased in a grocery store; food consumed in a restaurant is taxed but take-out food purchases are not. Hotel taxes vary widely by region, from about 8% to 15.5%.

▌TIME

California is in the Pacific time zone. Pacific daylight time (PDT) is in effect from mid-March through early November; the rest of the year the clock is set to Pacific standard time (PST).

▮ TIPPING

Most service workers in California are fairly well paid compared to those in the rest of the country, and extravagant tipping is not the rule here. Exceptions include wealthy enclaves such as Beverly Hills, La Jolla, and San Francisco as well as the most expensive resort areas.

TIPPING GUIDELINES FOR CALIFORNIA	
Bartender	$1 per drink, or 10%–15% of tab per round of drinks
Bellhop	$1–$5 per bag, depending on the level of the hotel
Hotel Concierge	$5 or more, if he/she performs a service for you
Hotel Doorman	$1–$2 if he/she helps you get a cab
Valet Parking Attendant	$2 when you get your car
Hotel Maid	$2–$3 per person, per day; more in high-end hotels
Waiter	15%–20% (20%-25% is standard in upscale restaurants); nothing additional if a service charge is added to the bill
Skycap at Airport	$1–$3 per bag
Hotel Room-Service Waiter	15%–20% per delivery, even if a service charge was added since that fee goes to the hotel, not the waiter
Taxi Driver	15%–20%, but round up the fare to the next dollar amount
Tour Guide	15% of the cost of the tour, more depending on quality

▮ TOURS

Guided tours are a good option when you don't want to do it all yourself. You travel along with a group (sometimes large, sometimes small), stay in prebooked hotels, eat with your fellow travelers (the cost of meals is sometimes included in the price of your tour, sometimes not), and follow a schedule.

But not all guided tours are an if-it's-Tuesday-this-must-be-Yosemite experience. A knowledgeable guide can take you places that you might never discover on your own, and you may be pushed to see more than you would have otherwise. Tours aren't for everyone, but they can be just the thing for trips to places where making travel arrangements is difficult or time-consuming.

Whenever you book a guided tour, find out what's included and what isn't. A "land-only" tour includes all your travel (by bus, in most cases) in the destination, but not necessarily your flights to and from or even within it. Also, in most cases prices in tour brochures don't include fees and taxes. And remember that you'll be expected to tip your guide (in cash) at the end of the tour.

▮ VISITOR INFORMATION

The California Travel and Tourism Commission's website takes you to each region of California, with digital visitor guides in multiple languages, driving tours, maps, welcome center locations, information on local tours, links to bed-and-breakfasts, and a complete booking center. It also links you—via the Explore California menu—to the websites of city and regional tourism offices and attractions. ⇨ *For the numbers and websites of regional and city visitor bureaus and chambers of commerce see the "Planning" sections in each chapter.*

Contacts California Travel and Tourism Commission ✉ *Sacramento* ☏ *916/444-4429 information, 800/862-2543 brochures* ⊕ *www.visitcalifornia.com.*

INDEX

PHOTO CREDITS

Front cover: Ty Milford/Masterfile [Description: Encinitas, San Diego County]. 1, Greg Epperson/Shutterstock. 2, 5, Som Vembar, Fodors.com member. Chapter 1: Experience Southern California: 8–9, Doug Lemke/Shutterstock. 11 (left), Valhalla I Design & Conquer, Fodors.com member. 11 (right), Lisa M. Hamilton. 12, Robert Holmes. 13 (left), Vincent Thompson, Fodors.com member. 13 (right), Charlie_Oregon, fodors.com member. 15, Robert Holmes. 16, Stas Volik/Shutterstock. 17 (left), Robert Holmes. 17 (right), dgassa, fodors.com member. 18 (left), Scott Frances/Esto/©2003 J. Paul Getty Trust. 18 (top right), Yenwen Lu/iStockphoto. 18 (bottom right), Robert Holmes. 19 (top left), Sheldon Kralstein/iStockphoto. 19 (bottom left), iStockphoto. 19 (right), Christophe Testi/iStockphoto. 21, twin65a, Fodors.com member. 22, Robert Holmes. 23, Geir Olav Lyngfjell/Shutterstock. 24, Robert Holmes. 27 (left), sebastien burel/iStockphoto. 27 (right), Mot the barber/Flickr. 28 (top), Janine Bolliger/iStockphoto. 28 (bottom), Lise Gagne/iStockphoto. 29, iStockphoto. 30 (top right), Evan Meyer/iStockphoto. 30 (center right), Kyle Maass/iStockphoto. 30 (left), iStockphoto. 30 (bottom right), Lise Gagne/iStockphoto. 31, Tom Baker/Shutterstock. 32 (left), SuperStock/age fotostock. 32 (top right), CURAphotography/Shutterstock. 32 (bottom right), Michael Almond/iStockphoto. 33 (top), iStockphoto. 33 (bottom), Lise Gagne/iStockphoto. 34 (left), TebNad/Shutterstock. 34 (top right), Ross Stapleton-Gray/iStockphoto. 34 (bottom right), Jay Spooner/iStockphoto. 35 (top), Jay Spooner/iStockphoto. 35 (bottom), Lise Gagne/iStockphoto. 36, John Elk III / Alamy. Chapter 2: San Diego: 37, Brett Shoaf/Artistic Visuals Photography. 38, frogger256, Fodors.com member. 39 (top), rkkwan, Fodors.com member. 39 (bottom), Steve Rabin/iStockphoto. 40 and 45, Brett Shoaf/Artistic Visuals Photography. 53 (top), Dreyer Peter / age fotostock. 53 (bottom), Epukas/Wikimedia Commons [Public Domain]. 54, Robert Holmes. 55, Steve Snodgrass/Flickr. 56 (left and top center), fPat/Flickr. 56 (top right), Jim Epler/Flickr. 56 (bottom center), Matthew Field/wikipedia.org. 56 (bottom right), RENAULT Philippe / age fotostock. 57, lora_313/Flickr. 58 (left), Cburnett/wikipedia.org. 58 (right), Susann Parker / age fotostock. 59 (top), George Ostertag / age fotostock. 59 (bottom), George Ostertag / age fotostock. 66 and 67, SeaWorld San Diego. 70, Howard Sandler/iStockphoto. 74, Brett Shoaf/Artistic Visuals Photography. 77, Janet Fullwood. 89, George's at the Cove. 93, Hotel Solamar. 95 (top), thalling55/Flickr. 95 (bottom), Hard Rock Hotel San Diego. 96 (top), Lodge at Torrey Pines. 96 (center left and center right), Hotel Solamar. 96 (bottom left), Grande Colonial Hotel. 96 (bottom right), Grande Colonial Hotel. 113, Merryl Edelstein, Fodors.com member. 114, Legoland California Resort. Chapter 3: Orange County and Catalina Island: 117, Robert Holmes. 118, Marc Pagani Photography/Shutterstock. 119 (top), Robert Holmes. 119 (bottom), Brent Reeves/Shutterstock. 120, Robert Holmes. 127, www.ericcastro.biz/Flickr. 138, Robert Holmes. 141, Scott Vickers/iStockphoto. 145, www.rwongphoto.com / Alamy. 148, Brett Shoaf/Artistic Visuals Photography. 152, Lowe Llaguno/Shutterstock. Chapter 4: Los Angeles: 159, Robert Holmes. 160, Kenna Love/LACVB. 161 (top), Wendy Connett/age fotostock. 161 (bottom), Scott Frances/Esto/J. Paul Getty Trust. 162, Jeff Morse/Stockphoto. 163 (top), Andrea Skjold/Shutterstock. 163 (bottom), wando studios inc/Stockphoto. 164, SIME/Giovanni Simeone/eStock Photo. 174, Alvaro Leiva/age footstock. 185, S. Greg Panosian/iStockphoto. 190, NOIZE Photography/Flickr. 203, Patina Restaurant Group. 211, LOOK Die Bildagentur der Fotografen GmbH/Alamy. 212 (left), Four Seasons Hotels & Resorts. 212 (right), Renaissance Hollywood Hotel & Spa. 214 (top), Farmer's Daughter Hotel. 214 (center left), Langham Hotels International. 214 (center right), The Crescent Beverly Hills. 214 (bottom left), The Peninsula Hotels. 214 (bottom right), Adam Policky. 224, Stepan Mazurov/Flickr. 226, Thomas Barrat/Shutterstock. Chapter 5: The Central Coast: 233, TweetieV, Fodors.com member. 234, Stephen Walls/iStockphoto. 235 (top), Bart Everett/iStockphoto. 235 (bottom), Robert Holmes. 236, David M. Schrader/Shutterstock. 246, S. Greg Panosian/iStockphoto. 247, Ruben G. Mendoza. 248 (top), Richard Wong/www.rwongphoto.com/Alamy. 248 (bottom), Ruben G. Mendoza. 249 (top left), Witold Skrypczak/Alamy. 249 (top right), S. Greg Panosian/iStockphoto. 249 (bottom), Janet Fullwood. 250 (top left), GIPhotoStock Z/Alamy. 250 (top right), Craig Lovell/Eagle Visions Photography/Alamy. 250 (bottom) and 251 (top), S. Greg Panosian/iStockphoto. 251 (bottom), Eugene Zelenko/wikipedia.org. 257, David M. Schrader/Shutterstock. 265, Doreen Miller, Fodors.com member. 276, Robert Holmes. 294–95, Valhalla I Design & Conquer, Fodors.com member. Chapter 6: Channel Islands National Park: 299, Christopher Russell/iStockphoto. 300 (top), Yenwen Lu/iStockphoto. 300 (bottom), NatalieJean/Shutterstock. 301, ZanyZeus/Shutterstock. 302, ZanyZeus/Shutterstock. Chapter 7: The Monterey Bay Area: 307, mellifluous, Fodors.com member. 308, Janet Fullwood. 309 (top), vittorio sciosia/age fotostock. 309 (bottom), Jeff Greenberg/age fotostock. 310, Brent Reeves/Shutterstock. 317, Robert Holmes. 324, Holger Mette/iStockphoto. 332, laurel stewart/iStockphoto. Chapter 8: The Inland Empire: 355, Mission Inn Hotel & Spa. 356, Hartford Family Wines. 357 (top), Robert Holmes. 357 (bottom), stevekc/Flickr. 358, Edward Lin/iStockphoto. 367, Glen Ivy Hot Springs. 378, Robert Holmes. 383, Brett Shoaf/Artistic Visuals Pho-

ABOUT OUR WRITERS

Freelance writer and editor **Tanvi Chheda,** who updated the Los Angeles chapter, has called California home for nearly five years now. A former Travel + Leisure editor, Chheda writes about travel and culture for publications including the New York Times' T magazine, Departures, AFAR, and Delta Sky, among others.

Seth Combs has spent some quality time obsessing over San Diego arts and nightlife, which he updated for this edition. He's the former Arts & Culture editor at the alt-weekly *San Diego CityBeat* and was also an Associate Editor at *Riviera Magazine*. Now a freelance writer and editor, he contributes to publications including *Spin* and *The Hollywood Reporter.*

Native Californian • **Cheryl Crabtree**— who updated the Central Coast, Channel Islands National Park, and Monterey Bay chapters—has worked as a freelance writer since 1987. Cheryl is editor of Montecito Magazine. Her articles have appeared in many regional and national publications, including US Airways inflight magazine and Santa Barbara Seasons, and annual visitor magazines in Santa Barbara and Ventura.

When **Maren Dougherty** moved to San Diego in 2005, she thought she'd stay for one year—maybe two. To her East Coast family's dismay, she fell in love with the year-round beach scene, perfectly mixed margaritas, and rooftop pool bars. Maren's freelance work has appeared in *San Diego Magazine* and *Alaska Airlines* magazine. She updated the Where to Eat and Where to Stay sections of San Diego.

Amanda Knoles has been a contributed to the Shopping and Beaches sections of San Diego. Amanda has been a travel writer for more than 15 years and lists San Diego as her favorite weekend getaway.

Finding the unexpected is Los Angeles freelance writer and frequent traveler **Kathy A. McDonald**'s favorite assignment. A writer with peripatetic beats, she covers the film business, design, and destinations, and is a frequent contributor to Variety, Los Angeles Confidential Magazine, and other publications. For this edition she updated our Orange County and Catalina Island chapter.

For more than 20 years **Reed Parsell** has written travel stories, for newspapers and magazines, about destinations throughout the world. Recently he has written mostly about California attractions, and has updated the Mojave, Southern Sierra, and Sacramento/Gold Country chapters for several years. He is the principal author of *Fodor's In Focus: Yosemite, Sequoia and Kings Canyon National Parks,* and frequently visits Death Valley.

A veteran traveler, **Claire Deeks van der Lee** feels lucky to call San Diego home. Claire loves playing tourist in her own city, exploring San Diego's cultural attractions as well as its myriad neighborhoods and Balboa Park—so it was a perfect fit for her to work on the neighborhoods of San Diego. She also updated the Sports section for this edition. Claire has traveled to more than 40 countries, and has contributed to *Everywhere* magazine.

Freelance writer **Christine Vovakes**—who updated the North Coast, Lake Tahoe, Far North, the Redwoods, and Travel Smart chapters—has contributed to Fodor's California since 2004. Her travel articles and photographs have appeared in many publications, including *The Washington Post, The Christian Science Monitor, The Sacramento Bee,* and the *San Francisco Chronicle.*

Bobbi Zane—who updated the Experience California, Inland Empire, Palm Springs, and The Joshua Tree National Parks chapters for this edition—grew up in Southern California. She now lives in historic Julian in San Diego County. Her articles on Palm Springs have appeared in the *Orange County Register* and *Westways* magazine. She has contributed to Fodor's *Complete Guide to the National Parks of the West* and *Fodor's San Diego.*

tography. Chapter 9: Palm Springs: 385, toby fraley/iStockphoto. 386, JustASC/Shutterstock. 387 (top and bottom), Robert Holmes. 388, iStockphoto. 391, William Royer/iStockphoto. 402, David Falk/iStockphoto. 422, Brett Shoaf/Artistic Visuals Photography. Chapter 10: Joshua Tree National Park: 427, Eric Foltz/iStockphoto. 428 (top), Loic Bernard/iStockphoto. 428 (bottom), Eric Foltz/iStockphoto. 429 (top), Justin Mair/Shutterstock. 429 (bottom), Mariusz S. Jurgielewicz/Shutterstock. 430, Eric Foltz/iStockphoto. Chapter 11: The Mojave Desert: 435, Robert Holmes. 436, amygdala imagery/Shutterstock. 437, Robert Holmes. 438, San Bernardino County Regional Parks. 445, Merryl Edelstein, Fodors.com member. 451, Robert Holmes. 461, Paul Erickson/iStockphoto. Chapter 12: Death Valley National Park: 463, Rodney Ee, Fodors.com member. 465 (top), Igor Karon/Shutterstock. 465 (bottom), iofoto/Shutterstock. 466, Paul D. Lemke/iStockphoto. 470-71, James Feliciano/iStockphoto. 474, Rodney Ee, Fodors.com member. Chapter 13: The Central Valley: 477, Kim Brogan, Fodors.com member. 478, Gary Allard/ iStockphoto. 479–99, Robert Holmes. Chapter 14: The Southern Sierra: 501, Randall Pugh, Fodors.com member. 502, Craig Cozart/iStock-photo. 503 (top), David T Gomez/iStockphoto. 503 (bottom left and bottom right), Robert Holmes. 504, christinea78, Fodors.com member. 509, moonjazz/Flickr. 516, Douglas Atmore/iStockphoto. Chapter 15: Yosemite National Park: 519, Sarah P. Corley, Fodors.com member. 520, Yosemite Concession Services. 521 (top), Andy Z./Shutterstock. 521 (bottom), Greg Epperson/age fotostock. 522, Doug Lemke/Shutterstock. 526, Rebalyn, Fodors.com member. 531, Nathan Jaskowiak/Shutterstock. 534, Greg Epperson/age fotostock. 538-39, Katrina Leigh/Shutterstock. Chapter 16: Sequoia and Kings Canyon National Parks: 541 and 542, Robert Holmes. 543 (top), Greg Epperson/age fotostock. 543 (bottom) and 544, Robert Holmes. 551, urosr/Shutterstock. 555, Robert Holmes. Back cover (left to right): Valhalla I Design & Conquer, Fodors.com member; Kimberly Beck Rubio/iStockphoto; © Salvador Ceja I Dreamstime.com. Spine: Ken Wolter/Shutterstock.